England

A1(M) Baldock — Extra MSA
A1(M) J10 • Northbound and southbound 29 E9 TL23443661
El Mexicana • Greggs • KFC • M&S Simply Food • McDonald's • MooDog • Sorriso café • Starbucks
Shell Days Inn 2hrs
A1(M), Junction 10, Baldock, Hertfordshire SG7 5TR
www.extraservices.co.uk
Forecourt shop, McDonald's and Starbucks open 24 hrs

A1(M) Peterborough — Extra MSA
A1(M) J17 • Northbound and southbound 37 F7 TL13939395
Costa • KFC • Le Petit Four • M&S Simply Food • McDonald's • WH Smith Shell, LPG Days Inn 2 hrs
Great North Road, Haddon, Peterborough PE7 8UQ
www.extraservices.co.uk
Forecourt shop open 24 hrs

A1(M) Blyth — Moto
A1(M) Junction 34 • Northbound and southbound 45 D10 SK62568827
Burger King • Costa • EDC • Krispy Kreme • M&S Simply Food • WH Smith Esso, LPG Travelodge
Hill Top Roundabout, Blyth S81 8HG 01909 591841
www.moto-way.co.uk

A1(M) Wetherby — Moto
A1(M): J46 • Northbound and southbound 51 D10 SE41525025
Burger King • Costa • EDC • M&S Simply Food • Upper Crust • West Cornish Pasty • WH Smith BP Days Inn 2 hrs
Kirk Deighton, North Yorkshire LS22 5GT
01937 545080
www.moto-way.co.uk
Forecourt outlets open 24 hrs

A1(M) Durham — RoadChef
A1(M) J61 • Northbound and southbound 58 C4 NZ30843718
Costa • McDonald's • WH Smith Total Days Inn 2 hrs Tursdale Road, Bowburn, County Durham DH6 5NP 0191 377 9222
www.roadchef.com
Fast food outlet and forecourt shop open 24 hrs

A1(M) Washington — Moto
A1(M) just north of J64 • Northbound and southbound 63 H8 NZ28375506
Burger King • Costa • EDC • WH Smith BP Travelodge 2 hrs
Portobello, Birtley, Tyne & Wear DH3 2SJ 0191 410 3436
www.moto-way.co.uk
WH Smith and forecourt outlets open 24 hrs

M1 London Gateway — Welcome Break
M1 between J2 and J4 • Northbound and southbound 19 B9 TQ20269369
Burger King • Eat In • Krispy Kreme • Starbucks • Waitrose • WH Smith Shell, LPG Days Hotel 2 hrs M1 J2/4, Mill Hill, London NW7 3HU 0208 906 0611 lgw.enquiry@welcomebreak.co.uk
www.welcomebreak.co.uk
WH Smith open 24 hrs

M1 Toddington — Moto
M1, 1 mile south of J12 • Northbound and southbound 29 F7 TL03092878
Burger King • Costa • Cotton Traders (northbound) • EDC • Greggs (northbound) • Krispy Kreme • M&S Simply Food • Starbucks • Upper Crust (northbound) • West Cornish Pasty Company (northbound) • WH Smith BP, LPG Travelodge 2 hrs
Toddington, Bedfordshire LU5 6HR 01525 878400
www.moto-way.co.uk
Forecourt outlets open 24 hrs

M1 Newport Pagnell — Welcome Break
M1, north of J14 • Northbound and southbound 28 D5 SP85834351
Burger King • Eat In • KFC • Starbucks • Waitrose • WH Smith Shell, electric car charge point Days Inn 2 hrs
M1 Motorway, J14/15, Newport Pagnell, Buckinghamshire MK16 8DS
01908 217722
newport.enquiry@welcomebreak.co.uk
www.welcomebreak.co.uk
WH Smith and forecourt shop open 24 hrs

M1 Northampton — RoadChef
M1 J15A • Northbound and southbound 28 C4 SP72285732
The Burger Company (northbound) • Costa • Hot Food Co (southbound) • McDonald's (southbound) • Restbite! (northbound) • WH Smith Shell, LPG 2 hrs
M1 Junction 15A, Northampton, Northamptonshire NN4 9QY 01604 831888
www.roadchef.com
WH Smith, forecourt shop and (southbound) McDonald's open 24 hrs

M1 Watford Gap — RoadChef
M1 between J16 and J17 • Northbound and southbound 28 B3 SP59956802
Northbound: Costa • Cotton Traders • Fresh Food Co • McDonald's • WH Smith • Southbound: • The Burger Company • Costa • Restbite! • WH Smith Shell Days Inn (southbound) 2 hrs
M1 Motorway, Northamptonshire NN6 7UZ
01327 879001
www.roadchef.com

M1 Leicester Forest East — Welcome Break
M1 between J21 and J21A • Northbound and southbound 35 E11 SK53860267
Burger King • Eat In • KFC • Starbucks • Waitrose • WH Smith Shell, LPG Days Inn 2 hrs
Leicester Forest East, M1, Leicester, Leicestershire LE3 3GB
0116 238 6801
lfe.enquiry@welcomebreak.co.uk
www.welcomebreak.co.uk
Eat In and WH Smith are open 24 hrs

M1 Donington Park — Moto
M1 J23A • Northbound and southbound 35 C10 SK46712513
Burger King • Costa • Cotton Traders • EDC • Krispy Kreme • M&S Simply Food • WH Smith BP, LPG Travelodge 2 hrs Castle Donington, Derby, East Midlands DE74 2TN
01509 672220
www.moto-way.co.uk
Forecourt shop and WH Smith open 24 hrs

M1 Trowell — Moto
M1 between J25 and J26 • Northbound and southbound 35 A10 SK49354073
Burger King • Costa • Krispy Kreme • EDC M&S Simply Food • WH Smith BP 2 hrs Ilkeston, Trowell, Nottinghamshire NG9 3PL
01159 320291
www.moto-way.co.uk
WH Smith and forecourt outlets are open 24 hrs

M1 Tibshelf — RoadChef
M1, 2 miles north of J28 • Northbound and southbound 45 F8 SK44856031
The Burger Company (northbound) • McDonald's (southbound) • Restbite! • WH Smith Shell, LPG Days Inn (northbound only) 2 hrs
Newton Wood Lane, Newton, Alfreton DE55 5TZ
01773 876600
www.roadchef.com
WH Smith and forecourt shop open 24 hrs

M1 Woodall — Welcome Break
M1, 2.5 miles north of J30 • Northbound and southbound 45 D8 SK47928006
Burger King • Eat In • KFC • Krispy Kreme • Starbucks • Waitrose • WH Smith Shell, LPG Days Inn 2 hrs
M1 Motorway, Sheffield, South Yorkshire S26 7XR
0114 248 7992
woodall.enquiry@welcomebreak.co.uk
www.welcomebreak.co.uk
Eat In, WH Smith and forecourt outlets open 24 hrs

M1 Woolley Edge — Moto
M1, just north of J38 • Northbound and southbound 45 A7 SE29841400
Burger King • Costa • EDC • Krispy Kreme • M&S Simply Food • WH Smith BP Travelodge 2 hrs
West Bretton, Wakefield, West Yorkshire WF4 4LQ
01924 830371
www.moto-way.co.uk
WH Smith and forecourt outlets open 24 hrs

M2 Medway — Moto
M2 between J4 and J5 • Eastbound and westbound 20 E5 TQ81756344
Burger King • Costa • Greggs • Krispy Kreme • WH Smith BP, LPG Travelodge 2 hrs M2, Rainham, Gillingham, Kent ME8 8PQ
01634 236900
www.moto-way.co.uk
WH Smith and forecourt shop open 24 hrs

M3 Fleet — Welcome Break
M3 between J4A/J5 • Eastbound and westbound 18 F4 SU79885583
Waitrose • WH Smith • Burger King • Eat In • KFC • Krispy Kreme • Starbucks Shell, LPG Days Inn 2 hrs
Fleet, Hampshire GU51 1AA
01252 788 500
fleet.enquiry@welcomebreak.co.uk
www.welcomebreak.co.uk
Eat In and WH Smith open 24 hrs

M3 Winchester — Moto
M3, 4 miles north of J9 • Northbound and southbound 18 H2 SU52303550
Burger King • Costa • EDC • Krispy Kreme • WH Smith BP, LPG Days Inn 2 hrs
Shroner Wood, Winchester, Hampshire SO21 1PP
01962 791140
www.moto-way.co.uk
Forecourt outlets open 24 hrs

M4 Heston — Moto
M4 1 mile east of J3 • Eastbound and westbound 19 D8 TQ11777778
Burger King • Costa • EDC (westbound) • Krispy Kreme • WH Smith BP, LPG Travelodge 2 hrs
Phoenix Way, Heston, Hounslow, London TW5 9NB
0208 5802152
www.moto-way.co.uk
WH Smith open 24 hrs

M4 Reading – eastbound — Moto
M4 Junctions 11-12 • Eastbound 18 E3 SU67177012
Burger King • Costa • EDC • Krispy Kreme • M&S Simply Food • West Cornish Pasty • WH Smith BP, LPG Travelodge 2 hrs Burghfield, Reading RG30 3UQ
01189 566966
www.moto-way.co.uk
WH Smith and forecourt outlets open 24 hrs

M4 Reading – westbound — Moto
M4 Junctions 11-12 • Westbound 18 E3 SU67046985
Burger King • Costa • EDC • Krispy Kreme • M&S Simply Food • Upper Crust • West Cornish Pasty • WH Smith BP, LPG Travelodge 2 hrs Burghfield, Reading RG30 3UQ 01189 566966
www.moto-way.co.uk
WH Smith and forecourt outlets open 24 hrs

M4 Chieveley — Moto
M4 J13 • Eastbound and westbound 17 D11 SU48157268
Burger King • Costa • EDC • Krispy Kreme • M&S Simply Food • West Cornish Pasty • WH Smith BP, LPG Travelodge 2 hrs
Oxford Road, Hermitage, Thatcham, Berkshire, RG18 9XX
01635 248024
www.moto-way.co.uk
WH Smith open 24 hrs

M4 Membury — Welcome Break
M4, 4 miles west of J14 • Eastbound and westbound 17 D10 SU30847601
Burger King • Eat In • KFC • Krispy Kreme • Starbucks • Waitrose • WH Smith Shell, LPG, electric car charge point Days Inn 2 hrs
Woodlands Road, Membury, near Lambourn, Berkshire RG17 7TZ
01488 674360 membury.enquiry@welcomebreak.co.uk
www.welcomebreak.co.uk
Eat In, WH Smith and forecourt shop open 24 hrs

M4 Leigh Delamere — Moto
M4 just west of J17 • Eastbound and westbound 16 D5 ST89077899
Burger King • Costa • Cotton Traders • EDC • Krispy Kreme • M&S Simply Food • West Cornish Pasty • WH Smith BP, LPG Travelodge 2 hrs
Chippenham, Wiltshire SN14 6LB
01666 837691 (eastbound); 01666 842015 (westbound)
www.moto.co.uk
WH Smith and shop and coffee shops in the forecourt open 24 hrs

M5 Frankley — Moto
M5 J3 • Northbound and southbound 34 G5 SO98938120
Burger King • Costa • EDC • Greggs (northbound) • Krispy Kreme • M&S Simply Food • WH Smith Esso Travelodge 2 hrs
Illey Lane, Birmingham, West Midlands B32 4AR
0121 550 3131
www.moto-way.co.uk
WH Smith and forecourt outlets open 24 hrs

M5 Strensham – southbound — RoadChef
M5 southbound, just before J8 • Southbound only 26 E6 SO90413993
Costa • Cotton Traders • Hot Food Co • McDonald's • Soho Coffee Company • WH Smith BP, LPG 2 hrs
M5 Motorway, Lower Strensham, Worcestershire WR8 9LJ
01684 290577
www.roadchef.com
McDonald's and forecourt outlet open 24 hrs

Symbols
- Accommodation
- Baby change
- Barber shop
- Bureau de change
- Cash machine
- Footbridge
- Fuel
- Meeting room
- Free parking
- Showers
- Toilets
- Disabled toilets
- RADAR key scheme
- Truckstop
- Truck wash
- Free WiFi
- Work space
- Address
- Telephone number
- e-mail address
- website
- Details of shops and catering outlets that are normally open 24 hours are listed at the end of each entry. Other listed outlets may not be open 24 hours.

M5 Strensham – northbound — RoadChef
M5, 1 mile north of J8 • Northbound only 26 D5 SO89344072
Costa • Cotton Traders • McDonald's • Pizza Hut Express • Subway • WH Smith Texaco, LPG Days Inn 2 hrs
M5 Motorway, Lower Strensham, Worcestershire WR8 9LJ
01684 293004
www.roadchef.com
McDonald's and forecourt outlets open 24 hrs

M5 Michaelwood — Welcome Break
M5, just north of J14 • Northbound and southbound 16 B4 ST70409541
Burger King • Eat In • KFC • Krispy Kreme • Starbucks • WH Smith Shell, electric car charge point Days Inn 2 hrs Lower Wick, Dursley, Gloucestershire GL11 6DD
01454 260631 michaelwood.enquiry@welcomebreak.co.uk
www.welcomebreak.co.uk
WH Smith and forecourt shop open 24 hrs

M5 Gordano — Welcome Break
M5 J19 • Northbound and southbound 16 D2 ST50977563
Burger King • Eat In • KFC • Krispy Kreme • Starbucks • Waitrose • WH Smith Shell, LPG Days Inn 2 hrs
Portbury, Bristol BS20 7XG
01275 373624 gordano.enquiry@welcomebreak.co.uk
www.welcomebreak.co.uk
WH Smith open 24 hrs

M5 Sedgemoor Southbound — RoadChef
M5, 7 miles south of J21 15 F9 ST35815259
The Burger Company • Costa • Restbite! • WH Smith Total 2 hrs
M5 Southbound Rooksbridge, Axbridge, Somerset BS26 2UF
01934 750888
www.roadchef.com
Forecourt shop open 24 hrs

M5 Sedgemoor Northbound — Welcome Break
M5, 3 miles north of J22 15 F9 ST35815259
Burger King • Eat In • Starbucks • WH Smith Shell, electric car charge point Days Inn 2 hrs
M5 Motorway Northbound, Bridgwater, Somerset BS24 0JL
01934 750730 sedgemoor.enquiry@welcomebreak.co.uk www.welcomebreak.co.uk WH Smith and shop on forecourt are open 24 hrs

M5 Bridgwater — Moto
M5, J24 • Northbound and southbound 8 A2 ST30403441
Burger King • Costa • EDC • Krispy Kreme • West Cornish Pasty • WH Smith BP Travelodge 2 hrs
Huntsworth Business Park, Bridgwater, Somerset TA6 6TS
01278 456800
www.moto-way.co.uk
WH Smith and forecourt shop open 24 hrs

M5 Taunton Deane — RoadChef
M5 between J25 and J26 • Northbound and southbound 7 D10 ST19592035
The Burger Company • Costa • Restbite! • WH Smith Shell Days Inn (southbound only) 2 hrs
Trull, Taunton, Somerset TA3 7PF 01823 271111
www.roadchef.com
Forecourt outlets are open 24 hrs

A38 / M5 Tiverton — Moto
M5 Junction 27 • Northbound and southbound 7 E9 ST04901386
Costa • Burger King Shell Travelodge 2 hrs. No HGVs
Tiverton EX16 7HD
01884 829423
www.moto-way.co.uk

M5 Cullompton — Extra MSA
M5, J28 • Northbound and southbound 7 F9 ST02660798
Costa • McDonald's • WH Smith Shell 2 hrs
Old Station Yard, Station Road, Cullompton, Devon EX15 1NS
01522 523737
www.extraservices.co.uk
WH Smith and forecourt shop open 24 hrs

M5 Exeter — Moto
M5 J30 • Northbound and southbound 7 G8 SX96779180
Burger King • Costa • EDS • Harry Ramsden • Krispy Kreme • M&S Simply Food • West Cornish Pasty • WH Smith BP Travelodge 2 hrs
Sandygate, Exeter, Devon EX2 7HF 01392 436266
www.moto-way.co.uk
WH Smith open 24 hrs

M6 Corley — Welcome Break
M6, 2.5 miles west of J3 • Eastbound and westbound 35 G9 SP30898604
Burger King • Eat In • KFC • Starbucks • Waitrose • WH Smith Shell, LPG, electric car charge point Days Inn 2 hrs
Highfield Lane, Corley, Staffordshire CV7 8NR
01676 540111
corleyenquiry@welcomebreak.co.uk
www.welcomebreak.co.uk
WH Smith open 24 hrs

M6 Norton Canes — Road Chef
M6 Toll between JT6 and JT7 • Eastbound and westbound 34 E6 SK02290745
The Burger Company • Costa • Restbite! • WH Smith Shell Days Inn 2 hrs
Betty's Lane, Norton Canes, Cannock, Staffordshire WS11 9UX
01543 272540
www.roadchef.co.uk
WH Smith and forecourt shop open 24 hrs

M6 Hilton Park Moto

M6 J10A and J11 • Northbound and southbound 34 E5 SJ96200500

Burger King • Costa • Cotton Traders (northbound) • EDC • KFC (northbound) • Krispy Kreme • M&S Simply Food • WH Smith

BP Travelodge 2 hrs Essington, Wolverhampton, Staffordshire WV11 2AT 01922 412237 www.moto-way.co.uk Coffee shops in forecourt and WH Smith are open 24 hrs

M6 Stafford – northbound Moto

M6, 3 miles north of J14 • Northbound only 34 B4 SJ88613186

Burger King • Costa • EDC • Krispy Kreme • M&S Simply Food • WH Smith

BP, LPG Travelodge 2 hrs Stone, Staffordshire ST15 0EU 01785 811188 www.moto-way.co.uk Forecourt outlets open 24 hrs

M6 Stafford South RoadChef

M6, 7.5 miles south of J15 • Southbound only 34 B4 SJ89243065

The Burger Company • Costa • Restbite! • WH Smith

Esso, LPG Days Inn 2 hrs M6 Southbound, Stone, Staffordshire ST15 0EU 01785 826300 www.roadchef.com

M6 Keele Welcome Break

M6, 6 miles north of J15 • Northbound and southbound 34 A4 SJ80624406

Burger King • Eat In • KFC • Krispy Kreme • Starbucks • Waitrose • WH Smith

Shell, LPG and electric car charge point (both southbound only) 2 hrs Three Mile Lane, Keele, Newcastle under Lyme, Staffordshire ST5 5HG 01782 626221 keele.enquiry@welcomebreak.co.uk www.welcomebreak.co.uk Eat In & WH Smith open 24 hrs

M6 Sandbach RoadChef

M6, just south of J17 • Northbound and southbound 43 F10 SJ02290745

Northbound: Costa • Restbite! • WH Smith • Southbound: Costa • Hot Food Co • McDonald's • WH Smith

Esso 2 hrs M6 Northbound, Sandbach, Cheshire CW11 2FZ 01270 767134 www.roadchef.co.uk Forecourt outlets and (southbound) McDonald's open 24 hrs

M6 Knutsford Moto

M6, between J18 and J19 • Northbound and southbound 43 E10 SJ73267826

Burger King • Costa • EDC • Krispy Kreme • M&S Simply Food • West Cornish Pasty (southbound) • WH Smith

BP, LPG Travelodge 2 hrs Northwich Road, Knutsford, Cheshire WA16 0TL 01565 634167 www.moto-way.co.uk Forecourt shop open 24 hrs

M6 Charnock Richard Welcome Break

M6, 2.5 miles north of J27 • Northbound and southbound 43 A8 SD54411521

Burger King • Eat In • KFC • Krispy Kreme • Starbucks • WH Smith

Shell, LPG (southbound only), electric car charge point Days Inn 2 hrs Mill Lane, Chorley, Lancashire PR7 5LR 01257 791494 charnock.enquiry@welcomebreak.co.uk www.welcomebreak.co.uk Eat In & WH Smith open 24 hrs

M6 Lancaster Moto

M6 south of J33 • Northbound and southbound 49 D5 SD50145198

Burger King • Costa • Cotton Traders (northbound) • EDC • Greggs (southbound) • M&S Simply Food • West Cornish Pasty Company (northbound) • WH Smith

BP, LPG Travelodge 2 hrs White Carr Lane, Bay Horse, Lancaster, Lancashire LA2 9DU 01524 791775 www.moto-way.co.uk WH Smith and forecourt shop are open 24 hrs

M6 Burton-in-Kendal Moto

M6 between J35 and J36 • Northbound only 49 B5 SD52207617

Burger King • Costa • EDC • WH Smith

BP 2 hrs Burton West, Carnforth, Lancashire LA6 1JF 01524 781234 www.moto-way.co.uk

M6 Killington Lake RoadChef

M6 just south of J37 • Southbound only 57 G7 SD58779111

The Burger Company • Costa • Restbite! • WH Smith

BP Days Inn 2 hrs M6 Southbound, near Kendal, Cumbria LA8 0NW 01539 620739 www.roadchef.com WH Smith and forecourt shop open 24 hrs

M6 Tebay – northbound Westmorland

M6, north of J38 • Northbound only 57 F8 NY60510626

Butcher's counter • cafe and coffee shop • farm shop • forecourt shop • takeaway snack bar

Total, LPG Westmorland Hotel Yes M6, Old Tebay, Cumbria CA10 3ZA 01539 624511 www.westmorland.com Petrol forecourt shop and takeaway open 24 hours

M6 Tebay – southbound Westmorland

M6, 4.5 miles south of J39 • Southbound only 57 F8 NY60790650

Butcher's counter • cafe and coffee shop • farm shop • forecourt shop • takeaway snack bar

Total, LPG Yes M6, Old Tebay, Cumbria CA10 3SB 01539 624511 www.westmorland.com Petrol forecourt shop and takeaway open 24 hours

M6 Southwaite Moto

M6 Junctions 41-42 • Northbound and southbound 56 B6 NY44164523

Burger King • Costa • Cotton Traders (northbound) • EDC • Greggs • M&S Simply Food (southbound) • West Cornish Pasty Company (southbound) • WH Smith

BP Travelodge 2 hrs Broadfield Road, Carlisle CA4 0NT 01697 473476 www.moto-way.co.uk WH Smith and outlets on the forecourts are open 24 hours

M11 Birchanger Green Welcome Break

M11 at J8/J8a • Northbound and southbound 30 F2 TL51202149

Burger King • Eat In • KFC • Krispy Kreme • Starbucks • Waitrose • WH Smith

Shell, LPG Days Hotel 2 hrs Old Dunmow Road, Bishop's Stortford, Hertfordshire CM23 5QZ 01279 653388 www.welcomebreak.co.uk WH Smith open 24 hrs

M18 Doncaster North Moto

M18 J5, at the western end of the M180 • Northbound and southbound 45 A10 SE66791104

Burger King • Costa • EDC • Greggs • Krispy Kreme • WH Smith

BP, LPG Travelodge 2 hrs Hatfield, Doncaster, South Yorkshire DN8 5GS 01302 847700 www.moto-way.co.uk WH Smith open 24 hrs

M20 Maidstone RoadChef

M20 J8 20 F5 TQ82455523

Costa • Cotton Traders • McDonald's • Restbite! • WH Smith

Esso Days Inn 2 hrs M20 J8, Hollingbourne, Maidstone, Kent ME17 1SS 01622 631100 www.roadchef.com McDonald's, WH Smith and forecourt outlets open 24 hrs

M20 Stop24 (Folkestone) Stop 24

M20 J11 21 H8 TR13283729

Coffee Stop • Haldane Express • Julian Graves • Just Spuds • KFC • Subway • WH Smith • Wimpy

Shell, LPG 2 hrs Junction 11 M20, Stanford Intersection, Stanford, Kent CT21 4BL 01303 760273 info@stop24.co.uk www.stop24.co.uk Forecourt outlets open 24 hrs

M23 Pease Pottage Moto

M23 J11 • Northbound and southbound 19 H9 TQ26183310

Burger King • Costa • EDC • Krispy Kreme • M&S Simply Food • West Cornish Pasty • WH Smith

BP, LPG 2 hrs Brighton Road, Pease Pottage, Crawley, West Sussex RH11 9AE 01293 562852 www.moto-way.co.uk WH Smith and forecourt outlets open 24 hrs

M25 Clacket Lane RoadChef

M25 between J5 and J6 • Eastbound and westbound 19 F11 TQ42335457

Costa • Cotton Traders • Hot Food Co • McDonald's • WH Smith

Total, electric car charge point Days Inn (westbound only) 2hrs M25 Westbound, Westerham, Kent TN16 2ER 01959 565577 www.roadchef.com McDonald's open 24 hrs

M25 Cobham Extra MSA

M25 J9-10 • Clockwise and anti-clockwise 19 F8 TQ11345768

Chozen Noodle • Eat In • El Mexicana • Greggs • KFC • M&S Simply Food • McDonald's • MooDog • Sorriso café • Starbucks • WH Smith

Shell, LPG Days Inn 2 hrs M25 J9/10, Downside, Cobham, Surrey KT11 3DB www.extraservices.co.uk Forecourt outlets open 24 hrs

M25 South Mimms Welcome Break

M25 J23 and A1(M) J1 • Clockwise and anti-clockwise 19 A9 TL23000023

Burger King • Eat In • KFC • Krispy Kreme • Starbucks • Waitrose • WH Smith

Shell, electric car charge point Days Inn 2 hrs Bignells Corner, Potters Bar, Hertfordshire EN6 3QQ 01707 621001 mimms.enquiry@welcomebreak.co.uk www.welcomebreak.co.uk Eat In, WH Smith and forecourt outlets open 24 hrs

M25 Thurrock Moto

M25, signposted from J30/J31 • Clockwise and anti-clockwise 20 D2 TQ57837947

Burger King • Costa • EDC • Krispy Kreme • M&S Simply Food • WH Smith

Esso Travelodge 2 hrs Arterial Road, West Thurrock, Grays, Essex RM16 3BG 01708 865487 www.moto-way.co.uk WH Smith and forecourt outlet open 24 hrs

M27 Rownhams RoadChef

M27, between J3 and J4 • Eastbound and westbound 10 C2 SU38791769

Costa • McDonald's (westbound) • Restbite! • WH Smith

Esso, LPG Days Inn (westbound) 2 hrs M27 Southbound, Southampton, Hampshire SO16 8AP 02380 734480 www.roadchef.com The outlets in the forecourts are open 24 hrs

M40 Beaconsfield Extra MSA

M40 J2 • Eastbound and westbound 18 C6 SU95098897

Carvery Express • Chozen Noodle • El Mexicana • Greggs • KFC • Le Petit Four • M&S Simply Food • McDonald's • MooDog • Starbucks

Shell, LPG Ibis 2 hrs A355 Windsor Drive, Beaconsfield, Buckinghamshire HP9 2SE www.extraservices.co.uk McDonald's and forecourt outlet open 24 hrs

M40 Oxford Welcome Break

M40 J8A • Northbound and southbound 18 A3 SP62440479

Burger King • Eat In • KFC • Krispy Kreme • Starbucks • Waitrose • WH Smith

Shell, electric car charge point Days Inn 2 hrs M40 Junction 8A, Waterstock, Oxfordshire OX33 1LJ 01865 877007 oxford.enquiry@welcomebreak.co.uk www.welcomebreak.co.uk McDonald's and Starbucks open 24 hours

M40 Cherwell Valley Moto

M40 J10 • Northbound and southbound 28 F2 SP55162822

Burger King • Costa • Cotton Traders • EDC • Krispy Kreme • M&S Simply Food • Upper Crust • West Cornish Pasty • WH Smith

Esso, electric car charge point Travelodge 2 hrs Northampton Road, Ardley, Bicester, Oxfordshire OX27 7RD 01869 346060 www.moto-way.co.uk WH Smith open 24 hrs

M40 Warwick South Welcome Break

M40 between J12 and J13 • Southbound 27 C10 SP34075801

Burger King • Eat In • Krispy Kreme • KFC • Starbucks • Waitrose • WH Smith

Shell Days Inn 2 hrs Banbury Road, Ashorne, Warwick CV35 0AA 01926 650168 warwicksouth.enquiry@welcomebreak.co.uk www.welcomebreak.co.uk Eat In, WH Smith and forecourt outlets open 24 hrs

M40 Warwick North Welcome Break

M40 between J12 and J13 • Northbound 57 F8 SP33885770

Burger King • Eat In • KFC • Krispy Kreme • Starbucks • Waitrose • WH Smith

Shell Days Inn 2 hrs Banbury Road, Ashorne, Warwick CV35 0AA 01926 650168 warwicknorth.enquiry@welcomebreak.co.uk www.welcomebreak.co.uk Eat In & WH Smith open 24 hrs

M42 Hopwood Park Welcome Break

M42 Junction 2 • Eastbound and westbound 27 A7 SP03637389

Burger King • Eat In • KFC • Krispy Kreme • Starbucks • Waitrose • WH Smith

Shell, LPG, electric car charge point 2 hrs Redditch Road, Alvechurch B48 7AU 0121 4474000 hopwood.enquiry@welcomebreak.co.uk www.welcomebreak.co.uk

M42 Tamworth Moto

M42, just north of J10 • Northbound and southbound 35 E8 SK2440112

Burger King • Costa • EDC • Krispy Kreme • M&S Simply Food • WH Smith

Esso Travelodge 2 hrs Green Lane, Tamworth, Staffordshire B77 5PS 01827 260120 www.moto-way.co.uk WH Smith and forecourt outlets are open 24 hrs

M48 Severn View Moto

M48 J1 • Eastbound and westbound 16 C2 ST57118959

Burger King • Costa • Krispy Kreme • WH Smith

BP Travelodge 2 hrs Aust, South Gloucestershire BS35 4BH 01454 623851 www.moto-way.co.uk Forecourt outlets open 24 hrs

M50/A40 Ross Spur Eurogarages

On A40, just west of M50 J4 • Southbound only 26 F3 SO6147125970

Coffee Nation • KFC • Spar • Starbucks • Subway

BP 2 hrs Trunk Road, Ross on Wye, Herefordshire HR9 7QJ 01989563493 (BP) www.eurogarages.com Forecourt outlets open 24 hours. KFC/Starbucks drive-thru only.

M54 Telford Welcome Break

M54 J4 • Eastbound and westbound 34 E3 SJ73050890

Burger King • Eat In • Starbucks • WH Smith

Shell, LPG available Days Inn 2 hrs Priorslee Road, Shifnal, Telford, Shropshire TF11 8TG 01952 238444 telford.enquiry@welcomebreak.co.uk www.welcomebreak.co.uk WH Smith and shop on forecourt open 24 hrs

M56 Chester RoadChef

M56 J14 • Eastbound and westbound 43 E7 SJ46537491

Costa • Cotton Traders • Hot Food Co • McDonald's • WH Smith

Shell Days Inn 2 hrs Elton, Chester, Cheshire CH2 4QZ 01928 728500 www.roadchef.com Costa and McDonald's open 24 hrs

M61 Rivington – northbound Euro Garages

M61 between J6 and J8 • Northbound and southbound 43 A9 SD62111168

Burger King • Spar • Starbucks • Subway

BP 2 hrs M61, Horwich, Bolton, Lancashire BL6 5UZ 01254 56070 enquiries@eurogarages.com www.eurogarages.com Forecourt outlets open 24 hrs

M61 Rivington – southbound Euro Garages

M61 between J8 and J6 • Northbound and southbound 43 A9 SD62111168

Burger King • Spar • Starbucks • Subway

BP Rivington Lodge 2 hrs M61, Horwich, Bolton, Lancashire BL6 5UZ 01254 56070 enquiries@eurogarages.com www.eurogarages.com Forecourt outlets open 24 hrs

M62 Burtonwood Welcome Break

M62 J8 • Eastbound and westbound 43 C8 SJ57749129

KFC • Starbucks • WH Smith

Shell 2 hrs M62 Great Sankey, Warrington, Cheshire WA5 3AX 01925 651656 burtonwood.enquiry@welcomebreak.co.uk www.welcomebreak.co.uk WH Smith open 24 hrs

M62 Birch – eastbound Moto

M62 1.5 miles east of J18 • Eastbound and westbound 43 B11 SD84700797

Burger King • Costa • EDC • Greggs • Krispy Kreme • M&S Simply Food • WH Smith

BP Travelodge 2 hrs Heywood, Lancashire OL10 2HQ 0161 643 0911 www.moto-way.co.uk WH Smith is open 24 hrs

M62 Birch – westbound Moto

M62 1.5 miles east of J18 • Eastbound and westbound 43 B11 SD84700797

Burger King • Costa • EDC • Krispy Kreme • M&S Simply Food • WH Smith

BP Travelodge 2 hrs Heywood, Lancashire OL10 2HQ 0161 643 0911 www.moto-way.co.uk WH Smith is open 24 hrs

M62 Hartshead Moor Welcome Break

M62, between J25 and J26 • Eastbound and westbound 51 G7 SE16892413

Burger King • Eat In • KFC • Krispy Kreme • Starbucks • WH Smith

Shell Days Inn 2 hrs Clifton, Brighouse, West Yorkshire HD6 4JX 01274 876584 hartshead.enquiry@welcomebreak.co.uk www.welcomebreak.co.uk Eat In and WH Smith open 24 hrs

M62 Ferrybridge Moto

M62 Junction 33. Also A1(M) J40 (northbound) or J41 (southbound) • Northbound and southbound 51 G10 SE48512262

Burger King • Costa • EDC • Greggs • Krispy Kreme • M&S Simply Food • WH Smith

BP Travelodge 2 hrs Ferrybridge, Knottingly, West Yorkshire WF11 0AF 01977 672767 www.moto-way.co.uk Coffee Nation and WH Smith open 24 hrs

M65 Blackburn with Darwen Extra MSA

M65 J4 • Eastbound and westbound 50 G2 SD68592414

Co-op • Costa • Greggs • McDonald's

Shell, LPG Travelodge 2 hrs Darwen Motorway Services Area, Darwen, Lancashire BB3 0AT www.extraservices.co.uk Forecourt shop is open 24 hrs

Scotland

M9 Stirling Moto

M9 J9 • Northbound and southbound 69 B7 NS80438870

Burger King • Costa • EDC • WH Smith

BP Travelodge 2 hrs Pirnhall, Stirling FK7 8EU 01786 813614 www.moto-way.co.uk WH Smith is open 24 hrs

M74 Bothwell RoadChef

M74, south of J4 • southbound only 68 E6 NS70855980

Costa • Restbite! • WH Smith

BP 2hrs M74 Southbound, Bothwell, Lanarkshire G71 8BG 01698 854123 www.roadchef.com Forecourt shop is open 24 hrs

M74 Hamilton RoadChef

M74, 1 mile north of J6 • northbound only 68 E6 NS72525672

Costa • Restbite! • WH Smith

BP Days Inn 2hrs M74 Northbound, Hamilton, South Lanarkshire ML3 6JW 01698 282176 www.roadchef.com Forecourt shop is open 24hrs

M74 Happendon Cairn Lodge

M74 between J11 and J12 on B7078 • Northbound and southbound 69 G7 NS85243364

Coffee shop • restaurant • retail shop

Shell 2hrs Cairn Lodge, Douglas, Lanark, South Lanarkshire ML11 0RJ 01555 851880

A74(M) Abington Welcome Break

A74(M) J13 • Northbound and southbound 69 H8 NS93022505

Burger King • Eat In • Starbucks • WH Smith

Shell, LPG Days Inn 2 hrs Abington, Biggar, South Lanarkshire ML12 6RG 01864 502637 abington.enquiry@welcomebreak.co.uk www.welcomebreak.co.uk Eat In open 24 hrs. Tourist information office

A74(M) Annandale Water Road Chef

A74(M) J16 • Northbound and southbound 61 D7 NY10389261

The Burger Company • Costa • Restbite! • WH Smith

BP Days Inn 2hrs Johnstone Bridge, near Lockerbie, Dumfries and Galloway DG11 1HD 01576 470870 www.roadchef.com Restbite and forecourt shop are open 24 hrs

A74(M) **Gretna Green**   Welcome Break

£ ♦♦ ♿ 🚻 (•) 🚂

A74(M), just north of J22 · Northbound and southbound
61 **G9** NY30746872
Burger King · Eat In · KFC · Krispy Kreme · Starbucks · Waitrose · WH Smith
⛽ Shell 🛏 Days Inn 🅿 2 hrs
✉ M74A Trunk Road, Gretna Green, Dumfries and Galloway DG16 5HQ 📞 01461 337567
@ gretna.enquiry@welcomebreak.co.uk
🖥 www.welcomebreak.co.uk
🕐 Eat In open 24 hrs

M80 **Old Inns**

♦♦

M80 · Eastbound and Westbound 68 **C6** NS77187671
Shell Select · Old Inns Cafe · Silk Cottage Cantonese buffet and takeaway ⛽ Shell
✉ Castlecary Road, Cumbernauld G68 0BJ 📞 0843 2590190 (filling station) 🖥 www.shell.co.uk · www.oldinnscafe.com

M90 **Kinross**   Moto

£ ♦♦ ♿ 😊 ♿ 🚲 (•)

M90 J6 · Northbound and southbound 76 **G4** NO10800282
Burger King · Costa · EDC · WH Smith
⛽ BP 🛏 Travelodge 🅿 2 hrs
✉ M90, Kinross KY13 7NQ
📞 01577 863123
🖥 www.moto-way.co.uk
🕐 WH Smith and forecourt shop open 24 hrs

Wales

M4 **Magor**   RoadChef

£ ♦♦ ♿ 🚲 (•)

M4 J23A · Eastbound and westbound 15 **C10** ST42068796
Costa · Cotton Traders · McDonald's · Restbite! · WH Smith ⛽ Esso 🛏 Days Inn
🅿 2 hrs ✉ M4 Magor, Caldicot, NP26 3YL 📞 01633 881515
@ info@firstmotorway.co.uk
🖥 www.roadchef.com
🕐 McDonald's open 24 hrs

M4 **Cardiff Gate**   Welcome Break

£ ♦♦ ♿ 🚻 (•) 🚂

M4 J30 · Eastbound and westbound 15 **C8** ST21658283
Burger King · Krispy Kreme · Starbucks · Waitrose · WH Smith ⛽ Shell 🅿 2 hrs
✉ Cardiff Gate Business Park, Cardiff, CF23 8RA 📞 02920 541122
@ cardiff.enquiry@welcomebreak.co.uk
🖥 www.welcomebreak.co.uk
🕐 Forecourt shop open 24 hrs

M4 **Cardiff West**   Moto

£ ♦♦ ♿ 😊 ♿ 🚲 (•)

M4, off J33 · Eastbound and westbound 14 **D6** ST09417967
Burger King · Costa · Krispy Kreme · WH Smith
⛽ Esso 🛏 Travelodge 🅿 2 hrs
✉ Pontyclun, Mid Glamorgan CF72 8SA 📞 02920 891141
🖥 www.moto-way.co.uk
🕐 WH Smith is open 24 hrs

M4 **Sarn Park**   Welcome Break

£ ♦♦ ♿ 🚲 (•) 🚂

M4 J36 · Eastbound and westbound 14 **C5** SS90688290
Burger King · Starbucks · WH Smith
⛽ Shell 🛏 Days Inn 🅿 2 hrs
✉ M4 Motorway, Junction 36, Sarn Park, Bridgend CF32 9RW
📞 01656 655332 @ sarn.enquiry@welcomebreak.co.uk
🖥 www.welcomebreak.co.uk
🕐 WH Smith and forecourt shop open 24 hrs

M4 **Swansea**   Moto

£ ♦♦ ♿ 😊 ♿ 🚲 (•)

M4 at J47 · Eastbound and westbound 14 **B2** SS62159969
Burger King · Costa · WH Smith
⛽ BP 🛏 Travelodge 🅿 2 hrs
✉ Penllergaer, Swansea, SA4 1GT
📞 01792 896222
🖥 www.moto-way.co.uk
🕐 Forecourt outlets open 24 hrs

M4 **Pont Abraham**   RoadChef

£ ♦♦ ♿ (•)

M4 J49 · Eastbound and westbound 23 **F10** SN57470743
Costa · Restbite! · WH Smith ⛽ Texaco
🅿 2 hrs ✉ Llanedi, Pontarddulais, SA4 0FU 📞 01792 884 663
🖥 www.roadchef.com
🕐 Forecourt outlets open 24 hrs

● Motorway service area

Restricted motorway junctions

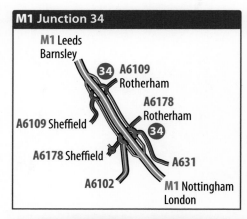

M1 Junction 34

M1 Leeds
Barnsley
34 A6109 Rotherham
A6178 Rotherham
A6109 Sheffield
A6178 Sheffield
34
A631
A6102
M1 Nottingham London

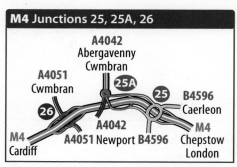

M1 Junctions 6, 6A
M25 Junctions 21, 21A

M1 The North Luton
A405 Hatfield St Albans
6A
21A
M25 (M40, M4) Heathrow
21
M25 (M11, M20) Dartford
6
A405 North Watford
M1 Watford Central London

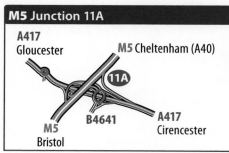

M4 Junctions 25, 25A, 26

A4042 Abergavenny Cwmbran
A4051 Cwmbran
25A
25 B4596 Caerleon
26
M4 Cardiff
A4042
A4051 Newport B4596
M4 Chepstow London

M5 Junction 11A

A417 Gloucester
M5 Cheltenham (A40)
11A
M5 Bristol
B4641
A417 Cirencester

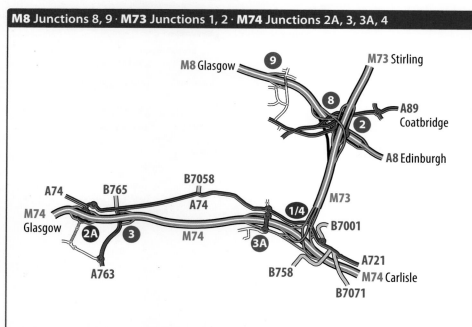

M8 Junctions 8, 9 · M73 Junctions 1, 2 · M74 Junctions 2A, 3, 3A, 4

M8 Glasgow
9
M73 Stirling
8
A89 Coatbridge
2
A8 Edinburgh
A74
B765
B7058
A74
M73
M74 Glasgow
1/4
B7001
2A
3
M74
3A
A721
A763
B758
M74 Carlisle
B7071

M1	Northbound	Southbound
2	No exit	No access
4	No exit	No access
6A	No exit. Access from M25 only	No access. Exit to M25 only
7	No exit. Access from A414 only	No access. Exit to A414 only
17	No access. Exit to M45 only	No exit. Access from M45 only
19	No exit to A14	No access from A14
21A	No access	No exit
23A		Exit to A42 only
24A	No exit	No access
35A	No access	No exit
43	No access. Exit to M621 only	No exit. Access from M621 only
48	No exit to A1(M) southbound	

M3	Eastbound	Westbound
8	No exit	No access
10	No access	No exit
13	No access to M27 eastbound	
14	No exit	No access

M4	Eastbound	Westbound
1	Exit to A4 eastbound only	Access from A4 westbound only
2	Access from A4 eastbound only	Access to A4 westbound only
21	No exit	No access
23	No access	No exit
25	No exit	No access
25A	No exit	No access
29	No exit	No access
38		No access
39	No exit or access	No exit
41	No access	No exit
41A	No access	No access
42	Access from A483 only	Exit to A483 only

M5	Northbound	Southbound
10	No exit	No access
11A	No access from A417 eastbound	No exit to A417 westbound

M6	Northbound	Southbound
3A	No access. Exit to M42 northbound only	No exit. Access from M6 eastbound only
4A	No exit. Access from M42 southbound only	No access. Exit to M42 only
5	No access	No exit
10A	No access. Exit to M54 only	No exit. Access from M54 only
11A	No exit. Access from M6 Toll only	No access. Exit to M6 Toll only
20	No exit to M56 eastbound	No access from M56 westbound
24	No exit	No access
25	No access	No exit
30	No exit. Access from M61 northbound only	No access. Exit to M61 southbound only
31A	No access	No exit
45	No access	No exit

M6 Toll	Northbound	Southbound
T1		No exit
T2	No exit, no access	No access
T5	No exit	No access
T7	No access	No access
T8	No access	No access

M8	Eastbound	Westbound
8	No exit to M73 northbound	No access from M73 southbound
9	No access	No exit
13	No exit southbound	Access from M73 southbound only
14	No access	No exit
16	No exit	No access
17	No exit	No access
18		No exit
19	No exit to A814 eastbound	No access from A814 westbound
20	No exit	No access
21	No access from M74	No exit
22	No exit. Access from M77 only	No access. Exit to M77 only
23	No exit	No access
25	Exit to A739 northbound only. Access from A739 southbound only	Access from A739 southbound only
25A	No exit	No access
28	No exit	No access
28A	No exit	No access

M9	Eastbound	Westbound
1A	No exit	No access
2	No access	No exit
3	No exit	No access
6	No access	No exit
8	No exit	No access

M11	Northbound	Southbound
4	No exit	No access
5	No access	No exit
9	No access	No exit
13	No access	No exit
14	No exit to A428 westbound	No exit. Access from A14 westbound only

M20	Eastbound	Westbound
2	No access	No exit
3	No exit Access from M26 eastbound only	No access Exit to M26 westbound only
11A	No access	No exit

M23	Northbound	Southbound
7	No exit to A23 southbound	No access from A23 northbound
10A	No exit	No access

M25	Clockwise	Anticlockwise
5	No exit to M26 eastbound	No access from M26 westbound
19	No access	No exit
21	No exit to M1 southbound. Access from M1 southbound only	No exit to M1 southbound. Access from M1. southbound only
31	No exit	No access

M27	Eastbound	Westbound
10	No exit	No access
12	No access	No exit

M40	Eastbound	Westbound
3	No exit	No access
7	No exit	No access
8	No exit	No access
13	No exit	No access
14	No access	No exit
16	No access	No exit

M42	Northbound	Southbound
1	No exit	No access
7	No access Exit to M6 northbound only	No exit Access from M6 northbound only
7A	No access. Exit to M6 southbound only	No exit
8	No exit. Access from M6 southbound only	Exit to M6 northbound only. Access from M6 southbound only

M45	Eastbound	Westbound
M1 J17	Access to M1 southbound only	No access from M1 southbound
With A45	No access	No exit

M48	Eastbound	Westbound
M4 J21	No exit to M4 westbound	No access from M4 eastbound
M4 J23	No access from M4 westbound	No exit to M4 eastbound

M49	Southbound	Northbound
18A	No exit to M5 northbound	No access from M5 southbound

M53	Northbound	Southbound
11	Exit to M56 eastbound only. Access from M56 westbound only	Exit to M56 eastbound only. Access from M56 westbound only

M56	Eastbound	Westbound
2	No exit	No access
3	No access	No exit
4	No exit	No access
7		No access
8	No exit or access	No exit
9	No access from M6 northbound	No access to M6 southbound
15	No exit to M53	No access from M53 northbound

M57	Northbound	Southbound
3	No exit	No access
5	No exit	No access

M58	Eastbound	Westbound
1	No exit	No access

M60	Clockwise	Anticlockwise
2	No exit	
3	No exit to A34 northbound	No exit to A34 northbound
4	No access from M56	No exit to M56
5	No exit to A5103 southbound	No exit to A5103 northbound
14	No exit	No access
16	No exit	No access
20	No access	No exit
22		No access
25	No access	
26		No exit or access
27	No exit	No access

M61	Northbound	Southbound
2	No access from A580 eastbound	No exit to A580 westbound
3	No access from A580 eastbound. No access from A666 southbound	No exit to A580 westbound
M6 J30	No exit to M6 southbound	No access from M6 northbound

M62	Eastbound	Westbound
23	No access	No exit

M65	Eastbound	Westbound
9	No access	No exit
11	No exit	No access

M66	Northbound	Southbound
1	No access	No exit

M67	Eastbound	Westbound
1A	No access	No exit
2	No exit	No access

M69	Northbound	Southbound
2	No exit	No access

M73	Northbound	Southbound
2	No access from M8 or A89 eastbound. No exit to A89	No exit to M8 or A89 westbound. No access from A89

M74	Northbound	Southbound
3	No access	No exit
3A	No exit	No access
7	No exit	No access
9	No exit or access	No access
10		No access
11	No exit	No access
12	No access	No exit

M77	Northbound	Southbound
4	No access	No access
6	No exit	No access
7	No exit or access	
8	No access	No access

M80	Northbound	Southbound
4A	No access	No exit
6A	No exit	
8	Exit to M876 northbound only. No access	Access from M876 southbound only. No exit

M90	Northbound	Southbound
2A	No access	No access
7	No exit	No access
8	No exit	No access
10	No access from A912	No exit to A912

M180	Eastbound	Westbound
1	No access	No exit

M621	Eastbound	Westbound
2A	No exit	No access
4	No exit	
5	No exit	No access
6	No access	No exit

M876	Northbound	Southbound
2	No access	No exit

A1(M)	Northbound	Southbound
2	No access	
3		No access
5	No exit	No access
14	No exit	No access
40	No access	No exit
43	No exit. Access from M1 only	No access. Exit to M1 only
57	No access	No exit
65	No access	No exit

A3(M)	Northbound	Southbound
1	No exit	No access
4	No access	No exit

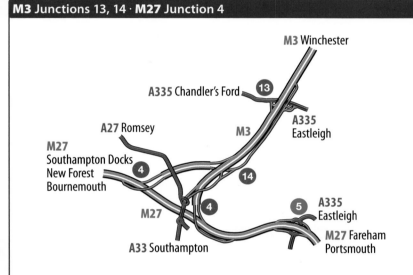

M3 Junctions 13, 14 · M27 Junction 4

A38(M)	Northbound	Southbound
With Victoria Rd, (Park Circus) Birmingham	No exit	No access

A48(M)	Northbound	Southbound
M4 Junc 29	Exit to M4 eastbound only	Access from M4 westbound only
29A	Access from A48 eastbound only	Exit to A48 westbound only

A57(M)	Eastbound	Westbound
With A5103	No access	No exit
With A34	No access	No exit

A58(M)		Southbound
With Park Lane and Westgate, Leeds		No access

A64(M)	Eastbound	Westbound
With A58 Clay Pit Lane, Leeds	No access	No exit
With Regent Street, Leeds	No access	No access

A74(M)	Northbound	Southbound
18	No access	No exit
22		No exit

A194(M)	Northbound	Southbound
A1(M) J65 Gateshead Western Bypass	Access from A1(M) northbound only	Exit to A1(M) southbound only

**M6 Junctions 3A, 4A · M42 Junctions 7, 7A, 8, 9
M6 Toll Junctions T1, T2**

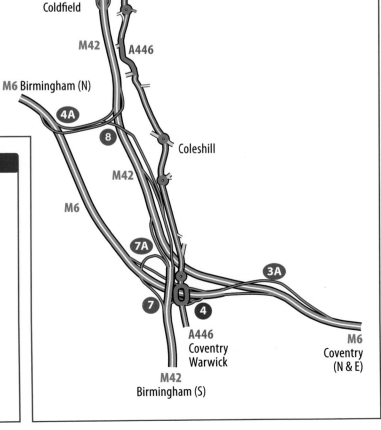

M62 Junctions 32A, 33 · A1(M) Junctions 40, 41

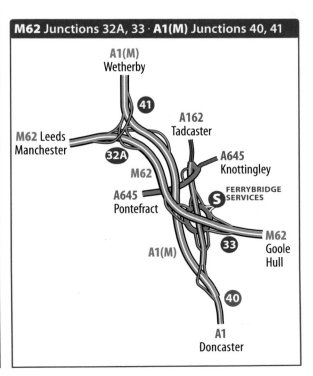

M6 Junction 20 · M56 Junction 4

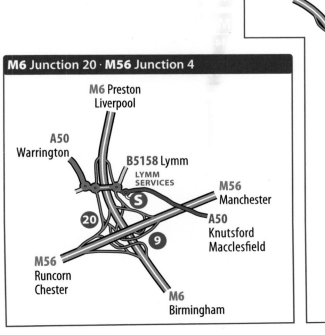

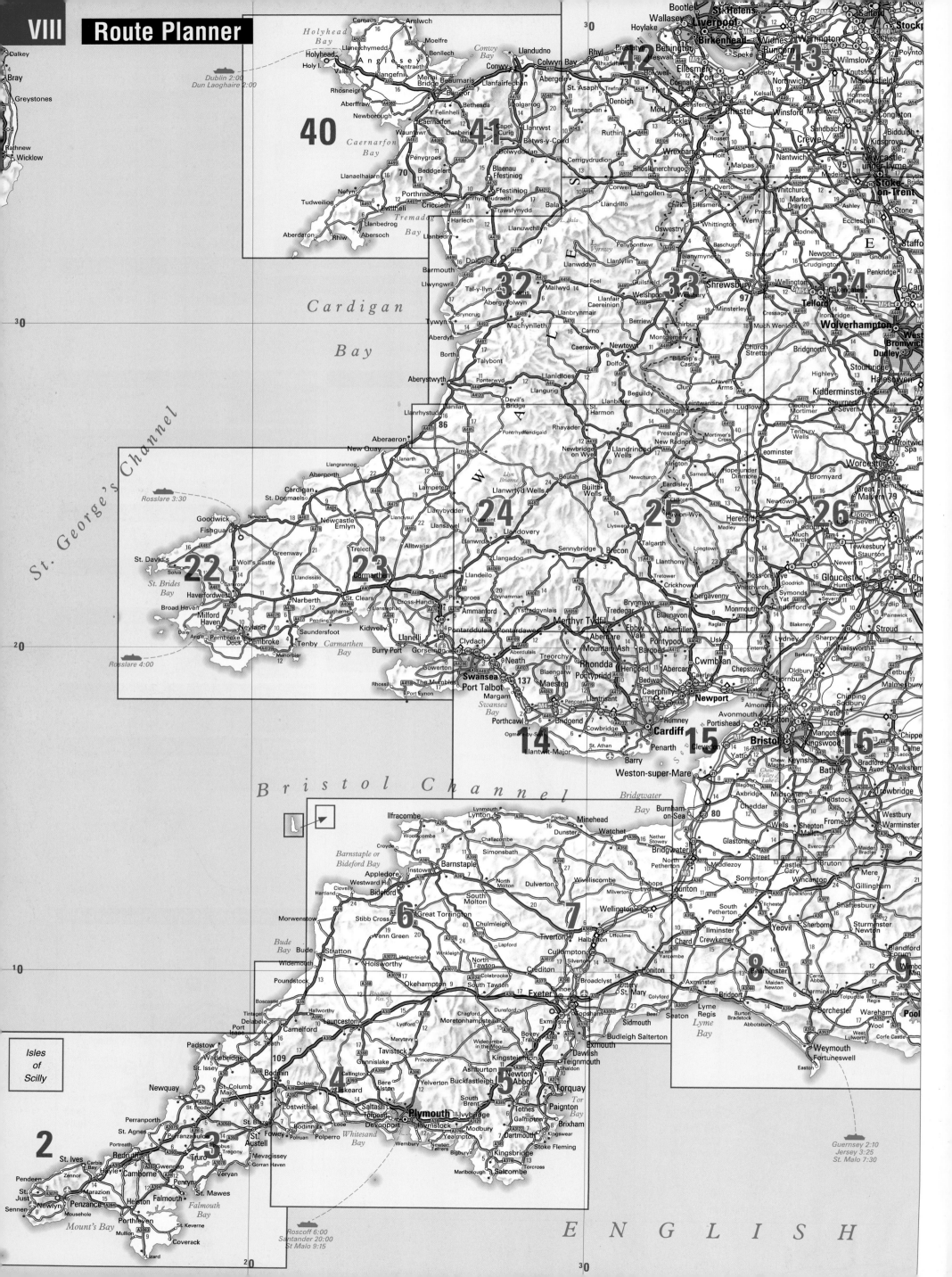

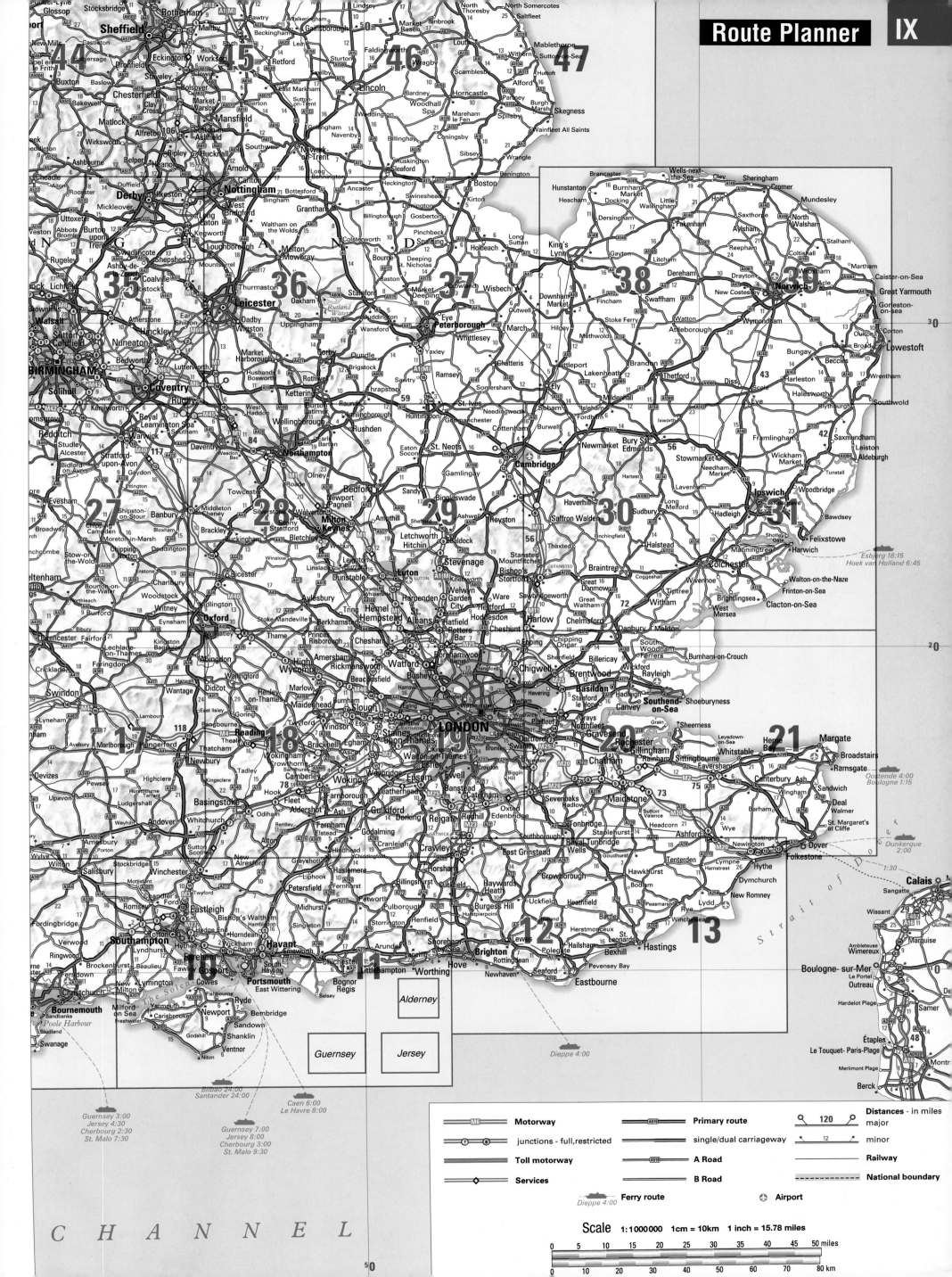

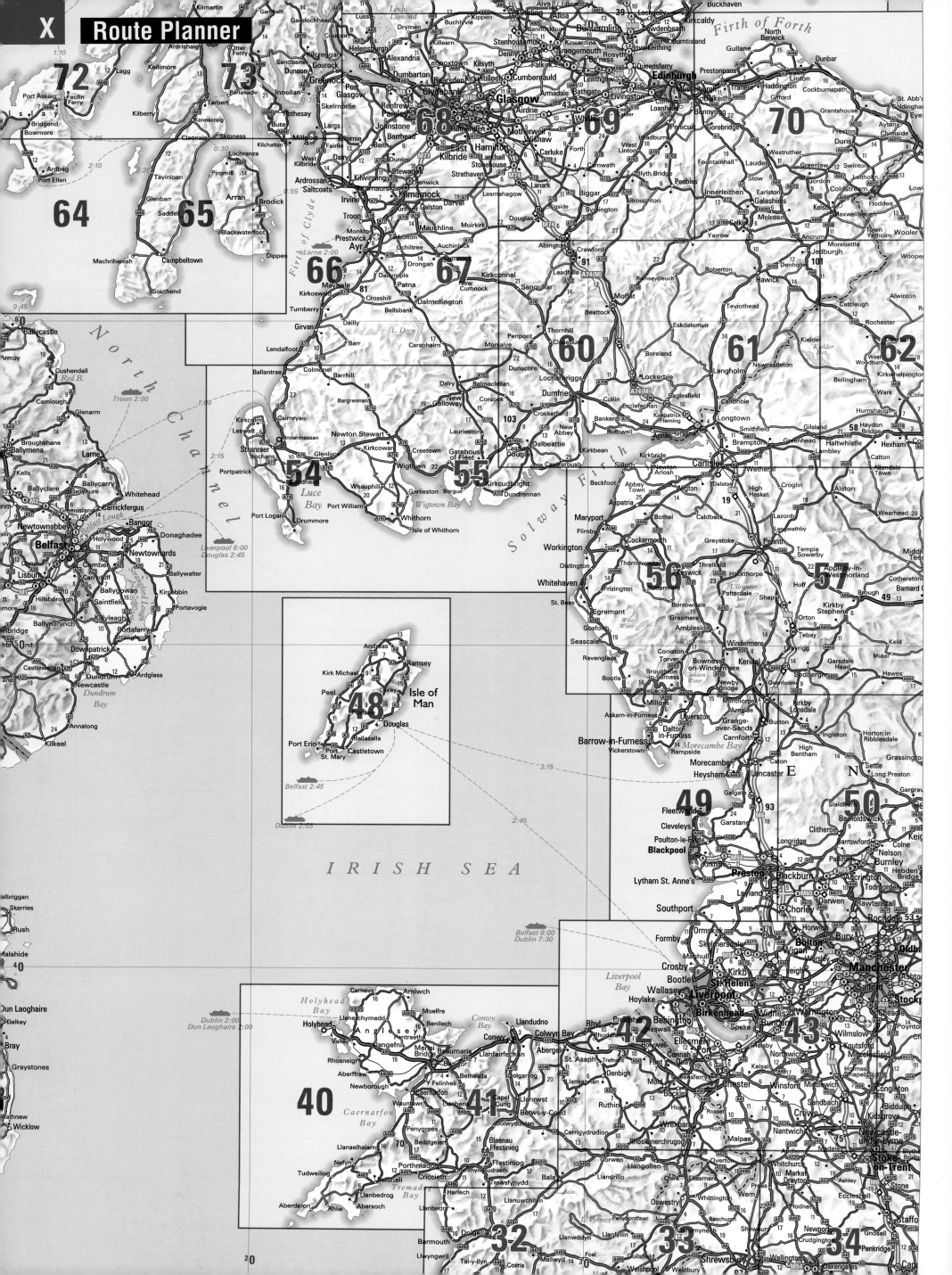

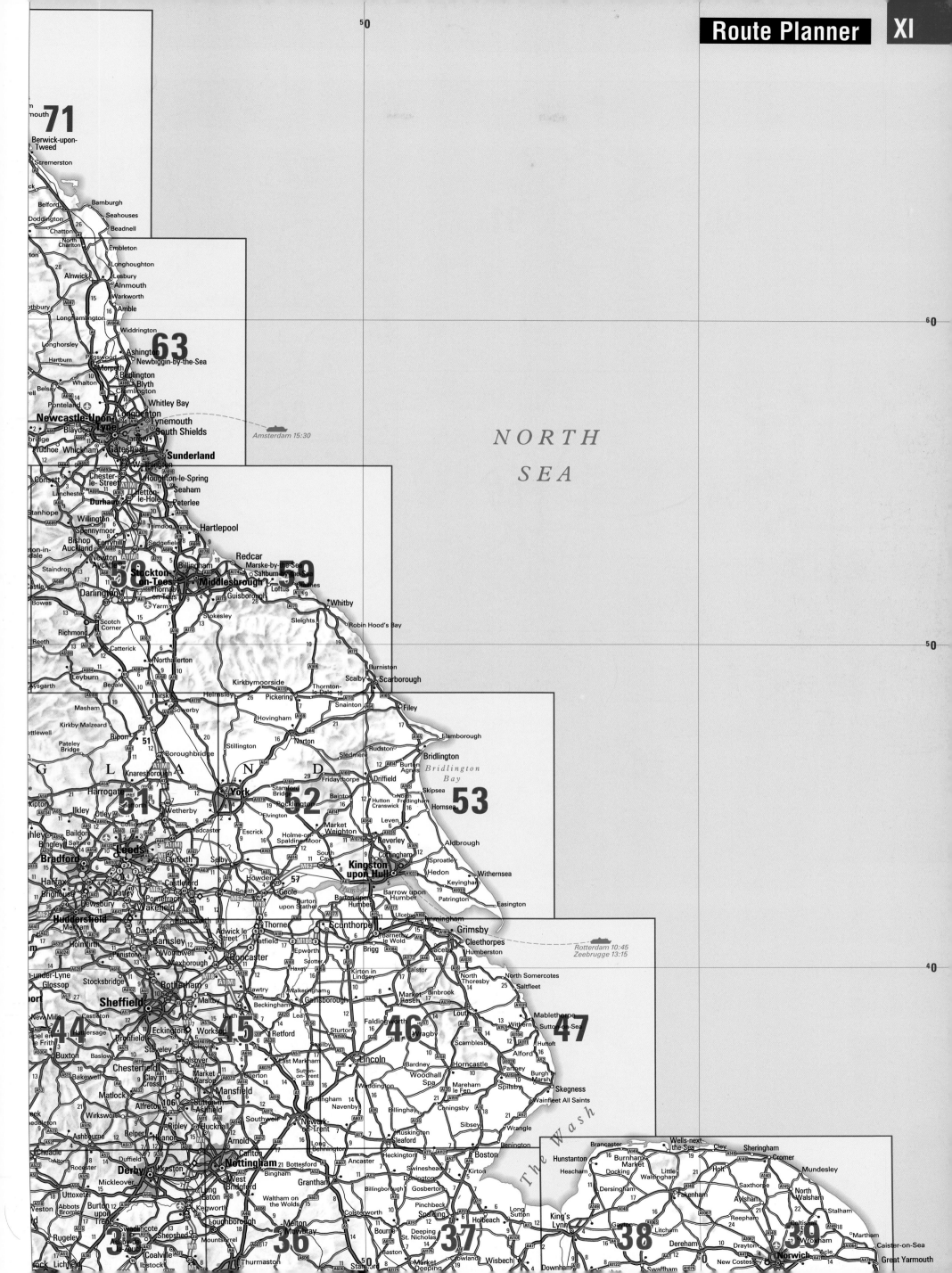

NORTH SEA

Amsterdam 15:30

Rotterdam 10:45
Zeebrugge 13:15

Bridlington Bay

The Wash

71

63

58 59

51 52 53

44 45 46 47

35 36 37 38 39

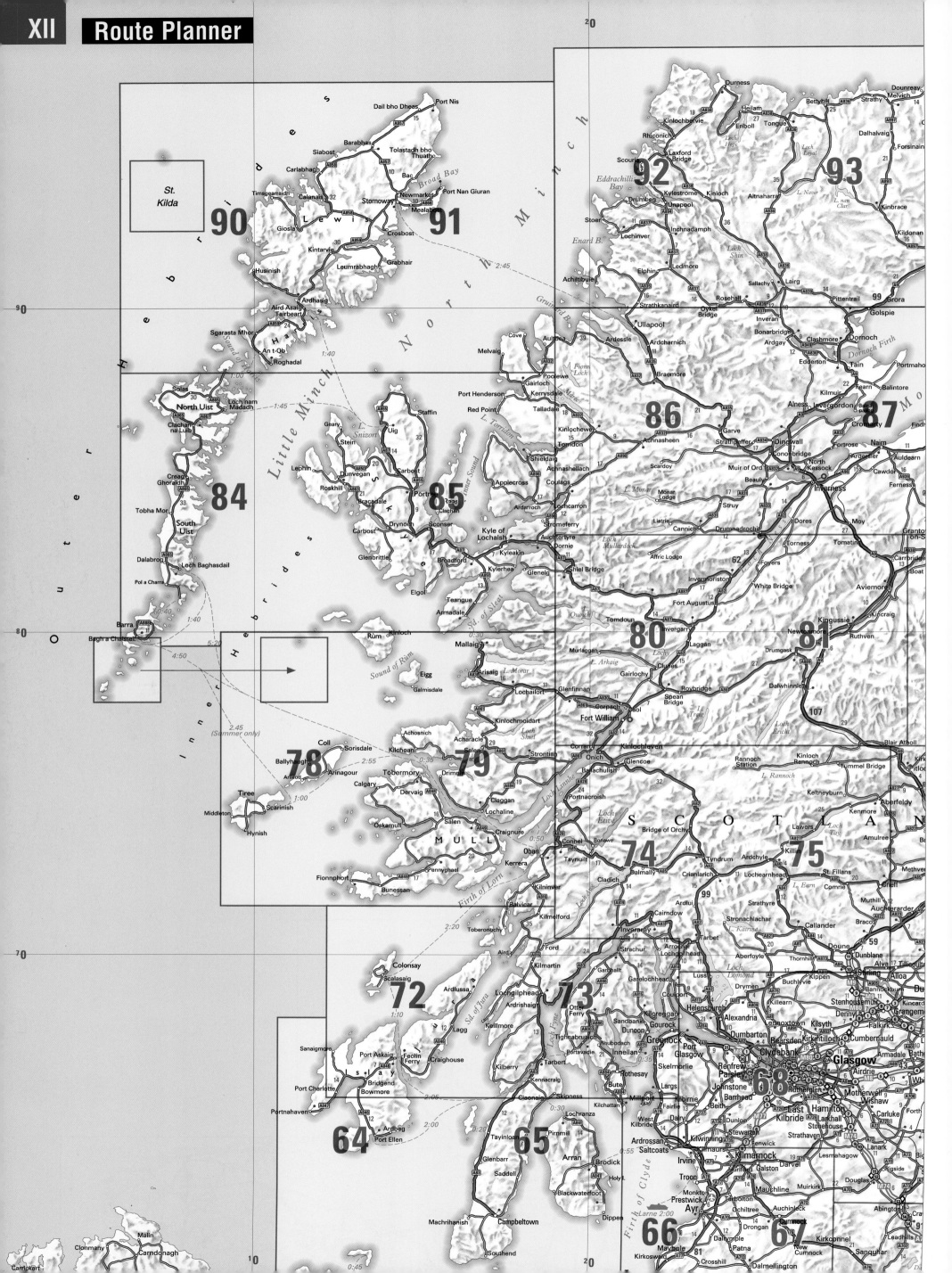

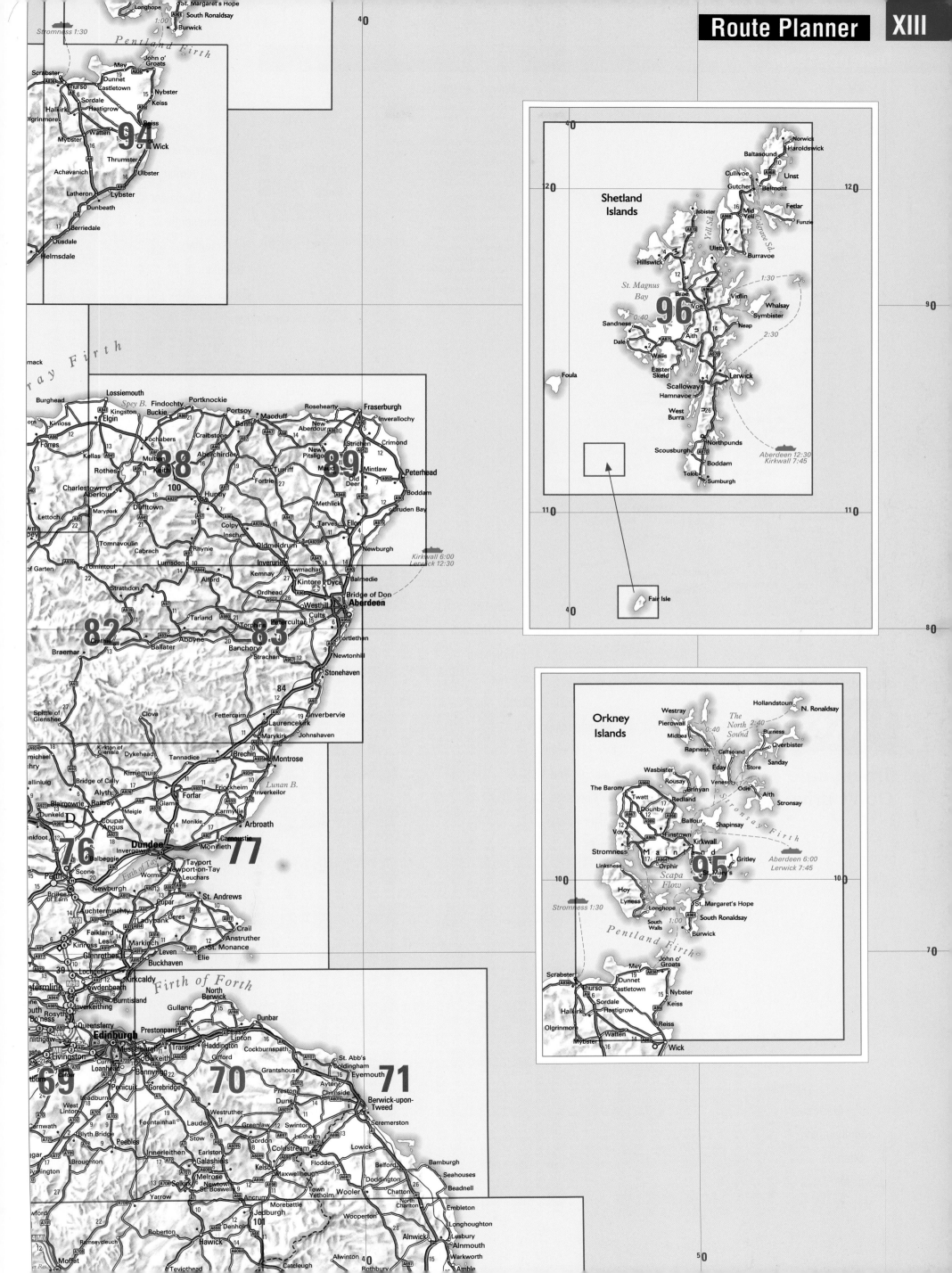

Distance table

How to use this table

Distances are shown in miles and kilometres with estimated journey times in hours and minutes.

For example: the distance between Dover and Fishguard is 331 miles or 533 kilometres with an estimated journey time of 6 hours, 20 minutes.

Estimated driving times are based on an average speed of 60mph on Motorways and 40mph on other roads. Drivers should allow extra time when driving at peak periods or through areas likely to be congested.

Example

	Dover	Dundee	Edinburgh	Exeter	Fishguard
Dover					
Dundee	523 / 842 / 9:10				
Edinburgh	462 / 744 / 8:10	56 / 90 / 1:30			
Exeter	450 / 724 / 8:00	518 / 834 / 9:10	248 / 399 / 4:40		
Fishguard	230 / 370 / 4:30	399 / 642 / 7:30	460 / 740 / 8:30	331 / 533 / 6:20	
Fort William	486 / 782 / 9:30	560 / 901 / 10:20	144 / 232 / 3:30	127 / 204 / 3:10	596 / 959 / 11:00

Map locations

John o' Groats · Kyle of Lochalsh · Inverness · Aberdeen · Braemar · Fort William · Dundee · Oban · Edinburgh · Glasgow · Ayr · Berwick-upon-Tweed · Stranraer · Carlisle · Newcastle upon Tyne · York · Kingston upon Hull · Blackpool · Leeds · Doncaster · Manchester · Liverpool · Sheffield · Lincoln · Holyhead · Nottingham · Norwich · Great Yarmouth · Shrewsbury · Leicester · Aberystwyth · Birmingham · Cambridge · Fishguard · Gloucester · Oxford · Harwich · Swansea · Cardiff · Bristol · London · Exeter · Bournemouth · Southampton · Brighton · Portsmouth · Plymouth · Dover · Land's End

Distance table (miles / kilometres / hours:minutes)

Columns in each row read right-to-left starting from London, then Aberdeen, Aberystwyth, Ayr, Berwick-upon-Tweed, Birmingham, … in the order of the diagonal city list.

Aberdeen — London: 517 / 832 / 11:20

Aberystwyth — Aberdeen: 445 / 716 / 8:40 · London: 211 / 340 / 4:40

Ayr — Aberystwyth: 317 / 510 / 6:10 · Aberdeen: 183 / 295 / 4:40 · London: 394 / 634 / 7:20

Berwick-upon-Tweed — Ayr: 134 / 216 / 4:40 · Aberystwyth: 311 / 501 / 7:30 · Aberdeen: 182 / 293 / 2:50 · London: 352 / 567 / 7:30

Birmingham — Berwick: 274 / 441 / 5:30 · Ayr: 289 / 465 / 5:30 · Aberystwyth: 114 / 183 / 2:50 · Aberdeen: 420 / 676 / 8:30 · London: 117 / 188 / 2:50

Blackpool — Birmingham: 123 / 198 / 3:50 · Berwick: 181 / 291 / 3:50 · Ayr: 153 / 290 / 3:20 · Aberystwyth: 148 / 238 / 3:50 · Aberdeen: 308 / 493 / 6:40 · London: 226 / 365 / 5:30

Bournemouth — Blackpool: 270 / 435 / 5:00 · Birmingham: 147 / 237 / 3:10 · Berwick: 412 / 663 / 7:50 · Ayr: 436 / 702 / 8:40 · Aberystwyth: 207 / 333 / 4:20 · Aberdeen: 564 / 908 / 10:40 · London: 107 / 172 / 2:40

Braemar — Bournemouth: 524 / 843 / 9:30 · Blackpool: 281 / 452 / 5:10 · Birmingham: 385 / 620 / 7:10 · Berwick: 148 / 238 / 3:20 · Ayr: 143 / 230 / 3:50 · Aberystwyth: 405 / 652 / 9:50 · Aberdeen: 59 / 95 / 1:50 · London: 482 / 775 / 7:50

Brighton — Braemar: 534 / 859 / 9:40 · Bournemouth: 92 / 148 / 2:10 · Blackpool: 286 / 460 / 5:20 · Birmingham: 163 / 262 / 3:20 · Berwick: 409 / 658 / 7:40 · Ayr: 446 / 718 / 8:00 · Aberystwyth: 253 / 407 / 4:30 · Aberdeen: 573 / 922 / 10:30 · London: 52 / 84 / 1:50

Bristol — Brighton: 147 / 237 / 4:10 · Braemar: 477 / 768 / 8:40 · Bournemouth: 82 / 132 / 2:30 · Blackpool: 204 / 328 / 3:40 · Birmingham: 81 / 130 / 2:40 · Berwick: 362 / 583 / 6:40 · Ayr: 370 / 595 / 5:00 · Aberystwyth: 125 / 201 / 3:40 · Aberdeen: 493 / 793 / 9:40 · London: 122 / 196 / 2:50

Cambridge — Bristol: 169 / 272 / 3:10 · Brighton: 116 / 187 / 2:20 · Braemar: 438 / 705 / 7:50 · Bournemouth: 154 / 248 / 3:00 · Blackpool: 208 / 335 / 3:50 · Birmingham: 100 / 161 / 2:10 · Berwick: 306 / 492 / 5:40 · Ayr: 357 / 575 / 6:20 · Aberystwyth: 214 / 344 / 4:00 · Aberdeen: 471 / 758 / 8:10 · London: 54 / 87 / 1:30

Cardiff — Cambridge: 190 / 306 / 3:30 · Bristol: 45 / 72 / 1:20 · Brighton: 182 / 293 / 4:00 · Braemar: 468 / 778 / 8:00 · Bournemouth: 117 / 188 / 3:00 · Blackpool: 209 / 336 / 3:50 · Birmingham: 103 / 166 / 2:40 · Berwick: 368 / 592 / 6:40 · Ayr: 382 / 615 / 5:00 · Aberystwyth: 105 / 169 / 4:30 · Aberdeen: 505 / 813 / 10:00 · London: 155 / 253 / 3:30

Carlisle — Cardiff: 289 / 465 / 5:20 · Cambridge: 264 / 425 / 4:40 · Bristol: 277 / 446 / 5:00 · Brighton: 370 / 596 / 6:40 · Braemar: 196 / 316 / 3:50 · Bournemouth: 343 / 552 / 6:20 · Blackpool: 87 / 140 / 1:50 · Birmingham: 196 / 315 / 3:50 · Berwick: 87 / 150 / 2:10 · Ayr: 93 / 150 / 2:10 · Aberystwyth: 224 / 360 / 4:30 · Aberdeen: 221 / 356 / 4:30 · London: 301 / 484 / 5:40

Doncaster — Carlisle: 142 / 229 / 3:00 · Cardiff: 209 / 336 / 4:10 · Cambridge: 116 / 187 / 2:10 · Bristol: 175 / 282 / 3:20 · Brighton: 236 / 380 / 4:10 · Braemar: 310 / 499 / 5:50 · Bournemouth: 235 / 378 / 4:40 · Blackpool: 94 / 151 / 2:00 · Birmingham: 84 / 151 / 2:00 · Berwick: 184 / 296 / 3:50 · Ayr: 235 / 378 / 4:20 · Aberystwyth: 176 / 283 / 4:00 · Aberdeen: 344 / 554 / 6:50 · London: 171 / 275 / 3:30

Dover — Doncaster: 242 / 390 / 4:30 · Carlisle: 389 / 626 / 7:00 · Cardiff: 238 / 383 / 4:30 · Cambridge: 125 / 201 / 2:30 · Bristol: 202 / 325 / 3:50 · Brighton: 82 / 132 / 2:20 · Braemar: 553 / 890 / 9:50 · Bournemouth: 174 / 280 / 4:30 · Blackpool: 312 / 502 / 5:40 · Birmingham: 194 / 312 / 3:50 · Berwick: 424 / 683 / 7:50 · Ayr: 478 / 769 / 8:30 · Aberystwyth: 297 / 478 / 7:10 · Aberdeen: 588 / 947 / 10:40 · London: 71 / 114 / 2:00

Dundee — Dover: 523 / 842 / 9:10 · Doncaster: 275 / 443 / 5:00 · Carlisle: 152 / 245 / 4:00 · Cardiff: 441 / 710 / 8:20 · Cambridge: 406 / 654 / 6:50 · Bristol: 430 / 692 / 6:20 · Brighton: 517 / 832 / 10:20 · Braemar: 52 / 84 / 1:40 · Bournemouth: 495 / 797 / 8:50 · Blackpool: 239 / 385 / 5:30 · Birmingham: 349 / 562 / 6:20 · Berwick: 117 / 182 / 2:40 · Ayr: 111 / 188 / 2:40 · Aberystwyth: 376 / 605 / 9:20 · Aberdeen: 67 / 108 / 1:40 · London: 448 / 721 / 7:50

Edinburgh — Dundee: 56 / 90 / 1:30 · Dover: 462 / 842 / 8:10 · Doncaster: 219 / 443 / 4:00 · Carlisle: 96 / 245 / 2:00 · Cardiff: 385 / 710 / 7:00 · Cambridge: 345 / 654 / 6:10 · Bristol: 373 / 692 / 6:50 · Brighton: 456 / 832 / 9:20 · Braemar: 91 / 84 / 2:10 · Bournemouth: 439 / 797 / 8:00 · Blackpool: 183 / 385 / 5:30 · Birmingham: 292 / 562 / 5:30 · Berwick: 57 / 182 / 1:40 · Ayr: 73 / 188 / 1:50 · Aberystwyth: 320 / 605 / 7:20 · Aberdeen: 125 / 108 / 3:10 · London: 390 / 628 / 7:20

Exeter — Edinburgh: 450 / 724 / 8:00 · Dundee: 518 / 834 / 9:10 · Dover: 248 / 399 / 4:40 · Doncaster: 251 / 404 / 4:40 · Carlisle: 353 / 568 / 5:40 · Cardiff: 121 / 195 / 4:00 · Cambridge: 249 / 401 / 4:20 · Bristol: 76 / 122 / 2:10 · Brighton: 184 / 296 / 4:10 · Braemar: 550 / 885 / 9:40 · Bournemouth: 82 / 132 / 2:20 · Blackpool: 282 / 454 / 5:10 · Birmingham: 157 / 253 / 3:50 · Berwick: 428 / 689 / 7:50 · Ayr: 446 / 718 / 7:50 · Aberystwyth: 201 / 323 / 4:20 · Aberdeen: 569 / 916 / 9:40 · London: 181 / 291 / 3:10

Fishguard — Exeter: 230 / 370 / 4:30 · Edinburgh: 399 / 642 / 7:30 · Dundee: 460 / 740 / 8:30 · Dover: 331 / 533 / 6:20 · Doncaster: 247 / 398 / 4:50 · Carlisle: 297 / 478 / 6:00 · Cardiff: 112 / 180 / 4:00 · Cambridge: 270 / 435 / 5:40 · Bristol: 154 / 248 / 3:40 · Brighton: 291 / 468 / 5:40 · Braemar: 493 / 794 / 9:10 · Bournemouth: 222 / 357 / 4:40 · Blackpool: 209 / 336 / 4:40 · Birmingham: 170 / 270 / 3:40 · Berwick: 371 / 597 / 7:20 · Ayr: 373 / 600 / 7:20 · Aberystwyth: 56 / 90 / 1:30 · Aberdeen: 504 / 811 / 10:10 · London: 260 / 418 / 5:20

Fort William — Fishguard: 486 / 782 / 9:30 · Exeter: 560 / 901 / 10:20 · Edinburgh: 144 / 232 / 3:30 · Dundee: 127 / 204 / 3:10 · Dover: 596 / 959 / 11:00 · Doncaster: 353 / 575 / 6:40 · Carlisle: 206 / 332 / 4:50 · Cardiff: 485 / 781 / 9:50 · Cambridge: 479 / 771 / 8:40 · Bristol: 466 / 782 / 8:00 · Brighton: 542 / 926 / 10:20 · Braemar: 125 / 201 / 2:40 · Bournemouth: 549 / 867 / 9:20 · Blackpool: 296 / 476 / 6:30 · Birmingham: 392 / 631 / 7:40 · Berwick: 187 / 306 / 4:10 · Ayr: 133 / 214 / 3:00 · Aberystwyth: 438 / 692 / 10:30 · Aberdeen: 149 / 240 / 3:10 · London: 510 / 821 / 10:40

Glasgow — Fort William: 101 / 163 / 2:50 · Fishguard: 376 / 605 / 7:10 · Exeter: 449 / 723 / 8:00 · Edinburgh: 96 / 219 / 1:20 · Dundee: 83 / 384 / 2:00 · Dover: 488 / 786 / 8:40 · Doncaster: 249 / 401 / 6:10 · Carlisle: 96 / 154 / 2:10 · Cardiff: 385 / 620 / 7:00 · Cambridge: 372 / 599 / 6:50 · Bristol: 373 / 600 / 6:30 · Brighton: 468 / 753 / 8:30 · Braemar: 110 / 177 / 2:30 · Bournemouth: 439 / 707 / 8:00 · Blackpool: 183 / 295 / 3:40 · Birmingham: 292 / 470 / 5:50 · Berwick: 101 / 163 / 2:40 · Ayr: 33 / 53 / 1:10 · Aberystwyth: 320 / 515 / 7:20 · Aberdeen: 145 / 233 / 3:30 · London: 397 / 639 / 7:30

Gloucester — Glasgow: 346 / 557 / 6:10 · Fort William: 454 / 731 / 8:30 · Fishguard: 153 / 246 / 3:10 · Exeter: 111 / 179 / 2:00 · Edinburgh: 149 / 562 / 6:10 · Dundee: 247 / 660 / 7:10 · Dover: 56 / 307 / 2:00 · Doncaster: 123 / 241 / 3:30 · Carlisle: 35 / 398 / 6:10 · Cardiff: 159 / 90 / 2:30 · Cambridge: 443 / 198 / 2:50 · Bristol: 99 / 56 / 1:50 · Brighton: 150 / 256 / 3:40 · Braemar: 318 / 713 / 6:30 · Bournemouth: 330 / 159 / 2:40 · Blackpool: 187 / 280 / 3:40 · Birmingham: 90 / 90 / 2:20 · Berwick: 317 / 512 / 6:40 · Ayr: 326 / 531 / 5:00 · Aberystwyth: 164 / 164 / 4:10 · Aberdeen: 446 / 753 / 9:20 · London: 109 / 175 / 2:40

Great Yarmouth — Gloucester: 225 / 362 / 4:40 · Glasgow: 419 / 674 / 8:00 · Fort William: 527 / 848 / 10:20 · Fishguard: 366 / 589 / 7:20 · Exeter: 335 / 539 / 6:30 · Edinburgh: 386 / 621 / 6:30 · Dundee: 484 / 779 / 9:00 · Dover: 185 / 298 / 3:40 · Doncaster: 167 / 269 / 3:40 · Carlisle: 320 / 515 / 5:50 · Cardiff: 284 / 457 / 5:10 · Cambridge: 82 / 132 / 4:10 · Bristol: 275 / 443 / 3:50 · Brighton: 180 / 290 / 4:10 · Braemar: 477 / 768 / 9:00 · Bournemouth: 240 / 386 / 4:40 · Blackpool: 252 / 406 / 5:10 · Birmingham: 180 / 290 / 4:10 · Berwick: 345 / 555 / 7:40 · Ayr: 402 / 647 / 6:20 · Aberystwyth: 294 / 473 / 5:00 · Aberdeen: 517 / 832 / 3:40 · London: 128 / 206 / 3:40

Harwich — Great Yarmouth: 82 / 132 / 2:10 · Gloucester: 196 / 316 / 4:00 · Glasgow: 432 / 695 / 8:10 · Fort William: 543 / 874 / 10:40 · Fishguard: 337 / 542 / 6:20 · Exeter: 279 / 449 / 4:40 · Edinburgh: 413 / 665 / 8:40 · Dundee: 469 / 755 / 9:10 · Dover: 125 / 201 / 2:50 · Doncaster: 194 / 312 / 3:40 · Carlisle: 388 / 541 / 6:40 · Cardiff: 187 / 396 / 4:20 · Cambridge: 67 / 108 / 2:30 · Bristol: 167 / 349 / 3:40 · Brighton: 122 / 206 / 3:20 · Braemar: 372 / 811 / 6:20 · Bournemouth: 185 / 301 / 4:30 · Blackpool: 281 / 443 / 5:10 · Birmingham: 167 / 269 / 3:40 · Berwick: 372 / 599 / 7:40 · Ayr: 425 / 684 / 6:20 · Aberystwyth: 269 / 452 / 5:10 · Aberdeen: 535 / 861 / 3:40 · London: 76 / 122 / 2:10

Holyhead — Harwich: 349 / 562 / 7:10 · Great Yarmouth: 334 / 538 / 7:00 · Gloucester: 191 / 307 / 4:00 · Glasgow: 330 / 531 / 6:40 · Fort William: 438 / 705 / 8:50 · Fishguard: 167 / 269 / 4:00 · Exeter: 282 / 454 / 5:40 · Edinburgh: 333 / 536 / 5:40 · Dundee: 394 / 634 / 6:40 · Dover: 360 / 580 / 7:30 · Doncaster: 181 / 297 / 3:50 · Carlisle: 231 / 348 / 4:30 · Cardiff: 216 / 435 / 4:50 · Cambridge: 270 / 332 / 3:50 · Bristol: 206 / 538 / 6:40 · Brighton: 334 / 686 / 6:10 · Braemar: 426 / 463 / 4:00 · Bournemouth: 288 / 227 / 2:30 · Blackpool: 141 / 238 / 3:50 · Birmingham: 148 / 501 / 3:10 · Berwick: 311 / 491 / 6:10 · Ayr: 305 / 179 / 2:40 · Aberystwyth: 111 / 707 / 4:00 · Aberdeen: 439 / 433 / 8:40 · London: 269 / 433 / 5:40

Inverness — Holyhead: 474 / 763 / 9:40 · Harwich: 569 / 916 / 11:00 · Great Yarmouth: 553 / 890 / 10:10 · Gloucester: 504 / 811 / 9:00 · Glasgow: 166 / 267 / 3:10 · Fort William: 66 / 106 / 1:40 · Fishguard: 542 / 872 / 10:30 · Exeter: 618 / 995 / 11:20 · Edinburgh: 158 / 254 / 3:50 · Dundee: 132 / 212 / 3:30 · Dover: 549 / 1001 / 10:40 · Doncaster: 348 / 617 / 6:20 · Carlisle: 215 / 422 / 5:00 · Cardiff: 199 / 884 / 10:30 · Cambridge: 148 / 813 / 11:30 · Bristol: 550 / 867 / 3:50 · Brighton: 617 / 993 / 3:30 · Braemar: 75 / 121 / 2:00 · Bournemouth: 961 / 961 / 3:40 · Blackpool: 215 / 560 / 6:20 · Birmingham: 437 / 737 / 7:50 · Berwick: 199 / 346 / 4:40 · Ayr: 169 / 320 / 3:50 · Aberystwyth: 485 / 782 / 11:30 · Aberdeen: 105 / 169 / 2:30 · London: 550 / 885 / 9:40

John o' Groats — Inverness: 129 / 208 / 3:20 · Holyhead: 603 / 970 / 12:40 · Harwich: 693 / 1116 / 14:00 · Great Yarmouth: 677 / 1090 / 14:00 · Gloucester: 628 / 1011 / 12:30 · Glasgow: 295 / 314 / 7:10 · Fort William: 195 / 1080 / 3:50 · Fishguard: 671 / 1197 / 13:40 · Exeter: 744 / 459 / 14:30 · Edinburgh: 285 / 417 / 7:10 · Dundee: 259 / 1201 / 6:30 · Dover: 746 / 816 / 14:30 · Doncaster: 507 / 629 / 10:00 · Carlisle: 391 / 1094 / 8:10 · Cardiff: 680 / 1014 / 10:00 · Cambridge: 630 / 1075 / 12:00 · Bristol: 668 / 1193 / 3:40 · Brighton: 741 / 325 / 3:50 · Braemar: 202 / 1165 / 4:40 · Bournemouth: 724 / 769 / 10:00 · Blackpool: 478 / 924 / 11:20 · Birmingham: 574 / 550 / 7:10 · Berwick: 342 / 787 / 8:10 · Ayr: 328 / 346 / 7:40 · Aberystwyth: 601 / 967 / 12:40 · Aberdeen: 232 / 373 / 5:10 · London: 663 / 1067 / 13:30

Kingston upon Hull — John o' Groats: 518 / 834 / 10:50 · Inverness: 394 / 634 / 7:50 · Holyhead: 231 / 372 / 4:50 · Harwich: 196 / 316 / 4:10 · Great Yarmouth: 207 / 333 / 5:20 · Gloucester: 169 / 272 / 4:00 · Glasgow: 254 / 409 / 5:50 · Fort William: 369 / 594 / 7:20 · Fishguard: 309 / 451 / 5:30 · Exeter: 282 / 497 / 5:40 · Edinburgh: 201 / 377 / 4:00 · Dundee: 295 / 475 / 6:10 · Dover: 249 / 296 / 4:10 · Doncaster: 46 / 67 / 1:30 · Carlisle: 154 / 254 / 3:50 · Cardiff: 233 / 393 / 4:40 · Cambridge: 245 / 224 / 3:40 · Bristol: 237 / 394 / 3:50 · Brighton: 307 / 526 / 4:20 · Braemar: 264 / 425 / 6:40 · Bournemouth: 207 / 359 / 4:30 · Blackpool: 124 / 216 / 2:40 · Birmingham: 130 / 298 / 3:20 · Berwick: 224 / 404 / 4:30 · Ayr: 184 / 359 / 4:10 · Aberystwyth: 238 / 586 / 5:40 · Aberdeen: 184 / 296 / 3:50 · London: 184 / 296 / 3:20

Kyle of Lochalsh — Kingston upon Hull: 445 / 716 / 9:00 · John o' Groats: 189 / 304 / 4:40 · Inverness: 84 / 135 / 2:10 · Holyhead: 514 / 827 / 10:40 · Harwich: 611 / 983 / 12:10 · Great Yarmouth: 602 / 969 / 10:20 · Gloucester: 528 / 850 / 10:00 · Glasgow: 179 / 288 / 4:40 · Fort William: 67 / 127 / 2:00 · Fishguard: 567 / 913 / 11:30 · Exeter: 628 / 1011 / 12:00 · Edinburgh: 216 / 348 / 5:00 · Dundee: 186 / 299 / 4:30 · Dover: 671 / 1080 / 12:00 · Doncaster: 432 / 695 / 7:20 · Carlisle: 270 / 443 / 5:10 · Cardiff: 564 / 908 / 11:10 · Cambridge: 555 / 893 / 8:30 · Bristol: 552 / 888 / 3:50 · Brighton: 651 / 1048 / 3:40 · Braemar: 159 / 256 / 3:30 · Bournemouth: 618 / 995 / 9:40 · Blackpool: 372 / 599 / 6:20 · Birmingham: 471 / 758 / 5:10 · Berwick: 263 / 423 / 4:20 · Ayr: 212 / 341 / 5:10 · Aberystwyth: 499 / 803 / 10:40 · Aberdeen: 189 / 304 / 3:00 · London: 586 / 943 / 11:40

Land's End — Kyle of Lochalsh: 763 / 1228 / 15:10 · Kingston upon Hull: 421 / 678 / 7:50 · John o' Groats: 868 / 1397 / 17:40 · Inverness: 741 / 1193 / 14:20 · Holyhead: 405 / 652 / 8:30 · Harwich: 390 / 628 / 9:10 · Great Yarmouth: 446 / 718 / 9:00 · Gloucester: 235 / 378 / 4:40 · Glasgow: 573 / 922 / 6:20 · Fort William: 686 / 1104 / 13:20 · Fishguard: 353 / 568 / 7:20 · Exeter: 121 / 198 / 12:00 · Edinburgh: 524 / 924 / 12:00 · Dundee: 374 / 1033 / 7:40 · Dover: 347 / 613 / 12:30 · Doncaster: 602 / 602 / 10:00 · Carlisle: 768 / 768 / 7:50 · Cardiff: 394 / 394 / 12:30 · Cambridge: 352 / 602 / 7:20 · Bristol: 200 / 652 / 4:30 · Brighton: 308 / 888 / 6:50 · Braemar: 281 / 330 / 5:10 · Bournemouth: 532 / 652 / 8:00 · Blackpool: 447 / 917 / 10:40 · Birmingham: 471 / 504 / 6:50 · Berwick: 263 / 758 / 3:10 · Ayr: 212 / 1114 / 13:40 · Aberystwyth: 499 / 478 / 13:40 · Aberdeen: 189 / 478 / 13:40 · London: 304 / 943 / 7:50

Leeds — Land's End: 405 / 652 / 8:00 · Kyle of Lochalsh: 394 / 634 / 8:40 · Kingston upon Hull: 55 / 89 / 1:30 · John o' Groats: 487 / 784 / 10:20 · Inverness: 360 / 579 / 7:10 · Holyhead: 176 / 283 / 3:50 · Harwich: 223 / 359 / 4:10 · Great Yarmouth: 196 / 280 / 3:20 · Gloucester: 174 / 346 / 4:10 · Glasgow: 215 / 381 / 6:40 · Fort William: 329 / 435 / 4:00 · Fishguard: 237 / 325 / 3:20 · Exeter: 270 / 415 / 3:50 · Edinburgh: 202 / 418 / 2:30 · Dundee: 258 / 419 / 3:30 · Dover: 145 / 472 / 2:30 · Doncaster: 194 / 410 / 1:40 · Carlisle: 293 / 116 / 2:30 · Cardiff: 255 / 182 / 3:40 · Cambridge: 72 / 251 / 3:40 · Bristol: 113 / 341 / 2:00 · Brighton: 212 / 272 / 4:30 · Braemar: 169 / 526 / 3:50 · Bournemouth: 327 / 526 / 3:50 · Blackpool: 189 / 304 / 3:50 · Birmingham: 184 / 296 / 3:50 · Berwick: 161 / 296 / 3:50 · Ayr: 212 / 341 / 3:40 · Aberystwyth: 204 / 359 / 3:50 · Aberdeen: 150 / 243 / 3:00 · London: 189 / 304 / 3:50

Leicester — Leeds: 95 / 153 / 2:00 · Land's End: 320 / 515 / 6:30 · Kyle of Lochalsh: 500 / 805 / 9:50 · Kingston upon Hull: 102 / 164 / 2:10 · John o' Groats: 588 / 947 / 11:50 · Inverness: 461 / 742 / 8:50 · Holyhead: 190 / 306 / 4:00 · Harwich: 147 / 197 / 3:10 · Great Yarmouth: 140 / 137 / 3:20 · Gloucester: 85 / 505 / 2:10 · Glasgow: 323 / 679 / 5:40 · Fort William: 437 / 196 / 4:00 · Fishguard: 196 / 315 / 4:00 · Exeter: 196 / 476 / 4:40 · Edinburgh: 349 / 298 / 2:40 · Dundee: 185 / 119 / 3:40 · Dover: 105 / 332 / 3:20 · Doncaster: 165 / 248 / 2:20 · Carlisle: 225 / 109 / 4:30 · Cardiff: 185 / 193 / 3:20 · Cambridge: 49 / 267 / 1:50 · Bristol: 99 / 264 / 2:40 · Brighton: 172 / 225 / 3:50 · Braemar: 161 / 63 / 3:40 · Bournemouth: 406 / 406 / 3:50 · Blackpool: 481 / 481 / 3:50 · Birmingham: 246 / 246 / 2:50 · Berwick: 666 / 666 / 3:40 · Ayr: 97 / 156 / 2:20 · London: 97 / 156 / 2:20

Lincoln — Leicester: 51 / 82 / 1:20 · Leeds: 68 / 109 / 2:00 · Land's End: 371 / 597 / 7:40 · Kyle of Lochalsh: 476 / 766 / 9:40 · Kingston upon Hull: 44 / 71 / 1:10 · John o' Groats: 554 / 892 / 8:30 · Inverness: 427 / 687 / 8:40 · Holyhead: 216 / 348 / 4:00 · Harwich: 155 / 249 / 3:20 · Great Yarmouth: 128 / 206 / 2:40 · Gloucester: 159 / 468 / 4:50 · Glasgow: 399 / 642 / 7:50 · Fort William: 272 / 438 / 5:30 · Fishguard: 247 / 398 / 4:40 · Exeter: 258 / 415 / 4:40 · Edinburgh: 314 / 505 / 6:00 · Dundee: 39 / 325 / 1:40 · Dover: 150 / 63 / 3:40 · Doncaster: 208 / 40 / 2:40 · Carlisle: 85 / 137 / 4:40 · Cardiff: 183 / 295 / 4:40 · Cambridge: 197 / 317 / 2:40 · Bristol: 357 / 575 / 4:40 · Brighton: 209 / 336 / 5:10 · Braemar: 90 / 206 / 3:40 · Bournemouth: 224 / 145 / 3:40 · Blackpool: 274 / 360 / 4:40 · Birmingham: 199 / 320 / 4:40 · Berwick: 383 / 616 / 3:40 · Ayr: 131 / 211 / 3:10 · London: 131 / 211 / 3:10

Liverpool — Lincoln: 129 / 208 / 3:20 · Leicester: 130 / 209 / 2:40 · Leeds: 75 / 121 / 1:50 · Land's End: 407 / 581 / 8:20 · Kyle of Lochalsh: 128 / 655 / 4:20 · Kingston upon Hull: 132 / 209 / 2:40 · John o' Groats: 511 / 822 / 7:40 · Inverness: 382 / 615 / 2:40 · Holyhead: 102 / 164 / 2:40 · Harwich: 265 / 427 / 6:40 · Great Yarmouth: 240 / 386 / 3:30 · Gloucester: 126 / 216 / 6:40 · Glasgow: 216 / 257 / 3:30 · Fort William: 330 / 381 / 4:00 · Fishguard: 160 / 348 / 4:00 · Exeter: 234 / 460 / 5:30 · Edinburgh: 219 / 481 / 2:40 · Dundee: 99 / 189 / 2:40 · Dover: 93 / 193 / 4:20 · Doncaster: 79 / 312 / 1:40 · Carlisle: 125 / 259 / 2:40 · Cardiff: 167 / 438 / 4:40 · Cambridge: 202 / 512 / 2:40 · Bristol: 149 / 377 / 4:40 · Brighton: 341 / 79 / 2:40 · Braemar: 202 / 352 / 4:40 · Bournemouth: 314 / 343 / 4:40 · Blackpool: 48 / 167 / 2:40 · Birmingham: 99 / 549 / 2:40 · Ayr: 212 / 325 / 3:50 · London: 212 / 325 / 3:50

Manchester — Liverpool: 35 / 56 / 1:10 · Lincoln: 84 / 135 / 2:00 · Leicester: 92 / 148 / 1:50 · Leeds: 42 / 64 / 2:00 · Land's End: 361 / 580 / 7:20 · Kyle of Lochalsh: 406 / 500 / 8:30 · Kingston upon Hull: 95 / 153 / 2:10 · John o' Groats: 500 / 605 / 10:30 · Inverness: 373 / 200 / 7:10 · Holyhead: 124 / 367 / 4:00 · Harwich: 228 / 367 / 5:10 · Great Yarmouth: 212 / 341 / 3:40 · Gloucester: 126 / 203 / 6:40 · Glasgow: 197 / 346 / 3:40 · Fort William: 236 / 317 / 4:00 · Fishguard: 215 / 380 / 4:00 · Exeter: 285 / 346 / 5:30 · Edinburgh: 276 / 459 / 2:40 · Dundee: 61 / 444 / 2:40 · Dover: 139 / 98 / 4:20 · Doncaster: 41 / 192 / 1:40 · Carlisle: 183 / 283 / 2:40 · Cardiff: 165 / 266 / 4:40 · Cambridge: 161 / 414 / 2:40 · Bristol: 101 / 512 / 4:40 · Brighton: 318 / 365 / 2:40 · Braemar: 227 / 77 / 4:40 · Bournemouth: 48 / 129 / 2:40 · Blackpool: 196 / 315 / 2:40 · Birmingham: 212 / 341 / 2:40 · Ayr: 208 / 340 / 3:50 · London: 185 / 340 / 3:50

Newcastle upon Tyne — Manchester: 132 / 212 / 2:50 · Liverpool: 168 / 270 / 3:20 · Lincoln: 159 / 256 / 3:20 · Leicester: 187 / 301 / 3:20 · Leeds: 92 / 148 / 1:50 · Land's End: 498 / 802 / 8:40 · Kyle of Lochalsh: 318 / 512 / 5:40 · Kingston upon Hull: 132 / 212 / 3:40 · John o' Groats: 395 / 636 / 5:50 · Inverness: 268 / 431 / 6:40 · Holyhead: 272 / 438 / 5:40 · Harwich: 326 / 496 / 6:40 · Great Yarmouth: 281 / 452 / 6:20 · Gloucester: 266 / 110 / 6:40 · Glasgow: 148 / 166 / 2:50 · Fort William: 238 / 576 / 4:00 · Fishguard: 407 / 183 / 4:00 · Exeter: 529 / 92 / 5:40 · Edinburgh: 586 / 523 / 2:40 · Dundee: 110 / 248 / 2:40 · Dover: 267 / 481 / 4:20 · Doncaster: 176 / 567 / 1:40 · Carlisle: 58 / 323 / 2:40 · Cardiff: 183 / 558 / 4:40 · Cambridge: 92 / 208 / 2:40 · Bristol: 523 / 333 / 4:40 · Brighton: 248 / 103 / 2:40 · Braemar: 208 / 240 / 4:40 · Bournemouth: 481 / 414 / 2:40 · Blackpool: 567 / 378 / 2:40 · Birmingham: 323 / 460 / 2:40 · Ayr: 286 / 460 / 2:40 · London: 286 / 460 / 2:40

Norwich — Newcastle upon Tyne: 264 / 425 / 5:20 · Manchester: 185 / 298 / 4:30 · Liverpool: 220 / 354 / 4:40 · Lincoln: 105 / 169 / 2:10 · Leicester: 119 / 192 / 3:20 · Leeds: 176 / 283 / 3:50 · Land's End: 421 / 678 / 11:50 · Kyle of Lochalsh: 582 / 937 / 10:30 · Kingston upon Hull: 149 / 240 / 6:10 · John o' Groats: 529 / 1053 / 10:40 · Inverness: 311 / 501 / 9:00 · Holyhead: 73 / 117 / 0:40 · Harwich: 204 / 32 / 4:10 · Great Yarmouth: 385 / 811 / 10:00 · Gloucester: 504 / 550 / 4:10 · Glasgow: 308 / 496 / 5:20 · Fort William: 366 / 589 / 6:40 · Fishguard: 402 / 280 / 4:40 · Exeter: 174 / 235 / 5:40 · Edinburgh: 147 / 344 / 3:20 · Dundee: 289 / 373 / 6:40 · Dover: 262 / 267 / 5:20 · Doncaster: 82 / 538 / 4:30 · Carlisle: 252 / 615 / 5:10 · Cardiff: 175 / 444 / 4:40 · Cambridge: 457 / 798 / 9:40 · Bristol: 214 / 183 / 3:30 · Brighton: 232 / 232 / 4:00 · Braemar: 166 / 166 / 4:00 · Bournemouth: 382 / 382 / 4:00 · Blackpool: 276 / 276 / 4:00 · Birmingham: 496 / 496 / 4:00 · Ayr: 114 / 183 / 3:30 · London: 114 / 183 / 3:30

Nottingham — Norwich: 130 / 209 / 3:10 · Newcastle upon Tyne: 157 / 253 / 3:40 · Manchester: 73 / 118 / 1:40 · Liverpool: 98 / 158 / 1:50 · Lincoln: 35 / 56 / 0:50 · Leicester: 25 / 40 / 0:40 · Leeds: 70 / 113 / 1:50 · Land's End: 345 / 555 / 7:10 · Kyle of Lochalsh: 479 / 771 / 9:50 · Kingston upon Hull: 90 / 145 / 2:10 · John o' Groats: 557 / 896 / 11:50 · Inverness: 430 / 692 / 8:50 · Holyhead: 185 / 298 / 4:00 · Harwich: 150 / 241 / 3:10 · Great Yarmouth: 153 / 246 / 4:00 · Gloucester: 110 / 110 / 2:40 · Glasgow: 372 / 472 / 5:30 · Fort William: 402 / 646 / 4:00 · Fishguard: 220 / 354 / 4:00 · Exeter: 223 / 356 / 5:30 · Edinburgh: 328 / 262 / 2:40 · Dundee: 163 / 328 / 3:40 · Dover: 205 / 49 / 4:20 · Doncaster: 31 / 312 / 1:40 · Carlisle: 172 / 134 / 2:40 · Cardiff: 181 / 233 / 4:40 · Cambridge: 77 / 311 / 2:40 · Bristol: 145 / 568 / 4:40 · Brighton: 179 / 295 / 2:40 · Braemar: 111 / 111 / 3:40 · Bournemouth: 50 / 356 / 3:40 · Blackpool: 221 / 441 / 3:40 · Birmingham: 274 / 264 / 2:40 · Ayr: 633 / 633 / 3:40 · London: 123 / 196 / 2:40

Oban — Nottingham: 390 / 628 / 7:30 · Norwich: 492 / 792 / 9:40 · Newcastle upon Tyne: 233 / 375 / 6:00 · Manchester: 307 / 494 / 6:10 · Liverpool: 308 / 496 / 6:20 · Lincoln: 387 / 623 / 7:30 · Leicester: 419 / 674 / 4:00 · Leeds: 307 / 494 / 3:20 · Land's End: 665 / 1070 / 13:20 · Kyle of Lochalsh: 128 / 206 / 6:00 · Kingston upon Hull: 346 / 557 / 8:10 · John o' Groats: 244 / 393 / 3:40 · Inverness: 117 / 188 / 3:10 · Holyhead: 427 / 687 / 10:00 · Harwich: 524 / 843 / 8:40 · Great Yarmouth: 515 / 829 / 10:00 · Gloucester: 441 / 710 / 4:00 · Glasgow: 99 / 148 / 4:00 · Fort William: 49 / 79 / 4:00 · Fishguard: 481 / 774 / 4:00 · Exeter: 549 / 884 / 5:40 · Edinburgh: 117 / 198 / 2:40 · Dundee: 585 / 182 / 2:40 · Dover: 346 / 942 / 4:20 · Doncaster: 188 / 650 / 1:40 · Carlisle: 477 / 4:40 · Cardiff: 468 / 763 / 4:40 · Cambridge: 465 / 748 / 2:40 · Bristol: 141 / 910 / 4:40 · Brighton: 590 / 227 / 2:40 · Braemar: 384 / 853 / 4:40 · Bournemouth: 180 / 459 / 4:40 · Blackpool: 94 / 618 / 4:40 · Birmingham: 412 / 290 / 4:40 · Ayr: 178 / 151 / 9:30 · London: 499 / 663 / 9:30

Oxford — Oban: 462 / 744 / 8:30 · Nottingham: 109 / 175 / 2:40 · Norwich: 145 / 233 / 3:10 · Newcastle upon Tyne: 260 / 418 / 5:20 · Manchester: 144 / 232 / 3:10 · Liverpool: 172 / 277 / 3:40 · Lincoln: 109 / 221 / 2:40 · Leicester: 73 / 117 / 1:40 · Leeds: 168 / 270 / 4:00 · Land's End: 274 / 441 / 6:40 · Kyle of Lochalsh: 550 / 885 / 9:40 · Kingston upon Hull: 168 / 309 / 4:50 · John o' Groats: 642 / 1056 / 5:10 · Inverness: 516 / 896 / 2:10 · Holyhead: 269 / 433 / 4:00 · Harwich: 132 / 233 / 3:20 · Great Yarmouth: 145 / 322 / 4:00 · Gloucester: 64 / 84 / 2:10 · Glasgow: 324 / 573 / 5:40 · Fort William: 438 / 760 / 4:00 · Fishguard: 141 / 330 / 4:00 · Exeter: 146 / 251 / 5:30 · Edinburgh: 324 / 599 / 2:40 · Dundee: 108 / 233 / 3:40 · Dover: 34 / 418 / 4:20 · Doncaster: 119 / 108 / 1:40 · Carlisle: 134 / 174 / 2:40 · Cardiff: 79 / 719 / 4:40 · Cambridge: 174 / 749 / 2:40 · Bristol: 145 / 145 / 4:40 · Brighton: 301 / 103 / 2:40 · Braemar: 103 / 521 / 4:40 · Bournemouth: 103 / 568 / 4:40 · Blackpool: 57 / 248 / 4:40 · Birmingham: 57 / 92 / 1:40 · Ayr: 777 / 777 / 9:30 · London: 57 / 92 / 1:40

Plymouth — Oxford: 199 / 320 / 4:00 · Oban: 587 / 552 / 11:00 · Nottingham: 267 / 430 / 5:10 · Norwich: 343 / 455 / 7:00 · Newcastle upon Tyne: 410 / 660 / 7:40 · Manchester: 283 / 455 / 5:50 · Liverpool: 283 / 455 / 5:40 · Lincoln: 293 / 509 / 5:40 · Leicester: 242 / 143 / 4:40 · Leeds: 316 / 1085 / 3:20 · Land's End: 674 / 571 / 13:20 · Kyle of Lochalsh: 355 / 1271 / 10:20 · Kingston upon Hull: 790 / 1069 / 5:40 · John o' Groats: 654 / 528 / 2:50 · Inverness: 48 / 97 / 4:00 · Holyhead: 445 / 550 / 4:10 · Harwich: 529 / 425 / 5:20 · Great Yarmouth: 264 / 798 / 10:00 · Gloucester: 46 / 528 / 4:10 · Glasgow: 552 / 327 / 5:20 · Fort William: 297 / 763 / 6:40 · Fishguard: 290 / 792 / 4:40 · Exeter: 193 / 382 / 5:40 · Edinburgh: 161 / 990 / 3:20 · Dundee: 945 / 351 / 6:40 · Dover: 206 / 206 / 4:20 · Doncaster: 528 / 528 / 1:40 · Carlisle: 327 / 327 / 2:40 · Cardiff: 763 / 763 / 4:40 · Cambridge: 792 / 792 / 2:40 · Bristol: 382 / 382 / 4:40 · Brighton: 990 / 990 / 2:40 · Aberdeen: 351 / 351 / 9:30 · London: 218 / 351 / 4:40

Portsmouth — Plymouth: 176 / 283 / 4:00 · Oxford: 77 / 124 / 1:20 · Oban: 545 / 877 / 10:50 · Nottingham: 191 / 307 / 4:00 · Norwich: 207 / 333 / 4:40 · Newcastle upon Tyne: 337 / 542 / 6:10 · Manchester: 236 / 380 / 4:40 · Liverpool: 215 / 409 / 4:40 · Lincoln: 162 / 323 / 4:10 · Leicester: 128 / 261 / 3:10 · Leeds: 269 / 414 / 4:40 · Land's End: 737 / 417 / 10:10 · Kyle of Lochalsh: 613 / 1019 / 11:40 · Kingston upon Hull: 311 / 433 / 6:40 · John o' Groats: 166 / 1186 / 3:40 · Inverness: 221 / 987 / 4:00 · Holyhead: 119 / 501 / 4:10 · Harwich: 448 / 192 / 5:20 · Great Yarmouth: 195 / 721 / 10:00 · Gloucester: 725 / 893 / 4:10 · Glasgow: 404 / 404 / 5:20 · Fort William: 217 / 217 / 6:40 · Fishguard: 729 / 729 / 4:40 · Exeter: 514 / 514 / 5:40 · Edinburgh: 209 / 209 / 3:20 · Dundee: 377 / 377 / 6:40 · Dover: 142 / 142 / 4:20 · Doncaster: 144 / 144 / 1:40 · Carlisle: 156 / 156 / 2:40 · Cardiff: 77 / 881 / 4:40 · Cambridge: 84 / 84 / 2:40 · Bristol: 425 / 425 / 4:40 · Brighton: 645 / 645 / 2:40 · Aberdeen: 692 / 692 / 9:30 · London: 113 / 357 / 3:10

Sheffield — Portsmouth: 230 / 370 / 4:30 · Plymouth: 283 / 455 / 5:30 · Oxford: 135 / 217 / 4:20 · Oban: 339 / 546 / 5:30 · Nottingham: 37 / 60 / 0:50 · Norwich: 146 / 235 / 4:00 · Newcastle upon Tyne: 36 / 201 / 2:00 · Manchester: 39 / 61 / 1:10 · Liverpool: 72 / 116 / 1:50 · Lincoln: 46 / 74 / 1:00 · Leicester: 57 / 100 / 1:40 · Leeds: 34 / 53 / 0:50 · Land's End: 361 / 580 / 7:10 · Kyle of Lochalsh: 427 / 687 / 9:10 · Kingston upon Hull: 61 / 105 / 1:40 · John o' Groats: 520 / 166 / 10:40 · Inverness: 160 / 188 / 8:10 · Holyhead: 166 / 166 / 3:20 · Harwich: 203 / 348 / 4:10 · Great Yarmouth: 216 / 216 / 4:40 · Gloucester: 86 / 399 / 2:00 · Glasgow: 76 / 560 / 3:50 · Fort William: 190 / 468 / 3:50 · Fishguard: 160 / 348 / 3:50 · Exeter: 245 / 159 / 4:40 · Edinburgh: 360 / 306 / 2:40 · Dundee: 394 / 394 / 3:30 · Dover: 159 / 579 / 4:20 · Doncaster: 18 / 256 / 0:50 · Carlisle: 194 / 18 / 2:40 · Cardiff: 194 / 194 / 4:40 · Cambridge: 161 / 161 / 2:40 · Bristol: 216 / 216 / 4:40 · Brighton: 86 / 86 / 2:40 · Aberdeen: 76 / 394 / 3:30 · London: 159 / 256 / 3:20

Shrewsbury — Sheffield: 82 / 132 / 2:20 · Portsmouth: 222 / 333 / 4:30 · Plymouth: 258 / 362 / 5:30 · Oxford: 120 / 171 / 4:20 · Oban: 364 / 586 / 5:30 · Nottingham: 100 / 150 / 2:00 · Norwich: 207 / 333 / 4:00 · Newcastle upon Tyne: 84 / 323 / 2:00 · Manchester: 109 / 111 / 1:10 · Liverpool: 58 / 214 / 1:50 · Lincoln: 135 / 135 / 1:00 · Leicester: 175 / 488 / 1:40 · Leeds: 108 / 726 / 0:50 · Land's End: 312 / 113 / 7:10 · Kyle of Lochalsh: 378 / 705 / 9:10 · Kingston upon Hull: 124 / 82 / 1:40 · John o' Groats: 438 / 615 / 10:40 · Inverness: 175 / 223 / 8:10 · Holyhead: 166 / 364 / 3:20 · Harwich: 256 / 597 / 4:10 · Great Yarmouth: 166 / 298 / 4:40 · Gloucester: 72 / 158 / 2:00 · Glasgow: 425 / 425 / 3:50 · Fort William: 433 / 433 / 3:50 · Fishguard: 124 / 124 / 3:50 · Exeter: 642 / 642 / 4:40 · Edinburgh: 259 / 259 / 2:40 · Dundee: 258 / 258 / 3:30 · Aberdeen: 82 / 132 / 3:30 · London: 159 / 258 / 3:10

Southampton — Shrewsbury: 185 / 298 / 3:30 · Sheffield: 199 / 320 / 4:10 · Portsmouth: 21 / 34 / 0:50 · Plymouth: 151 / 243 / 4:40 · Oxford: 64 / 103 / 1:30 · Oban: 530 / 853 / 10:40 · Nottingham: 176 / 289 / 4:00 · Norwich: 206 / 521 / 4:10 · Newcastle upon Tyne: 221 / 356 / 6:20 · Manchester: 239 / 385 / 5:00 · Liverpool: 204 / 328 / 4:40 · Lincoln: 137 / 373 / 4:10 · Leicester: 120 / 373 / 3:20 · Leeds: 258 / 240 / 4:40 · Land's End: 723 / 995 / 10:10 · Kyle of Lochalsh: 598 / 1000 / 11:40 · Kingston upon Hull: 256 / 411 / 6:40 · John o' Groats: 314 / 1118 / 3:40 · Inverness: 105 / 969 / 4:00 · Holyhead: 433 / 705 / 4:10 · Harwich: 541 / 805 / 5:20 · Great Yarmouth: 105 / 871 / 10:00 · Gloucester: 420 / 315 / 4:10 · Glasgow: 169 / 169 / 5:20 · Fort William: 238 / 238 / 6:40 · Fishguard: 727 / 727 / 4:40 · Exeter: 112 / 112 / 5:40 · Edinburgh: 404 / 404 / 3:20 · Dundee: 206 / 206 / 6:40 · Dover: 124 / 124 / 4:20 · Aberdeen: 204 / 204 / 9:30 · London: 77 / 124 / 2:00

Stranraer — Southampton: 445 / 716 / 8:20 · Shrewsbury: 277 / 446 / 4:20 · Sheffield: 263 / 423 / 4:50 · Portsmouth: 460 / 742 / 8:00 · Plymouth: 151 / 805 / 6:20 · Oxford: 330 / 610 / 6:10 · Oban: 209 / 238 / 4:20 · Nottingham: 187 / 467 / 4:30 · Norwich: 158 / 649 / 5:50 · Newcastle upon Tyne: 354 / 354 / 4:30 · Manchester: 329 / 480 / 5:50 · Liverpool: 331 / 531 / 5:40 · Lincoln: 343 / 942 / 5:30 · Leicester: 195 / 420 / 5:40 · Leeds: 314 / 417 / 3:20 · Land's End: 631 / 610 / 13:40 · Kyle of Lochalsh: 731 / 422 / 10:20 · Kingston upon Hull: 167 / 544 / 6:40 · John o' Groats: 448 / 660 / 10:00 · Inverness: 269 / 686 / 9:00 · Holyhead: 168 / 798 / 4:40 · Harwich: 414 / 525 / 5:20 · Great Yarmouth: 163 / 367 / 10:00 · Gloucester: 628 / 647 / 4:10 · Glasgow: 610 / 312 / 5:20 · Fort William: 765 / 765 / 6:40 · Fishguard: 444 / 444 / 4:40 · Exeter: 303 / 274 / 5:40 · Edinburgh: 82 / 82 / 3:20 · Dundee: 523 / 523 / 6:40 · Dover: 367 / 367 / 4:20 · Aberdeen: 647 / 647 / 9:30 · London: 402 / 647 / 7:10

Swansea — Stranraer: 417 / 671 / 7:50 · Southampton: 161 / 259 / 3:40 · Shrewsbury: 118 / 259 / 2:20 · Sheffield: 217 / 349 / 6:20 · Portsmouth: 132 / 206 / 4:00 · Plymouth: 191 / 283 / 4:00 · Oxford: 141 / 506 / 3:20 · Oban: 192 / 559 / 9:25 · Nottingham: 301 / 301 / 6:00 · Norwich: 347 / 559 / 6:00 · Newcastle upon Tyne: 126 / 375 / 2:40 · Manchester: 195 / 195 / 3:40 · Liverpool: 233 / 399 / 3:40 · Lincoln: 177 / 459 / 4:40 · Leicester: 248 / 425 / 4:40 · Leeds: 285 / 658 / 3:20 · Land's End: 264 / 108 / 13:40 · Kyle of Lochalsh: 696 / 425 / 10:20 · Kingston upon Hull: 572 / 663 / 6:40 · John o' Groats: 184 / 761 / 10:00 · Inverness: 267 / 441 / 9:00 · Holyhead: 89 / 365 / 4:40 · Harwich: 304 / 137 / 5:20 · Great Yarmouth: 496 / 269 / 10:00 · Gloucester: 161 / 207 / 4:10 · Glasgow: 412 / 412 / 5:20 · Fort William: 222 / 222 / 6:40 · Fishguard: 505 / 505 / 4:40 · Exeter: 167 / 167 / 5:40 · Edinburgh: 216 / 216 / 3:20 · Dundee: 383 / 383 / 6:40 · Dover: 379 / 379 / 4:20 · Doncaster: 73 / 117 / 7:10 · Carlisle: 507 / 816 / 6:50 · Cardiff: 194 / 312 / 3:30 · London: 194 / 312 / 3:30

York — Swansea: 272 / 438 / 5:10 · Stranraer: 222 / 357 / 4:40 · Southampton: 258 / 415 / 5:40 · Shrewsbury: 128 / 214 / 2:40 · Sheffield: 54 / 84 / 1:10 · Portsmouth: 333 / 536 / 6:20 · Plymouth: 181 / 309 / 5:10 · Oxford: 309 / 497 / 4:40 · Oban: 291 / 124 / 6:20 · Nottingham: 86 / 291 / 1:40 · Norwich: 103 / 64 / 3:20 · Newcastle upon Tyne: 159 / 661 / 2:10 · Manchester: 121 / 174 / 2:40 · Liverpool: 174 / 407 / 3:20 · Lincoln: 24 / 57 / 0:50 · Leicester: 411 / 771 / 1:40 · Leeds: 60 / 566 / 2:40 · Land's End: 387 / 521 / 8:00 · Kyle of Lochalsh: 323 / 454 / 9:30 · Kingston upon Hull: 189 / 55 / 4:40 · John o' Groats: 207 / 195 / 5:50 · Inverness: 349 / 393 / 6:30 · Holyhead: 531 / 266 / 5:40 · Harwich: 287 / 443 / 4:40 · Great Yarmouth: 202 / 459 / 5:10 · Gloucester: 312 / 154 / 4:00 · Glasgow: 402 / 209 / 5:40 · Fort William: 454 / 344 / 5:40 · Fishguard: 55 / 314 / 5:40 · Exeter: 195 / 513 / 5:40 · Edinburgh: 393 / 333 / 2:40 · Dundee: 266 / 266 / 3:30 · Dover: 238 / 238 / 4:10 · Doncaster: 34 / 194 / 3:10 · Carlisle: 159 / 159 / 4:10 · Cardiff: 209 / 209 / 4:10 · London: 207 / 333 / 4:10

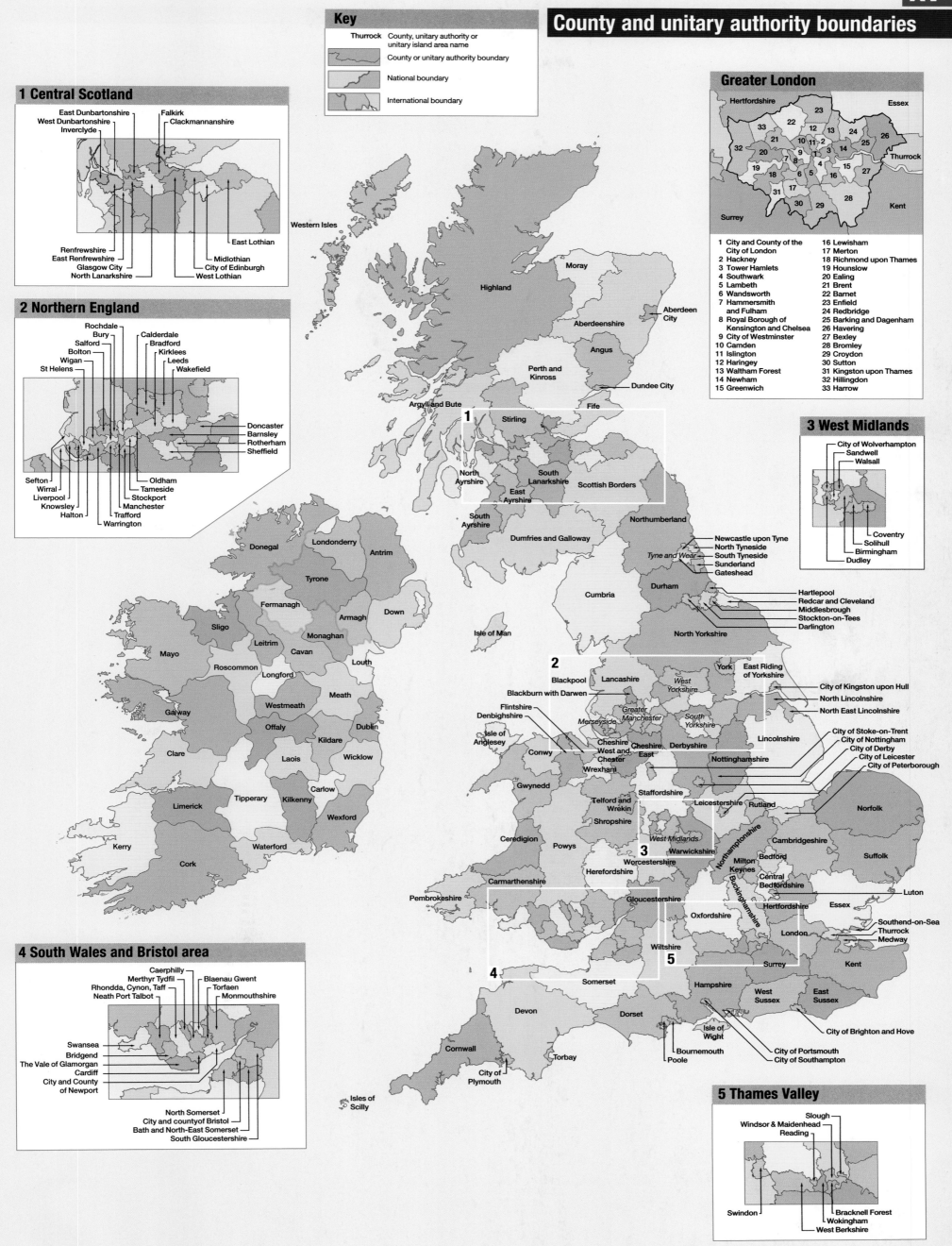

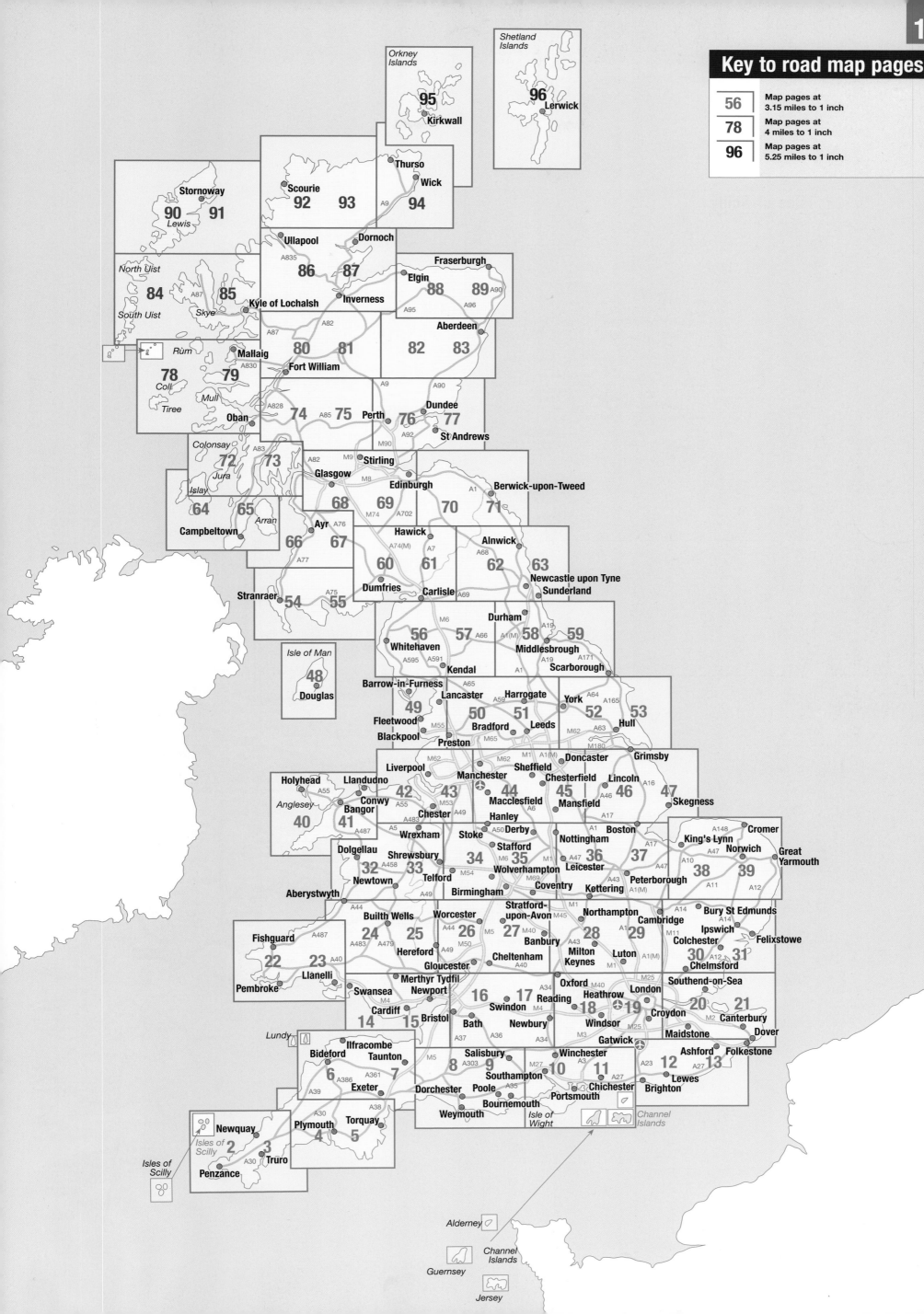

Key to road map pages

56	Map pages at 3.15 miles to 1 inch
78	Map pages at 4 miles to 1 inch
96	Map pages at 5.25 miles to 1 inch

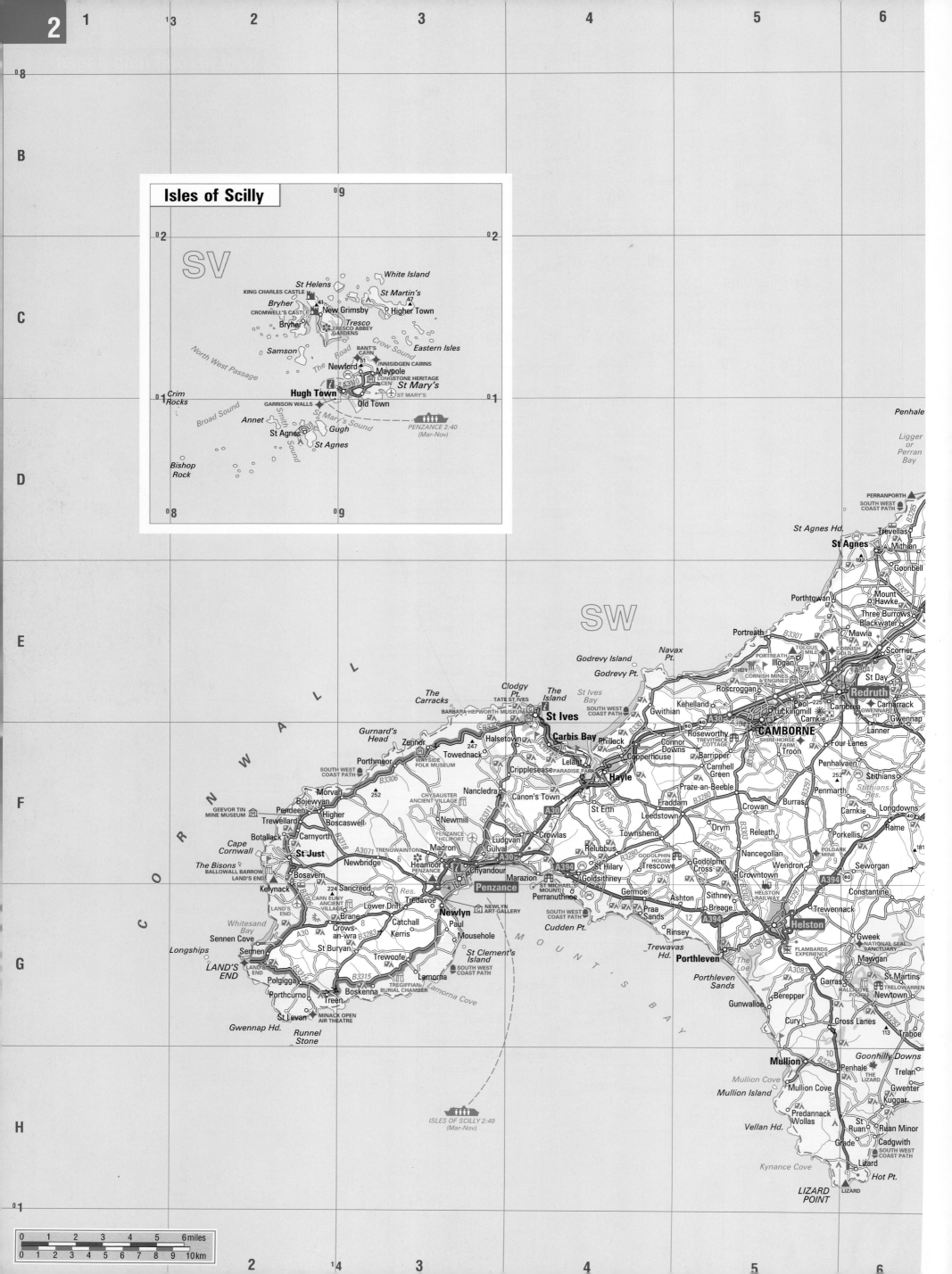

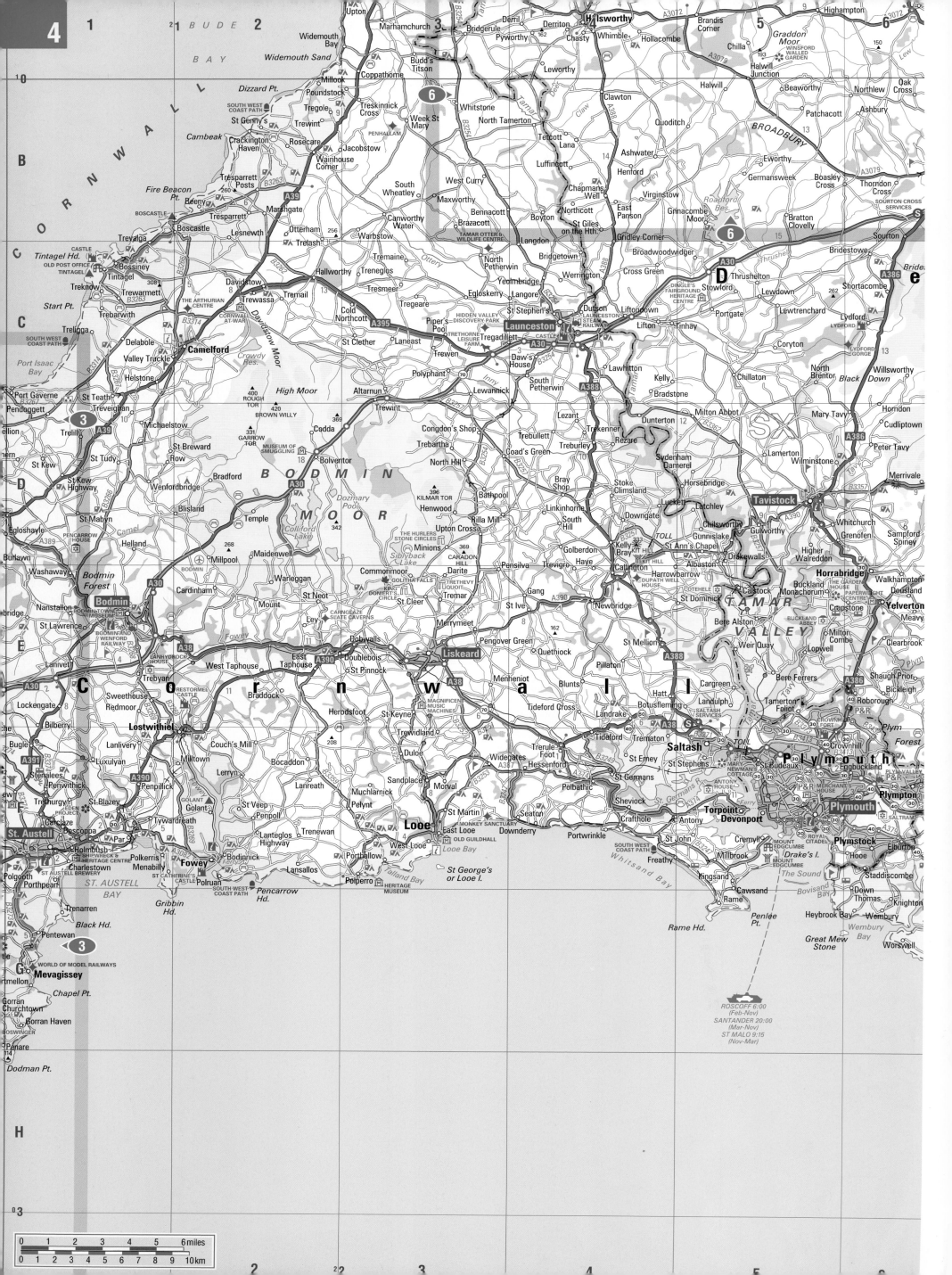

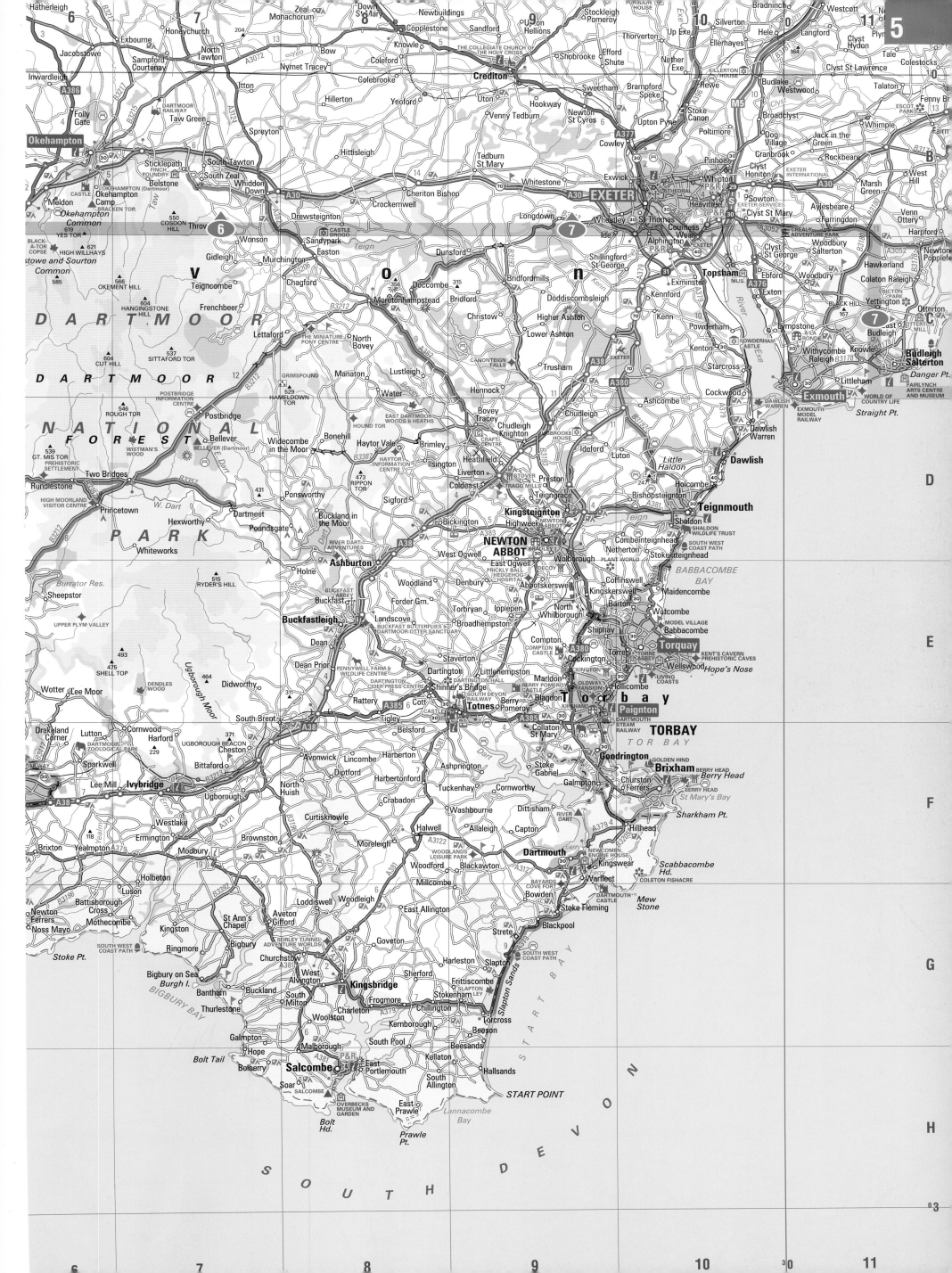

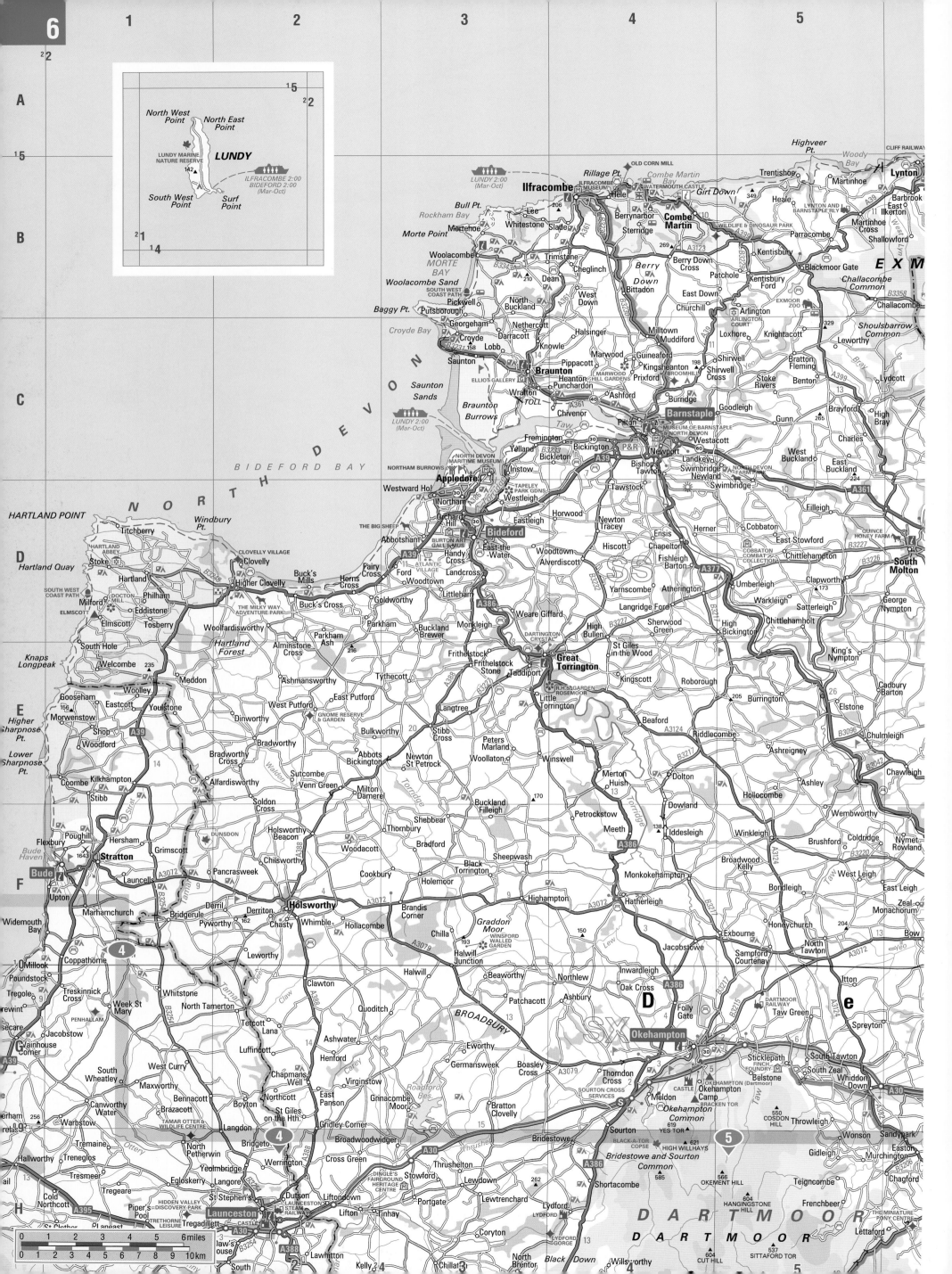

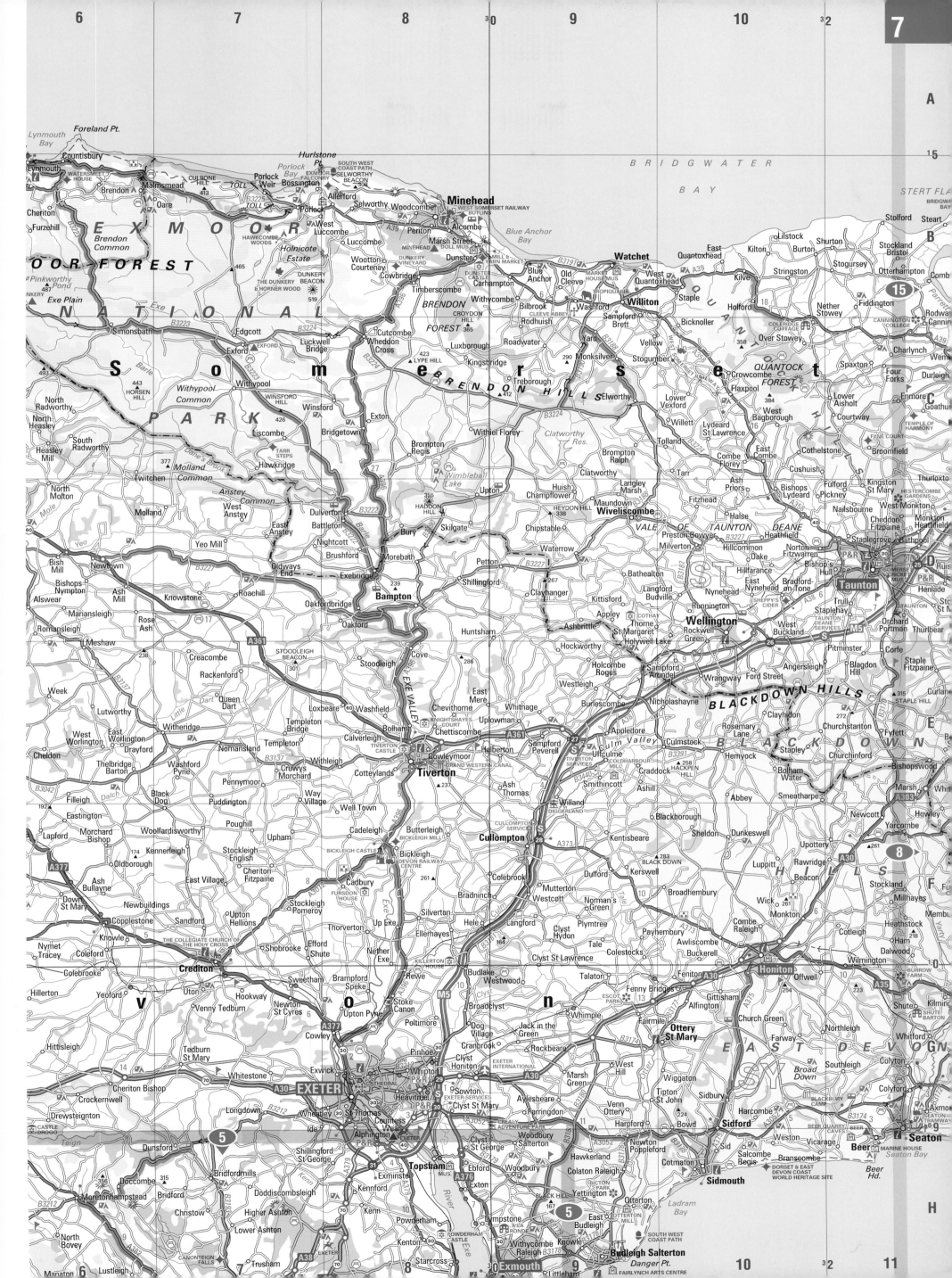

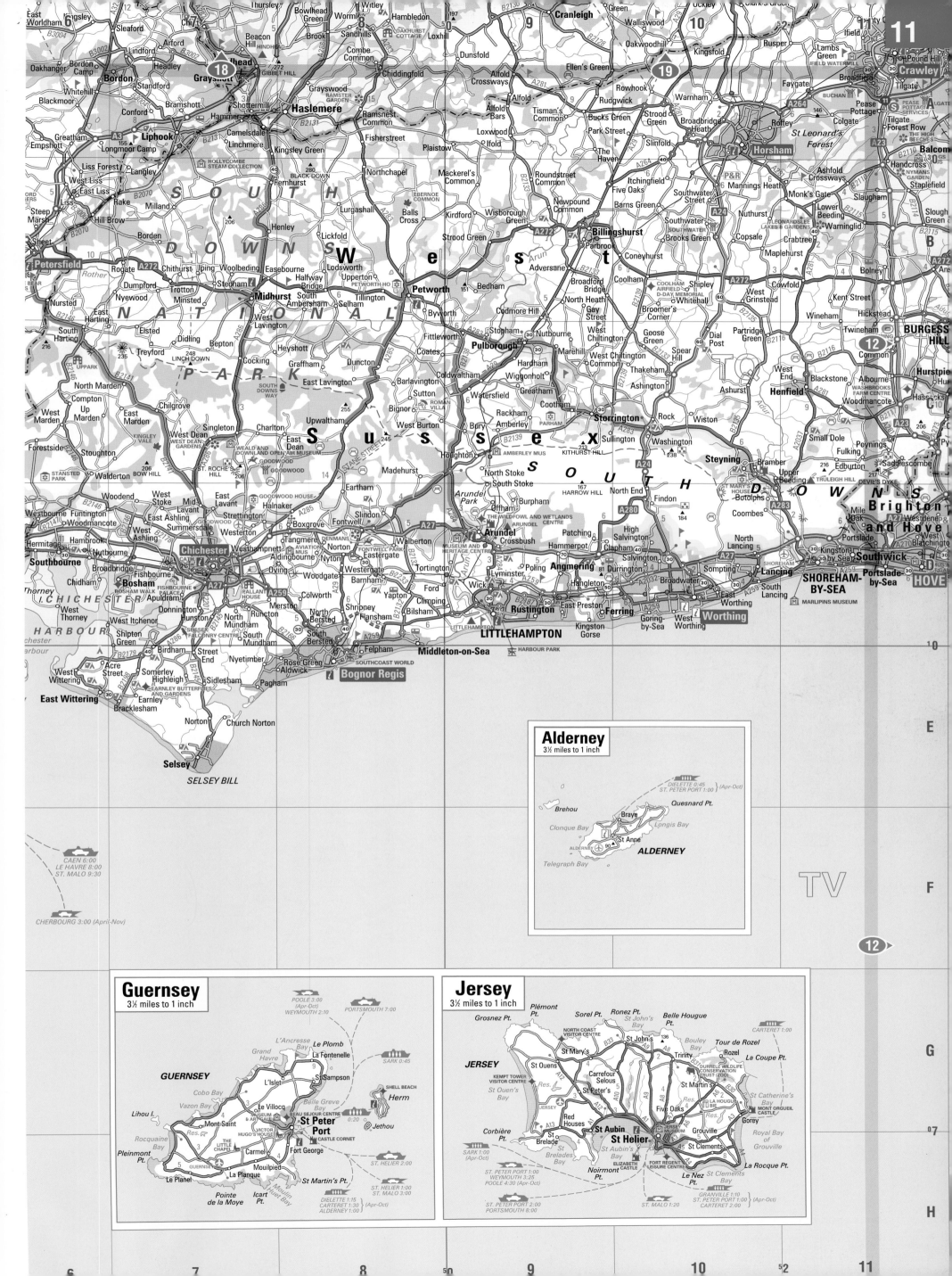

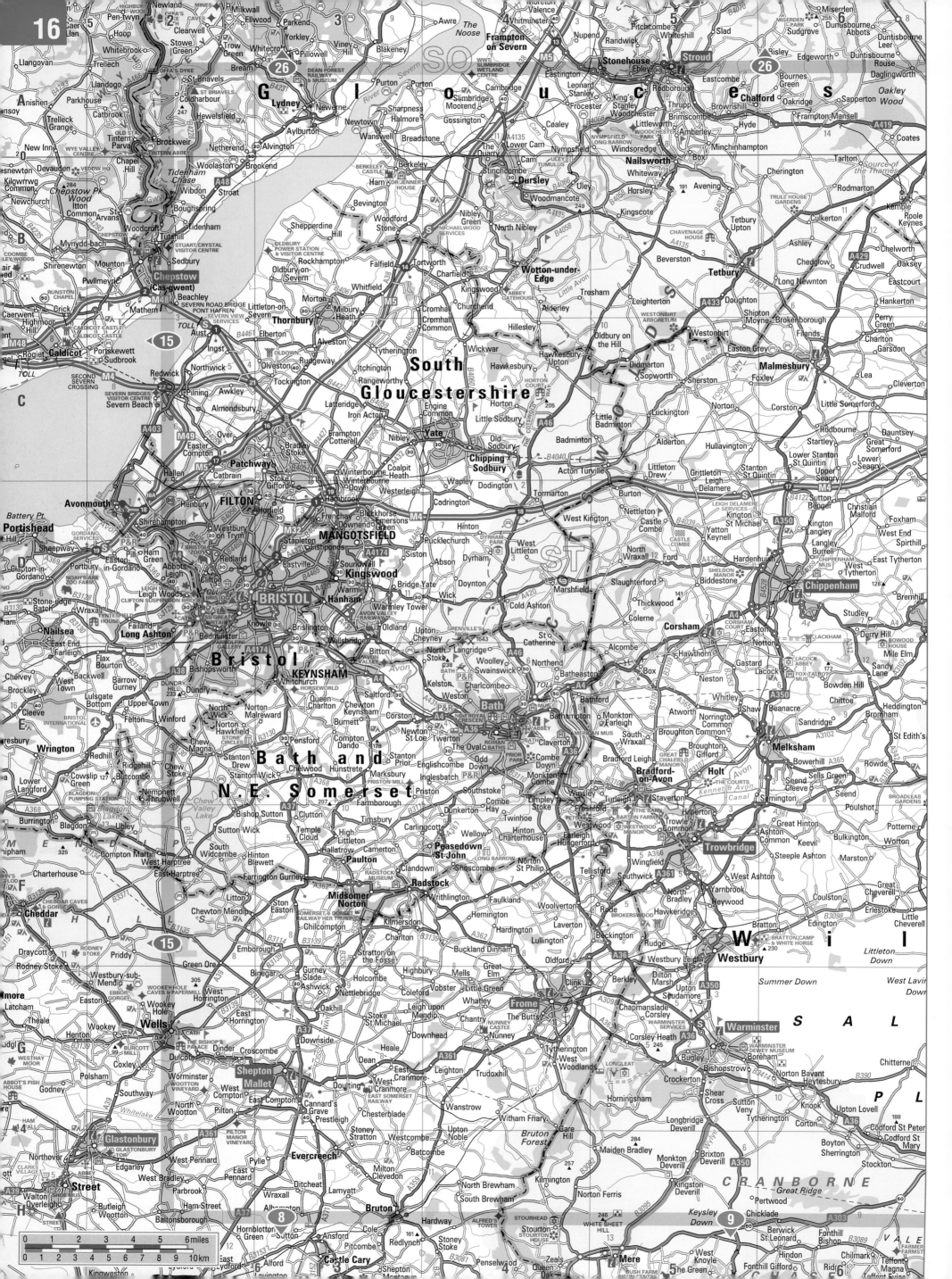

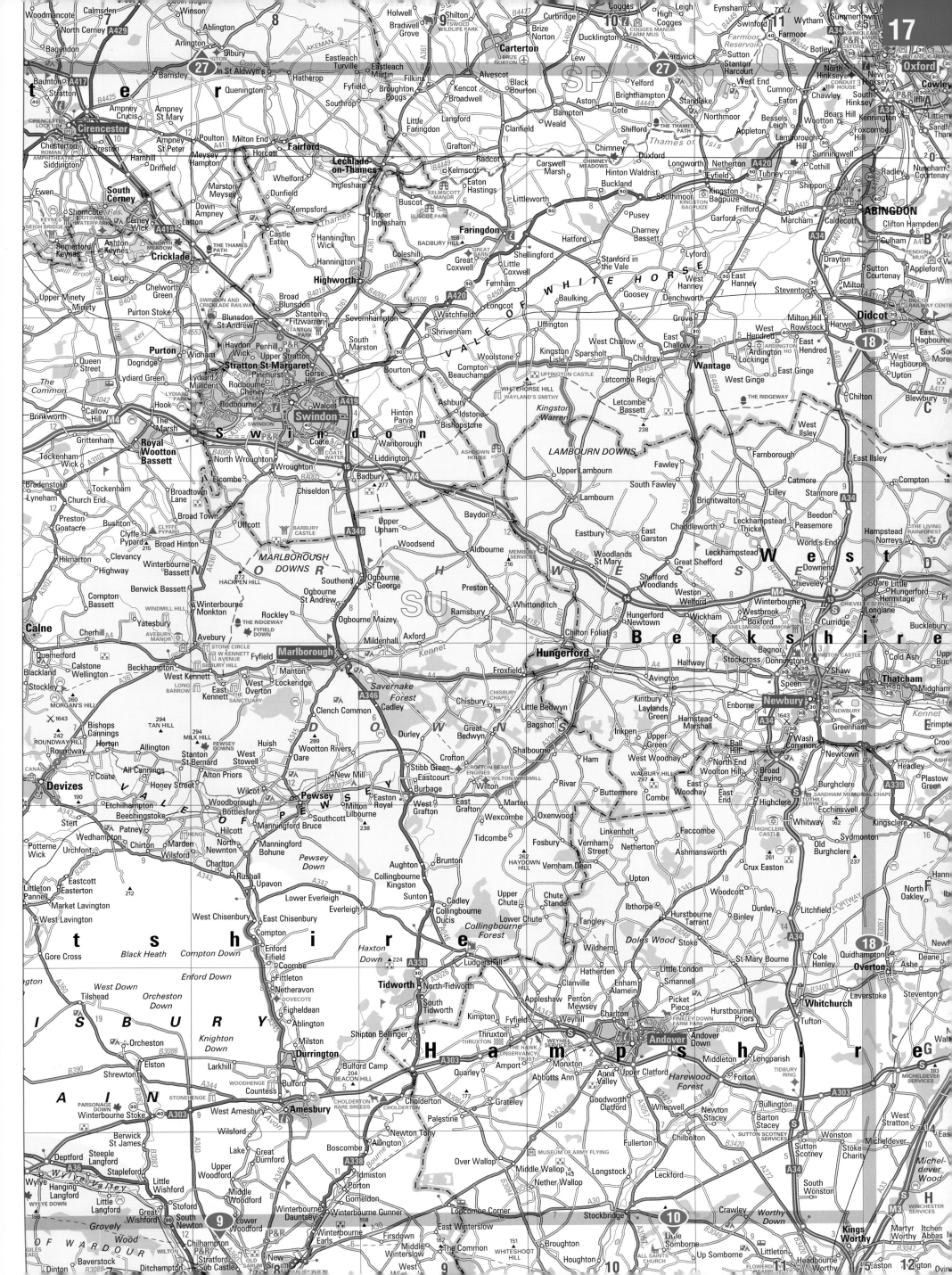

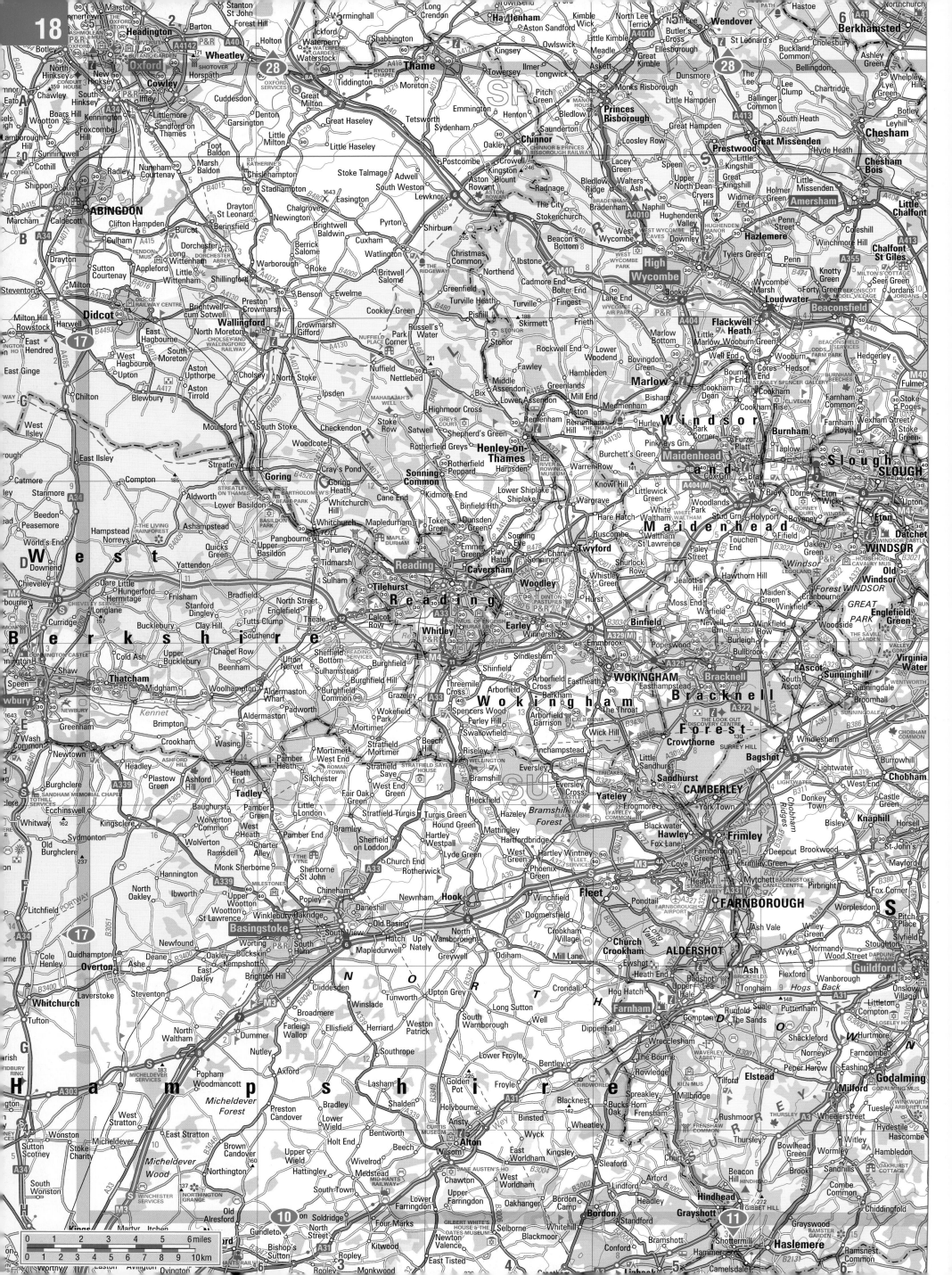

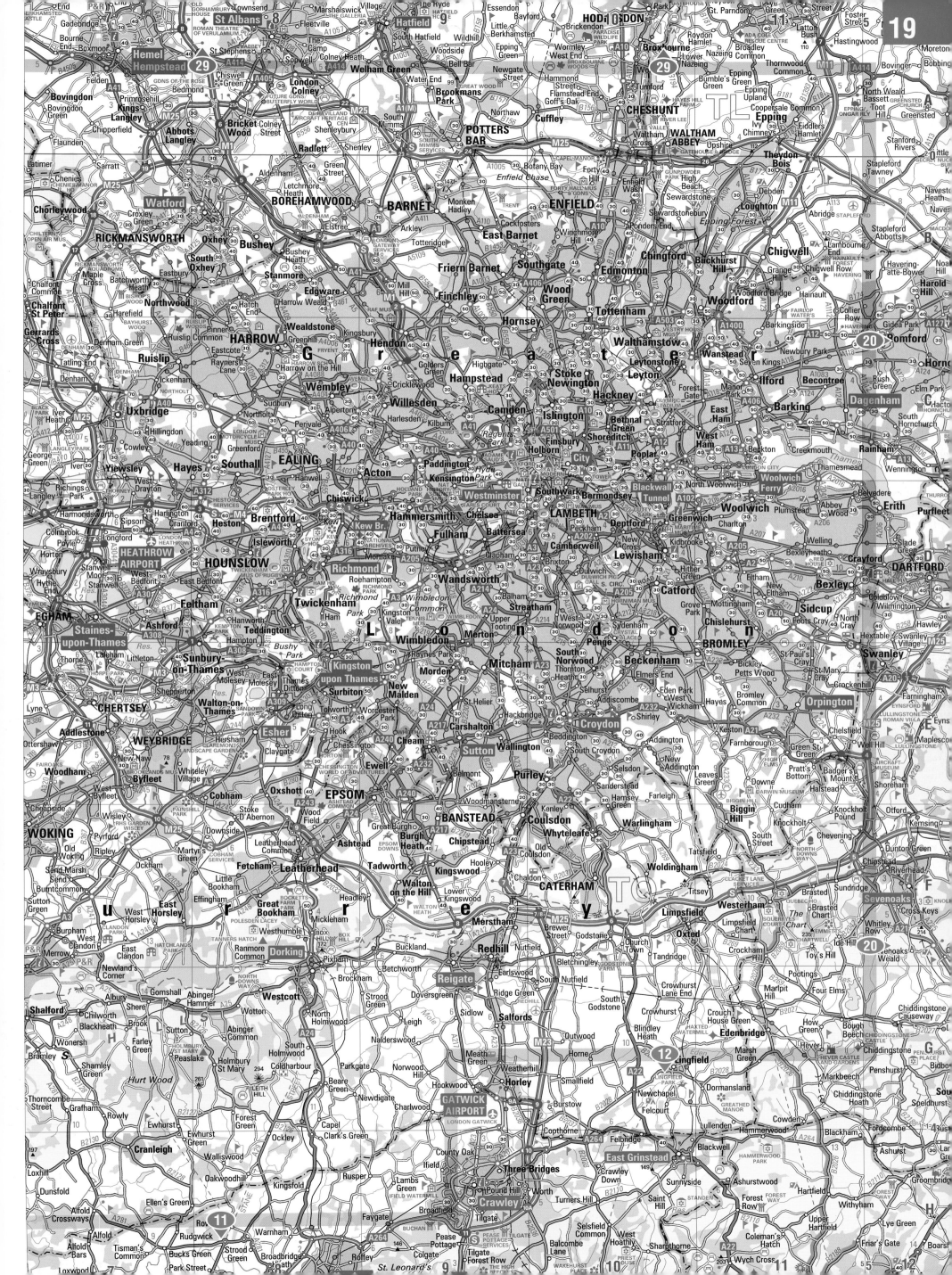

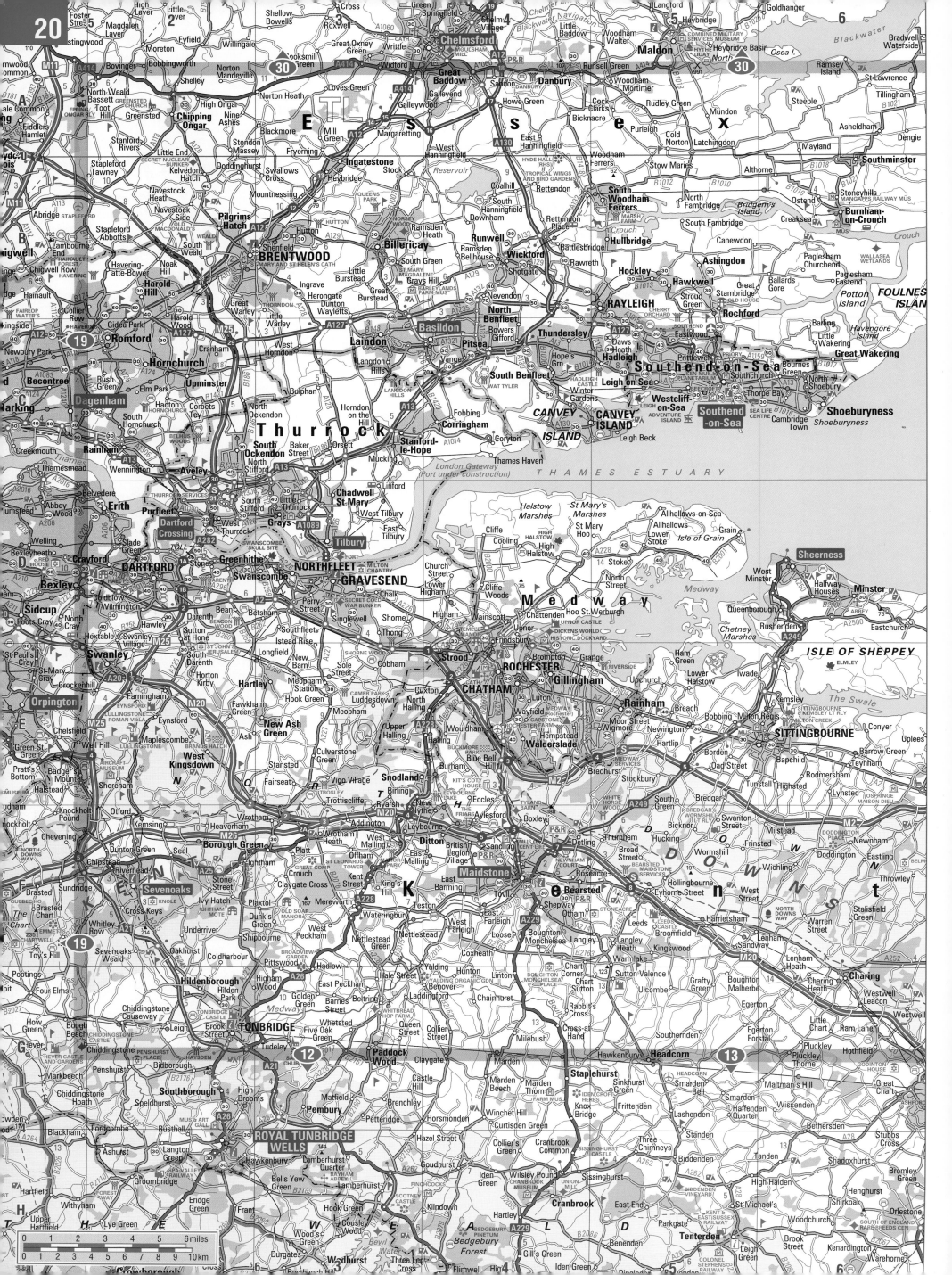

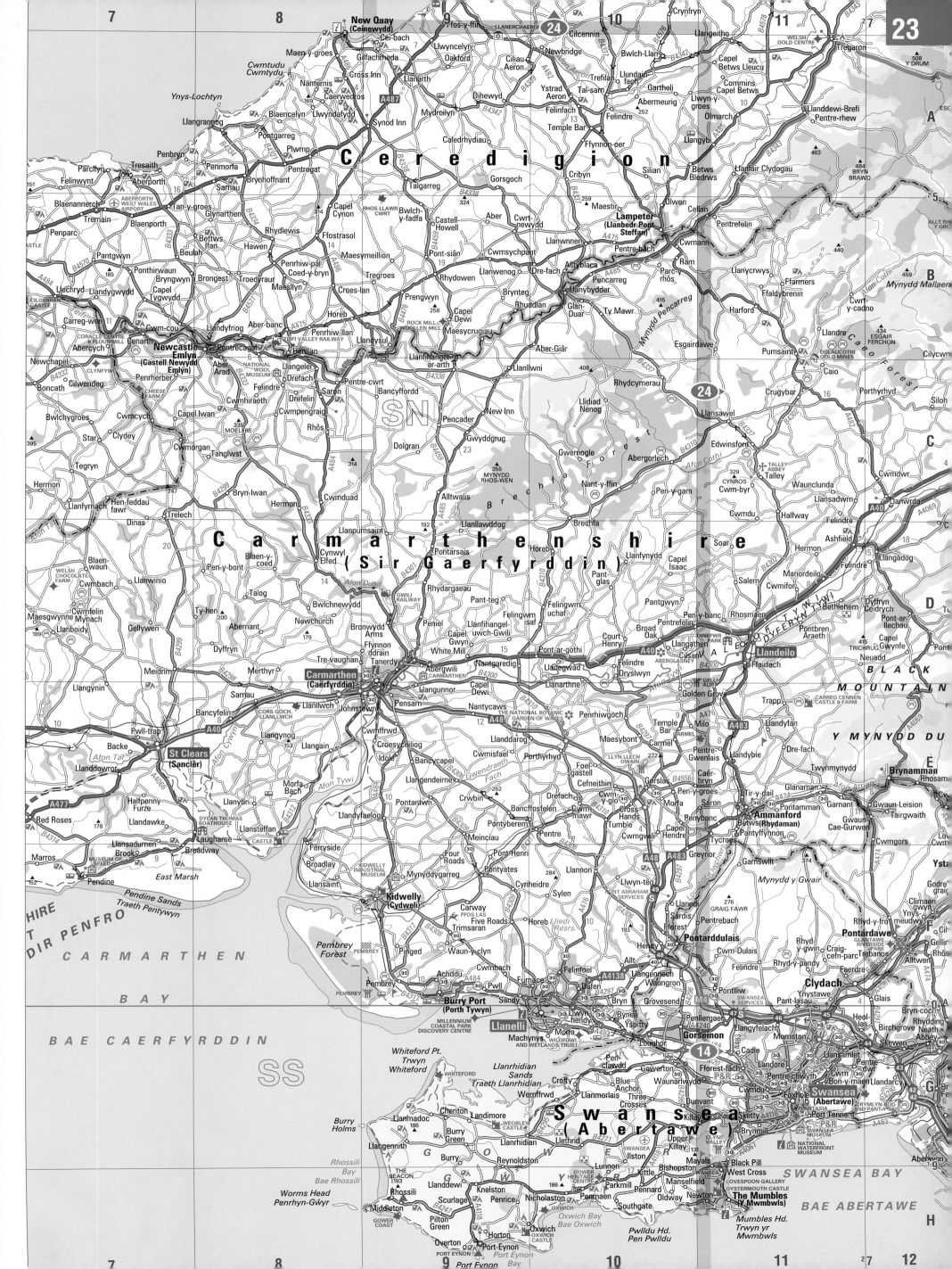

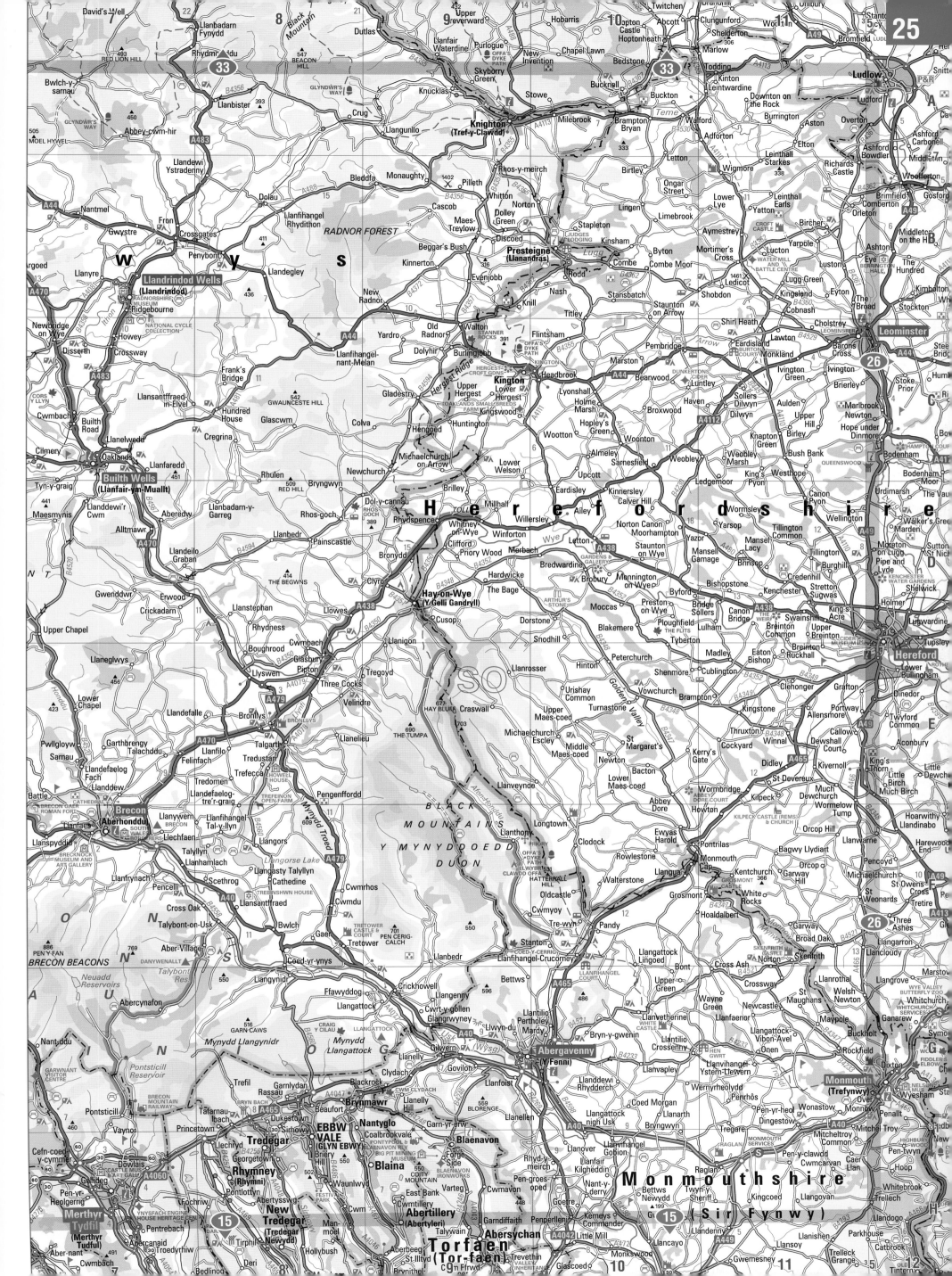

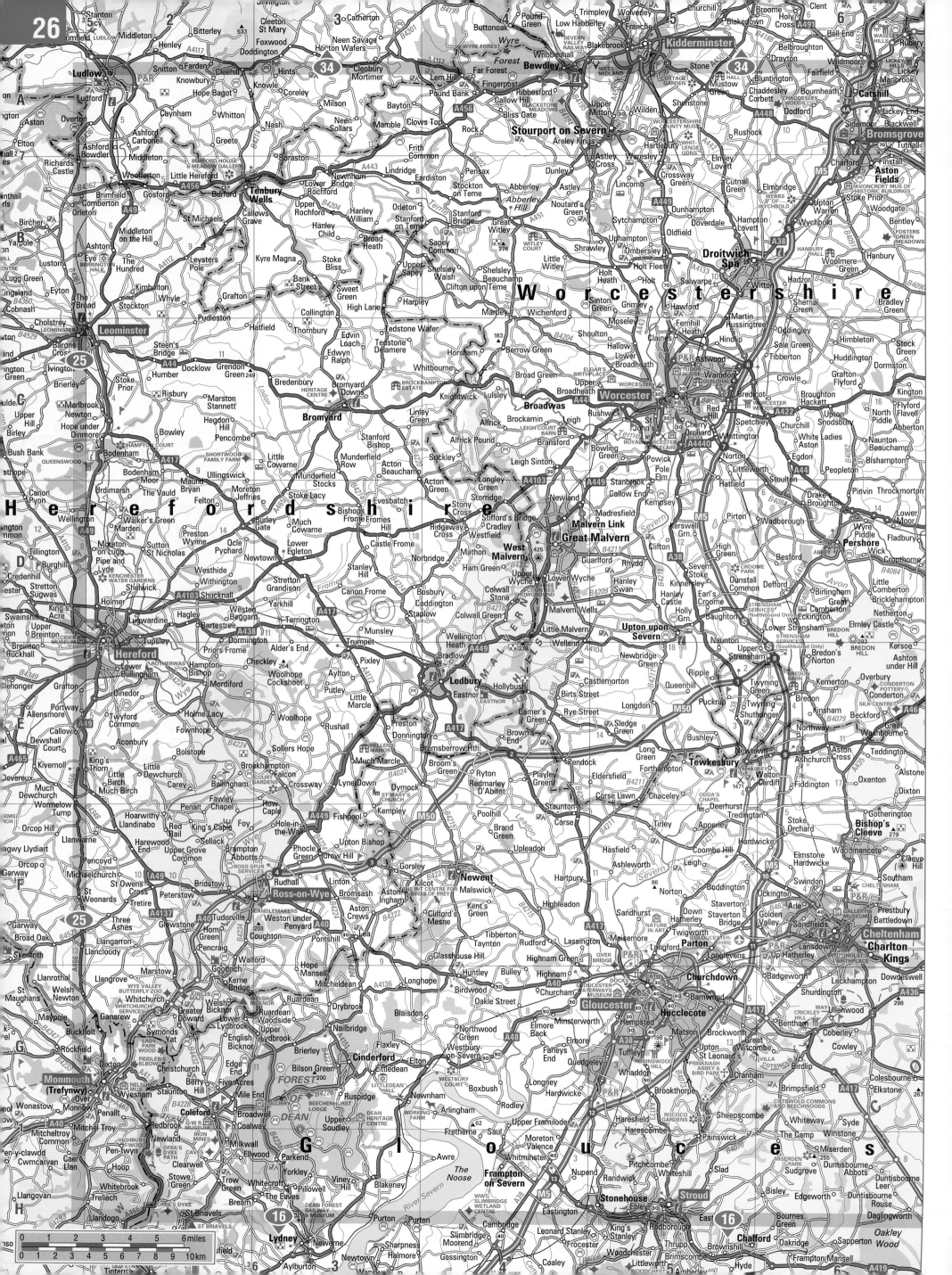

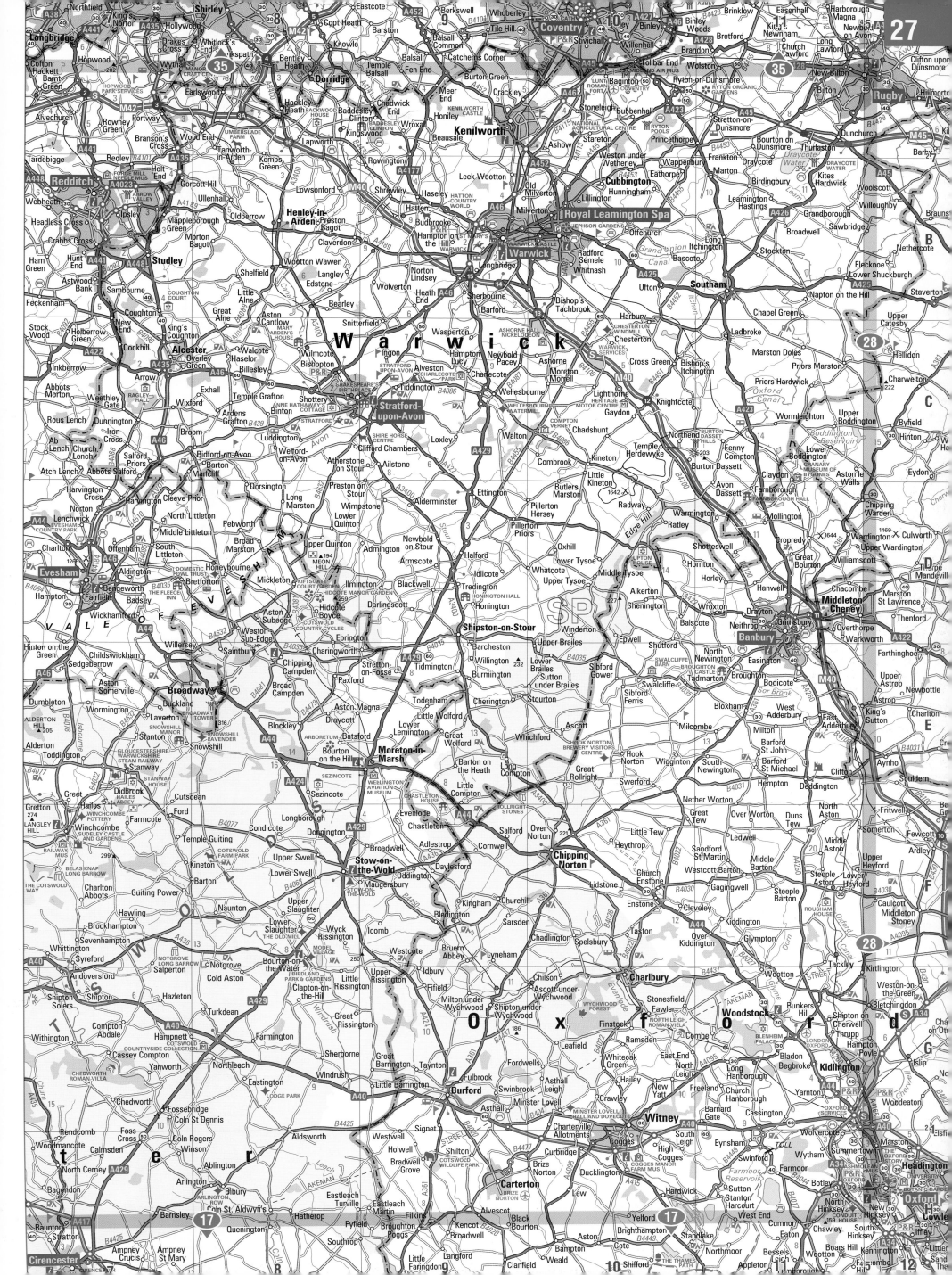

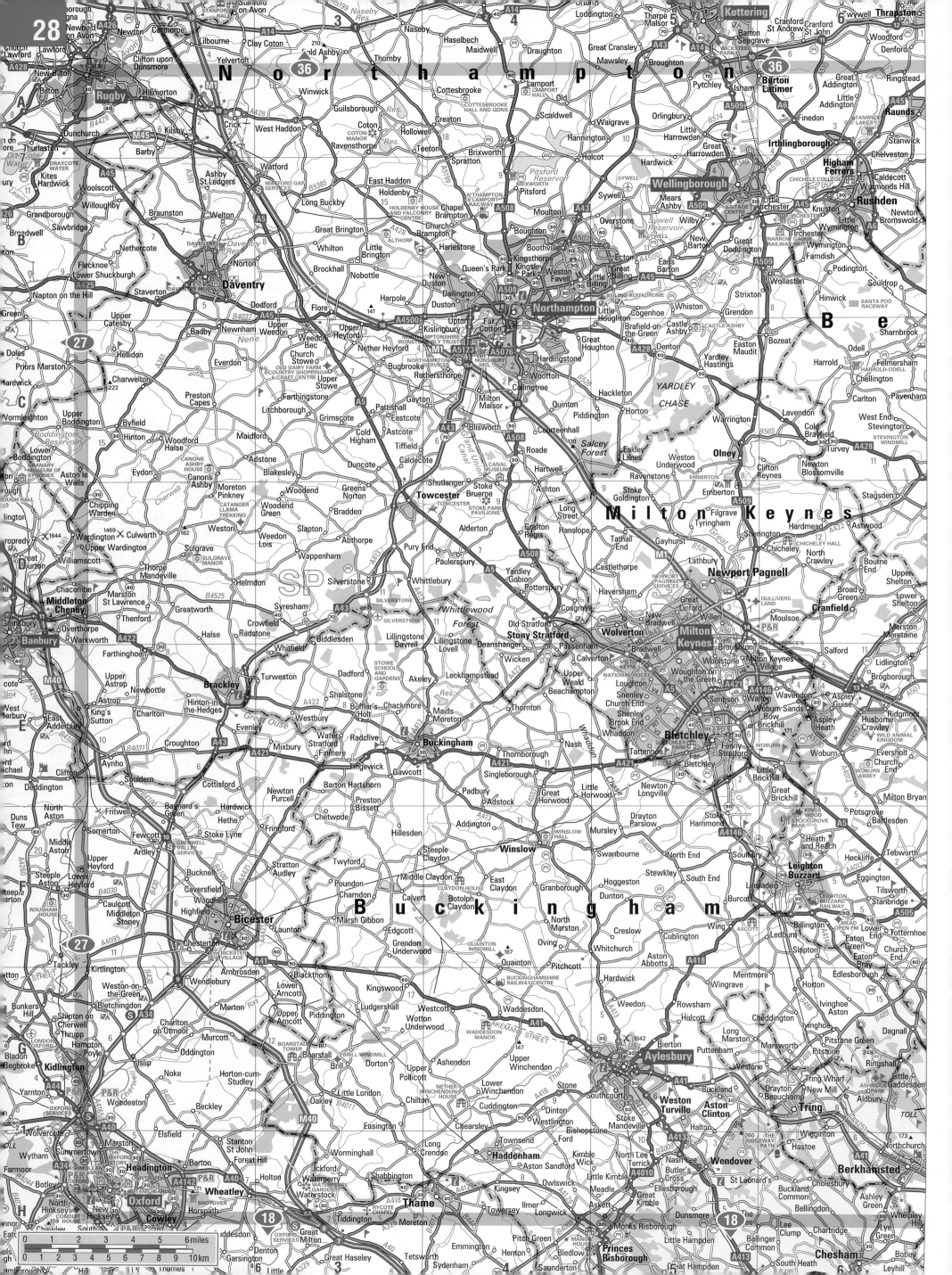

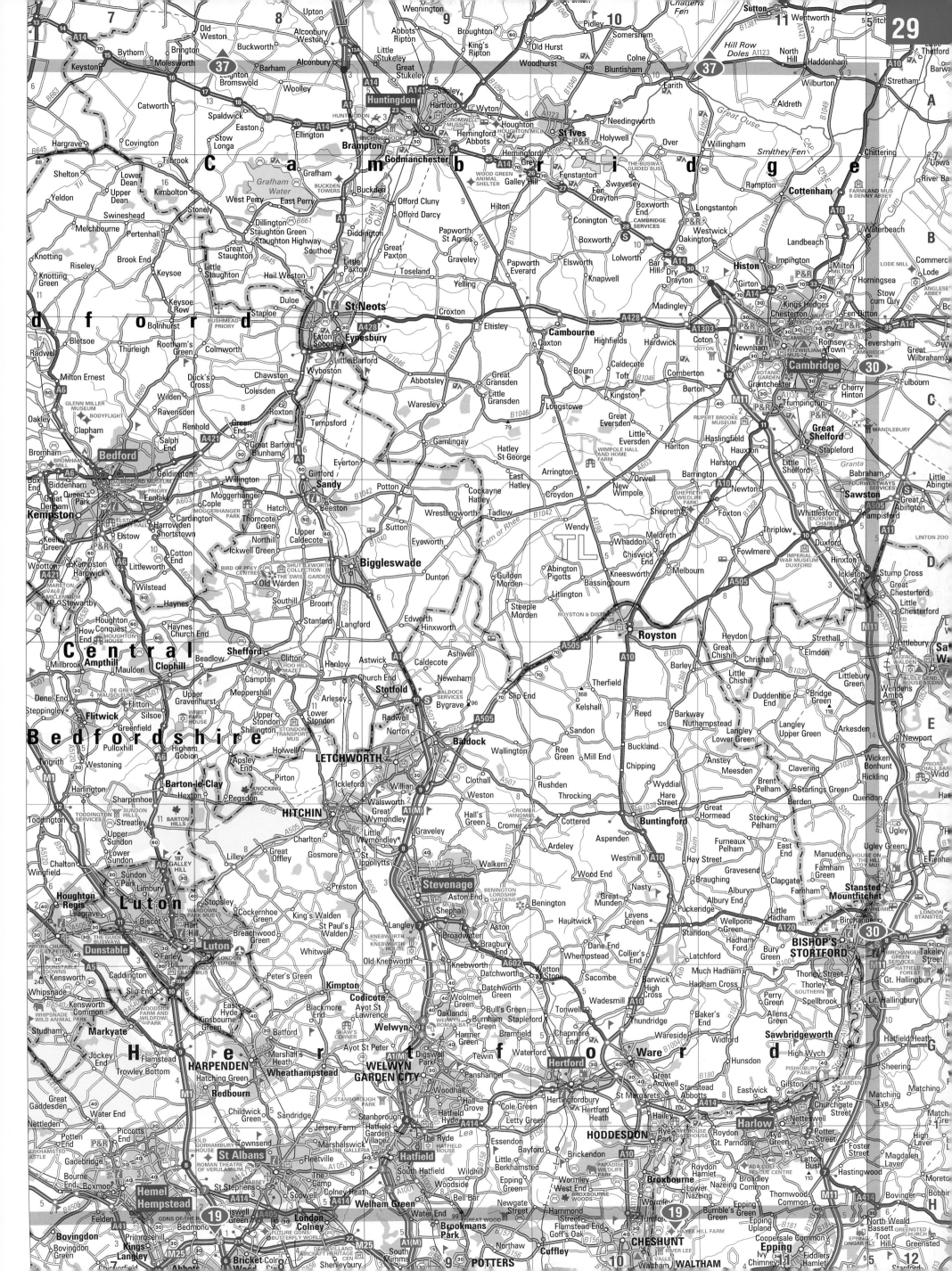

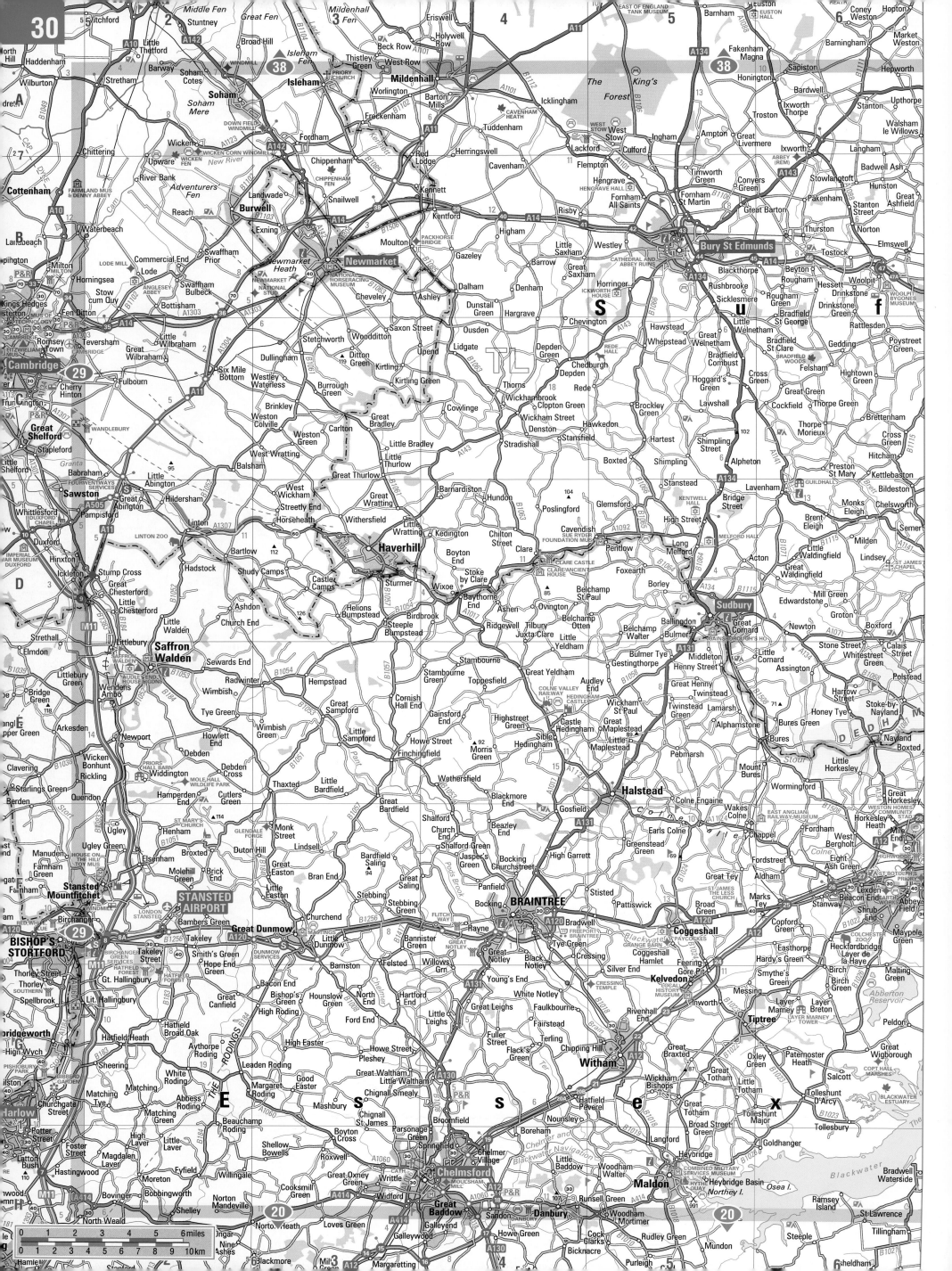

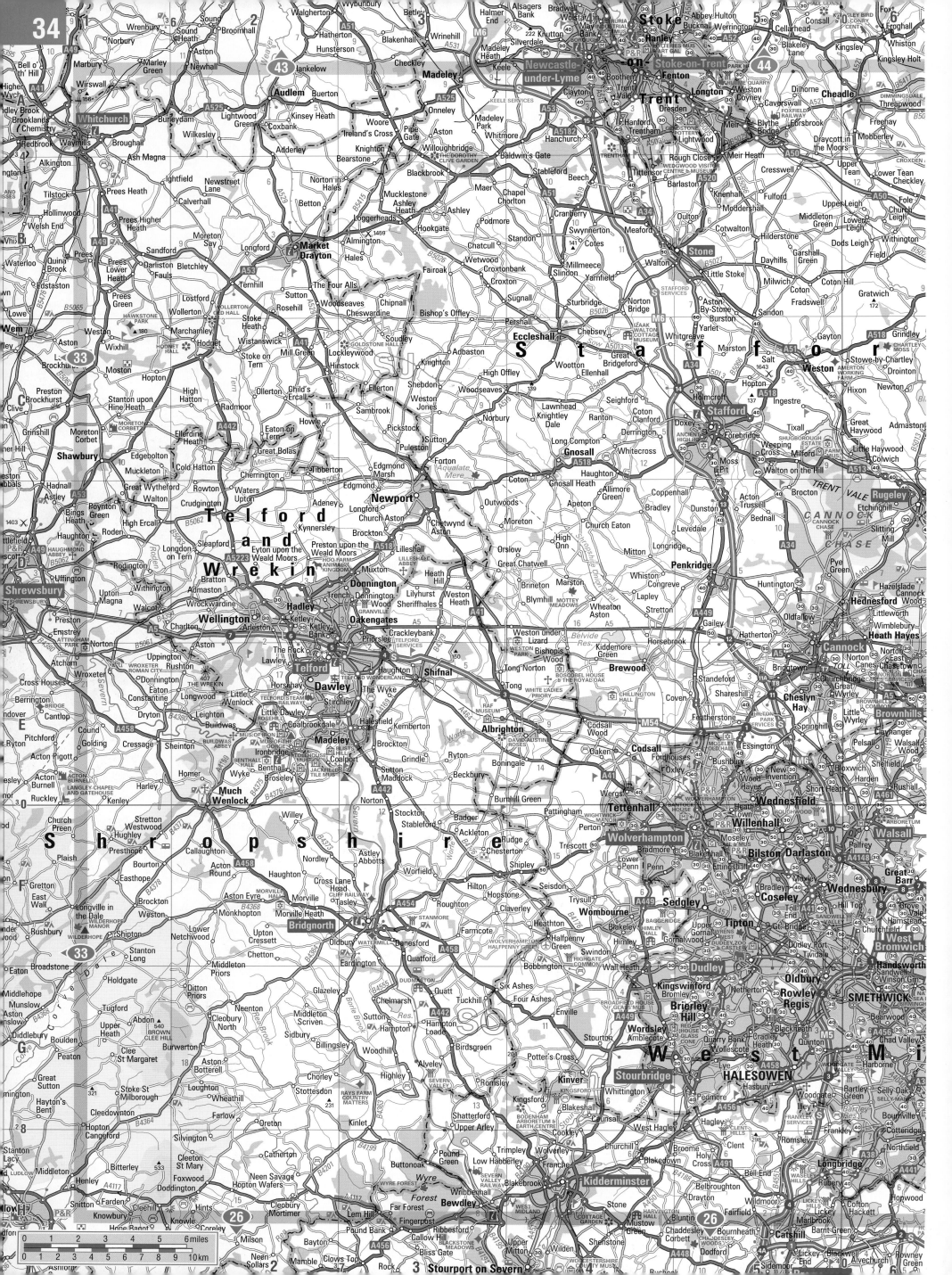

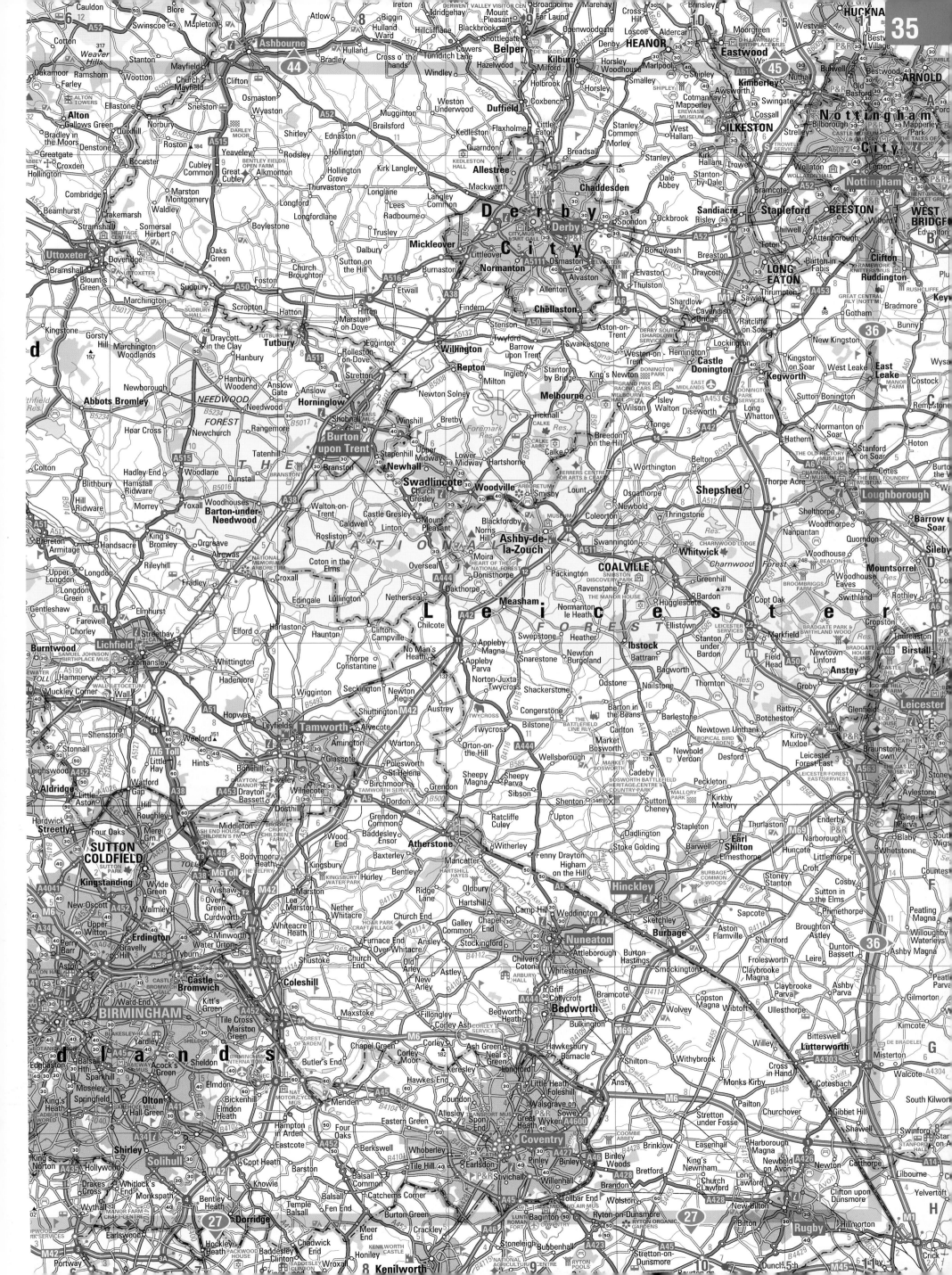

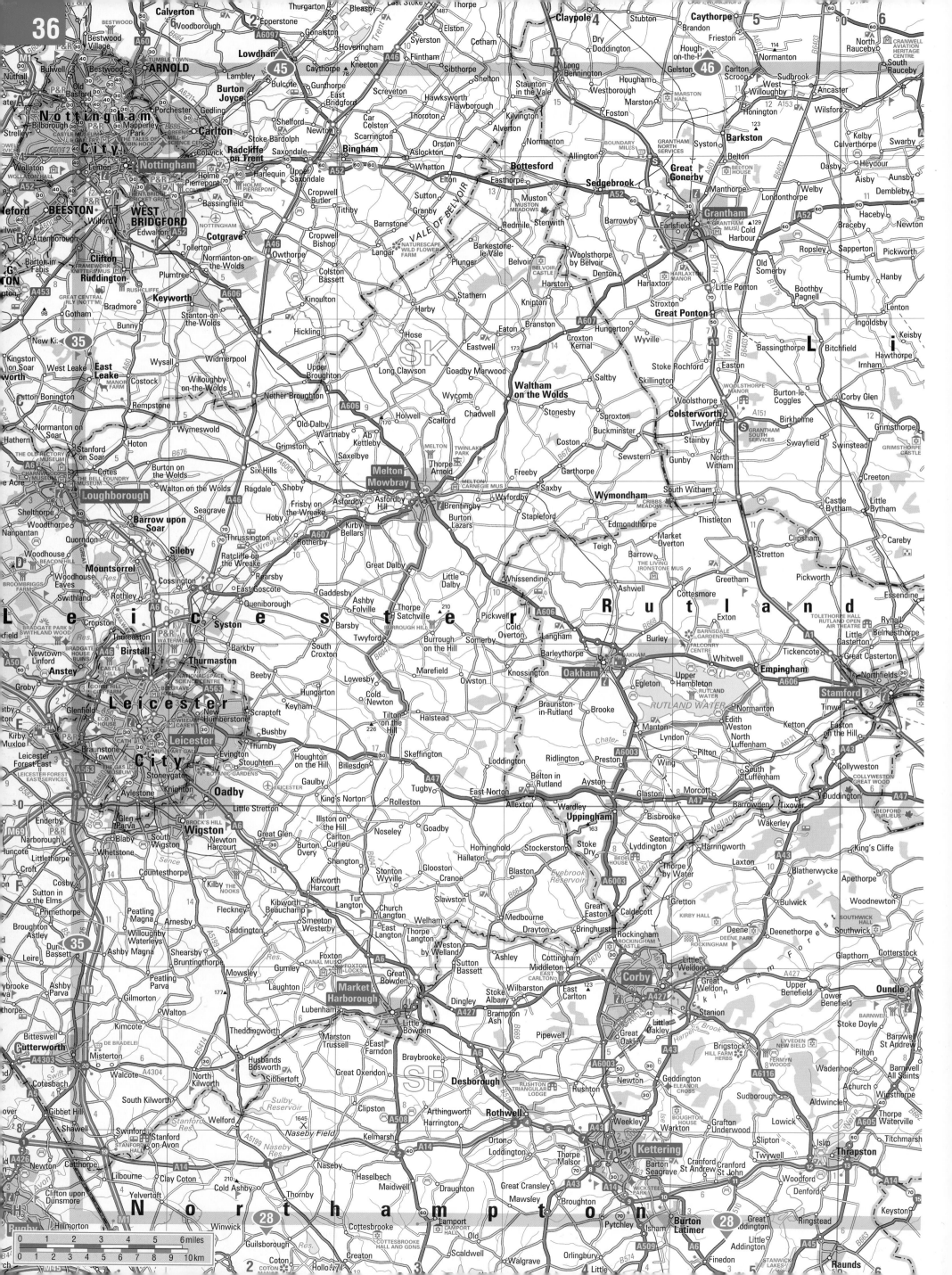

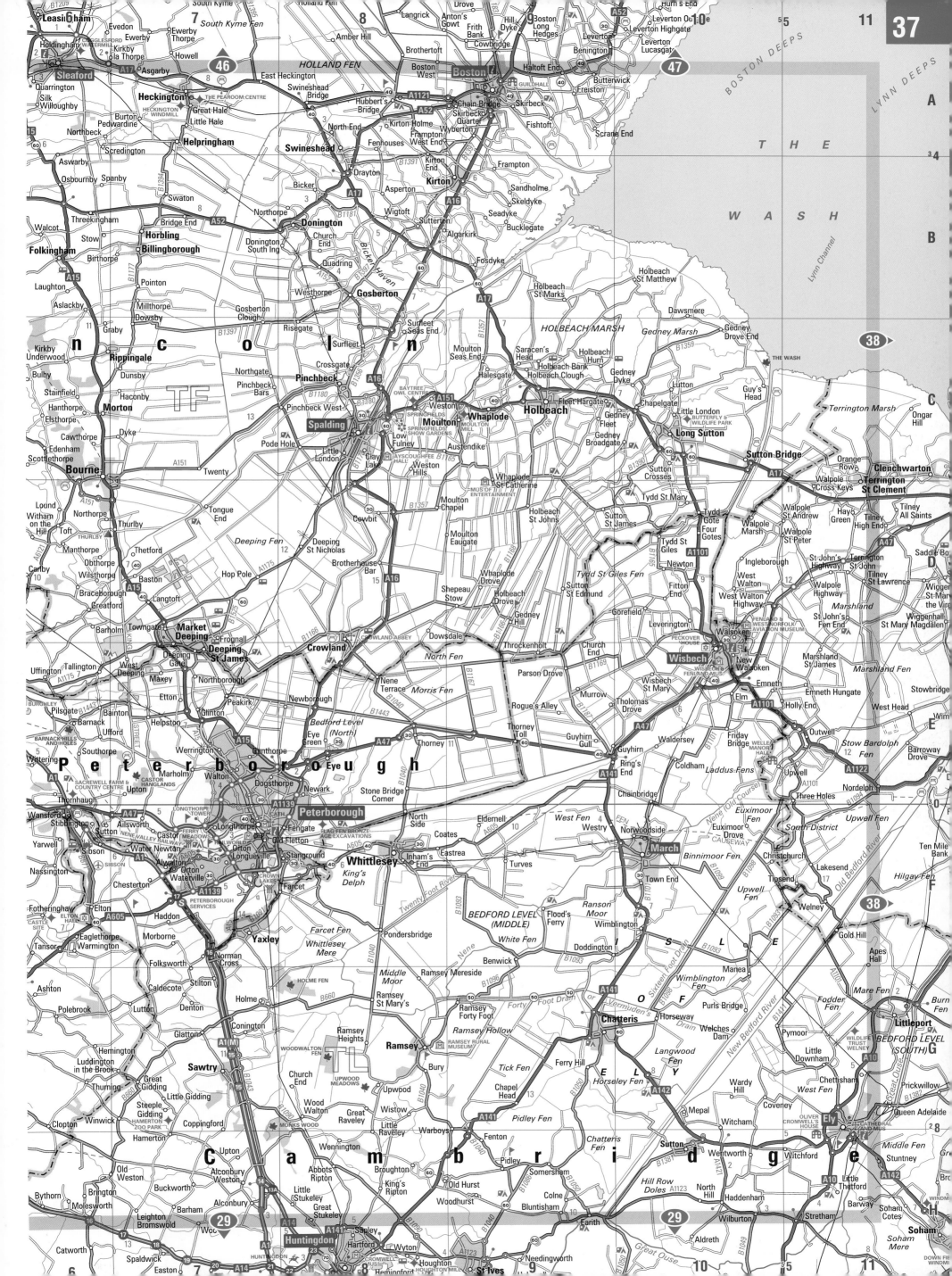

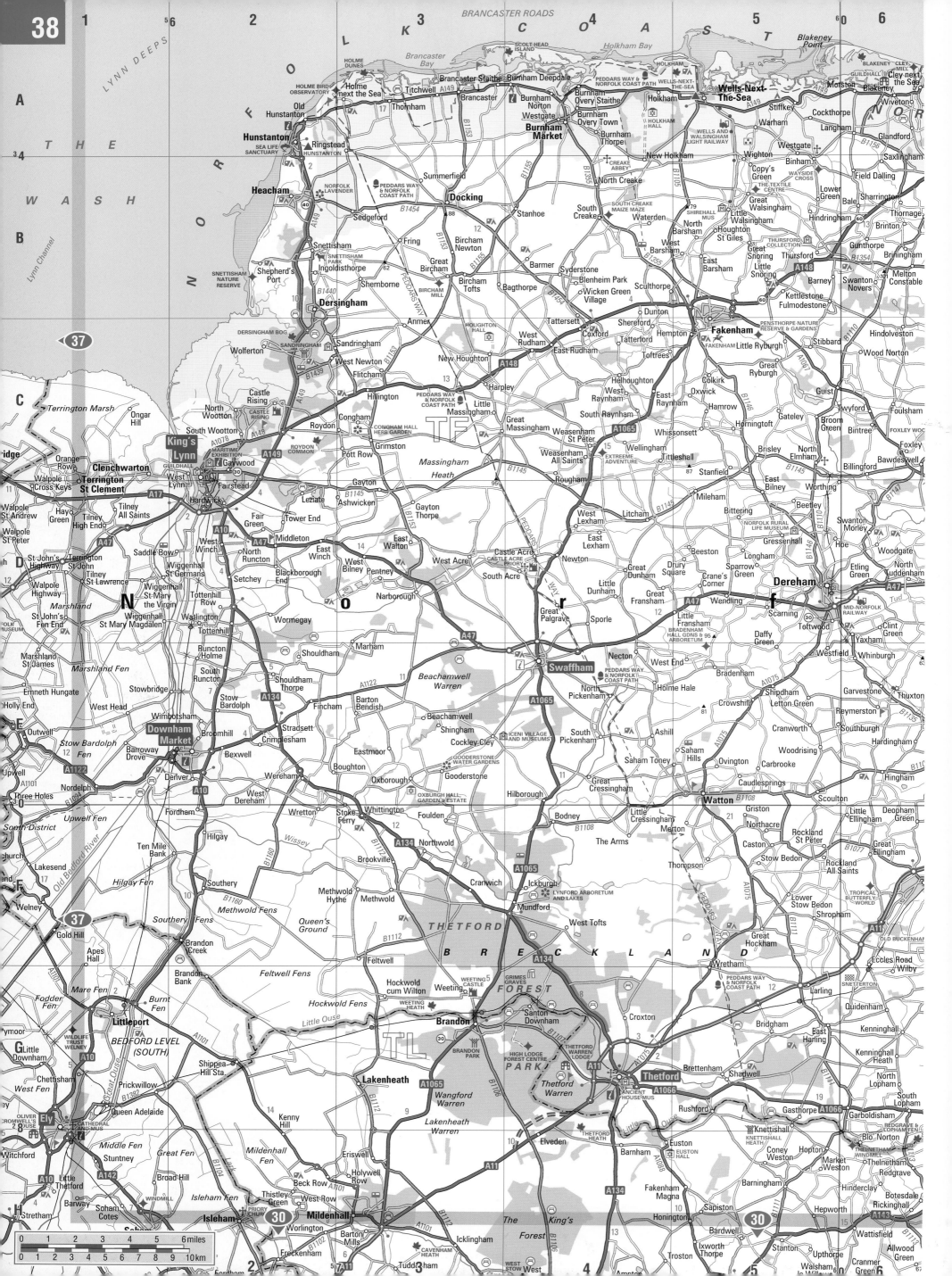

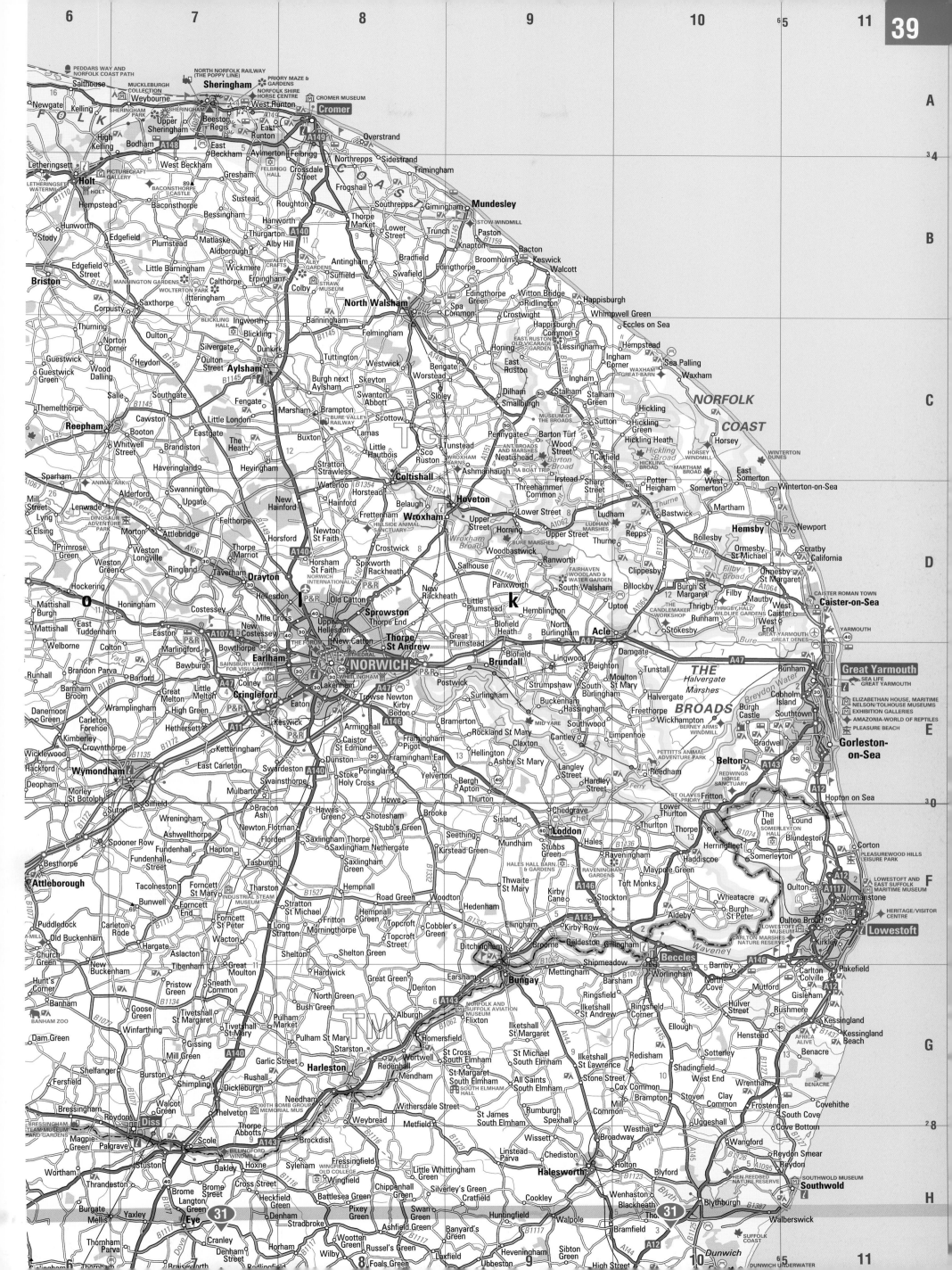

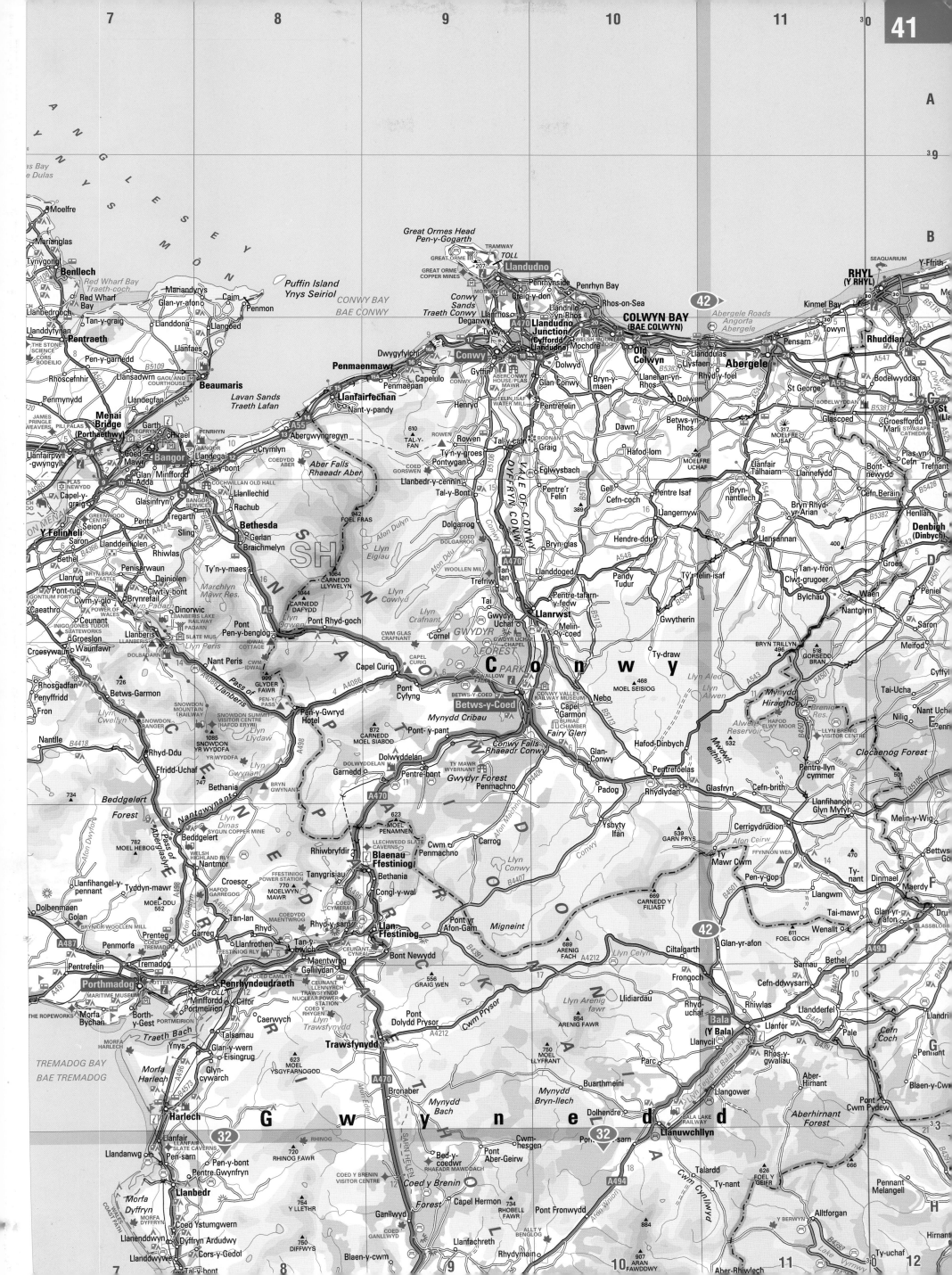

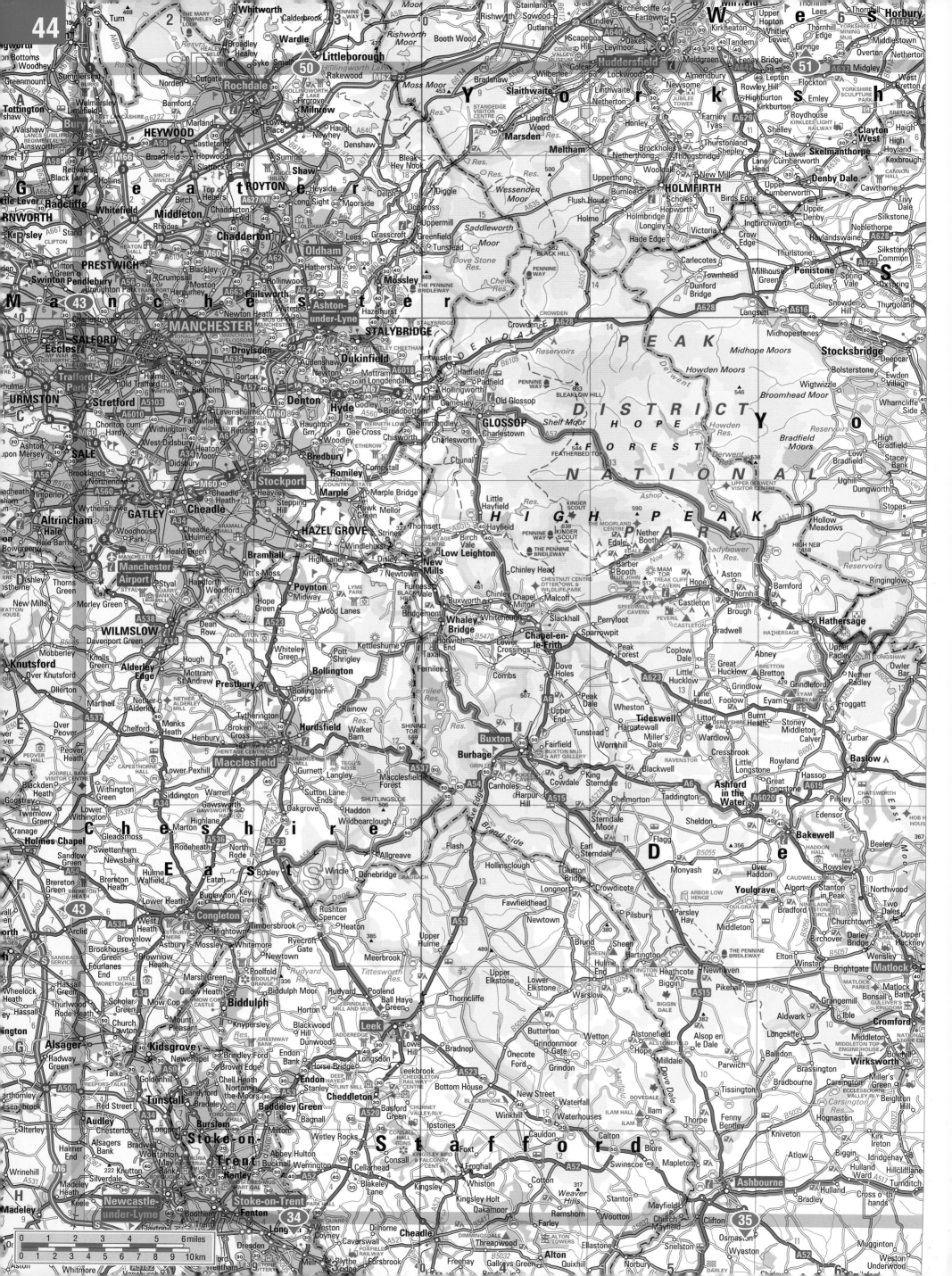

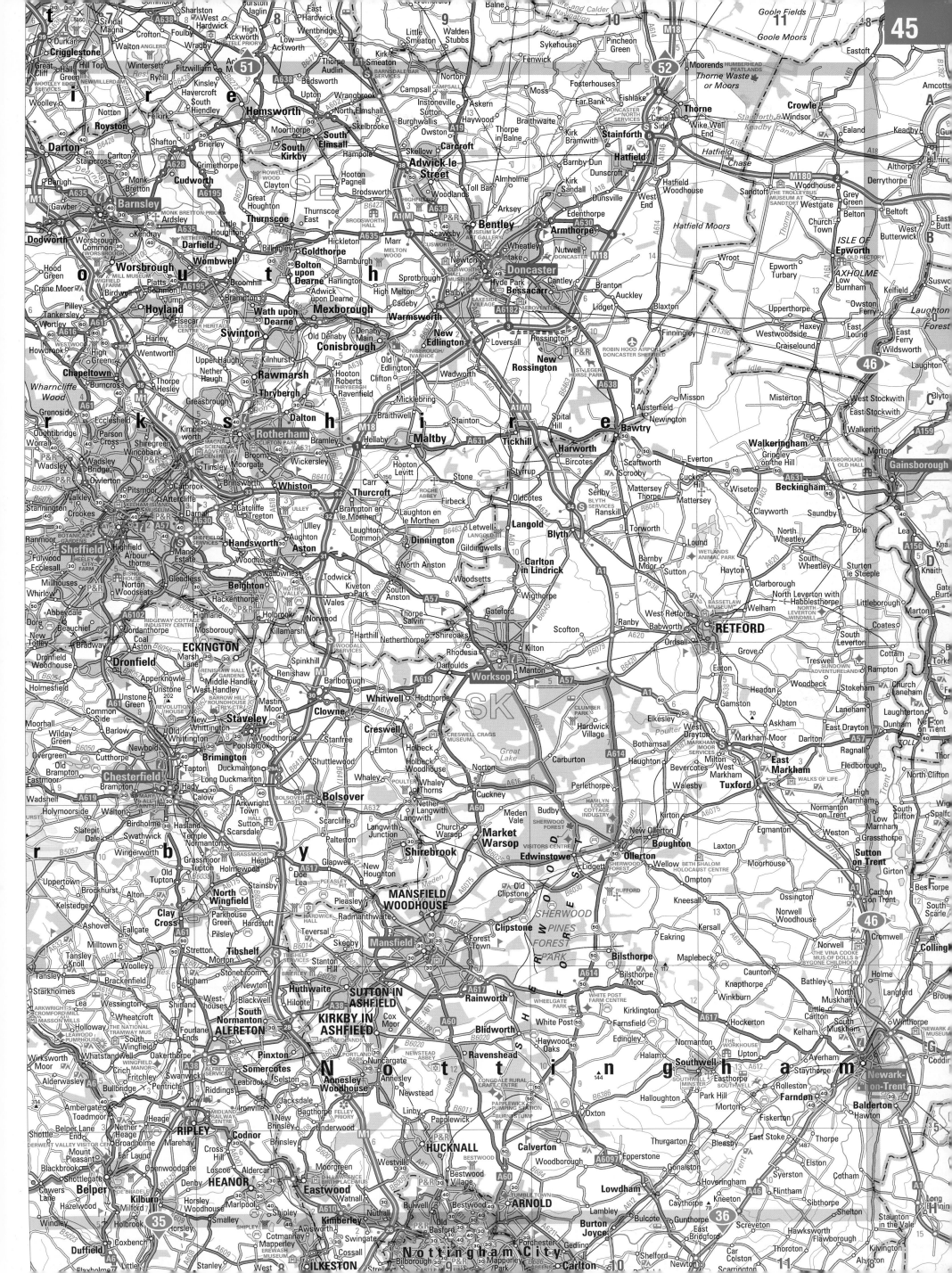

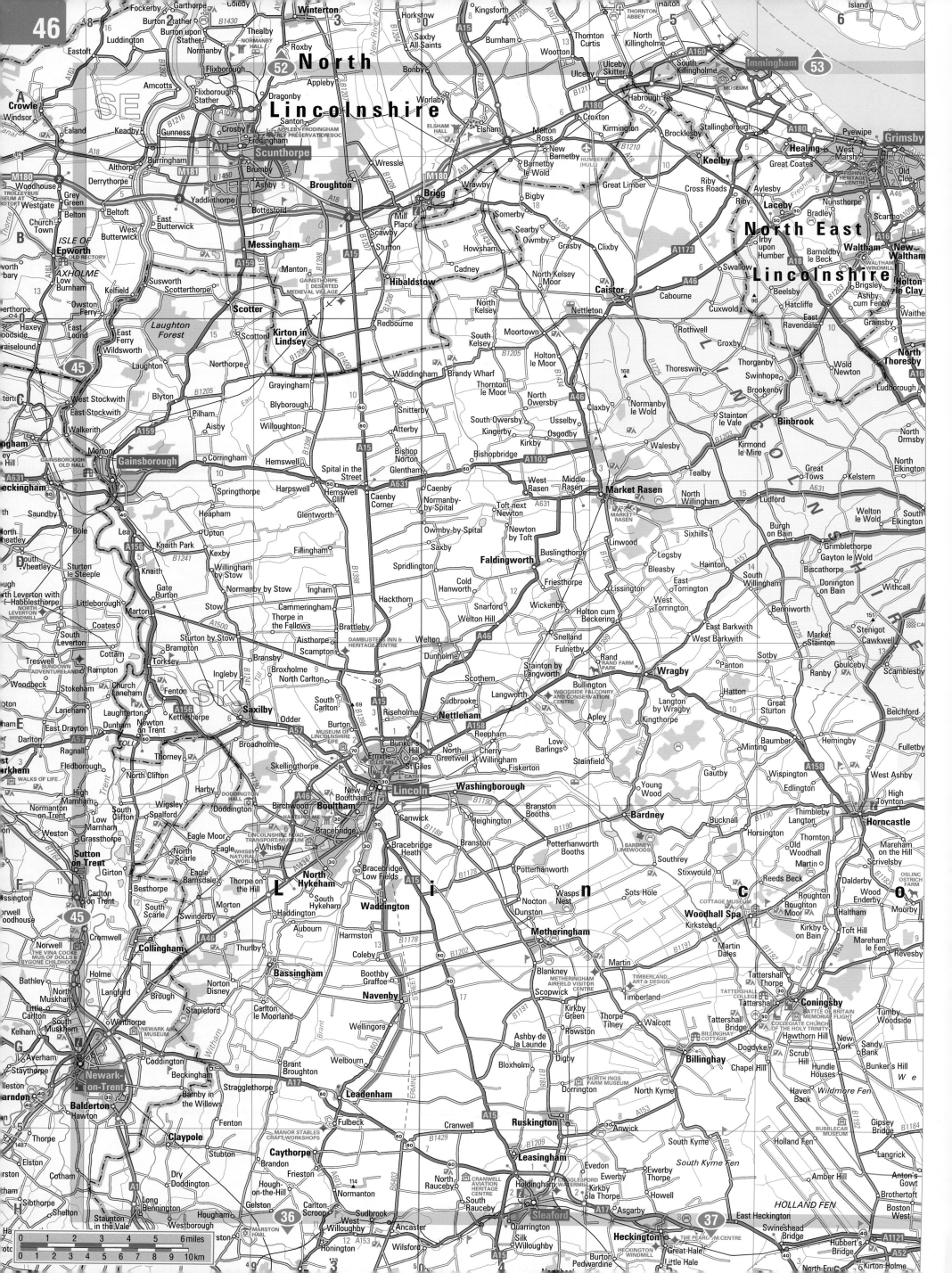

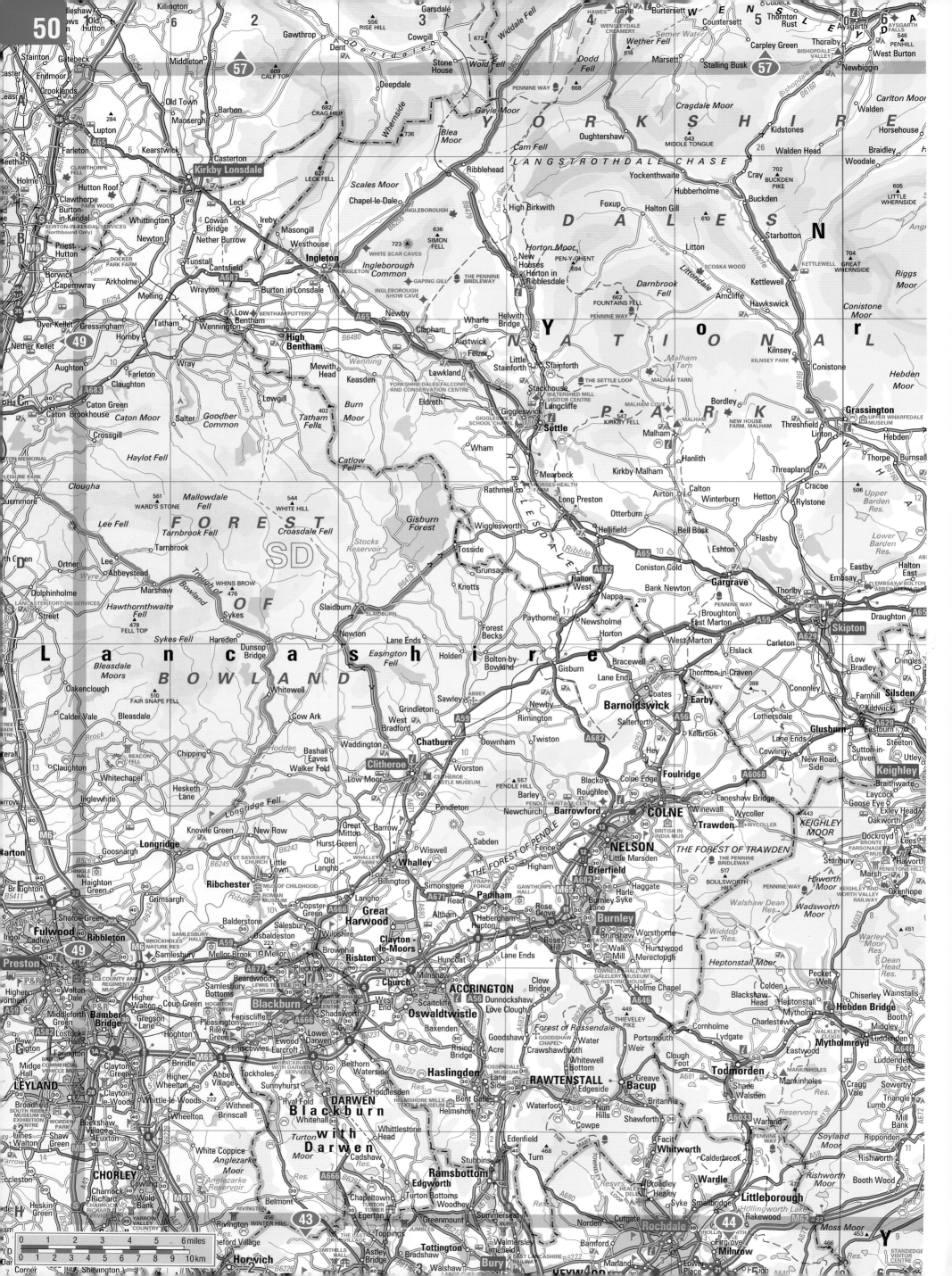

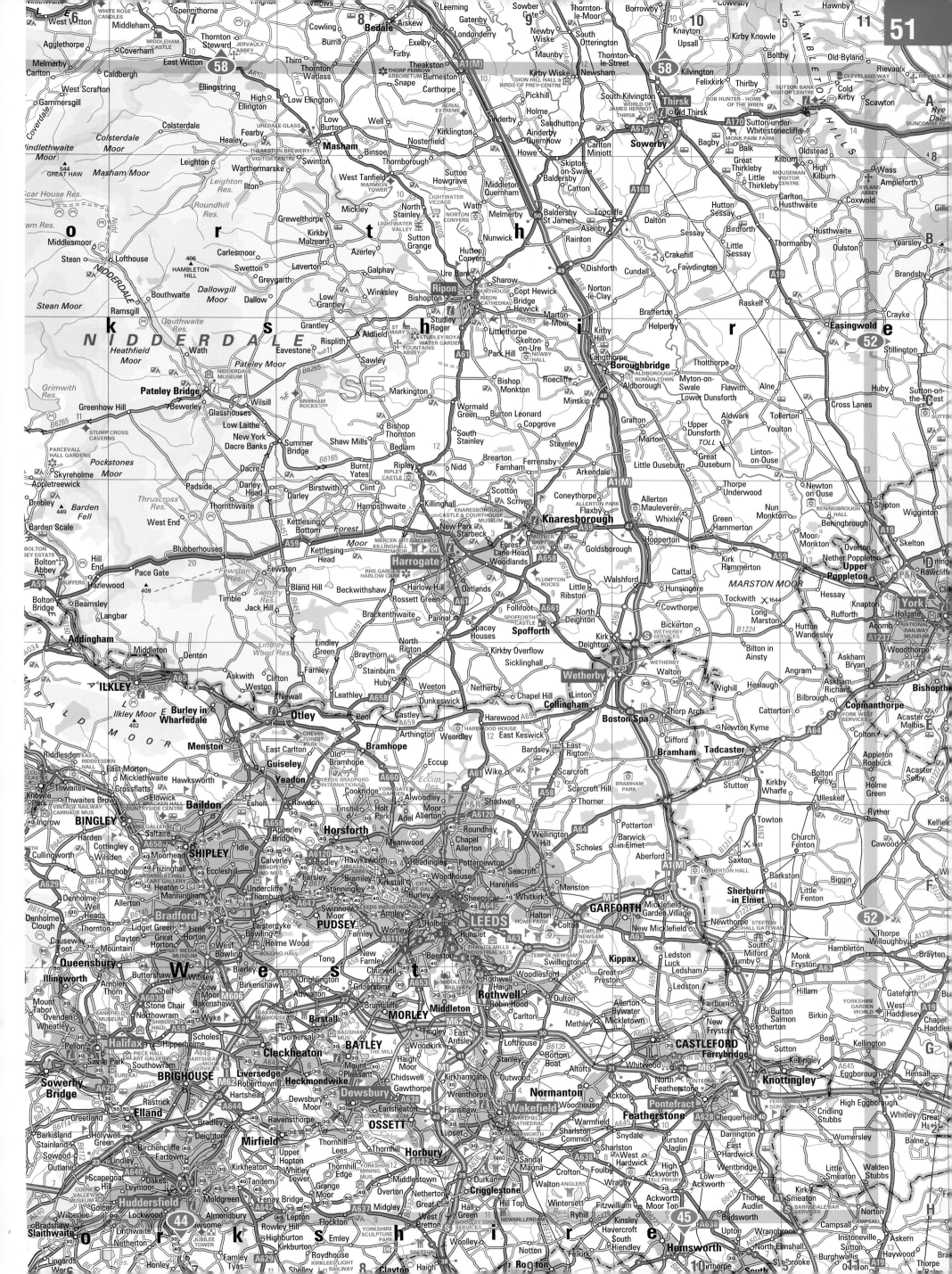

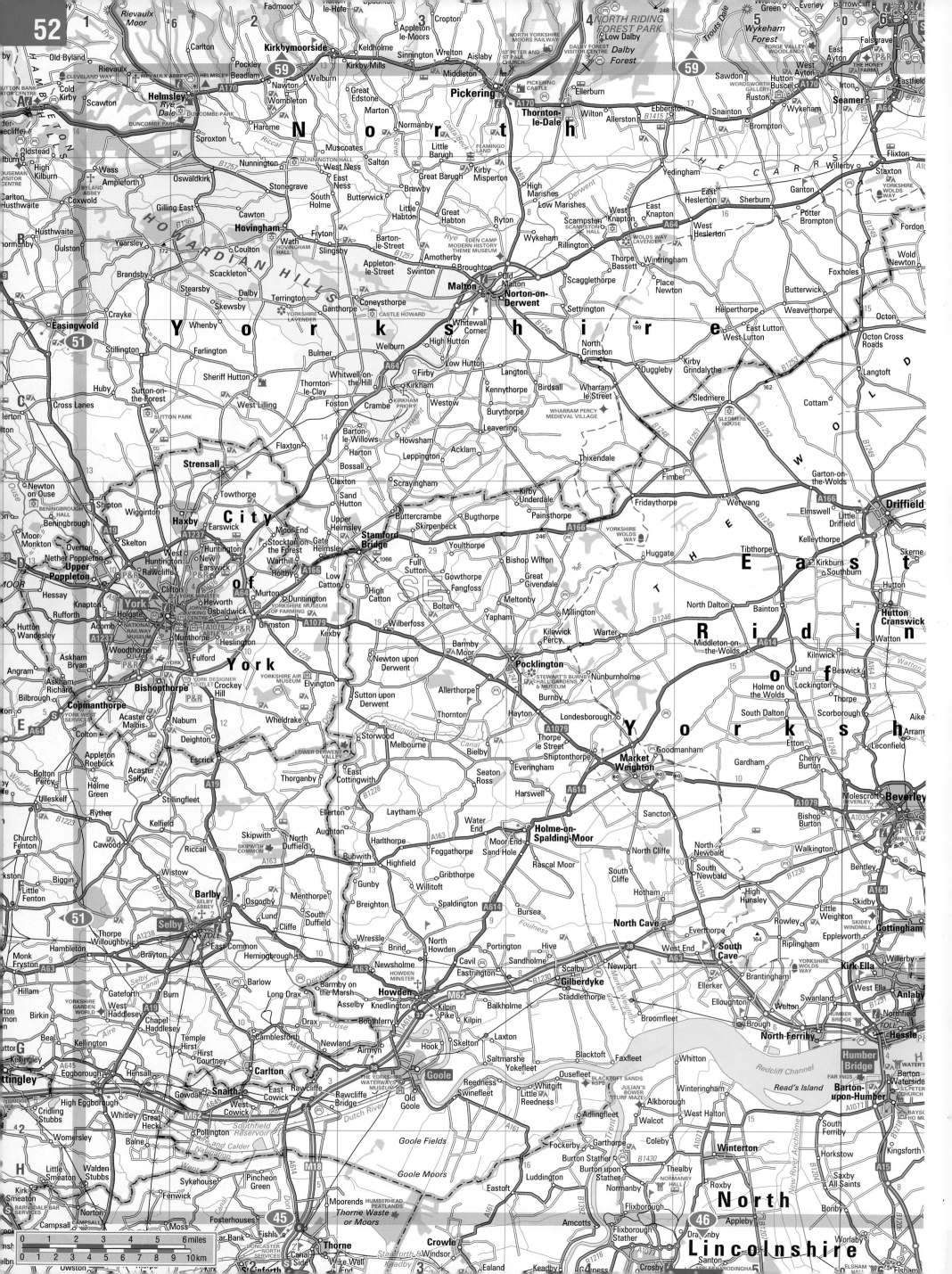

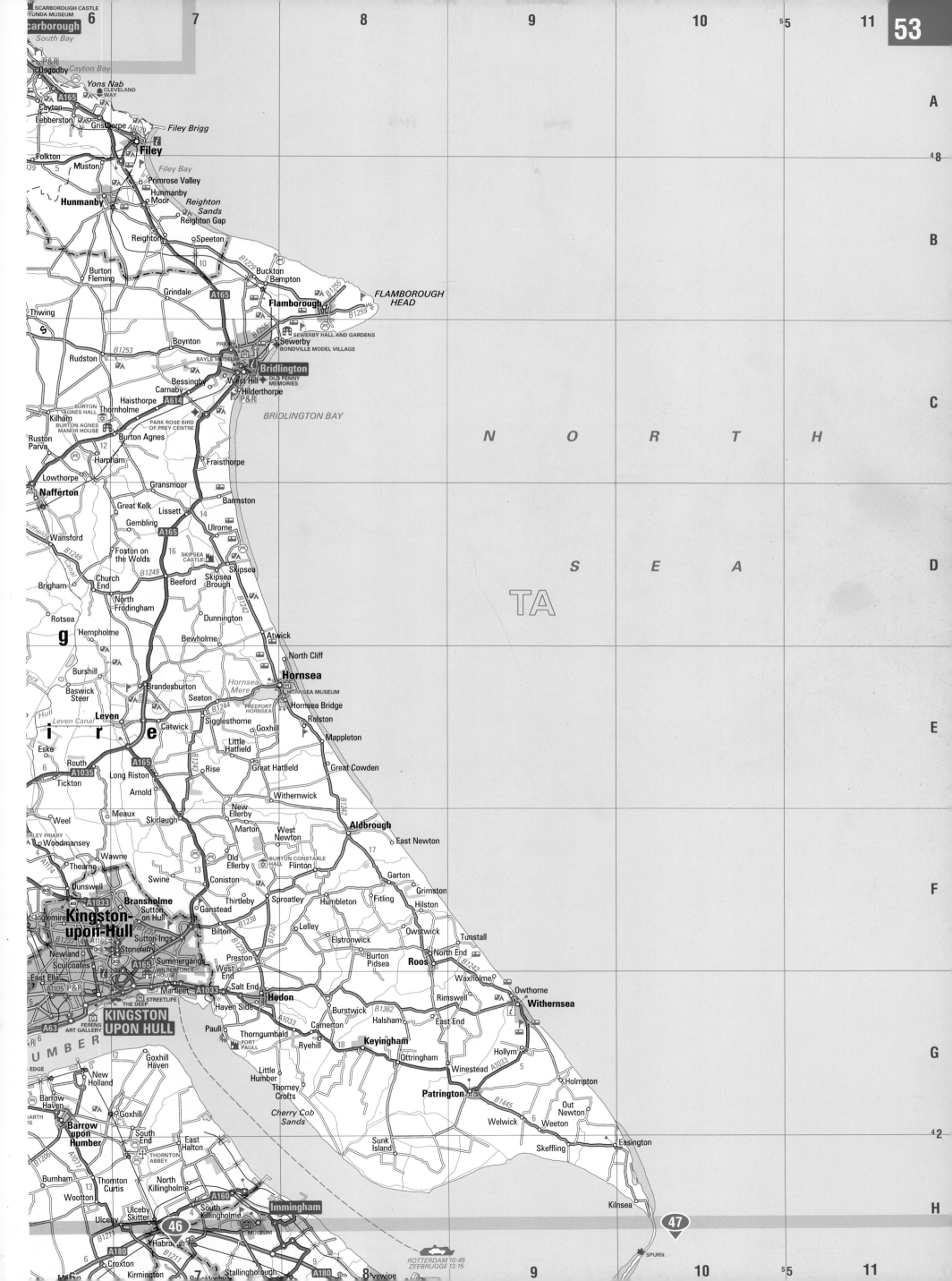

Scarborough

Rotunda Museum
Scarborough Castle

South Bay

6   7   8   9   10   11

A

Osgodby   Cayton Bay
P&R
Cayton
Lebberston   A165
Folkton   Gristhorpe   A1039   Filey Brigg
Muston   **Filey**   i

B

Yons Nab   CLEVELAND WAY

Filey Bay
Primrose Valley
Hunmanby Moor
Hunmanby   Reighton Sands
Reighton Gap
Reighton   Speeton

Burton Fleming   Buckton
Bempton
Grindale   A165
Thwing   **Flamborough**   B1255
   B1259

FLAMBOROUGH HEAD

Rudston   B1253   Boynton
PRIORY   SEWERBY HALL AND GARDENS
BAYLE MUSEUM   Sewerby
BONDVILLE MODEL VILLAGE

C

Bessingby   **Bridlington**
Carnaby   West Hill   OLD PENNY MEMORIES
Haisthorpe   A614   Hilderthorpe
Kilham   Thornholme   P&R
BURTON AGNES HALL   Burton Agnes
Ruston Parva   MANOR HOUSE   PARK ROSE BIRD OF PREY CENTRE

N O R T H

12   Harpham   Fraisthorpe

BRIDLINGTON BAY

Nafferton   Lowthorpe   Gransmoor
Great Kelk   Barmston
Wansford   Gembling   Lissett   14
A165   Ulrome

S E A

Foston on the Wolds   16   SKIPSEA CASTLE
Brigham   B1249   Skipsea
Church End   Beeford   Skipsea Brough
North Frodingham   B1242

TA

D

Rotsea   Dunnington
g   Hempholme   Bewholme   Atwick

Burshill   North Cliff
Baswick Steer   Brandesburton   **Hornsea**
Hornsea Mere   HORNSEA MUSEUM

E

i   r   e   **Leven**   Seaton   B1244
Leven Canal   Catwick   Sigglesthorne   FREEPORT HORNSEA   Hornsea Bridge
Eske   Goxhill   Rolston
Routh   A165   Little Hatfield   Mappleton
6   A1035   Long Riston   Rise   Great Hatfield
Tickton   Arnold   Great Cowden
Weel   Meaux   B1243   Withernwick

F

Woodmansey   Skirlaugh   New Ellerby
Thearne   Marton   West Newton   **Aldbrough**
Wawne   B1242   East Newton
Dunswell   Old Ellerby   Flinton   Garton
13   BURTON CONSTABLE HALL   Grimston
A1033   **Bransholme**   Swine   Coniston   Fitling   Hilston
40   Sutton on Hull   Thirtleby   Sproatley   Humbleton
Kingston-upon-Hull   Ganstead   Lelley   Owstwick
Inglemire   Bilton   B1238   B1240   Elstronwick   Tunstall
Newland   Sutton Ings   Preston   Burton Pidsea   North End
Sculcoates   Stoneferry   A165   **Roos**   B1242
East Ella   Summergangs   West End   Waxholme

G

WILBERFORCE HOUSE   A1033   Salt End   Rimswell   Owthorne
A1105   P&R   Marfleet   **Withernsea**   i
THE DEEP   STREETLIFE   **Hedon**   Burstwick   East End
FERENS ART GALLERY   Haven Side   B1362   Halsham   Hollym
KINGSTON UPON HULL   A1033   Camerton
A63   Paull   Thorngumbald   **Keyingham**   Winestead   A1033
H U M B E R   FORT PAULL   Ryehill   18   Ottringham   Holmpton
  Goxhill Haven   Little Humber   **Patrington**   Out Newton
New Holland   Thorney Crofts   B1445   Welwick   Weeton

H

Barrow Haven   Cherry Cob Sands
Barrow upon Humber   Goxhill   South End   East Halton   Sunk Island   Skeffling   Easington
Burnham   Thornton Curtis   North Killingholme   THORNTON ABBEY
Wootton   Ulceby   A160   South Killingholme   Kilnsea
B1206   Ulceby Skitter   **Immingham**   47
A1077   46   MUSEUM
B1211   Habrough   SPURN
A180   Croxton   Kirmington   Stallingborough   A180   Yawthorpe
B1211   ROTTERDAM 10:45
ZEEBRUGGE 13:15

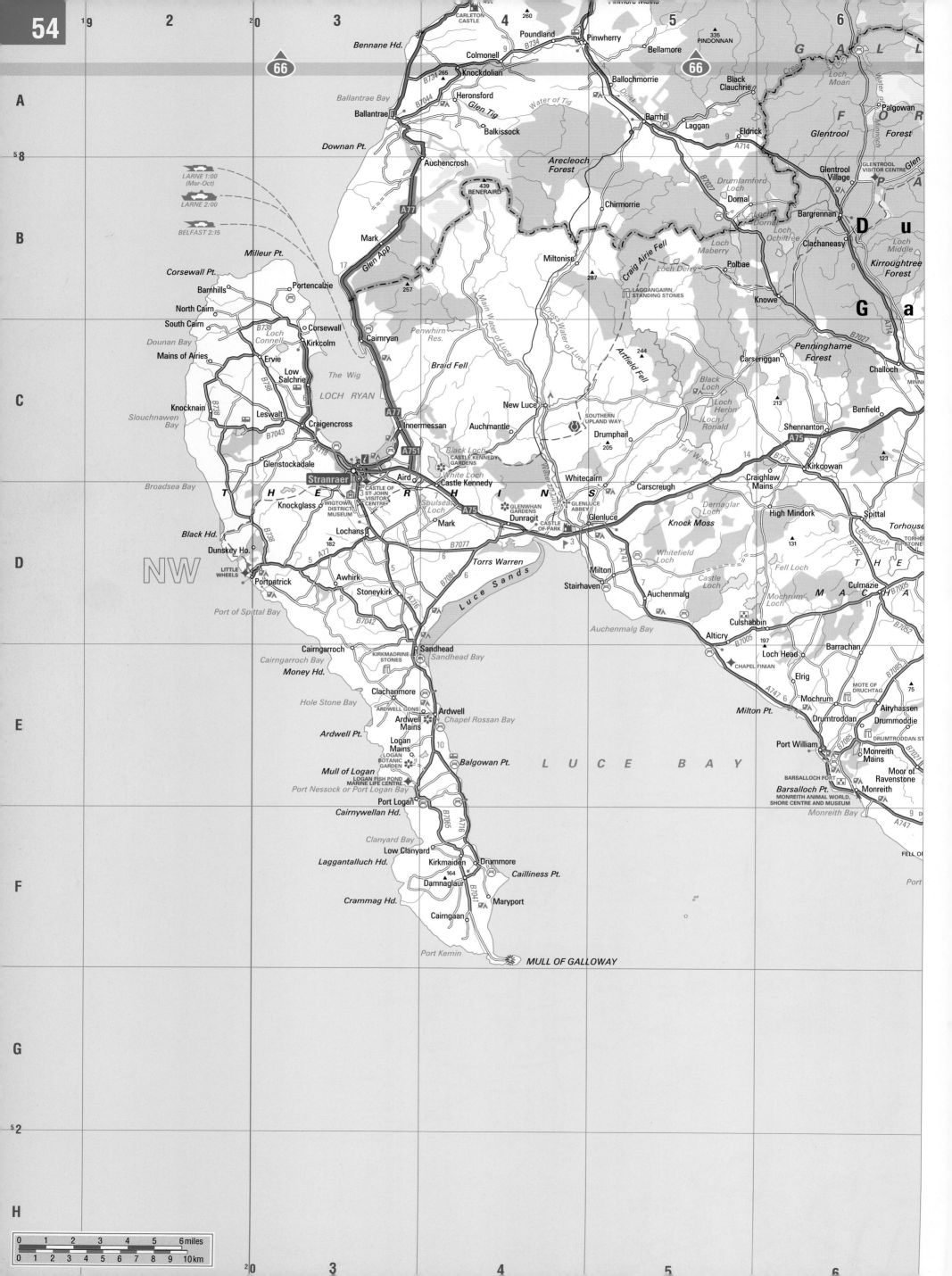

GALL...

FOR...

DU...

G a...

66

66

Carleton Castle
Poundland
Pinwherry
Bellamore
260
335 PINDONNAN
Bennane Hd.
Colmonell
B734
Milmore Mains
Ballochmorrie
Black Clauchrie
Palgowan
Knockdolian
B734 265
Heronsford
Barrhill
Laggan
Eldrick
Glentrool
Ballantrae Bay
B7044
Glen Tig
Water of Tig
A714
Ballantrae
Balkissock
Glentrool Village
GLENTROOL VISITOR CENTRE
Glen...

Downan Pt.
Auchencrosh
Arecleoch Forest
Drumlamford Loch
Dornal
Bargrennan
PA...

439 BENERAIRD
Chirmorrie
Loch Dornal
Clachaneasy
Loch Middle
Kirroughtree Forest

A77
Mark
Glen App
Miltonise
Craig Airie Fell
Loch Maberry
Polbae
Knowe
Loch Derry

Milleur Pt.
257
Loch Ochiltree

Corsewall Pt.
Portencalzie
LAGGANGAIRN STANDING STONES
287
B7027

Barnhills
North Cairn
South Cairn
Dounan Bay
B738 Loch Connell
Corsewall
Kirkcolm
Cairnryan
Penwhirn Res.
Main Water of Luce
Cross Water of Luce
244 Artfield Fell
Carseriggan
Penninghame Forest
Challoch

Mains of Airies
Ervie
Low Salchrie
The Wig
Braid Fell
Black Loch
Loch Heron
Loch Ronald
Shennanton
Benfield

Slouchnawen Bay
Knocknain
Leswalt
LOCH RYAN
New Luce
SOUTHERN UPLAND WAY
Drumphail
205
213
A75
123

B7043
Craigencross
A77
Innermessan
Auchmantle
Tar Water
14
B733
Kirkcowan
Craighlaw Mains

Glenstockadale
A751
Aird
Black Lochs
White Loch
CASTLE KENNEDY GARDENS
Whitecairn
Carscreugh
Dernaglar Loch
High Mindork
Spittal
Torhouse

Broadsea Bay
THE
Stranraer
WIGTOWN DISTRICT MUSEUM
CASTLE OF ST JOHN VISITOR CENTRE
Castle Kennedy
GLENWHAN GARDENS
Dunragit
GLENLUCE ABBEY
Glenluce
Knock Moss
131
THE

Black Hd.
Dunskey Ho.
Knockglass
RHI
Mark
Soulseat Loch
A75
CASTLE OF PARK
Whitefield Loch
Milton
Fell Loch
Castle Loch
Culmazie
B7005
11

NW
LITTLE WHEELS
Lochans
182
N
Torrs Warren
S
Stairhaven
Auchenmalg
Mochrum Loch
MACH...
B7005

Portpatrick
Awhirk
Stoneykirk
Luce Sands
Auchenmalg Bay
Alticry
197
Loch Head
Barrachan

Port of Spittal Bay
8
B7042
A716
Culshabbin
B7005
CHAPEL FINIAN
Elrig
MOTE OF DRUCHTAG
75
Airyhassen

Cairngarroch
KIRKMADRINE STONES
Sandhead
A747
Mochrum
Drummoddie

Cairngarroch Bay
Money Hd.
Sandhead Bay
Milton Pt.
Drumtroddan
DRUMTRODDAN ST...

Clachanmore
ARDWELL GDNS.
Ardwell
Port William
Monreith Mains

Hole Stone Bay
Ardwell Mains
Chapel Rossan Bay
B7085
Moor of Ravenstone

Ardwell Pt.
Logan Mains
LOGAN BOTANIC GARDEN
10
Balgowan Pt.
LUCE BAY
BARSALLOCH FORT
Monreith
MONREITH ANIMAL WORLD, SHORE CENTRE AND MUSEUM

Mull of Logan
LOGAN FISH POND MARINE LIFE CENTRE
Barsalloch Pt.
Monreith Bay
A747
9

Port Nessock or Port Logan Bay
Port Logan
FELL O...

Cairnywellan Hd.
B7085
A716
Port...

Clanyard Bay
Low Clanyard

Laggantalluch Hd.
Kirkmaiden
Drummore
Cailliness Pt.

Crammag Hd.
164
Damnaglaur
B7041
Maryport

Cairngaan

Port Kemin
MULL OF GALLOWAY

LARNE 1:00 (Mar-Oct)
LARNE 2:00
BELFAST 2:15

0 1 2 3 4 5 6 miles
0 1 2 3 4 5 6 7 8 9 10km

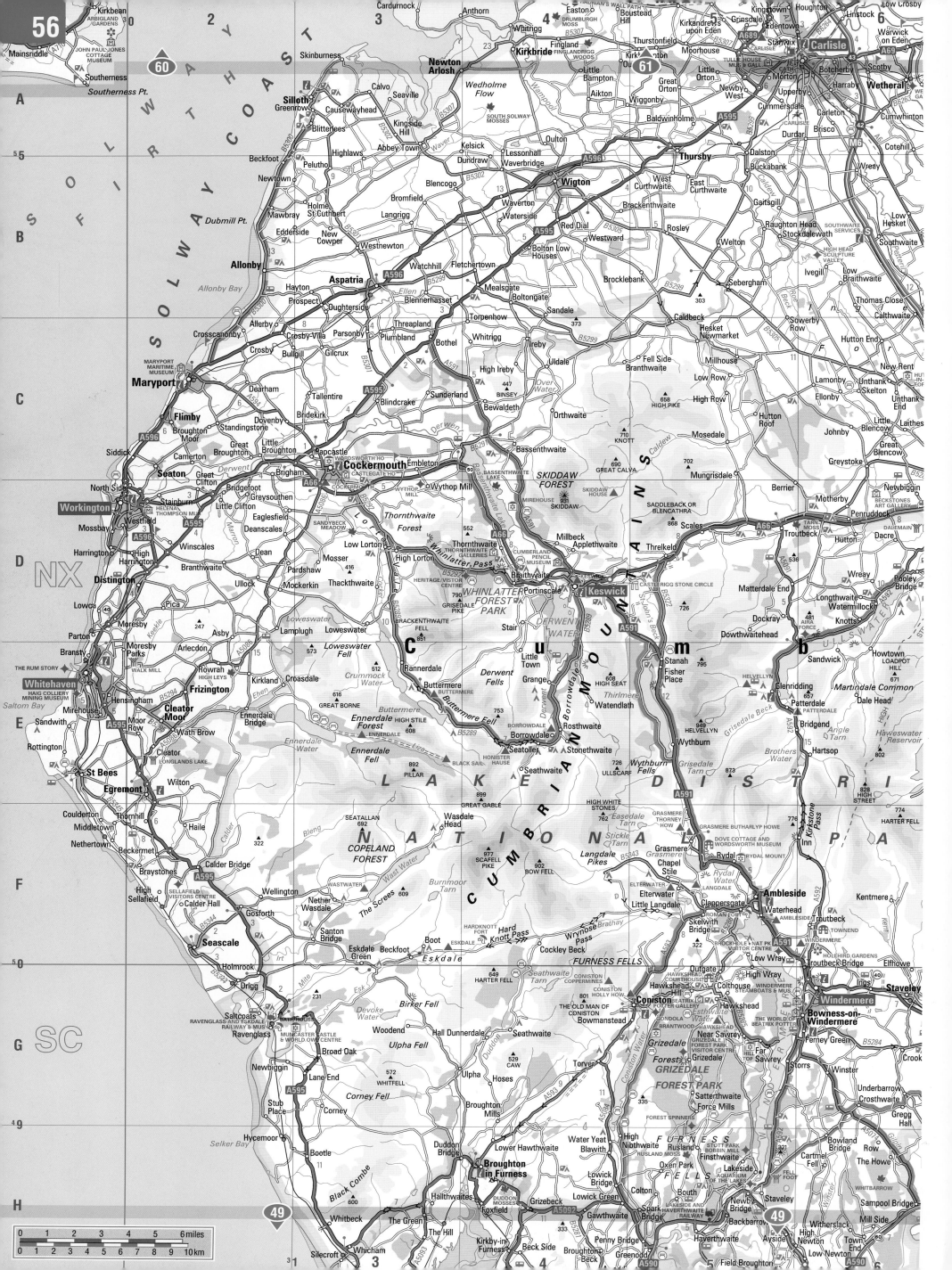

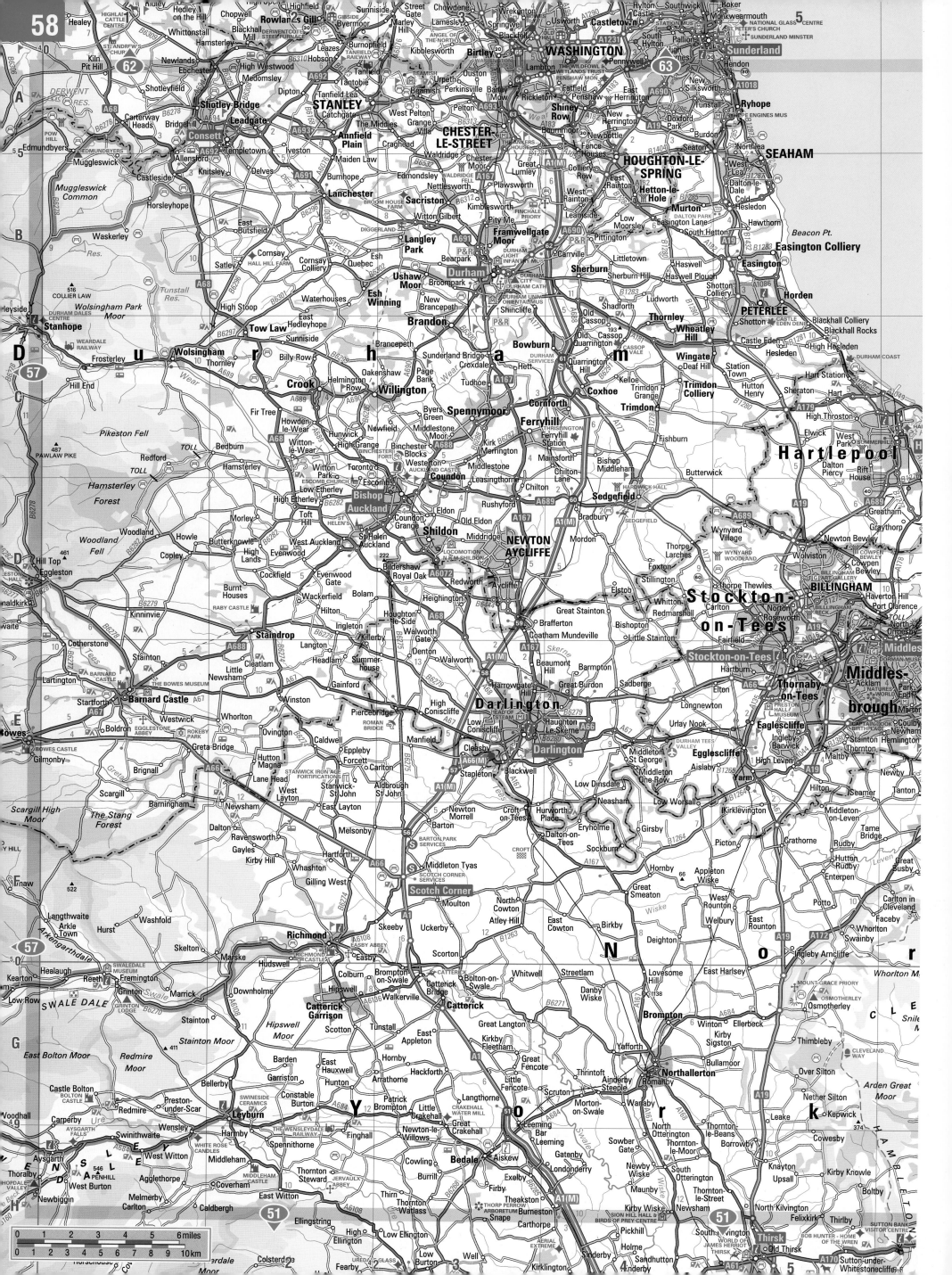

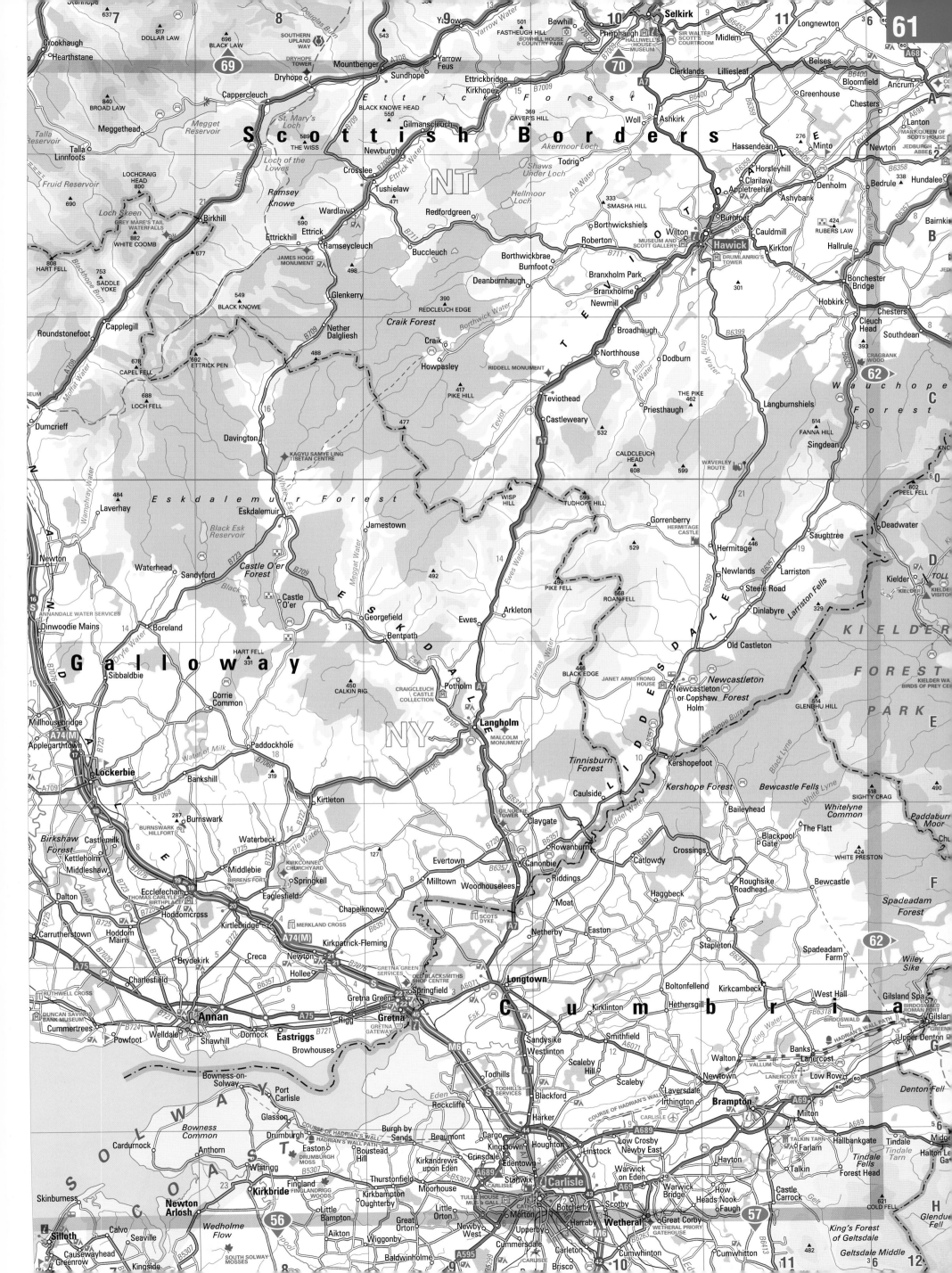

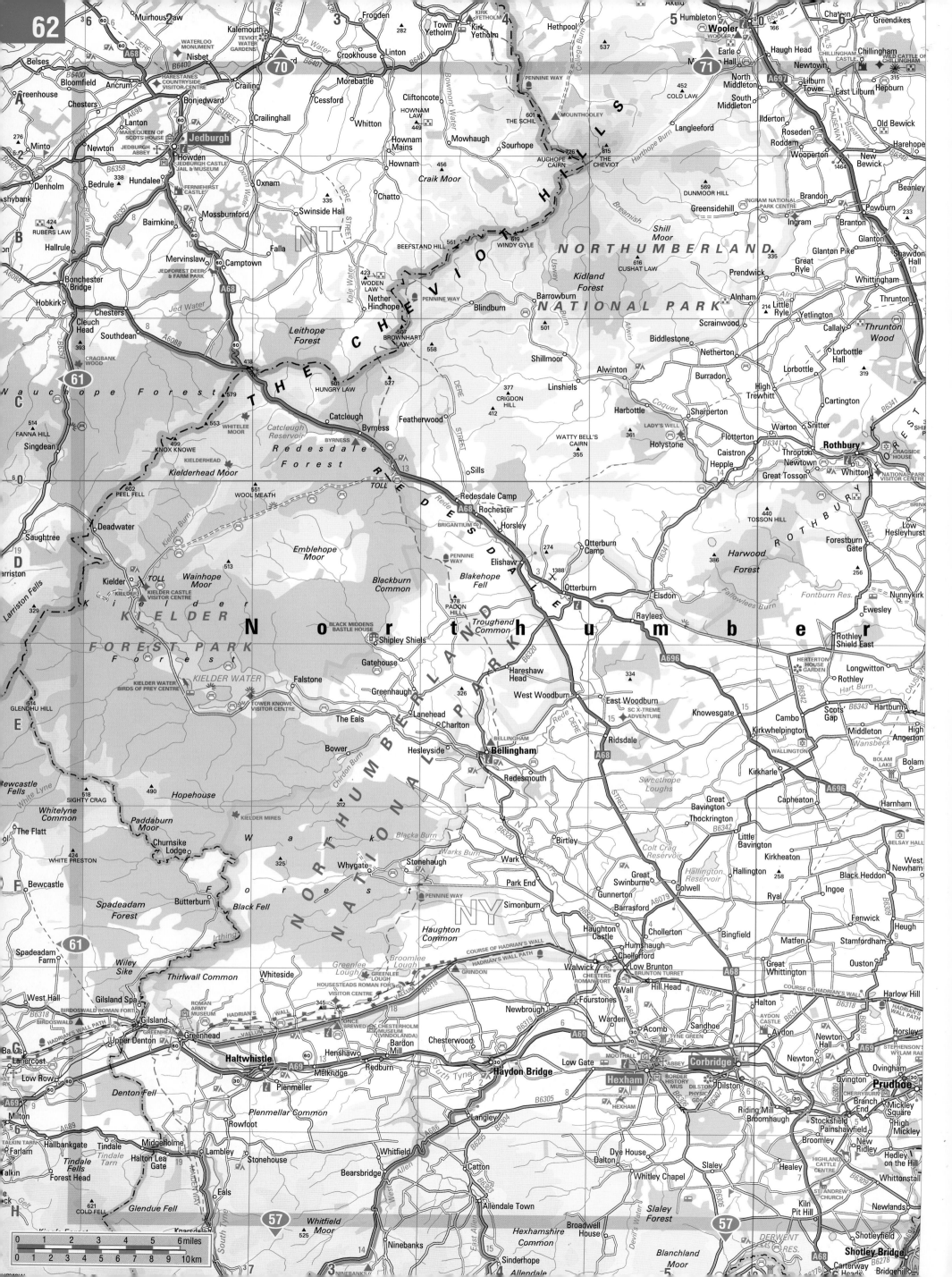

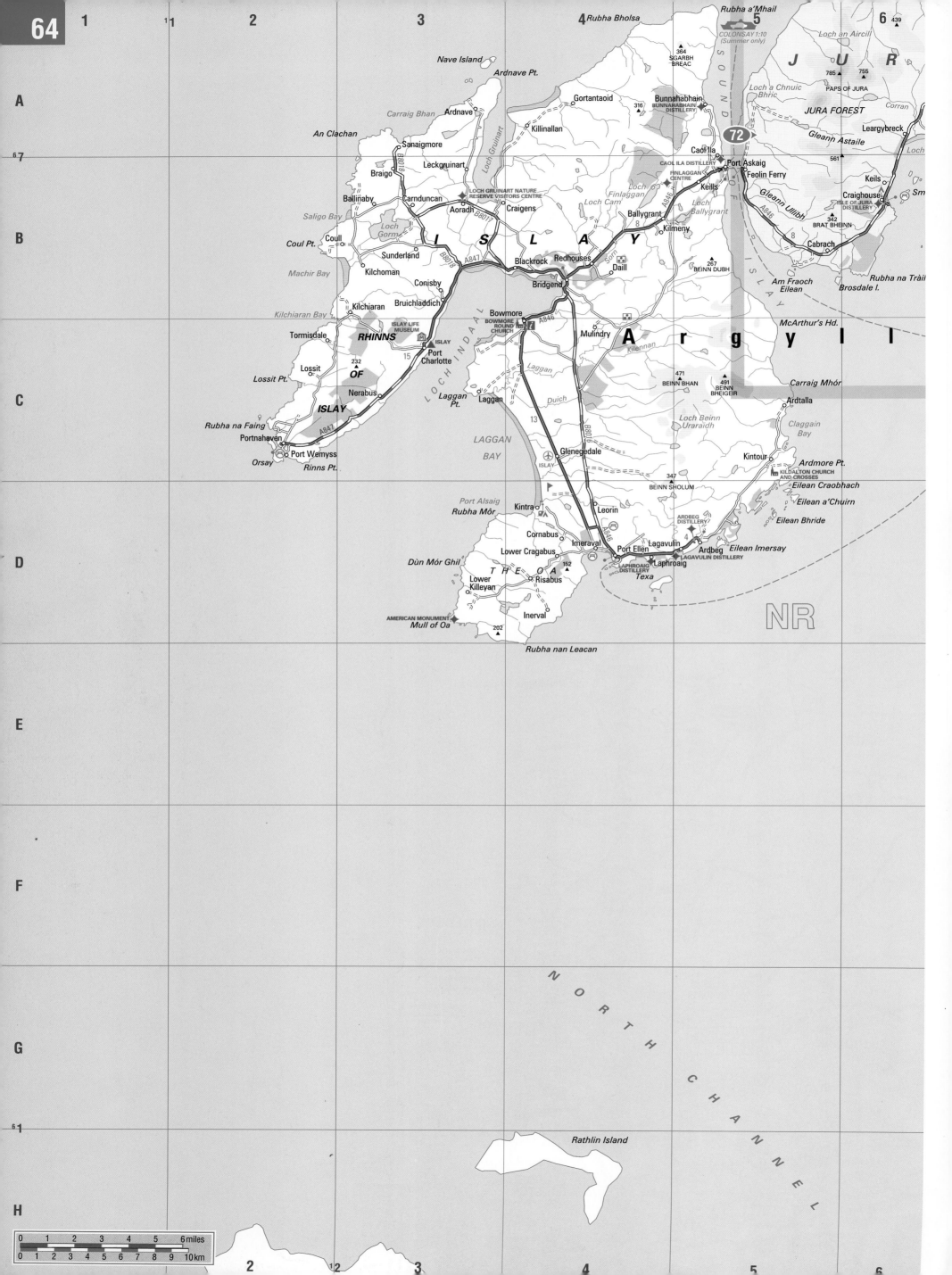

1 1 2 3 4 5 6 439

A

Rubha Bholsa
Rubha a'Mhail
COLONSAY 1:10
(Summer only)
Loch an Aircill

JURA
Loch a Chnuic Bhric
785 755
PAPS OF JURA
JURA FOREST
Corran

Nave Island
Ardnave Pt.
Gortantaoid
316
Bunnahabhain
BUNNAHABHAIN DISTILLERY
561
Leargybreck
Gleann Astaile

Carraig Bhan
Ardnave
Killinallan
SGARBH BREAC 364

An Clachan
Sanaigmore
72

B

Braigo
Leckgruinart
CAOL ILA DISTILLERY
Caol Ila
Port Askaig
Feolin Ferry
Keils
Craighouse
ISLE OF JURA DISTILLERY

Ballinaby
Carnduncan
LOCH GRUINART NATURE RESERVE VISITORS CENTRE
Loch Gruinart
Craigens
FINLAGGAN CENTRE
Loch Finlaggan
Keills
Gleann Ullibh
342
BRAT BHEINN

Coull Pt.
Coull
Sunderland
Loch Gorm
Aoradh
Loch Cam
Ballygrant
Kilmeny
Cabrach
Am Fraoch Eilean

ISLAY ISLAY
Blackrock Redhouses
Daill
Sorn
8
267
BEINN DUBH
Rubha na Tràili
Brosdale I.

Machir Bay
Kilchoman
Conisby
Bridgend

Kilchiaran
Bruichladdich
Kilchiaran Bay
McArthur's Hd.

C

Tormisdale
RHINNS
ISLAY LIFE MUSEUM
Bowmore
BOWMORE ROUND CHURCH
Mulindry
Kilennan
Argyll

Lossit
232
OF
ISLAY
Port Charlotte
15
471
BEINN BHAN
491
BEINN BHEIGEIR
Carraig Mhór

Lossit Pt.
Nerabus
Laggan
Duich
Loch Beinn Uraraidh
Ardtalla
Claggain Bay

Rubha na Faing
ISLAY
Laggan Pt.
Laggan
13
Kintour
Ardmore Pt.

Portnahaven
A847
Port Wemyss
Orsay
Rinns Pt.
LAGGAN BAY
ISLAY
Glenegedale
347
BEINN SHOLUM
Eilean Craobhach
Eilean a'Chuirn
Eilean Bhride

D

Port Alsaig
Rubha Mór
Kintra
Cornabus
Leorin
ARDBEG DISTILLERY
KILDALTON CHURCH AND CROSSES

Dùn Mór Ghil
Lower Cragabus
Imeraval
Port Ellen
Lagavulin
4
Ardbeg
Eilean Imersay

THE OA
152
LAPHROAIG DISTILLERY
Laphroaig
LAGAVULIN DISTILLERY

Lower Killeyan
Risabus
Texa

AMERICAN MONUMENT
Inerval
NR

Mull of Oa
202

Rubha nan Leacan

E

F

G

NORTH

6 1

Rathlin Island

CHANNEL

H

0 1 2 3 4 5 6 miles
0 1 2 3 4 5 6 7 8 9 10km

2 2 3 4 5 6

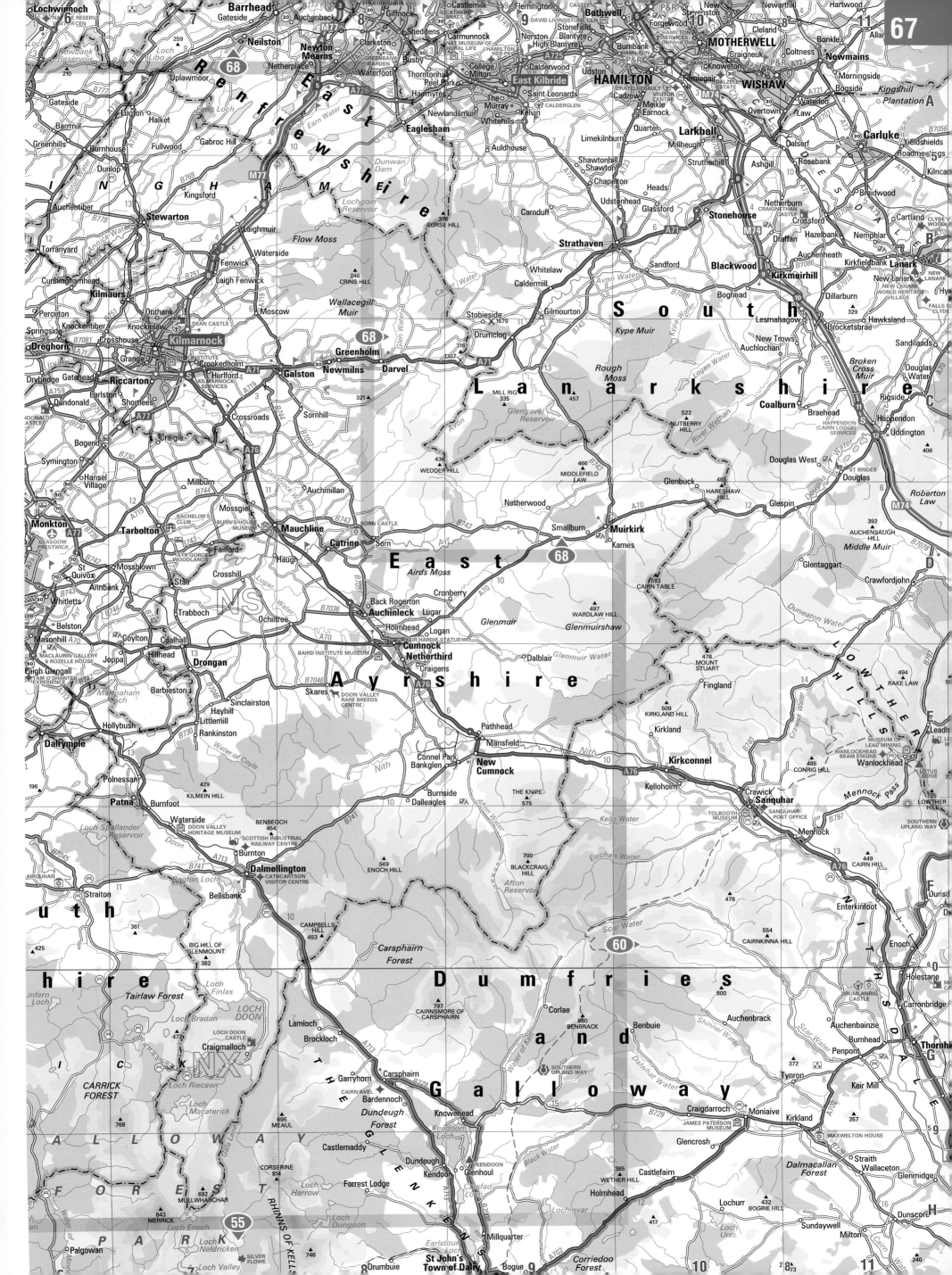

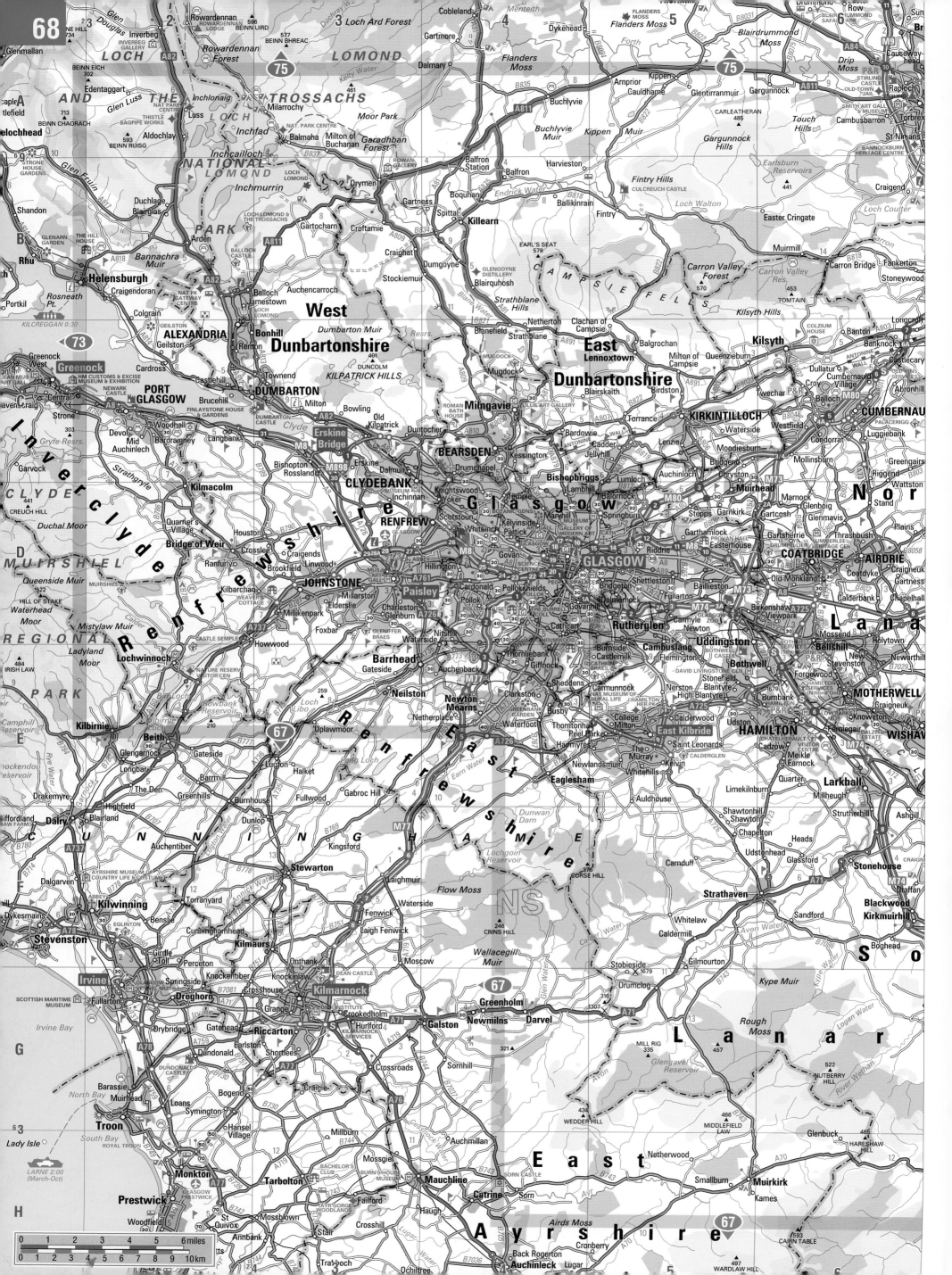

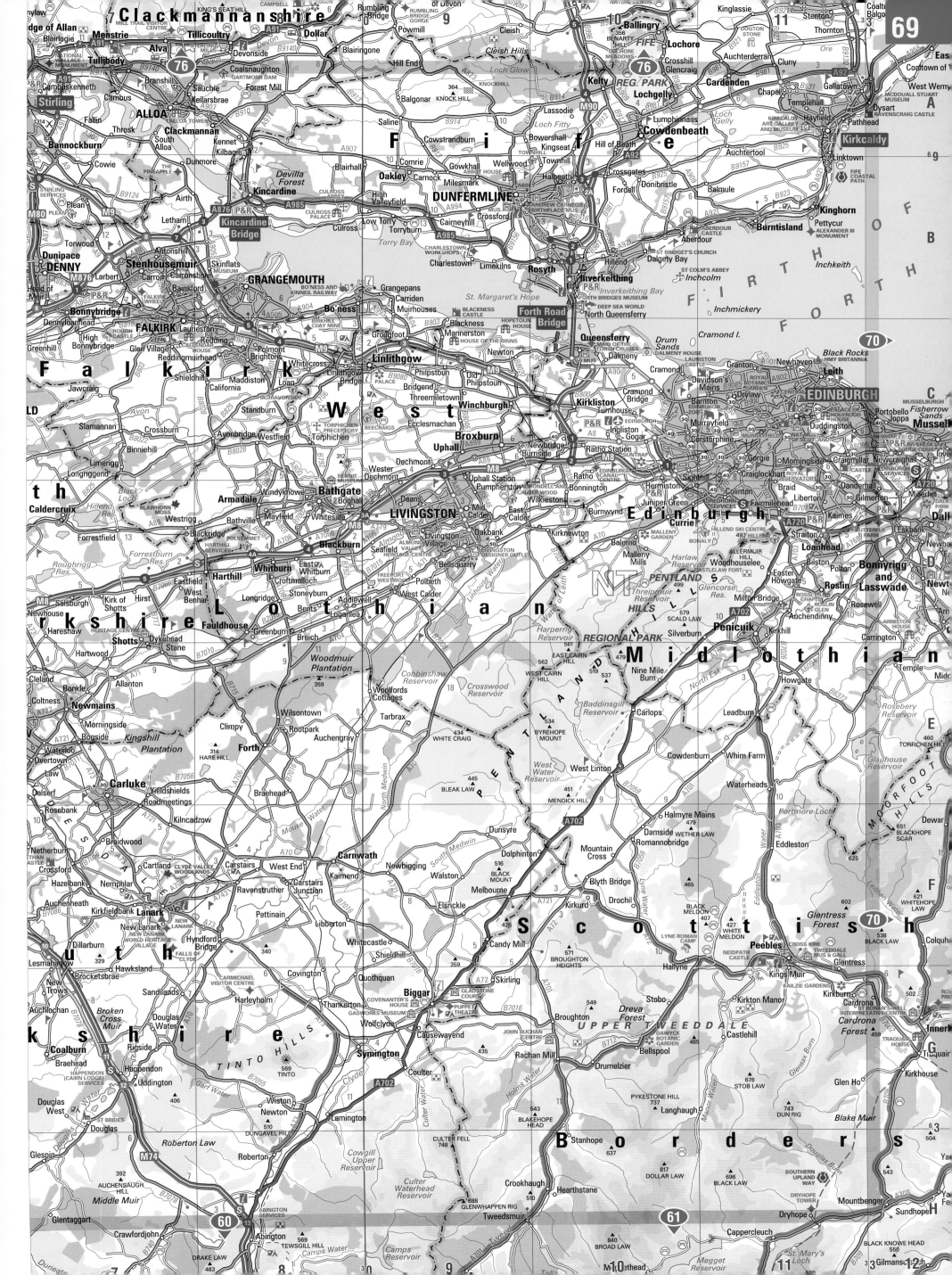

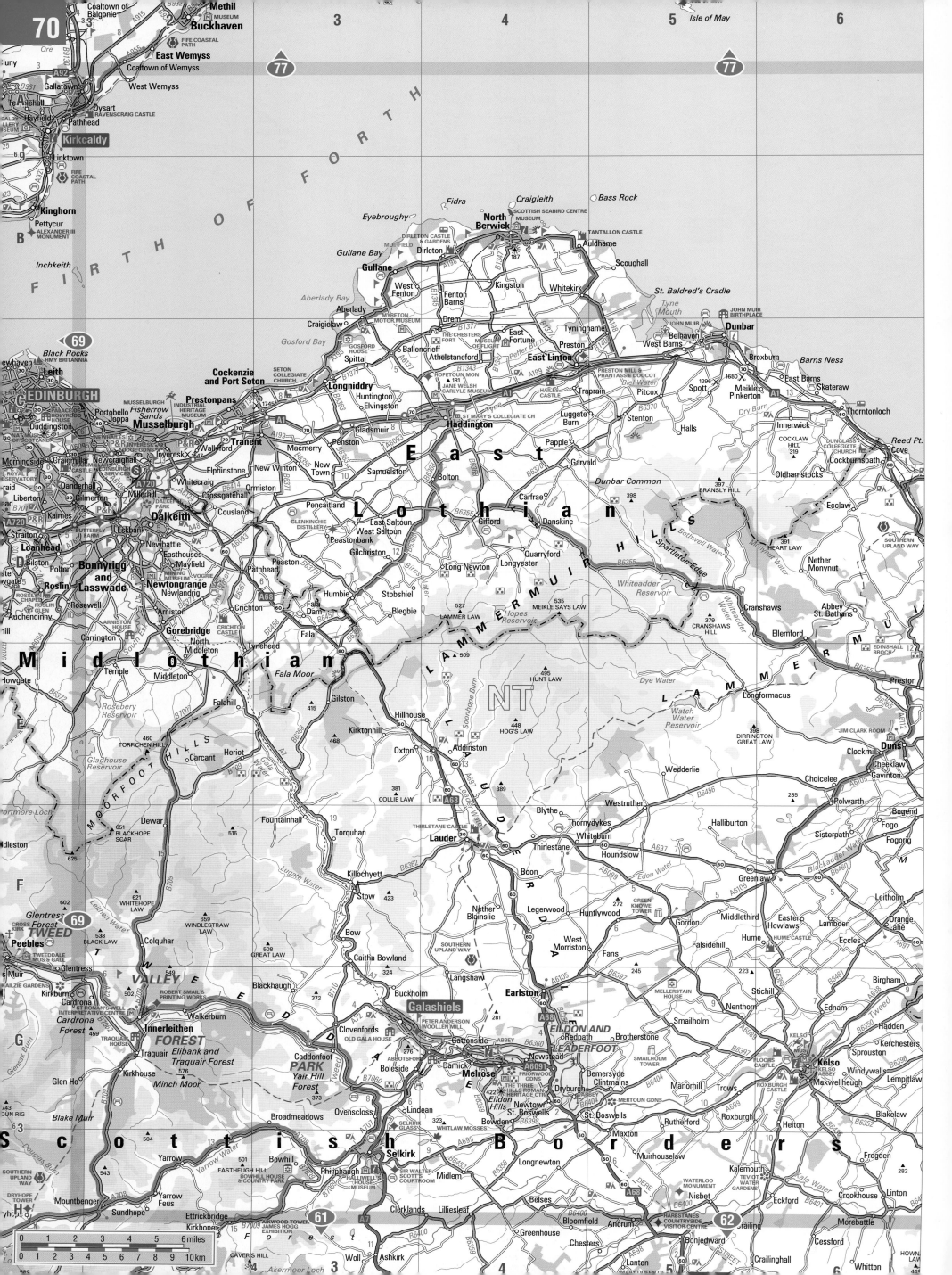

NORTH SEA

NU

Siccar Pt.   Wheat Stack
FAST CASTLE
ST ABB'S HEAD
St. Abb's Head
KITTIWAKE GALLERY
Lumsdaine
Northfield
St Abbs
Coldingham Bay
St. Abb's Haven
COLDINGHAM PRIORY
Coldingham Moor
Huxton   Coldingham
Grantshouse
Houndwood
Caimcross
Eyemouth
EYEMOUTH MUSEUM
Auchencrow   Reston   Ayton
AYTON CASTLE
Burnmouth
Prenderguest
Lamberton Beach
Lintlaw   Lamberton
Chirnside   Foulden   Clappers
Chirnsidebridge   FOULDEN TITHE BARN   Highfields
Edrom   Berwick-upon-Tweed
Buxley   BARRACKS MUSEUM & RAMPARTS BERWICK
MANDERSTON   Hutton   Paxton   East   Tweedmouth
SCRUMSTANE FARM PARK   Ord   Spittal
Blackadder West   PAXTON HOUSE   Prior Park
Allanton   Loanend
Sinclair's Hill   Whitsome   FISHWICK UNION SUSPENSION BRIDGE   Redshin Cove
Swinton   Horncliffe   Murton   Scremerston
SWINTON KIRK   Thornton Park   Thornton
Swintonmill   Horndean   NORHAM CASTLE   West Allerdean   Cheswick
Simprim   Norham   Shoreswood   Goswick
Ladykirk   Grindon   Shoresdean   Ancroft   Haggerston   LINDISFARNE
Felkington   Berrington   Emmanuel Hd.
Shellacres   Duddo   Bowsden   Beal   Holy Island (Lindisfarne)
Lennel   Castle Heaton   Barmoor Lane End   Causeway Holy Island   LINDISFARNE CASTLE
Coldstream   Cornhill-on-Tweed   Lowick   Sands   Castle Pt.
THE HIRSEL   HEATHERSLAW LIGHT RAILWAY   ERROL HUT SMITHY AND WOOD WORKSHOP   Barmoor Castle   West Kyloe   Fenham   LINDISFARNE PRIORY   Guile Pt.
Carham   Etal   HEATHERSLAW CORNMILL   East Kyloe   LINDISFARNE HERITAGE CENTRE
Wark   East Learmouth   Crookham   LADY WATERFORD HALL   Kyloe Hills   Buckton   Farne Islands
West Learmouth   Branxton   Ford   ST CUTHBERTS WAY   Elwick   Ross   Budle Bay   Staple Sound   FARNE ISLANDS
Holefield   Pressen   Flodden   Kimmerston   Holburn   Detchant   Budle   BAMBURGH CASTLE   Inner Sound   Bamburgh
Downham   Howtel   Nesbit   Hetton Steads   Middleton   Easington   Waren Mill   Glororum   Burton
Mindrum   Milfield   Fenton Town   North Hazelrigg   Belford   Spindlestone   Seahouses
KIRK YETHOLM   Pawston   Kilham   Lanton   Doddington   South Hazelrigg   Mousen   Bradford   Elford   North Sunderland
Hoselaw   Coupland   West Horton   Warenton   Bellshill   Adderstone   Newham   Beadnell
Town Yetholm   Kirknewton   Akeld   Newtown   East Horton   Warenford   Hall   Swinhoe   Benthall
Kirk Yetholm   Westnewton   Weetwood Hall   Newstead   Newham   Fleetham
Shotton   Humbleton   Chatton   Greendikes   Rosebrough   Ellingham   Preston   High Newton-by-the-Sea
PENNINE WAY   Wooler   WOOLER   Haugh Head   Chillingham   Chathill   Low Newton-by-the-Sea
Earle   CHILLINGHAM CASTLE   WILD CATTLE OF CHILLINGHAM   PRESTON TOWER   Beadnell Bay
Cliftoncote   THE SCHIL   COLD LAW   North Middleton   Newtown   Brownyside   North Charlton   Christon Bank   Embleton Bay
MOUNTHOOLEY   South Middleton   Lilburn Tower   East Lilburn   Hepburn   Old Bewick   Dunstan Steads   Castle Point
angleeford   Roseden   West   DUNSTANBURGH CASTLE
Ilderton

Eye Water
Ale Water
Whiteadder Water
Leet Water
Tweed
DEVIL'S CAUSEWAY
NORTHUMBERLAND COAST
North Low
South Low

62   63

Iona

MACLEAN'S CROSS

Eilean Annraidh
Rubha nan Cearc
IONA ABBEY AND CATHEDRAL
Kintra
IONA HERITAGE CENTRE
Baile Mor
ST COLUMBA EXHIBITION & WELCOME CENTRE
Fionnphort
Aridhglas
Eorabus
Lee
Fidden
Tiraghoil
Bunessan
A849
Loch na Lathaich
Loch Assapol
CRUACHAN MIN 376

Erraid
ROSS OF MULL
Ardalanish
Uisken
Scoor
Ardchiavaig
125
Malcolm's Pt.
Rubha nam Braithrean

Eilean a'Chalmain
Rubh Ardalanish

ARDMEANACH
Killiemore House
Aird of Kinloch
THE BURG
Kilfinichen Bay
Pennycross
Torrans
BROLASS
Loch Fuaron
503 BEINN NA CROISE
Carsaig
376
Loch Buie
Carsaig Bay
Rubha Dubh
CARSAIG ARCHES
Leidle
Beach

248
Loch Airdeglais
Loch Spelve
Ben Buie 717
698 CREACH BEINN
Kinlochspelve
Lochbuie
Barachandroman
Loch Uisg
405 DRUIM FADA
Laggan Deer Forest
LORD LOVAT'S CAVE
Frank Lockwood's Island

Croggan
Rubha nan Sailthean
Bach I.
Rubha Seanach
Ardmore

INSH I.
Sound of Insh
Clachan-Seil
AN CALA GARDENS
Easdale
EASDALE ISLAND FOLK MUSEUM
Dubh-fheith

Seil
B844
Easdale
Balvicar
Cuan
Kilchoan

FIRTH OF LORN

78

79

NM

Torran Rocks

Garbh Eileach
Garvellachs
Eileach an Naoimh
SCARBA, Eilean Dubh Mor
LUNGA AND THE GARVELLACHS
Lunga
CRUACH SCARBA 449
Scarba
Gulf of Corryvreckan

OBAN 2:20

Ferry
Torsa
Cullipool
94
Luing
Achafolla
ARDUAINE GARDEN
Arduaine

Toberonochy
Shuna Sound
Shuna
Lunga
Shuna Pt.

Craobh Haven

Rubha Aird Luing
Aird
Rèisa an t-Sruith
Craignish Pt.
Kinuachdrachd Harbour

Island Macaskin
SCULPTURED

0

Kiloran Bay
Rubh 'a' Geadha
Balnahard

KILORAN GARDENS
Kilchattan
Kiloran
COLONSAY
Scalasaig
B8086
B8085

Garvard
Rubha Dubh
Loch Staosnaig

PRIORY
Dubh Eilean
Oronsay

Eilean nan Ron

Glengarrisdale Bay
Kinuachdrachd
296 CRUACH NA SEILCHEIG
Glendebadel Bay

365 BEN GARRISDALE
Corpach Bay

Lealt Burn
Lealt
Lussa

J
U
R
A

Crinan
Killmahumaig
Bellanoch

KNAPD
265
Gallachoille
Carsaig
Tayvallich
Achanamara
Kilmichael of Inverlussa

E

Rubh'an t-Sàilein
1:10 (Summer Only)
Rubha Lang-aoinidh

Shian Bay
453 RAINBERG MOR
Shian
Loch Righ Mòr
318

467 BEINN BHREAC

Ardlussa
Inverlussa
Lussagiven
Ardlussa Bay
Barrahormid

TAYNISH
466 CRUACH LUSACH
Taynish
Dunrostan

Rubha a'Mhail
Rubha Bholsa

Loch Tarbert
Tarbert
Lagg

KEILLS CHAPEL
Keillmore
New Ulva
Island of Danna
ST COLUMBA'S CAVE
CASTLE SWEEN
Lochead
Achahoish

439

Nave Island
Ardnave Pt.
Ardnave
364 SGARBH BREAC
Bunnahabhain
BUNNAHABHAIN DISTILLERY
316
Gortantaoid
Killinallan

785
755
PAPS OF JURA
Corran
Loch an Aircill
JURA
JURA FOREST
Leargybreck
Gleann Astaile
Loch na Mile
Knockrome

An Dùnan
Lowlandman's Bay

SOUND OF JURA

Eilean Mòr
ST CORMAC'S CHAPEL
CHAPEL
Kilmory Bay
Kilmory
Ellary
Clachbreck

Baile Boidheach
Ormsary
241
305
Druimdrishaig

Pt. of Knap

Leckgruinart
LOCH GRUINART NATURE RESERVE VISITORS CENTRE
Aoradh
B8017
Craigens

Caol Ila
CAOL ILA DISTILLERY
FINLAGGAN CENTRE
Keills
Port Askaig
Feolin Ferry
Loch Finlaggan
Loch Cam
Ballygrant
Kilmeny
561
Keils

Craighouse
ISLE OF JURA DISTILLERY
Small Isles
342 BRAT BHEINN
Gleann Ullibh
Cabrach

64

NR

Miller's Bay
Cretshengan
CRUACH LAGAIN 264
Coulaghailtro
Kilberry

ISLAY
I
S
L
A
Y
Blackrock
Redhouses
Daill
Bridgend
8

Bowmore
BOWMORE ROUND CHURCH
A846
Mulindry
Kilennan
Loch Ballygrant

267 BEINN DUBH
Am Fraoch Eilean
Brosdale I.
Rubha na Tràille
McArthur's Hd.

KILBERRY HD.
SCULPTURED STONES
N

DUN
305
15

Islay
Port Charlotte
Port Ellen
nisby
ddich
LOCH INDAAL

471 BEINN BHAN
491 BEINN BHEIGEIR
Ardtalla
Loch Beinn Uraraidh

Carraig Mhòr
Claggain Bay

Carraig Bheag

2:05

PORT ELLEN 2:10

Eilean Garbh
West Tarbert Bay
East Tarbert Bay
Gigha
65

Ardpatrick
Ardpatrick Ho.
Portachoillan
Ardpatrick Pt.
Eilean Tràighe
Ronachan Pt.

Loch Stornoway
Carse Ho.
Dunmore
Loch nan Torran

A83
Clachan
WEST LOCH
Gartnagrenach
Balochroy

Laggan
Laggan Pt.
Duich
Loch
Kintour

0 1 2 3 4 5 6 miles
0 1 2 3 4 5 6 7 8 9 10km

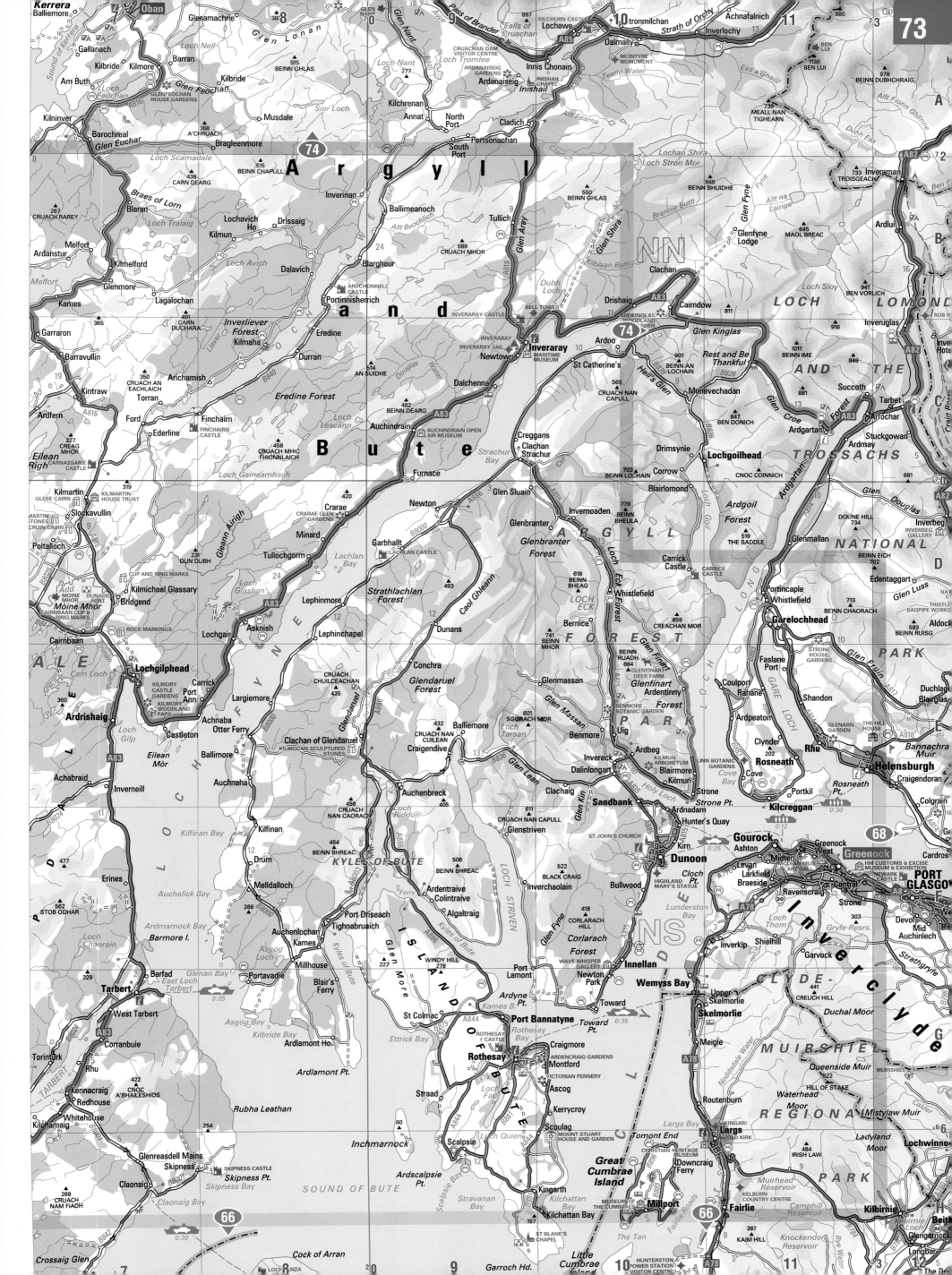

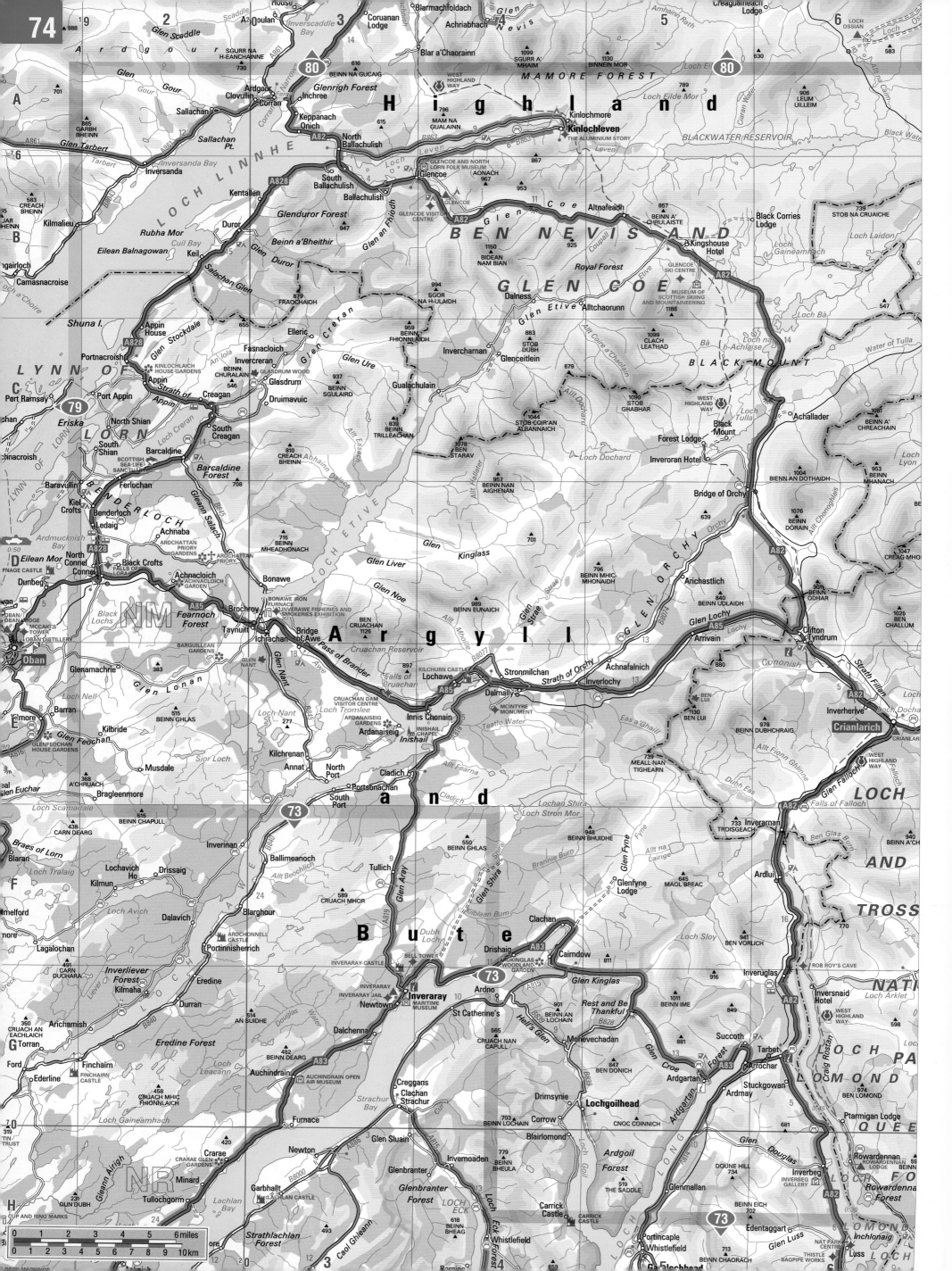

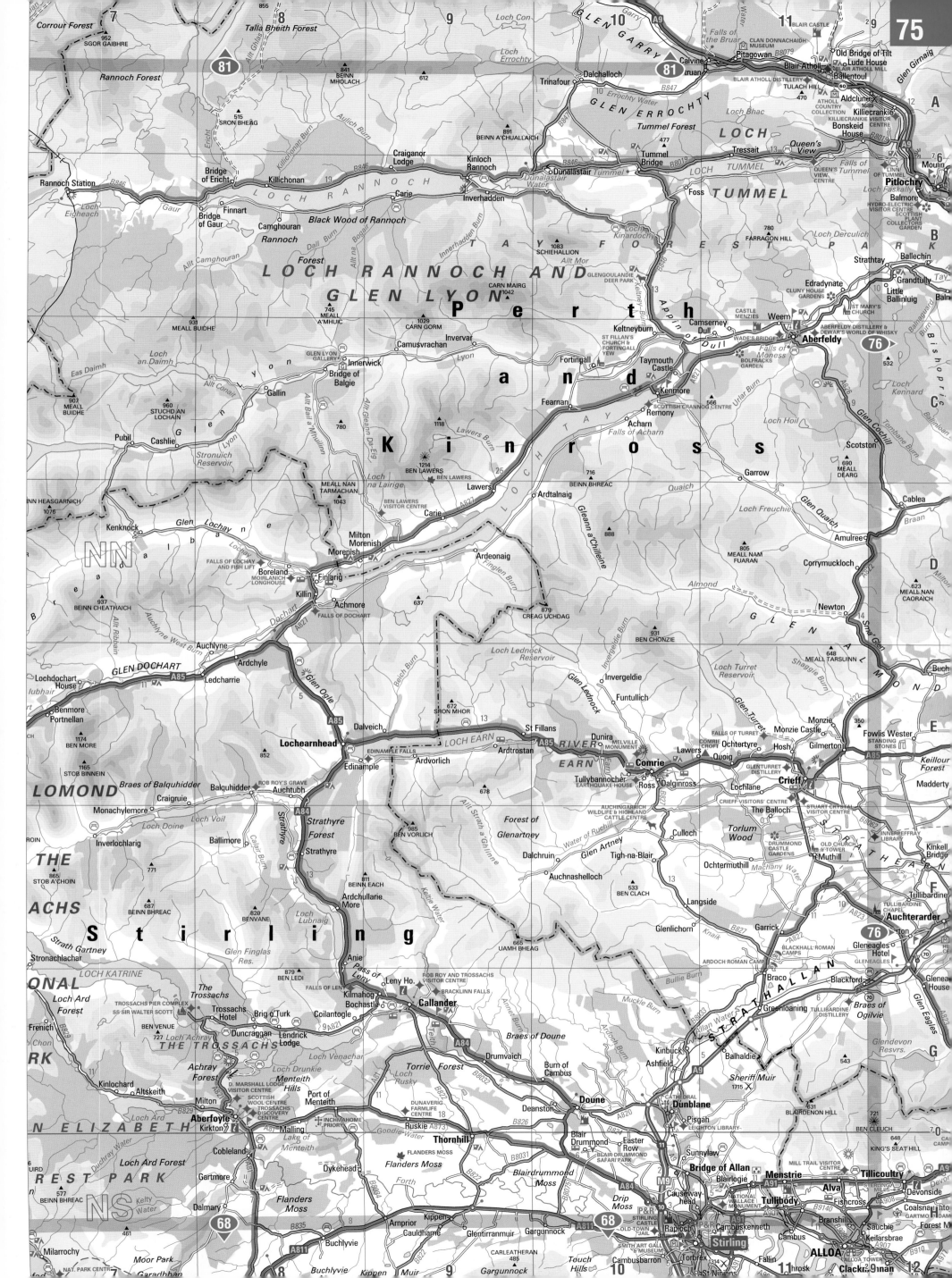

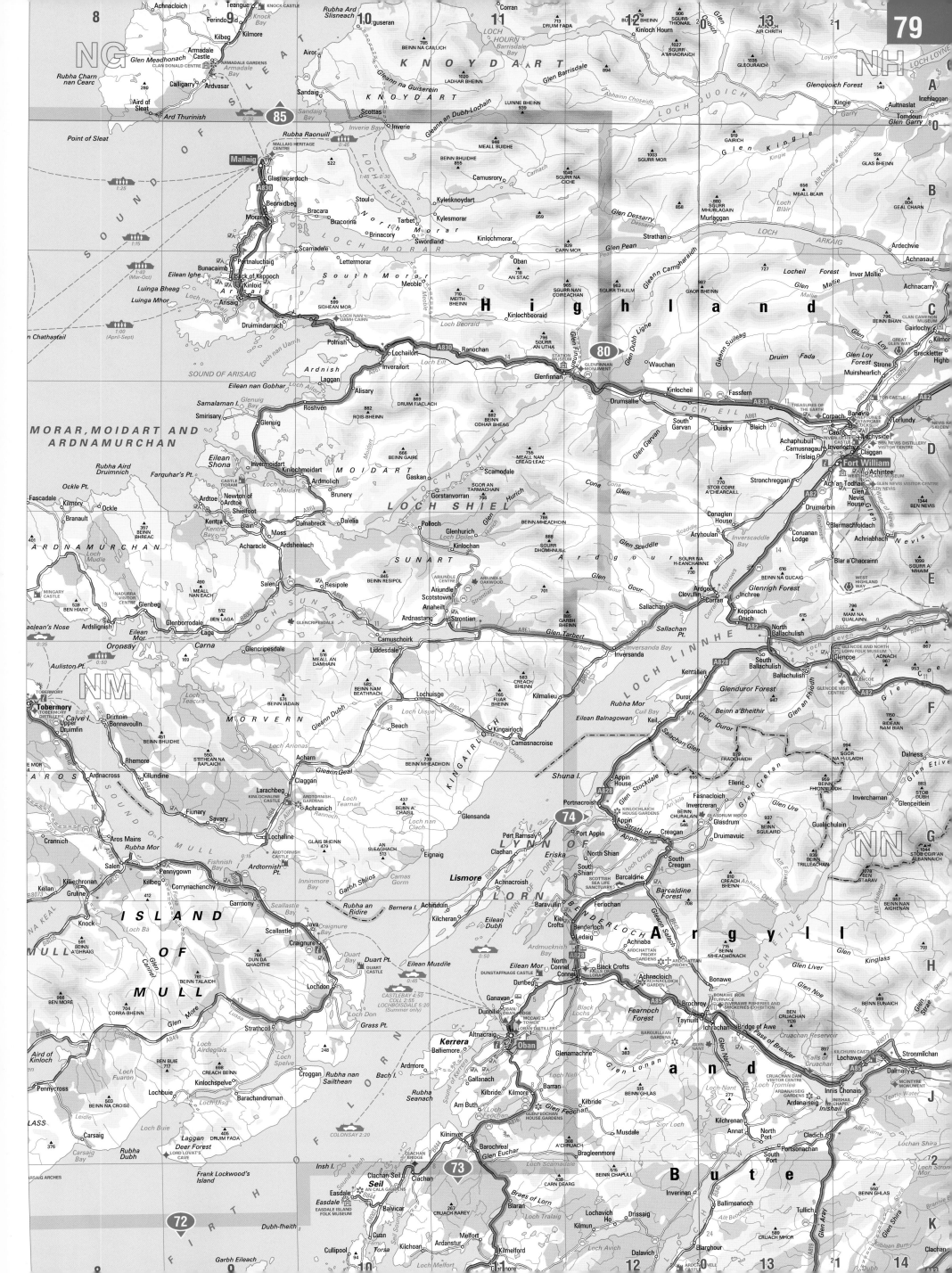

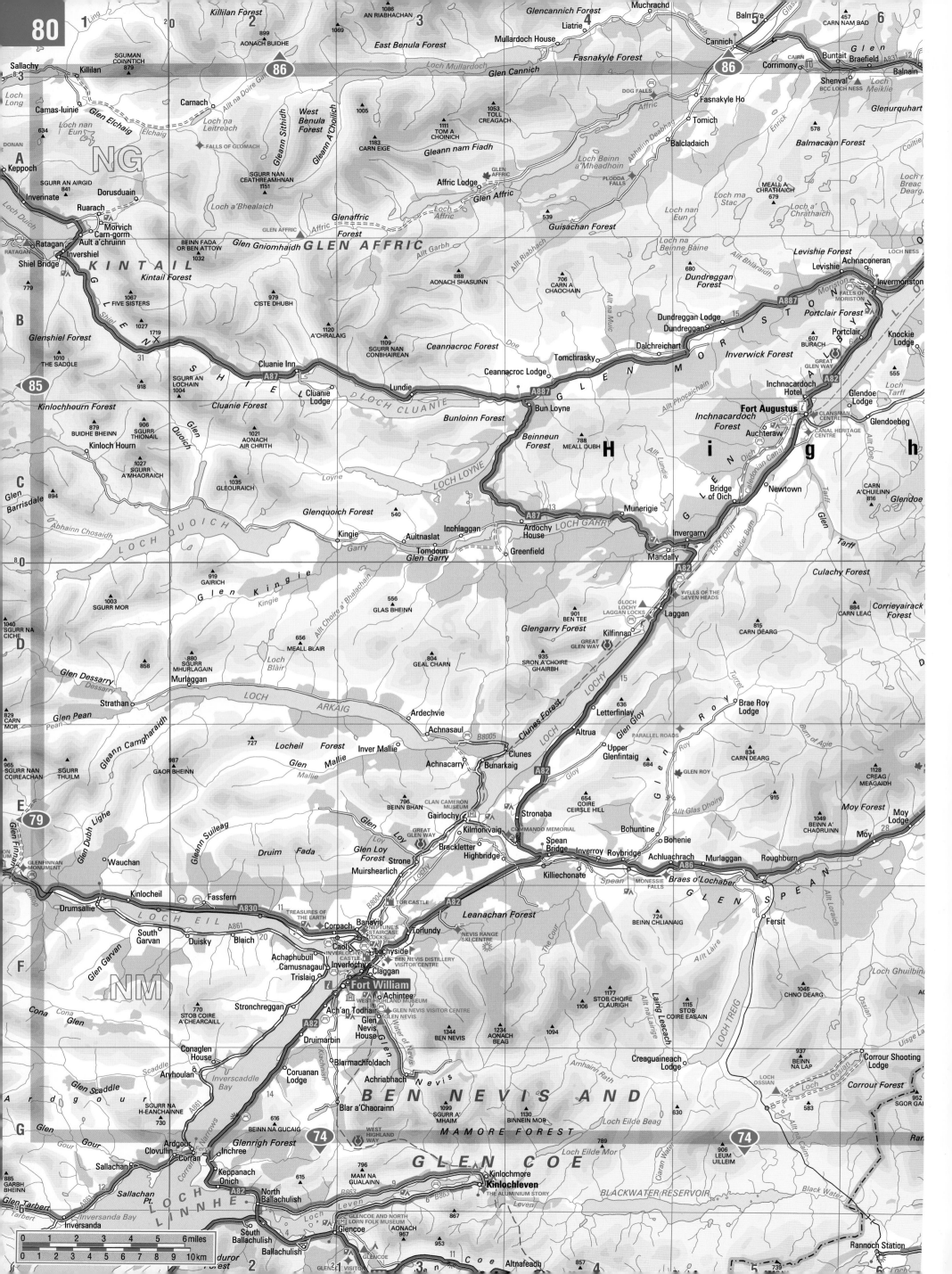

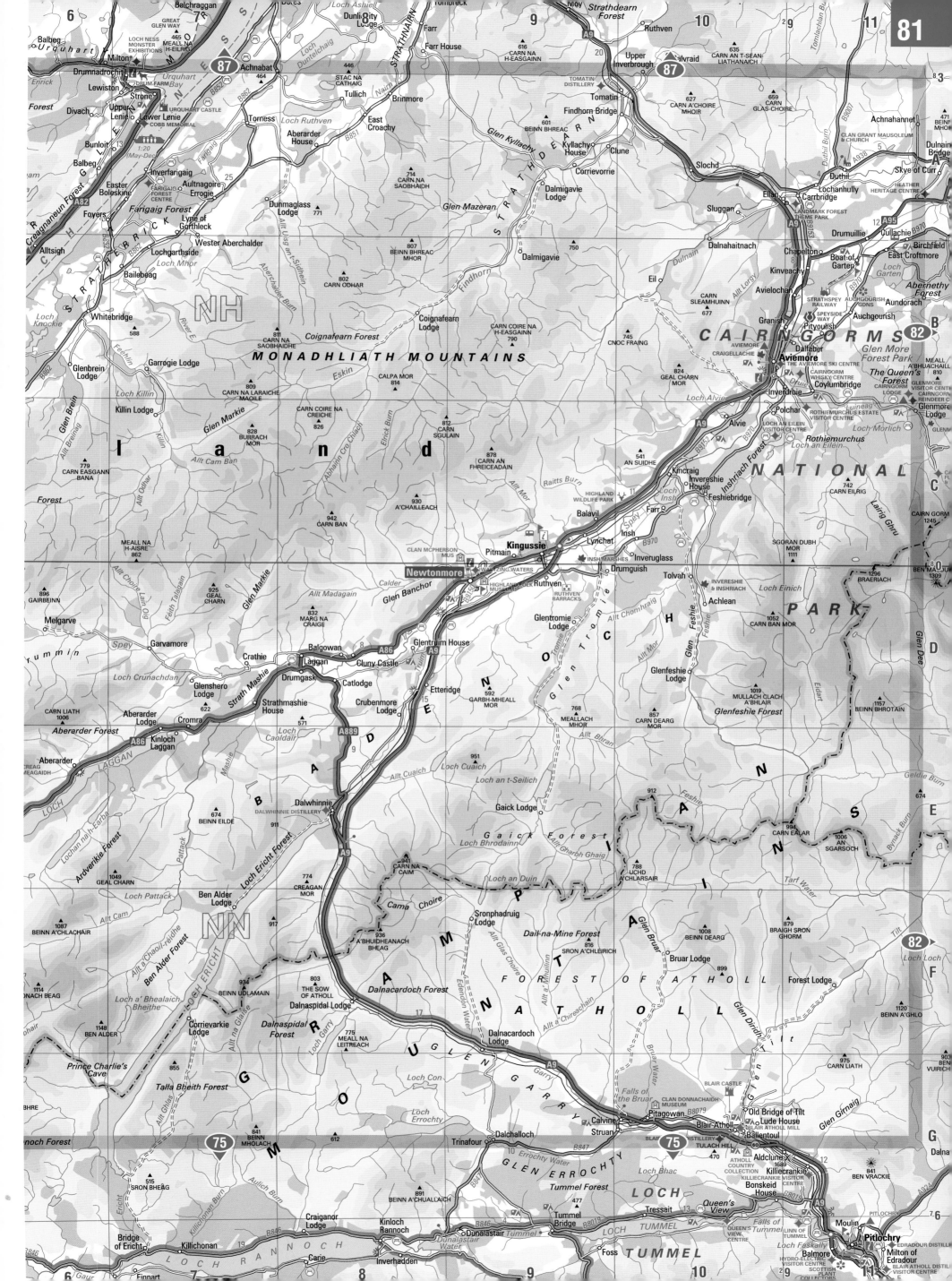

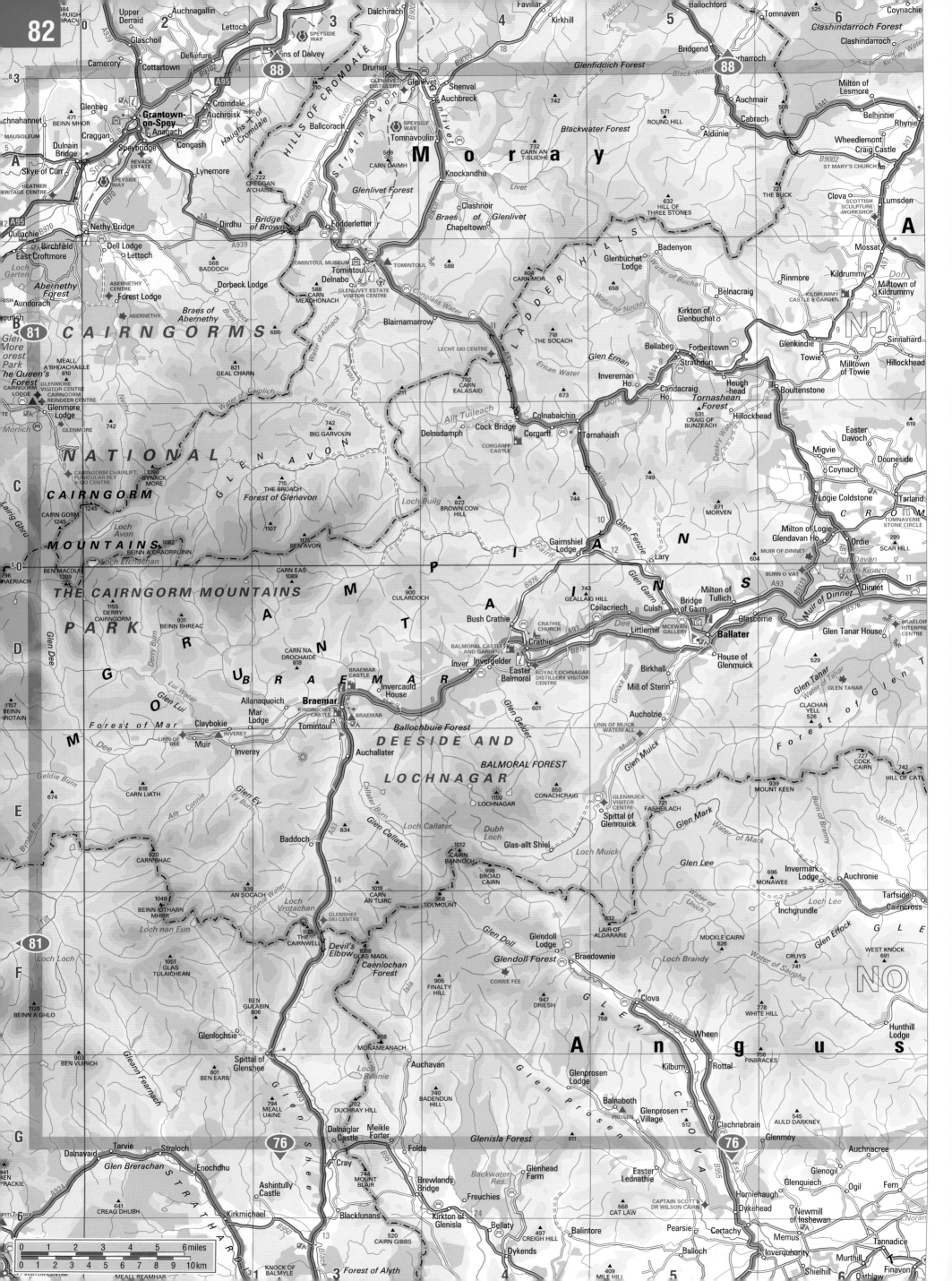

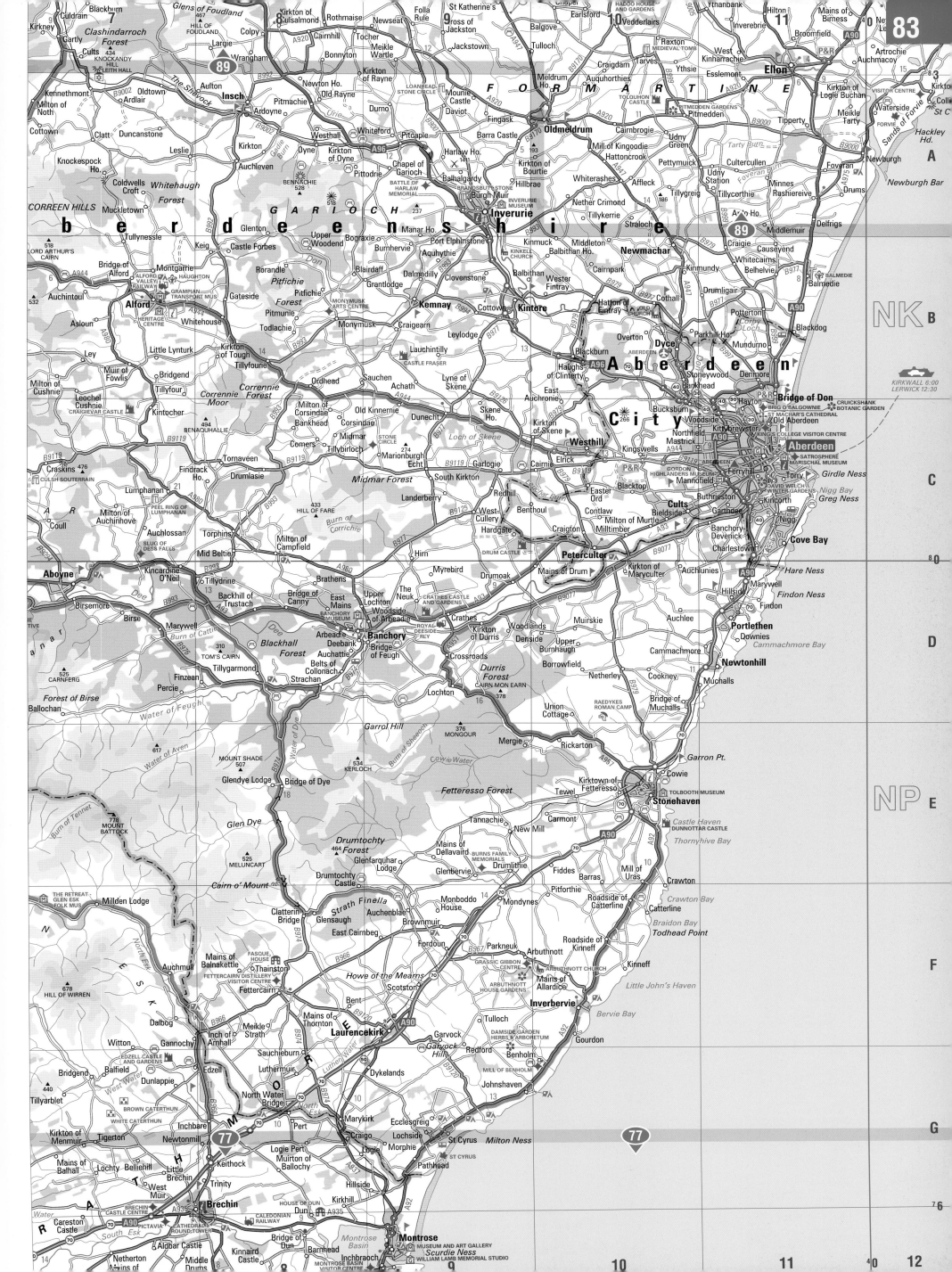

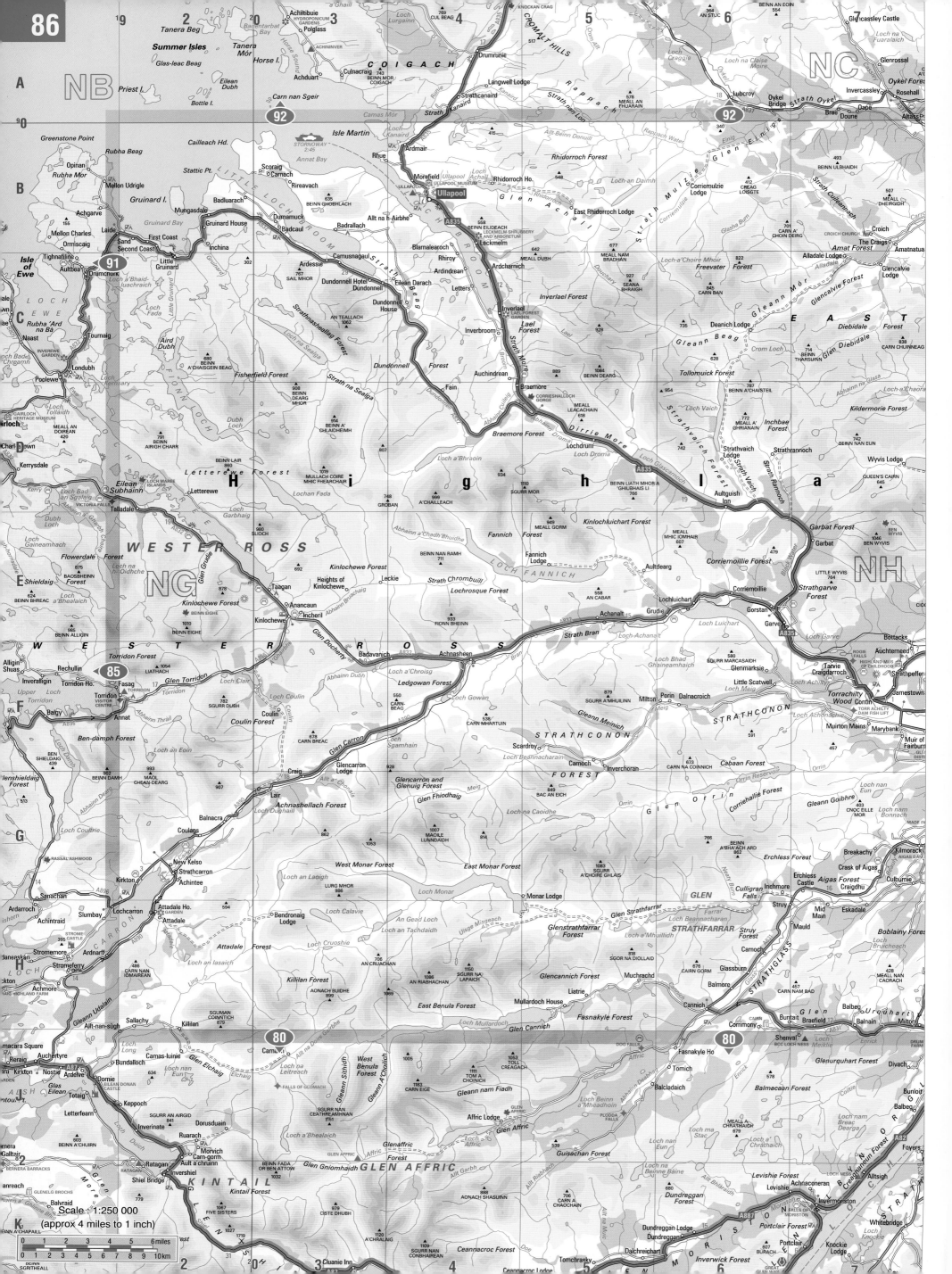

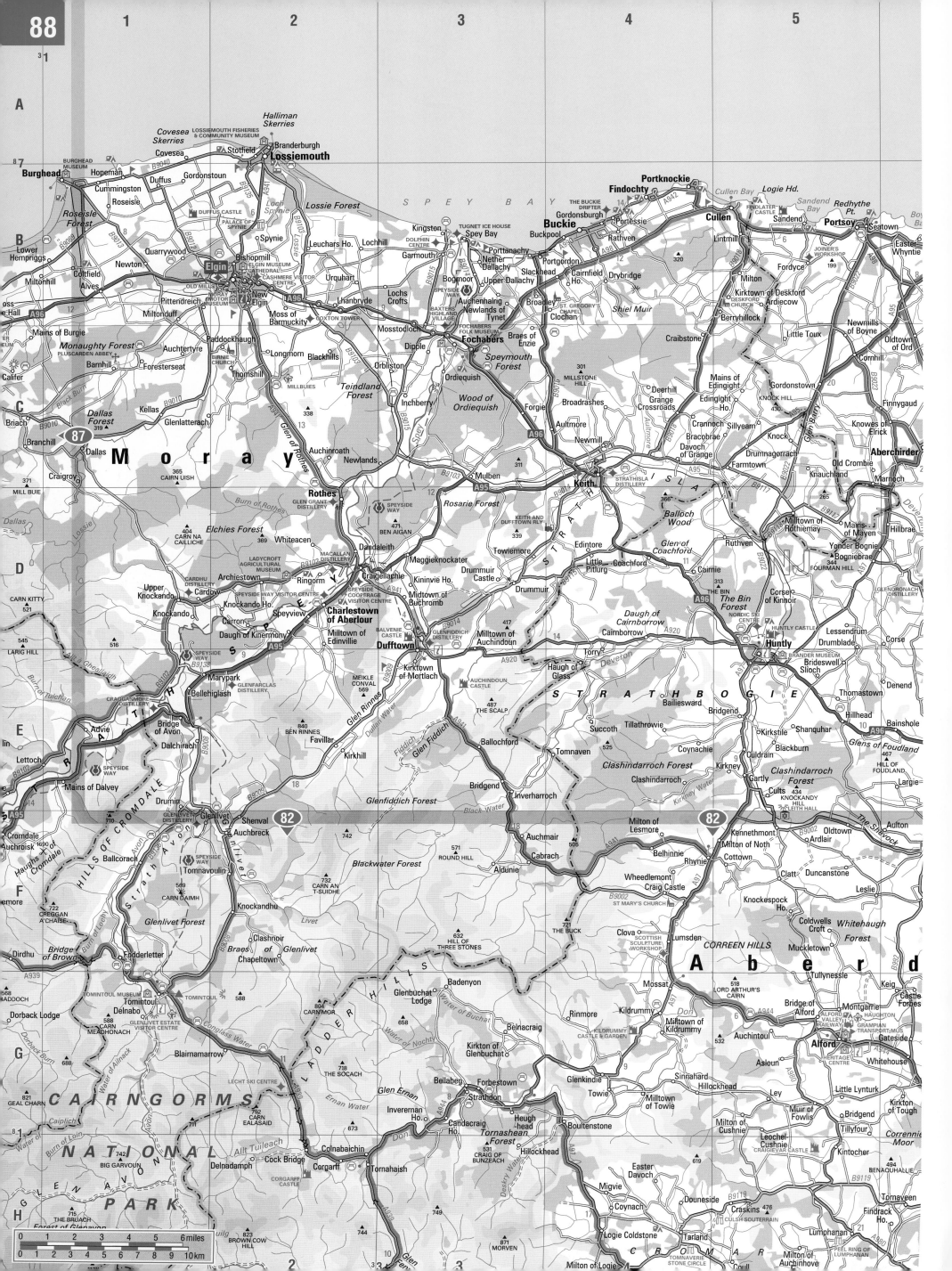

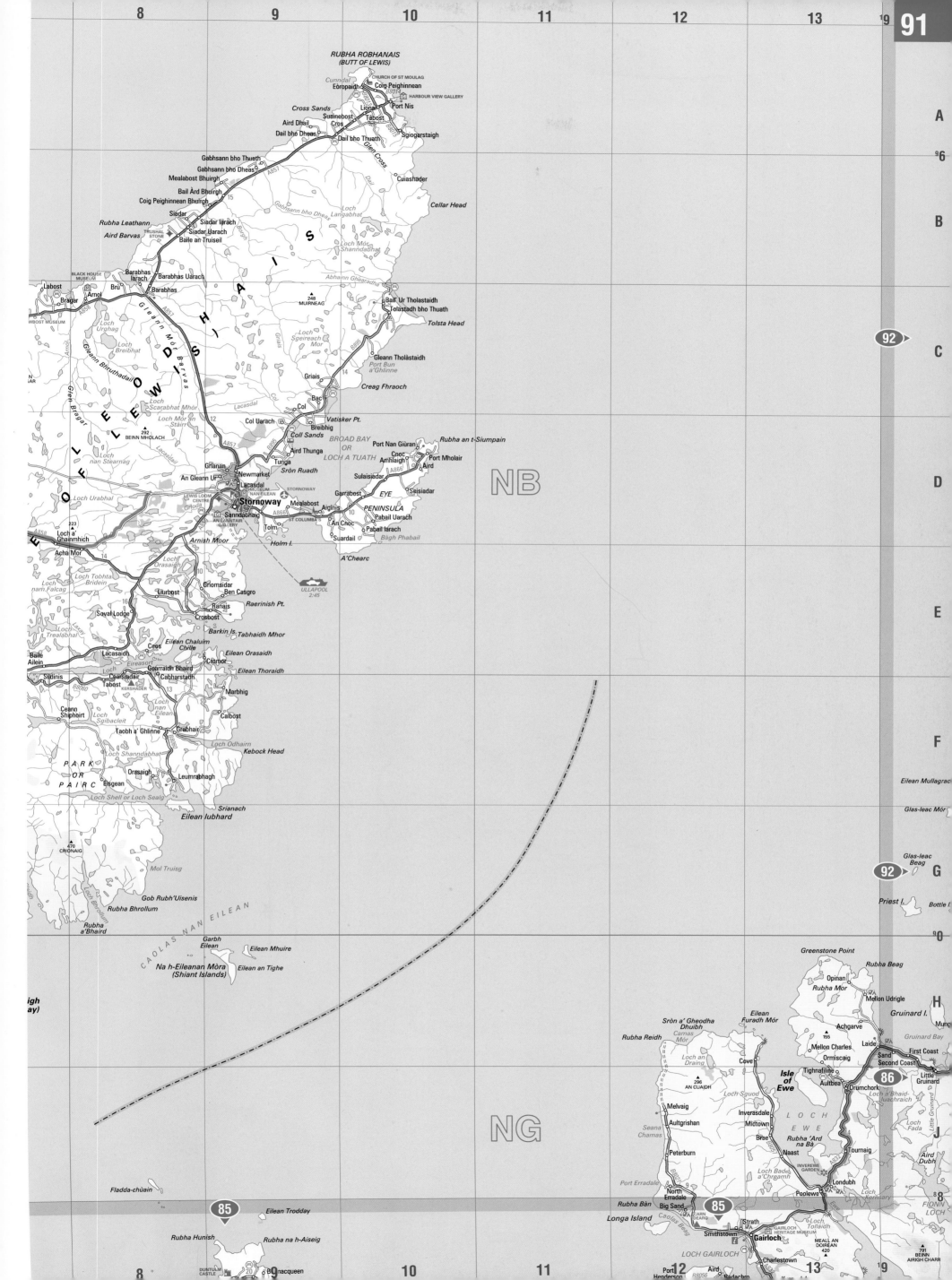

**RUBHA ROBHANAIS
(BUTT OF LEWIS)**

Cunndal · CHURCH OF ST MOULAG
Eòropaidh · Coig Peighinnean
· B8014
· Port Nis · HARBOUR VIEW GALLERY
Lional
Cross Sands · Suainebost · Tabost
Aird Dhail · Cros
Dail bho Dheas · Dail bho Thuath · Sgiogarstaigh

Gabhsann bho Thuath
Gabhsann bho Dheas · A857
Mealabost Bhuirgh · Glen Cross
Bail Àrd Bhuirgh · Dail
Coig Peighinnean Bhuirgh · 15 · Cuiashader
Siadar · LEWIS · Cellar Head
Rubha Leathann · Siadar Iarach · Loch
Aird Barvas · TRUSHAL · Siadar Uarach · Langabhat
STONE · Baile an Truiseil

BLACK HOUSE · Gabhsann bho Dheas
MUSEUM · Barabhas Iarach · Loch Mòr
Labost · Brù · Barabhas Uarach · Shanndabhat
Bragar · Arnol · Barabhas · Abhainn Ghearadha
WBOST MUSEUM · A858 · 248 · Bail' Ur Tholastaidh
· MUIRNEAG · Tolastadh bho Thuath
Loch · Gruais · Tolsta Head
Urghag · Gleann Mòr Barvas · A857
Loch Breibhat · Loch
Gleann Bhruthadail · Sgeireach
Loch · Mor
Scarabhat Mhòr · Gleann Tholàstaidh
Glen Bragar · Port Bun
Loch Mòr an · a'Ghlinne
Stàirr · 14 · Creag Fhraoch
Loch · 292 · Griais
nan Stearnag · BEINN MHOLACH · Bac
Acha Mòr · A857 · Col
· Col Uarach · Vatisker Pt.
Loch a' · Breibhig
Ghainmhich · Coll Sands · BROAD BAY · Rubha an t-Siumpain
· Aird Thunga · OR · Port Nan Giùran
Loch · Griomsidar · Grianan · LOCH A TUATH · Cnoc
Tobhta · Newmarket · Tunga · Amhlaigh · Port Mholair
Bridein · An Gleann Ur · Sròn Ruadh · Sulaisiadar · Aird
Loch · Ben Casgro · Lacasdal · A866 · Garrabost · Seisiadar
nam Falcag · Ranais · MUSEUM · Stornoway · EYE · A866
Soval Lodge · Crosbost · NAN EILEAN · STORNOWAY · An Cnoc · PENINSULA
· Liurbost · LEWIS LODGE · Mealabost · Aiginis · Pabail Uarach
· CENTRE · STORNOWAY · ST COLUMBA'S · Pabail Iarach
Loch · Raerinish Pt. · AN LANNTAIR · Tolm · A'Chearc
Trealabhal · GALLERY · 223 · Suardail · Bàgh Phabail
Baile · Arnish Moor · Holm I.
Ailein · Barkin Is. · Tabhaidh Mhor
Lacasaidh · Ceos · Eilean Chaluim · Cille
Sildinis · Gearraidh Bhaird · Cabharstadh · Eilean Orasaidh
Tabost · Cearsadar · B8060 · Cromor · Eilean Thoraidh
· KERSHADER · 13 · ULLAPOOL
Ceann · Loch · Marbhig · 2:45
Shiphoirt · nan · Eilean
· Loch Sgibacleit · Calbost
· Taobh a' Ghlinne
· Grabhair
PARK · Loch Odhairn · Kebock Head
OR · Orasaigh
PAIRC · Leumrabhagh
· Eisgean
Loch Shell or Loch Sealg
· Srianach
· Eilean Iubhard
· 470
· CRIONAIG
· Mol Truisg

· Gob Rubh'Uisenis
· Rubha Bhrollum
Rubha
a'Bhaird

CAOLAS NAN EILEAN
· Garbh
· Eilean
· Eilean Mhuire
Na h-Eileanan Mòra · Eilean an Tighe
(Shiant Islands)

NB

NG

Eilean Mullagrach
Glas-leac Mòr
Glas-leac
Beag
Priest I. · Bottle I.

Greenstone Point
· Rubha Beag
Opinan · Rubha Mòr
· Mellon Udrigle
Sròn a' Gheodha · Eilean · Gruinard I.
Dhuibh · Furadh Mòr
Camas Mòr · Achgarve · Mung
Rubha Reidh · 155 · Gruinard Bay
· Mellon Charles · Laide · First Coast
Loch an · Ormiscaig · Sand · Second Coast
Draing · Cove · Aultbea · 86
· 296 · Isle · Little
· AN CUAIDH · of · Drumchork · Gruinard
· Loch Sguod · Ewe · Loch a'Bhaid-
Melvaig · · luachraich
· Inverasdale · LOCH
Seana · Midtown · EWE · Loch
Chamas · Brae · Fada
· Aultgrishan · Rubha 'Ard
· na Bà · Tournaig · Aird
· Naast · INVEREWE · Dubh
Peterburn · GARDEN
· Londubh
Port Erradale · A832 · Loch
North · Poolewe · Kernsary
Erradale · Big Sand · FIONN
Rubha Bàn · CARN · LOCH
· DEARG · Loch
Fladda-chùain · Caolas Beag · Tollaidh
· 85 · GAIRLOCH · MEALL AN
Eilean Trodday · Strath · HERITAGE · DOIREAN
· MUSEUM · 420
· Smithstown · BEINN
Longa Island · Gairloch · 791 · AIRIGH CHARR
Rubha Hunish · Rubha na h-Aiseig · Charlestown
· LOCH GAIRLOCH
DUNTULM · 20 · Port · Aird
CASTLE · Bornacqueen · Henderson · B8056 · Redachro

92 ▶
92 ▶
86
85 ▼
85 ▼

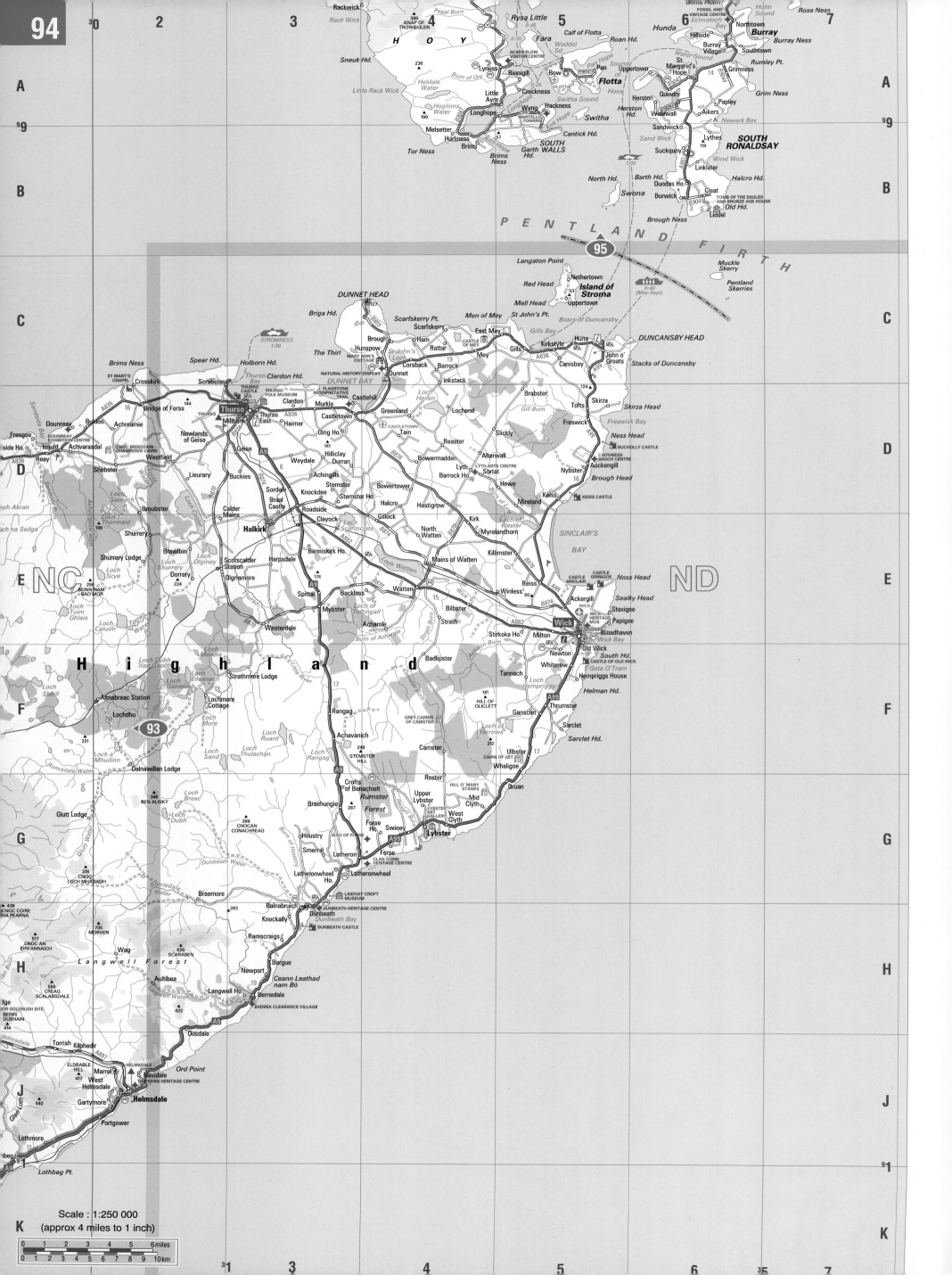

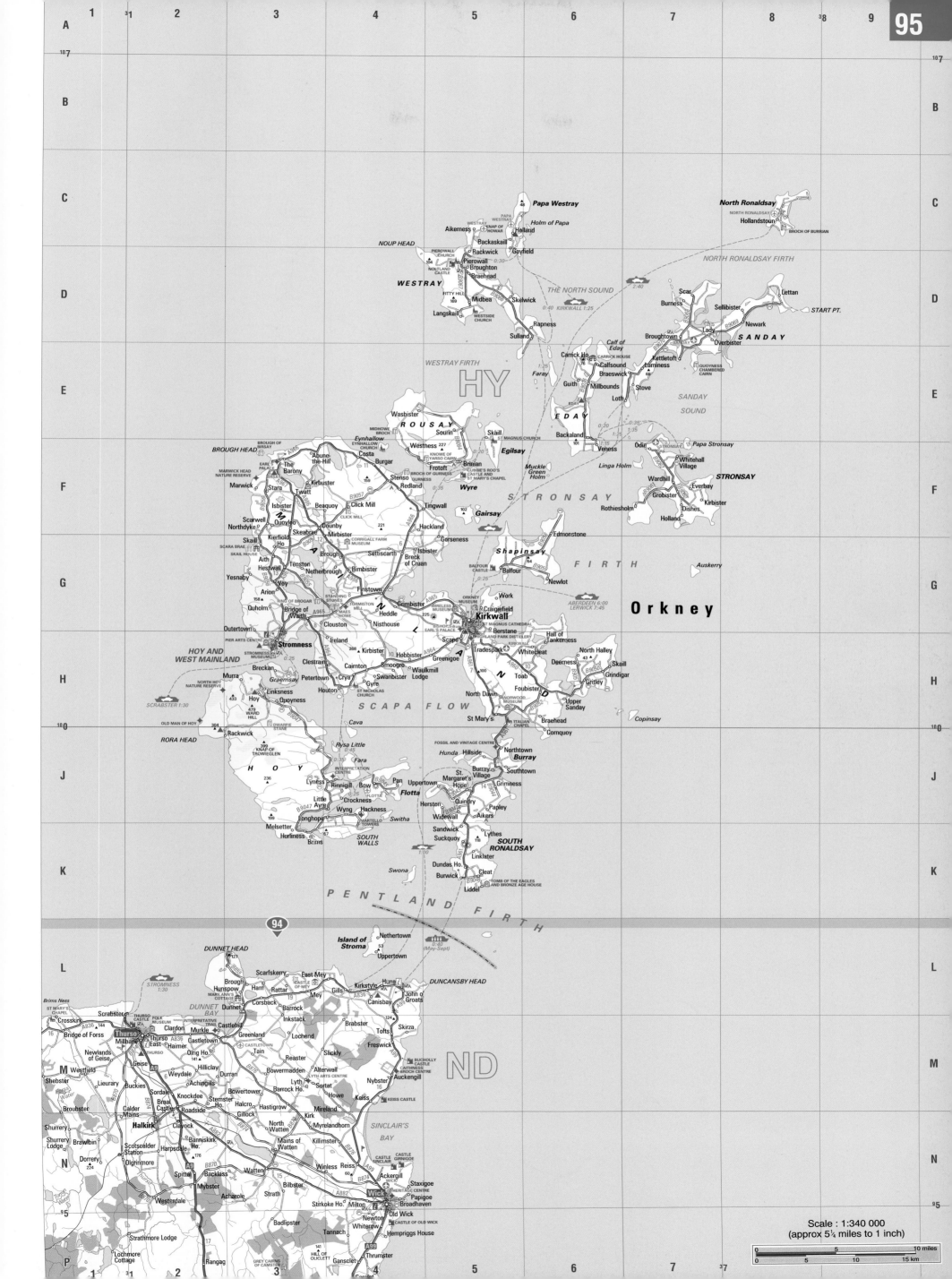

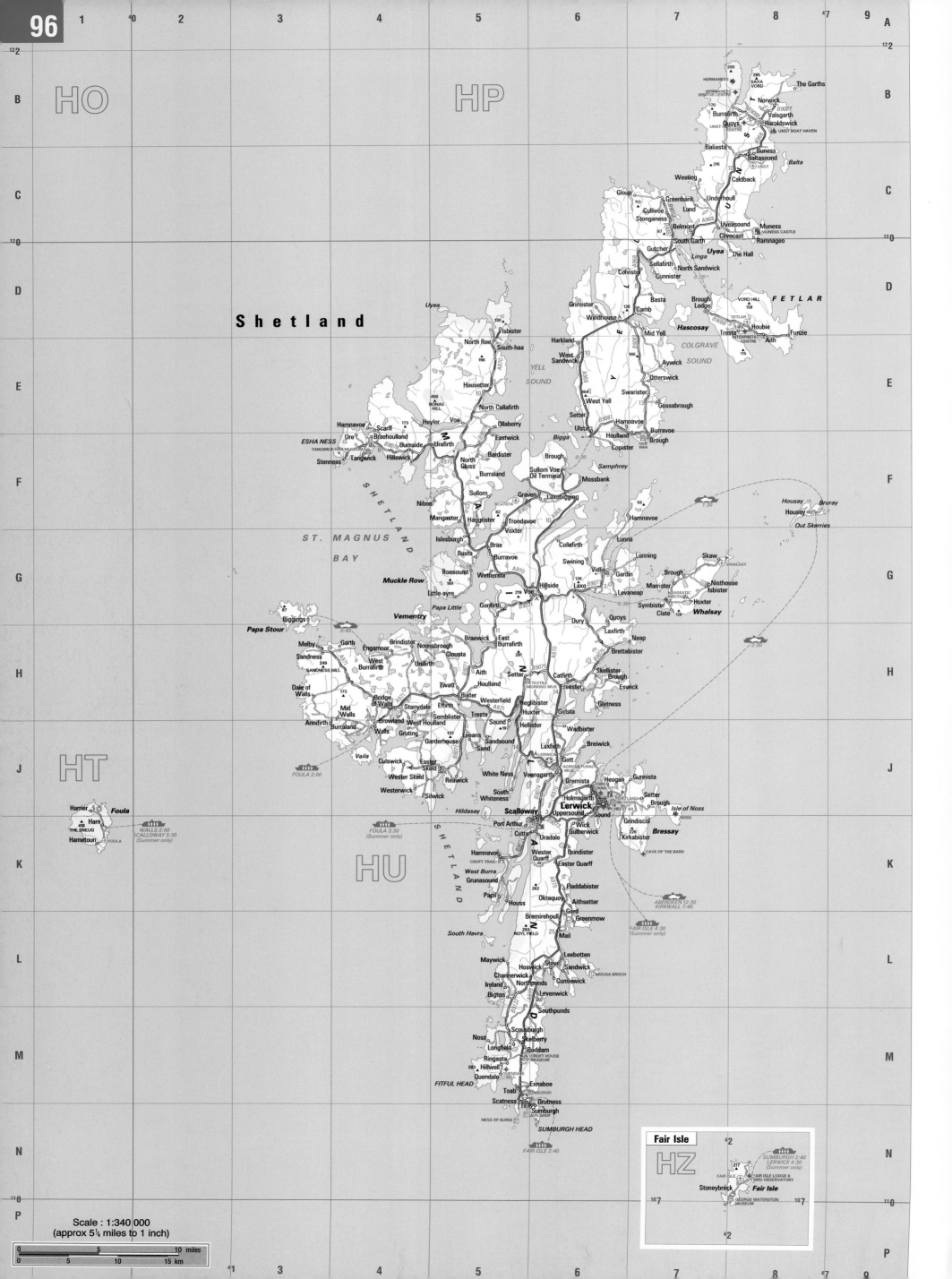

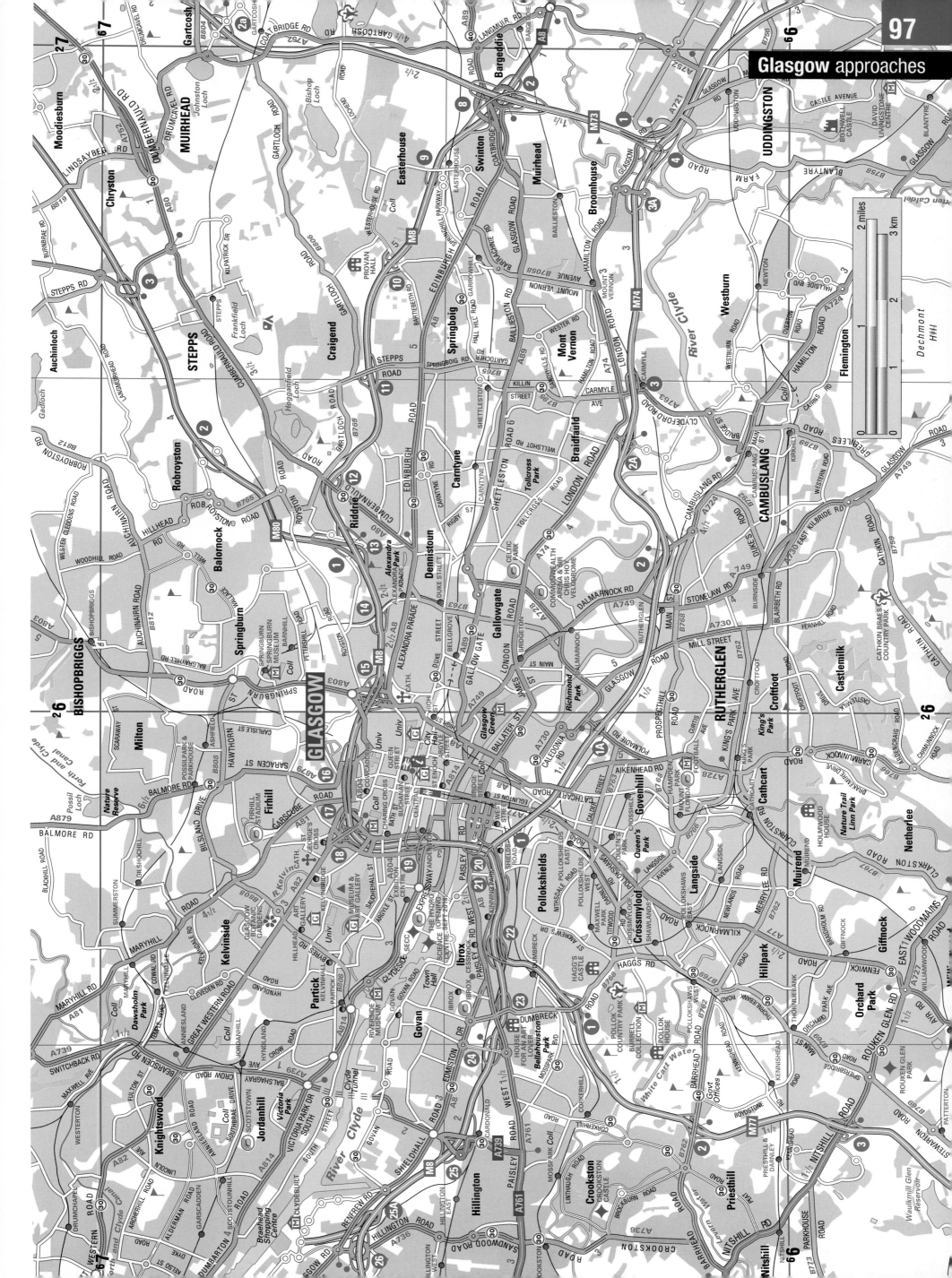

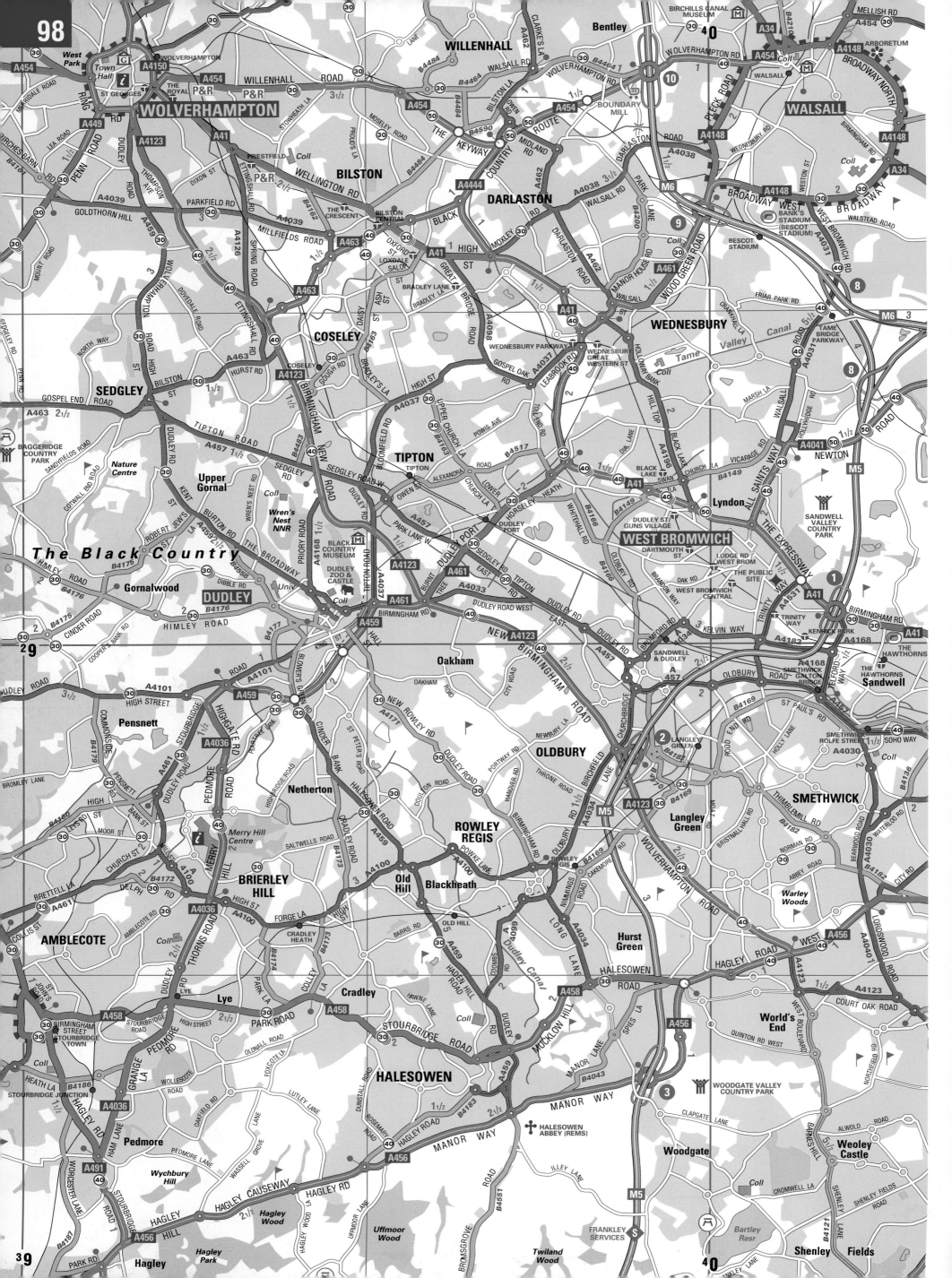

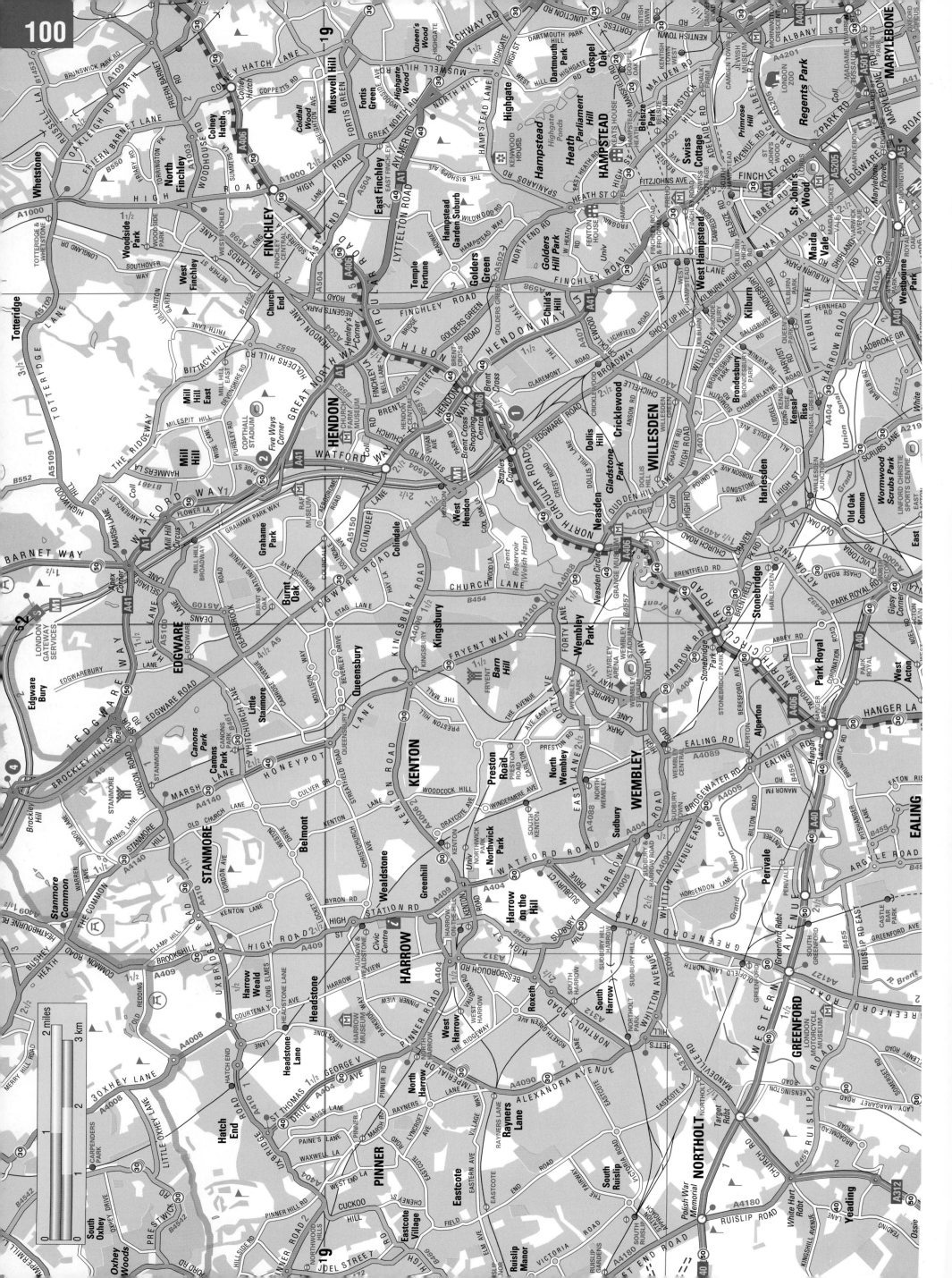

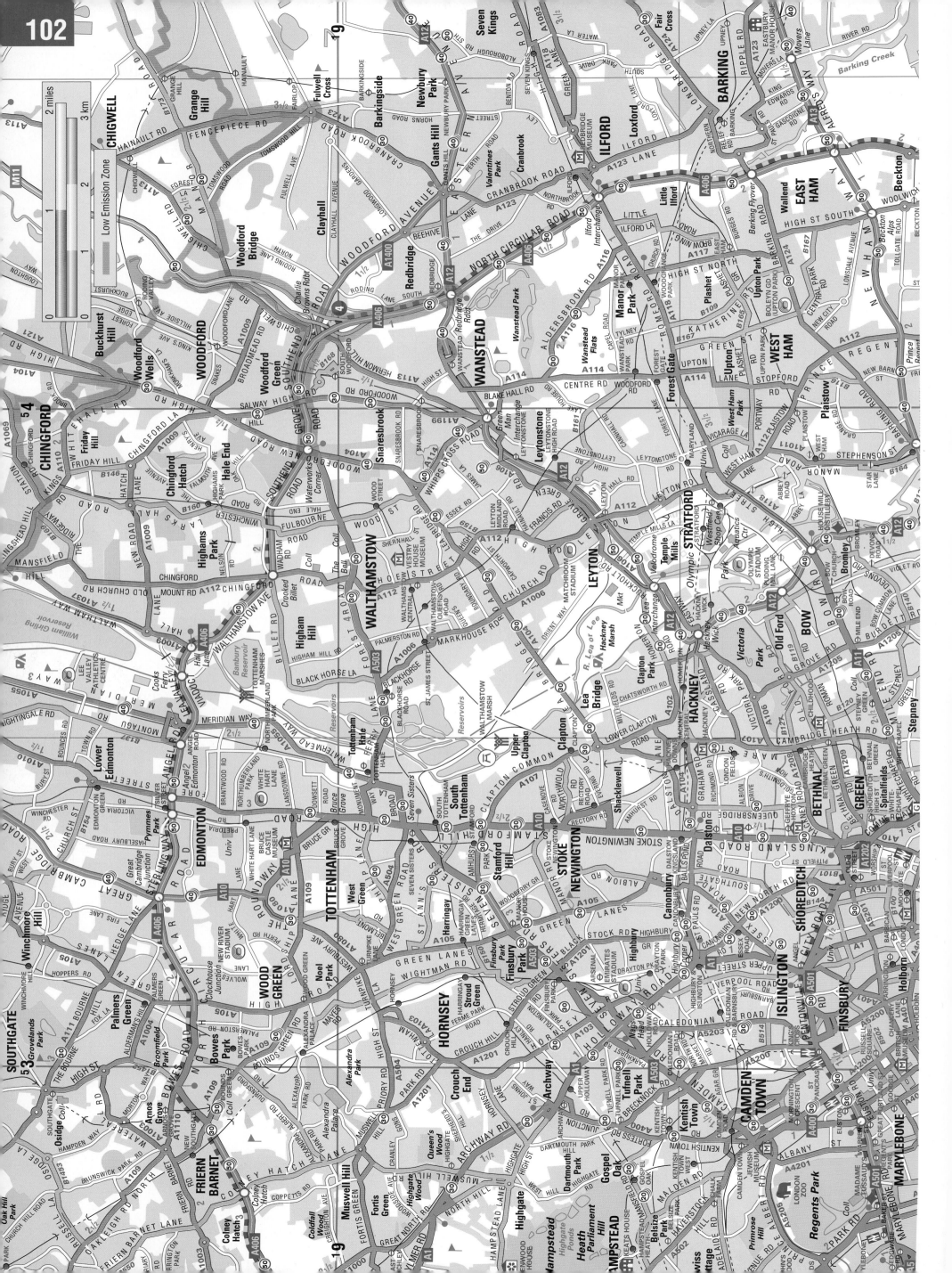

Aberdeen page 83 ● Bath page 16 ● Birmingham page 35 ● Blackpool page 49 ● Bournemouth page 9 ● Bradford page 51 ● Brighton page 12

105

Town plan symbols

	Motorway
	Primary route – dual, single carriageway
	A road – dual, single carriageway
	B road – dual, single carriageway
	Minor through road
	One-way street
	Pedestrian roads
	Shopping streets
	Railway with station
	Tramway with station
	Underground or Metro station
H	Hospital
P	Parking
	Police, Post Office
	Shopmobility
▲	Youth hostel
	Bus or railway station building
	Shopping precinct or retail park
	Park
	Congestion charge zone

✝	Abbey or cathedral
	Ancient monument
	Aquarium
	Art gallery
	Bird collection or aviary
	Building of interest
	Castle
	Church of interest
	Cinema
	Garden
	Historic ship
	House
	House and garden
	Museum
	Preserved railway
	Roman antiquity
	Safari park
	Theatre
	Tourist information centre
	Zoo
✦	Other place of interest

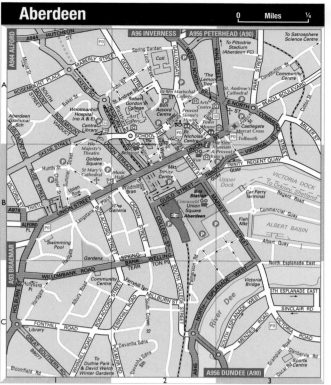

Aberdeen

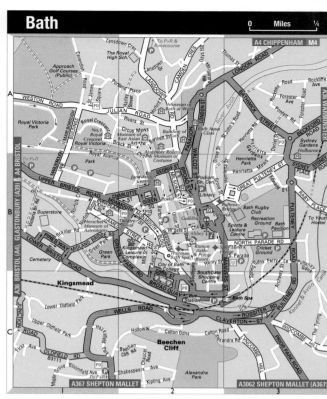

Bath

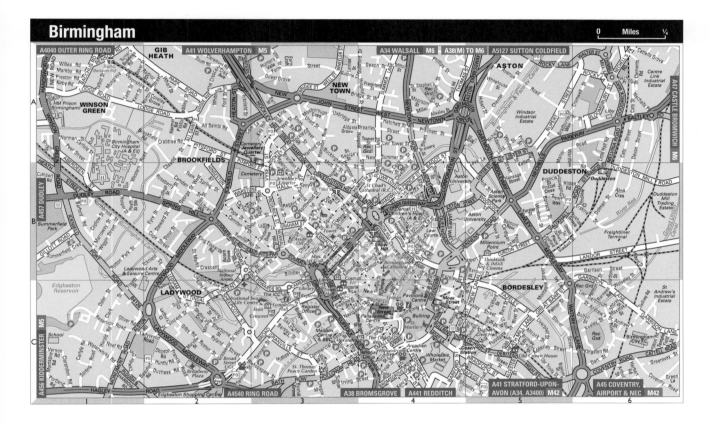

Birmingham

Blackpool

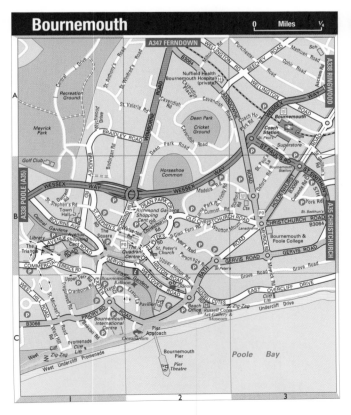

Bournemouth

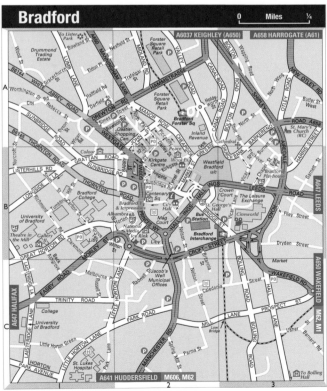

Bradford

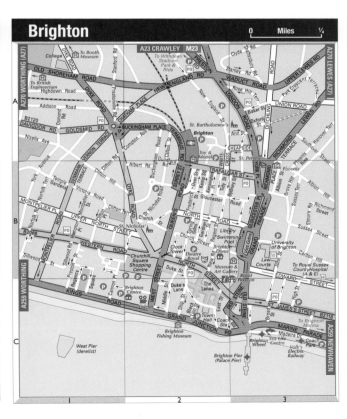

Brighton

Bristol

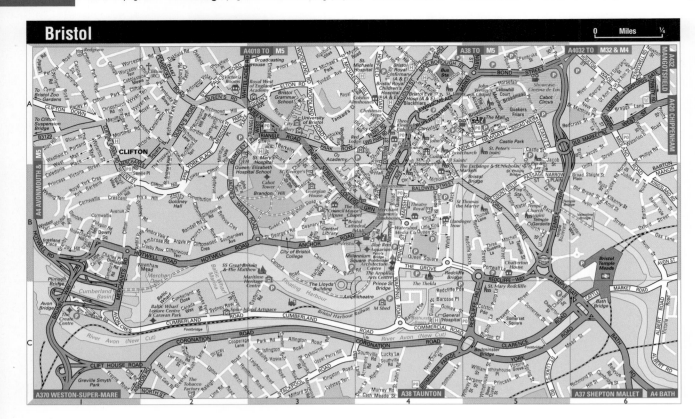

Cambridge

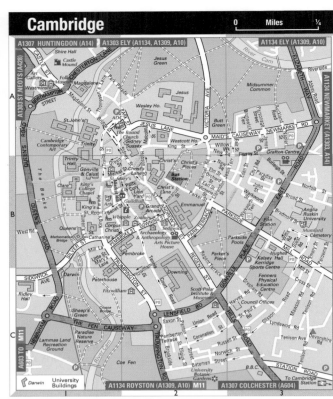

Canterbury

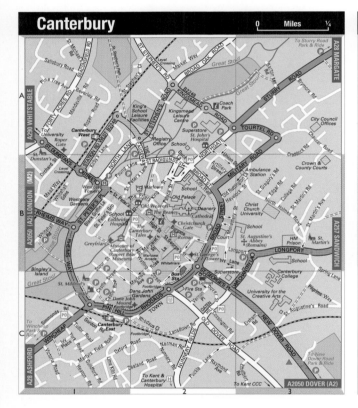

Cardiff / Caerdydd

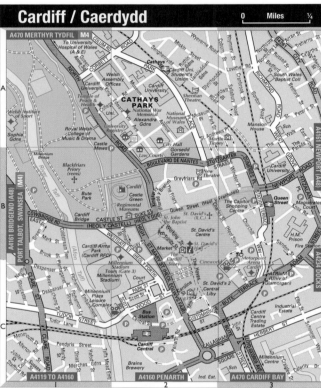

Chester

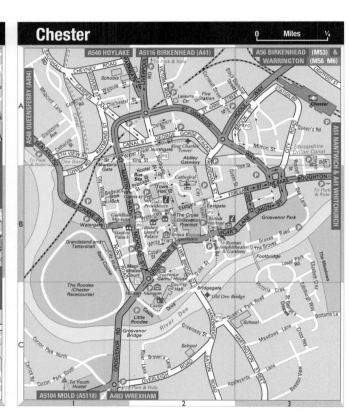

Colchester

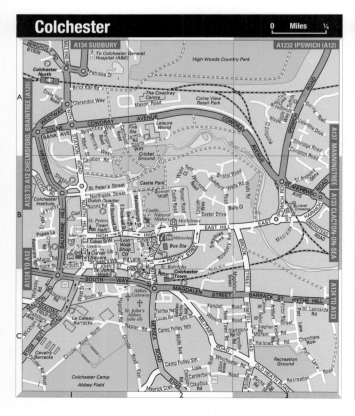

Coventry

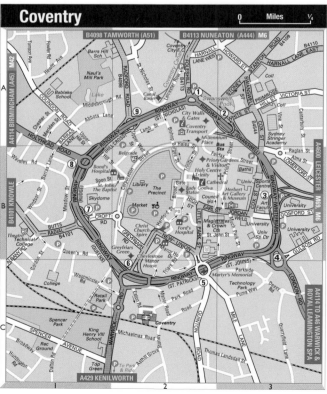

Derby

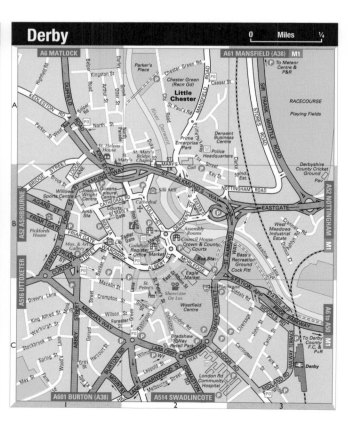

Durham page 58 • **Edinburgh** page 69 • **Exeter** page 7 • **Glasgow** page 68 • **Gloucester** page 26 • **Hull** page 53 • **Ipswich** page 31

107

Durham

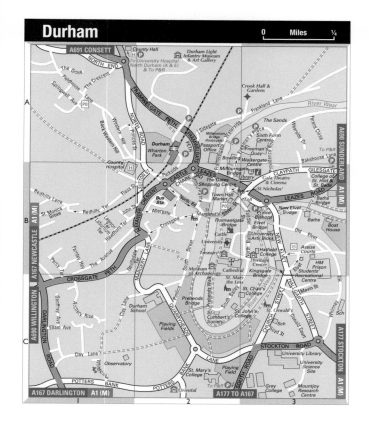

Edinburgh

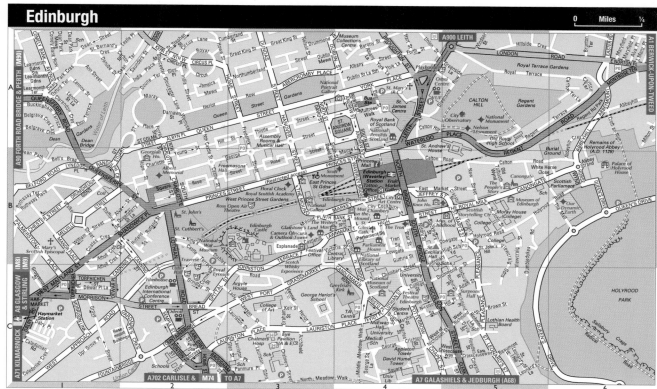

Exeter

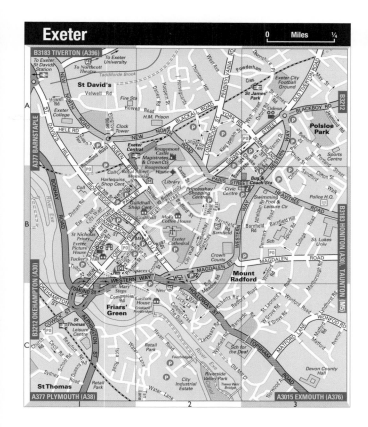

Glasgow

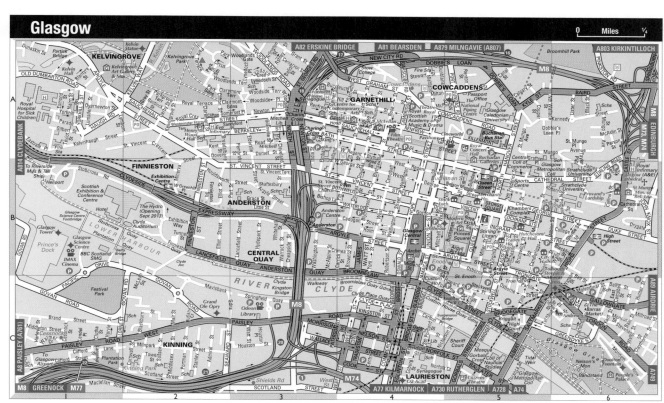

Gloucester

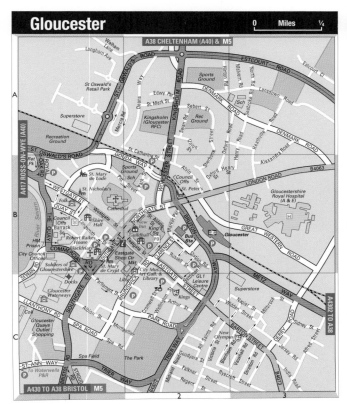

Hull

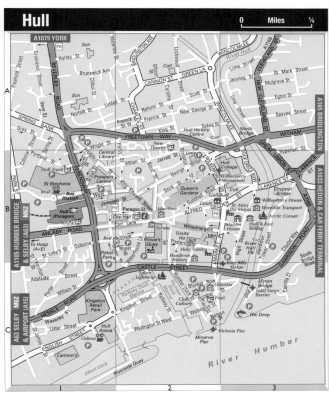

Ipswich

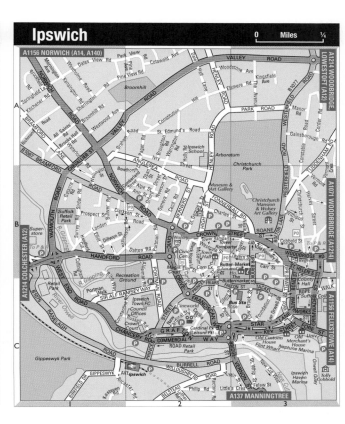

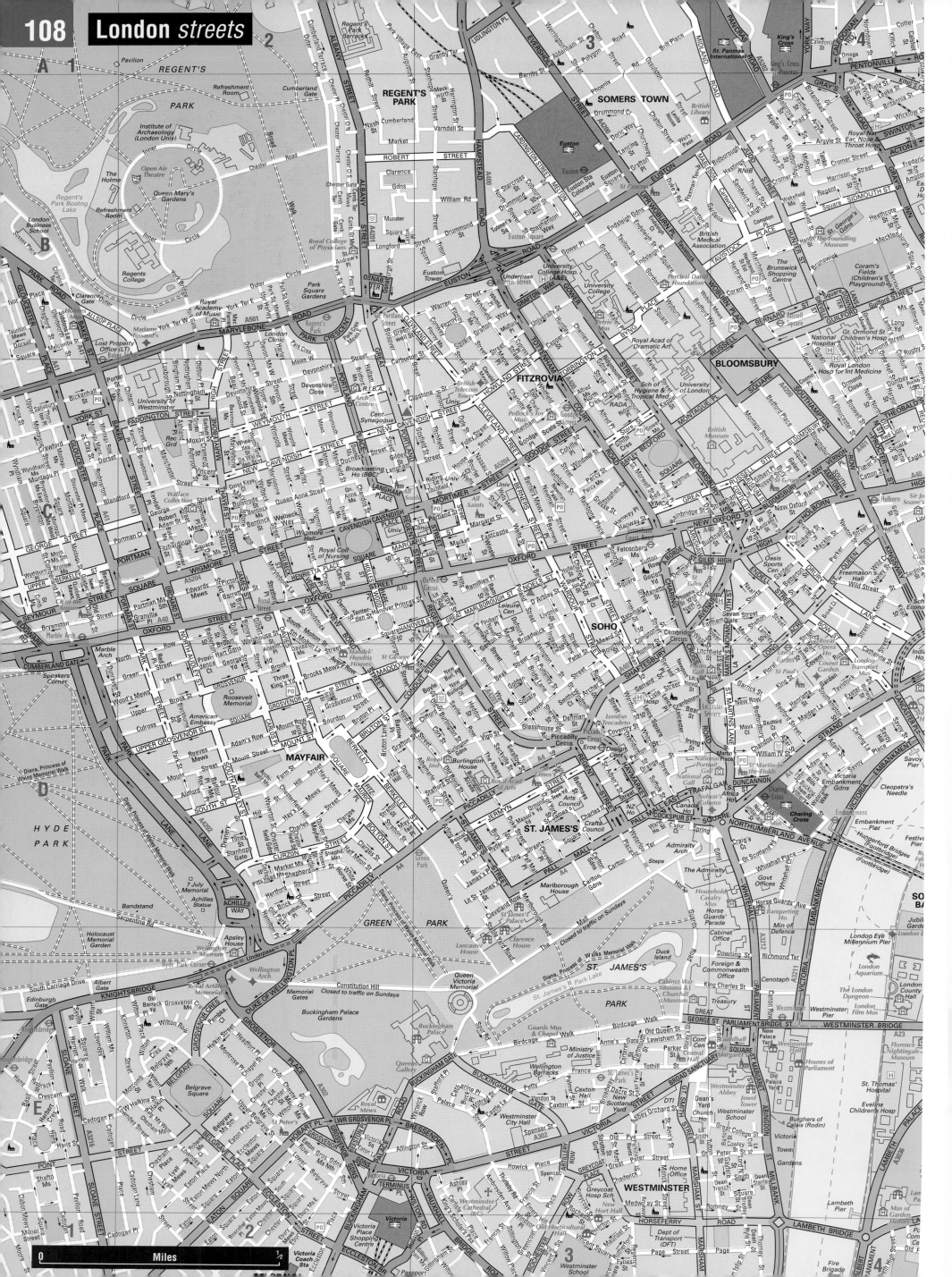

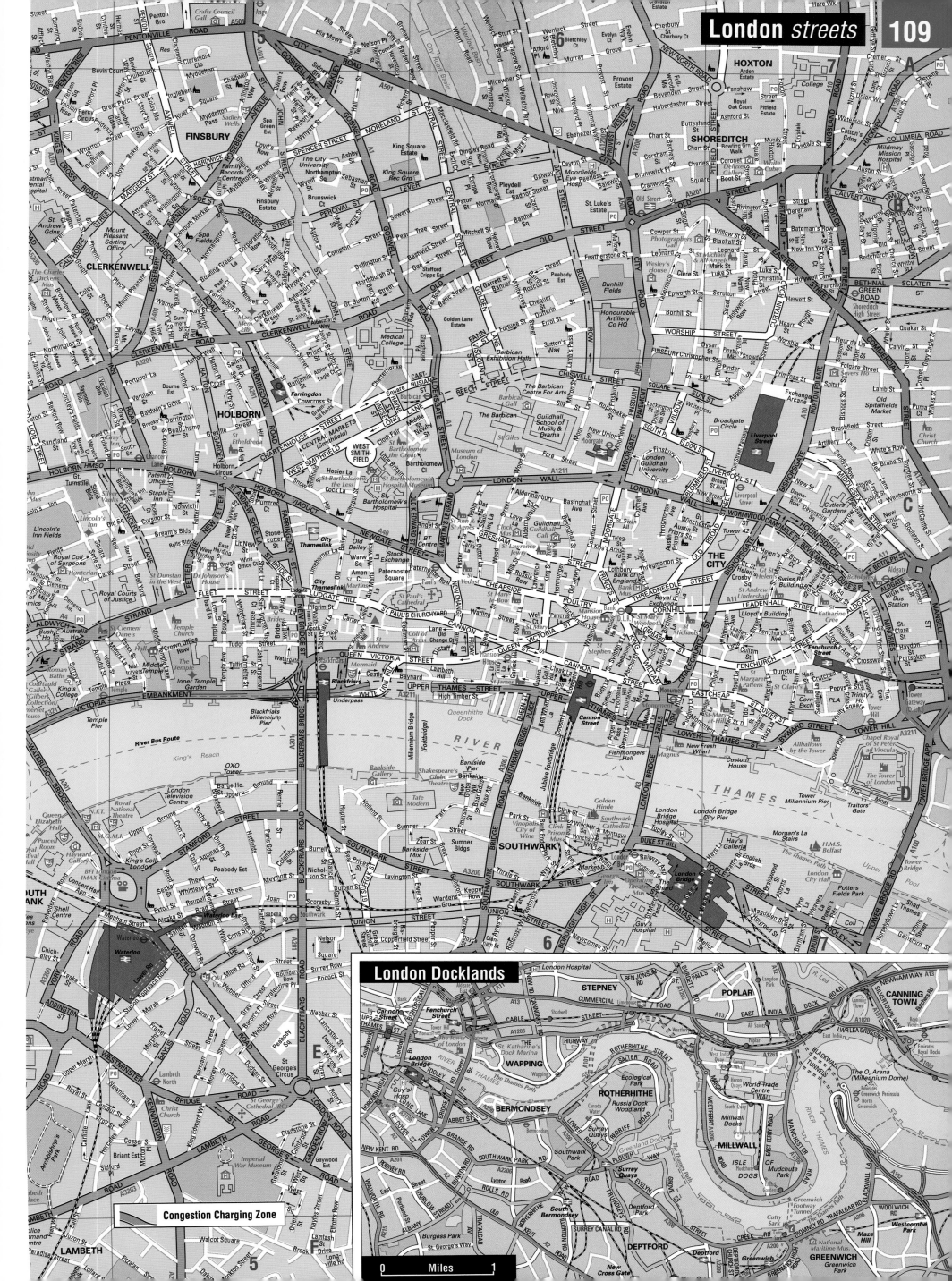

London Docklands

Congestion Charging Zone

0 Miles 1

Leeds

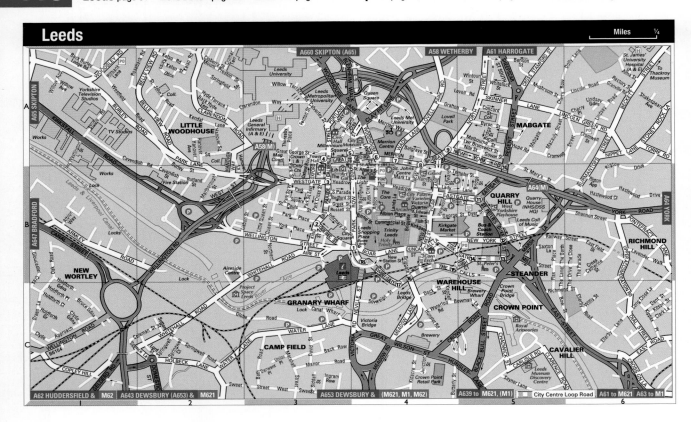

Leicester

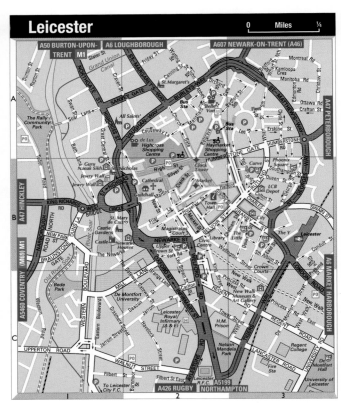

Lincoln

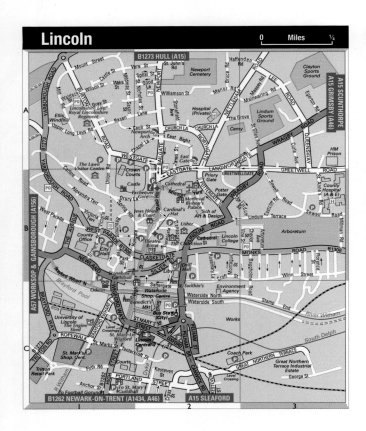

Liverpool

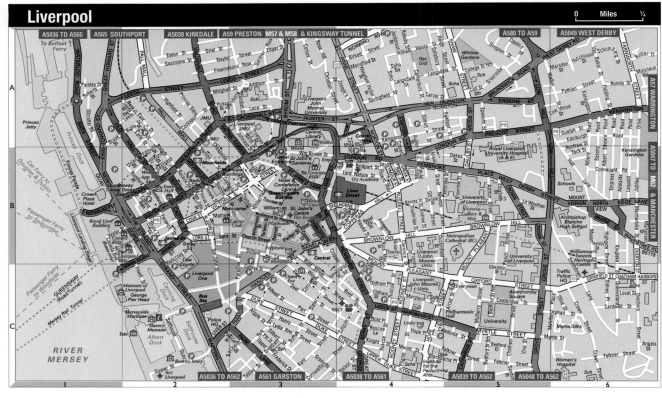

Manchester

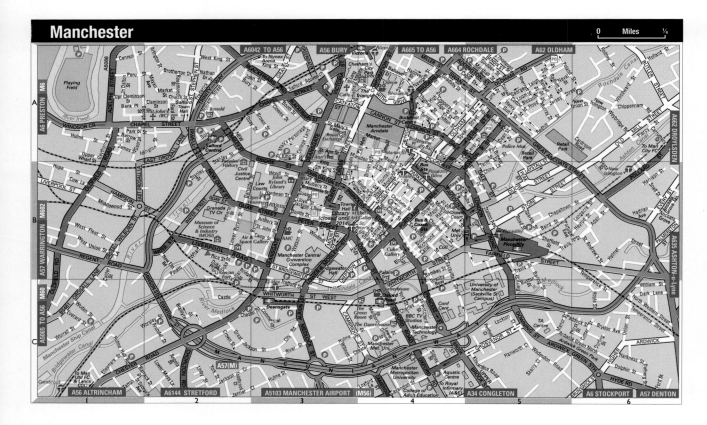

Middlesbrough

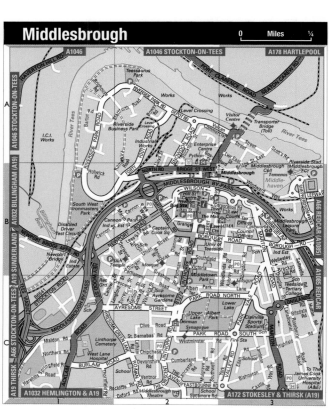

Newcastle page 63 • Northampton page 28 • Norwich page 39 • Nottingham page 36 • Oxford page 28 • Plymouth page 4 • Portsmouth page 10 • Reading page 18 • Salisbury page 9

111

Newcastle upon Tyne
0 Miles ¼

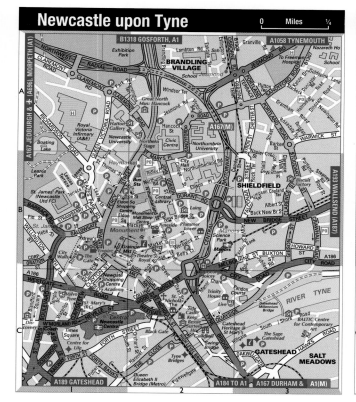

Northampton
0 Miles ¼

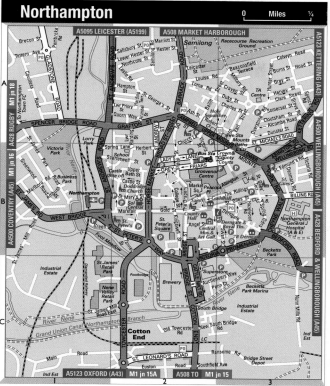

Norwich
0 Miles ¼

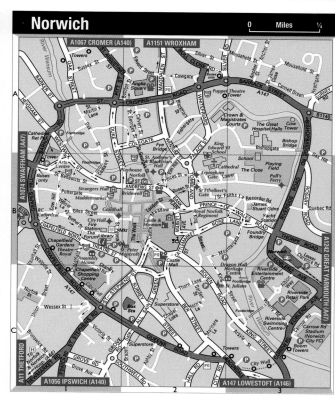

Nottingham
0 Miles ¼

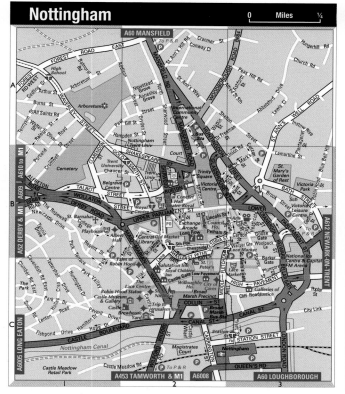

Oxford
0 Miles ¼

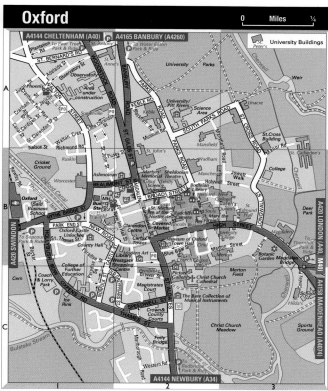

Plymouth
0 Miles ¼

Portsmouth
0 Miles ¼

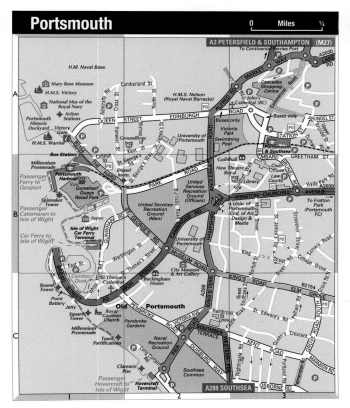

Reading
0 Miles ¼

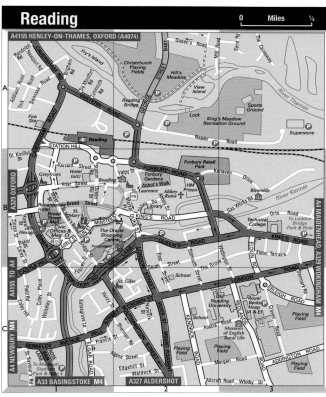

Salisbury
0 Miles ¼

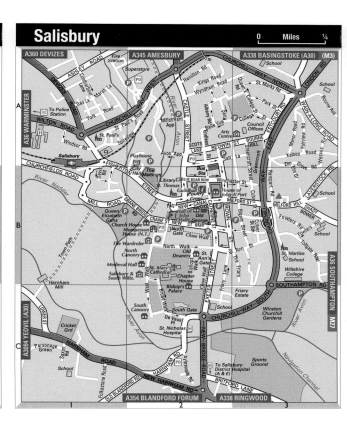

Sheffield
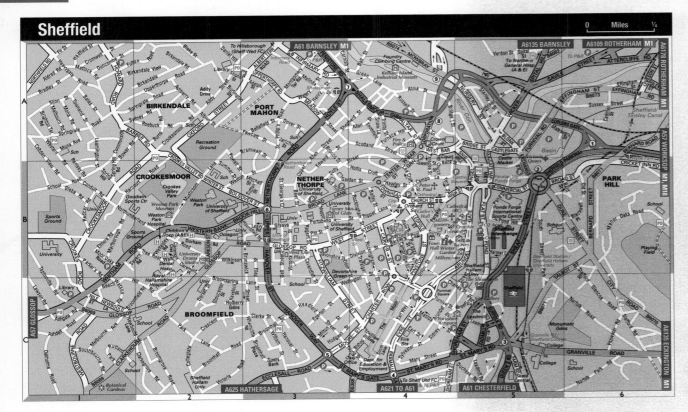

Southampton
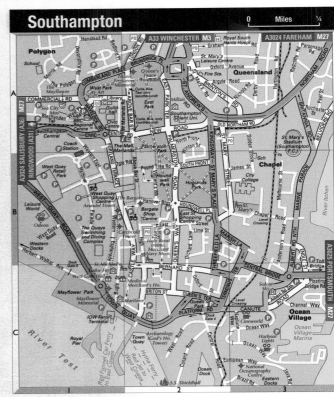

Stratford-upon-Avon
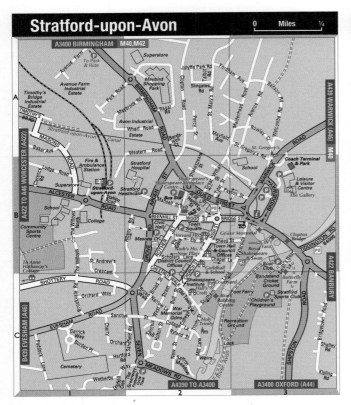

Sunderland
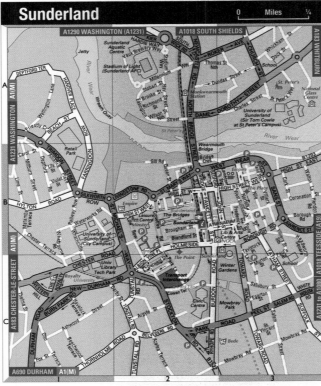

Swansea / Abertawe
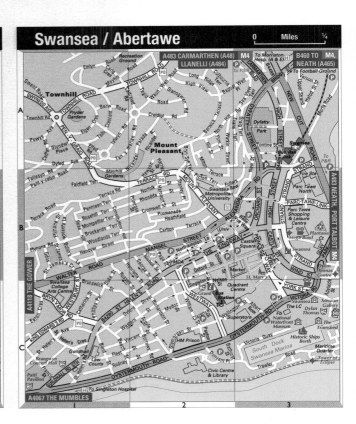

Winchester
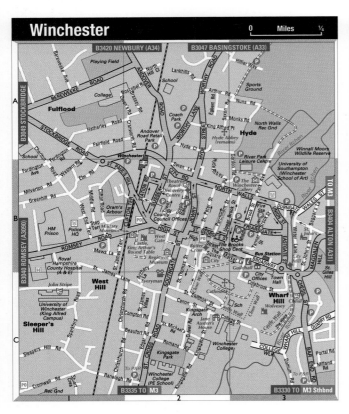

Worcester
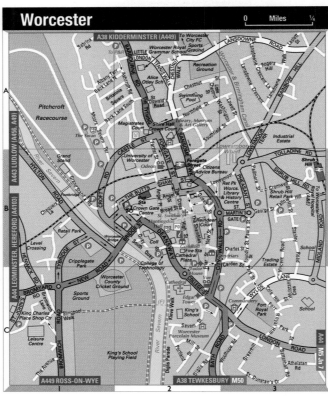

York
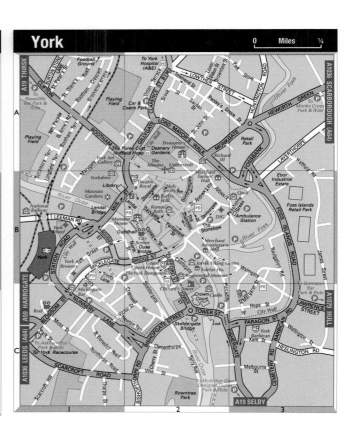

Map of Britain showing county and unitary authority boundaries with labels including: W Isles, Highland, Moray, Aberds, Aberdeen, Perth and Kinross, Angus, Dundee, Argyll and Bute, Stirling, Fife, Glasgow, Edin, Midloth, E Loth, N Ayrs, S Lanark, E Ayrs, Borders, S Ayrs, Dumfries and Galloway, Northumberland, Tyne and Wear, Cumbria, Durham, Hartlepool, Redcar and Cleveland, Middlesbrough, Darlington, Stockton-on-Tees, IoM, North Yorkshire, York, E Yorks, Blackpool, Lancs, W Yorks, N Lincs, NE Lincs, Anglesey, Mers, Gtr Man, S Yorks, Lincolnshire, Conwy, Flint, Denb, Wrex, Ches, Derbys, Notts, Gwyn, Telford, Shrops, Staffs, Leics, Rutland, Norfolk, Ceredig, Powys, Worcs, Warks, Northants, Cambs, Suffolk, Bedford, C Beds, Pembs, Carms, Hereford, Glos, Oxon, Bucks, Herts, Essex, Swansea, Cardiff, Mon, Bristol, Wilts, London, Southend, Medway, Somerset, Hants, Surrey, Kent, Devon, Dorset, IoW, Bmouth, Poole, Ptsmth, Brighton, W Sus, E Sus, Cornwall, Torbay, Plymouth, Scilly.

Abbreviations used in the index

Aberdeen	Aberdeen City	Dumfries	Dumfries and Galloway
Aberds	Aberdeenshire	Dundee	Dundee City
Ald	Alderney	Durham	Durham
Anglesey	Isle of Anglesey	E Ayrs	East Ayrshire
Angus	Angus	E Dunb	East Dunbartonshire
Argyll	Argyll and Bute	E Loth	East Lothian
Bath	Bath and North East Somerset	E Renf	East Renfrewshire
Bedford	Bedford	E Sus	East Sussex
Bl Gwent	Blaenau Gwent	E Yorks	East Riding of Yorkshire
Blackburn	Blackburn with Darwen	Edin	City of Edinburgh
Blackpool	Blackpool	Essex	Essex
Borders	Scottish Borders	Falk	Falkirk
Brack	Bracknell	Fife	Fife
Bridgend	Bridgend	Flint	Flintshire
Brighton	City of Brighton and Hove	Glasgow	City of Glasgow
Bristol	City and County of Bristol	Glos	Gloucestershire
Bucks	Buckinghamshire	Gtr Man	Greater Manchester
C Beds	Central Bedfordshire	Guern	Guernsey
Caerph	Caerphilly	Gwyn	Gwynedd
Cambs	Cambridgeshire	Halton	Halton
Cardiff	Cardiff	Hants	Hampshire
Carms	Carmarthenshire	Hereford	Herefordshire
Ceredig	Ceredigion	Herts	Hertfordshire
Ches E	Cheshire East	Highld	Highland
Ches W	Cheshire West and Chester	Hrtlpl	Hartlepool
Clack	Clackmannanshire	Hull	Hull
Conwy	Conwy	IoM	Isle of Man
Corn	Cornwall	IoW	Isle of Wight
Cumb	Cumbria	Invclyd	Inverclyde
Darl	Darlington	Jersey	Jersey
Denb	Denbighshire	Kent	Kent
Derby	City of Derby	Lancs	Lancashire
Derbys	Derbyshire	Leicester	City of Leicester
Devon	Devon	Leics	Leicestershire
Dorset	Dorset	Lincs	Lincolnshire
		London	Greater London
		Luton	Luton
		M Keynes	Milton Keynes
		M Tydf	Merthyr Tydfil

Mbro	Middlesbrough	Poole	Poole
Medway	Medway	Powys	Powys
Mers	Merseyside	Ptsmth	Portsmouth
Midloth	Midlothian	Reading	Reading
Mon	Monmouthshire	Redcar	Redcar and Cleveland
Moray	Moray	Renfs	Renfrewshire
N Ayrs	North Ayrshire	Rhondda	Rhondda Cynon Taff
N Lanark	North Lanarkshire	Rutland	Rutland
N Lincs	North Lincolnshire	S Ayrs	South Ayrshire
N Som	North Somerset	S Glos	South Gloucestershire
N Yorks	North Yorkshire	S Lanark	South Lanarkshire
NE Lincs	North East Lincolnshire	S Yorks	South Yorkshire
Neath	Neath Port Talbot	Scilly	Scilly
Newport	City and County of Newport	Shetland	Shetland
Norf	Norfolk	Shrops	Shropshire
Northants	Northamptonshire	Slough	Slough
Northumb	Northumberland	Som	Somerset
Notts	Nottinghamshire	Soton	Southampton
Nottingham	City of Nottingham	Staffs	Staffordshire
Orkney	Orkney	Stirling	Stirling
Oxon	Oxfordshire	Stockton	Stockton-on-Tees
Pboro	Peterborough	Stoke	Stoke-on-Trent
Pembs	Pembrokeshire	Suff	Suffolk
Perth	Perth and Kinross	Sur	Surrey
Plym	Plymouth		

Swansea	Swansea
Swindon	Swindon
T&W	Tyne and Wear
Telford	Telford and Wrekin
Thurrock	Thurrock
Torbay	Torbay
Torf	Torfaen
V Glam	The Vale of Glamorgan
W Berks	West Berkshire
W Dunb	West Dunbartonshire
W Isles	Western Isles
W Loth	West Lothian
W Mid	West Midlands
W Sus	West Sussex
W Yorks	West Yorkshire
Warks	Warwickshire
Warr	Warrington
Wilts	Wiltshire
Windsor	Windsor and Maidenhead
Wokingham	Wokingham
Worcs	Worcestershire
Wrex	Wrexham
York	City of York

Index to road maps of Britain

How to use the index

Example: **Thornton-le-Beans** N Yorks **58 G4**

- grid square
- page number
- county or unitary authority

Austrey Warks 35 E8
Austwick N Yorks 50 C3
Authorpe Lincs 47 D8
Authorpe Row Lincs 47 E9
Avebury Wilts 17 E8
Aveley Thurrock 20 C2
Avening Glos 16 B5
Averham Notts 45 G11
Aveton Gifford Devon 5 G7
Avielochan Highld 81 B11
Aviemore Highld 81 B10
Avington Hants 10 A4
Avington W Berks 17 E10
Avoch Highld 87 F10
Avon Hants 9 E10
Avon Dassett Warks 27 D11
Avonbridge Falk 69 C8
Avonmouth Bristol 15 D11
Avonwick Devon 5 F8
Awbridge Hants 10 B2
Awhirk Dumfries 54 D3
Awkley S Glos 16 C2
Awliscombe Devon 7 F10
Awre Glos 26 H4
Awsworth Notts 35 A10
Axbridge Som 15 F10
Axford Hants 18 G3
Axford Wilts 17 D9
Axminster Devon 8 E1
Axmouth Devon 8 E1
Axton Flint 42 D4
Aycliff Kent 21 G10
Aycliffe Durham 58 D3
Aydon Northumb 62 G6
Aylburton Glos 16 A3
Ayle Northumb 57 B9
Aylesbeare Devon 7 G9
Aylesbury Bucks 28 G5
Aylesby NE Lincs 46 B6
Aylesford Kent 20 F4
Aylesham Kent 21 F9
Aylestone Leicester 36 E1
Aylmerton Norf 39 B7
Aylsham Norf 39 C7
Aylton Hereford 26 E3
Aymestrey Hereford 25 B11
Aynho Northants 28 E2
Ayot St Lawrence Herts 29 G8
Ayot St Peter Herts 29 G9
Ayr S Ayrs 66 D6
Aysgarth N Yorks 58 H1
Ayside Cumb 49 A3
Ayston Rutland 36 E4
Aythorpe Roding Essex 30 G2
Ayton Borders 71 D8
Aywick Shetland 96 E7
Azerley N Yorks 51 B8

B

Babbacombe Torbay 5 E10
Babbinswood Shrops 33 B9
Babcary Som 8 B4
Babel Carms 24 E5
Babell Flint 42 E4
Babraham Cambs 30 C2
Babworth Notts 45 D10
Bac W Isles 91 C9
Bachau Anglesey 40 B6
Back of Keppoch Highld 79 C9
Back Rogerton E Ayrs 67 D8
Backaland Orkney 95 E6
Backaskaill Orkney 95 C5
Backbarrow Cumb 49 A3
Backe Carms 23 E7
Backfolds Aberds 89 C10
Backford Ches W 43 E7
Backford Cross Ches W 43 E6
Backhill Aberds 89 E10
Backhill Aberds 89 E7
Backhill of Clackriach Aberds 89 D9
Backhill of Fortree Aberds 89 D9
Backhill of Trustach Aberds 83 D8
Backies Highld 93 J11
Backlass Highld 94 E4
Backwell N Som 15 E10
Backworth T&W 63 F9
Bacon End Essex 30 G3
Baconsthorpe Norf 39 B7
Bacton Hereford 25 E10
Bacton Norf 39 B9
Bacton Suff 31 B7
Bacton Green Suff 31 B7
Bacup Lancs 50 G4
Badachro Highld 85 A12
Badanloch Lodge Highld 93 F10
Badavanich Highld 86 F4
Badbury Swindon 17 C8
Badby Northants 28 C2
Badcall Highld 92 D5
Badcaul Highld 86 B3
Baddeley Green Stoke 44 G3
Baddesley Clinton Warks 27 A9
Baddesley Ensor Warks 35 F8
Baddidarach Highld 92 G3
Baddoch Aberds 82 E3
Baddock Highld 87 F10
Badenscoth Aberds 89 E7
Badenyon Aberds 82 B5
Badger Shrops 34 F3
Badger's Mount Kent 19 E11
Badgeworth Glos 26 G6
Badgworth Som 15 F9
Badicaul Highld 85 F12
Badingham Suff 31 B10
Badlesmere Kent 21 F7
Badlipster Highld 94 F4
Badluarach Highld 86 B2
Badminton S Glos 16 C5
Badnaban Highld 92 G3
Badninish Highld 87 B10
Badrallach Highld 86 B3
Badsey Worcs 27 D7
Badshot Lea Sur 18 G5
Badsworth W Yorks 45 A8
Badwell Ash Suff 30 B6
Bae Colwyn = Colwyn Bay Conwy 41 C10
Bag Enderby Lincs 47 E7
Bagby N Yorks 51 A10
Bagendon Glos 27 H7
Bagh a Chaisteil = Castlebay W Isles 84 J1
Bagh Mor W Isles 84 C3
Bagh Shiarabhagh W Isles 84 H2
Baghasdal W Isles 84 G2
Bagillt Flint 42 E5
Baginton Warks 27 A10
Baglan Neath 14 B3
Bagley Shrops 33 C10
Bagnall Staffs 44 G3
Bagnor W Berks 17 E11
Bagshot Sur 18 E6
Bagshot Wilts 17 E10
Bagthorpe Norf 38 B3
Bagthorpe Notts 45 G8
Bagworth Leics 35 E10
Bagwy Llydiart Hereford 25 F11
Bail àrd Bhuirgh W Isles 91 B9
Bail' lochdrach W Isles 84 C3
Bail Uachdraich W Isles 84 B3
Bail' Ur Tholastaidh W Isles 91 C10
Baildon W Yorks 51 F7
Baile W Isles 90 J4
Baile a Mhanaich W Isles 84 C2
Baile Ailein W Isles 91 E7
Baile an Truiseil W Isles 91 B8
Baile Boidheach Argyll 72 F6
Baile Glas W Isles 84 C3
Baile Mhartainn W Isles 84 A2
Baile Mhic Phail W Isles 84 A3
Baile Mor Argyll 78 J5
Baile Mor W Isles 84 B2
Baile na Creige W Isles 84 H1
Baile nan Cailleach W Isles 84 C2
Baile Raghaill W Isles 84 A2
Bailebeag Highld 81 B7
Baileyhead Cumb 61 F11
Bailiesward Aberds 88 E4
Baillieston Glasgow 68 D5
Bainbridge N Yorks 57 G11
Bainsford Falk 69 B7
Bainshole Aberds 88 E6
Bainton E Yorks 52 D5
Bainton Pboro 37 E6
Bairnkine Borders 62 B2
Baker Street Thurrock 20 C3
Baker's End Herts 29 G10
Bakewell Derbys 44 F6
Bala = Y Bala Gwyn 32 B5
Balachuirn Highld 85 D10
Balavil Highld 81 C9
Balbeg Highld 81 A6
Balbeg Highld 86 H7
Balbeggie Perth 76 E4
Balbithan Aberds 83 B9
Balbithan Ho. Aberds 83 B10
Balblair Highld 87 B8
Balblair Highld 87 E10
Balby S Yorks 45 B9
Balchladich Highld 92 F3
Balchraggan Highld 87 G8
Balchraggan Highld 87 H8
Balchrick Highld 92 D4
Balchrystie Fife 77 G7
Balcladaich Highld 80 A4
Balcombe W Sus 12 C2
Balcombe Lane W Sus 12 C2
Balcomie Fife 77 F9
Balcurvie Fife 76 G6
Baldersby N Yorks 51 B9
Baldersby St James N Yorks 51 B9
Balderstone Lancs 50 F2
Balderton Ches W 42 F6
Balderton Notts 46 G2
Baldhu Corn 3 E6
Baldinnie Fife 77 F7
Baldock Herts 29 E9
Baldovie Dundee 77 D7
Baldrine IoM 48 D4
Baldslow E Sus 13 E6
Baldwin IoM 48 D3
Baldwinholme Cumb 56 A5
Baldwin's Gate Staffs 34 A3
Bale Norf 38 B6
Balearn Aberds 89 C10
Balemartine Argyll 78 G2
Balephuil Argyll 78 G2
Balerno Edin 69 D10
Balevullin Argyll 78 G2
Balfield Angus 83 G7
Balfour Orkney 95 G5
Balfron Stirling 68 B4
Balfron Station Stirling 68 B4
Balgaveny Aberds 89 D6
Balgavies Angus 77 B8
Balgonar Fife 69 A9
Balgove Aberds 89 E8
Balgowan Highld 81 D8
Balgown Highld 85 B8
Balgrochan E Dunb 68 C5
Balgy Highld 85 C13
Balhaldie Stirling 75 G11
Balhalgardy Aberds 83 A9
Balham London 19 D9
Balhary Perth 76 C5
Baliasta Shetland 96 C8
Baligill Highld 93 C11
Balintore Angus 76 B5
Balintore Highld 87 D11
Balintraid Highld 87 D10
Balk N Yorks 51 A10
Balkeerie Angus 76 C6
Balkemback Angus 76 D6
Balkholme E Yorks 52 G3
Balkissock S Ayrs 54 A4
Ball Shrops 33 C9
Ball Haye Green Staffs 44 G3
Ball Hill Hants 17 E11
Ballabeg IoM 48 E2
Ballacannel IoM 48 D4
Ballachulish Highld 74 B3
Ballajora IoM 48 C4
Ballaleigh IoM 48 D3
Ballamodha IoM 48 E2
Ballantrae S Ayrs 54 A3
Ballaquine IoM 48 D4
Ballards Gore Essex 20 B6
Ballasalla IoM 48 C3
Ballasalla IoM 48 E2
Ballater Aberds 82 D5
Ballaugh IoM 48 C3
Ballaveare IoM 48 E3
Ballcorach Moray 82 A3
Ballechin Perth 76 B2
Balleigh Highld 87 C10
Ballencrieff E Loth 70 C3
Ballentoul Perth 81 G10
Ballidon Derbys 44 G6
Balliemore Argyll 73 E9
Balliemore Argyll 79 J11
Ballikinrain Stirling 68 B4
Ballimeanoch Argyll 73 B9
Ballimore Argyll 73 E8
Ballimore Stirling 75 F8
Ballinaby Argyll 64 B3
Ballindean Perth 76 E5
Ballingdon Suff 30 D5
Ballinger Common Bucks 18 A6
Ballingham Hereford 26 E2
Ballingry Fife 76 H4
Ballinlick Perth 76 C2
Ballinluig Perth 76 B2
Ballintuim Perth 76 B4
Balloch Angus 76 B6
Balloch Highld 87 G10
Balloch N Lanark 68 C6
Balloch W Dunb 68 B2
Ballochan Aberds 83 D7
Ballochford Moray 88 E3
Ballochmorrie S Ayrs 54 A5
Balls Cross W Sus 11 B8
Balls Green Essex 31 F7
Ballygown Argyll 78 G7
Ballygrant Argyll 64 B4
Ballyhaugh Argyll 78 F4
Balmacara Highld 85 F13
Balmacara Square Highld 85 F13
Balmaclellan Dumfries 55 B9
Balmacneil Perth 76 B2
Balmacqueen Highld 85 A9
Balmae Dumfries 55 E9
Balmaha Stirling 68 A3
Balmalcolm Fife 76 G6
Balmeanach Highld 85 D10
Balmedie Aberds 83 B11
Balmer Heath Shrops 33 B10
Balmerino Fife 76 E6
Balmerlawn Hants 10 D2
Balmichael N Ayrs 66 C2
Balmirmer Angus 77 D8
Balmore Highld 85 D7
Balmore Highld 86 H6
Balmore Highld 87 G11
Balmore Perth 76 B2
Balmule Fife 69 B11
Balmullo Fife 77 E7
Balmungie Highld 87 F10
Balnaboth Angus 82 G5
Balnabruaich Highld 87 E10
Balnabruich Highld 94 H3
Balnacoil Highld 93 H11
Balnacra Highld 86 G2
Balnafoich Highld 87 H9
Balnagall Highld 87 C11
Balnaguard Perth 76 B2
Balnahard Argyll 72 D3
Balnahard Argyll 78 H7
Balnain Highld 86 H7
Balnakeil Highld 92 C6
Balnaknock Highld 85 B9
Balnapaling Highld 87 E10
Balne N Yorks 52 H1
Balochroy Argyll 65 C8
Balone Fife 77 F7
Balornock Glasgow 68 D5
Balquharn Perth 76 D3
Balquhidder Stirling 75 E8
Balsall W Mid 35 H8
Balsall Common W Mid 35 H8
Balsall Hth. W Mid 35 G6
Balscott Oxon 27 D10
Balsham Cambs 30 C2
Baltasound Shetland 96 C8
Balterley Staffs 43 G10
Baltersan Dumfries 55 C7
Balthangie Aberds 89 C8
Baltonsborough Som 8 A4
Balvaird Highld 87 F8
Balvicar Argyll 72 B6
Balvraid Highld 85 G13
Balvraid Highld 87 H11
Bamber Bridge Lancs 50 G1
Bambers Green Essex 30 F2
Bamburgh Northumb 71 G10
Bamff Perth 76 B5
Bamford Derbys 44 D6
Bamford Gtr Man 44 A2
Bampton Cumb 57 E7
Bampton Devon 7 D8
Bampton Oxon 17 A10
Bampton Grange Cumb 57 E7
Banavie Highld 80 F3
Banbury Oxon 27 D11
Bancffosfelen Carms 23 E9
Banchory Aberds 83 D8
Banchory-Devenick Aberds 83 C11
Bancycapel Carms 23 E9
Bancyfelin Carms 23 E8
Bancyffordd Carms 23 C9
Bandirran Perth 76 D5
Banff Aberds 89 B6
Bangor Gwyn 41 C7
Bangor-is-y-coed Wrex 43 H6
Banham Norf 39 G6
Bank Hants 10 D1
Bank Newton N Yorks 50 D5
Bank Street Worcs 26 B3
Bankend Dumfries 60 G6
Bankfoot Perth 76 D3
Bankglen E Ayrs 67 E9
Bankhead Aberdeen 83 B10
Bankhead Aberds 83 C8
Banknock Falk 68 C6
Banks Cumb 61 G11
Banks Lancs 49 G3
Bankshill Dumfries 61 E7
Banningham Norf 39 C8
Banniskirk Ho. Highld 94 E3
Bannister Green Essex 30 F3
Bannockburn Stirling 69 A7
Banstead Sur 19 F9
Bantham Devon 5 G7
Banton N Lanark 68 C6
Banwell N Som 15 F9
Banyard's Green Suff 31 A9
Bapchild Kent 20 E6
Bar Hill Cambs 29 B10
Barabhas W Isles 91 C8
Barabhas Iarach W Isles 91 C8
Barabhas Uarach W Isles 91 B8
Barachandroman Argyll 79 J9
Barassie S Ayrs 66 C6
Baravullin Argyll 79 H11
Barbaraville Highld 87 D10
Barber Booth Derbys 44 D5
Barbieston S Ayrs 67 E7
Barbon Cumb 50 A2
Barbridge Ches E 43 G9
Barbrook Devon 6 B6
Barby Northants 28 A2
Barcaldine Argyll 74 C2
Barcheston Warks 27 E9
Barcombe E Sus 12 E3
Barcombe Cross E Sus 12 E3
Barden N Yorks 58 G2
Barden Scale N Yorks 51 D6
Bardennoch Dumfries 67 G8
Bardfield Saling Essex 30 F3
Bardister Shetland 96 F5
Bardney Lincs 46 F5
Bardon Leics 35 D10
Bardon Mill Northumb 62 G3
Bardowie E Dunb 68 C4
Bardrainney Invclyd 68 C2
Bardsea Cumb 49 B3
Bardsey W Yorks 51 E9
Bardwell Suff 30 A6
Bare Lancs 49 C4
Barfad Argyll 73 G7
Barford Norf 39 E7
Barford Warks 27 B9
Barford St John Oxon 27 E11
Barford St Martin Wilts 9 A9
Barford St Michael Oxon 27 E11
Barfrestone Kent 21 F9
Bargod = Bargoed Caerph 15 B7
Bargoed = Bargod Caerph 15 B7
Bargrennan Dumfries 54 B6
Barham Cambs 37 H7
Barham Kent 21 F9
Barham Suff 31 C8
Barharrow Dumfries 55 D9
Barhill Dumfries 55 C11
Barholm Lincs 37 D6
Barkby Leics 36 E2
Barkestone-le-Vale Leics 36 B3
Barkham Wokingham 18 E4
Barking London 19 C11
Barking Suff 31 C7
Barking Tye Suff 31 C7
Barkingside London 19 C11
Barkisland W Yorks 51 H6
Barkston Lincs 36 A5
Barkston N Yorks 51 F10
Barkway Herts 29 E10
Barlaston Staffs 34 B4
Barlavington W Sus 11 C8
Barlborough Derbys 45 E8
Barlby N Yorks 52 F2
Barlestone Leics 35 E10
Barley Herts 29 E10
Barley Lancs 50 E4
Barley Mow T&W 58 A3
Barleythorpe Rutland 36 E4
Barling Essex 20 C6
Barlow Derbys 45 E7
Barlow N Yorks 52 G2
Barlow T&W 63 G7
Barmby Moor E Yorks 52 E3
Barmby on the Marsh E Yorks 52 G2
Barmer Norf 38 B4
Barmoor Castle Northumb 71 G8
Barmoor Lane End Northumb 71 G9
Barmouth = Abermaw Gwyn 32 D2
Barmpton Darl 58 E4
Barmston E Yorks 53 D7
Barnack Pboro 37 E6
Barnacle Warks 35 G9
Barnard Castle Durham 58 E1
Barnard Gate Oxon 27 G11
Barnardiston Suff 30 D4
Barnbarroch Dumfries 55 D11
Barnburgh S Yorks 45 B8
Barnby Suff 39 G10
Barnby Dun S Yorks 45 B10
Barnby in the Willows Notts 46 G2
Barnby Moor Notts 45 D10
Barnes Street Kent 20 G3
Barnet London 19 B9
Barnetby le Wold N Lincs 46 B4
Barney Norf 38 B5
Barnham Suff 38 H4
Barnham W Sus 11 D8
Barnham Broom Norf 39 E6
Barnhead Angus 77 B9
Barnhill Ches W 43 G7
Barnhill Dundee 77 D7
Barnhill Moray 88 C1
Barnhills Dumfries 54 B2
Barningham Durham 58 E1
Barningham Suff 38 H5
Barnoldby le Beck NE Lincs 46 B6
Barnoldswick Lancs 50 E4
Barns Green W Sus 11 B10
Barnsley Glos 27 H7
Barnsley S Yorks 45 B7
Barnstaple Devon 6 C4
Barnston Essex 30 G3
Barnston Mers 42 D5
Barnstone Notts 36 B3
Barnt Green Worcs 27 A7
Barnton Ches W 43 E9
Barnton Edin 69 C10
Barnwell All Saints Northants 36 G6
Barnwell St Andrew Northants 36 G6
Barnwood Glos 26 G5
Barochreal Argyll 79 J11
Barons Cross Hereford 25 C11
Barr S Ayrs 66 G5
Barra Castle Aberds 83 A9
Barrachan Dumfries 54 E6
Barrack Aberds 89 D8
Barraglom W Isles 90 D6
Barrahormid Argyll 72 E6
Barran Argyll 79 J11
Barrapol Argyll 78 G2
Barras Aberds 83 E10
Barras Cumb 57 E10
Barrasford Northumb 62 F5
Barravullin Argyll 73 C7
Barregarrow IoM 48 D3
Barrhead E Renf 68 E3
Barrhill S Ayrs 54 A5
Barrington Cambs 29 D10
Barrington Som 8 C2
Barripper Corn 2 F5
Barrmill N Ayrs 67 A6
Barrock Highld 94 C4
Barrock Ho. Highld 94 D4
Barrow Lancs 50 F3
Barrow Rutland 36 D4
Barrow Suff 30 B4
Barrow Green Kent 20 E6
Barrow Gurney N Som 15 E11
Barrow Haven N Lincs 53 G6
Barrow-in-Furness Cumb 49 C2
Barrow Island Cumb 49 C1
Barrow Nook Lancs 43 B7
Barrow Street Wilts 9 A7
Barrow upon Humber N Lincs 53 G6
Barrow upon Soar Leics 36 D1
Barrow upon Trent Derbys 35 C9
Barroway Drove Norf 38 E1
Barrowburn Northumb 62 B4
Barrowby Lincs 36 B4
Barrowcliff N Yorks 59 H11
Barrowden Rutland 36 E5
Barrowford Lancs 50 F4
Barrows Green Ches E 43 G9
Barrows Green Cumb 57 H7
Barrow's Green Mers 43 D8
Barry Angus 77 D8
Barry = Y Barri V Glam 15 E7
Barry Island V Glam 15 E7
Barsby Leics 36 D2
Barsham Suff 39 G9
Barston W Mid 35 H8
Bartestree Hereford 26 D2
Barthol Chapel Aberds 89 E8
Barthomley Ches E 43 G10
Bartley Hants 10 C2
Bartley Green W Mid 34 G6
Bartlow Cambs 30 D2
Barton Cambs 29 C11
Barton Ches W 43 G7
Barton Glos 27 F8
Barton Lancs 42 B6
Barton Lancs 49 F5
Barton N Yorks 58 F3
Barton Oxon 28 H2
Barton Torbay 5 E10
Barton Warks 27 C8
Barton Bendish Norf 38 E3
Barton Hartshorn Bucks 28 E3
Barton in Fabis Notts 35 B11
Barton in the Beans Leics 35 E9
Barton-le-Clay C Beds 29 E7
Barton-le-Street N Yorks 52 B3
Barton-le-Willows N Yorks 52 C3
Barton Mills Suff 30 A4
Barton on Sea Hants 9 E11
Barton on the Heath Warks 27 E9
Barton St David Som 8 A4
Barton Seagrave Northants 36 H4
Barton Stacey Hants 17 G11
Barton Turf Norf 39 C9
Barton-under-Needwood Staffs 35 D7
Barton-upon-Humber N Lincs 52 G6
Barton Waterside N Lincs 52 G6
Barugh S Yorks 45 B7
Barway Cambs 37 H11
Barwell Leics 35 F10
Barwick Herts 29 G10
Barwick Som 8 C4
Barwick in Elmet W Yorks 51 F9
Baschurch Shrops 33 C10
Bascote Warks 27 B11
Basford Green Staffs 44 G3
Bashall Eaves Lancs 50 E2
Bashley Hants 9 E11
Basildon Essex 20 C4
Basingstoke Hants 18 F3
Baslow Derbys 44 E6
Bason Bridge Som 15 G9
Bassaleg Newport 15 C8
Bassenthwaite Cumb 56 C4
Bassett Soton 10 C3
Bassingbourn Cambs 29 D10
Bassingfield Notts 36 B2
Bassingham Lincs 46 F3
Bassingthorpe Lincs 36 C5
Basta Shetland 96 D7
Baston Lincs 37 D7
Bastwick Norf 39 D10
Baswick Steer E Yorks 53 E6
Batchworth Heath Herts 19 B7
Batcombe Dorset 8 D5
Batcombe Som 16 H3
Bate Heath Ches E 43 E9
Batford Herts 29 G8
Bath Bath 16 E4
Bathampton Bath 16 E4
Bathealton Som 7 D9
Batheaston Bath 16 E4
Bathford Bath 16 E4
Bathgate W Loth 69 D8
Bathley Notts 45 G11
Bathpool Corn 4 D3
Bathpool Som 8 B1
Bathville W Loth 69 D8
Batley W Yorks 51 G8
Batsford Glos 27 E8
Battersby N Yorks 59 F6
Battersea London 19 D9
Battisborough Cross Devon 5 G6
Battisford Suff 31 C7
Battisford Tye Suff 31 C7
Battle E Sus 12 E6
Battle Powys 25 E7
Battledown Glos 26 F6
Battlefield Shrops 33 D11
Battlesbridge Essex 20 B4
Battlesden C Beds 28 F6
Battlesea Green Suff 39 H8
Battleton Som 7 D8
Battram Leics 35 E10
Battramsley Hants 10 E2
Baughton Worcs 26 D5
Baughurst Hants 18 F2
Baulking Oxon 17 B10
Baumber Lincs 46 E6
Baunton Glos 17 A7
Baverstock Wilts 9 A9
Bawburgh Norf 39 E7
Bawdeswell Norf 38 C6
Bawdrip Som 15 H9
Bawdsey Suff 31 D10
Bawtry S Yorks 45 C10
Baxenden Lancs 50 G3
Baxterley Warks 35 F8
Baybridge Hants 10 B4
Baycliff Cumb 49 B2
Baydon Wilts 17 D9
Bayford Herts 29 H10
Bayford Som 8 B6
Bayles Cumb 57 B9
Baylham Suff 31 C8
Baynard's Green Oxon 28 F2
Bayston Hill Shrops 33 E10
Baythorn End Essex 30 D4
Bayton Worcs 26 A3
Beach Highld 79 F10
Beachampton Bucks 28 E4
Beachamwell Norf 38 E3
Beachans Moray 87 G13
Beacharr Argyll 65 D7
Beachborough Kent 21 H8
Beachley Glos 16 B2
Beacon Devon 7 F10
Beacon End Essex 30 F6
Beacon Hill Sur 18 H5
Beacon's Bottom Bucks 18 B4
Beaconsfield Bucks 18 C6
Beacrabhaic W Isles 90 H6
Beadlam N Yorks 52 A2
Beadlow C Beds 29 E8
Beadnell Northumb 71 H11
Beaford Devon 6 E4
Beal N Yorks 51 G11
Beal Northumb 71 F9
Beamhurst Staffs 35 B6
Beaminster Dorset 8 D3
Beamish Durham 58 A3
Beamsley N Yorks 51 D6
Bean Kent 20 D2
Beanacre Wilts 16 E6
Beanley Northumb 62 B6
Beaquoy Orkney 95 F4
Bear Cross Bmouth 9 E9
Beardwood Blackburn 50 G2
Beare Green Sur 19 G8
Bearley Warks 27 B8
Bearnus Argyll 78 G6
Bearpark Durham 58 B3
Bearsbridge Northumb 62 H3
Bearsden E Dunb 68 C4
Bearsted Kent 20 F4
Bearstone Shrops 34 B3
Bearwood Hereford 25 C10
Bearwood Poole 9 E9
Bearwood W Mid 34 G6
Beattock Dumfries 60 C6
Beauchamp Roding Essex 30 G2
Beauchief S Yorks 45 D7
Beaufort Bl Gwent 25 G8
Beaufort Castle Highld 87 G8
Beaulieu Hants 10 D2
Beauly Highld 87 G8
Beaumaris Anglesey 41 C8
Beaumont Cumb 61 H9
Beaumont Essex 31 F8
Beaumont Hill Darl 58 E3
Beausale Warks 27 A9
Beauworth Hants 10 B4
Beaworthy Devon 6 G3
Beazley End Essex 30 F4
Bebington Mers 42 D6
Bebside Northumb 63 E8
Beccles Suff 39 F10
Becconsall Lancs 49 G4
Beck Foot Cumb 57 G8
Beck Hole N Yorks 59 F9
Beck Row Suff 38 H2
Beck Side Cumb 49 A2
Beckbury Shrops 34 E3
Beckenham London 19 E10
Beckermet Cumb 56 F2
Beckfoot Cumb 56 B2
Beckfoot Cumb 56 F3
Beckford Worcs 26 E6
Beckhampton Wilts 17 E7
Beckingham Lincs 46 G2
Beckingham Notts 45 D11
Beckington Som 16 F5
Beckley E Sus 13 D7
Beckley Hants 9 E11
Beckley Oxon 28 G2
Beckton London 19 C11
Beckwithshaw N Yorks 51 D8
Becontree London 19 C11
Bed-y-coedwr Gwyn 32 C3
Bedale N Yorks 58 H3
Bedburn Durham 58 C2
Bedchester Dorset 9 C7
Beddau Rhondda 14 C6
Beddgelert Gwyn 41 F7
Beddingham E Sus 12 F3
Beddington London 19 E10
Bedfield Suff 31 B9
Bedford Bedford 29 C7
Bedham W Sus 11 B9
Bedhampton Hants 10 D6
Bedingfield Suff 31 B8
Bedlam N Yorks 51 C8
Bedlington Northumb 63 E8
Bedlington Station Northumb 63 E8
Bedlinog M Tydf 14 A6
Bedminster Bristol 16 D2
Bedmond Herts 19 A7
Bednall Staffs 34 D5
Bedrule Borders 62 B2
Bedstone Shrops 33 H9
Bedwas Caerph 15 C7
Bedworth Warks 35 G9
Bedworth Heath Warks 35 G9
Beeby Leics 36 E2
Beech Hants 18 H3
Beech Staffs 34 B4
Beech Hill Gtr Man 43 B8
Beech Hill W Berks 18 E3
Beechingstoke Wilts 17 F7
Beedon W Berks 17 D11
Beeford E Yorks 53 D7
Beeley Derbys 44 F6
Beelsby NE Lincs 46 B6
Beenham W Berks 18 E2
Beeny Corn 4 B2
Beer Devon 8 F1
Beer Hackett Dorset 8 C4
Beercrocombe Som 8 B2
Beesands Devon 5 G9
Beesby Lincs 47 D8
Beeson Devon 5 G9
Beeston C Beds 29 D8
Beeston Ches W 43 G8
Beeston Norf 38 D5
Beeston Notts 35 B11
Beeston W Yorks 51 F8
Beeston Regis Norf 39 A7
Beeswing Dumfries 55 C11
Beetham Cumb 49 B4
Beetley Norf 38 D5
Begbroke Oxon 27 G11
Begelly Pembs 22 F6
Beggar's Bush Powys 25 B9
Beguildy Powys 33 H7
Beighton Norf 39 E9
Beighton S Yorks 45 D8
Beighton Hill Derbys 44 G6
Beith N Ayrs 66 A6
Bekesbourne Kent 21 F8
Belaugh Norf 39 D8
Belbroughton Worcs 34 H5
Belchamp Otten Essex 30 D5
Belchamp St Paul Essex 30 D4
Belchamp Walter Essex 30 D5
Belchford Lincs 46 E6
Belford Northumb 71 G10
Belhaven E Loth 70 C5
Belhelvie Aberds 83 B11
Belhinnie Aberds 82 A6
Bell Bar Herts 29 H9
Bell Busk N Yorks 50 D5
Bell End Worcs 34 H5
Bell o' th' Hill Ches W 43 H8
Bellabeg Aberds 82 B5
Bellamore S Ayrs 66 H5
Bellanoch Argyll 72 D6
Bellaty Angus 76 B5
Belleau Lincs 47 E8
Bellehiglash Moray 88 E1
Bellerby N Yorks 58 G2
Bellever Devon 5 D7
Belliehill Angus 77 A8
Bellingdon Bucks 28 H6
Bellingham Northumb 62 E4
Belloch Argyll 65 E7
Bellochantuy Argyll 65 E7
Bells Yew Green E Sus 12 C5
Bellsbank E Ayrs 67 F7
Bellshill N Lanark 68 D6
Bellshill Northumb 71 G10
Bellspool Borders 69 G10
Bellsquarry W Loth 69 D9
Belmaduthy Highld 87 F9
Belmesthorpe Rutland 36 D6
Belmont Blackburn 50 H2
Belmont London 19 E9
Belmont S Ayrs 66 D6
Belmont Shetland 96 C7
Belnacraig Aberds 82 B5
Belowda Corn 3 C8
Belper Derbys 45 H7
Belper Lane End Derbys 45 H7
Belsay Northumb 63 F7
Belses Borders 70 H4
Belsford Devon 5 F8
Belstead Suff 31 D8
Belston S Ayrs 67 D6
Belstone Devon 6 G5
Belthorn Blackburn 50 G3
Beltinge Kent 21 E8
Beltoft N Lincs 46 B2
Belton Leics 35 C10
Belton Lincs 36 B5
Belton N Lincs 45 B11
Belton Norf 39 E10
Belton in Rutland Rutland 36 E4
Beltring Kent 20 G3
Belts of Collonach Aberds 83 D8
Belvedere London 19 D11
Belvoir Leics 36 B4
Bembridge IoW 10 F5
Bemersyde Borders 70 G4
Bemerton Wilts 9 A10
Bempton E Yorks 53 B7
Ben Alder Lodge Highld 81 F7
Ben Armine Lodge Highld 93 H10
Ben Casgro W Isles 91 E9
Benacre Suff 39 G11
Benbuie Dumfries 60 D3
Benderloch Argyll 74 D2
Bendronaig Lodge Highld 86 H3
Benenden Kent 13 C7
Benfield Dumfries 54 C6
Bengate Norf 39 C9
Bengeworth Worcs 27 D7
Benhall Green Suff 31 B10
Benhall Street Suff 31 B10
Benholm Aberds 83 G10
Beningbrough N Yorks 51 D11
Benington Herts 29 F9
Benington Lincs 47 H7
Benllech Anglesey 41 B7
Benmore Argyll 73 E10
Benmore Stirling 75 E7
Benmore Lodge Highld 92 H6
Bennacott Corn 6 G1
Bennan N Ayrs 66 D2
Benniworth Lincs 46 D6
Benover Kent 20 G4
Bensham T&W 63 G8
Benslie N Ayrs 66 B6
Benson Oxon 18 B3
Bent Aberds 83 F8
Bent Gate Lancs 50 G3
Benthall Northumb 71 H11
Benthall Shrops 34 E2
Bentham Glos 26 G6
Benthoul Aberdeen 83 C10
Bentlawnt Shrops 33 E9
Bentley E Yorks 52 F6
Bentley Hants 18 G4
Bentley S Yorks 45 B9
Bentley Suff 31 E8
Bentley Warks 35 F8
Bentley Worcs 26 B6
Bentley Heath W Mid 35 H7
Benton Devon 6 C5
Bentpath Dumfries 61 D9
Bents W Loth 69 D8
Bentworth Hants 18 G3
Benvie Dundee 76 D6
Benwick Cambs 37 F9
Beoley Worcs 27 B7
Beoraidbeg Highld 79 B9
Bepton W Sus 11 C7
Berden Essex 29 F11
Bere Alston Devon 4 E5
Bere Ferrers Devon 4 E5
Bere Regis Dorset 9 E7
Berepper Corn 2 G5
Bergh Apton Norf 39 E9
Berinsfield Oxon 18 B2
Berkeley Glos 16 B3
Berkhamsted Herts 28 H6
Berkley Som 16 G5
Berkswell W Mid 35 H8
Bermondsey London 19 D10
Bernera Highld 85 F13
Bernice Argyll 73 D10
Bernisdale Highld 85 C9
Berrick Salome Oxon 18 B3
Berriedale Highld 94 H3
Berrier Cumb 56 D5
Berriew Powys 33 E7
Berrington Northumb 71 F9
Berrington Shrops 33 E11
Berrow Som 15 F9
Berrow Green Worcs 26 C4
Berry Down Cross Devon 6 B4
Berry Hill Glos 26 G2
Berry Hill Pembs 22 B5
Berry Pomeroy Devon 5 E9
Berryhillock Moray 88 B5
Berrynarbor Devon 6 B4
Bersham Wrex 42 H6
Berstane Orkney 95 G5
Berwick E Sus 12 F4
Berwick Bassett Wilts 17 D7
Berwick Hill Northumb 63 F7
Berwick St James Wilts 17 H7
Berwick St John Wilts 9 B8
Berwick St Leonard Wilts 9 A8
Berwick-upon-Tweed Northumb 71 E8
Bescar Lancs 43 A6
Besford Worcs 26 D6
Bessacarr S Yorks 45 B10
Bessels Leigh Oxon 17 A11
Bessingby E Yorks 53 C7
Bessingham Norf 39 B7
Bestbeech Hill E Sus 12 C5
Besthorpe Norf 39 F6
Besthorpe Notts 46 F2
Bestwood Nottingham 36 A1
Bestwood Village Notts 45 H9
Beswick E Yorks 52 E6
Betchworth Sur 19 G9
Bethania Ceredig 24 B2
Bethania Gwyn 41 E8
Bethania Gwyn 41 F9
Bethel Anglesey 40 C5
Bethel Gwyn 32 B5
Bethel Gwyn 41 D7
Bethersden Kent 13 B8
Bethesda Gwyn 41 D8
Bethesda Pembs 22 E5
Bethlehem Carms 24 F3
Bethnal Green London 19 C10
Betley Staffs 43 H10
Betsham Kent 20 D3
Betteshanger Kent 21 F10
Bettiscombe Dorset 8 E2
Bettisfield Wrex 33 B10
Betton Shrops 33 E9
Betton Shrops 34 B2
Bettws Bridgend 14 C5
Bettws Mon 25 G9
Bettws Newport 15 B8
Bettws Cedewain Powys 33 F7
Bettws Gwerfil Goch Denb 42 H3
Bettws Ifan Ceredig 23 B8
Bettws Newydd Mon 25 H10
Bettws-y-crwyn Shrops 33 G8
Bettyhill Highld 93 C10
Betws Carms 24 G3
Betws Bledrws Ceredig 23 A10
Betws-Garmon Gwyn 41 E7
Betws-y-Coed Conwy 41 E9
Betws-yn-Rhos Conwy 42 E2
Beulah Ceredig 23 B7
Beulah Powys 24 C6
Bevendean Brighton 12 F2
Bevercotes Notts 45 E10
Beverley E Yorks 52 F6
Beverston Glos 16 B5
Bevington Glos 16 B3
Bewaldeth Cumb 56 C4
Bewcastle Cumb 61 F11
Bewdley Worcs 34 H3
Bewerley N Yorks 51 C7
Bewholme E Yorks 53 D7
Bexhill E Sus 12 F6
Bexley London 19 D11
Bexleyheath London 19 D11
Bexwell Norf 38 E2
Beyton Suff 30 B6
Bhaltos W Isles 90 D5
Bhatarsaigh W Isles 84 J1
Bibury Glos 27 H8
Bicester Oxon 28 F2
Bickenhall Som 8 C1
Bickenhill W Mid 35 G7
Bicker Lincs 37 B8
Bickershaw Gtr Man 43 B9
Bickerstaffe Lancs 43 B7
Bickerton Ches E 43 G8
Bickerton N Yorks 51 D10
Bickington Devon 5 D8
Bickington Devon 6 C4
Bickleigh Devon 4 E6
Bickleigh Devon 7 F8
Bickleton Devon 6 C4
Bickley London 19 E11
Bickley Moss Ches W 43 H8
Bicknacre Essex 20 A4
Bicknoller Som 7 C10
Bicknor Kent 20 F5
Bickton Hants 9 C10
Bicton Shrops 33 D10
Bicton Shrops 33 G8
Bidborough Kent 12 B4
Biddenden Kent 13 C7
Biddenham Bedford 29 D7
Biddestone Wilts 16 D5
Biddisham Som 15 F9
Biddlesden Bucks 28 D3
Biddlestone Northumb 62 C5
Biddulph Staffs 44 G2
Biddulph Moor Staffs 44 G3
Bideford Devon 6 D3
Bidford-on-Avon Warks 27 C8
Bidston Mers 42 C5
Bielby E Yorks 52 E3
Bieldside Aberdeen 83 C10
Bierley IoW 10 G4
Bierley W Yorks 51 F7
Bierton Bucks 28 G5
Big Sand Highld 85 A12
Bigbury Devon 5 G7
Bigbury on Sea Devon 5 G7
Bigby Lincs 46 B4
Biggar Cumb 49 C1
Biggar S Lanark 69 G9
Biggin Derbys 44 G5
Biggin Derbys 44 H6
Biggin N Yorks 51 F11
Biggin Hill London 19 F11
Biggings Shetland 96 G3
Biggleswade C Beds 29 D8
Bighouse Highld 93 C11
Bighton Hants 10 A5
Bignor W Sus 11 C8
Bigton Shetland 96 L5
Bilberry Corn 3 C9
Bilborough Nottingham 35 A11
Bilbrook Som 7 B9
Bilbrough N Yorks 51 E11
Bilbster Highld 94 E4
Bildershaw Durham 58 D3
Bildeston Suff 30 D6
Billericay Essex 20 B3
Billesdon Leics 36 E3
Billesley Warks 27 C8
Billingborough Lincs 37 B7
Billinge Mers 43 B8
Billingford Norf 38 C6
Billingham Stockton 58 D5
Billinghay Lincs 46 G5
Billingley S Yorks 45 B8
Billingshurst W Sus 11 B9
Billingsley Shrops 34 G3
Billington C Beds 28 F6
Billington Lancs 50 F3
Billockby Norf 39 D10
Billy Row Durham 58 C2
Bilsborrow Lancs 49 F5
Bilsby Lincs 47 E8
Bilsham W Sus 11 D8
Bilsington Kent 13 C9
Bilson Green Glos 26 G3
Bilsthorpe Notts 45 F10
Bilsthorpe Moor Notts 45 G10
Bilston Midloth 69 D11
Bilston W Mid 34 F5
Bilstone Leics 35 E9
Bilting Kent 21 G7
Bilton E Yorks 53 F7
Bilton Northumb 63 B8
Bilton Warks 27 A11
Bilton in Ainsty N Yorks 51 E10
Bimbister Orkney 95 G4
Binbrook Lincs 46 C6
Binchester Blocks Durham 58 C3
Bincombe Dorset 8 F5
Bindal Highld 87 C12
Binegar Som 16 G3
Binfield Brack 18 D5
Binfield Hth. Oxon 18 D4
Bingfield Northumb 62 F5
Bingham Notts 36 B3
Bingley W Yorks 51 F7
Bings Heath Shrops 33 D11
Binham Norf 38 B5
Binley Hants 17 F11
Binley W Mid 35 H9
Binley Woods Warks 35 H9
Binniehill Falk 69 C7
Binsoe N Yorks 51 B8
Binstead IoW 10 E4
Binsted Hants 18 G4
Binton Warks 27 C8
Bintree Norf 38 C6
Binweston Shrops 33 E9
Birch Essex 30 G6
Birch Gtr Man 44 B2
Birch Green Essex 30 G6
Birch Heath Ches W 43 F8
Birch Hill Ches W 43 E8
Birch Vale Derbys 44 D4
Bircham Newton Norf 38 B3
Bircham Tofts Norf 38 B3
Birchanger Essex 30 F2
Birchencliffe W Yorks 51 H7
Bircher Hereford 25 B11
Birchfield Highld 82 A1
Birchgrove Cardiff 15 D7
Birchgrove Swansea 14 B3
Birchington Kent 21 E9
Birchmoor Warks 35 E8
Birchover Derbys 44 F6
Birchwood Lincs 46 F3
Birchwood Warr 43 C9
Bircotes Notts 45 C10
Birdbrook Essex 30 D4
Birdforth N Yorks 51 B10
Birdham W Sus 11 E7
Birdholme Derbys 45 F7
Birdingbury Warks 27 B11
Birdlip Glos 26 G6
Birds Edge W Yorks 44 B6
Birdsall N Yorks 52 C4
Birdsgreen Shrops 34 G3
Birdsmoor Gate Dorset 8 D2
Birdston E Dunb 68 C5
Birdwell S Yorks 45 B7
Birdwood Glos 26 G4
Birgham Borders 70 G6
Birkby N Yorks 58 F4
Birkdale Mers 49 H3
Birkenhead Mers 42 D6
Birkenhills Aberds 89 D7
Birkenshaw N Lanark 68 D5
Birkenshaw W Yorks 51 G8
Birkhall Aberds 82 D5
Birkhill Angus 76 D6
Birkhill Borders 61 B8
Birkholme Lincs 36 C5
Birkin N Yorks 51 G11
Birley Hereford 25 C11
Birling Kent 20 E3
Birling Northumb 63 C8
Birling Gap E Sus 12 G4
Birlingham Worcs 26 D6
Birmingham W Mid 35 G6
Birnam Perth 76 C3
Birse Aberds 83 D7
Birsemore Aberds 83 D7
Birstall Leics 36 E1
Birstall W Yorks 51 G8
Birstwith N Yorks 51 D8
Birthorpe Lincs 37 B7
Birtley Hereford 25 B10
Birtley Northumb 62 F4
Birtley T&W 63 H8
Birts Street Worcs 26 E4
Bisbrooke Rutland 36 F4
Biscathorpe Lincs 46 D6
Biscot Luton 29 F7
Bish Mill Devon 7 D6
Bisham Windsor 18 C5
Bishampton Worcs 26 C6
Bishop Auckland Durham 58 D3
Bishop Burton E Yorks 52 F5
Bishop Middleham Durham 58 C4
Bishop Monkton N Yorks 51 C9
Bishop Norton Lincs 46 C3
Bishop Sutton Bath 16 F2
Bishop Thornton N Yorks 51 C8
Bishop Wilton E Yorks 52 D3
Bishopbridge Lincs 46 C4
Bishopbriggs E Dunb 68 D5
Bishopmill Moray 88 B2
Bishops Cannings Wilts 17 E7
Bishop's Castle Shrops 33 G9
Bishop's Caundle Dorset 8 C5
Bishop's Cleeve Glos 26 F6
Bishops Frome Hereford 26 D3
Bishop's Green Essex 30 G3
Bishop's Hull Som 7 D11
Bishop's Itchington Warks 27 C10
Bishops Lydeard Som 7 D10
Bishops Nympton Devon 7 D6
Bishop's Offley Staffs 34 C3
Bishop'S Stortford Herts 29 F11
Bishop's Sutton Hants 10 A5
Bishop's Tachbrook Warks 27 B10
Bishops Tawton Devon 6 C4
Bishop's Waltham Hants 10 C4
Bishop's Wood Staffs 34 E4
Bishopsbourne Kent 21 F8
Bishopsteignton Devon 5 D10
Bishopstoke Hants 10 C3
Bishopston Swansea 23 H10
Bishopstone Bucks 28 G5
Bishopstone E Sus 12 F3
Bishopstone Hereford 25 D11
Bishopstone Swindon 17 C9
Bishopstone Wilts 9 B9
Bishopstrow Wilts 16 G5
Bishopswood Som 8 C1
Bishopsworth Bristol 16 E2
Bishopthorpe York 52 E1
Bishopton Darl 58 D4
Bishopton Dumfries 55 E7
Bishopton N Yorks 51 B9
Bishopton Renfs 68 C3
Bishopton Warks 27 C8
Bishton Newport 15 C9
Bisley Glos 26 H6
Bisley Sur 18 F6
Bispham Blackpool 49 E3
Bispham Green Lancs 43 A7
Bissoe Corn 3 E6
Bisterne Close Hants 9 D11
Bitchfield Lincs 36 C5
Bittadon Devon 6 B4
Bittaford Devon 5 F7
Bittering Norf 38 D5
Bitterley Shrops 34 H1
Bitterne Soton 10 C3
Bitteswell Leics 35 G11
Bitton S Glos 16 E3
Bix Oxon 18 C4
Bixter Shetland 96 H5
Blaby Leics 36 F1
Black Bourton Oxon 17 A9
Black Callerton T&W 63 G7
Black Clauchrie S Ayrs 54 A5
Black Corries Lodge Highld 74 B5
Black Crofts Argyll 74 D2
Black Dog Devon 7 F7
Black Heddon Northumb 62 F6
Black Lane Gtr Man 43 B10
Black Marsh Shrops 33 F9
Black Mount Argyll 74 C5
Black Notley Essex 30 F4
Black Pill Swansea 14 B2
Black Tar Pembs 22 F4
Black Torrington Devon 6 F3
Blackacre Dumfries 60 D6
Blackadder West Borders 71 E7
Blackawton Devon 5 F9
Blackborough Devon 7 F9
Blackborough End Norf 38 D2
Blackboys E Sus 12 D4
Blackbrook Derbys 45 H7
Blackbrook Mers 43 C8
Blackbrook Staffs 34 B3
Blackburn Aberds 83 B10
Blackburn Aberds 88 E5
Blackburn Blackburn 50 G2
Blackburn W Loth 69 D8
Blackcraig Dumfries 60 E3
Blackden Heath Ches E 43 E10
Blackdog Aberds 83 B11
Blackfell T&W 63 H8
Blackfield Hants 10 D3
Blackford Cumb 61 G9
Blackford Perth 75 G11
Blackford Som 8 B5
Blackford Som 15 G10
Blackfordby Leics 35 D9
Blackgang IoW 10 G3
Blackhall Colliery Durham 58 C5
Blackhall Mill T&W 63 H7
Blackhall Rocks Durham 58 C5
Blackham E Sus 12 C3
Blackhaugh Borders 70 G3
Blackheath Essex 31 F7
Blackheath Suff 31 A11
Blackheath Sur 19 G7
Blackheath W Mid 34 G5
Blackhill Aberds 89 C10
Blackhill Aberds 89 D10
Blackhill Highld 85 C8
Blackhills Highld 87 F12
Blackhills Moray 88 C2
Blackhorse S Glos 16 D3
Blackland Wilts 17 E7
Blacklaw Aberds 89 C6
Blackley Gtr Man 44 B2
Blacklunans Perth 76 A4
Blackmill Bridgend 14 C5
Blackmoor Hants 11 A6
Blackmoor Gate Devon 6 B5
Blackmore Essex 20 A3
Blackmore End Essex 30 E4
Blackmore End Herts 29 G8
Blackness Falk 69 C9
Blacknest Hants 18 G4
Blacko Lancs 50 E4
Blackpool Blackpool 49 F3
Blackpool Devon 5 G9
Blackpool Pembs 22 E5
Blackpool Gate Cumb 61 F11
Blackridge W Loth 69 D7
Blackrock Argyll 64 B4
Blackrock Mon 25 G9
Blackrod Gtr Man 43 A9
Blackshaw Dumfries 60 G6
Blackshaw Head W Yorks 50 G5
Blacksmith's Green Suff 31 B8
Blackstone W Sus 11 C11
Blackthorn Oxon 28 G3
Blackthorpe Suff 30 B6
Blacktoft E Yorks 52 G4
Blacktop Aberdeen 83 C10
Blacktown Newport 15 C8
Blackwall Tunnel London 19 C10
Blackwater Corn 2 E6
Blackwater Hants 18 F5
Blackwater IoW 10 F4
Blackwaterfoot N Ayrs 66 D1
Blackwell Darl 58 E3
Blackwell Derbys 44 E5
Blackwell Derbys 45 G8
Blackwell W Sus 12 C2
Blackwell Warks 27 D9
Blackwell Worcs 26 A6
Blackwood = Coed Duon Caerph 15 B7
Blackwood S Lanark 68 F6
Blackwood Hill Staffs 44 G3
Blacon Ches W 43 F6
Bladnoch Dumfries 55 D7
Bladon Oxon 27 G11
Blaen-gwynfi Neath 14 B4
Blaen-waun Carms 23 D7
Blaen-y-coed Carms 23 D8
Blaen-y-Cwm Denb 32 B6
Blaen-y-cwm Gwyn 32 C3
Blaen-y-cwm Powys 33 C6
Blaenannerch Ceredig 23 B7
Blaenau Ffestiniog Gwyn 41 F9
Blaenavon Torf 25 H9
Blaencelyn Ceredig 23 A8
Blaendyryn Powys 24 E6
Blaenffos Pembs 22 C6
Blaengarw Bridgend 14 B5
Blaengwrach Neath 24 H5
Blaenpennal Ceredig 24 B3
Blaenplwyf Ceredig 32 H1
Blaenporth Ceredig 23 B7
Blaenrhondda Rhondda 14 A5
Blaenycwm Ceredig 32 H4
Blagdon N Som 15 F11
Blagdon Torbay 5 E9
Blagdon Hill Som 7 E11
Blagill Cumb 57 B9
Blaguegate Lancs 43 B7
Blaich Highld 80 F2
Blain Highld 79 E9
Blaina Bl Gwent 25 H9
Blair Atholl Perth 81 G10
Blair Drummond Stirling 75 H10
Blairbeg N Ayrs 66 C3
Blairdaff Aberds 83 B8
Blairglas Argyll 68 B2
Blairgowrie Perth 76 C4
Blairhall Fife 69 B9
Blairingone Perth 76 H2
Blairland N Ayrs 66 B6
Blairlogie Stirling 75 H11
Blairlomond Argyll 74 H4
Blairmore Argyll 73 E10
Blairnamarrow Moray 82 B4
Blairquhosh Stirling 68 B4
Blair's Ferry Argyll 73 G8
Blairskaith E Dunb 68 C4
Blaisdon Glos 26 G4
Blakebrook Worcs 34 H4
Blakedown Worcs 34 H4
Blakelaw Borders 70 G6
Blakeley Staffs 34 F4
Blakeley Lane Staffs 44 H3
Blakemere Hereford 25 D10
Blakeney Glos 26 H3
Blakeney Norf 38 A6
Blakenhall Ches E 43 H10
Blakenhall W Mid 34 F5
Blakeshall Worcs 34 G4
Blakesley Northants 28 C3
Blanchland Northumb 57 A11
Bland Hill N Yorks 51 D8
Blandford Forum Dorset 9 D7
Blandford St Mary Dorset 9 D7
Blanefield Stirling 68 C4
Blankney Lincs 46 F4
Blantyre S Lanark 68 E5
Blar a'Chaorainn Highld 80 G3
Blaran Argyll 73 B7
Blarghour Argyll 73 B8
Blarmachfoldach Highld 80 G2
Blarnalearoch Highld 86 B4
Blashford Hants 9 D10
Blaston Leics 36 F4
Blatherwycke Northants 36 F5
Blawith Cumb 56 H4
Blaxhall Suff 31 C10
Blaxton S Yorks 45 B10
Blaydon T&W 63 G7
Bleadon N Som 15 F9
Bleak Hey Nook Gtr Man 44 B4
Blean Kent 21 E8
Bleasby Lincs 46 D5
Bleasby Notts 45 H11
Bleasdale Lancs 50 E1
Bleatarn Cumb 57 E9
Blebocraigs Fife 77 F7
Bleddfa Powys 25 B9
Bledington Glos 27 F9
Bledlow Bucks 18 A4
Bledlow Ridge Bucks 18 B4
Blegbie E Loth 70 D3
Blencarn Cumb 57 C8
Blencogo Cumb 56 B3
Blendworth Hants 10 C6
Blenheim Park Norf 38 B4
Blennerhasset Cumb 56 B3
Blervie Castle Moray 87 F13
Bletchingdon Oxon 28 G2
Bletchingley Sur 19 F10
Bletchley M Keynes 28 E5
Bletchley Shrops 34 B2
Bletherston Pembs 22 D5
Bletsoe Bedford 29 C7
Blewbury Oxon 18 C2
Blickling Norf 39 C7
Blidworth Notts 45 G9
Blindburn Northumb 62 B4
Blindcrake Cumb 56 C3
Blindley Heath Sur 19 G10
Blisland Corn 4 D2
Bliss Gate Worcs 26 A4
Blissford Hants 9 C10
Blisworth Northants 28 C4
Blithbury Staffs 35 C6
Blitterlees Cumb 56 A3
Blo' Norton Norf 38 H6
Blockley Glos 27 E8
Blofield Norf 39 E9
Blofield Heath Norf 39 D9
Bloomfield Borders 61 A11
Blore Staffs 44 H5
Blount's Green Staffs 35 B6
Blowick Mers 49 H3
Bloxham Oxon 27 E11
Bloxholm Lincs 46 G4
Bloxwich W Mid 34 E5
Bloxworth Dorset 9 E7
Blubberhouses N Yorks 51 D7
Blue Anchor Som 7 B9
Blue Anchor Swansea 23 G10
Blue Row Essex 31 G7
Blundeston Suff 39 F11
Blunham C Beds 29 C8
Blunsdon St Andrew Swindon 17 C8
Bluntington Worcs 26 A5
Bluntisham Cambs 29 A10
Blunts Corn 4 E4
Blyborough Lincs 46 C3
Blyford Suff 39 H10
Blymhill Staffs 34 D4
Blyth Northumb 63 E9
Blyth Notts 45 D10
Blyth Bridge Borders 69 F10
Blythburgh Suff 39 H10
Blythe Borders 70 F4
Blythe Bridge Staffs 34 A5
Blyton Lincs 46 C2
Boarhills Fife 77 F8
Boarhunt Hants 10 D5
Boars Head Gtr Man 43 B8
Boars Hill Oxon 17 A11
Boarshead E Sus 12 C4
Boarstall Bucks 28 G3
Boasley Cross Devon 6 G3
Boat of Garten Highld 81 B11
Boath Highld 87 D8
Bobbing Kent 20 E5
Bobbington Staffs 34 F4
Bobbingworth Essex 30 H2
Bocaddon Corn 4 F2
Bochastle Stirling 75 G9
Bocking Essex 30 F4
Bocking Churchstreet Essex 30 F4
Boddam Aberds 89 D11
Boddam Shetland 96 M5
Boddington Glos 26 F5
Bodedern Anglesey 40 B5
Bodelwyddan Denb 42 E3
Bodenham Hereford 26 C2
Bodenham Wilts 9 B10
Bodenham Moor Hereford 26 C2
Bodermid Gwyn 40 H3
Bodewryd Anglesey 40 A5
Bodfari Denb 42 E3
Bodffordd Anglesey 40 C6
Bodham Norf 39 A7
Bodiam E Sus 13 D6
Bodicote Oxon 27 E11
Bodieve Corn 3 B8
Bodinnick Corn 4 F2
Bodle Street Green E Sus 12 E5
Bodmin Corn 4 E1
Bodney Norf 38 F4
Bodorgan Anglesey 40 D5
Bodsham Kent 21 G8
Boduan Gwyn 40 G5
Bodymoor Heath Warks 35 F7
Bogallan Highld 87 F9
Bogbrae Aberds 89 E10
Bogend Borders 70 F6
Bogend S Ayrs 67 C6
Boghall W Loth 69 D8
Boghead S Lanark 68 F6
Bogmoor Moray 88 B3
Bogniebrae Aberds 88 D5
Bognor Regis W Sus 11 E8
Bograxie Aberds 83 B9
Bogside N Lanark 69 E7
Bogton Aberds 89 C6
Bogue Dumfries 55 A9
Bohenie Highld 80 E4
Bohortha Corn 3 F7
Bohuntine Highld 80 E4
Boirseam W Isles 90 J5
Bojewyan Corn 2 F2
Bolam Durham 58 D2
Bolam Northumb 62 E6
Bolberry Devon 5 H7
Bold Heath Mers 43 D8
Boldon T&W 63 G9
Boldon Colliery T&W 63 G9
Boldre Hants 10 E2
Boldron Durham 58 E1
Bole Notts 45 D11
Bolehill Derbys 44 G6
Boleside Borders 70 G3
Bolham Devon 7 E8
Bolham Water Devon 7 E10
Bolingey Corn 3 D6
Bollington Ches E 44 E3
Bollington Cross Ches E 44 E3
Bolney W Sus 12 D1
Bolnhurst Bedford 29 C7
Bolshan Angus 77 B9
Bolsover Derbys 45 E8
Bolsterstone S Yorks 44 C6
Bolstone Hereford 26 E2
Boltby N Yorks 58 H5
Bolter End Bucks 18 B4
Bolton Cumb 57 D8
Bolton E Loth 70 C4
Bolton E Yorks 52 D3
Bolton Gtr Man 43 B10
Bolton Northumb 63 B7
Bolton Abbey N Yorks 51 D6
Bolton Bridge N Yorks 51 D6
Bolton-by-Bowland Lancs 50 E3
Bolton-le-Sands Lancs 49 C4
Bolton Low Houses Cumb 56 B4
Bolton-on-Swale N Yorks 58 G3
Bolton Percy N Yorks 51 E11
Bolton Town End Lancs 49 C4
Bolton upon Dearne S Yorks 45 B8
Boltonfellend Cumb 61 G10
Boltongate Cumb 56 B4
Bolventor Corn 4 D2
Bomere Heath Shrops 33 D10
Bon-y-maen Swansea 14 B2
Bonar Bridge Highld 87 B9
Bonawe Argyll 74 D3
Bonby N Lincs 52 H6
Boncath Pembs 23 C7
Bonchester Bridge Borders 61 B11
Bonchurch IoW 10 G4
Bondleigh Devon 6 F5
Bonehill Devon 5 D8
Bonehill Staffs 35 E7
Bo'ness Falk 69 B8
Bonhill W Dunb 68 C2
Boningale Shrops 34 E4
Bonjedward Borders 62 A2
Bonkle N Lanark 69 E7
Bonnavoulin Highld 79 F8
Bonnington Edin 69 D10
Bonnington Kent 13 C9
Bonnybank Fife 76 G6
Bonnybridge Falk 69 B7
Bonnykelly Aberds 89 C8
Bonnyrigg and Lasswade Midloth 70 D2
Bonnyton Aberds 89 E6
Bonnyton Angus 76 D6
Bonnyton Angus 77 B9
Bonsall Derbys 44 G6
Bonskeid House Perth 75 A11
Bont Mon 25 G10
Bont-Dolgadfan Powys 32 E4
Bont-goch Ceredig 32 G2
Bont-newydd Conwy 42 E3
Bont Newydd Gwyn 32 C3
Bont Newydd Gwyn 41 F9
Bontddu Gwyn 32 D2
Bonthorpe Lincs 47 E8
Bontnewydd Ceredig 24 B3
Bontnewydd Gwyn 40 E6
Bontuchel Denb 42 G3
Bonvilston V Glam 14 D6
Booker Bucks 18 B5
Boon Borders 70 F4
Boosbeck Redcar 59 E7
Boot Cumb 56 F3
Boot Street Suff 31 D9
Booth W Yorks 50 G6
Booth Wood W Yorks 50 H6
Boothby Graffoe Lincs 46 G3
Boothby Pagnell Lincs 36 B5
Boothen Stoke 34 A4
Boothferry E Yorks 52 G3
Boothville Northants 28 B4
Bootle Cumb 56 H3
Bootle Mers 42 C6
Booton Norf 39 C7
Boquhan Stirling 68 B4
Boraston Shrops 26 A3
Borden Kent 20 E5
Borden W Sus 11 B7
Bordley N Yorks 50 C5
Bordon Hants 18 H5
Bordon Camp Hants 18 H4
Boreham Essex 30 H4
Boreham Wilts 16 G5
Boreham Street E Sus 12 E5
Borehamwood Herts 19 B8
Boreland Dumfries 61 D7
Boreland Stirling 75 D8
Borgh W Isles 84 H1
Borgh W Isles 90 J4
Borghastan W Isles 90 C7
Borgie Highld 93 D9
Borgue Dumfries 55 E9
Borgue Highld 94 H3
Borley Essex 30 D5
Bornais W Isles 84 F2
Bornesketaig Highld 85 A8
Borness Dumfries 55 E9
Borough Green Kent 20 F3
Boroughbridge N Yorks 51 C9
Borras Head Wrex 42 G6
Borreraig Highld 84 C6
Borrobol Lodge Highld 93 G11
Borrowash Derbys 35 B10
Borrowby N Yorks 58 H5
Borrowdale Cumb 56 E4
Borrowfield Aberds 83 D10
Borth Ceredig 32 F2
Borth-y-Gest Gwyn 41 G7
Borthwickbrae Borders 61 B10
Borthwickshiels Borders 61 B10
Borve Highld 85 D9
Borve Lodge W Isles 90 H5
Borwick Lancs 49 B5
Bosavern Corn 2 F2
Bosbury Hereford 26 D3
Boscastle Corn 4 B2
Boscombe Bmouth 9 E10
Boscombe Wilts 17 H9
Boscoppa Corn 3 D9
Bosham W Sus 11 D7
Bosherston Pembs 22 G4
Boskenna Corn 2 G3
Bosley Ches E 44 F3
Bossall N Yorks 52 C3
Bossiney Corn 4 C1
Bossingham Kent 21 G8
Bossington Som 7 B7
Bostock Green Ches W 43 F9
Boston Lincs 37 A9
Boston Long Hedges Lincs 47 H7
Boston Spa W Yorks 51 E10
Boston West Lincs 46 H6
Boswinger Corn 3 E8
Botallack Corn 2 F2
Botany Bay London 19 B9
Botcherby Cumb 61 H10
Botcheston Leics 35 E10
Botesdale Suff 38 H6
Bothal Northumb 63 E8
Bothamsall Notts 45 E10
Bothel Cumb 56 C3
Bothenhampton Dorset 8 E3
Bothwell S Lanark 68 E6
Botley Bucks 18 A6
Botley Hants 10 C4
Botley Oxon 27 H11
Botolph Claydon Bucks 28 F4
Botolphs W Sus 11 D10
Bottacks Highld 86 E7
Bottesford Leics 36 B4
Bottesford N Lincs 46 B2
Bottisham Cambs 30 B2
Bottlesford Wilts 17 F8
Bottom Boat W Yorks 51 G9
Bottom House Staffs 44 G4
Bottom o' th' Moor Gtr Man 43 A9
Bottom of Hutton Lancs 49 G4
Bottomcraig Fife 76 E6
Botusfleming Corn 4 E5
Botwnnog Gwyn 40 G4
Bough Beech Kent 19 G11
Boughrood Powys 25 E8
Boughspring Glos 16 B2
Boughton Norf 38 E2
Boughton Northants 28 B4
Boughton Notts 45 F10
Boughton Aluph Kent 21 G7
Boughton Lees Kent 21 G7
Boughton Malherbe Kent 20 G5
Boughton Monchelsea Kent 20 F4
Boughton Street Kent 21 F7
Boulby Redcar 59 E8
Boulden Shrops 33 G11
Boulmer Northumb 63 B8
Boulston Pembs 22 E4
Boultenstone Aberds 82 B6
Boultham Lincs 46 F3
Bourn Cambs 29 C10
Bourne Lincs 37 C6
Bourne End Bucks 18 C5
Bourne End C Beds 28 D6
Bourne End Herts 29 H7
Bournemouth Bmouth 9 E9
Bournes Green Glos 16 A6
Bournes Green Southend 20 C6
Bournheath Worcs 26 A6
Bournmoor Durham 58 A4
Bournville W Mid 34 G6
Bourton Dorset 9 A6
Bourton N Som 15 E9
Bourton Oxon 17 C9
Bourton Shrops 34 F1
Bourton on Dunsmore Warks 27 A11
Bourton on the Hill Glos 27 E8
Bourton-on-the-Water Glos 27 F8
Bousd Argyll 78 E5
Boustead Hill Cumb 61 H8
Bouth Cumb 56 H5
Bouthwaite N Yorks 51 B7
Boveney Bucks 18 D6
Boverton V Glam 14 E5
Bovey Tracey Devon 5 D9
Bovingdon Herts 19 A7
Bovingdon Green Bucks 18 C5
Bovingdon Green Herts 19 A7
Bovinger Essex 30 H2
Bovington Camp Dorset 9 F7
Bow Borders 70 F3
Bow Devon 6 F6
Bow Orkney 95 J4
Bow Brickhill M Keynes 28 E6
Bow of Fife Fife 76 F6
Bow Street Ceredig 32 G2
Bowbank Durham 57 D11
Bowburn Durham 58 C4
Bowcombe IoW 10 F3
Bowd Devon 7 G10
Bowden Borders 70 G4
Bowden Devon 5 G9
Bowden Hill Wilts 16 E6

Bowderdale Cumb 57 F8
Bowdon Gtr Man 43 D10
Bower Northumb 62 E3
Bower Hinton Som 8 C3
Bowerchalke Wilts 9 B9
Bowerhill Wilts 16 E6
Bowermadden Highld 94 D4
Bowers Gifford Essex 20 C4
Bowershall Fife 69 A9
Bowertower Highld 94 D4
Bowes Durham 57 E11
Bowgreave Lancs 49 E4
Bowgreen Gtr Man 43 D10
Bowhill Borders 70 H3
Bowhouse Dumfries 60 G6
Bowland Bridge Cumb 56 H6
Bowley Hereford 26 C2
Bowlhead Green Sur 18 H6
Bowling W Dunb 68 C3
Bowling W Yorks 51 F7
Bowling Bank Wrex 43 H6
Bowling Green Worcs 26 C5
Bowmanstead Cumb 56 G5
Bowmore Argyll 64 C4
Bowness-on-Solway Cumb 61 G8
Bowness-on-Windermere Cumb 56 G6
Bowsden Northumb 71 F8
Bowside Lodge Highld 93 C11
Bowston Cumb 57 G6
Bowthorpe Norf 39 E7
Box Glos 16 A5
Box Wilts 16 E5
Box End Bedford 29 D7
Boxbush Glos 26 G4
Boxford Suff 30 D6
Boxford W Berks 17 D11
Boxgrove W Sus 11 D8
Boxley Kent 20 F4
Boxmoor Herts 29 H7
Boxted Essex 30 E6
Boxted Suff 30 C5
Boxted Cross Essex 31 E7
Boxted Heath Essex 31 E7
Boxworth Cambs 29 B10
Boxworth End Cambs 29 B10
Boyden Gate Kent 21 E9
Boylestone Derbys 35 B7
Boyndie Aberds 89 B6
Boynton E Yorks 53 C7
Boysack Angus 77 C9
Boyton Corn 6 G2
Boyton Suff 31 D10
Boyton Wilts 16 H6
Boyton Cross Essex 30 H3
Boyton End Suff 30 D4
Bozeat Northants 28 C6
Brù W Isles 91 C8
Braaid IoM 48 E3
Braal Castle Highld 94 D3
Brabling Green Suff 31 B9
Brabourne Kent 13 B9
Brabourne Lees Kent 13 B9
Brabster Highld 94 D5
Bracadale Highld 85 E8
Bracara Highld 79 B10
Braceborough Lincs 37 D6
Bracebridge Lincs 46 F3
Bracebridge Heath Lincs 46 F3
Bracebridge Low Fields Lincs 46 F3
Braceby Lincs 36 B6
Bracewell Lancs 50 E4
Brackenfield Derbys 45 G7
Brackenthwaite Cumb 56 B4
Brackenthwaite N Yorks 51 D8
Bracklesham W Sus 11 E7
Brackletter Highld 80 E3
Brackley Argyll 65 D8
Brackley Northants 28 E2
Brackloch Highld 92 G4
Bracknell Brack 18 E5
Braco Perth 75 G11
Bracobrae Moray 88 C5
Bracon Ash Norf 39 F7
Bracorina Highld 79 B10
Bradbourne Derbys 44 G6
Bradbury Durham 58 D4
Bradda IoM 48 F1
Bradden Northants 28 D3
Braddock Corn 4 E2
Bradeley Stoke 44 G2
Bradenham Bucks 18 B5
Bradenham Norf 38 E5
Bradenstoke Wilts 17 D7
Bradfield Essex 31 E8
Bradfield Norf 39 B8
Bradfield W Berks 18 D3
Bradfield Combust Suff 30 C5
Bradfield Green Ches E 43 G9
Bradfield Heath Essex 31 F8
Bradfield St Clare Suff 30 C6
Bradfield St George Suff 30 B6
Bradford Corn 4 D2
Bradford Derbys 44 F6
Bradford Devon 6 F3
Bradford Northumb 71 G10
Bradford W Yorks 51 F7
Bradford Abbas Dorset 8 C4
Bradford Leigh Wilts 16 E5
Bradford-on-Avon Wilts 16 E5
Bradford-on-Tone Som 7 D10
Bradford Peverell Dorset 8 E5
Brading IoW 10 F5
Bradley Derbys 44 H6
Bradley Hants 18 G3
Bradley NE Lincs 46 B6
Bradley Staffs 34 D4
Bradley W Mid 34 F5
Bradley W Yorks 51 G7
Bradley Green Worcs 26 B6
Bradley in the Moors Staffs 35 A6
Bradley Stoke S Glos 16 C3
Bradlow Hereford 26 E4
Bradmore Notts 36 B1
Bradmore W Mid 34 F4
Bradninch Devon 7 F9
Bradnop Staffs 44 G4
Bradpole Dorset 8 E3
Bradshaw Gtr Man 43 A10
Bradshaw W Yorks 44 A4
Bradstone Devon 4 C4
Bradwall Green Ches E 43 F10
Bradway S Yorks 45 D7
Bradwell Derbys 44 D5
Bradwell Essex 30 F5
Bradwell M Keynes 28 E5
Bradwell Norf 39 E11
Bradwell Staffs 44 H2
Bradwell Grove Oxon 27 H9
Bradwell on Sea Essex 31 H7
Bradwell Waterside Essex 30 H6
Bradworthy Devon 6 E2
Bradworthy Cross Devon 6 E2
Brae Dumfries 60 F4
Brae Highld 91 J13
Brae Highld 92 J7
Brae Shetland 96 G5
Brae of Achnahaird Highld 92 H3
Brae Roy Lodge Highld 80 D5
Braeantra Highld 87 D8
Braedownie Angus 82 F4
Braefield Highld 86 H7
Braegrum Perth 76 E3
Braehead Dumfries 55 D7
Braehead Orkney 95 D5
Braehead Orkney 95 H6
Braehead S Lanark 69 E8
Braehead S Lanark 69 G7
Braehead of Lunan Angus 77 B9
Braehoulland Shetland 96 F4
Braehungie Highld 94 G3
Braelangwell Lodge Highld 87 B8
Braemar Aberds 82 D3
Braemore Highld 86 D4
Braemore Highld 94 G2
Braes of Enzie Moray 88 C3
Braeside Invclyd 73 F11
Braeswick Orkney 95 E7
Braewick Shetland 96 H5
Brafferton Darl 58 D3
Brafferton N Yorks 51 B10
Brafield-on-the-Green Northants 28 C5
Bragar W Isles 91 C7
Bragbury End Herts 29 F9
Bragleenmore Argyll 74 E2
Braichmelyn Gwyn 41 D8
Braid Edin 69 D11
Braides Lancs 49 D4
Braidley N Yorks 50 A6
Braidwood S Lanark 69 F7
Braigo Argyll 64 B3
Brailsford Derbys 35 A8
Brainshaugh Northumb 63 C8
Braintree Essex 30 F4
Braiseworth Suff 31 A8
Braishfield Hants 10 B2
Braithwaite Cumb 56 D4
Braithwaite S Yorks 45 A10
Braithwaite W Yorks 50 E6
Braithwell S Yorks 45 C9
Bramber W Sus 11 C10
Bramcote Notts 35 B11
Bramcote Warks 35 G10
Bramdean Hants 10 B5
Bramerton Norf 39 E8
Bramfield Herts 29 G9
Bramfield Suff 31 A10
Bramford Suff 31 D8
Bramhall Gtr Man 44 D2
Bramham W Yorks 51 E10
Bramhope W Yorks 51 E8
Bramley Hants 18 F3
Bramley S Yorks 45 C8
Bramley Sur 19 G7
Bramley W Yorks 51 F8
Bramling Kent 21 F9
Brampford Speke Devon 7 G8
Brampton Cambs 29 A9
Brampton Cumb 57 D8
Brampton Cumb 61 G11
Brampton Derbys 45 E7
Brampton Hereford 25 E11
Brampton Lincs 46 E2
Brampton Norf 39 C8
Brampton S Yorks 45 B8
Brampton Suff 39 G10
Brampton Abbotts Hereford 26 F3
Brampton Ash Northants 36 G3
Brampton Bryan Hereford 25 A10
Brampton en le Morthen S Yorks 45 D8
Bramshall Staffs 35 B6
Bramshaw Hants 10 C1
Bramshill Hants 18 E4
Bramshott Hants 11 A7
Bran End Essex 30 F3
Branault Highld 79 E8
Brancaster Norf 38 A3
Brancaster Staithe Norf 38 A3
Brancepeth Durham 58 C3
Branch End Northumb 62 G6
Branchill Moray 87 F13
Brand Green Glos 26 F4
Branderburgh Moray 88 A2
Brandesburton E Yorks 53 E7
Brandeston Suff 31 B9
Brandhill Shrops 33 H10
Brandis Corner Devon 6 F3
Brandiston Norf 39 C7
Brandon Durham 58 C3
Brandon Lincs 46 H3
Brandon Northumb 62 B6
Brandon Suff 38 G3
Brandon Warks 35 H10
Brandon Bank Cambs 38 G2
Brandon Creek Norf 38 F2
Brandon Parva Norf 39 E6
Brandsby N Yorks 52 B1
Brandy Wharf Lincs 46 C4
Brane Corn 2 G3
Branksome Poole 9 E9
Branksome Park Poole 9 E9
Bransby Lincs 46 E2
Branscombe Devon 7 H10
Bransford Worcs 26 C4
Bransgore Hants 9 E10
Branshill Clack 69 A7
Bransholme Hull 53 F7
Branson's Cross Worcs 27 A7
Branston Leics 36 C4
Branston Lincs 46 F4
Branston Staffs 35 C8
Branston Booths Lincs 46 F4
Branstone IoW 10 F4
Bransty Cumb 56 E1
Brant Broughton Lincs 46 G3
Brantham Suff 31 E8
Branthwaite Cumb 56 C4
Branthwaite Cumb 56 D2
Brantingham E Yorks 52 G5
Branton Northumb 62 B6
Branton S Yorks 45 B10
Branxholm Park Borders 61 B10
Branxholme Borders 61 B10
Branxton Northumb 71 G7
Brassey Green Ches W 43 F8
Brassington Derbys 44 G6
Brasted Kent 19 F11
Brasted Chart Kent 19 F11
Brathens Aberds 83 D8
Bratoft Lincs 47 F8
Brattleby Lincs 46 D3
Bratton Telford 34 D2
Bratton Wilts 16 F6
Bratton Clovelly Devon 6 G3
Bratton Fleming Devon 6 C5
Bratton Seymour Som 8 B5
Braughing Herts 29 F10
Braunston Northants 28 B2
Braunston-in-Rutland Rutland 36 E4
Braunstone Town Leicester 36 E1
Braunton Devon 6 C3
Brawby N Yorks 52 B3
Brawl Highld 93 C11
Brawlbin Highld 94 E2
Bray Windsor 18 D6
Bray Shop Corn 4 D4
Bray Wick Windsor 18 D5
Braybrooke Northants 36 G3
Braye Ald 11
Brayford Devon 6 C5
Braystones Cumb 56 F2
Braythorn N Yorks 51 E8
Brayton N Yorks 52 F2
Brazacott Corn 6 G1
Breach Kent 20 E5
Breachacha Castle Argyll 78 F4
Breachwood Green Herts 29 F8
Breacleit W Isles 90 D6
Breaden Heath Shrops 33 B10
Breadsall Derbys 35 B9
Breadstone Glos 16 A4
Breage Corn 2 G5
Breakachy Highld 86 G7
Bream Glos 26 H3
Breamore Hants 9 C10
Brean Som 15 F8
Breanais W Isles 90 E4
Brearton N Yorks 51 C9
Breascleit W Isles 90 D7
Breaston Derbys 35 B10
Brechfa Carms 23 C10
Brechin Angus 77 A8
Breck of Cruan Orkney 95 G4
Breckan Orkney 95 H3
Breckrey Highld 85 B10
Brecon = Aberhonddu Powys 25 F7
Bredbury Gtr Man 44 C3
Brede E Sus 13 E7
Bredenbury Hereford 26 C3
Bredfield Suff 31 C9
Bredgar Kent 20 E5
Bredhurst Kent 20 E4
Bredicot Worcs 26 C6
Bredon Worcs 26 E6
Bredon's Norton Worcs 26 E6
Bredwardine Hereford 25 D10
Breedon on the Hill Leics 35 C10
Breibhig W Isles 84 J1
Breibhig W Isles 91 D9
Breich W Loth 69 D8
Breightmet Gtr Man 43 B10
Breighton E Yorks 52 F3
Breinton Hereford 25 E11
Breinton Common Hereford 25 D11
Breiwick Shetland 96 J6
Bremhill Wilts 16 D6
Bremirehoull Shetland 96 L6
Brenchley Kent 12 B5
Brendon Devon 7 B6
Brenkley T&W 63 F8
Brent Eleigh Suff 30 D6
Brent Knoll Som 15 F9
Brent Pelham Herts 29 E11
Brentford London 19 D8
Brentingby Leics 36 D3
Brentwood Essex 20 B2
Brenzett Kent 13 D9
Brereton Staffs 35 D6
Brereton Green Ches E 43 F10
Brereton Heath Ches E 44 F2
Bressingham Norf 39 G6
Bretby Derbys 35 C8
Bretford Warks 35 H10
Bretforton Worcs 27 D7
Bretherdale Head Cumb 57 F7
Bretherton Lancs 49 G4
Brettabister Shetland 96 H6
Brettenham Norf 38 G5
Brettenham Suff 30 C6
Bretton Derbys 44 E6
Bretton Flint 42 F6
Brewer Street Sur 19 F10
Brewlands Bridge Angus 76 A4
Brewood Staffs 34 E4
Briach Moray 87 F13
Briants Puddle Dorset 9 E7
Brick End Essex 30 F2
Brickendon Herts 29 H10
Bricket Wood Herts 19 A8
Bricklehampton Worcs 26 D6
Bride IoM 48 B4
Bridekirk Cumb 56 C3
Bridell Pembs 22 B6
Bridestowe Devon 4 C6
Brideswell Aberds 88 E5
Bridford Devon 5 C9
Bridfordmills Devon 5 C9
Bridge Kent 21 F8
Bridge End Lincs 37 B7
Bridge Green Essex 29 E11
Bridge Hewick N Yorks 51 B9
Bridge of Alford Aberds 83 B7
Bridge of Allan Stirling 75 H10
Bridge of Avon Moray 88 E1
Bridge of Awe Argyll 74 E3
Bridge of Balgie Perth 75 C8
Bridge of Cally Perth 76 B4
Bridge of Canny Aberds 83 D8
Bridge of Craigisla Angus 76 B5
Bridge of Dee Dumfries 55 D10
Bridge of Don Aberdeen 83 B11
Bridge of Dun Angus 77 B9
Bridge of Dye Aberds 83 E8
Bridge of Earn Perth 76 F4
Bridge of Ericht Perth 75 B8
Bridge of Feugh Aberds 83 D9
Bridge of Forss Highld 93 C13
Bridge of Gairn Aberds 82 D5
Bridge of Gaur Perth 75 B8
Bridge of Muchalls Aberds 83 D10
Bridge of Oich Highld 80 C5
Bridge of Orchy Argyll 74 D5
Bridge of Waith Orkney 95 G3
Bridge of Walls Shetland 96 H4
Bridge of Weir Renfs 68 D2
Bridge Sollers Hereford 25 D11
Bridge Street Suff 30 D5
Bridge Trafford Ches W 43 E7
Bridge Yate S Glos 16 D3
Bridgefoot Angus 76 D6
Bridgefoot Cumb 56 D2
Bridgehampton Som 8 B4
Bridgehill Durham 58 A1
Bridgemary Hants 10 D4
Bridgemont Derbys 44 D4
Bridgend Aberds 83 B7
Bridgend Aberds 88 E5
Bridgend Angus 83 G7
Bridgend Argyll 64 B4
Bridgend Argyll 65 E8
Bridgend Argyll 73 D7
Bridgend = Pen-y-bont ar Ogwr Bridgend 14 D5
Bridgend Cumb 56 E5
Bridgend Fife 76 F6
Bridgend Moray 88 E3
Bridgend N Lanark 68 C5
Bridgend Pembs 22 B6
Bridgend W Loth 69 C9
Bridgend of Lintrathen Angus 76 B5
Bridgerule Devon 6 F1
Bridges Shrops 33 F9
Bridgeton Glasgow 68 D5
Bridgetown Corn 4 C4
Bridgetown Som 7 C8
Bridgham Norf 38 G5
Bridgnorth Shrops 34 F3
Bridgtown Staffs 34 E5
Bridgwater Som 15 H9
Bridlington E Yorks 53 C7
Bridport Dorset 8 E3
Bridstow Hereford 26 F2
Brierfield Lancs 50 F4
Brierley Glos 26 G3
Brierley Hereford 25 C11
Brierley S Yorks 45 A8
Brierley Hill W Mid 34 G5
Briery Hill Bl Gwent 25 H8
Brig o'Turk Stirling 75 G8
Brigg N Lincs 46 B4
Briggswath N Yorks 59 F9
Brigham Cumb 56 C2
Brigham E Yorks 53 D6
Brighouse W Yorks 51 G7
Brighstone IoW 10 F3
Brightgate Derbys 44 G6
Brighthampton Oxon 17 A10
Brightling E Sus 12 D5
Brightlingsea Essex 31 G7
Brighton Brighton 12 F2
Brighton Corn 3 D8
Brighton Hill Hants 18 G3
Brightons Falk 69 C8
Brightwalton W Berks 17 D11
Brightwell Suff 31 D9
Brightwell Baldwin Oxon 18 B3
Brightwell cum Sotwell Oxon 18 B2
Brignall Durham 58 E1
Brigsley NE Lincs 46 B6
Brigsteer Cumb 57 H6
Brigstock Northants 36 G5
Brill Bucks 28 G3
Brilley Hereford 25 D9
Brimaston Pembs 22 D4
Brimfield Hereford 26 B2
Brimington Derbys 45 E8
Brimley Devon 5 D8
Brimpsfield Glos 26 G6
Brimpton W Berks 18 E2
Brims Orkney 95 K3
Brimscombe Glos 16 A5
Brimstage Mers 42 D6
Brinacory Highld 79 B10
Brind E Yorks 52 F3
Brindister Shetland 96 H4
Brindister Shetland 96 K6
Brindle Lancs 50 G2
Brindley Ford Stoke 44 G2
Brineton Staffs 34 D4
Bringhurst Leics 36 F4
Brington Cambs 37 H6
Brinian Orkney 95 F5
Briningham Norf 38 B6
Brinkhill Lincs 47 E7
Brinkley Cambs 30 C3
Brinklow Warks 35 H10
Brinkworth Wilts 17 C7
Brinmore Highld 81 A8
Brinscall Lancs 50 G2
Brinsea N Som 15 E10
Brinsley Notts 45 H8
Brinsop Hereford 25 D11
Brinsworth S Yorks 45 D8
Brinton Norf 38 B6
Brisco Cumb 56 A6
Brisley Norf 38 C5
Brislington Bristol 16 D3
Bristol Bristol 16 D2
Briston Norf 39 B6
Britannia Lancs 50 G4
Britford Wilts 9 B10
Brithdir Gwyn 32 D3
British Legion Village Kent 20 F4
Briton Ferry Neath 14 B3
Britwell Salome Oxon 18 B3
Brixham Torbay 5 F10
Brixton Devon 5 F6
Brixton London 19 D10
Brixton Deverill Wilts 16 H5
Brixworth Northants 28 A4
Brize Norton Oxon 27 H10
Broad Blunsdon Swindon 17 B8
Broad Campden Glos 27 E8
Broad Chalke Wilts 9 B9
Broad Green C Beds 28 D6
Broad Green Essex 30 F5
Broad Green Worcs 26 C4
Broad Haven Pembs 22 E3
Broad Heath Worcs 26 B3
Broad Hill Cambs 38 H1
Broad Hinton Wilts 17 D8
Broad Laying Hants 17 E11
Broad Marston Worcs 27 D8
Broad Oak Carms 23 D10
Broad Oak Cumb 56 G3
Broad Oak Dorset 8 E3
Broad Oak Dorset 9 C6
Broad Oak E Sus 12 D5
Broad Oak E Sus 13 E7
Broad Oak Hereford 25 F11
Broad Oak Mers 43 C8
Broad Street Kent 20 F5
Broad Street Green Essex 30 H5
Broad Town Wilts 17 D7
Broadbottom Gtr Man 44 C3
Broadbridge W Sus 11 D7
Broadbridge Heath W Sus 11 A10
Broadclyst Devon 7 G8
Broadfield Gtr Man 44 A2
Broadfield Lancs 49 G5
Broadfield Pembs 22 F6
Broadfield W Sus 12 C1
Broadford Highld 85 F11
Broadford Bridge W Sus 11 B9
Broadhaugh Borders 61 C10
Broadhaven Highld 94 E5
Broadheath Gtr Man 43 D10
Broadhembury Devon 7 F10
Broadhempston Devon 5 E9
Broadholme Derbys 45 H7
Broadholme Lincs 46 E2
Broadland Row E Sus 13 E7
Broadlay Carms 23 F8
Broadley Lancs 50 H4
Broadley Moray 88 B3
Broadley Common Essex 29 H11
Broadmayne Dorset 8 F6
Broadmeadows Borders 70 G3
Broadmere Hants 18 G3
Broadmoor Pembs 22 F5
Broadoak Kent 21 E8
Broadrashes Moray 88 C4
Broadsea Aberds 89 B9
Broadstairs Kent 21 E10
Broadstone Poole 9 E9
Broadstone Shrops 33 G11
Broadtown Lane Wilts 17 D7
Broadwas Worcs 26 C4
Broadwater Herts 29 F9
Broadwater W Sus 11 D10
Broadway Carms 23 F7
Broadway Pembs 22 E3
Broadway Som 8 C2
Broadway Suff 39 H9
Broadway Worcs 27 E7
Broadwell Glos 26 G2
Broadwell Glos 27 F9
Broadwell Oxon 17 A9
Broadwell Warks 27 B11
Broadwell House Northumb 57 A11
Broadwey Dorset 8 F5
Broadwindsor Dorset 8 D3
Broadwood Kelly Devon 6 F5
Broadwoodwidger Devon 4 C5
Brobury Hereford 25 D10
Brochel Highld 85 D10
Brochloch Dumfries 67 G8
Brochroy Argyll 74 D3
Brockamin Worcs 26 C4
Brockbridge Hants 10 C5
Brockdam Northumb 63 A7
Brockdish Norf 39 H8
Brockenhurst Hants 10 D2
Brocketsbrae S Lanark 69 G7
Brockford Street Suff 31 B8
Brockhall Northants 28 B3
Brockham Sur 19 G8
Brockhampton Glos 27 F7
Brockhampton Hereford 26 E2
Brockholes W Yorks 44 A5
Brockhurst Derbys 45 F7
Brockhurst Hants 10 D5
Brocklebank Cumb 56 B5
Brocklesby Lincs 46 A5
Brockley N Som 15 E10
Brockley Green Suff 30 C5
Brockleymoor Cumb 57 C6
Brockton Shrops 33 E9
Brockton Shrops 33 G9
Brockton Shrops 34 E3
Brockton Shrops 34 F1
Brockton Telford 34 D3
Brockweir Glos 15 A11
Brockwood Hants 10 B5
Brockworth Glos 26 G5
Brocton Staffs 34 D5
Brodick N Ayrs 66 C3
Brodsworth S Yorks 45 B9
Brogaig Highld 85 B9
Brogborough C Beds 28 E6
Broken Cross Ches E 44 E2
Broken Cross Ches W 43 E9
Brokenborough Wilts 16 C6
Bromborough Mers 42 D6
Brome Suff 39 H7
Brome Street Suff 39 H7
Bromeswell Suff 31 C10
Bromfield Cumb 56 B3
Bromfield Shrops 33 H10
Bromham Bedford 29 C7
Bromham Wilts 16 E6
Bromley London 19 E11
Bromley W Mid 34 G5
Bromley Common London 19 E11
Bromley Green Kent 13 C8
Brompton Medway 20 E4
Brompton N Yorks 52 A5
Brompton N Yorks 58 G4
Brompton-on-Swale N Yorks 58 G3
Brompton Ralph Som 7 C9
Brompton Regis Som 7 C8
Bromsash Hereford 26 F3
Bromsberrow Hth. Glos 26 E4
Bromsgrove Worcs 26 A6
Bromyard Hereford 26 C3
Bromyard Downs Hereford 26 C3
Bronaber Gwyn 41 G9
Brongest Ceredig 23 B8
Bronington Wrex 33 B10
Bronllys Powys 25 E8
Bronnant Ceredig 24 B3
Bronwydd Arms Carms 23 D9
Bronydd Powys 25 D9
Bronygarth Shrops 33 B8
Brook Carms 23 F7
Brook Hants 10 B2
Brook Hants 10 C1
Brook IoW 10 F2
Brook Kent 13 B9
Brook Sur 18 H6
Brook Sur 19 G7
Brook End Bedford 29 B7
Brook Hill Hants 10 C1
Brook Street Kent 13 C8
Brook Street Kent 20 G2
Brook Street W Sus 12 D2
Brooke Norf 39 F8
Brooke Rutland 36 E4
Brookenby Lincs 46 C6
Brookend Glos 16 B2
Brookfield Renfs 68 D3
Brookhouse Lancs 49 C5
Brookhouse Green Ches E 44 F2
Brookland Kent 13 D8
Brooklands Dumfries 60 F4
Brooklands Gtr Man 43 C10
Brooklands Shrops 33 A11
Brookmans Park Herts 19 A9
Brooks Powys 33 F7
Brooks Green W Sus 11 B10
Brookthorpe Glos 26 G5
Brookville Norf 38 F3
Brookwood Sur 18 F6
Broom C Beds 29 D8
Broom S Yorks 45 C8
Broom Warks 27 C7
Broom Worcs 34 H5
Broom Green Norf 38 C5
Broom Hill Dorset 9 D9
Broome Norf 39 F9
Broome Shrops 33 G10
Broome Park Northumb 63 B7
Broomedge Warr 43 D10
Broomer's Corner W Sus 11 B10
Broomfield Aberds 89 E9
Broomfield Essex 30 G4
Broomfield Kent 20 F5
Broomfield Kent 21 E8
Broomfield Som 7 C11
Broomfleet E Yorks 52 G4
Broomhall Ches E 43 H9
Broomhall Windsor 18 E6
Broomhaugh Northumb 62 G6
Broomhill Norf 38 E2
Broomhill Northumb 63 C8
Broomhill S Yorks 45 B8
Broomholm Norf 39 B9
Broomley Northumb 62 G6
Broompark Durham 58 B3
Broom's Green Glos 26 E4
Broomy Lodge Hants 9 C11
Brora Highld 93 J12
Broseley Shrops 34 E2
Brotherhouse Bar Lincs 37 D8
Brotherstone Borders 70 G5
Brothertoft Lincs 46 H6
Brotherton N Yorks 51 G10
Brotton Redcar 59 E7
Broubster Highld 93 C13
Brough Cumb 57 E9
Brough Derbys 44 D5
Brough E Yorks 52 G5
Brough Highld 94 C4
Brough Notts 46 G2
Brough Orkney 95 G4
Brough Shetland 96 F7
Brough Shetland 96 F6
Brough Shetland 96 G7
Brough Shetland 96 H6
Brough Shetland 96 J7
Brough Lodge Shetland 96 D7
Brough Sowerby Cumb 57 E9
Broughall Shrops 34 A1
Broughton Borders 69 G10
Broughton Cambs 37 H8
Broughton Flint 42 F6
Broughton Hants 10 A2
Broughton Lancs 49 F5
Broughton M Keynes 28 D5
Broughton N Lincs 46 B3
Broughton N Yorks 50 D5
Broughton N Yorks 52 B3
Broughton Northants 36 H4
Broughton Orkney 95 D5
Broughton Oxon 27 E11
Broughton V Glam 14 D5
Broughton Astley Leics 35 F11
Broughton Beck Cumb 49 A2
Broughton Common Wilts 16 E5
Broughton Gifford Wilts 16 E5
Broughton Hackett Worcs 26 C6
Broughton in Furness Cumb 56 H4
Broughton Mills Cumb 56 G4
Broughton Moor Cumb 56 C2
Broughton Park Gtr Man 44 B2
Broughton Poggs Oxon 17 A9
Broughtown Orkney 95 D7
Broughty Ferry Dundee 77 D7
Browhouses Dumfries 61 G8
Browland Shetland 96 H4
Brown Candover Hants 18 H2
Brown Edge Lancs 42 A6
Brown Edge Staffs 44 G3
Brown Heath Ches W 43 F7
Brownhill Aberds 89 D8
Brownhill Aberds 89 D6
Brownhill Blackburn 50 F2
Brownhill Shrops 33 C10
Brownhills Fife 77 F8
Brownhills W Mid 34 E6
Brownlow Ches E 44 F2
Brownlow Heath Ches E 44 F2
Brownmuir Aberds 83 F9
Brown's End Glos 26 E4
Brownshill Glos 16 A5
Brownston Devon 5 F7
Brownyside Northumb 63 A7
Broxa N Yorks 59 G10
Broxbourne Herts 29 H10
Broxburn E Loth 70 C5
Broxburn W Loth 69 C9
Broxholme Lincs 46 E3
Broxted Essex 30 F2
Broxton Ches W 43 G7
Broxwood Hereford 25 C10
Broyle Side E Sus 12 E3
Bruairnis W Isles 84 H2
Bruan Highld 94 G5
Bruar Lodge Perth 81 F10
Brucehill W Dunb 68 C2
Bruera Ches W 43 F7
Bruern Abbey Oxon 27 F9
Bruichladdich Argyll 64 B3
Bruisyard Suff 31 B10
Brumby N Lincs 46 B2
Brund Staffs 44 F5
Brundall Norf 39 E9
Brundish Suff 31 B9
Brundish Street Suff 31 A9
Brunery Highld 79 D10
Brunshaw Lancs 50 F4
Brunswick Village T&W 63 F8
Bruntcliffe W Yorks 51 G8
Bruntingthorpe Leics 36 F2
Brunton Fife 76 E6
Brunton Northumb 63 A8
Brunton Wilts 17 F9
Brushford Devon 6 F5
Brushford Som 7 D8
Bruton Som 8 A5
Bryanston Dorset 9 D7
Brydekirk Dumfries 61 F7
Bryher Scilly 2 C2
Brymbo Wrex 42 G5
Brympton Som 8 C4
Bryn Carms 23 F10
Bryn Gtr Man 43 B8
Bryn Neath 14 B4
Bryn Shrops 33 G8
Bryn-coch Neath 14 B3
Bryn Du Anglesey 40 C5
Bryn Gates Gtr Man 43 B8
Bryn-glas Conwy 41 D10
Bryn Golau Rhondda 14 C5
Bryn-Iwan Carms 23 C8
Bryn-mawr Gwyn 40 G4
Bryn-nantllech Conwy 42 F2
Bryn-penarth Powys 33 E7
Bryn Rhyd-yr-Arian Conwy 42 F2
Bryn Saith Marchog Denb 42 G3
Bryn Sion Gwyn 32 D4
Bryn-y-gwenin Mon 25 G10
Bryn-y-maen Conwy 41 C10
Bryn-yr-eryr Gwyn 40 F5
Brynamman Carms 24 G4
Brynberian Pembs 22 C6
Brynbryddan Neath 14 B3
Brynbuga = Usk Mon 15 A9
Bryncae Rhondda 14 C5
Bryncethin Bridgend 14 C5
Bryncir Gwyn 40 F6
Bryncroes Gwyn 40 G4
Bryncrug Gwyn 32 E2
Bryneglwys Denb 42 H4
Brynford Flint 42 E4
Bryngwran Anglesey 40 C5
Bryngwyn Ceredig 23 B7
Bryngwyn Mon 25 H10
Bryngwyn Powys 25 D8
Brynhenllan Pembs 22 C5
Brynhoffnant Ceredig 23 A8
Brynithel Bl Gwent 15 A8
Brynmawr Bl Gwent 25 G8
Brynmenyn Bridgend 14 C5
Brynmill Swansea 14 B2
Brynna Rhondda 14 C5
Brynrefail Anglesey 40 B6
Brynrefail Gwyn 41 D7
Brynsadler Rhondda 14 C6
Brynsiencyn Anglesey 40 D6
Brynteg Anglesey 40 B6
Brynteg Ceredig 23 B9
Buaile nam Bodach W Isles 84 H2
Bualintur Highld 85 F9
Buarthmeini Gwyn 41 G10
Bubbenhall Warks 27 A10
Bubwith E Yorks 52 F3
Buccleuch Borders 61 B9
Buchanhaven Aberds 89 D11
Buchanty Perth 76 E2
Buchlyvie Stirling 68 A4
Buckabank Cumb 56 B5
Buckden Cambs 29 B8
Buckden N Yorks 50 B5
Buckenham Norf 39 E9
Buckerell Devon 7 F10
Buckfast Devon 5 E8
Buckfastleigh Devon 5 E8
Buckhaven Fife 76 H6
Buckholm Borders 70 G3
Buckholt Mon 26 G2
Buckhorn Weston Dorset 9 B6
Buckhurst Hill Essex 19 B11
Buckie Moray 88 B4
Buckies Highld 94 D3
Buckingham Bucks 28 E3
Buckland Bucks 28 G5
Buckland Devon 5 G7
Buckland Glos 27 E7
Buckland Hants 10 E2
Buckland Herts 29 E10
Buckland Kent 21 G10
Buckland Oxon 17 B10
Buckland Sur 19 F9
Buckland Brewer Devon 6 D3
Buckland Common Bucks 28 H6
Buckland Dinham Som 16 F4
Buckland Filleigh Devon 6 F3
Buckland in the Moor Devon 5 D8
Buckland Monachorum Devon 4 E5
Buckland Newton Dorset 8 D5
Buckland St Mary Som 8 C1
Bucklebury W Berks 18 D2
Bucklegate Lincs 37 B9
Bucklerheads Angus 77 D7
Bucklers Hard Hants 10 E3
Bucklesham Suff 31 D9
Buckley = Bwcle Flint 42 F5
Bucklow Hill Ches E 43 D10
Buckminster Leics 36 C4
Bucknall Lincs 46 F5
Bucknall Stoke 44 H3
Bucknell Oxon 28 F2
Bucknell Shrops 25 A10
Buckpool Moray 88 B4
Buck's Cross Devon 6 D2
Bucks Green W Sus 11 A9
Bucks Horn Oak Hants 18 G5
Buck's Mills Devon 6 D2
Bucksburn Aberdeen 83 C10
Buckshaw Village Lancs 50 G1
Buckskin Hants 18 F3
Buckton E Yorks 53 B7
Buckton Hereford 25 A10
Buckton Northumb 71 G9
Buckworth Cambs 37 H7
Budbrooke Warks 27 B9
Budby Notts 45 F10
Budd's Titson Corn 4 A3
Bude Corn 6 F1
Budlake Devon 7 G8
Budle Northumb 71 G10
Budleigh Salterton Devon 7 H9
Budock Water Corn 3 F6
Buerton Ches E 34 A2
Buffler's Holt Bucks 28 E3
Bugbrooke Northants 28 C3
Buglawton Ches E 44 F2
Bugle Corn 3 D9
Bugley Wilts 16 G5
Bugthorpe E Yorks 52 D3
Buildwas Shrops 34 E2
Builth Road Powys 25 C7
Builth Wells = Llanfair-ym-Muallt Powys 25 C7
Buirgh W Isles 90 H5
Bulby Lincs 37 C6
Bulcote Notts 36 A2
Buldoo Highld 93 C12
Bulford Wilts 17 G8
Bulford Camp Wilts 17 G8
Bulkeley Ches E 43 G8
Bulkington Warks 35 G9
Bulkington Wilts 16 F6
Bulkworthy Devon 6 E2
Bull Hill Hants 10 E2
Bullamoor N Yorks 58 G4
Bullbridge Derbys 45 G7
Bullbrook Brack 18 E5
Bulley Glos 26 G4
Bullgill Cumb 56 C2
Bullington Hants 17 G11
Bullington Lincs 46 E4
Bull's Green Herts 29 G9
Bullwood Argyll 73 F10
Bulmer Essex 30 D5
Bulmer N Yorks 52 C2
Bulmer Tye Essex 30 E5
Bulphan Thurrock 20 C3
Bulverhythe E Sus 13 F6
Bulwark Aberds 89 D9
Bulwell Nottingham 45 H9
Bulwick Northants 36 F5
Bumble's Green Essex 29 H11
Bun Abhainn Eadarra W Isles 90 G6
Bun a'Mhuillin W Isles 84 G2
Bun Loyne Highld 80 C4
Bunacaimb Highld 79 C9
Bunarkaig Highld 80 E3
Bunbury Ches E 43 G8
Bunbury Heath Ches E 43 G8
Bunchrew Highld 87 G9
Bundalloch Highld 85 F13
Buness Shetland 96 C8
Bunessan Argyll 78 J6
Bungay Suff 39 G9
Bunker's Hill Lincs 46 E3
Bunker's Hill Lincs 46 G6
Bunkers Hill Oxon 27 G11
Bunloit Highld 81 A7
Bunnahabhain Argyll 64 A5
Bunny Notts 36 C1
Buntait Highld 86 H6
Buntingford Herts 29 F10
Bunwell Norf 39 F7
Burbage Derbys 44 E4
Burbage Leics 35 F10
Burbage Wilts 17 E9
Burchett's Green Windsor 18 C5
Burcombe Wilts 9 A9
Burcot Oxon 18 B2
Burcott Bucks 28 F5
Burdon T&W 58 A4
Bures Suff 30 E6
Bures Green Suff 30 E6
Burford Ches E 43 G9
Burford Oxon 27 G9
Burford Shrops 26 B2
Burg Argyll 78 G6
Burgar Orkney 95 F4
Burgate Hants 9 C10
Burgate Suff 39 H6
Burgess Hill W Sus 12 E2
Burgh Suff 31 C9
Burgh by Sands Cumb 61 H9
Burgh Castle Norf 39 E10
Burgh Heath Sur 19 F9
Burgh le Marsh Lincs 47 F9
Burgh Muir Aberds 83 A9
Burgh next Aylsham Norf 39 C8
Burgh on Bain Lincs 46 D6
Burgh St Margaret Norf 39 D10
Burgh St Peter Norf 39 F10
Burghclere Hants 17 E11
Burghead Moray 87 E14
Burghfield W Berks 18 E3
Burghfield Common W Berks 18 E3
Burghfield Hill W Berks 18 E3
Burghill Hereford 25 D11
Burghwallis S Yorks 45 A9
Burham Kent 20 E4
Buriton Hants 10 B6
Burland Ches E 43 G9
Burlawn Corn 3 B8
Burleigh Brack 18 E5
Burlescombe Devon 7 E9
Burleston Dorset 9 E6
Burley Hants 9 D11
Burley Rutland 36 D4
Burley W Yorks 51 F8
Burley Gate Hereford 26 D2
Burley in Wharfedale W Yorks 51 E7
Burley Lodge Hants 9 D11
Burley Street Hants 9 D11
Burleydam Ches E 34 A2
Burlingjobb Powys 25 C9
Burlow E Sus 12 E4
Burlton Shrops 33 C10
Burmarsh Kent 13 C9
Burmington Warks 27 E9
Burn N Yorks 52 G1
Burn of Cambus Stirling 75 G10
Burnaston Derbys 35 B8
Burnbank S Lanark 68 E6
Burnby E Yorks 52 E4
Burncross S Yorks 45 C7
Burneside Cumb 57 G7
Burness Orkney 95 D7
Burneston N Yorks 58 H4
Burnett Bath 16 E3
Burnfoot Borders 61 B11
Burnfoot Borders 61 B10
Burnfoot E Ayrs 67 F7
Burnfoot Perth 76 G2
Burnham Bucks 18 C6
Burnham N Lincs 53 H6
Burnham Deepdale Norf 38 A4
Burnham Green Herts 29 G9
Burnham Market Norf 38 A4
Burnham Norton Norf 38 A4
Burnham-on-Crouch Essex 20 B6
Burnham-on-Sea Som 15 G9
Burnham Overy Staithe Norf 38 A4
Burnham Overy Town Norf 38 A4
Burnham Thorpe Norf 38 A4
Burnhead Dumfries 60 D4
Burnhead S Ayrs 66 F5
Burnhervie Aberds 83 B9
Burnhill Green Staffs 34 E3
Burnhope Durham 58 B2
Burnhouse N Ayrs 67 A6
Burniston N Yorks 59 G11
Burnlee W Yorks 44 B5
Burnley Lancs 50 F4
Burnley Lane Lancs 50 F4
Burnmouth Borders 71 D8
Burnopfield Durham 63 H7
Burnsall N Yorks 50 C6
Burnside Angus 77 B8
Burnside E Ayrs 67 E8
Burnside Fife 76 G4
Burnside S Lanark 68 D5
Burnside Shetland 96 F4
Burnside W Loth 69 C9
Burnside of Duntrune Angus 77 D7
Burnswark Dumfries 61 F7
Burnt Heath Derbys 44 E6
Burnt Houses Durham 58 D2
Burnt Yates N Yorks 51 C8
Burntcommon Sur 19 F7
Burnthouse Corn 3 F6
Burntisland Fife 69 B11
Burnton E Ayrs 67 F7
Burntwood Staffs 35 E6
Burnwynd Edin 69 D10
Burpham Sur 19 F7
Burpham W Sus 11 D9
Burradon Northumb 62 C5
Burradon T&W 63 F8
Burrafirth Shetland 96 B8
Burraland Shetland 96 F5
Burraland Shetland 96 J4
Burras Corn 2 F5
Burravoe Shetland 96 F7
Burravoe Shetland 96 G5
Burray Village Orkney 95 J5
Burrells Cumb 57 E8
Burrelton Perth 76 D5
Burridge Devon 6 C4
Burridge Hants 10 C4
Burrill N Yorks 58 H3
Burringham N Lincs 46 B2
Burrington Devon 6 E5
Burrington Hereford 25 A11
Burrington N Som 15 F10
Burrough Green Cambs 30 C3
Burrough on the Hill Leics 36 D3
Burrow-bridge Som 8 B2
Burrowhill Sur 18 E6
Burry Swansea 23 G9
Burry Green Swansea 23 G9
Burry Port = Porth Tywyn Carms 23 F9
Burscough Lancs 43 A7
Burscough Bridge Lancs 43 A7
Bursea E Yorks 52 F4
Burshill E Yorks 53 E6
Bursledon Hants 10 D3
Burslem Stoke 44 H2
Burstall Suff 31 D7
Burstock Dorset 8 D3
Burston Norf 39 G7
Burston Staffs 34 B5
Burstow Sur 12 B2
Burstwick E Yorks 53 G8
Burtersett N Yorks 57 H10
Burtle Som 15 G9
Burton Ches W 42 E6
Burton Ches W 43 F8
Burton Dorset 9 E10
Burton Lincs 46 E3
Burton Northumb 71 G10
Burton Pembs 22 F4
Burton Som 7 B10
Burton Wilts 16 D5
Burton Agnes E Yorks 53 C7
Burton Bradstock Dorset 8 F3
Burton Dassett Warks 27 C10
Burton Fleming E Yorks 53 B6
Burton Green W Mid 35 H8
Burton Green Wrex 42 G6
Burton Hastings Warks 35 F10
Burton-in-Kendal Cumb 49 B5
Burton in Lonsdale N Yorks 50 B2
Burton Joyce Notts 36 A2
Burton Latimer Northants 28 A6
Burton Lazars Leics 36 D3
Burton-le-Coggles Lincs 36 C5
Burton Leonard N Yorks 51 C9
Burton on the Wolds Leics 36 C1
Burton Overy Leics 36 F2
Burton Pedwardine Lincs 37 A7
Burton Pidsea E Yorks 53 F8
Burton Salmon N Yorks 51 G10
Burton Stather N Lincs 52 H4
Burton upon Stather N Lincs 52 H4
Burton upon Trent Staffs 35 C8
Burtonwood Warr 43 C8
Burwardsley Ches W 43 G8
Burwarton Shrops 34 G2
Burwash E Sus 12 D5
Burwash Common E Sus 12 D5
Burwash Weald E Sus 12 D5
Burwell Cambs 30 B2
Burwell Lincs 47 E7
Burwen Anglesey 40 A6
Burwick Orkney 95 K5
Bury Cambs 37 G8
Bury Gtr Man 44 A2
Bury Som 7 D8
Bury W Sus 11 C9
Bury Green Herts 29 F11
Bury St Edmunds Suff 30 B5
Burythorpe N Yorks 52 C3
Busby E Renf 68 E4
Buscot Oxon 17 B9
Bush Bank Hereford 25 C11
Bush Crathie Aberds 82 D4
Bush Green Norf 39 G8
Bushbury W Mid 34 E5
Bushby Leics 36 E2
Bushey Herts 19 B8
Bushey Heath Herts 19 B8
Bushley Worcs 26 E5
Bushton Wilts 17 D7
Buslingthorpe Lincs 46 D4
Busta Shetland 96 G5
Butcher's Cross E Sus 12 D4
Butcombe N Som 15 E11
Butetown Cardiff 15 D7
Butleigh Som 8 A4
Butleigh Wootton Som 15 H11
Butler's Cross Bucks 28 H5
Butler's End Warks 35 G8
Butlers Marston Warks 27 C11
Butley Suff 31 C10
Butley High Corner Suff 31 D10
Butt Green Ches E 43 G9
Butterburn Cumb 62 F2
Buttercrambe N Yorks 52 D3
Butterknowle Durham 58 D2
Butterleigh Devon 7 F8
Buttermere Cumb 56 E3
Buttermere Wilts 17 E10
Buttershaw W Yorks 51 G7
Butterstone Perth 76 C3
Butterton Staffs 44 G4
Butterwick Durham 58 D4
Butterwick Lincs 47 H7
Butterwick N Yorks 52 B5
Butterwick N Yorks 52 B3
Buttington Powys 33 E8
Buttonoak Worcs 34 H3
Butt's Green Hants 10 B2
Buttsash Hants 10 D3
Buxhall Suff 31 C7
Buxhall Fen Street Suff 31 C7
Buxley Borders 71 E7
Buxted E Sus 12 D3
Buxton Derbys 44 E4
Buxton Norf 39 C8
Buxworth Derbys 44 D4
Bwcle = Buckley Flint 42 F5
Bwlch Powys 25 F8
Bwlch-Llan Ceredig 23 A10
Bwlch-y-cibau Powys 33 D7
Bwlch-y-fadfa Ceredig 23 B9
Bwlch-y-ffridd Powys 33 F6
Bwlch-y-sarnau Powys 25 A7
Bwlchgwyn Wrex 42 G5
Bwlchnewydd Carms 23 D8
Bwlchtocyn Gwyn 40 H5
Bwlchyddar Powys 33 C7
Bwlchygroes Pembs 23 C7
Byermoor T&W 63 H7
Byers Green Durham 58 C3
Byfield Northants 28 C2
Byfleet Sur 19 E7
Byford Hereford 25 D10
Bygrave Herts 29 E9
Byker T&W 63 G8
Bylchau Conwy 42 F2
Byley Ches W 43 F10
Bynea Carms 23 G10
Byrness Northumb 62 C3
Bythorn Cambs 37 H6
Byton Hereford 25 B10
Byworth W Sus 11 B8

C

Cabharstadh W Isles 91 E8
Cablea Perth 76 D2
Cabourne Lincs 46 B5
Cabrach Argyll 72 G3
Cabrach Moray 82 A5
Cabrich Highld 87 G8
Cabus Lancs 49 E4
Cackle Street E Sus 12 D3
Cadbury Devon 7 F8
Cadbury Barton Devon 6 E5
Cadder E Dunb 68 C5
Caddington C Beds 29 G7
Caddonfoot Borders 70 G3
Cade Street E Sus 12 D5
Cadeby Leics 35 E10
Cadeby S Yorks 45 B9
Cadeleigh Devon 7 F8
Cadgwith Corn 2 H6
Cadham Fife 76 G5
Cadishead Gtr Man 43 C10
Cadle Swansea 14 B2
Cadley Lancs 49 F5
Cadley Wilts 17 E9
Cadley Wilts 17 F9
Cadmore End Bucks 18 B4
Cadnam Hants 10 C1
Cadney N Lincs 46 B4
Cadole Flint 42 F5
Cadoxton V Glam 15 E7
Cadoxton-Juxta-Neath Neath 14 B3
Cadshaw Blackburn 50 H3
Cadzow S Lanark 68 E6
Caeathro Gwyn 41 D7
Caehopkin Powys 24 G5
Caenby Lincs 46 D4
Caenby Corner Lincs 46 D3
Caér-bryn Carms 23 E10
Caer Llan Mon 25 H11
Caerau Bridgend 14 B4
Caerau Cardiff 15 D7
Caerdeon Gwyn 32 D2
Caerdydd = Cardiff Cardiff 15 D7
Caerfarchell Pembs 22 D2
Caerffili = Caerphilly Caerph 15 C7
Caerfyrddin = Carmarthen Carms 23 D9
Caergeiliog Anglesey 40 C5
Caergwrle Flint 42 G6
Caergybi = Holyhead Anglesey 40 B4
Caerleon = Caerllion Newport 15 B9
Caerllion = Caerleon Newport 15 B9
Caernarfon Gwyn 40 D6
Caerphilly = Caerffili Caerph 15 C7
Caersws Powys 32 F6
Caerwedros Ceredig 23 A8
Caerwent Mon 15 B10
Caerwych Gwyn 41 G8
Caerwys Flint 42 E4
Caethle Gwyn 32 F2
Caim Anglesey 41 B8
Caio Carms 24 E3
Cairinis W Isles 84 B3
Cairisiadar W Isles 90 D5
Cairminis W Isles 90 J5
Cairnbaan Argyll 73 D7
Cairnbanno Ho. Aberds 89 D8
Cairnborrow Aberds 88 D4
Cairnbrogie Aberds 89 F8
Cairnbulg Castle Aberds 89 B10
Cairncross Angus 82 F6
Cairncross Borders 71 D7
Cairndow Argyll 74 F4
Cairness Aberds 89 B10
Cairneyhill Fife 69 B9
Cairnfield Ho. Moray 88 B4
Cairngaan Dumfries 54 F4
Cairngarroch Dumfries 54 E3
Cairnhill Aberds 89 E6
Cairnie Aberds 83 C10
Cairnie Aberds 88 D4
Cairnorrie Aberds 89 D8
Cairnpark Aberds 83 B10
Cairnryan Dumfries 54 C3
Cairnton Orkney 95 H4
Caister-on-Sea Norf 39 D11
Caistor Lincs 46 B5
Caistor St Edmund Norf 39 E8
Caistron Northumb 62 C5
Caitha Bowland Borders 70 F3
Calais Street Suff 30 E6
Calanais W Isles 90 D7
Calbost W Isles 91 F9
Calbourne IoW 10 F3
Calceby Lincs 47 E7
Calcot Row W Berks 18 D3
Calcott Kent 21 E8
Caldback Shetland 96 C8
Caldbeck Cumb 56 C5
Caldbergh N Yorks 58 H1
Caldecote Cambs 29 C10
Caldecote Cambs 37 G7
Caldecote Herts 29 E9
Caldecote Northants 28 C3
Caldecott Northants 28 B6
Caldecott Oxon 17 B11
Caldecott Rutland 36 F4
Calder Bridge Cumb 56 F2
Calder Hall Cumb 56 F2
Calder Mains Highld 94 E2
Calder Vale Lancs 49 E5
Calderbank N Lanark 68 D6
Calderbrook Gtr Man 50 H5
Caldercruix N Lanark 69 D7
Caldermill S Lanark 68 F5
Calderwood S Lanark 68 E5
Caldhame Angus 77 C7
Caldicot Mon 15 C10
Caldwell Derbys 35 D8
Caldwell N Yorks 58 E2
Caldy Mers 42 D5
Caledrhydiau Ceredig 23 A9
Calfsound Orkney 95 E6
Calgary Argyll 78 F6
Califer Moray 87 F13
California Falk 69 C8
California Norf 39 D11
Calke Derbys 35 C9
Callakille Highld 85 C11
Callaly Northumb 62 C6
Callander Stirling 75 G9
Callaughton Shrops 34 F2
Callestick Corn 3 D6
Calligarry Highld 85 H11
Callington Corn 4 E4
Callow Hereford 25 E11
Callow End Worcs 26 D5
Callow Hill Wilts 17 C7
Callow Hill Worcs 26 A4
Callows Grave Worcs 26 B2
Calmore Hants 10 C2
Calmsden Glos 27 H7
Calne Wilts 17 D7
Calow Derbys 45 E8
Calshot Hants 10 D3
Calstock Corn 4 E5
Calstone Wellington Wilts 17 E7
Calthorpe Norf 39 B7
Calthwaite Cumb 56 B6
Calton N Yorks 50 D5
Calton Staffs 44 G5
Calveley Ches E 43 G8
Calver Derbys 44 E6
Calver Hill Hereford 25 D10
Calverhall Shrops 34 B2
Calverleigh Devon 7 E8
Calverley W Yorks 51 F8
Calvert Bucks 28 F3
Calverton M Keynes 28 E4
Calverton Notts 45 H10
Calvine Perth 81 G10
Calvo Cumb 56 A3
Cam Glos 16 B4
Camas-luinie Highld 80 A1
Camasnacroise Highld 79 F11
Camastianavaig Highld 85 E10
Camasunary Highld 85 G10
Camault Muir Highld 87 G8
Camb Shetland 96 D7
Camber E Sus 13 E8
Camberley Sur 18 E5
Camberwell London 19 D10
Camblesforth N Yorks 52 G2
Cambo Northumb 62 E6
Cambois Northumb 63 E9
Camborne Corn 2 E5
Cambourne Cambs 29 C10
Cambridge Cambs 29 C11
Cambridge Glos 16 A4
Cambridge Town Southend 20 C6
Cambus Clack 69 A7
Cambusavie Farm Highld 87 B10
Cambusbarron Stirling 68 A6
Cambuskenneth Stirling 69 A7
Cambuslang S Lanark 68 D5
Cambusmore Lodge Highld 87 B10
Camden London 19 C9
Camelford Corn 4 C2
Camelsdale Sur 11 A7
Camerory Highld 87 H13
Camer's Green Worcs 26 E4
Camerton Bath 16 F3
Camerton Cumb 56 C2
Camerton E Yorks 53 G8
Camghouran Perth 75 B8
Cammachmore Aberds 83 D11
Cammeringham Lincs 46 D3
Camore Highld 87 B10
Camp Hill Warks 35 F9
Campbeltown Argyll 65 F8
Camperdown T&W 63 F8
Campmuir Perth 76 D5
Campsall S Yorks 45 A9
Campsey Ash Suff 31 C10
Campton C Beds 29 E8
Camptown Borders 62 B2
Camrose Pembs 22 D4
Camserney Perth 75 C11
Camster Highld 94 F4
Camuschoirk Highld 79 E10
Camuscross Highld 85 G11
Camusnagaul Highld 80 F2
Camusnagaul Highld 86 C3
Camusrory Highld 79 B11
Camusteel Highld 85 D12
Camusterrach Highld 85 D12
Camusvrachan Perth 75 C9
Canada Hants 10 C1
Canadia E Sus 12 E6
Canal Side S Yorks 45 A10
Candacraig Ho. Aberds 82 B5
Candlesby Lincs 47 F8
Candy Mill S Lanark 69 F9
Cane End Oxon 18 D3
Canewdon Essex 20 B5
Canford Bottom Dorset 9 D9
Canford Cliffs Poole 9 F9
Canford Magna Poole 9 E9
Canham's Green Suff 31 B7
Canholes Derbys 44 E4
Canisbay Highld 94 C5
Cann Dorset 9 B7
Cann Common Dorset 9 B7
Cannard's Grave Som 16 G3
Cannich Highld 86 H6
Cannington Som 15 H8
Cannock Staffs 34 E5
Cannock Wood Staffs 34 D6
Canon Bridge Hereford 25 D11
Canon Frome Hereford 26 D3
Canon Pyon Hereford 25 D11
Canonbie Dumfries 61 F9
Canons Ashby Northants 28 C2
Canonstown Corn 2 F4
Canterbury Kent 21 F8
Cantley Norf 39 E9
Cantley S Yorks 45 B10
Cantlop Shrops 33 E11
Canton Cardiff 15 D7
Cantraybruich Highld 87 G10
Cantraydoune Highld 87 G10
Cantraywood Highld 87 G10
Cantsfield Lancs 50 B2
Canvey Island Essex 20 C4
Canwick Lincs 46 F3
Canworthy Water Corn 4 B3
Caol Highld 80 F3
Caol Ila Argyll 64 A5
Caolas Argyll 78 G3
Caolas Scalpaigh W Isles 90 H7
Caolas Stocinis W Isles 90 H6
Capel Sur 19 G8
Capel Bangor Ceredig 32 G2
Capel Betws Lleucu Ceredig 24 C3
Capel Carmel Gwyn 40 H3
Capel Coch Anglesey 40 B6
Capel Curig Conwy 41 E9
Capel Cynon Ceredig 23 B8
Capel Dewi Carms 23 D9
Capel Dewi Ceredig 23 B9
Capel Dewi Ceredig 32 G2
Capel Garmon Conwy 41 E10
Capel-gwyn Anglesey 40 C5
Capel Gwyn Carms 23 D9
Capel Gwynfe Carms 24 F4
Capel Hendre Carms 23 E10
Capel Hermon Gwyn 32 C3
Capel Isaac Carms 23 D10
Capel Iwan Carms 23 C7
Capel le Ferne Kent 21 H9
Capel Llanilltern Cardiff 14 C6
Capel Mawr Anglesey 40 C6
Capel St Andrew Suff 31 D10
Capel St Mary Suff 31 E7
Capel Seion Ceredig 32 H2
Capel Tygwydd Ceredig 23 B7
Capel Uchaf Gwyn 40 F6
Capel-y-graig Gwyn 41 D7
Capelulo Conwy 41 C9
Capenhurst Ches W 42 E6
Capernwray Lancs 49 B5
Capheaton Northumb 62 E6
Cappercleuch Borders 61 A8
Capplegill Dumfries 61 C7
Capton Devon 5 F9
Caputh Perth 76 D3
Car Colston Notts 36 A3
Carbis Bay Corn 2 F4
Carbost Highld 85 D9
Carbost Highld 85 E8
Carbrook S Yorks 45 D7
Carbrooke Norf 38 E5
Carburton Notts 45 E10
Carcant Borders 70 E2
Carcary Angus 77 B9
Carclaze Corn 3 D9
Carcroft S Yorks 45 A9
Cardenden Fife 69 A11
Cardeston Shrops 33 D9
Cardiff = Caerdydd Cardiff 15 D7
Cardigan = Aberteifi Ceredig 22 B6
Cardington Bedford 29 D7
Cardington Shrops 33 F11
Cardinham Corn 4 E2
Cardonald Glasgow 68 D4
Cardow Moray 88 D1
Cardrona Borders 70 G2
Cardross Argyll 68 C2
Cardurnock Cumb 61 H7
Careby Lincs 36 D6
Careston Castle Angus 77 B8
Carew Pembs 22 F5
Carew Cheriton Pembs 22 F5
Carew Newton Pembs 22 F5
Carey Hereford 26 E2
Carfrae E Loth 70 D4
Cargenbridge Dumfries 60 F5
Cargill Perth 76 D4
Cargo Cumb 61 H9
Cargreen Corn 4 E5
Carham Northumb 71 G7
Carhampton Som 7 B9
Carharrack Corn 2 E6
Carie Perth 75 B9
Carie Perth 75 D9
Carines Corn 3 D6
Carisbrooke IoW 10 F3
Cark Cumb 49 B3
Carlabhagh W Isles 90 C7
Carland Cross Corn 3 D7
Carlby Lincs 37 D6
Carlecotes S Yorks 44 B5
Carlesmoor N Yorks 51 B7
Carleton Cumb 56 A6
Carleton Cumb 57 D7
Carleton Lancs 49 F3
Carleton N Yorks 50 E5
Carleton Forehoe Norf 39 E6
Carleton Rode Norf 39 F7
Carlin How Redcar 59 E8
Carlingcott Bath 16 F3
Carlisle Cumb 61 H10
Carlops Borders 69 E10
Carlton Bedford 28 C6
Carlton Cambs 30 C3
Carlton Leics 35 E9
Carlton N Yorks 51 A6
Carlton N Yorks 52 G2
Carlton N Yorks 58 E2
Carlton N Yorks 59 H7
Carlton Notts 36 A2
Carlton S Yorks 45 A7
Carlton Stockton 58 D4
Carlton Suff 31 B10
Carlton W Yorks 51 G9
Carlton Colville Suff 39 G11
Carlton Curlieu Leics 36 F2
Carlton Husthwaite N Yorks 51 B10
Carlton in Cleveland N Yorks 58 F6
Carlton in Lindrick Notts 45 D9
Carlton le Moorland Lincs 46 G3
Carlton Miniott N Yorks 51 A9
Carlton on Trent Notts 45 F11
Carlton Scroop Lincs 36 A5
Carluke S Lanark 69 E7
Carmarthen = Caerfyrddin Carms 23 D9
Carmel Anglesey 40 B5
Carmel Carms 23 E10
Carmel Flint 42 E4
Carmel Guern 11
Carmel Gwyn 40 E6
Carmont Aberds 83 E10
Carmunnock Glasgow 68 E5
Carmyle Glasgow 68 D5
Carmyllie Angus 77 C8
Carn-gorm Highld 80 A1
Carnaby E Yorks 53 C7
Carnach Highld 80 A2
Carnach Highld 86 B3
Carnach W Isles 90 H7
Carnachy Highld 93 D10
Càrnais W Isles 90 D5
Carnbee Fife 77 G8
Carnbo Perth 76 G3
Carnbrea Corn 2 E5
Carnduff S Lanark 68 F5
Carnduncan Argyll 64 B3
Carne Corn 3 F8
Carnforth Lancs 49 B4
Carnhedryn Pembs 22 D3
Carnhell Green Corn 2 F5
Carnkie Corn 2 F5
Carnkie Corn 2 F6
Carno Powys 32 F5
Carnoch Highld 86 F5
Carnoch Highld 86 H6
Carnock Fife 69 B9
Carnon Downs Corn 3 E6
Carnousie Aberds 89 C6
Carnoustie Angus 77 D8
Carnwath S Lanark 69 F8
Carnyorth Corn 2 F2
Carperby N Yorks 58 H1
Carpley Green N Yorks 57 H11
Carr S Yorks 45 C9
Carr Hill T&W 63 G8
Carradale Argyll 65 E9
Carragraich W Isles 90 H6
Carrbridge Highld 81 A11
Carrefour Selous Jersey 11
Carreg-wen Pembs 23 B7
Carreglefn Anglesey 40 B5
Carrick Argyll 73 E8
Carrick Fife 77 E7
Carrick Castle Argyll 73 D10
Carrick Ho. Orkney 95 E6
Carriden Falk 69 B9
Carrington Gtr Man 43 C10
Carrington Lincs 47 G7
Carrington Midloth 70 D2
Carrog Conwy 41 F9
Carrog Denb 33 A7
Carron Falk 69 B7
Carron Moray 88 D2
Carron Bridge Stirling 68 B6
Carronbridge Dumfries 60 D4
Carronshore Falk 69 B7
Carrshield Northumb 57 B10
Carrutherstown Dumfries 61 F7
Carrville Durham 58 B4
Carsaig Argyll 72 E6
Carsaig Argyll 79 J8
Carscreugh Dumfries 54 D5
Carse Gray Angus 77 B7
Carse Ho. Argyll 72 G6
Carsegowan Dumfries 55 D7
Carseriggan Dumfries 54 C6
Carsethorn Dumfries 60 H5
Carshalton London 19 E9
Carsington Derbys 44 G6
Carskiey Argyll 65 H7
Carsluith Dumfries 55 D7
Carsphairn Dumfries 67 G8
Carstairs S Lanark 69 F8
Carstairs Junction S Lanark 69 F8
Carswell Marsh Oxon 17 B10
Carter's Clay Hants 10 B2
Carterton Oxon 27 H9
Carterway Heads Northumb 58 A1
Carthew Corn 3 D9
Carthorpe N Yorks 51 A9
Cartington Northumb 62 C6
Cartland S Lanark 69 F7
Cartmel Cumb 49 B3
Cartmel Fell Cumb 56 H6
Carway Carms 23 F9
Cary Fitzpaine Som 8 B4
Cas-gwent = Chepstow Mon 15 B11
Cascob Powys 25 B9
Cashlie Perth 75 C7
Cashmoor Dorset 9 C8
Casnewydd = Newport Newport 15 C9
Cassey Compton Glos 27 G7
Cassington Oxon 27 G11
Cassop Durham 58 C4
Castell Denb 42 F4
Castell-Howell Ceredig 23 B9

Castell-Nedd = Neath Neath 14 B3
Castell Newydd Emlyn = Newcastle Emlyn Carms 23 B8
Castell-y-bwch Torf 15 B8
Castellau Rhondda 14 C6
Casterton Cumb 50 B2
Castle Acre Norf 38 D4
Castle Ashby Northants 28 C5
Castle Bolton N Yorks 58 G1
Castle Bromwich W Mid 35 G7
Castle Bytham Lincs 36 D5
Castle Caereinion Powys 33 E7
Castle Camps Cambs 30 D3
Castle Carrock Cumb 61 H11
Castle Cary Som 8 A5
Castle Combe Wilts 16 D5
Castle Donington Leics 35 C10
Castle Douglas Dumfries 55 C10
Castle Eaton Swindon 17 B8
Castle Eden Durham 58 C5
Castle Forbes Aberds 83 B8
Castle Frome Hereford 26 D3
Castle Green Sur 18 E6
Castle Gresley Derbys 35 D8
Castle Heaton Northumb 71 F8
Castle Hedingham Essex 30 E4
Castle Hill Kent 12 B5
Castle Huntly Perth 76 E6
Castle Kennedy Dumfries 54 D4
Castle O'er Dumfries 61 D8
Castle Pulverbatch Shrops 33 E10
Castle Rising Norf 38 C2
Castle Stuart Highld 87 G10
Castlebay = Bagh a Chaisteil W Isles 84 J1
Castlebythe Pembs 22 D5
Castlecary N Lanark 68 C6
Castlecraig Highld 87 E11
Castlefairn Dumfries 60 E3
Castleford W Yorks 51 G10
Castlehill Borders 69 G11
Castlehill Highld 94 D3
Castlehill W Dunb 68 C2
Castlemaddy Dumfries 67 H8
Castlemartin Pembs 22 G4
Castlemilk Dumfries 61 F7
Castlemilk Glasgow 68 E5
Castlemorris Pembs 22 C4
Castlemorton Worcs 26 E4
Castleside Durham 58 B1
Castlethorpe M Keynes 28 D5
Castleton Angus 76 C6
Castleton Argyll 73 E7
Castleton Derbys 44 D5
Castleton Gtr Man 44 A2
Castleton N Yorks 59 F7
Castleton Newport 15 C8
Castletown Ches W 43 G7
Castletown Highld 87 G10
Castletown Highld 94 D3
Castletown IoM 48 F2
Castletown T&W 63 H9
Castleweary Borders 61 C10
Castley N Yorks 51 E8
Caston Norf 38 F5
Castor Pboro 37 F7
Catacol N Ayrs 66 B2
Catbrain S Glos 16 C2
Catbrook Mon 15 A11
Catchall Corn 2 G3
Catchems Corner W Mid 35 H8
Catchgate Durham 58 A2
Catcleugh Northumb 62 C3
Catcliffe S Yorks 45 D8
Catcott Som 15 H9
Caterham Sur 19 F10
Catfield Norf 39 C9
Catfirth Shetland 96 H6
Catford London 19 D10
Catforth Lancs 49 F4
Cathays Cardiff 15 D7
Cathcart Glasgow 68 D4
Cathedine Powys 25 F8
Catherington Hants 10 C5
Catherton Shrops 34 H2
Catlodge Highld 81 D8
Catlowdy Cumb 61 F10
Catmore W Berks 17 C11
Caton Lancs 49 C5
Caton Green Lancs 49 C5
Catrine E Ayrs 67 D8
Cat's Ash Newport 15 B9
Catsfield E Sus 12 E6
Catshill Worcs 26 A6
Cattal N Yorks 51 D10
Cattawade Suff 31 E8
Catterall Lancs 49 E4
Catterick N Yorks 58 G3
Catterick Bridge N Yorks 58 G3
Catterick Garrison N Yorks 58 G2
Catterlen Cumb 57 C6
Catterline Aberds 83 F10
Catterton N Yorks 51 E11
Catthorpe Leics 36 H1
Cattistock Dorset 8 E4
Catton N Yorks 51 B9
Catton Northumb 62 H4
Catwick E Yorks 53 E7
Catworth Cambs 29 A7
Caudlesprings Norf 38 E5
Caulcott Oxon 28 F2
Cauldcots Angus 77 C9
Cauldhame Stirling 68 A5
Cauldmill Borders 61 B11
Cauldon Staffs 44 H4
Caulkerbush Dumfries 60 H5
Caulside Dumfries 61 E10
Caunsall Worcs 34 G4
Caunton Notts 45 G11
Causeway End Dumfries 55 C7
Causeway Foot W Yorks 51 F6
Causeway-head Stirling 75 H10
Causewayend S Lanark 69 G9
Causewayhead Cumb 56 A3
Causey Park Bridge Northumb 63 D7
Causeyend Aberds 83 B11
Cautley Cumb 57 G8
Cavendish Suff 30 D5
Cavendish Bridge Leics 35 C10
Cavenham Suff 30 B4
Caversfield Oxon 28 F2
Caversham Reading 18 D4
Caverswall Staffs 34 A5
Cavil E Yorks 52 F3
Cawdor Highld 87 F11
Cawkwell Lincs 46 E6
Cawood N Yorks 52 F1
Cawsand Corn 4 F5
Cawston Norf 39 C7
Cawthorne S Yorks 44 B6
Cawthorpe Lincs 37 C6
Cawton N Yorks 52 B2
Caxton Cambs 29 C10
Caynham Shrops 26 A2
Caythorpe Lincs 46 H3
Caythorpe Notts 45 H10
Cayton N Yorks 53 A6
Ceann a Bhaigh W Isles 84 B2
Ceann a Deas Loch Baghasdail W Isles 84 G2
Ceann Shiphoirt W Isles 91 F7
Ceann Tarabhaigh W Isles 90 F7
Ceannacroc Lodge Highld 80 B4
Cearsiadair W Isles 91 E8
Cefn Berain Conwy 42 F2
Cefn-brith Conwy 42 G2
Cefn Canol Powys 33 B8
Cefn-coch Conwy 41 D10
Cefn Coch Powys 33 C7
Cefn-coed-y-cymmer M Tydf 25 H7
Cefn Cribbwr Bridgend 14 C4
Cefn Cross Bridgend 14 C4
Cefn-ddwysarn Gwyn 32 B5
Cefn Einion Shrops 33 G8
Cefn-gorwydd Powys 24 D6
Cefn-mawr Wrex 33 A8
Cefn-y-bedd Flint 42 G6
Cefn-y-pant Carms 22 D6
Cefneithin Carms 23 E10
Cei-bach Ceredig 23 A9
Ceinewydd = New Quay Ceredig 23 A8
Ceint Anglesey 40 C6
Cellan Ceredig 24 D3
Cellarhead Staffs 44 H3
Cemaes Anglesey 40 A5
Cemmaes Powys 32 E4
Cemmaes Road Powys 32 E4
Cenarth Carms 23 B7
Cenin Gwyn 40 F6
Central Invclyd 73 F11
Ceos W Isles 91 E8
Ceres Fife 77 F7
Cerne Abbas Dorset 8 D5
Cerney Wick Glos 17 B7
Cerrigceinwen Anglesey 40 C6
Cerrigydrudion Conwy 42 H2
Cessford Borders 62 A3
Ceunant Gwyn 41 D7
Chaceley Glos 26 E5
Chacewater Corn 3 E6
Chackmore Bucks 28 E3
Chacombe Northants 27 D11
Chad Valley W Mid 34 G6
Chadderton Gtr Man 44 B3
Chadderton Fold Gtr Man 44 B2
Chaddesden Derby 35 B9
Chaddesley Corbett Worcs 26 A5
Chaddleworth W Berks 17 D11
Chadlington Oxon 27 F10
Chadshunt Warks 27 C10
Chadwell Leics 36 C3
Chadwell St Mary Thurrock 20 D3
Chadwick End W Mid 27 A9
Chadwick Green Mers 43 C8
Chaffcombe Som 8 C2
Chagford Devon 5 C8
Chailey E Sus 12 E2
Chain Bridge Lincs 37 A9
Chainbridge Cambs 37 E10
Chainhurst Kent 20 G4
Chalbury Dorset 9 D9
Chalbury Common Dorset 9 D9
Chaldon Sur 19 F10
Chaldon Herring Dorset 9 F6
Chale IoW 10 G3
Chale Green IoW 10 G3
Chalfont Common Bucks 19 B7
Chalfont St Giles Bucks 18 B6
Chalfont St Peter Bucks 19 B7
Chalford Glos 16 A5
Chalgrove Oxon 18 B3
Chalk Kent 20 D3
Challacombe Devon 6 B5
Challoch Dumfries 54 C6
Challock Kent 21 F7
Chalton C Beds 29 F7
Chalton Hants 10 C6
Chalvington E Sus 12 F4
Chancery Ceredig 32 H1
Chandler's Ford Hants 10 B3
Channel Tunnel Kent 21 H8
Channerwick Shetland 96 L6
Chantry Som 16 G4
Chantry Suff 31 D8
Chapel Fife 69 A11
Chapel Allerton Som 15 F10
Chapel Allerton W Yorks 51 F9
Chapel Amble Corn 3 B8
Chapel Brampton Northants 28 B4
Chapel Chorlton Staffs 34 B4
Chapel-en-le-Frith Derbys 44 D4
Chapel End Warks 35 F9
Chapel Green Warks 27 B11
Chapel Green Warks 35 G8
Chapel Haddlesey N Yorks 52 G1
Chapel Head Cambs 37 G9
Chapel Hill Aberds 89 E10
Chapel Hill Lincs 46 G6
Chapel Hill Mon 15 B11
Chapel Hill N Yorks 51 E9
Chapel Lawn Shrops 33 H9
Chapel-le-Dale N Yorks 50 B3
Chapel Milton Derbys 44 D4
Chapel of Garioch Aberds 83 A9
Chapel Row W Berks 18 E2
Chapel St Leonards Lincs 47 E9
Chapel Stile Cumb 56 F5
Chapelgate Lincs 37 C10
Chapelhall N Lanark 68 D6
Chapelhill Dumfries 60 D6
Chapelhill Highld 87 D11
Chapelhill N Ayrs 66 B5
Chapelhill Perth 76 D3
Chapelhill Perth 76 E5
Chapelknowe Dumfries 61 F9
Chapelton Angus 77 C9
Chapelton Devon 6 D4
Chapelton Highld 81 B11
Chapelton S Lanark 68 F5
Chapeltown Blackburn 50 H3
Chapeltown Moray 82 A4
Chapeltown S Yorks 45 C7
Chapmans Well Devon 6 G2
Chapmanslade Wilts 16 G5
Chapmore End Herts 29 G10
Chappel Essex 30 F5
Chard Som 8 D2
Chardstock Devon 8 D2
Charfield S Glos 16 B4
Charford Worcs 26 B6
Charing Kent 20 G6
Charing Cross Dorset 9 C10
Charing Heath Kent 20 G6
Charingworth Glos 27 E9
Charlbury Oxon 27 G10
Charlcombe Bath 16 E4
Charlecote Warks 27 C9
Charles Devon 6 C5
Charles Tye Suff 31 C7
Charlesfield Dumfries 61 G7
Charleston Angus 76 C6
Charleston Renfs 68 D3
Charlestown Aberdeen 83 C11
Charlestown Corn 3 D9
Charlestown Derbys 44 C4
Charlestown Dorset 8 G5
Charlestown Fife 69 B9
Charlestown Gtr Man 44 B2
Charlestown Highld 85 A13
Charlestown Highld 87 G9
Charlestown W Yorks 50 G5
Charlestown of Aberlour Moray 88 D2
Charlesworth Derbys 44 C4
Charleton Devon 5 G8
Charlton Hants 17 G10
Charlton Herts 29 F8
Charlton London 19 D11
Charlton Northants 28 E2
Charlton Northumb 62 E4
Charlton Som 16 F3
Charlton Telford 34 D1
Charlton W Sus 11 C7
Charlton Wilts 9 B8
Charlton Wilts 16 C6
Charlton Wilts 17 F8
Charlton Worcs 27 D7
Charlton Abbots Glos 27 F7
Charlton Adam Som 8 B4
Charlton-All-Saints Wilts 9 B10
Charlton Down Dorset 8 E5
Charlton Horethorne Som 8 B5
Charlton Kings Glos 26 F6
Charlton Mackerell Som 8 B4
Charlton Marshall Dorset 9 D7
Charlton Musgrove Som 8 B6
Charlton on Otmoor Oxon 28 G2
Charltons Redcar 59 E7
Charlwood Sur 19 G9
Charlynch Som 7 C11
Charminster Dorset 8 E5
Charmouth Dorset 8 E2
Charndon Bucks 28 F3
Charney Bassett Oxon 17 B10
Charnock Richard Lancs 50 H1
Charsfield Suff 31 C9
Chart Corner Kent 20 F4
Chart Sutton Kent 20 G5
Charter Alley Hants 18 F2
Charterhouse Som 15 F10
Charterville Allotments Oxon 27 G10
Chartham Kent 21 F8
Chartham Hatch Kent 21 F8
Chartridge Bucks 18 A6
Charvil Wokingham 18 D4
Charwelton Northants 28 C2
Chasetown Staffs 34 E6
Chastleton Oxon 27 F9
Chasty Devon 6 F2
Chatburn Lancs 50 E3
Chatcull Staffs 34 B3
Chatham Medway 20 E4
Chathill Northumb 71 H10
Chattenden Medway 20 D4
Chatteris Cambs 37 G9
Chattisham Suff 31 D7
Chatto Borders 62 B3
Chatton Northumb 71 H9
Chawleigh Devon 6 E6
Chawley Oxon 17 A11
Chawston Bedford 29 C8
Chawton Hants 18 H4
Cheadle Gtr Man 44 D2
Cheadle Staffs 34 A6
Cheadle Heath Gtr Man 44 D2
Cheadle Hulme Gtr Man 44 D2
Cheam London 19 E9
Cheapside Sur 19 F7
Chearsley Bucks 28 G4
Chebsey Staffs 34 C4
Checkendon Oxon 18 C3
Checkley Ches E 43 H10
Checkley Hereford 26 E2
Checkley Staffs 34 B6
Chedburgh Suff 30 C4
Cheddar Som 15 F10
Cheddington Bucks 28 G6
Cheddleton Staffs 44 G3
Cheddon Fitzpaine Som 8 B1
Chedglow Wilts 16 B6
Chedgrave Norf 39 F9
Chedington Dorset 8 D3
Chediston Suff 39 H9
Chedworth Glos 27 G7
Chedzoy Som 15 H9
Cheeklaw Borders 70 E6
Cheeseman's Green Kent 13 C9
Cheglinch Devon 6 B4
Cheldon Devon 7 E6
Chelford Ches E 44 E2
Chell Heath Stoke 44 G2
Chellaston Derby 35 B9
Chellington Bedford 28 C6
Chelmarsh Shrops 34 G3
Chelmer Village Essex 30 H4
Chelmondiston Suff 31 E9
Chelmorton Derbys 44 F5
Chelmsford Essex 30 H4
Chelsea London 19 D9
Chelsfield London 19 E11
Chelsworth Suff 30 D6
Cheltenham Glos 26 F6
Chelveston Northants 28 B6
Chelvey N Som 15 E10
Chelwood Bath 16 E3
Chelwood Common E Sus 12 D3
Chelwood Gate E Sus 12 D3
Chelworth Wilts 16 B6
Chelworth Green Wilts 17 B7
Chemistry Shrops 33 A11
Chenies Bucks 19 B7
Cheny Longville Shrops 33 G10
Chepstow = Cas-gwent Mon 15 B11
Chequerfield W Yorks 51 G10
Cherhill Wilts 17 D7
Cherington Glos 16 B6
Cherington Warks 27 E9
Cheriton Devon 7 B6
Cheriton Hants 10 B4
Cheriton Kent 21 H8
Cheriton Swansea 23 G9
Cheriton Bishop Devon 7 G6
Cheriton Fitzpaine Devon 7 F7
Cheriton or Stackpole Elidor Pembs 22 G4
Cherrington Telford 34 C2
Cherry Burton E Yorks 52 E5
Cherry Hinton Cambs 29 C11
Cherry Orchard Worcs 26 C5
Cherry Willingham Lincs 46 E4
Cherrybank Perth 76 E4
Chertsey Sur 19 E7
Cheselbourne Dorset 9 E6
Chesham Bucks 18 A6
Chesham Bois Bucks 18 B6
Cheshunt Herts 19 A10
Cheslyn Hay Staffs 34 E5
Chessington London 19 E8
Chester Ches W 43 F7
Chester-Le-Street Durham 58 A3
Chester Moor Durham 58 B3
Chesterblade Som 16 G3
Chesterfield Derbys 45 E7
Chesters Borders 62 A2
Chesters Borders 62 B2
Chesterton Cambs 29 B11
Chesterton Cambs 37 F7
Chesterton Glos 17 A7
Chesterton Oxon 28 F2
Chesterton Shrops 34 F3
Chesterton Staffs 44 H2
Chesterton Warks 27 C10
Chesterwood Northumb 62 G4
Chestfield Kent 21 E8
Cheston Devon 5 F7
Cheswardine Shrops 34 C3
Cheswick Northumb 71 F9
Chetnole Dorset 8 D5
Chettiscombe Devon 7 E8
Chettisham Cambs 37 G11
Chettle Dorset 9 C8
Chetton Shrops 34 F2
Chetwode Bucks 28 F3
Chetwynd Aston Telford 34 D3
Cheveley Cambs 30 B3
Chevening Kent 19 F11
Chevington Suff 30 C4
Chevithorne Devon 7 E8
Chew Magna Bath 16 E2
Chew Stoke Bath 16 E2
Chewton Keynsham Bath 16 E3
Chewton Mendip Som 16 F2
Chicheley M Keynes 28 D6
Chichester W Sus 11 D7
Chickerell Dorset 8 F5
Chicklade Wilts 9 A8
Chicksgrove Wilts 9 A8
Chidden Hants 10 C5
Chiddingfold Sur 18 H6
Chiddingly E Sus 12 E4
Chiddingstone Kent 19 G11
Chiddingstone Causeway Kent 20 G2
Chiddingstone Hoath Kent 12 B3
Chideock Dorset 8 E3
Chidham W Sus 11 D6
Chidswell W Yorks 51 G8
Chieveley W Berks 17 D11
Chignall St James Essex 30 H3
Chignall Smealy Essex 30 G3
Chigwell Essex 19 B11
Chigwell Row Essex 19 B11
Chilbolton Hants 17 H10
Chilcomb Hants 10 B4
Chilcombe Dorset 8 E4
Chilcompton Som 16 F3
Chilcote Leics 35 D8
Child Okeford Dorset 9 C7
Childer Thornton Ches W 42 E6
Childrey Oxon 17 C10
Child's Ercall Shrops 34 C2
Childswickham Worcs 27 E7
Childwall Mers 43 D7
Childwick Green Herts 29 G8
Chilfrome Dorset 8 E4
Chilgrove W Sus 11 C7
Chilham Kent 21 F7
Chilhampton Wilts 9 A9
Chilla Devon 6 F3
Chillaton Devon 4 C5
Chillenden Kent 21 F9
Chillerton IoW 10 F3
Chillesford Suff 31 C10
Chillingham Northumb 71 H9
Chillington Devon 5 G8
Chillington Som 8 C2
Chilmark Wilts 9 A8
Chilson Oxon 27 G10
Chilsworthy Corn 4 D5
Chilsworthy Devon 6 F2
Chilthorne Domer Som 8 C4
Chiltington E Sus 12 E2
Chilton Bucks 28 G3
Chilton Durham 58 D3
Chilton Oxon 17 C11
Chilton Cantelo Som 8 B4
Chilton Foliat Wilts 17 D10
Chilton Lane Durham 58 C4
Chilton Polden Som 15 H9
Chilton Street Suff 30 D4
Chilton Trinity Som 15 H8
Chilvers Coton Warks 35 F9
Chilwell Notts 35 B11
Chilworth Hants 10 C3
Chilworth Sur 19 G7
Chimney Oxon 17 A10
Chineham Hants 18 F3
Chingford London 19 B10
Chinley Derbys 44 D4
Chinley Head Derbys 44 D4
Chinnor Oxon 18 A4
Chipnall Shrops 34 B3
Chippenhall Green Suff 39 H8
Chippenham Cambs 30 B3
Chippenham Wilts 16 D6
Chipperfield Herts 19 A7
Chipping Herts 29 E10
Chipping Lancs 50 E2
Chipping Campden Glos 27 E8
Chipping Hill Essex 30 G5
Chipping Norton Oxon 27 F10
Chipping Ongar Essex 20 A2
Chipping Sodbury S Glos 16 C4
Chipping Warden Northants 27 D11
Chipstable Som 7 D9
Chipstead Kent 19 F11
Chipstead Sur 19 F9
Chirbury Shrops 33 F8
Chirk = Y Waun Wrex 33 B8
Chirk Bank Shrops 33 B8
Chirmorrie S Ayrs 54 B5
Chirnside Borders 71 E7
Chirnsidebridge Borders 71 E7
Chirton Wilts 17 F7
Chisbury Wilts 17 E9
Chiselborough Som 8 C3
Chiseldon Swindon 17 D8
Chiserley W Yorks 50 G6
Chislehampton Oxon 18 B2
Chislehurst London 19 D11
Chislet Kent 21 E9
Chiswell Green Herts 19 A8
Chiswick London 19 D9
Chiswick End Cambs 29 D10
Chisworth Derbys 44 C3
Chithurst W Sus 11 B7
Chittering Cambs 29 A11
Chitterne Wilts 16 G6
Chittlehamholt Devon 6 D5
Chittlehampton Devon 6 D5
Chittoe Wilts 16 E6
Chivenor Devon 6 C4
Chobham Sur 18 E6
Choicelee Borders 70 E6
Cholderton Wilts 17 G9
Cholesbury Bucks 28 H6
Chollerford Northumb 62 F5
Chollerton Northumb 62 F5
Cholmondeston Ches E 43 F9
Cholsey Oxon 18 C2
Cholstrey Hereford 25 C11
Chop Gate N Yorks 59 G6
Choppington Northumb 63 E8
Chopwell T&W 63 H7
Chorley Ches E 43 G8
Chorley Lancs 50 H1
Chorley Shrops 34 G2
Chorley Staffs 35 D6
Chorleywood Herts 19 B7
Chorlton cum Hardy Gtr Man 44 C2
Chorlton Lane Ches W 43 H7
Choulton Shrops 33 G9
Chowdene T&W 63 H8
Chowley Ches W 43 G7
Chrishall Essex 29 E11
Christchurch Cambs 37 F10
Christchurch Dorset 9 E10
Christchurch Glos 26 G2
Christchurch Newport 15 C9
Christian Malford Wilts 16 D6
Christleton Ches W 43 F7
Christmas Common Oxon 18 B4
Christon N Som 15 F9
Christon Bank Northumb 63 A8
Christow Devon 5 C9
Chryston N Lanark 68 C5
Chudleigh Devon 5 D9
Chudleigh Knighton Devon 5 D9
Chulmleigh Devon 6 E5
Chunal Derbys 44 C4
Church Lancs 50 G3
Church Aston Telford 34 D3
Church Brampton Northants 28 B4
Church Broughton Derbys 35 B8
Church Crookham Hants 18 F5
Church Eaton Staffs 34 D4
Church End C Beds 28 E6
Church End C Beds 28 F6
Church End C Beds 29 E8
Church End Cambs 37 E9
Church End Cambs 37 G8
Church End E Yorks 53 D6
Church End Essex 30 D2
Church End Essex 30 F4
Church End Hants 18 F3
Church End Lincs 37 B8
Church End Warks 35 F8
Church End Warks 35 F8
Church End Wilts 17 D7
Church Enstone Oxon 27 F10
Church Fenton N Yorks 51 F11
Church Green Devon 7 G10
Church Green Norf 39 F6
Church Gresley Derbys 35 D8
Church Hanborough Oxon 27 G11
Church Hill Ches W 43 F9
Church Houses N Yorks 59 G7
Church Knowle Dorset 9 F8
Church Laneham Notts 46 E2
Church Langton Leics 36 F3
Church Lawford Warks 35 H10
Church Lawton Ches E 44 G2
Church Leigh Staffs 34 B6
Church Lench Worcs 27 C7
Church Mayfield Staffs 35 A7
Church Minshull Ches E 43 F9
Church Norton W Sus 11 E7
Church Preen Shrops 33 F11
Church Pulverbatch Shrops 33 E10
Church Stoke Powys 33 F8
Church Stowe Northants 28 C3
Church Street Kent 20 D4
Church Stretton Shrops 33 F10
Church Town N Lincs 45 B11
Church Town Sur 19 F10
Church Village Rhondda 14 C6
Church Warsop Notts 45 F9
Churcham Glos 26 G4
Churchbank Shrops 33 H8
Churchbridge Staffs 34 E5
Churchdown Glos 26 G5
Churchend Essex 21 B7
Churchend Essex 30 F3
Churchend S Glos 16 B4
Churchfield W Mid 34 F6
Churchgate Street Essex 29 G11
Churchill Devon 6 B4
Churchill Devon 8 D2
Churchill N Som 15 F10
Churchill Oxon 27 F9
Churchill Worcs 26 C6
Churchill Worcs 34 H4
Churchinford Som 7 E11
Churchover Warks 35 G11
Churchstanton Som 7 E10
Churchstow Devon 5 G8
Churchtown Derbys 44 F6
Churchtown IoM 48 C4
Churchtown Lancs 49 E4
Churchtown Mers 49 H3
Churnsike Lodge Northumb 62 F2
Churston Ferrers Torbay 5 F10
Churt Sur 18 H5
Churton Ches W 43 G7
Churwell W Yorks 51 G8
Chute Standen Wilts 17 F10
Chwilog Gwyn 40 G6
Chyandour Corn 2 F3
Cilan Uchaf Gwyn 40 H4
Cilcain Flint 42 F4
Cilcennin Ceredig 24 B2
Cilfor Gwyn 41 G8
Cilfrew Neath 14 A3
Cilfynydd Rhondda 14 B6
Cilgerran Pembs 22 B6
Cilgwyn Carms 24 F4
Cilgwyn Gwyn 40 E6
Cilgwyn Pembs 22 C5
Ciliau Aeron Ceredig 23 A9
Cill Donnain W Isles 84 F2
Cille Bhrighde W Isles 84 G2
Cille Pheadair W Isles 84 G2
Cilmery Powys 25 C7
Cilsan Carms 23 D10
Ciltalgarth Gwyn 41 F10
Cilwendeg Pembs 23 C7
Cilybebyll Neath 14 A3
Cilycwm Carms 24 E4
Cimla Neath 14 B3
Cinderford Glos 26 G3
Cippyn Pembs 22 B6
Circebost W Isles 90 D6
Cirencester Glos 17 A7
Ciribhig W Isles 90 C6
City London 19 C10
City Powys 33 G8
City Dulas Anglesey 40 B6
Clachaig Argyll 73 E10
Clachan Argyll 72 B6
Clachan Argyll 72 H6
Clachan Argyll 74 F4
Clachan Argyll 79 G11
Clachan Highld 85 E10
Clachan W Isles 84 D2
Clachan na Luib W Isles 84 B3
Clachan of Campsie E Dunb 68 C5
Clachan of Glendaruel Argyll 73 E8
Clachan-Seil Argyll 72 B6
Clachan Strachur Argyll 73 C9
Clachaneasy Dumfries 54 B6
Clachanmore Dumfries 54 E3
Clachbreck Argyll 72 F6
Clachnabrain Angus 82 G5
Clachtoll Highld 92 G3
Clackmannan Clack 69 A8
Clacton-on-Sea Essex 31 G8
Cladach Chireboist W Isles 84 B2
Claddach-knockline W Isles 84 B2
Cladich Argyll 74 E3
Claggan Highld 79 G9
Claggan Highld 80 F3
Claigan Highld 84 C7
Claines Worcs 26 C5
Clandown Bath 16 F3
Clanfield Hants 10 C5
Clanfield Oxon 17 A9
Clanville Hants 17 G10
Claonaig Argyll 73 H7
Claonel Highld 93 J8
Clap Hill Kent 13 C9
Clapgate Dorset 9 D9
Clapgate Herts 29 F11
Clapham Bedford 29 C7
Clapham London 19 D9
Clapham N Yorks 50 C3
Clapham W Sus 11 D9
Clappers Borders 71 E8
Clappersgate Cumb 56 F5
Clapton Som 8 D3
Clapton-in-Gordano N Som 15 D10
Clapton-on-the-Hill Glos 27 G8
Clapworthy Devon 6 D5
Clara Vale T&W 63 G7
Clarach Ceredig 32 G2
Clarbeston Pembs 22 D5
Clarbeston Road Pembs 22 D5
Clarborough Notts 45 D11
Clardon Highld 94 D3
Clare Suff 30 D4
Clarebrand Dumfries 55 C10
Clarencefield Dumfries 60 G6
Clarilaw Borders 61 B11
Clark's Green Sur 19 H8
Clarkston E Renf 68 E4
Clashandorran Highld 87 G8
Clashcoig Highld 87 B9
Clashindarroch Aberds 88 E4
Clashmore Highld 87 C10
Clashmore Highld 92 F3
Clashnessie Highld 92 F3
Clashnoir Moray 82 A4
Clate Shetland 96 G7
Clathy Perth 76 F2
Clatt Aberds 83 A7
Clatter Powys 32 F5
Clatterford IoW 10 F3
Clatterin Bridge Aberds 83 F8
Clatworthy Som 7 C9
Claughton Lancs 49 E5
Claughton Lancs 50 C1
Claughton Mers 42 D6
Claverdon Warks 27 B8
Claverham N Som 15 E10
Clavering Essex 29 E11
Claverley Shrops 34 F3
Claverton Bath 16 E4
Clawdd-newydd Denb 42 G3
Clawthorpe Cumb 49 B5
Clawton Devon 6 G2
Claxby Lincs 46 C5
Claxby Lincs 47 E8
Claxton N Yorks 52 C2
Claxton Norf 39 E9
Clay Common Suff 39 G10
Clay Coton Northants 36 H1
Clay Cross Derbys 45 F7
Clay Hill W Berks 18 D2
Clay Lake Lincs 37 C8
Claybokie Aberds 82 D2
Claybrooke Magna Leics 35 G10
Claybrooke Parva Leics 35 G10
Claydon Oxon 27 C11
Claydon Suff 31 C8
Claygate Dumfries 61 F9
Claygate Kent 12 B6
Claygate Sur 19 E8
Claygate Cross Kent 20 F3
Clayhanger Devon 7 D9
Clayhanger W Mid 34 E6
Clayhidon Devon 7 E10
Clayhill E Sus 13 D7
Clayhill Hants 10 D2
Clayock Highld 94 E3
Claypole Lincs 46 H2
Clayton S Yorks 45 B8
Clayton Staffs 34 A4
Clayton W Sus 12 E1
Clayton W Yorks 51 F7
Clayton Green Lancs 50 G1
Clayton-le-Moors Lancs 50 F3
Clayton-le-Woods Lancs 50 G1
Clayton West W Yorks 44 A6
Clayworth Notts 45 D11
Cleadale Highld 78 C7
Cleadon T&W 63 G9
Clearbrook Devon 4 E6
Clearwell Glos 26 H2
Cleasby N Yorks 58 E3
Cleat Orkney 95 K5
Cleatlam Durham 58 E2
Cleator Cumb 56 E2
Cleator Moor Cumb 56 E2
Clebrig Highld 93 F8
Cleckheaton W Yorks 51 G7
Clee St Margaret Shrops 34 G1
Cleedownton Shrops 34 G1
Cleehill Shrops 34 H1
Cleethorpes NE Lincs 47 B7
Cleeton St Mary Shrops 34 H2
Cleeve N Som 15 E10
Cleeve Hill Glos 26 F6
Cleeve Prior Worcs 27 D7
Clegyrnant Powys 32 E5
Clehonger Hereford 25 E11
Cleish Perth 76 H3
Cleland N Lanark 69 E7
Clench Common Wilts 17 E8
Clenchwarton Norf 38 C1
Clent Worcs 34 H5
Cleobury Mortimer Shrops 34 H2
Cleobury North Shrops 34 G2
Cleongart Argyll 65 E7
Clephanton Highld 87 F11
Clerklands Borders 61 A11
Clestrain Orkney 95 H4
Cleuch Head Borders 61 B11
Cleughbrae Dumfries 60 F6
Clevancy Wilts 17 D7
Clevedon N Som 15 D10
Cleveley Oxon 27 F10
Cleveleys Lancs 49 E3
Cleverton Wilts 16 C6
Clevis Bridgend 14 D4
Clewer Som 15 F10
Cley next the Sea Norf 38 A6
Cliaid W Isles 84 H1
Cliasmol W Isles 90 G5
Cliburn Cumb 57 D7
Click Mill Orkney 95 F4
Cliddesden Hants 18 G3
Cliff End E Sus 13 E7
Cliffburn Angus 77 C9
Cliffe Medway 20 D4
Cliffe N Yorks 52 F2
Cliffe Woods Medway 20 D4
Clifford Hereford 25 D9
Clifford W Yorks 51 E10
Clifford Chambers Warks 27 C8
Clifford's Mesne Glos 26 F4
Cliffsend Kent 21 E10
Clifton Bristol 16 D2
Clifton C Beds 29 E8
Clifton Cumb 57 D7
Clifton Derbys 35 A7
Clifton Lancs 49 F4
Clifton N Yorks 51 E7
Clifton Northumb 63 E8
Clifton Nottingham 36 B1
Clifton Oxon 27 E11
Clifton S Yorks 45 C9
Clifton Stirling 74 D6
Clifton Worcs 26 D5
Clifton York 52 D1
Clifton Campville Staffs 35 D8
Clifton Green Gtr Man 43 B10
Clifton Hampden Oxon 18 B2
Clifton Reynes M Keynes 28 C6
Clifton upon Dunsmore Warks 35 H11
Clifton upon Teme Worcs 26 B4
Cliftoncote Borders 62 A4
Cliftonville Kent 21 D10
Climaen gwyn Neath 24 H4
Climping W Sus 11 D9
Climpy S Lanark 69 E8
Clink Som 16 G4
Clint N Yorks 51 D8
Clint Green Norf 38 D6
Clintmains Borders 70 G5
Cliobh W Isles 90 D5
Clippesby Norf 39 D10
Clipsham Rutland 36 D5
Clipston Northants 36 G3
Clipstone Notts 45 F9
Clitheroe Lancs 50 E3
Cliuthar W Isles 90 H6
Clive Shrops 33 C11
Clivocast Shetland 96 C8
Clixby Lincs 46 B5
Clocaenog Denb 42 G3
Clochan Moray 88 B4
Clock Face Mers 43 C8
Clockmill Borders 70 E6
Cloddiau Powys 33 E8
Clodock Hereford 25 F10
Clola Aberds 89 D10
Clophill C Beds 29 E7
Clopton Northants 37 G6
Clopton Suff 31 C9
Clopton Corner Suff 31 C9
Clopton Green Suff 30 C4
Close Clark IoM 48 E2
Closeburn Dumfries 60 D4
Closworth Som 8 C4
Clothall Herts 29 E9
Clotton Ches W 43 F8
Clough Foot W Yorks 50 G5
Cloughton N Yorks 59 G11
Cloughton Newlands N Yorks 59 G11
Clousta Shetland 96 H5
Clouston Orkney 95 G3
Clova Aberds 82 A6
Clova Angus 82 F5
Clove Lodge Durham 57 E11
Clovelly Devon 6 D2
Clovenfords Borders 70 G3
Clovenstone Aberds 83 B9
Clovullin Highld 74 A3
Clow Bridge Lancs 50 G4
Clowne Derbys 45 E8
Clows Top Worcs 26 A4
Cloy Wrex 33 A9
Cluanie Inn Highld 80 B2
Cluanie Lodge Highld 80 B2
Clun Shrops 33 G9
Clunbury Shrops 33 G9
Clunderwen Carms 22 E6
Clune Highld 81 A9
Clunes Highld 80 E4
Clungunford Shrops 33 H9
Clunie Aberds 89 C6
Clunie Perth 76 C4
Clunton Shrops 33 G9
Cluny Fife 76 H5
Cluny Castle Highld 81 D8
Clutton Bath 16 F3
Clutton Ches W 43 G7
Clwt-grugoer Conwy 42 F2
Clwt-y-bont Gwyn 41 D7
Clydach Mon 25 G9
Clydach Swansea 14 A2
Clydach Vale Rhondda 14 B5
Clydebank W Dunb 68 C3
Clydey Pembs 23 C7
Clyffe Pypard Wilts 17 D7
Clynder Argyll 73 E11
Clyne Neath 14 A4
Clynelish Highld 93 J11
Clynnog-fawr Gwyn 40 E6
Clyro Powys 25 D9
Clyst Honiton Devon 7 G8
Clyst Hydon Devon 7 F9
Clyst St George Devon 5 C10
Clyst St Lawrence Devon 7 F9
Clyst St Mary Devon 7 G8
Cnoc Amhlaigh W Isles 91 D10
Cnwch-coch Ceredig 32 H2
Coachford Aberds 88 D4
Coad's Green Corn 4 D3
Coal Aston Derbys 45 E7
Coalbrookdale Telford 34 E2
Coalbrookvale Bl Gwent 25 H8
Coalburn S Lanark 69 G7
Coalburns T&W 63 G7
Coalcleugh Northumb 57 B10
Coaley Glos 16 A4
Coalhall E Ayrs 67 E7
Coalhill Essex 20 B4
Coalpit Heath S Glos 16 C3
Coalport Telford 34 E2
Coalsnaughton Clack 76 H2
Coaltown of Balgonie Fife 76 H5
Coaltown of Wemyss Fife 76 H6
Coalville Leics 35 D10
Coalway Glos 26 G2
Coat Som 8 B3
Coatbridge N Lanark 68 D6
Coatdyke N Lanark 68 D6
Coate Swindon 17 C8
Coate Wilts 17 E7
Coates Cambs 37 F9
Coates Glos 16 A6
Coates Lancs 50 E4
Coates Notts 46 D2
Coates W Sus 11 C8
Coatham Redcar 59 D6
Coatham Mundeville Darl 58 D3
Coatsgate Dumfries 60 C6
Cobbaton Devon 6 D5
Cobbler's Green Norf 39 F8
Coberley Glos 26 G6
Cobham Kent 20 E3
Cobham Sur 19 E8
Cobholm Island Norf 39 E11
Cobleland Stirling 75 H8
Cobnash Hereford 25 B11
Coburty Aberds 89 B9
Cock Bank Wrex 42 H6
Cock Bridge Aberds 82 C4
Cock Clarks Essex 20 A5
Cockayne N Yorks 59 G7
Cockayne Hatley Cambs 29 D9
Cockburnspath Borders 70 C6
Cockenzie and Port Seton E Loth 70 C3
Cockerham Lancs 49 D4
Cockermouth Cumb 56 C3
Cockernhoe Green Herts 29 F8
Cockfield Durham 58 D2
Cockfield Suff 30 C6
Cockfosters London 19 B9
Cocking W Sus 11 C7
Cockington Torbay 5 E9
Cocklake Som 15 G10
Cockley Beck Cumb 56 F4
Cockley Cley Norf 38 E3
Cockshutt Shrops 33 C10
Cockthorpe Norf 38 A5
Cockwood Devon 5 C10
Cockyard Hereford 25 E11
Codda Corn 4 D2
Coddenham Suff 31 C8
Coddington Ches W 43 G7
Coddington Hereford 26 D4
Coddington Notts 46 G2
Codford St Mary Wilts 16 H6
Codford St Peter Wilts 16 H6
Codicote Herts 29 G9
Codmore Hill W Sus 11 B9
Codnor Derbys 45 H8
Codrington S Glos 16 D4
Codsall Staffs 34 E4
Codsall Wood Staffs 34 E4
Coed Duon = Blackwood Caerph 15 B7
Coed Mawr Gwyn 41 C7
Coed Morgan Mon 25 G10
Coed-Talon Flint 42 G5
Coed-y-bryn Ceredig 23 B8
Coed-y-paen Mon 15 B9
Coed-yr-ynys Powys 25 F8
Coed Ystumgwern Gwyn 32 C1
Coedely Rhondda 14 C6
Coedkernew Newport 15 C8
Coedpoeth Wrex 42 G5
Coedway Powys 33 D9
Coelbren Powys 24 G5
Coffinswell Devon 5 E9
Cofton Hackett Worcs 34 H6
Cogan V Glam 15 D7
Cogenhoe Northants 28 B5
Cogges Oxon 27 H10
Coggeshall Essex 30 F5
Coggeshall Hamlet Essex 30 F5
Coggins Mill E Sus 12 D4
Coig Peighinnean W Isles 91 A10
Coig Peighinnean Bhuirgh W Isles 91 B9
Coignafearn Lodge Highld 81 B8
Coilacriech Aberds 82 D5
Coilantogle Stirling 75 G8
Coilleag W Isles 84 G2
Coillore Highld 85 E8
Coity Bridgend 14 C5
Col W Isles 91 C9
Col Uarach W Isles 91 D9
Colaboll Highld 93 H8
Colan Corn 3 C7
Colaton Raleigh Devon 7 H9
Colbost Highld 84 D7
Colburn N Yorks 58 G2
Colby Cumb 57 D8
Colby IoM 48 E2
Colby Norf 39 B8
Colchester Essex 31 F7
Colcot V Glam 15 E7
Cold Ash W Berks 18 E2
Cold Ashby Northants 36 H2
Cold Ashton S Glos 16 D4
Cold Aston Glos 27 G8
Cold Blow Pembs 22 E6
Cold Brayfield M Keynes 28 C6
Cold Hanworth Lincs 46 D4
Cold Harbour Lincs 36 B5
Cold Hatton Telford 34 C2
Cold Hesledon Durham 58 B5
Cold Higham Northants 28 C3
Cold Kirby N Yorks 51 A11
Cold Newton Leics 36 E3
Cold Northcott Corn 4 C3
Cold Norton Essex 20 A5
Cold Overton Leics 36 D4
Coldbackie Highld 93 D9
Coldbeck Cumb 57 F9
Coldblow London 20 D2
Coldean Brighton 12 F2
Coldeast Devon 5 D9
Colden W Yorks 50 G5
Colden Common Hants 10 B3
Coldfair Green Suff 31 B11
Coldham Cambs 37 E10
Coldharbour Glos 16 A2
Coldharbour Kent 20 F2
Coldharbour Sur 19 G8
Coldingham Borders 71 D8
Coldrain Perth 76 G3
Coldred Kent 21 G9
Coldridge Devon 6 F5
Coldstream Angus 76 D6
Coldstream Borders 71 G7
Coldwaltham W Sus 11 C9
Coldwells Aberds 89 D11
Coldwells Croft Aberds 83 A7
Coldyeld Shrops 33 F9
Cole Som 8 A5
Cole Green Herts 29 G9
Cole Henley Hants 17 F11
Colebatch Shrops 33 G9
Colebrook Devon 7 F9
Colebrooke Devon 7 G6
Coleby Lincs 46 F3
Coleby N Lincs 52 H4
Coleford Devon 7 F6
Coleford Glos 26 G2
Coleford Som 16 G3
Colehill Dorset 9 D9
Coleman's Hatch E Sus 12 C3
Colemere Shrops 33 B10
Colemore Hants 10 A6
Coleorton Leics 35 D10
Colerne Wilts 16 D5
Cole's Green Suff 31 B9
Coles Green Suff 31 D7
Colesbourne Glos 26 G6
Colesden Bedford 29 C8
Coleshill Bucks 18 B6
Coleshill Oxon 17 B9
Coleshill Warks 35 G8
Colestocks Devon 7 F9
Colgate W Sus 11 A11
Colgrain Argyll 68 B2
Colinsburgh Fife 77 G7
Colinton Edin 69 D11
Colintraive Argyll 73 F9
Colkirk Norf 38 C5
Collace Perth 76 D5
Collafirth Shetland 96 G6
Collaton St Mary Torbay 5 F9
College Milton S Lanark 68 E5
Collessie Fife 76 F5
Collier Row London 20 B2
Collier Street Kent 20 G4
Collier's End Herts 29 F10
Collier's Green Kent 13 C6
Colliery Row T&W 58 B4
Collieston Aberds 89 F10
Collin Dumfries 60 F6
Collingbourne Ducis Wilts 17 F9
Collingbourne Kingston Wilts 17 F9
Collingham Notts 46 F2
Collingham W Yorks 51 E9
Collington Hereford 26 B3
Collingtree Northants 28 C4
Collins Green Warr 43 C8
Colliston Angus 77 C9
Collycroft Warks 35 G9
Collynie Aberds 89 E8
Collyweston Northants 36 E5
Colmonell S Ayrs 66 H4
Colmworth Bedford 29 C8
Coln Rogers Glos 27 H7
Coln St Aldwyn's Glos 27 H8
Coln St Dennis Glos 27 G7
Colnabaichin Aberds 82 C4
Colnbrook Slough 19 D7
Colne Cambs 37 H9
Colne Lancs 50 E4
Colne Edge Lancs 50 E4
Colne Engaine Essex 30 E5
Colney Norf 39 E7
Colney Heath Herts 29 H9
Colney Street Herts 19 A8
Colpy Aberds 89 E6
Colquhar Borders 70 F2
Colsterdale N Yorks 51 A7
Colsterworth Lincs 36 C5
Colston Bassett Notts 36 B2
Coltfield Moray 87 E14
Colthouse Cumb 56 G5
Coltishall Norf 39 D8
Coltness N Lanark 69 E7
Colton Cumb 56 H5
Colton N Yorks 51 E11
Colton Norf 39 E7
Colton Staffs 35 C6
Colton W Yorks 51 F9
Colva Powys 25 C9
Colvend Dumfries 55 D11
Colvister Shetland 96 D7
Colwall Green Hereford 26 D4
Colwall Stone Hereford 26 D4
Colwell Northumb 62 F5
Colwich Staffs 34 C6
Colwick Notts 36 A2
Colwinston V Glam 14 D5
Colworth W Sus 11 D8
Colwyn Bay = Bae Colwyn Conwy 41 C10
Colyford Devon 8 E1
Colyton Devon 8 E1
Combe Hereford 25 B10
Combe Oxon 27 G11
Combe W Berks 17 E10
Combe Common Sur 18 H6
Combe Down Bath 16 E4
Combe Florey Som 7 C10
Combe Hay Bath 16 F4
Combe Martin Devon 6 B4
Combe Moor Hereford 25 B10
Combe Raleigh Devon 7 F10
Combe St Nicholas Som 8 C2
Combeinteignhead Devon 5 D10
Comberbach Ches W 43 E9
Comberton Cambs 29 C10
Comberton Hereford 25 B11
Combpyne Devon 8 E1
Combridge Staffs 35 B6
Combrook Warks 27 C10
Combs Derbys 44 E4
Combs Suff 31 C7
Combs Ford Suff 31 C7
Combwich Som 15 G8
Comers Aberds 83 C8
Comins Coch Ceredig 32 G2
Commercial End Cambs 30 B2
Commins Capel Betws Ceredig 24 C3
Commins Coch Powys 32 E4
Common Edge Blackpool 49 F3
Common Side Derbys 45 E7
Commondale N Yorks 59 E7
Commonmoor Corn 4 E3
Commonside Ches W 43 E8
Compstall Gtr Man 44 C3
Compton Devon 5 E9
Compton Hants 10 B3
Compton Sur 18 G5
Compton Sur 18 G6
Compton W Berks 18 D2
Compton W Sus 11 C6
Compton Wilts 17 F8
Compton Abbas Dorset 9 C7
Compton Abdale Glos 27 G7
Compton Bassett Wilts 17 D7
Compton Beauchamp Oxon 17 C9
Compton Bishop Som 15 F9
Compton Chamberlayne Wilts 9 B9
Compton Dando Bath 16 E3
Compton Dundon Som 8 A3
Compton Martin Bath 15 F11
Compton Pauncefoot Som 8 B5
Compton Valence Dorset 8 E4
Comrie Fife 69 B9
Comrie Perth 75 E10
Conaglen House Highld 80 G2
Conchra Argyll 73 E9
Concraigie Perth 76 C4
Conder Green Lancs 49 D4
Conderton Worcs 26 E6
Condicote Glos 27 F8
Condorrat N Lanark 68 C6
Condover Shrops 33 E10
Coney Weston Suff 38 H5
Coneyhurst W Sus 11 B10
Coneysthorpe N Yorks 52 B3
Coneythorpe N Yorks 51 D9
Conford Hants 11 A7
Congash Highld 82 A2
Congdon's Shop Corn 4 D3
Congerstone Leics 35 E9
Congham Norf 38 C3
Congl-y-wal Gwyn 41 F9
Congleton Ches E 44 F2
Congresbury N Som 15 E10
Congreve Staffs 34 D5
Conicavel Moray 87 F12
Coningsby Lincs 46 G6
Conington Cambs 29 B10
Conington Cambs 37 G7
Conisbrough S Yorks 45 C9
Conisby Argyll 64 B3
Conisholme Lincs 47 C8
Coniston Cumb 56 G5
Coniston E Yorks 53 F7
Coniston Cold N Yorks 50 D5
Conistone N Yorks 50 C5
Connah's Quay Flint 42 F5
Connel Argyll 74 D2
Connel Park E Ayrs 67 E9
Connor Downs Corn 2 F4
Conon Bridge Highld 87 F8
Conon House Highld 87 F8
Cononley N Yorks 50 E5
Conordan Highld 85 E10
Consall Staffs 44 H3
Consett Durham 58 A2
Constable Burton N Yorks 58 G2
Constantine Corn 2 G6
Constantine Bay Corn 3 B7
Contin Highld 86 F7
Contlaw Aberdeen 83 C10
Conwy Conwy 41 C9
Conyer Kent 20 E6
Conyers Green Suff 30 B5
Cooden E Sus 12 F6
Cooil IoM 48 E3
Cookbury Devon 6 F3
Cookham Windsor 18 C5
Cookham Dean Windsor 18 C5
Cookham Rise Windsor 18 C5
Cookhill Worcs 27 C7
Cookley Suff 39 H9
Cookley Worcs 34 G4
Cookley Green Oxon 18 B3
Cookney Aberds 83 D10
Cookridge W Yorks 51 E8
Cooksbridge E Sus 12 E3
Cooksmill Green Essex 30 H3
Coolham W Sus 11 B10
Cooling Medway 20 D4
Coombe Corn 3 D8
Coombe Corn 6 E1
Coombe Hants 10 B5
Coombe Wilts 17 F8
Coombe Bissett Wilts 9 B10
Coombe Hill Glos 26 F5
Coombe Keynes Dorset 9 F7
Coombes W Sus 11 D10
Coopersale Common Essex 19 A11
Cootham W Sus 11 C9
Copdock Suff 31 D8
Copford Green Essex 30 F6
Copgrove N Yorks 51 C9
Copister Shetland 96 F6
Cople Bedford 29 D8
Copley Durham 58 D1
Coplow Dale Derbys 44 E5
Copmanthorpe York 52 E1
Coppathorne Corn 4 A3
Coppenhall Staffs 34 D5
Coppenhall Moss Ches E 43 G10
Copperhouse Corn 2 F4
Coppingford Cambs 37 G7
Copplestone Devon 7 F6
Coppull Lancs 43 A8
Coppull Moor Lancs 43 A8
Copsale W Sus 11 B10
Copster Green Lancs 50 F2
Copston Magna Warks 35 G10
Copt Heath W Mid 35 H7
Copt Hewick N Yorks 51 B9
Copt Oak Leics 35 D10
Copthorne Shrops 33 D10
Copthorne Sur 12 C2
Copy's Green Norf 38 B5
Copythorne Hants 10 C2
Corbets Tey London 20 C2
Corbridge Northumb 62 G5
Corby Northants 36 G4
Corby Glen Lincs 36 C5
Cordon N Ayrs 66 C3
Coreley Shrops 26 A3
Cores End Bucks 18 C6
Corfe Som 7 E11
Corfe Castle Dorset 9 F8
Corfe Mullen Dorset 9 E8
Corfton Shrops 33 G10
Corgarff Aberds 82 C4
Corhampton Hants 10 B5
Corlae Dumfries 67 G9
Corley Warks 35 G9
Corley Ash Warks 35 G8
Corley Moor Warks 35 G8
Cornaa IoM 48 D4
Cornabus Argyll 64 D4
Cornel Conwy 41 D9
Corner Row Lancs 49 F4
Corney Cumb 56 G3
Cornforth Durham 58 C4
Cornhill Aberds 88 C5
Cornhill-on-Tweed Northumb 71 G7
Cornholme W Yorks 50 G5
Cornish Hall End Essex 30 E3
Cornquoy Orkney 95 J6
Cornsay Durham 58 B2
Cornsay Colliery Durham 58 B2
Corntown Highld 87 F8
Corntown V Glam 14 D5
Cornwell Oxon 27 F9
Cornwood Devon 5 F7
Cornworthy Devon 5 F9
Corpach Highld 80 F2
Corpusty Norf 39 B7
Corran Highld 74 A3
Corran Highld 85 H13
Corranbuie Argyll 73 G7
Corrany IoM 48 D4
Corrie N Ayrs 66 B3
Corrie Common Dumfries 61 E8
Corriecravie N Ayrs 66 D2
Corriemoillie Highld 86 E6
Corriemulzie Lodge Highld 86 B6
Corrievarkie Lodge Perth 81 F7
Corrievorrie Highld 81 A9
Corrimony Highld 86 H6
Corringham Lincs 46 C2
Corringham Thurrock 20 C4
Corris Gwyn 32 E3
Corris Uchaf Gwyn 32 E3
Corrour Shooting Lodge Highld 80 G6
Corrow Argyll 74 G4
Corry Highld 85 F11
Corry of Ardnagrask Highld 87 G8
Corrykinloch Highld 92 G6
Corrymuckloch Perth 75 D11
Corrynachenchy Argyll 79 G9
Cors-y-Gedol Gwyn 32 C1
Corsback Highld 94 C4
Corscombe Dorset 8 D4
Corse Aberds 88 D6
Corse Glos 26 F4
Corse Lawn Worcs 26 E5
Corse of Kinnoir Aberds 88 D5
Corsewall Dumfries 54 C3
Corsham Wilts 16 D5
Corsindae Aberds 83 C8
Corsley Wilts 16 G5
Corsley Heath Wilts 16 G5
Corsock Dumfries 60 F3
Corston Bath 16 E3
Corston Wilts 16 C6
Corstorphine Edin 69 C10
Cortachy Angus 76 B6
Corton Suff 39 F11
Corton Wilts 16 G6
Corton Denham Som 8 B5
Coruanan Lodge Highld 80 G2
Corunna W Isles 84 B3
Corwen Denb 33 A6
Coryton Devon 4 C5
Coryton Thurrock 20 C4
Cosby Leics 35 F11
Coseley W Mid 34 F5
Cosgrove Northants 28 D4
Cosham Ptsmth 10 D5
Cosheston Pembs 22 F5
Cossall Notts 35 A10
Cossington Leics 36 D2
Cossington Som 15 G9
Costa Orkney 95 F4
Costessey Norf 39 D7
Costock Notts 36 C1
Coston Leics 36 C4
Cote Oxon 17 A10
Cotebrook Ches W 43 F8
Cotehill Cumb 56 A6
Cotes Cumb 57 H6
Cotes Leics 36 C1
Cotes Staffs 34 B4
Cotesbach Leics 35 G11
Cotgrave Notts 36 B2
Cothall Aberds 83 B10
Cotham Notts 45 H11
Cothelstone Som 7 C10
Cotherstone Durham 58 E1
Cothill Oxon 17 B11
Cotleigh Devon 7 F11
Cotmanhay Derbys 35 A10
Cotmaton Devon 7 H10
Coton Cambs 29 C11
Coton Northants 28 A3
Coton Staffs 34 B5
Coton Staffs 34 C4
Coton Clanford Staffs 34 C4
Coton Hill Shrops 33 D10
Coton Hill Staffs 34 B5
Coton in the Elms Derbys 35 D8
Cott Devon 5 E8
Cottam E Yorks 52 C5
Cottam Lancs 49 F5
Cottam Notts 46 E2
Cottartown Highld 87 H13
Cottenham Cambs 29 B11
Cotterdale N Yorks 57 G10
Cottered Herts 29 F10
Cotteridge W Mid 34 H6
Cotterstock Northants 36 F6
Cottesbrooke Northants 28 A4
Cottesmore Rutland 36 D5
Cotteylands Devon 7 E8
Cottingham E Yorks 52 F6
Cottingham Northants 36 F4
Cottingley W Yorks 51 F7
Cottisford Oxon 28 E2
Cotton Staffs 44 H4
Cotton Suff 31 B7
Cotton End Bedford 29 D7
Cottown Aberds 83 A7
Cottown Aberds 83 B9
Cottown Aberds 89 D8
Cotwalton Staffs 34 B5
Couch's Mill Corn 4 F2
Coughton Hereford 26 F2
Coughton Warks 27 B7
Coulaghailtro Argyll 72 G6
Coulags Highld 86 G2
Coulby Newham Mbro 58 E6
Coulderton Cumb 56 F1
Coulin Highld 86 F3
Coull Aberds 83 C7
Coull Argyll 64 B3
Coulport Argyll 73 E11
Coulsdon London 19 F9
Coulston Wilts 16 F6
Coulter S Lanark 69 G9
Coulton N Yorks 52 B2
Cound Shrops 34 E1
Coundon Durham 58 D3
Coundon W Mid 35 G9
Coundon Grange Durham 58 D3
Countersett N Yorks 57 H11
Countess Wilts 17 G8
Countess Wear Devon 5 C10
Countesthorpe Leics 36 F1
Countisbury Devon 7 B6
County Oak W Sus 12 C1
Coup Green Lancs 50 G1
Coupar Angus Perth 76 C5
Coupland Northumb 71 G8
Cour Argyll 65 D9
Courance Dumfries 60 D6
Court-at-Street Kent 13 C9
Court Henry Carms 23 D10
Courteenhall Northants 28 C4
Courtsend Essex 21 B7
Courtway Som 7 C11
Cousland Midloth 70 D2
Cousley Wood E Sus 12 C5
Cove Argyll 73 E11
Cove Borders 70 C6
Cove Devon 7 E8
Cove Hants 18 F5
Cove Highld 91 H13
Cove Bay Aberdeen 83 C11
Cove Bottom Suff 39 H10
Covehithe Suff 39 G11
Coven Staffs 34 E5
Coveney Cambs 37 G10
Covenham St Bartholomew Lincs 47 C7
Covenham St Mary Lincs 47 C7
Coventry W Mid 35 H9
Coverack Corn 3 H6
Coverham N Yorks 58 H2
Covesea Moray 88 A1
Covington Cambs 29 A7
Covington S Lanark 69 G8
Cow Ark Lancs 50 E2
Cowan Bridge Lancs 50 B2
Cowbeech E Sus 12 E5
Cowbit Lincs 37 D8
Cowbridge Lincs 47 H7
Cowbridge Som 7 B8
Cowbridge = Y Bont-Faen V Glam 14 D5
Cowdale Derbys 44 E4
Cowden Kent 12 B3
Cowdenbeath Fife 69 A10
Cowdenburn Borders 69 E11
Cowers Lane Derbys 45 H7
Cowes IoW 10 E3
Cowesby N Yorks 58 H5
Cowfold W Sus 11 B11
Cowgill Cumb 57 H9
Cowie Aberds 83 E10
Cowie Stirling 69 B7
Cowley Devon 7 G8
Cowley Glos 26 G6
Cowley London 19 C7
Cowley Oxon 18 A2
Cowleymoor Devon 7 E8
Cowling Lancs 50 H1
Cowling N Yorks 50 E5
Cowling N Yorks 58 H3
Cowlinge Suff 30 C4
Cowpe Lancs 50 G4
Cowpen Northumb 63 E8
Cowpen Bewley Stockton 58 D5
Cowplain Hants 10 C5
Cowshill Durham 57 B10
Cowslip Green N Som 15 E10
Cowstrandburn Fife 69 A9
Cowthorpe N Yorks 51 D10
Cox Common Suff 39 G9
Cox Green Windsor 18 D5
Cox Moor Notts 45 G9
Coxbank Ches E 34 A2
Coxbench Derbys 35 A9
Coxford Norf 38 C4
Coxford Soton 10 C2
Coxheath Kent 20 F4
Coxhill Kent 21 G9
Coxhoe Durham 58 C4
Coxley Som 15 G11
Coxwold N Yorks 51 B11
Coychurch Bridgend 14 D5
Coylton S Ayrs 67 D7
Coylumbridge Highld 81 B11
Coynach Aberds 82 C6
Coynachie Aberds 88 E4
Coytrahen Bridgend 14 C4
Crabadon Devon 5 F8
Crabbs Cross Worcs 27 B7
Crabtree W Sus 11 B11
Crackenthorpe Cumb 57 D8
Crackington Haven Corn 4 B2
Crackley Warks 27 A9
Crackleybank Shrops 34 D3
Crackpot N Yorks 57 G11
Cracoe N Yorks 50 C5
Craddock Devon 7 E9
Cradhlastadh W Isles 90 D5
Cradley Hereford 26 D4
Cradley Heath W Mid 34 G5
Crafthole Corn 4 F4
Cragg Vale W Yorks 50 G6
Craggan Highld 82 A2
Craggie Highld 87 H10
Craggie Highld 93 H11
Craghead Durham 58 A3
Crai Powys 24 F5
Craibstone Moray 88 C4
Craichie Angus 77 C8
Craig Dumfries 55 B9
Craig Dumfries 55 C9
Craig Highld 86 G3
Craig Castle Aberds 82 A6
Craig-cefn-parc Swansea 14 A2
Craig Penllyn V Glam 14 D5
Craig-y-don Conwy 41 B9
Craig-y-nos Powys 24 G5
Craiganor Lodge Perth 75 B9
Craigdam Aberds 89 E8
Craigdarroch Dumfries 60 D3
Craigdarroch Highld 86 F7
Craigdhu Highld 86 G7
Craigearn Aberds 83 B9
Craigellachie Moray 88 D2
Craigencross Dumfries 54 C3
Craigend Perth 76 E4
Craigend Stirling 68 B6
Craigendive Argyll 73 E9
Craigendoran Argyll 68 B2
Craigends Renfs 68 D3
Craigens Argyll 64 B3
Craigens E Ayrs 67 E8
Craighat Stirling 68 B3
Craighead Fife 77 G9
Craighlaw Mains Dumfries 54 C6
Craighouse Argyll 72 G4
Craigie Aberds 83 B11
Craigie Dundee 77 D7
Craigie Perth 76 C4
Craigie Perth 76 E4
Craigie S Ayrs 67 C7
Craigiefield Orkney 95 G5
Craigielaw E Loth 70 C3
Craiglockhart Edin 69 C11
Craigmalloch E Ayrs 67 G7
Craigmaud Aberds 89 C8
Craigmillar Edin 69 C11
Craigmore Argyll 73 G10
Craignant Shrops 33 B8
Craigneuk N Lanark 68 D6
Craigneuk N Lanark 68 E6
Craignure Argyll 79 H10
Craigo Angus 77 A9
Craigow Perth 76 G3
Craigrothie Fife 76 F6
Craigroy Moray 87 F14
Craigruie Stirling 75 E7
Craigston Castle Aberds 89 C7
Craigton Aberdeen 83 C10
Craigton Angus 76 B6
Craigton Angus 77 D8
Craigton Highld 87 B9
Craigtown Highld 93 D11
Craik Borders 61 C9
Crail Fife 77 G9
Crailing Borders 62 A2
Crailinghall Borders 62 A2
Craiselound N Lincs 45 C11
Crakehill N Yorks 51 B10
Crakemarsh Staffs 35 B6
Crambe N Yorks 52 C3
Cramlington Northumb 63 F8
Cramond Edin 69 C10
Cramond Bridge Edin 69 C10
Cranage Ches E 43 F10
Cranberry Staffs 34 B4
Cranborne Dorset 9 C9
Cranbourne Brack 18 D6
Cranbrook Devon 7 G9
Cranbrook Kent 13 C6
Cranbrook Common Kent 13 C6
Crane Moor S Yorks 45 B7
Crane's Corner Norf 38 D5
Cranfield C Beds 28 D6
Cranford London 19 D8
Cranford St Andrew Northants 36 H5
Cranford St John Northants 36 H5
Cranham Glos 26 G5
Cranham London 20 C2
Crank Mers 43 C8
Crank Wood Gtr Man 43 B9
Cranleigh Sur 19 H7
Cranley Suff 31 A8
Cranmer Green Suff 31 A7
Cranmore IoW 10 F2

D

E

Easterton Wilts 17 F7
Eastertown Som 15 F9
Eastertown of Auchleuchries Aberds 89 E10
Eastfield N Lanark 69 D7
Eastfield N Yorks 52 A6
Eastfield Hall Northumb 63 C8
Eastgate Durham 57 C11
Eastgate Norf 39 C7
Eastham Mers 42 D6
Eastham Ferry Mers 42 D6
Easthampstead Brack 18 E5
Eastheath Wokingham 18 E5
Easthope Shrops 34 F1
Easthorpe Essex 30 F6
Easthorpe Leics 36 B4
Easthorpe Notts 45 G11
Easthouses Midloth 70 D2
Eastington Devon 7 F6
Eastington Glos 26 H4
Eastington Glos 27 G8
Eastleach Martin Glos 27 H9
Eastleach Turville Glos 27 H8
Eastleigh Devon 6 D3
Eastleigh Hants 10 C3
Eastling Kent 20 F6
Eastmoor Derbys 45 E7
Eastmoor Norf 38 E3
Eastney Ptsmth 10 E5
Eastnor Hereford 26 E4
Eastoft N Lincs 52 H4
Eastoke Hants 10 E6
Easton Cambs 29 A8
Easton Cumb 61 F10
Easton Cumb 61 H8
Easton Devon 5 C8
Easton Dorset 8 G5
Easton Hants 10 A4
Easton Lincs 36 C5
Easton Norf 39 D7
Easton Som 15 G11
Easton Suff 31 C9
Easton Wilts 16 D5
Easton Grey Wilts 16 C5
Easton-in-Gordano N Som 15 D11
Easton Maudit Northants 28 C5
Easton on the Hill Northants 36 E6
Easton Royal Wilts 17 E9
Eastpark Dumfries 60 G6
Eastrea Cambs 37 F8
Eastriggs Dumfries 61 G8
Eastrington E Yorks 52 F3
Eastry Kent 21 F10
Eastville Bristol 16 D3
Eastville Lincs 47 G8
Eastwell Leics 36 C3
Eastwick Herts 29 G11
Eastwick Shetland 96 F5
Eastwood Notts 45 H8
Eastwood Southend 20 C5
Eastwood W Yorks 50 G5
Eathorpe Warks 27 B10
Eaton Ches E 44 F2
Eaton Ches W 43 F8
Eaton Leics 36 C3
Eaton Norf 39 E8
Eaton Notts 45 E11
Eaton Oxon 17 A11
Eaton Shrops 33 G9
Eaton Shrops 33 G11
Eaton Bishop Hereford 25 E11
Eaton Bray C Beds 28 F6
Eaton Constantine Shrops 34 E1
Eaton Green C Beds 28 F6
Eaton Hastings Oxon 17 B9
Eaton on Tern Shrops 34 C2
Eaton Socon Cambs 29 C8
Eavestone N Yorks 51 C8
Ebberston N Yorks 52 A4
Ebbesbourne Wake Wilts 9 B8
Ebbw Vale = Glyn Ebwy Bl Gwent 25 H8
Ebchester Durham 63 H7
Ebford Devon 5 C10
Ebley Glos 26 H5
Ebnal Ches W 43 H7
Ebrington Glos 27 D8
Ecchinswell Hants 17 F11
Ecclaw Borders 70 D6
Ecclefechan Dumfries 61 F7
Eccles Borders 70 F6
Eccles Gtr Man 43 C10
Eccles Kent 20 E4
Eccles on Sea Norf 39 C10
Eccles Road Norf 38 F6
Ecclesall S Yorks 45 D7
Ecclesfield S Yorks 45 C7
Ecclesgreig Aberds 83 G9
Eccleshall Staffs 34 C4
Eccleshill W Yorks 51 F7
Ecclesmachan W Loth 69 C9
Eccleston Ches W 43 F7
Eccleston Lancs 49 H5
Eccleston Mers 43 C7
Eccleston Park Mers 43 C7
Eccup W Yorks 51 E8
Echt Aberds 83 C9
Eckford Borders 70 H6
Eckington Derbys 45 E8
Eckington Worcs 26 D6
Ecton Northants 28 B5
Edale Derbys 44 D5
Edburton W Sus 11 C11
Edderside Cumb 56 B2
Edderton Highld 87 C10
Eddistone Devon 6 D1
Eddleston Borders 69 F11
Eden Park London 19 E10
Edenbridge Kent 19 G11
Edenfield Lancs 50 H3
Edenhall Cumb 57 C7
Edenham Lincs 37 C6
Edensor Derbys 44 F6
Edentaggart Argyll 68 A2
Edenthorpe S Yorks 45 B10
Edentown Cumb 61 H9
Ederline Argyll 73 C7
Edern Gwyn 40 G4
Edgarley Som 15 H11
Edgbaston W Mid 35 G6
Edgcott Bucks 28 F3
Edgcott Som 7 C7
Edge Shrops 33 E9
Edge End Glos 26 G2
Edge Green Ches W 43 G7
Edge Hill Mers 42 C6
Edgebolton Shrops 34 C1
Edgefield Norf 39 B6
Edgefield Street Norf 39 B6
Edgeside Lancs 50 G4
Edgeworth Glos 26 H6
Edgmond Telford 34 D3
Edgmond Marsh Telford 34 C3
Edgton Shrops 33 G9
Edgware London 19 B8
Edgworth Blackburn 50 H3
Edinample Stirling 75 E8
Edinbane Highld 85 C8
Edinburgh Edin 69 C11
Edingale Staffs 35 D8
Edingight Ho. Moray 88 C5
Edingley Notts 45 G10
Edingthorpe Norf 39 B9
Edingthorpe Green Norf 39 B9
Edington Som 15 H9
Edington Wilts 16 F6
Edintore Moray 88 D4
Edith Weston Rutland 36 E5
Edithmead Som 15 G9
Edlesborough Bucks 28 G6
Edlingham Northumb 63 C7
Edlington Lincs 46 E6
Edmondsham Dorset 9 C9
Edmondsley Durham 58 B3
Edmondthorpe Leics 36 D4
Edmonstone Orkney 95 F6
Edmonton London 19 B10
Edmundbyers Durham 58 A1
Ednam Borders 70 G6
Ednaston Derbys 35 A8
Edradynate Perth 75 B11
Edrom Borders 71 E7
Edstaston Shrops 33 B11
Edstone Warks 27 B8
Edvin Loach Hereford 26 C3
Edwalton Notts 36 B1
Edwardstone Suff 30 D6
Edwinsford Carms 24 E3
Edwinstowe Notts 45 F10
Edworth C Beds 29 D9
Edwyn Ralph Hereford 26 C3
Edzell Angus 83 G7
Efail Isaf Rhondda 14 C6
Efailnewydd Gwyn 40 G5
Efailwen Carms 22 D6
Efenechtyd Denb 42 G4
Effingham Sur 19 F8
Effirth Shetland 96 H5
Efford Devon 7 F7
Egdon Worcs 26 C6
Egerton Gtr Man 43 A10
Egerton Kent 20 G6
Egerton Forstal Kent 20 G5
Eggborough N Yorks 52 G1
Eggbuckland Plym 4 F6
Eggington C Beds 28 F6
Egginton Derbys 35 C8
Egglescliffe Stockton 58 E5
Eggleston Durham 57 D11
Egham Sur 19 D7
Egleton Rutland 36 E4
Eglingham Northumb 63 B7
Egloshayle Corn 3 B8
Egloskerry Corn 4 C3
Eglwys-Brewis V Glam 14 E6
Eglwys Cross Wrex 33 A10
Eglwys Fach Ceredig 32 F2
Eglwysbach Conwy 41 C10
Eglwyswen Pembs 22 C6
Eglwyswrw Pembs 22 C6
Egmanton Notts 45 F11
Egremont Cumb 56 E2
Egremont Mers 42 C6
Egton N Yorks 59 F9
Egton Bridge N Yorks 59 F9
Eight Ash Green Essex 30 F6
Eignaig Highld 79 G10
Eil Highld 81 B10
Eilanreach Highld 85 G13
Eilean Darach Highld 86 C4
Eileanach Lodge Highld 87 E8
Einacleite W Isles 90 E6
Eisgean W Isles 91 F8
Eisingrug Gwyn 41 G8
Elan Village Powys 24 B6
Elberton S Glos 16 C3
Elburton Plym 4 F6
Elcho Perth 76 E4
Elcombe Swindon 17 C8
Eldernell Cambs 37 F9
Eldersfield Worcs 26 E5
Elderslie Renfs 68 D3
Eldon Durham 58 D3
Eldrick S Ayrs 54 A5
Eldroth N Yorks 50 C3
Eldwick W Yorks 51 E7
Elfhowe Cumb 56 G6
Elford Northumb 71 G10
Elford Staffs 35 D7
Elgin Moray 88 B2
Elgol Highld 85 G10
Elham Kent 21 G8
Elie Fife 77 G7
Elim Anglesey 40 B5
Eling Hants 10 C2
Elishader Highld 85 B10
Elishaw Northumb 62 D4
Elkesley Notts 45 E10
Elkstone Glos 26 G6
Ellan Highld 81 A10
Elland W Yorks 51 G7
Ellary Argyll 72 F6
Ellastone Staffs 35 A7
Ellemford Borders 70 D6
Ellenbrook IoM 48 E3
Ellenhall Staffs 34 C4
Ellen's Green Sur 19 H7
Ellerbeck N Yorks 58 G5
Ellerburn N Yorks 52 A4
Ellerby N Yorks 59 E8
Ellerdine Heath Telford 34 C2
Ellerhayes Devon 7 F8
Elleric Argyll 74 C3
Ellerker E Yorks 52 G5
Ellerton E Yorks 52 F3
Ellerton Shrops 34 C3
Ellesborough Bucks 28 H5
Ellesmere Shrops 33 B10
Ellesmere Port Ches W 43 E7
Ellingham Norf 39 F9
Ellingham Northumb 71 H10
Ellingstring N Yorks 51 A7
Ellington Cambs 29 A8
Ellington Northumb 63 D8
Elliot Angus 77 D9
Ellisfield Hants 18 G3
Ellistown Leics 35 D10
Ellon Aberds 89 E9
Ellonby Cumb 56 C6
Ellough Suff 39 G10
Elloughton E Yorks 52 G5
Ellwood Glos 26 H2
Elm Cambs 37 E10
Elm Hill Dorset 9 B7
Elm Park London 20 C2
Elmbridge Worcs 26 B6
Elmdon Essex 29 E11
Elmdon W Mid 35 G7
Elmdon Heath W Mid 35 G7
Elmers End London 19 E10
Elmesthorpe Leics 35 F10
Elmfield IoW 10 E5
Elmhurst Staffs 35 D7
Elmley Castle Worcs 26 D6
Elmley Lovett Worcs 26 B5
Elmore Glos 26 G4
Elmore Back Glos 26 G4
Elmscott Devon 6 D1
Elmsett Suff 31 D7
Elmstead Market Essex 31 F7
Elmsted Kent 21 G8
Elmstone Kent 21 E9
Elmstone Hardwicke Glos 26 F6
Elmswell E Yorks 52 D5
Elmswell Suff 30 B6
Elmton Derbys 45 E9
Elphin Highld 92 H5
Elphinstone E Loth 70 C2
Elrick Aberds 83 C10
Elrig Dumfries 54 E6
Elsdon Northumb 62 D5
Elsecar S Yorks 45 C7
Elsenham Essex 30 F2
Elsfield Oxon 28 G2
Elsham N Lincs 46 A4
Elsing Norf 39 D6
Elslack N Yorks 50 E5
Elson Shrops 33 B9
Elsrickle S Lanark 69 F9
Elstead Sur 18 G6
Elsted W Sus 11 C7
Elsthorpe Lincs 37 C6
Elstob Durham 58 D4
Elston Notts 45 H11
Elston Wilts 17 G7
Elstone Devon 6 E5
Elstow Bedford 29 D7
Elstree Herts 19 B8
Elstronwick E Yorks 53 F8
Elswick Lancs 49 F4
Elsworth Cambs 29 B10
Elterwater Cumb 56 F5
Eltham London 19 D11
Eltisley Cambs 29 C9
Elton Cambs 37 F6
Elton Ches W 43 E7
Elton Derbys 44 F6
Elton Glos 26 G4
Elton Hereford 25 A11
Elton Notts 36 B3
Elton Stockton 58 E5
Elton Green Ches W 43 E7
Elvanfoot S Lanark 60 B5
Elvaston Derbys 35 B10
Elveden Suff 38 H4
Elvingston E Loth 70 C3
Elvington Kent 21 F9
Elvington York 52 E2
Elwick Hrtlpl 58 C5
Elwick Northumb 71 G10
Elworth Ches E 43 F10
Elworthy Som 7 C9
Ely Cambs 37 G11
Ely Cardiff 15 D7
Emberton M Keynes 28 D5
Embleton Cumb 56 C3
Embleton Northumb 63 A8
Embo Highld 87 B11
Embo Street Highld 87 B11
Emborough Som 16 F3
Embsay N Yorks 50 D6
Emersons Green S Glos 16 D3
Emery Down Hants 10 D1
Emley W Yorks 44 A6
Emmbrook Wokingham 18 E4
Emmer Green Reading 18 D4
Emmington Oxon 18 A4
Emneth Norf 37 E10
Emneth Hungate Norf 37 E11
Empingham Rutland 36 E5
Empshott Hants 11 A6
Emstrey Shrops 33 D11
Emsworth Hants 10 D6
Enborne W Berks 17 E11
Enchmarsh Shrops 33 F11
Enderby Leics 35 F11
Endmoor Cumb 49 A5
Endon Staffs 44 G3
Endon Bank Staffs 44 G3
Enfield London 19 B10
Enfield Wash London 19 B10
Enford Wilts 17 F8
Engamoor Shetland 96 H4
Engine Common S Glos 16 C3
Englefield W Berks 18 D3
Englefield Green Sur 18 D6
Englesea-brook Ches E 43 G10
English Bicknor Glos 26 G2
English Frankton Shrops 33 C10
Englishcombe Bath 16 E4
Enham Alamein Hants 17 G10
Enmore Som 8 A1
Ennerdale Bridge Cumb 56 E2
Enoch Dumfries 60 C4
Enochdhu Perth 76 A3
Ensay Argyll 78 G6
Ensbury Bmouth 9 E9
Ensdon Shrops 33 D10
Ensis Devon 6 D4
Enstone Oxon 27 F10
Enterkinfoot Dumfries 60 C4
Enterpen N Yorks 58 F5
Enville Staffs 34 G4
Eolaigearraidh W Isles 84 H2
Eorabus Argyll 78 J6
Eòropaidh W Isles 91 A10
Epperstone Notts 45 H10
Epping Essex 19 A11
Epping Green Essex 29 H11
Epping Green Herts 29 H9
Epping Upland Essex 19 A11
Eppleby N Yorks 58 E2
Eppleworth E Yorks 52 F6
Epsom Sur 19 E9
Epwell Oxon 27 D10
Epworth N Lincs 45 B11
Epworth Turbary N Lincs 45 B11
Erbistock Wrex 33 A9
Erbusaig Highld 85 F12
Erchless Castle Highld 86 G7
Erdington W Mid 35 F7
Eredine Argyll 73 C8
Eriboll Highld 92 D7
Ericstane Dumfries 60 B6
Eridge Green E Sus 12 C4
Erines Argyll 73 F7
Eriswell Suff 38 H3
Erith London 20 D2
Erlestoke Wilts 16 F6
Ermine Lincs 46 E3
Ermington Devon 5 F7
Erpingham Norf 39 B7
Errogie Highld 81 A7
Errol Perth 76 E5
Erskine Renfs 68 C3
Erskine Bridge Renfs 68 C3
Ervie Dumfries 54 C3
Erwarton Suff 31 E9
Erwood Powys 25 D7
Eryholme N Yorks 58 F4
Eryrys Denb 42 G5
Escomb Durham 58 D2
Escrick N Yorks 52 E2
Esgairdawe Carms 24 D3
Esgairgeiliog Powys 32 E3
Esh Durham 58 B2
Esh Winning Durham 58 B2
Esher Sur 19 E8
Esholt W Yorks 51 E7
Eshott Northumb 63 D8
Eshton N Yorks 50 D5
Esk Valley N Yorks 59 F9
Eskadale Highld 86 H7
Eskbank Midloth 70 D2
Eskdale Green Cumb 56 F3
Eskdalemuir Dumfries 61 D8
Eske E Yorks 53 E6
Eskham Lincs 47 C7
Esprick Lancs 49 F4
Essendine Rutland 36 D6
Essendon Herts 29 H9
Essich Highld 87 H9
Essington Staffs 34 E5
Esslemont Aberds 89 F9
Eston Redcar 59 E6
Eswick Shetland 96 H6
Etal Northumb 71 G8
Etchilhampton Wilts 17 E7
Etchingham E Sus 12 D6
Etchinghill Kent 21 H8
Etchinghill Staffs 34 D6
Ethie Castle Angus 77 C9
Ethie Mains Angus 77 C9
Etling Green Norf 38 D6
Eton Windsor 18 D6
Eton Wick Windsor 18 D6
Etteridge Highld 81 D8
Ettersgill Durham 57 D10
Ettingshall W Mid 34 F5
Ettington Warks 27 D9
Etton E Yorks 52 E5
Etton Pboro 37 E7
Ettrick Borders 61 B8
Ettrickbridge Borders 61 A9
Ettrickhill Borders 61 B8
Etwall Derbys 35 B8
Euston Suff 38 H4
Euximoor Drove Cambs 37 F10
Euxton Lancs 50 H1
Evanstown Bridgend 14 C5
Evanton Highld 87 E9
Evedon Lincs 46 H4
Evelix Highld 87 B10
Evenjobb Powys 25 B9
Evenley Northants 28 E2
Evenlode Glos 27 F9
Evenwood Durham 58 D2
Evenwood Gate Durham 58 D2
Everbay Orkney 95 F7
Evercreech Som 16 H3
Everdon Northants 28 C2
Everingham E Yorks 52 E4
Everleigh Wilts 17 F9
Everley N Yorks 59 H10
Eversholt C Beds 28 E6
Evershot Dorset 8 D4
Eversley Hants 18 E4
Eversley Cross Hants 18 E4
Everthorpe E Yorks 52 F5
Everton C Beds 29 C9
Everton Hants 10 E1
Everton Mers 42 C6
Everton Notts 45 C10
Evertown Dumfries 61 F9
Evesbatch Hereford 26 D3
Evesham Worcs 27 D7
Evington Leicester 36 E2
Ewden Village S Yorks 44 C6
Ewell Sur 19 E9
Ewell Minnis Kent 21 G9
Ewelme Oxon 18 B3
Ewen Glos 17 B7
Ewenny V Glam 14 D5
Ewerby Lincs 46 H5
Ewerby Thorpe Lincs 46 H5
Ewes Dumfries 61 D9
Ewesley Northumb 62 D6
Ewhurst Sur 19 G7
Ewhurst Green E Sus 13 D6
Ewhurst Green Sur 19 H7
Ewloe Flint 42 F6
Ewloe Grn. Flint 42 F5
Ewood Blackburn 50 G2
Eworthy Devon 6 G3
Ewshot Hants 18 G5
Ewyas Harold Hereford 25 F10
Exbourne Devon 6 F5
Exbury Hants 10 E3
Exebridge Devon 7 D8
Exelby N Yorks 58 H3
Exeter Devon 7 G8
Exford Som 7 C7
Exhall Warks 27 C8
Exley Head W Yorks 50 F6
Exminster Devon 5 C10
Exmouth Devon 5 C11
Exnaboe Shetland 96 M5
Exning Suff 30 B3
Exton Devon 5 C10
Exton Hants 10 B5
Exton Rutland 36 D5
Exton Som 7 C8
Exwick Devon 7 G8
Eyam Derbys 44 E6
Eydon Northants 28 C2
Eye Hereford 25 B11
Eye Pboro 37 E8
Eye Suff 31 A8
Eye Green Pboro 37 E8
Eyemouth Borders 71 D8
Eyeworth C Beds 29 D9
Eyhorne Street Kent 20 F5
Eyke Suff 31 C10
Eynesbury Cambs 29 C8
Eynort Highld 85 F8
Eynsford Kent 20 E2
Eynsham Oxon 27 H11
Eype Dorset 8 E3
Eyre Highld 85 C9
Eyre Highld 85 E10
Eythorne Kent 21 G9
Eyton Hereford 25 B11
Eyton Shrops 33 G9
Eyton Wrex 33 A9
Eyton upon the Weald Moors Telford 34 D2

F

Faccombe Hants 17 F10
Faceby N Yorks 58 F5
Facit Lancs 50 H4
Faddiley Ches E 43 G8
Fadmoor N Yorks 59 H7
Faerdre Swansea 14 A2
Failand N Som 15 D11
Failford S Ayrs 67 D7
Failsworth Gtr Man 44 B2
Fain Highld 86 D4
Fair Green Norf 38 D2
Fair Hill Cumb 57 C7
Fair Oak Hants 10 C3
Fair Oak Green Hants 18 E3
Fairbourne Gwyn 32 D2
Fairburn N Yorks 51 G10
Fairfield Derbys 44 E4
Fairfield Stockton 58 E5
Fairfield Worcs 34 H5
Fairfield Worcs 27 D7
Fairford Glos 17 A8
Fairhaven Lancs 49 G3
Fairlie N Ayrs 73 H11
Fairlight E Sus 13 E7
Fairlight Cove E Sus 13 E7
Fairmile Devon 7 G9
Fairmilehead Edin 69 D11
Fairoak Staffs 34 B3
Fairseat Kent 20 E3
Fairstead Essex 30 G4
Fairstead Norf 38 C2
Fairwarp E Sus 12 D3
Fairy Cottage IoM 48 D4
Fairy Cross Devon 6 D3
Fakenham Norf 38 C5
Fakenham Magna Suff 38 H5
Fala Midloth 70 D3
Fala Dam Midloth 70 D3
Falahill Borders 70 E2
Falcon Hereford 26 E3
Faldingworth Lincs 46 D4
Falfield S Glos 16 B3
Falkenham Suff 31 E9
Falkirk Falk 69 C7
Falkland Fife 76 G5
Falla Borders 62 B3
Fallgate Derbys 45 F7
Fallin Stirling 69 A7
Fallowfield Gtr Man 44 C2
Fallsidehill Borders 70 F5
Falmer E Sus 12 F2
Falmouth Corn 3 F7
Falsgrave N Yorks 59 H11
Falstone Northumb 62 E3
Fanagmore Highld 92 E4
Fangdale Beck N Yorks 59 G6
Fangfoss E Yorks 52 D3
Fankerton Falk 68 B6
Fanmore Argyll 78 G7
Fannich Lodge Highld 86 E5
Fans Borders 70 F5
Far Bank S Yorks 45 A10
Far Bletchley M Keynes 28 E5
Far Cotton Northants 28 C4
Far Forest Worcs 26 A4
Far Laund Derbys 45 H7
Far Sawrey Cumb 56 G5
Farcet Cambs 37 F8
Farden Shrops 34 H1
Fareham Hants 10 D4
Farewell Staffs 35 E6
Farforth Lincs 47 E7
Faringdon Oxon 17 B9
Farington Lancs 49 G5
Farlam Cumb 61 H11
Farlary Highld 93 J10
Farleigh N Som 15 E10
Farleigh Sur 19 E10
Farleigh Hungerford Som 16 F5
Farleigh Wallop Hants 18 G3
Farlesthorpe Lincs 47 E8
Farleton Cumb 49 A5
Farleton Lancs 50 C1
Farley Shrops 33 E9
Farley Staffs 35 A6
Farley Wilts 9 B11
Farley Green Sur 19 G7
Farley Hill Luton 29 F7
Farley Hill Wokingham 18 E4
Farleys End Glos 26 G4
Farlington N Yorks 52 C2
Farlow Shrops 34 G2
Farmborough Bath 16 E3
Farmcote Glos 27 F7
Farmcote Shrops 34 F3
Farmington Glos 27 G8
Farmoor Oxon 27 H11
Farmtown Moray 88 C5
Farnborough London 19 E11
Farnborough Hants 18 F5
Farnborough W Berks 17 C11
Farnborough Warks 27 D11
Farnborough Green Hants 18 F5
Farncombe Sur 18 G6
Farndish Bedford 28 B6
Farndon Ches W 43 G7
Farndon Notts 45 G11
Farnell Angus 77 B9
Farnham Dorset 9 C8
Farnham Essex 29 F11
Farnham N Yorks 51 C9
Farnham Suff 31 B10
Farnham Sur 18 G5
Farnham Common Bucks 18 C6
Farnham Green Essex 29 F11
Farnham Royal Bucks 18 C6
Farnhill N Yorks 50 E6
Farningham Kent 20 E2
Farnley N Yorks 51 E8
Farnley W Yorks 51 F8
Farnley Tyas W Yorks 44 A5
Farnsfield Notts 45 G10
Farnworth Gtr Man 43 B10
Farnworth Halton 43 D8
Farr Highld 81 C10
Farr Highld 87 H9
Farr Highld 93 C10
Farr House Highld 87 H9
Farringdon Devon 7 G9
Farrington Gurney Bath 16 F3
Farsley W Yorks 51 F8
Farthinghoe Northants 28 E2
Farthingloe Kent 21 G9
Farthingstone Northants 28 C3
Fartown W Yorks 51 H7
Farway Devon 7 G10
Fasag Highld 85 C13
Fascadale Highld 79 D8
Faslane Port Argyll 73 E11
Fasnacloich Argyll 74 C3
Fasnakyle Ho Highld 80 A5
Fassfern Highld 80 F2
Fatfield T&W 58 A4
Fattahead Aberds 89 C6
Faugh Cumb 57 A7
Fauldhouse W Loth 69 D8
Faulkbourne Essex 30 G4
Faulkland Som 16 F4
Fauls Shrops 34 B1
Faversham Kent 21 E7
Favillar Moray 88 E2
Fawdington N Yorks 51 B10
Fawfieldhead Staffs 44 F4
Fawkham Green Kent 20 E2
Fawler Oxon 27 G10
Fawley Bucks 18 C4
Fawley Hants 10 D3
Fawley W Berks 17 C10
Fawley Chapel Hereford 26 F2
Faxfleet E Yorks 52 G4
Faygate W Sus 11 A11
Fazakerley Mers 43 C6
Fazeley Staffs 35 E8
Fearby N Yorks 51 A7
Fearn Highld 87 D11
Fearn Lodge Highld 87 C9
Fearn Station Highld 87 D11
Fearnan Perth 75 C10
Fearnbeg Highld 85 C12
Fearnhead Warr 43 C9
Fearnmore Highld 85 B12
Featherstone Staffs 34 E5
Featherstone W Yorks 51 G10
Featherwood Northumb 62 C4
Feckenham Worcs 27 B7
Feering Essex 30 F5
Feetham N Yorks 57 G11
Feizor N Yorks 50 C3
Felbridge Sur 12 C2
Felbrigg Norf 39 B8
Felcourt Sur 12 B2
Felden Herts 19 A7
Felin-Crai Powys 24 F5
Felindre Carms 23 C8
Felindre Carms 23 D10
Felindre Carms 24 E3
Felindre Carms 24 F4
Felindre Ceredig 23 A10
Felindre Powys 33 G7
Felindre Swansea 14 A2
Felindre Farchog Pembs 22 C6
Felinfach Ceredig 23 A10
Felinfach Powys 25 E7
Felinfoel Carms 23 F10
Felingwm isaf Carms 23 D10
Felingwm uchaf Carms 23 D10
Felinwynt Ceredig 23 A7
Felixkirk N Yorks 51 A10
Felixstowe Suff 31 E9
Felixstowe Ferry Suff 31 E10
Felkington Northumb 71 F8
Felkirk W Yorks 45 A7
Fell Side Cumb 56 C5
Felling T&W 63 G8
Felmersham Bedford 28 C6
Felmingham Norf 39 C8
Felpham W Sus 11 E8
Felsham Suff 30 C6
Felsted Essex 30 F3
Feltham London 19 D8
Felthorpe Norf 39 D7
Felton Hereford 26 D2
Felton N Som 15 E11
Felton Northumb 63 C7
Felton Butler Shrops 33 D9
Feltwell Norf 38 F3
Fen Ditton Cambs 29 B11
Fen Drayton Cambs 29 B10
Fen End W Mid 35 H8
Fen Side Lincs 47 G7
Fenay Bridge W Yorks 51 H7
Fence Lancs 50 F4
Fence Houses T&W 58 A4
Fengate Norf 39 C7
Fengate Pboro 37 F8
Fenham Northumb 71 F9
Fenhouses Lincs 37 A8
Feniscliffe Blackburn 50 G2
Feniscowles Blackburn 50 G2
Feniton Devon 7 G10
Fenlake Bedford 29 D7
Fenny Bentley Derbys 44 G5
Fenny Bridges Devon 7 G10
Fenny Compton Warks 27 C11
Fenny Drayton Leics 35 F9
Fenny Stratford M Keynes 28 E5
Fenrother Northumb 63 D7
Fenstanton Cambs 29 B10
Fenton Cambs 37 H9
Fenton Lincs 46 E2
Fenton Lincs 46 G2
Fenton Stoke 34 A4
Fenton Barns E Loth 70 B4
Fenton Town Northumb 71 G8
Fenwick E Ayrs 67 B7
Fenwick Northumb 62 F6
Fenwick Northumb 71 F9
Fenwick S Yorks 52 H1
Feochaig Argyll 65 G8
Feock Corn 3 F7
Feolin Ferry Argyll 72 G3
Ferindonald Highld 85 H11
Feriniquarrie Highld 84 C6
Ferlochan Argyll 74 C2
Fern Angus 77 A8
Ferndale Rhondda 14 B6
Ferndown Dorset 9 D9
Ferness Highld 87 G12
Ferney Green Cumb 56 G6
Fernham Oxon 17 B9
Fernhill Heath Worcs 26 C5
Fernhurst W Sus 11 B7
Fernie Fife 76 F6
Ferniegair S Lanark 68 E6
Fernilea Highld 85 E8
Fernilee Derbys 44 E4
Ferrensby N Yorks 51 C9
Ferring W Sus 11 D9
Ferry Hill Cambs 37 G9
Ferry Point Highld 87 C10
Ferrybridge W Yorks 51 G10
Ferryden Angus 77 B10
Ferryhill Aberdeen 83 C11
Ferryhill Durham 58 C3
Ferryhill Station Durham 58 C4
Ferryside Carms 23 E8
Fersfield Norf 39 G6
Fersit Highld 80 F5
Feshiebridge Highld 81 C10
Fetcham Sur 19 F8
Fetlar Airport Shetland 96 D8
Fetterangus Aberds 89 C9
Fettercairn Aberds 83 F8
Fettes Highld 87 F8
Fewcott Oxon 28 F2
Fewston N Yorks 51 D7
Ffair-Rhos Ceredig 24 B4
Ffairfach Carms 24 F3
Ffaldybrenin Carms 24 D3
Ffarmers Carms 24 D3
Ffawyddog Powys 25 G9
Fforest Carms 23 F10
Fforest-fâch Swansea 14 B2
Ffos-y-ffin Ceredig 24 B1
Ffostrasol Ceredig 23 B8
Ffridd-Uchaf Gwyn 41 E7
Ffrith Wrex 42 G5
Ffrwd Gwyn 40 E6
Ffynnon ddrain Carms 23 D9
Ffynnon-oer Ceredig 23 A10
Ffynnongroyw Flint 42 D4
Fidden Argyll 78 J6
Fiddes Aberds 83 E10
Fiddington Glos 26 E6
Fiddington Som 7 B11
Fiddleford Dorset 9 C7
Fiddlers Hamlet Essex 19 A11
Field Staffs 34 B6
Field Broughton Cumb 49 A3
Field Dalling Norf 38 B6
Field Head Leics 35 E10
Fifehead Magdalen Dorset 9 B6
Fifehead Neville Dorset 9 C6
Fifield Oxon 27 G9
Fifield Wilts 17 F8
Fifield Windsor 18 D6
Fifield Bavant Wilts 9 B9
Figheldean Wilts 17 G8
Filands Wilts 16 C6
Filby Norf 39 D10
Filey N Yorks 53 A7
Filgrave M Keynes 28 D5
Filkins Oxon 17 A9
Filleigh Devon 6 D5
Filleigh Devon 7 E6
Fillingham Lincs 46 D3
Fillongley Warks 35 G8
Filton S Glos 16 D3
Fimber E Yorks 52 C4
Finavon Angus 77 B7
Finchairn Argyll 73 C8
Fincham Norf 38 E2
Finchampstead Wokingham 18 E4
Finchdean Hants 10 C6
Finchingfield Essex 30 E3
Finchley London 19 B9
Findern Derbys 35 B9
Findhorn Moray 87 E13
Findhorn Bridge Highld 81 A10
Findo Gask Perth 76 E3
Findochty Moray 88 B4
Findon Aberds 83 D11
Findon W Sus 11 D10
Findon Mains Highld 87 E9
Findrack Ho. Aberds 83 C8
Finedon Northants 28 A6
Fingal Street Suff 31 B9
Fingask Aberds 89 F7
Fingerpost Worcs 26 A4
Fingest Bucks 18 B4
Finghall N Yorks 58 H2
Fingland Cumb 61 H8
Fingland Dumfries 60 B3
Finglesham Kent 21 F10
Fingringhoe Essex 31 F7
Finlarig Stirling 75 D8
Finmere Oxon 28 E3
Finnart Perth 75 B8
Finningham Suff 31 B8
Finningley S Yorks 45 C10
Finnygaud Aberds 88 C5
Finsbury London 19 C10
Finstall Worcs 26 B6
Finsthwaite Cumb 56 H5
Finstock Oxon 27 G10
Finstown Orkney 95 G4
Fintry Aberds 89 C7
Fintry Dundee 77 D7
Fintry Stirling 68 B5
Finzean Aberds 83 D8
Fionnphort Argyll 78 J6
Fionnsbhagh W Isles 90 J5
Fir Tree Durham 58 C2
Firbeck S Yorks 45 D9
Firby N Yorks 52 C3
Firby N Yorks 58 H3
Firgrove Gtr Man 44 A3
Firsby Lincs 47 F8
Firsdown Wilts 9 A11
First Coast Highld 86 B2
Fishbourne IoW 10 E4
Fishbourne W Sus 11 D7
Fishburn Durham 58 C4
Fishcross Clack 75 H11
Fisher Place Cumb 56 E5
Fisherford Aberds 89 E6
Fisher's Pond Hants 10 B3
Fisherstreet W Sus 11 A8
Fisherton Highld 87 F10
Fisherton S Ayrs 66 E5
Fishguard = Abergwaun Pembs 22 C4
Fishlake S Yorks 45 A10
Fishleigh Barton Devon 6 D4
Fishponds Bristol 16 D3
Fishpool Glos 26 F3
Fishtoft Lincs 37 A9
Fishtoft Drove Lincs 47 H7
Fishtown of Usan Angus 77 B10
Fishwick Borders 71 E8
Fiskavaig Highld 85 E8
Fiskerton Lincs 46 E4
Fiskerton Notts 45 G11
Fitling E Yorks 53 F8
Fittleton Wilts 17 G8
Fittleworth W Sus 11 C9
Fitton End Cambs 37 D10
Fitz Shrops 33 D10
Fitzhead Som 7 D10
Fitzwilliam W Yorks 45 A8
Fiunary Highld 79 G9
Five Acres Glos 26 G2
Five Ashes E Sus 12 D4
Five Oak Green Kent 20 G3
Five Oaks Jersey 11
Five Oaks W Sus 11 B9
Five Roads Carms 23 F9
Fivecrosses Ches W 43 E8
Fivehead Som 8 B2
Flack's Green Essex 30 G4
Flackwell Heath Bucks 18 C5
Fladbury Worcs 26 D6
Fladdabister Shetland 96 K6
Flagg Derbys 44 F5
Flamborough E Yorks 53 B8
Flamstead Herts 29 G7
Flamstead End Herts 19 A10
Flansham W Sus 11 D8
Flanshaw W Yorks 51 G9
Flasby N Yorks 50 D5
Flash Staffs 44 F4
Flashader Highld 85 C8
Flask Inn N Yorks 59 F10
Flaunden Herts 19 A7
Flawborough Notts 36 A3
Flawith N Yorks 51 C10
Flax Bourton N Som 15 E11
Flaxby N Yorks 51 D9
Flaxholme Derbys 35 A9
Flaxley Glos 26 G3
Flaxpool Som 7 C10
Flaxton N Yorks 52 C2
Fleckney Leics 36 F2
Flecknoe Warks 28 B2
Fledborough Notts 46 E2
Fleet Hants 10 D6
Fleet Hants 18 F5
Fleet Lincs 37 C9
Fleet Hargate Lincs 37 C9
Fleetham Northumb 71 H10
Fleetlands Hants 10 D4
Fleetville Herts 29 H8
Fleetwood Lancs 49 E3
Flemingston V Glam 14 E6
Flemington S Lanark 68 E5
Flempton Suff 30 B5
Fleoideabhagh W Isles 90 J5
Fletchertown Cumb 56 B4
Fletching E Sus 12 D3
Flexbury Corn 4 A3
Flexford Sur 18 G6
Flimby Cumb 56 C2
Flimwell E Sus 12 C6
Flint = Y Fflint Flint 42 E5
Flint Mountain Flint 42 E5
Flintham Notts 45 H11
Flinton E Yorks 53 F8
Flintsham Hereford 25 C10
Flitcham Norf 38 C3
Flitton C Beds 29 E7
Flitwick C Beds 29 E7
Flixborough N Lincs 52 H4
Flixborough Stather N Lincs 46 A2
Flixton Gtr Man 43 C10
Flixton N Yorks 52 B6
Flixton Suff 39 G9
Flockton W Yorks 44 A6
Flodaigh W Isles 84 C3
Flodden Northumb 71 G8
Flodigarry Highld 85 A9
Flood's Ferry Cambs 37 F9
Flookburgh Cumb 49 B3
Florden Norf 39 F7
Flore Northants 28 B3
Flotterton Northumb 62 C5
Flowton Suff 31 D7
Flush House W Yorks 44 B5
Flushing Aberds 89 D10
Flushing Corn 3 F7
Flyford Flavell Worcs 26 C6
Foals Green Suff 31 A9
Fobbing Thurrock 20 C4
Fochabers Moray 88 C3
Fochriw Caerph 25 H8
Fockerby N Lincs 52 H4
Fodderletter Moray 82 A3
Fodderty Highld 87 F8
Foel Powys 32 D5
Foel-gastell Carms 23 E10
Foffarty Angus 77 C7
Foggathorpe E Yorks 52 F3
Fogo Borders 70 F6
Fogorig Borders 70 F6
Foindle Highld 92 E4
Folda Angus 76 A4
Fole Staffs 34 B6
Foleshill W Mid 35 G9
Folke Dorset 8 C5
Folkestone Kent 21 H9
Folkingham Lincs 37 B6
Folkington E Sus 12 F4
Folksworth Cambs 37 G7
Folkton N Yorks 53 B6
Folla Rule Aberds 89 E7
Follifoot N Yorks 51 D9
Folly Gate Devon 6 G4
Fonthill Bishop Wilts 9 A8
Fonthill Gifford Wilts 9 A8
Fontmell Magna Dorset 9 C7
Fontwell W Sus 11 D8
Foolow Derbys 44 E5
Foots Cray London 19 D11
Forbestown Aberds 82 B5
Force Mills Cumb 56 G5
Forcett N Yorks 58 E2
Ford Argyll 73 C7
Ford Bucks 28 H4
Ford Devon 6 D3
Ford Glos 27 F7
Ford Northumb 71 G8
Ford Shrops 33 D10
Ford Staffs 44 G4
Ford W Sus 11 D9
Ford Wilts 16 D5
Ford End Essex 30 G3
Ford Street Som 7 E10
Fordcombe Kent 12 B4
Fordell Fife 69 B10
Forden Powys 33 E8
Forder Green Devon 5 E8
Fordham Cambs 30 A3
Fordham Essex 30 F6
Fordham Norf 38 F2
Fordhouses W Mid 34 E5
Fordingbridge Hants 9 C10
Fordon E Yorks 52 B6
Fordoun Aberds 83 F9
Ford's Green Suff 31 B7
Fordstreet Essex 30 F6
Fordwells Oxon 27 G10
Fordwich Kent 21 F8
Fordyce Aberds 88 B5
Forebridge Staffs 34 C5
Forest Durham 57 C10
Forest Becks Lancs 50 D3
Forest Gate London 19 C11
Forest Green Sur 19 G8
Forest Hall Cumb 57 F7
Forest Head Cumb 61 H11
Forest Hill Oxon 28 H2
Forest Lane Head N Yorks 51 D9
Forest Lodge Argyll 74 C5
Forest Lodge Highld 82 B2
Forest Lodge Perth 81 F11
Forest Mill Clack 69 A8
Forest Row E Sus 12 C3
Forest Town Notts 45 F9
Forestburn Gate Northumb 62 D6
Foresterseat Moray 88 C1
Forestside W Sus 11 C6
Forfar Angus 77 B7
Forgandenny Perth 76 F3
Forge Powys 32 F3
Forge Side Torf 25 H9
Forgewood N Lanark 68 E6
Forgie Moray 88 C3
Forglen Ho. Aberds 89 C6
Formby Mers 42 B6
Forncett End Norf 39 F7
Forncett St Mary Norf 39 F7
Forncett St Peter Norf 39 F7
Forneth Perth 76 C3
Fornham All Saints Suff 30 B5
Fornham St Martin Suff 30 B5
Forres Moray 87 F13
Forrest Lodge Dumfries 67 H8
Forrestfield N Lanark 69 D7
Forsbrook Staffs 34 A5
Forse Highld 94 G4
Forse Ho. Highld 94 G4
Forsinain Highld 93 E12
Forsinard Highld 93 E11
Forsinard Station Highld 93 E11
Forston Dorset 8 E5
Fort Augustus Highld 80 C5
Fort George Guern 11
Fort George Highld 87 F10
Fort William Highld 80 F3
Forteviot Perth 76 F3
Forth S Lanark 69 E8
Forth Road Bridge Edin 69 C10
Forthampton Glos 26 E5
Fortingall Perth 75 C10
Forton Hants 17 G11
Forton Lancs 49 D4
Forton Shrops 33 D10
Forton Som 8 D2
Forton Staffs 34 C3
Forton Heath Shrops 33 D10
Fortrie Aberds 89 D6
Fortrose Highld 87 F10
Fortuneswell Dorset 8 G5
Forty Green Bucks 18 B6
Forty Hill London 19 B10
Forward Green Suff 31 C7
Fosbury Wilts 17 F10
Fosdyke Lincs 37 B9
Foss Perth 75 B10
Foss Cross Glos 27 H7
Fossebridge Glos 27 G7
Foster Street Essex 29 H11
Fosterhouses S Yorks 45 A10
Foston Derbys 35 B7
Foston Lincs 36 A4
Foston N Yorks 52 C2
Foston on the Wolds E Yorks 53 D7
Fotherby Lincs 47 C7
Fotheringhay Northants 37 F6
Foubister Orkney 95 H6
Foul Mile E Sus 12 E5
Foulby W Yorks 51 H9
Foulden Borders 71 E8
Foulden Norf 38 F3
Foulis Castle Highld 87 E8
Foulridge Lancs 50 E4
Foulsham Norf 39 C6
Fountainhall Borders 70 F3
Four Ashes Staffs 34 G4
Four Ashes Suff 31 A7
Four Crosses Powys 33 D8
Four Crosses Powys 33 E6
Four Crosses Wrex 42 G5
Four Elms Kent 19 G11
Four Forks Som 7 C11
Four Gotes Cambs 37 D10
Four Lane Ends Ches W 43 F8
Four Lanes Corn 2 F5
Four Marks Hants 10 A5
Four Mile Bridge Anglesey 40 C4
Four Oaks E Sus 13 D7
Four Oaks W Mid 35 F7
Four Oaks W Mid 35 G8
Four Roads Carms 23 F9
Four Roads IoM 48 F2
Four Throws Kent 13 D6
Fourlane Ends Derbys 45 G7
Fourlanes End Ches E 44 G2
Fourpenny Highld 87 B11
Fourstones Northumb 62 G4
Fovant Wilts 9 B9
Foveran Aberds 89 F9
Fowey Corn 4 F2
Fowley Common Warr 43 C9
Fowlis Angus 76 D6
Fowlis Wester Perth 76 E2
Fowlmere Cambs 29 D11
Fownhope Hereford 26 E2
Fox Corner Sur 18 F6
Fox Lane Hants 18 F5
Fox Street Essex 31 F7
Foxbar Renfs 68 D3
Foxcombe Hill Oxon 17 A11
Foxdale IoM 48 E2
Foxearth Essex 30 D5
Foxfield Cumb 56 H4
Foxham Wilts 16 D6
Foxhole Corn 3 D8
Foxhole Swansea 14 B2
Foxholes N Yorks 52 B6
Foxhunt Green E Sus 12 E4
Foxley Norf 38 C6
Foxley Wilts 16 C5
Foxt Staffs 44 H4
Foxton Cambs 29 D11
Foxton Durham 58 D4
Foxton Leics 36 F3
Foxup N Yorks 50 B4
Foxwist Green Ches W 43 F9
Foxwood Shrops 34 H2
Foy Hereford 26 F2
Foyers Highld 81 A6
Fraddam Corn 2 F4
Fraddon Corn 3 D8
Fradley Staffs 35 D7
Fradswell Staffs 34 B5
Fraisthorpe E Yorks 53 C7
Framfield E Sus 12 D3
Framingham Earl Norf 39 E8
Framingham Pigot Norf 39 E8
Framlingham Suff 31 B9
Frampton Dorset 8 E5
Frampton Lincs 37 B9
Frampton Cotterell S Glos 16 C3
Frampton Mansell Glos 16 A6
Frampton on Severn Glos 26 H4
Frampton West End Lincs 37 A8
Framsden Suff 31 C8
Framwellgate Moor Durham 58 B3
Franche Worcs 34 H4
Frankby Mers 42 D5
Frankley Worcs 34 G5
Frank's Bridge Powys 25 C8
Frankton Warks 27 A11
Frant E Sus 12 C4
Fraserburgh Aberds 89 B9
Frating Green Essex 31 F7
Fratton Ptsmth 10 E5
Freathy Corn 4 F4
Freckenham Suff 30 A3
Freckleton Lancs 49 G4
Freeby Leics 36 C4
Freehay Staffs 34 A6
Freeland Oxon 27 G11
Freester Shetland 96 H6
Freethorpe Norf 39 E10
Freiston Lincs 37 A9
Fremington Devon 6 C4
Fremington N Yorks 58 G1
Frenchay S Glos 16 D3
Frenchbeer Devon 5 C7
Frenich Stirling 75 G7
Frensham Sur 18 G5
Fresgoe Highld 93 C12
Freshfield Mers 42 B5
Freshford Bath 16 E4
Freshwater IoW 10 F2
Freshwater Bay IoW 10 F2
Freshwater East Pembs 22 G5
Fressingfield Suff 39 H8
Freston Suff 31 E8
Freswick Highld 94 D5
Fretherne Glos 26 H4
Frettenham Norf 39 D8
Freuchie Fife 76 G5
Freuchies Angus 76 A5
Freystrop Pembs 22 E4
Friar's Gate E Sus 12 C3
Friarton Perth 76 E4
Friday Bridge Cambs 37 E10
Friday Street E Sus 12 F5
Fridaythorpe E Yorks 52 D4
Friern Barnet London 19 B9
Friesland Argyll 78 F4
Friesthorpe Lincs 46 D4
Frieston Lincs 46 H3
Frieth Bucks 18 B4
Frilford Oxon 17 B11
Frilsham W Berks 18 D2
Frimley Sur 18 F5
Frimley Green Sur 18 F5
Frindsbury Medway 20 D4
Fring Norf 38 B3
Fringford Oxon 28 F3
Frinsted Kent 20 F5
Frinton-on-Sea Essex 31 F9
Friockheim Angus 77 C8
Friog Gwyn 32 D2
Frisby on the Wreake Leics 36 D2
Friskney Lincs 47 G8
Friskney Eaudike Lincs 47 G8
Friskney Tofts Lincs 47 G8
Friston E Sus 12 G4
Friston Suff 31 B11
Fritchley Derbys 45 G7
Frith Bank Lincs 47 H7
Frith Common Worcs 26 B3
Fritham Hants 9 C11
Frithelstock Devon 6 E3
Frithelstock Stone Devon 6 E3
Frithville Lincs 47 G7
Frittenden Kent 13 B7
Frittiscombe Devon 5 G9
Fritton Norf 39 E10
Fritton Norf 39 F8
Fritwell Oxon 28 F2
Frizinghall W Yorks 51 F7
Frizington Cumb 56 E2
Frocester Glos 16 A4
Frodesley Shrops 33 E11
Frodingham N Lincs 46 A2
Frodsham Ches W 43 E8
Frogden Borders 70 H6
Froggatt Derbys 44 E6
Froghall Staffs 44 H4
Frogmore Devon 5 G8
Frogmore Hants 18 F5
Frognall Lincs 37 E7
Frogshail Norf 39 B8
Frolesworth Leics 35 F11
Frome Som 16 G4
Frome St Quintin Dorset 8 D4
Fromes Hill Hereford 26 D3
Fron Denb 42 F3
Fron Gwyn 40 G5
Fron Gwyn 41 E7
Fron Powys 25 B7
Fron Powys 33 E8
Fron Powys 33 F7
Froncysyllte Wrex 33 A8
Frongoch Gwyn 32 B5
Frostenden Suff 39 G10
Frosterley Durham 58 C1
Frotoft Orkney 95 F5
Froxfield Wilts 17 E9
Froxfield Green Hants 10 B6
Froyle Hants 18 G4
Fryerning Essex 20 A3
Fryton N Yorks 52 B2
Fulbeck Lincs 46 G3
Fulbourn Cambs 30 C2
Fulbrook Oxon 27 G9
Fulford Som 7 D11
Fulford Staffs 34 B5
Fulford York 52 E2
Fulham London 19 D9
Fulking W Sus 11 C11
Full Sutton E Yorks 52 D3
Fullarton Glasgow 68 D5
Fullarton N Ayrs 66 C6
Fuller Street Essex 30 G4
Fuller's Moor Ches W 43 G7
Fullerton Hants 17 H10
Fulletby Lincs 46 E6
Fullwood E Ayrs 67 A7
Fulmer Bucks 18 C6
Fulmodestone Norf 38 B5
Fulnetby Lincs 46 E4
Fulstow Lincs 47 C7
Fulwell T&W 63 H9
Fulwood Lancs 49 F5
Fulwood S Yorks 45 D7
Fundenhall Norf 39 F7
Fundenhall Street Norf 39 F7
Funtington W Sus 11 D6
Funtley Hants 10 D4
Funtullich Perth 75 E10
Funzie Shetland 96 D8
Furley Devon 8 D1
Furnace Argyll 73 C9
Furnace Carms 23 F10
Furnace End Warks 35 F8
Furneaux Pelham Herts 29 F11
Furness Vale Derbys 44 D4
Furze Platt Windsor 18 C5
Furzehill Devon 7 B6
Fyfett Som 7 E11
Fyfield Essex 30 H2
Fyfield Glos 17 A9
Fyfield Hants 17 G9
Fyfield Oxon 17 B11
Fyfield Wilts 17 E8
Fylingthorpe N Yorks 59 F10
Fyvie Aberds 89 E7

G

Gabhsann bho Dheas W Isles 91 B9
Gabhsann bho Thuath W Isles 91 B9
Gablon Highld 87 B10
Gabroc Hill E Ayrs 67 A7
Gaddesby Leics 36 D2
Gadebridge Herts 29 H7
Gaer Powys 25 F8
Gaerllwyd Mon 15 B10
Gaerwen Anglesey 40 C6
Gagingwell Oxon 27 F11
Gaick Lodge Highld 81 E9
Gailey Staffs 34 D5
Gainford Durham 58 E2
Gainsborough Lincs 46 C2
Gainsborough Suff 31 D8
Gainsford End Essex 30 E4
Gairloch Highld 85 A13
Gairlochy Highld 80 E3
Gairney Bank Perth 76 H4
Gairnshiel Lodge Aberds 82 C4
Gaisgill Cumb 57 F8
Gaitsgill Cumb 56 B5
Galashiels Borders 70 G3
Galgate Lancs 49 D4
Galhampton Som 8 B5
Gallaberry Dumfries 60 E5
Gallachoille Argyll 72 E6
Gallanach Argyll 74 E2
Gallanach Argyll 78 E5
Gallantry Bank Ches E 43 G8
Gallatown Fife 69 A11
Galley Common Warks 35 F9
Galley Hill Cambs 29 B10
Galleyend Essex 20 A4
Galleywood Essex 20 A4
Gallin Perth 75 C8
Gallowfauld Angus 77 C7
Gallows Green Staffs 35 A6
Galltair Highld 85 F13
Galmisdale Highld 78 C7
Galmpton Devon 5 G7
Galmpton Torbay 5 F9
Galphay N Yorks 51 B8
Galston E Ayrs 67 C8
Galtrigill Highld 84 C6
Gamblesby Cumb 57 C8
Gamesley Derbys 44 C4
Gamlingay Cambs 29 C9
Gammersgill N Yorks 51 A6
Gamston Notts 45 E11
Ganarew Hereford 26 G2
Ganavan Argyll 79 H11
Gang Corn 4 E4
Ganllwyd Gwyn 32 C3
Gannochy Angus 83 F7
Gannochy Perth 76 E4
Gansclet Highld 94 F5
Ganstead E Yorks 53 F7
Ganthorpe N Yorks 52 B2
Ganton N Yorks 52 B5
Garbat Highld 86 E7
Garbhallt Argyll 73 D9
Garboldisham Norf 38 G6
Garden City Flint 42 F6
Garden Village W Yorks 51 F10
Garden Village Wrex 42 G6
Gardenstown Aberds 89 B7
Garderhouse Shetland 96 J5
Gardham E Yorks 52 E5
Gardin Shetland 96 G6
Gare Hill Som 16 G4
Garelochhead Argyll 73 D11
Garford Oxon 17 B11
Garforth W Yorks 51 F10
Gargrave N Yorks 50 D5
Gargunnock Stirling 68 A6
Garlic Street Norf 39 G8
Garlieston Dumfries 55 E7
Garlinge Green Kent 21 F8
Garlogie Aberds 83 C9
Garmond Aberds 89 C8
Garmony Argyll 79 G9
Garmouth Moray 88 B3
Garn-yr-erw Torf 25 G9
Garnant Carms 24 G3
Garndiffaith Torf 15 A8
Garndolbenmaen Gwyn 40 F6
Garnedd Conwy 41 E9
Garnett Bridge Cumb 57 G7
Garnfadryn Gwyn 40 G4
Garnkirk N Lanark 68 D5
Garnlydan Bl Gwent 25 G8
Garnswllt Swansea 24 H3
Garrabost W Isles 91 D10
Garraron Argyll 73 C7
Garras Corn 2 G6
Garreg Gwyn 41 F8
Garrick Perth 75 F11
Garrigill Cumb 57 B9
Garriston N Yorks 58 G2
Garroch Dumfries 67 H8
Garrogie Lodge Highld 81 B7
Garros Corn 3 C7
Garrow Perth 75 C11
Garryhorn Dumfries 67 G8
Garsdale Cumb 57 H9
Garsdale Head Cumb 57 G9
Garsdon Wilts 16 C6
Garshall Green Staffs 34 B5
Garsington Oxon 18 A2
Garstang Lancs 49 E4
Garston Mers 43 D7
Garswood Mers 43 C8
Gartcosh N Lanark 68 D5
Garth Bridgend 14 B5
Garth Gwyn 41 C7
Garth Powys 24 D6
Garth Shetland 96 H4
Garth Wrex 33 A8
Garth Row Cumb 57 G7
Garthamlock Glasgow 68 D5
Garthbrengy Powys 25 E7
Garthdee Aberdeen 83 C11
Garthelli Ceredig 23 A10
Garthmyl Powys 33 F7
Garthorpe Leics 36 C4
Garthorpe N Lincs 52 H4
Gartly Aberds 88 E5
Gartmore Stirling 75 H8
Gartnagrenach Argyll 72 H6
Gartness N Lanark 68 D6
Gartness Stirling 68 B4
Gartocharn W Dunb 68 B3
Garton E Yorks 53 F8
Garton-on-the-Wolds E Yorks 52 D5
Gartsherrie N Lanark 68 D6
Gartymore Highld 93 H13
Garvald E Loth 70 C4
Garvamore Highld 81 D7
Garvard Argyll 72 D2
Garvault Hotel Highld 93 F10
Garve Highld 86 E6
Garvestone Norf 38 E6
Garvock Aberds 83 F9
Garvock Involyd 73 F11
Garway Hereford 25 F11
Garway Hill Hereford 25 F11
Gaskan Highld 79 D10
Gastard Wilts 16 E5
Gasthorpe Norf 38 G5
Gatcombe IoW 10 F3
Gate Burton Lincs 46 D2
Gate Helmsley N Yorks 52 D2
Gateacre Mers 43 D7
Gatebeck Cumb 57 H7
Gateford Notts 45 D9
Gateforth N Yorks 52 G1
Gatehead E Ayrs 67 C6
Gatehouse Northumb 62 E3
Gatehouse of Fleet Dumfries 55 D9
Gatelawbridge Dumfries 60 D5
Gateley Norf 38 C5
Gatenby N Yorks 58 H4
Gateshead T&W 63 G8
Gatesheath Ches W 43 F7
Gateside Aberds 83 B8
Gateside Angus 77 C7
Gateside E Renf 68 E3
Gateside Fife 76 G4
Gateside N Ayrs 67 A6
Gathurst Gtr Man 43 B8
Gatley Gtr Man 44 D2
Gattonside Borders 70 G4
Gatwick Airport W Sus 12 B1
Gaufron Powys 24 B6
Gaulby Leics 36 E2
Gauldry Fife 76 E6
Gaunt's Common Dorset 9 D9
Gautby Lincs 46 E5
Gavinton Borders 70 E6
Gawber S Yorks 45 B7
Gawcott Bucks 28 E3
Gawsworth Ches E 44 F2
Gawthorpe W Yorks 51 G8
Gawthrop Cumb 57 H8
Gawthwaite Cumb 49 A2
Gay Street W Sus 11 B9
Gaydon Warks 27 C10
Gayfield Orkney 95 C5
Gayhurst M Keynes 28 D5
Gayle N Yorks 57 H10
Gayles N Yorks 58 F2
Gayton Mers 42 D5
Gayton Norf 38 D3
Gayton Northants 28 C4
Gayton Staffs 34 C5
Gayton le Marsh Lincs 47 D8
Gayton le Wold Lincs 46 D6
Gayton Thorpe Norf 38 D3
Gaywood Norf 38 C2
Gazeley Suff 30 B4
Geanies House Highld 87 D11
Gearraidh Bhailteas W Isles 84 F2
Gearraidh Bhaird W Isles 91 E8
Gearraidh na h-Aibhne W Isles 90 D7
Gearraidh na Monadh W Isles 84 G2
Geary Highld 84 B7
Geddes House Highld 87 F11
Gedding Suff 30 C6
Geddington Northants 36 G4
Gedintailor Highld 85 E10
Gedling Notts 36 A2
Gedney Lincs 37 C10
Gedney Broadgate Lincs 37 C10
Gedney Drove End Lincs 37 C10
Gedney Dyke Lincs 37 C10
Gedney Hill Lincs 37 D9
Gee Cross Gtr Man 44 C3
Geilston Argyll 68 C2
Geirinis W Isles 84 D2
Geise Highld 94 D3
Geisiadar W Isles 90 D6
Geldeston Norf 39 F9
Gell Conwy 41 D10
Gelli Pembs 22 E5
Gelli Rhondda 14 B5
Gellideg M Tydf 25 H7
Gellifor Denb 42 F4
Gelligaer Caerph 15 B7
Gellilydan Gwyn 41 G8
Gellinudd Neath 14 A3
Gellyburn Perth 76 D3
Gellywen Carms 23 D7
Gelston Dumfries 55 D10
Gelston Lincs 36 A5
Gembling E Yorks 53 D7
Gentleshaw Staffs 35 D6
Geocrab W Isles 90 H6
George Green Bucks 19 C7
George Nympton Devon 6 D6
Georgefield Dumfries 61 D7
Georgeham Devon 6 C3
Georgetown Bl Gwent 25 H8
Gerlan Gwyn 41 D8
Germansweek Devon 6 G3
Germoe Corn 2 G4
Gerrans Corn 3 F7
Gerrards Cross Bucks 19 C7
Gestingthorpe Essex 30 E5
Geuffordd Powys 33 D8
Gib Hill Ches W 43 E9
Gibbet Hill Warks 35 G11
Gibbshill Dumfries 60 F3
Gidea Park London 20 C2
Gidleigh Devon 5 C7
Giffnock E Renf 68 E4
Gifford E Loth 70 D4
Giffordland N Ayrs 66 B5
Giffordtown Fife 76 F5
Giggleswick N Yorks 50 C4
Gilberdyke E Yorks 52 G4
Gilchriston E Loth 70 D3
Gilcrux Cumb 56 C3
Gildersome W Yorks 51 G8
Gildingwells S Yorks 45 D9
Gileston V Glam 14 E6
Gilfach Caerph 15 B7
Gilfach Goch Rhondda 14 C5
Gilfachrheda Ceredig 23 A9
Gillamoor N Yorks 59 G7
Gillar's Green Mers 43 C7
Gillen Highld 84 C7
Gilling East N Yorks 52 B2
Gilling West N Yorks 58 F2
Gillingham Dorset 9 B7
Gillingham Medway 20 E4
Gillingham Norf 39 F10
Gillock Highld 94 E4
Gillow Heath Staffs 44 G2
Gills Highld 94 C5
Gill's Green Kent 13 C6
Gilmanscleuch Borders 61 A9
Gilmerton Edin 69 D11
Gilmerton Perth 75 E11
Gilmonby Durham 57 E11
Gilmorton Leics 36 G1
Gilmourton S Lanark 68 F5
Gilsland Northumb 62 G2
Gilsland Spa Cumb 62 G2
Gilston Borders 70 E3
Gilston Herts 29 G11
Gilwern Mon 25 G9
Gimingham Norf 39 B8
Giosla W Isles 90 E6
Gipping Suff 31 B7
Gipsey Bridge Lincs 46 H6
Girdle Toll N Ayrs 66 B6
Girlsta Shetland 96 H6
Girsby N Yorks 58 F4
Girtford C Beds 29 C8
Girthon Dumfries 55 D9
Girton Cambs 29 B11
Girton Notts 46 F2
Girvan S Ayrs 66 G4
Gisburn Lancs 50 E4
Gisleham Suff 39 G11
Gislingham Suff 31 A7
Gissing Norf 39 G7
Gittisham Devon 7 G10
Gladestry Powys 25 C9
Gladsmuir E Loth 70 C3
Glais Swansea 14 A3
Glaisdale N Yorks 59 F8
Glame Highld 85 D10
Glamis Angus 76 C6
Glan Adda Gwyn 41 C7
Glan Conwy Conwy 41 C10
Glan-Conwy Conwy 41 E10
Glan-Duar Carms 23 B10
Glan-Dwyfach Gwyn 40 F6
Glan Gors Anglesey 40 C6
Glan-rhyd Gwyn 40 E6
Glan-traeth Anglesey 40 C4
Glan-y-don Flint 42 E4
Glan-y-nant Powys 32 G5
Glan-y-wern Gwyn 41 G8
Glan-yr-afon Anglesey 41 B8
Glan-yr-afon Gwyn 32 A5
Glan-yr-afon Gwyn 32 A6
Glanaman Carms 24 G3
Glandford Norf 38 A6
Glandwr Pembs 22 D6
Glandy Cross Carms 22 D6
Glandyfi Ceredig 32 F3
Glangrwyney Powys 25 G9
Glanmule Powys 33 F7
Glanrafon Ceredig 32 G2
Glanrhyd Gwyn 40 G4
Glanrhyd Pembs 22 B6
Glanton Northumb 62 B6
Glanton Pike Northumb 62 B6
Glanvilles Wootton Dorset 8 D5
Glapthorn Northants 36 F6
Glapwell Derbys 45 F8
Glas-allt Shiel Aberds 82 E4
Glasbury Powys 25 E8
Glaschoil Highld 87 H13
Glascoed Denb 42 E2
Glascoed Mon 15 A9
Glascoed Powys 33 D7
Glascorrie Aberds 82 D5
Glascote Staffs 35 E8
Glascwm Powys 25 C8
Glasdrum Argyll 74 C3
Glasfryn Conwy 42 G2
Glasgow Glasgow 68 D4
Glashvin Highld 85 B9
Glasinfryn Gwyn 41 D7
Glasnacardoch Highld 79 B9
Glasnakille Highld 85 G10
Glasphein Highld 84 D6
Glaspwll Powys 32 F3
Glassburn Highld 86 H6
Glasserton Dumfries 55 F7
Glassford S Lanark 68 F6
Glasshouse Hill Glos 26 F4
Glasshouses N Yorks 51 C7
Glasslie Fife 76 G5
Glasson Cumb 61 G8
Glasson Lancs 49 D4
Glassonby Cumb 57 C7
Glasterlaw Angus 77 B8
Glaston Rutland 36 E4
Glastonbury Som 15 H11
Glatton Cambs 37 G7
Glazebrook Warr 43 C9
Glazebury Warr 43 C9
Glazeley Shrops 34 G3
Gleadless S Yorks 45 D7
Gleadsmoss Ches E 44 F2
Gleann Tholàstaidh W Isles 91 C10
Gleaston Cumb 49 B2
Gleiniant Powys 32 F5
Glemsford Suff 30 D5
Glen Dumfries 55 D8
Glen Dumfries 60 F4
Glen Auldyn IoM 48 C4
Glen Bernisdale Highld 85 D9
Glen Ho Borders 69 G11
Glen Mona IoM 48 D4
Glen Nevis House Highld 80 F3
Glen Parva Leics 36 F1
Glen Sluain Argyll 73 D9
Glen Tanar House Aberds 82 D6
Glen Trool Lodge Dumfries 55 A7
Glen Village Falk 69 C7
Glen Vine IoM 48 E3
Glenamachrie Argyll 74 E2
Glenbarr Argyll 65 E7
Glenbeg Highld 79 E8
Glenbeg Highld 88 E1
Glenbervie Aberds 83 E9
Glenboig N Lanark 68 D6
Glenborrodale Highld 79 E9
Glenbranter Argyll 73 D10
Glenbreck Borders 60 A6
Glenbrein Lodge Highld 81 B6
Glenbrittle House Highld 85 F9
Glenbuchat Lodge Aberds 82 B5
Glenbuck E Ayrs 68 H6
Glenburn Renfs 68 D3
Glencalvie Lodge Highld 86 C7
Glencanisp Lodge Highld 92 G4
Glencaple Dumfries 60 G5
Glencarron Lodge Highld 86 F3
Glencarse Perth 76 E4
Glencassley Castle Highld 92 J7
Glenceitlein Highld 74 C4
Glencoe Highld 74 B3
Glencraig Fife 76 H4
Glencripesdale Highld 79 F9
Glencrosh Dumfries 60 E3
Glendavan Ho. Aberds 82 C6
Glendevon Perth 76 G2
Glendoe Lodge Highld 80 C6
Glendoebeg Highld 80 C6
Glendoick Perth 76 E5
Glendoll Lodge Angus 82 F4
Glendoune S Ayrs 66 G4
Glenduckie Fife 76 F5
Glendye Lodge Aberds 83 E8
Gleneagles Hotel Perth 76 F2
Gleneagles House Perth 76 G2
Glenegedale Argyll 64 C4
Glenelg Highld 85 G13
Glenernie Moray 87 G13
Glenfarg Perth 76 F4
Glenfarquhar Lodge Aberds 83 E9
Glenferness House Highld 87 G12
Glenfeshie Lodge Highld 81 D10
Glenfield Leics 35 E11
Glenfinnan Highld 79 C11
Glenfoot Perth 76 F4
Glenfyne Lodge Argyll 74 F5
Glengap Dumfries 55 D9
Glengarnock N Ayrs 66 A6
Glengorm Castle Argyll 78 F7
Glengrasco Highld 85 D9
Glenhead Farm Angus 76 A5
Glenhoul Dumfries 67 H9

Glenhurich Highld 79 E11
Glenkerry Borders 61 B8
Glenkiln Dumfries 60 F4
Glenkindie Aberds 82 B6
Glenlatterach Moray 88 C1
Glenlee Dumfries 55 A9
Glenlichorn Perth 75 F10
Glenlivet Moray 82 A3
Glenlochsie Perth 82 F2
Glenloig N Ayrs 66 C2
Glenluce Dumfries 54 D5
Glenmallan Argyll 74 H5
Glenmarksie Highld 86 F6
Glenmassan Argyll 73 E10
Glenmavis N Lanark 68 D6
Glenmaye IoM 48 E2
Glenmidge Dumfries 60 E4
Glenmore Argyll 73 B7
Glenmore Highld 85 D9
Glenmore Lodge Highld 82 C1
Glenmoy Angus 77 A7
Glenogil Angus 77 A7
Glenprosen Lodge Angus 82 G4
Glenprosen Village Angus 82 G5
Glenquiech Angus 77 A7
Glenreasdell Mains Argyll 73 H7
Glenree N Ayrs 66 D2
Glenridding Cumb 56 E5
Glenrossal Highld 92 J7
Glenrothes Fife 76 G5
Glensanda Highld 79 G11
Glensaugh Aberds 83 F8
Glenshero Lodge Highld 81 D7
Glenstockadale Dumfries 54 C3
Glenstriven Argyll 73 F9
Glentaggart S Lanark 69 H7
Glentham Lincs 46 C4
Glentirranmuir Stirling 68 A5
Glenton Aberds 83 A8
Glentress Borders 69 G11
Glentromie Lodge Highld 81 D9
Glentrool Village Dumfries 54 B6
Glentruan IoM 48 B4
Glentruim House Highld 81 D8
Glentworth Lincs 46 D3
Glenuig Highld 79 D9
Glenurquhart Highld 87 E10
Glespin S Lanark 69 H7
Gletness Shetland 96 H6
Glewstone Hereford 26 F2
Glinton Pboro 37 E7
Glooston Leics 36 F3
Glororum Northumb 71 G10
Glossop Derbys 44 C4
Gloster Hill Northumb 63 C8
Gloucester Glos 26 G5
Gloup Shetland 96 C7
Glusburn N Yorks 50 E6
Glutt Lodge Highld 93 F12
Glutton Bridge Staffs 44 F4
Glympton Oxon 27 F11
Glyn-Ceiriog Wrex 33 B8
Glyn-cywarch Gwyn 41 G8
Glyn Ebwy = Ebbw Vale Bl Gwent 25 H8
Glyn-neath = Glynedd Neath 24 H5
Glynarthen Ceredig 23 B8
Glynbrochan Powys 32 G5
Glyncoch Rhondda 14 B6
Glyncorrwg Neath 14 B4
Glynde E Sus 12 F3
Glyndebourne E Sus 12 E3
Glyndyfrdwy Denb 33 A7
Glynedd = Glyn-neath Neath 24 H5
Glynogwr Bridgend 14 C5
Glyntaff Rhondda 14 C6
Glyntawe Powys 24 G5
Gnosall Staffs 34 C4
Gnosall Heath Staffs 34 C4
Goadby Leics 36 F3
Goadby Marwood Leics 36 C3
Goat Lees Kent 21 G7
Goatacre Wilts 17 D7
Goathill Dorset 8 C5
Goathland N Yorks 59 F9
Goathurst Som 8 A1
Gobernuisgach Lodge Highld 92 E7
Gobhaig W Isles 90 G5
Gobowen Shrops 33 B9
Godalming Sur 18 G6
Godley Gtr Man 44 C3
Godmanchester Cambs 29 A9
Godmanstone Dorset 8 E5
Godmersham Kent 21 F7
Godney Som 15 G10
Godolphin Cross Corn 2 F5
Godre'r-graig Neath 24 H4
Godshill Hants 9 C10
Godshill IoW 10 F4
Godstone Sur 19 F10
Godwinscroft Hants 9 E10
Goetre Mon 25 H10
Goferydd Anglesey 40 B4
Goff's Oak Herts 19 A10
Gogar Edin 69 C10
Goginan Ceredig 32 G2
Golan Gwyn 41 F7
Golant Corn 4 F2
Golberdon Corn 4 D4
Golborne Gtr Man 43 C9
Golcar W Yorks 51 H7
Gold Hill Norf 37 F11
Goldcliff Newport 15 C9
Golden Cross E Sus 12 E4
Golden Green Kent 20 G3
Golden Grove Carms 23 E10
Golden Hill Hants 10 E1
Golden Pot Hants 18 G4
Golden Valley Glos 26 F6
Goldenhill Stoke 44 G2
Golders Green London 19 C9
Goldhanger Essex 30 H6
Golding Shrops 33 E11
Goldington Bedford 29 C7
Goldsborough N Yorks 51 D9
Goldsborough N Yorks 59 E9
Goldsithney Corn 2 F4
Goldsworthy Devon 6 D2
Goldthorpe S Yorks 45 B8
Gollanfield Highld 87 F11
Golspie Highld 93 J11
Golval Highld 93 C11
Gomeldon Wilts 17 H8
Gomersal W Yorks 51 G8
Gomshall Sur 19 G7
Gonalston Notts 45 H10
Gonfirth Shetland 96 G5
Good Easter Essex 30 G3
Gooderstone Norf 38 E3
Goodleigh Devon 6 C5
Goodmanham E Yorks 52 E4
Goodnestone Kent 21 E7
Goodnestone Kent 21 F9
Goodrich Hereford 26 G2
Goodrington Torbay 5 F9
Goodshaw Lancs 50 G4
Goodwick = Wdig Pembs 22 C4
Goodworth Clatford Hants 17 G10
Goole E Yorks 52 G3
Goonbell Corn 2 E6
Goonhavern Corn 3 D6
Goose Eye W Yorks 50 E6
Goose Green Gtr Man 43 B8
Goose Green Norf 39 G7
Goose Green W Sus 11 C10
Gooseham Corn 6 E1
Goosey Oxon 17 B10
Goosnargh Lancs 50 F1
Goostrey Ches E 43 E10
Gorcott Hill Warks 27 B7
Gord Shetland 96 L6
Gordon Borders 70 F5
Gordonbush Highld 93 J11
Gordonsburgh Moray 88 B4
Gordonstoun Moray 88 B1
Gordonstown Aberds 88 C5
Gordonstown Aberds 89 E7
Gore Kent 21 F10
Gore Cross Wilts 17 F7
Gore Pit Essex 30 G5
Gorebridge Midloth 70 D2
Gorefield Cambs 37 D10
Gorey Jersey 11
Gorgie Edin 69 C11
Goring Oxon 18 C3
Goring-by-Sea W Sus 11 D10
Goring Heath Oxon 18 D3
Gorleston-on-Sea Norf 39 E11
Gornalwood W Mid 34 F5
Gorrachie Aberds 89 C7
Gorran Churchtown Corn 3 E8
Gorran Haven Corn 3 E9
Gorrenberry Borders 61 D10
Gors Ceredig 32 H2
Gorse Hill Swindon 17 C8
Gorsedd Flint 42 E4
Gorseinon Swansea 23 G10
Gorseness Orkney 95 G5
Gorsgoch Ceredig 23 A9
Gorslas Carms 23 E10
Gorsley Glos 26 F3
Gorstan Highld 86 E6
Gorstanvorran Highld 79 D11
Gorsteyhill Staffs 43 G10
Gorsty Hill Staffs 35 C7
Gortantaoid Argyll 64 A4
Gorton Gtr Man 44 C2
Gosbeck Suff 31 C8
Gosberton Lincs 37 B8
Gosberton Clough Lincs 37 C7
Gosfield Essex 30 F4
Gosford Hereford 26 B2
Gosforth Cumb 56 F2
Gosforth T&W 63 G8
Gosmore Herts 29 F8
Gosport Hants 10 E5
Gossabrough Shetland 96 E7
Gossington Glos 16 A4
Goswick Northumb 71 F9
Gotham Notts 35 B11
Gotherington Glos 26 F6
Gott Shetland 96 J6
Goudhurst Kent 12 C6
Goulceby Lincs 46 E6
Gourdas Aberds 89 D7
Gourdon Aberds 83 F10
Gourock Invclyd 73 F11
Govan Glasgow 68 D4
Govanhill Glasgow 68 D4
Goveton Devon 5 G8
Govilon Mon 25 G9
Gowanhill Aberds 89 B10
Gowdall E Yorks 52 G2
Gowerton Swansea 23 G10
Gowkhall Fife 69 B9
Gowthorpe E Yorks 52 D3
Goxhill E Yorks 53 E7
Goxhill N Lincs 53 G7
Goxhill Haven N Lincs 53 G7
Goybre Neath 14 C3
Grabhair W Isles 91 F8
Graby Lincs 37 C6
Grade Corn 2 H6
Graffham W Sus 11 C8
Grafham Cambs 29 B8
Grafham Sur 19 G7
Grafton Hereford 25 E11
Grafton N Yorks 51 C10
Grafton Oxon 17 A9
Grafton Shrops 33 D10
Grafton Worcs 26 B2
Grafton Flyford Worcs 26 C6
Grafton Regis Northants 28 D4
Grafton Underwood Northants 36 G5
Grafty Green Kent 20 G5
Graianrhyd Denb 42 G5
Graig Conwy 41 C10
Graig Denb 42 E3
Graig-fechan Denb 42 G4
Grain Medway 20 D5
Grainsby Lincs 46 C6
Grainthorpe Lincs 47 C7
Grampound Corn 3 E8
Grampound Road Corn 3 D8
Gramsdal W Isles 84 C3
Granborough Bucks 28 F4
Granby Notts 36 B3
Grandborough Warks 27 B11
Grandtully Perth 76 B2
Grange Cumb 56 E4
Grange E Ayrs 67 C7
Grange Medway 20 E4
Grange Mers 42 D5
Grange Perth 76 E5
Grange Crossroads Moray 88 C4
Grange Hall Moray 87 E13
Grange Hill Essex 19 B11
Grange Moor W Yorks 51 H8
Grange of Lindores Fife 76 F5
Grange-over-Sands Cumb 49 B4
Grange Villa Durham 58 A3
Grangemill Derbys 44 G6
Grangemouth Falk 69 B8
Grangepans Falk 69 B9
Grangetown Cardiff 15 D7
Grangetown Redcar 59 D6
Granish Highld 81 B11
Gransmoor E Yorks 53 D7
Granston Pembs 22 C3
Grantchester Cambs 29 C11
Grantham Lincs 36 B5
Grantley N Yorks 51 C8
Grantlodge Aberds 83 B9
Granton Dumfries 60 C6
Granton Edin 69 C11
Grantown-on-Spey Highld 82 A2
Grantshouse Borders 71 D7
Grappenhall Warr 43 D9
Grasby Lincs 46 B4
Grasmere Cumb 56 F5
Grasscroft Gtr Man 44 B3
Grassendale Mers 43 D6
Grassholme Durham 57 D11
Grassington N Yorks 50 C6
Grassmoor Derbys 45 F8
Grassthorpe Notts 45 F11
Grateley Hants 17 G9
Gratwich Staffs 34 B6
Graveley Cambs 29 B9
Graveley Herts 29 F9
Gravelly Hill W Mid 35 F7
Gravels Shrops 33 E9
Graven Shetland 96 F6
Graveney Kent 21 E7
Gravesend Herts 29 F11
Gravesend Kent 20 D3
Grayingham Lincs 46 C3
Grayrigg Cumb 57 G7
Grays Thurrock 20 D3
Grayshott Hants 18 H5
Grayswood Sur 11 A8
Graythorp Hrtlpl 58 D6
Grazeley Wokingham 18 E3
Greasbrough S Yorks 45 C8
Greasby Mers 42 D5
Great Abington Cambs 30 D2
Great Addington Northants 28 A6
Great Alne Warks 27 C8
Great Altcar Lancs 42 B6
Great Amwell Herts 29 G10
Great Asby Cumb 57 E8
Great Ashfield Suff 30 B6
Great Ayton N Yorks 59 E6
Great Baddow Essex 20 A4
Great Bardfield Essex 30 E3
Great Barford Bedford 29 C8
Great Barr W Mid 34 F6
Great Barrington Glos 27 G9
Great Barrow Ches W 43 F7
Great Barton Suff 30 B5
Great Barugh N Yorks 52 B3
Great Bavington Northumb 62 E5
Great Bealings Suff 31 D9
Great Bedwyn Wilts 17 E9
Great Bentley Essex 31 F8
Great Billing Northants 28 B5
Great Bircham Norf 38 B3
Great Blakenham Suff 31 C8
Great Blencow Cumb 56 C6
Great Bolas Telford 34 C2
Great Bookham Sur 19 F8
Great Bourton Oxon 27 D11
Great Bowden Leics 36 G3
Great Bradley Suff 30 C3
Great Braxted Essex 30 G5
Great Bricett Suff 31 C7
Great Brickhill Bucks 28 E6
Great Bridge W Mid 34 F5
Great Bridgeford Staffs 34 C4
Great Brington Northants 28 B3
Great Bromley Essex 31 F7
Great Broughton Cumb 56 C2
Great Broughton N Yorks 59 F6
Great Budworth Ches W 43 E9
Great Burdon Darl 58 E4
Great Burgh Sur 19 F9
Great Burstead Essex 20 B3
Great Busby N Yorks 58 F6
Great Canfield Essex 30 G2
Great Carlton Lincs 47 D8
Great Casterton Rutland 36 E6
Great Chart Kent 13 B8
Great Chatwell Staffs 34 D3
Great Chesterford Essex 30 D2
Great Cheverell Wilts 16 F6
Great Chishill Cambs 29 E11
Great Clacton Essex 31 G8
Great Cliff W Yorks 51 H9
Great Clifton Cumb 56 D2
Great Coates NE Lincs 46 B6
Great Comberton Worcs 26 D6
Great Corby Cumb 56 A6
Great Cornard Suff 30 D5
Great Cowden E Yorks 53 E8
Great Coxwell Oxon 17 B9
Great Crakehall N Yorks 58 G3
Great Cransley Northants 36 H4
Great Cressingham Norf 38 E4
Great Crosby Mers 42 C6
Great Cubley Derbys 35 B7
Great Dalby Leics 36 D3
Great Denham Bedford 29 D7
Great Doddington Northants 28 B5
Great Dunham Norf 38 D4
Great Dunmow Essex 30 F3
Great Durnford Wilts 17 H8
Great Easton Essex 30 F3
Great Easton Leics 36 F4
Great Eccleston Lancs 49 E4
Great Edstone N Yorks 52 A3
Great Ellingham Norf 38 F6
Great Elm Som 16 G4
Great Eversden Cambs 29 C10
Great Fencote N Yorks 58 G3
Great Finborough Suff 31 C7
Great Fransham Norf 38 D4
Great Gaddesden Herts 29 G7
Great Gidding Cambs 37 G7
Great Givendale E Yorks 52 D4
Great Glemham Suff 31 B10
Great Glen Leics 36 F2
Great Gonerby Lincs 36 B4
Great Gransden Cambs 29 C9
Great Green Norf 39 G8
Great Green Suff 30 C6
Great Habton N Yorks 52 B3
Great Hale Lincs 37 A7
Great Hallingbury Essex 30 G2
Great Hampden Bucks 18 A5
Great Harrowden Northants 28 A5
Great Harwood Lancs 50 F3
Great Haseley Oxon 18 A3
Great Hatfield E Yorks 53 E7
Great Haywood Staffs 34 C6
Great Heath W Mid 35 G9
Great Heck N Yorks 52 G1
Great Henny Essex 30 E5
Great Hinton Wilts 16 F6
Great Hockham Norf 38 F5
Great Holland Essex 31 G9
Great Horkesley Essex 30 E6
Great Hormead Herts 29 F10
Great Horton W Yorks 51 F7
Great Horwood Bucks 28 E4
Great Houghton Northants 28 C4
Great Houghton S Yorks 45 B8
Great Hucklow Derbys 44 E5
Great Kelk E Yorks 53 D7
Great Kimble Bucks 28 H5
Great Kingshill Bucks 18 B5
Great Langton N Yorks 58 G3
Great Leighs Essex 30 G4
Great Lever Gtr Man 43 B10
Great Limber Lincs 46 B5
Great Linford M Keynes 28 D5
Great Livermere Suff 30 A5
Great Longstone Derbys 44 E6
Great Lumley Durham 58 B3
Great Lyth Shrops 33 E10
Great Malvern Worcs 26 D4
Great Maplestead Essex 30 E5
Great Marton Blackpool 49 F3
Great Massingham Norf 38 C3
Great Melton Norf 39 E7
Great Milton Oxon 18 A3
Great Missenden Bucks 18 A5
Great Mitton Lancs 50 F3
Great Mongeham Kent 21 F10
Great Moulton Norf 39 F7
Great Munden Herts 29 F10
Great Musgrave Cumb 57 E9
Great Ness Shrops 33 D9
Great Notley Essex 30 F4
Great Oakley Essex 31 F8
Great Oakley Northants 36 G4
Great Offley Herts 29 F8
Great Ormside Cumb 57 E9
Great Orton Cumb 56 A5
Great Ouseburn N Yorks 51 C10
Great Oxendon Northants 36 G3
Great Oxney Green Essex 30 H3
Great Palgrave Norf 38 D4
Great Parndon Essex 29 H11
Great Paxton Cambs 29 B9
Great Plumpton Lancs 49 F3
Great Plumstead Norf 39 D9
Great Ponton Lincs 36 B5
Great Preston W Yorks 51 G10
Great Raveley Cambs 37 G8
Great Rissington Glos 27 G8
Great Rollright Oxon 27 E10
Great Ryburgh Norf 38 C5
Great Ryle Northumb 62 B6
Great Ryton Shrops 33 E10
Great Saling Essex 30 F4
Great Salkeld Cumb 57 C7
Great Sampford Essex 30 E3
Great Sankey Warr 43 D8
Great Saxham Suff 30 B4
Great Shefford W Berks 17 D10
Great Shelford Cambs 29 C11
Great Smeaton N Yorks 58 F4
Great Snoring Norf 38 B5
Great Somerford Wilts 16 C6
Great Stainton Darl 58 D4
Great Stambridge Essex 20 B5
Great Staughton Cambs 29 B8
Great Steeping Lincs 47 F8
Great Stonar Kent 21 F10
Great Strickland Cumb 57 D7
Great Stukeley Cambs 29 A9
Great Sturton Lincs 46 E6
Great Sutton Ches W 43 E6
Great Sutton Shrops 33 G11
Great Swinburne Northumb 62 F5
Great Tew Oxon 27 F10
Great Tey Essex 30 F5
Great Thurkleby N Yorks 51 B10
Great Thurlow Suff 30 C3
Great Torrington Devon 6 E3
Great Tosson Northumb 62 C6
Great Totham Essex 30 G5
Great Totham Essex 30 G5
Great Tows Lincs 46 C6
Great Urswick Cumb 49 B2
Great Wakering Essex 20 C6
Great Waldingfield Suff 30 D6
Great Walsingham Norf 38 B5
Great Waltham Essex 30 G3
Great Warley Essex 20 B2
Great Washbourne Glos 26 E6
Great Weldon Northants 36 G5
Great Welnetham Suff 30 C5
Great Wenham Suff 31 E7
Great Whittington Northumb 62 F6
Great Wigborough Essex 30 G6
Great Wilbraham Cambs 30 C2
Great Wishford Wilts 17 H7
Great Witcombe Glos 26 G6
Great Witley Worcs 26 B4
Great Wolford Warks 27 E9
Great Wratting Suff 30 D3
Great Wymondley Herts 29 F9
Great Wyrley Staffs 34 E5
Great Wytheford Shrops 34 D1
Great Yarmouth Norf 39 E11
Great Yeldham Essex 30 E4
Greater Doward Hereford 26 G2
Greatford Lincs 37 D6
Greatgate Staffs 35 A6
Greatham Hants 11 A6
Greatham Hrtlpl 58 D5
Greatham W Sus 11 C9
Greatstone on Sea Kent 13 D9
Greatworth Northants 28 D2
Greave Lancs 50 G4
Greeba IoM 48 D3
Green Denb 42 F3
Green End Bedford 29 C8
Green Hammerton N Yorks 51 D10
Green Lane Powys 33 F7
Green Ore Som 16 F2
Green St Green London 19 E11
Green Street Herts 19 B8
Greenbank Shetland 96 C7
Greenburn W Loth 69 D8
Greendikes Northumb 71 H9
Greenfield C Beds 29 E7
Greenfield Flint 42 E4
Greenfield Gtr Man 44 B3
Greenfield Highld 80 C4
Greenfield Oxon 18 B4
Greenford London 19 C8
Greengairs N Lanark 68 C6
Greenham W Berks 17 E11
Greenhaugh Northumb 62 E3
Greenhead Northumb 62 G2
Greenhill Falk 69 C7
Greenhill Kent 21 E8
Greenhill Leics 35 D10
Greenhill London 19 C8
Greenhills N Ayrs 67 A6
Greenhithe Kent 20 D2
Greenholm E Ayrs 67 C8
Greenholme Cumb 57 F7
Greenhouse Borders 61 A11
Greenhow Hill N Yorks 51 C7
Greenigoe Orkney 95 H5
Greenland Highld 94 D4
Greenlands Bucks 18 C4
Greenlaw Aberds 89 C6
Greenlaw Borders 70 F6
Greenlea Dumfries 60 F6
Greenloaning Perth 75 G11
Greenmount Gtr Man 43 A10
Greenmow Shetland 96 L6
Greenock Invclyd 73 F11
Greenock West Invclyd 73 F11
Greenodd Cumb 49 A3
Greenrow Cumb 56 A3
Greens Norton Northants 28 D3
Greenside T&W 63 G7
Greensidehill Northumb 62 B5
Greenstead Green Essex 30 F5
Greensted Essex 20 A2
Greenwich London 19 D10
Greet Glos 27 E7
Greete Shrops 26 A2
Greetham Lincs 47 E7
Greetham Rutland 36 D5
Greetland W Yorks 51 G6
Gregg Hall Cumb 56 G6
Gregson Lane Lancs 50 G1
Greinetobht W Isles 84 A3
Greinton Som 15 H10
Gremista Shetland 96 J6
Grenaby IoM 48 E2
Grendon Northants 28 B5
Grendon Warks 35 E8
Grendon Common Warks 35 F8
Grendon Green Hereford 26 C2
Grendon Underwood Bucks 28 F3
Grenofen Devon 4 D5
Grenoside S Yorks 45 C7
Greosabhagh W Isles 90 H6
Gresford Wrex 42 G6
Gresham Norf 39 B7
Greshornish Highld 85 C8
Gressenhall Norf 38 D5
Gressingham Lancs 50 C1
Gresty Green Ches E 43 G10
Greta Bridge Durham 58 E1
Gretna Dumfries 61 G9
Gretna Green Dumfries 61 G9
Gretton Glos 27 E7
Gretton Northants 36 F4
Gretton Shrops 33 F11
Grewelthorpe N Yorks 51 B8
Grey Green N Lincs 45 B11
Greygarth N Yorks 51 B7
Greynor Carms 23 F10
Greysouthen Cumb 56 D2
Greystoke Cumb 56 C6
Greystone Angus 77 C8
Greystone Dumfries 60 F5
Greywell Hants 18 F4
Griais W Isles 91 C9
Grianan W Isles 91 D9
Gribthorpe E Yorks 52 F3
Gridley Corner Devon 6 G2
Griff Warks 35 G9
Griffithstown Torf 15 B8
Grimbister Orkney 95 G4
Grimblethorpe Lincs 46 D6
Grimeford Village Lancs 43 A9
Grimethorpe S Yorks 45 B8
Griminis W Isles 84 C2
Grimister Shetland 96 D6
Grimley Worcs 26 B5
Grimness Orkney 95 J5
Grimoldby Lincs 47 D7
Grimpo Shrops 33 C9
Grimsargh Lancs 50 F1
Grimsbury Oxon 27 D11
Grimsby NE Lincs 46 A6
Grimscote Northants 28 C3
Grimscott Corn 6 F1
Grimsthorpe Lincs 36 C6
Grimston E Yorks 53 F8
Grimston Leics 36 C2
Grimston Norf 38 C3
Grimston York 52 D2
Grimstone Dorset 8 E5
Grinacombe Moor Devon 6 G3
Grindale E Yorks 53 B7
Grindigar Orkney 95 H6
Grindiscol Shetland 96 K6
Grindle Shrops 34 E3
Grindleford Derbys 44 E6
Grindleton Lancs 50 E3
Grindley Staffs 34 C6
Grindley Brook Shrops 33 A11
Grindlow Derbys 44 E5
Grindon Northumb 71 F8
Grindon Staffs 44 G4
Grindonmoor Gate Staffs 44 G4
Gringley on the Hill Notts 45 C11
Grinsdale Cumb 61 H9
Grinshill Shrops 33 C11
Grinton N Yorks 58 G1
Griomsidar W Isles 91 E8
Grishipoll Argyll 78 F4
Grisling Common E Sus 12 D3
Gristhorpe N Yorks 53 A6
Griston Norf 38 F5
Gritley Orkney 95 H6
Grittenham Wilts 17 C7
Grittleton Wilts 16 C5
Grizebeck Cumb 49 A2
Grizedale Cumb 56 G5
Grobister Orkney 95 F7
Groby Leics 35 E11
Groes Conwy 42 F3
Groes Neath 14 C3
Groes-faen Rhondda 14 C6
Groes-lwyd Powys 33 D8
Groesffordd Marli Denb 42 E3
Groeslon Gwyn 40 E6
Groeslon Gwyn 41 D7
Grogport Argyll 65 D9
Gromford Suff 31 C10
Gronant Flint 42 D3
Groombridge E Sus 12 C4
Grosmont Mon 25 F11
Grosmont N Yorks 59 F9
Groton Suff 30 D6
Grougfoot Falk 69 C9
Grouville Jersey 11
Grove Dorset 8 G6
Grove Kent 21 E9
Grove Notts 45 E11
Grove Oxon 17 B11
Grove Park London 19 D11
Grove Vale W Mid 34 F6
Grovesend Swansea 23 F10
Grudie Highld 86 E6
Gruids Highld 93 J8
Gruinard House Highld 86 B2
Grula Highld 85 F8
Gruline Argyll 79 G8
Grunasound Shetland 96 K5
Grundisburgh Suff 31 C9
Grunsagill Lancs 50 D3
Gruting Shetland 96 J4
Grutness Shetland 96 N6
Gualachulain Highld 74 C4
Gualin Ho. Highld 92 D6
Guardbridge Fife 77 F7
Guarlford Worcs 26 D5
Guay Perth 76 C3
Guestling Green E Sus 13 E7
Guestling Thorn E Sus 13 E7
Guestwick Norf 39 C6
Guestwick Green Norf 39 C6
Guide Blackburn 50 G3
Guide Post Northumb 63 E8
Guilden Morden Cambs 29 D9
Guilden Sutton Ches W 43 F7
Guildford Sur 18 G6
Guildtown Perth 76 D4
Guilsborough Northants 28 A3
Guilsfield Powys 33 D8
Guilton Kent 21 F9
Guineaford Devon 6 C4
Guisborough Redcar 59 E7
Guiseley W Yorks 51 E7
Guist Norf 38 C5
Guith Orkney 95 E6
Guiting Power Glos 27 F7
Gulberwick Shetland 96 K6
Gullane E Loth 70 B3
Gulval Corn 2 F3
Gulworthy Devon 4 D5
Gumfreston Pembs 22 F6
Gumley Leics 36 F2
Gummow's Shop Corn 3 D7
Gun Hill E Sus 12 E4
Gunby E Yorks 52 F3
Gunby Lincs 36 C5
Gundleton Hants 10 A5
Gunn Devon 6 C5
Gunnerside N Yorks 57 G11
Gunnerton Northumb 62 F5
Gunness N Lincs 46 A2
Gunnislake Corn 4 D5
Gunnista Shetland 96 J7
Gunthorpe Norf 38 B6
Gunthorpe Notts 36 A2
Gunthorpe Pboro 37 E7
Gunville IoW 10 F3
Gunwalloe Corn 2 G5
Gurnard IoW 10 E3
Gurnett Ches E 44 E3
Gurney Slade Som 16 G3
Gurnos Powys 24 H4
Gussage All Saints Dorset 9 C9
Gussage St Michael Dorset 9 C8
Guston Kent 21 G10
Gutcher Shetland 96 D7
Guthrie Angus 77 B8
Guyhirn Cambs 37 E9
Guyhirn Gull Cambs 37 E9
Guy's Head Lincs 37 C10
Guy's Marsh Dorset 9 B7
Guyzance Northumb 63 C8
Gwaenysgor Flint 42 D3
Gwalchmai Anglesey 40 C5
Gwaun-Cae-Gurwen Neath 24 G4
Gwaun-Leision Neath 24 G4
Gwbert Ceredig 22 B6
Gweek Corn 2 G6
Gwehelog Mon 15 A9
Gwenddwr Powys 25 D7
Gwennap Corn 2 F6
Gwenter Corn 2 H6
Gwernaffield Flint 42 F5
Gwernesney Mon 15 A10
Gwernogle Carms 23 C10
Gwernymynydd Flint 42 F5
Gwersyllt Wrex 42 G6
Gwespyr Flint 42 D4
Gwithian Corn 2 E4
Gwredog Anglesey 40 B6
Gwyddelwern Denb 42 H3
Gwyddgrug Carms 23 C9
Gwydyr Uchaf Conwy 41 D9
Gwynfryn Wrex 42 G5
Gwystre Powys 25 B7
Gwytherin Conwy 41 D10
Gyfelia Wrex 42 H6
Gyffin Conwy 41 C9
Gyre Orkney 95 H4
Gyrn-goch Gwyn 40 F6

H

Habberley Shrops 33 E9
Habergham Lancs 50 F4
Habrough NE Lincs 46 A5
Haceby Lincs 36 B6
Hacheston Suff 31 C10
Hackbridge London 19 E9
Hackenthorpe S Yorks 45 D8
Hackford Norf 39 E6
Hackforth N Yorks 58 G3
Hackland Orkney 95 F4
Hackleton Northants 28 C5
Hackness N Yorks 59 G10
Hackness Orkney 95 J4
Hackney London 19 C10
Hackthorn Lincs 46 D3
Hackthorpe Cumb 57 D7
Haconby Lincs 37 C7
Hacton London 20 C2
Hadden Borders 70 G6
Haddenham Bucks 28 H4
Haddenham Cambs 37 H10
Haddington E Loth 70 C4
Haddington Lincs 46 F3
Haddiscoe Norf 39 F10
Haddon Cambs 37 F7
Haddon Ches E 44 F3
Hade Edge W Yorks 44 B5
Hademore Staffs 35 E7
Hadfield Derbys 44 C4
Hadham Cross Herts 29 G11
Hadham Ford Herts 29 F11
Hadleigh Essex 20 C5
Hadleigh Suff 31 D7
Hadley Telford 34 D2
Hadley End Staffs 35 C7
Hadlow Kent 20 G3
Hadlow Down E Sus 12 D4
Hadnall Shrops 33 D11
Hadstock Essex 30 D2
Hady Derbys 45 E7
Hadzor Worcs 26 B6
Haffenden Quarter Kent 13 B7
Hafod-Dinbych Conwy 41 E10
Hafod-lom Conwy 41 C10
Haggate Lancs 50 F4
Haggbeck Cumb 61 F10
Haggerston Northumb 71 F9
Haggrister Shetland 96 F5
Hagley Hereford 26 D2
Hagley Worcs 34 G5
Hagworthingham Lincs 47 F7
Haigh Gtr Man 43 B9
Haigh S Yorks 44 A6
Haigh Moor W Yorks 51 G8
Haighton Green Lancs 50 F1
Hail Weston Cambs 29 B8
Haile Cumb 56 F2
Hailes Glos 27 E7
Hailey Herts 29 G10
Hailey Oxon 27 G10
Hailsham E Sus 12 F4
Haimer Highld 94 D3
Hainault London 19 B11
Hainford Norf 39 D8
Hainton Lincs 46 D5
Hairmyres S Lanark 68 E5
Haisthorpe E Yorks 53 C7
Hakin Pembs 22 F3
Halam Notts 45 G10
Halbeath Fife 69 B10
Halberton Devon 7 E9
Halcro Highld 94 D4
Hale Gtr Man 43 D10
Hale Halton 43 D7
Hale Hants 9 C10
Hale Bank Halton 43 D7
Hale Street Kent 20 G3
Halebarns Gtr Man 43 D10
Hales Norf 39 F9
Hales Staffs 34 B3
Hales Place Kent 21 F8
Halesfield Telford 34 E3
Halesgate Lincs 37 C9
Halesowen W Mid 34 G5
Halesworth Suff 39 H9
Halewood Mers 43 D7
Halford Shrops 33 G10
Halford Warks 27 D9
Halfpenny Furze Carms 23 E7
Halfpenny Green Staffs 34 F4
Halfway Carms 24 E3
Halfway Carms 24 E5
Halfway W Berks 17 E11
Halfway Bridge W Sus 11 B8
Halfway House Shrops 33 D9
Halfway Houses Kent 20 D6
Halifax W Yorks 51 G6
Halket E Ayrs 67 A7
Halkirk Highld 94 E3
Halkyn Flint 42 E5
Hall Dunnerdale Cumb 56 G4
Hall Green W Mid 35 G7
Hall Green W Yorks 51 H9
Hall Grove Herts 29 G9
Hall of Tankerness Orkney 95 H6
Hall of the Forest Shrops 33 G8
Halland E Sus 12 E3
Hallaton Leics 36 F3
Hallatrow Bath 16 F3
Hallbankgate Cumb 61 H11
Hallen S Glos 15 C11
Halliburton Borders 70 F5
Hallin Highld 84 C7
Halling Medway 20 E4
Hallington Lincs 47 D7
Hallington Northumb 62 F5
Halliwell Gtr Man 43 A10
Halloughton Notts 45 G10
Hallow Worcs 26 C5
Hallrule Borders 61 B11
Halls E Loth 70 C5
Hall's Green Herts 29 F9
Hallsands Devon 5 H9
Hallthwaites Cumb 56 H3
Hallworthy Corn 4 C2
Hallyburton House Perth 76 D5
Hallyne Borders 69 F10
Halmer End Staffs 43 H10
Halmore Glos 16 A3
Halmyre Mains Borders 69 F10
Halnaker W Sus 11 D8
Halsall Lancs 42 A6
Halse Northants 28 D2
Halse Som 7 D10
Halsetown Corn 2 F4
Halsham E Yorks 53 G8
Halsinger Devon 6 C4
Halstead Essex 30 E5
Halstead Kent 19 E11
Halstead Leics 36 E3
Halstock Dorset 8 D4
Haltham Lincs 46 F6
Haltoft End Lincs 47 H7
Halton Bucks 28 G5
Halton Halton 43 D8
Halton Lancs 49 C5
Halton Northumb 62 G5
Halton W Yorks 51 F9
Halton Wrex 33 B9
Halton East N Yorks 50 D6
Halton Gill N Yorks 50 B4
Halton Holegate Lincs 47 F8
Halton Lea Gate Northumb 62 H2
Halton West N Yorks 50 D4
Haltwhistle Northumb 62 G3
Halvergate Norf 39 E10
Halwell Devon 5 F8
Halwill Devon 6 G3
Halwill Junction Devon 6 F3
Ham Devon 7 F11
Ham Glos 16 B3
Ham Highld 94 C4
Ham Kent 21 F10
Ham London 19 D8
Ham Shetland 96 K1
Ham Wilts 17 E10
Ham Common Dorset 9 B7
Ham Green Hereford 26 D4
Ham Green Kent 13 D7
Ham Green Kent 20 E5
Ham Green N Som 15 D11
Ham Green Worcs 27 B7
Ham Street Som 8 A4
Hamble-le-Rice Hants 10 D3
Hambleden Bucks 18 C4
Hambledon Hants 10 C5
Hambledon Sur 18 H6
Hambleton Lancs 49 E3
Hambleton N Yorks 52 F1
Hambridge Som 8 B2
Hambrook S Glos 16 D3
Hambrook W Sus 11 D6
Hameringham Lincs 47 F7
Hamerton Cambs 37 H7
Hametoun Shetland 96 K1
Hamilton S Lanark 68 E6
Hammer W Sus 11 A7
Hammerpot W Sus 11 D9
Hammersmith London 19 D9
Hammerwich Staffs 35 E6
Hammerwood E Sus 12 C3
Hammond Street Herts 19 A10
Hammoon Dorset 9 C7
Hamnavoe Shetland 96 E4
Hamnavoe Shetland 96 E6
Hamnavoe Shetland 96 F6
Hamnavoe Shetland 96 K5
Hampden Park E Sus 12 F5
Hamperden End Essex 30 E2
Hampnett Glos 27 G7
Hampole S Yorks 45 A9
Hampreston Dorset 9 E9
Hampstead London 19 C9
Hampstead Norreys W Berks 18 D2
Hampsthwaite N Yorks 51 D8
Hampton London 19 E8
Hampton Shrops 34 G3
Hampton Worcs 27 D7
Hampton Bishop Hereford 26 E2
Hampton Heath Ches W 43 H7
Hampton in Arden W Mid 35 G8
Hampton Loade Shrops 34 G3
Hampton Lovett Worcs 26 B5
Hampton Lucy Warks 27 C9
Hampton on the Hill Warks 27 B9
Hampton Poyle Oxon 28 G2
Hamrow Norf 38 C5
Hamsey E Sus 12 E3
Hamsey Green London 19 F10
Hamstall Ridware Staffs 35 D7
Hamstead IoW 10 E3
Hamstead W Mid 34 F6
Hamstead Marshall W Berks 17 E11
Hamsterley Durham 58 C2
Hamsterley Durham 63 H7
Hamstreet Kent 13 C9
Hamworthy Poole 9 E8
Hanbury Staffs 35 C7
Hanbury Worcs 26 B6
Hanbury Woodend Staffs 35 C7
Hanby Lincs 36 B6
Hanchurch Staffs 34 A4
Handbridge Ches W 43 F7
Handcross W Sus 12 D1
Handforth Ches E 44 D2
Handley Ches W 43 G7
Handsacre Staffs 35 D6
Handsworth S Yorks 45 D8
Handsworth W Mid 34 F6
Handy Cross Devon 6 D3
Hanford Stoke 34 A4
Hanging Langford Wilts 17 H7
Hangleton W Sus 11 D9
Hanham S Glos 16 D3
Hankelow Ches E 43 H9
Hankerton Wilts 16 B6
Hankham E Sus 12 F5
Hanley Stoke 44 H2
Hanley Castle Worcs 26 D5
Hanley Child Worcs 26 B3
Hanley Swan Worcs 26 D5
Hanley William Worcs 26 B3
Hanlith N Yorks 50 C5
Hanmer Wrex 33 B10
Hannah Lincs 47 E9
Hannington Hants 18 F2
Hannington Northants 28 A5
Hannington Swindon 17 B8
Hannington Wick Swindon 17 B8
Hansel Village S Ayrs 67 C6
Hanslope M Keynes 28 D5
Hanthorpe Lincs 37 C6
Hanwell London 19 C8
Hanwell Oxon 27 D11
Hanwood Shrops 33 E10
Hanworth London 19 D8
Hanworth Norf 39 B7
Happendon S Lanark 69 G7
Happisburgh Norf 39 B9
Happisburgh Common Norf 39 C9
Hapsford Ches W 43 E7
Hapton Lancs 50 F3
Hapton Norf 39 F7
Harberton Devon 5 F8
Harbertonford Devon 5 F8
Harbledown Kent 21 F8
Harborne W Mid 34 G6
Harborough Magna Warks 35 H10
Harbottle Northumb 62 C5
Harbury Warks 27 C10
Harby Leics 36 B3
Harby Notts 46 E2
Harcombe Devon 7 G10
Harden W Mid 34 E6
Harden W Yorks 51 F6
Hardenhuish Wilts 16 D6
Hardgate Aberds 83 C9
Hardham W Sus 11 C9
Hardingham Norf 38 E6
Hardingstone Northants 28 C4
Hardington Som 16 F4
Hardington Mandeville Som 8 C4
Hardington Marsh Som 8 D4
Hardley Hants 10 D3
Hardley Street Norf 39 E9
Hardmead M Keynes 28 D6
Hardrow N Yorks 57 G10
Hardstoft Derbys 45 F8
Hardway Hants 10 D5
Hardway Som 8 A6
Hardwick Bucks 28 G5
Hardwick Cambs 29 C10
Hardwick Norf 38 D2
Hardwick Norf 39 G8
Hardwick Northants 28 B5
Hardwick Notts 45 E10
Hardwick Oxon 27 H10
Hardwick Oxon 28 F2
Hardwick W Mid 35 F6
Hardwicke Glos 26 F6
Hardwicke Glos 26 G4
Hardwicke Hereford 25 D9
Hardy's Green Essex 30 F6
Hare Green Essex 31 F7
Hare Hatch Wokingham 18 D5
Hare Street Herts 29 F10
Hareby Lincs 47 F7
Hareden Lancs 50 D2
Harefield London 19 B7
Harehills W Yorks 51 F9
Harehope Northumb 62 A6
Haresceugh Cumb 57 B8
Harescombe Glos 26 G5
Haresfield Glos 26 G5
Hareshaw N Lanark 69 D7
Hareshaw Head Northumb 62 E4
Harewood W Yorks 51 E9
Harewood End Hereford 26 F2
Harford Carms 24 D3
Harford Devon 5 F7
Hargate Norf 39 F7
Hargatewall Derbys 44 E5
Hargrave Ches W 43 F7
Hargrave Northants 29 A7
Hargrave Suff 30 C4
Harker Cumb 61 G9
Harkland Shetland 96 E6
Harkstead Suff 31 E8
Harlaston Staffs 35 D8
Harlaw Ho. Aberds 83 A9
Harlaxton Lincs 36 B4
Harle Syke Lancs 50 F4
Harlech Gwyn 41 G7
Harlequin Notts 36 B2
Harlescott Shrops 33 D11
Harlesden London 19 C9
Harleston Devon 5 G8
Harleston Norf 39 G8
Harleston Suff 31 C7
Harlestone Northants 28 B4
Harley S Yorks 45 C7
Harley Shrops 34 E1
Harleyholm S Lanark 69 G8
Harlington C Beds 29 E7
Harlington London 19 D7
Harlington S Yorks 45 B8
Harlosh Highld 85 D7
Harlow Essex 29 G11
Harlow Hill N Yorks 51 D8
Harlow Hill Northumb 62 G6
Harlthorpe E Yorks 52 F3
Harlton Cambs 29 C10
Harman's Cross Dorset 9 F8
Harmby N Yorks 58 H2
Harmer Green Herts 29 G9
Harmer Hill Shrops 33 C10
Harmondsworth London 19 D7
Harmston Lincs 46 F3
Harnham Northumb 62 F6
Harnhill Glos 17 A7
Harold Hill London 20 B2
Harold Wood London 20 B2
Haroldston West Pembs 22 E3
Haroldswick Shetland 96 B8
Harome N Yorks 52 A2
Harpenden Herts 29 G8
Harpford Devon 7 G9
Harpham E Yorks 53 C6
Harpley Norf 38 C3
Harpley Worcs 26 B3
Harpole Northants 28 B3
Harpsdale Highld 94 E3
Harpsden Oxon 18 C4
Harpswell Lincs 46 D3
Harpur Hill Derbys 44 E4
Harpurhey Gtr Man 44 B2
Harraby Cumb 56 A6
Harrapool Highld 85 F11
Harrier Shetland 96 J1
Harrietfield Perth 76 E2
Harrietsham Kent 20 F5
Harrington Cumb 56 D1
Harrington Lincs 47 E7
Harrington Northants 36 G3
Harringworth Northants 36 F5
Harris Highld 78 B6
Harrogate N Yorks 51 D9
Harrold Bedford 28 C6
Harrow London 19 C8
Harrow on the Hill London 19 C8
Harrow Street Suff 30 E6
Harrow Weald London 19 B8
Harrowbarrow Corn 4 E4
Harrowden Bedford 29 D7
Harrowgate Hill Darl 58 E3
Harston Cambs 29 C11
Harston Leics 36 B4
Harswell E Yorks 52 E4
Hart Hrtlpl 58 C5
Hart Common Gtr Man 43 B9
Hart Hill Luton 29 F8
Hart Station Hrtlpl 58 C5
Hartburn Northumb 62 E6
Hartburn Stockton 58 E5
Hartest Suff 30 C5
Hartfield E Sus 12 C3
Hartford Cambs 29 A9
Hartford Ches W 43 E9
Hartford End Essex 30 G3
Hartfordbridge Hants 18 F4
Hartforth N Yorks 58 F2
Harthill Ches W 43 G8
Harthill N Lanark 69 D8
Harthill S Yorks 45 D8
Hartington Derbys 44 F5
Hartland Devon 6 D1
Hartlebury Worcs 26 A5
Hartlepool Hrtlpl 58 C6
Hartley Cumb 57 F9
Hartley Kent 13 C6
Hartley Kent 20 E3
Hartley Northumb 63 F9
Hartley Westpall Hants 18 F3
Hartley Wintney Hants 18 F4
Hartlip Kent 20 E5
Hartoft End N Yorks 59 G8
Harton N Yorks 52 C3
Harton Shrops 33 G10
Harton T&W 63 G9
Hartpury Glos 26 F4
Hartshead W Yorks 51 G7
Hartshill Warks 35 F9
Hartshorne Derbys 35 C9
Hartsop Cumb 56 E6
Hartwell Northants 28 C4
Hartwood N Lanark 69 E7
Harvieston Stirling 68 B4
Harvington Worcs 27 D7
Harvington Cross Worcs 27 D7
Harwell Oxon 17 C11
Harwich Essex 31 E9
Harwood Durham 57 C10
Harwood Gtr Man 43 A10
Harwood Dale N Yorks 59 G10
Harworth Notts 45 C10
Hasbury W Mid 34 G5
Hascombe Sur 18 G6
Haselbech Northants 36 H3
Haselbury Plucknett Som 8 C3
Haseley Warks 27 B9
Haselor Warks 27 C8
Hasfield Glos 26 F5
Hasguard Pembs 22 F3
Haskayne Lancs 42 B6
Hasketon Suff 31 C9
Hasland Derbys 45 F7
Haslemere Sur 11 A8
Haslingden Lancs 50 G3
Haslingfield Cambs 29 C11
Haslington Ches E 43 G10
Hassall Ches E 43 G10
Hassall Green Ches E 43 G10
Hassell Street Kent 21 G7
Hassendean Borders 61 A11
Hassingham Norf 39 E9
Hassocks W Sus 12 E1
Hassop Derbys 44 E6
Hastigrow Highld 94 D4
Hastingleigh Kent 13 B9
Hastings E Sus 13 F7
Hastingwood Essex 29 H11
Hastoe Herts 28 H6
Haswell Durham 58 B4
Haswell Plough Durham 58 B4
Hatch C Beds 29 D8
Hatch Hants 18 F3
Hatch Wilts 9 B8
Hatch Beauchamp Som 8 B2
Hatch End London 19 B8
Hatch Green Som 8 C2
Hatchet Gate Hants 10 D2
Hatching Green Herts 29 G8
Hatchmere Ches W 43 E8
Hatcliffe NE Lincs 46 B6
Hatfield Hereford 26 C2
Hatfield Herts 29 H9
Hatfield S Yorks 45 B10
Hatfield Worcs 26 C5
Hatfield Broad Oak Essex 30 G2
Hatfield Garden Village Herts 29 H9
Hatfield Heath Essex 30 G2
Hatfield Hyde Herts 29 G9
Hatfield Peverel Essex 30 G4
Hatfield Woodhouse S Yorks 45 B10
Hatford Oxon 17 B10
Hatherden Hants 17 F10
Hatherleigh Devon 6 F4
Hathern Leics 35 C10
Hatherop Glos 27 H8
Hathersage Derbys 44 D6
Hathershaw Gtr Man 44 B3
Hatherton Ches E 43 H9
Hatherton Staffs 34 D5
Hatley St George Cambs 29 C9
Hatt Corn 4 E4
Hattingley Hants 18 H3
Hatton Aberds 89 E10
Hatton Derbys 35 C8
Hatton Lincs 46 E5
Hatton Shrops 33 F10
Hatton Warks 27 B9
Hatton Warr 43 D8
Hatton Castle Aberds 89 D7
Hatton Heath Ches W 43 F7
Hatton of Fintray Aberds 83 B10
Hattoncrook Aberds 89 F8
Haugh E Ayrs 67 D7
Haugh Gtr Man 44 A3
Haugh Lincs 47 E8
Haugh Head Northumb 71 H9
Haugh of Glass Moray 88 E4
Haugh of Urr Dumfries 55 C11
Haugham Lincs 47 D7
Haughley Suff 31 B7
Haughley Green Suff 31 B7
Haughs of Clinterty Aberdeen 83 B10
Haughton Notts 45 E10
Haughton Shrops 33 C9
Haughton Shrops 34 D1
Haughton Shrops 34 E3
Haughton Shrops 34 F2
Haughton Staffs 34 C4
Haughton Castle Northumb 62 F5
Haughton Green Gtr Man 44 C3
Haughton Moss Ches E 43 G8
Haultwick Herts 29 F10
Haunn Argyll 78 G6
Haunn W Isles 84 G2
Haunton Staffs 35 D8
Hauxley Northumb 63 C8
Hauxton Cambs 29 C11
Havant Hants 10 D6
Haven Hereford 25 C11
Haven Bank Lincs 46 G6
Haven Side E Yorks 53 G7
Havenstreet IoW 10 E4
Havercroft W Yorks 45 A7
Haverfordwest = Hwlffordd Pembs 22 E4
Haverhill Suff 30 D3
Haverigg Cumb 49 B1
Havering-atte-Bower London 20 B2
Haveringland Norf 39 C7
Haversham M Keynes 28 D5
Haverthwaite Cumb 49 A3
Haverton Hill Stockton 58 D5
Hawarden = Penarlâg Flint 42 F6
Hawcoat Cumb 49 B2
Hawen Ceredig 23 B8
Hawes N Yorks 57 H10
Hawes' Green Norf 39 F8
Hawes Side Blackpool 49 F3
Hawford Worcs 26 B5
Hawick Borders 61 B11
Hawk Green Gtr Man 44 D3
Hawkchurch Devon 8 D2
Hawkedon Suff 30 C4
Hawkenbury Kent 12 C4
Hawkenbury Kent 13 B7
Hawkeridge Wilts 16 F5
Hawkerland Devon 7 H9
Hawkes End W Mid 35 G9
Hawkesbury S Glos 16 C4
Hawkesbury Warks 35 G9
Hawkesbury Upton S Glos 16 C4
Hawkhill Northumb 63 B8
Hawkhurst Kent 13 C6
Hawkinge Kent 21 H9
Hawkley Hants 10 B6
Hawkridge Som 7 C7
Hawkshead Cumb 56 G5
Hawkshead Hill Cumb 56 G5
Hawksland S Lanark 69 G7
Hawkswick N Yorks 50 B5
Hawksworth Notts 36 A3
Hawksworth W Yorks 51 E7
Hawksworth W Yorks 51 F8
Hawkwell Essex 20 B5
Hawley Hants 18 F5
Hawley Kent 20 D2
Hawling Glos 27 F7
Hawnby N Yorks 59 H6
Haworth W Yorks 50 F6
Hawstead Suff 30 C5
Hawthorn Durham 58 B5
Hawthorn Rhondda 15 C7
Hawthorn Wilts 16 E5
Hawthorn Hill Brack 18 D5
Hawthorn Hill Lincs 46 G6
Hawthorpe Lincs 36 C6
Hawton Notts 45 G11
Haxby York 52 D2
Haxey N Lincs 45 C11
Hay Green Norf 37 D11
Hay-on-Wye = Y Gelli Gandryll Powys 25 D9
Hay Street Herts 29 F10
Haydock Mers 43 C8
Haydon Dorset 8 C5
Haydon Bridge Northumb 62 G4
Haydon Wick Swindon 17 C8
Haye Corn 4 E4
Hayes London 19 C8
Hayes London 19 E11
Hayfield Derbys 44 D4
Hayfield Fife 69 A11
Hayhill E Ayrs 67 E7
Hayhillock Angus 77 C8
Hayle Corn 2 F4
Haynes C Beds 29 D7
Haynes Church End C Beds 29 D7
Hayscastle Pembs 22 D3
Hayscastle Cross Pembs 22 D4
Hayshead Angus 77 C9
Hayton Aberdeen 83 C11
Hayton Cumb 56 B3
Hayton Cumb 61 H11
Hayton E Yorks 52 E4
Hayton Notts 45 D11
Hayton's Bent Shrops 33 G11
Haytor Vale Devon 5 D8
Haywards Heath W Sus 12 D2
Haywood S Yorks 45 A9
Haywood Oaks Notts 45 G10
Hazel Grove Gtr Man 44 D3
Hazel Street Kent 12 C5
Hazelbank S Lanark 69 F7
Hazelbury Bryan Dorset 8 D6
Hazeley Hants 18 F4
Hazelhurst Gtr Man 44 B3
Hazelslade Staffs 34 D6
Hazelton Glos 27 G7
Hazelton Walls Fife 76 E6
Hazelwood Derbys 45 H7
Hazlemere Bucks 18 B5
Hazlerigg T&W 63 F8
Hazlewood N Yorks 51 D6
Hazon Northumb 63 C7
Heacham Norf 38 B2
Head of Muir Falk 69 B7
Headbourne Worthy Hants 10 A3
Headbrook Hereford 25 C10
Headcorn Kent 13 B7
Headingley W Yorks 51 F8
Headington Oxon 28 H2
Headlam Durham 58 E2
Headless Cross Worcs 27 B7
Headley Hants 18 E2
Headley Hants 18 H5
Headley Sur 19 F9
Headon Notts 45 E11
Heads S Lanark 68 F6
Heads Nook Cumb 61 H10
Heage Derbys 45 G7
Healaugh N Yorks 51 E10
Healaugh N Yorks 58 G1
Heald Green Gtr Man 44 D2
Heale Devon 6 B5
Heale Som 16 G3
Healey Gtr Man 50 H4
Healey N Yorks 51 A7
Healey Northumb 62 H6
Healing NE Lincs 46 A6
Heamoor Corn 2 F3
Heanish Argyll 78 G3
Heanor Derbys 45 H8
Heanton Punchardon Devon 6 C4
Heapham Lincs 46 D2
Hearthstane Borders 69 H10
Heasley Mill Devon 7 C6
Heast Highld 85 G11
Heath Cardiff 15 D7
Heath Derbys 45 F8
Heath and Reach C Beds 28 F6
Heath End Hants 18 E2
Heath End Sur 18 G5
Heath End Warks 27 B9
Heath Hayes Staffs 34 D6
Heath Hill Shrops 34 D3
Heath House Som 15 G10
Heath Town W Mid 34 F5
Heathcote Derbys 44 F5
Heather Leics 35 D9
Heatherfield Highld 85 D9
Heathfield Devon 5 D9
Heathfield E Sus 12 D4
Heathfield Som 7 D10
Heathhall Dumfries 60 F5
Heathrow Airport London 19 D7
Heathstock Devon 8 D1
Heathton Shrops 34 F4
Heatley Warr 43 D10
Heaton Lancs 49 C4
Heaton Staffs 44 F3
Heaton T&W 63 G8
Heaton W Yorks 51 F7
Heaton Moor Gtr Man 44 C2
Heaverham Kent 20 F2
Heaviley Gtr Man 44 D3
Heavitree Devon 7 G8
Hebburn T&W 63 G9
Hebden N Yorks 50 C6
Hebden Bridge W Yorks 50 G5
Hebron Anglesey 40 B6
Hebron Carms 22 D6
Hebron Northumb 63 E7
Heck Dumfries 60 E6
Heckfield Hants 18 E4
Heckfield Green Suff 39 H7
Heckfordbridge Essex 30 F6
Heckington Lincs 37 A7
Heckmondwike W Yorks 51 G8
Heddington Wilts 16 E6
Heddle Orkney 95 G4
Heddon-on-the-Wall Northumb 63 G7
Hedenham Norf 39 F9
Hedge End Hants 10 C3
Hedgerley Bucks 18 C6
Hedging Som 8 B2
Hedley on the Hill Northumb 62 H6
Hednesford Staffs 34 D6
Hedon E Yorks 53 G7
Hedsor Bucks 18 C6
Hedworth T&W 63 G9
Hegdon Hill Hereford 26 C2
Heggerscales Cumb 57 E10
Heglibister Shetland 96 H5
Heighington Darl 58 D3
Heighington Lincs 46 F4
Heights of Brae Highld 87 E8
Heights of Kinlochewe Highld 86 E3
Heilam Highld 92 C7
Heiton Borders 70 G6
Hele Devon 6 B4
Hele Devon 7 F8
Helensburgh Argyll 73 E11
Helford Corn 3 G6
Helford Passage Corn 3 G6
Helhoughton Norf 38 C4
Helions Bumpstead Essex 30 D3
Hellaby S Yorks 45 C9
Helland Corn 4 D1
Hellesdon Norf 39 D8
Hellidon Northants 28 C2
Hellifield N Yorks 50 D4
Hellingly E Sus 12 E4
Hellington Norf 39 E9
Hellister Shetland 96 J5
Helm Northumb 63 D7
Helmdon Northants 28 D2
Helmingham Suff 31 C8
Helmington Row Durham 58 C2
Helmsdale Highld 93 H13
Helmshore Lancs 50 G3
Helmsley N Yorks 52 A2
Helperby N Yorks 51 C10
Helperthorpe N Yorks 52 B5
Helpringham Lincs 37 A7
Helpston Pboro 37 E7
Helsby Ches W 43 E7
Helsey Lincs 47 E9
Helston Corn 2 G5
Helstone Corn 4 C1
Helton Cumb 57 D7
Helwith Bridge N Yorks 50 C4
Hemblington Norf 39 D9
Hemel Hempstead Herts 29 H7
Hemingbrough N Yorks 52 F2
Hemingby Lincs 46 E6
Hemingford Abbots Cambs 29 A9
Hemingford Grey Cambs 29 A9
Hemingstone Suff 31 C8
Hemington Leics 35 C10
Hemington Northants 37 G6
Hemington Som 16 F4
Hemley Suff 31 D9
Hemlington Mbro 58 E6
Hemp Green Suff 31 B10
Hempholme E Yorks 53 D6
Hempnall Norf 39 F8
Hempnall Green Norf 39 F8
Hempriggs House Highld 94 F5
Hempstead Essex 30 E3
Hempstead Medway 20 E4
Hempstead Norf 39 B7
Hempstead Norf 39 C10
Hempsted Glos 26 G5
Hempton Norf 38 C5
Hempton Oxon 27 E11
Hemsby Norf 39 D10
Hemswell Lincs 46 C3
Hemswell Cliff Lincs 46 D3
Hemsworth W Yorks 45 A8
Hemyock Devon 7 E10
Hen-feddau fawr Pembs 23 C7
Henbury Bristol 16 D2
Henbury Ches E 44 E2
Hendon London 19 C9
Hendon T&W 63 H10
Hendre Flint 42 F4
Hendre-ddu Conwy 41 D10
Hendreforgan Rhondda 14 C5
Hendy Carms 23 F10
Heneglwys Anglesey 40 C6
Henfield W Sus 11 C11
Henford Devon 6 G2
Henghurst Kent 13 C8
Hengoed Caerph 15 B7
Hengoed Powys 25 C9
Hengoed Shrops 33 B8
Hengrave Suff 30 B5
Henham Essex 30 F2
Heniarth Powys 33 E7
Henlade Som 8 B1
Henley Shrops 33 H11
Henley Som 8 A3
Henley Suff 31 C8
Henley W Sus 11 B7
Henley-in-Arden Warks 27 B8
Henley-on-Thames Oxon 18 C4
Henley's Down E Sus 12 E6
Henllan Ceredig 23 B8
Henllan Denb 42 F3
Henllan Amgoed Carms 22 D6
Henllys Torf 15 B8
Henlow C Beds 29 E8
Hennock Devon 5 C9
Henny Street Essex 30 E5
Henryd Conwy 41 C9
Henry's Moat Pembs 22 D5
Hensall N Yorks 52 G1
Henshaw Northumb 62 G3
Hensingham Cumb 56 E1
Henstead Suff 39 G10
Henstridge Som 8 C6
Henstridge Ash Som 8 B6
Henstridge Marsh Som 8 B6
Henton Oxon 18 A4
Henton Som 15 G10
Henwood Corn 4 D3
Heogan Shetland 96 J6
Heol-las Swansea 14 B2
Heol Senni Powys 24 F6
Heol-y-Cyw Bridgend 14 C5
Hepburn Northumb 62 A6
Hepple Northumb 62 C5
Hepscott Northumb 63 E8
Heptonstall W Yorks 50 G5
Hepworth Suff 30 A6
Hepworth W Yorks 44 B5
Herbrandston Pembs 22 F3
Hereford Hereford 26 D2
Heriot Borders 70 E2
Hermiston Edin 69 C10
Hermitage Borders 61 D11
Hermitage Dorset 8 D5
Hermitage W Berks 18 D2
Hermitage W Sus 11 D6
Hermon Anglesey 40 D5
Hermon Carms 23 C8
Hermon Carms 24 F3
Hermon Pembs 23 C7
Herne Kent 21 E8
Herne Bay Kent 21 E8
Herner Devon 6 D4
Hernhill Kent 21 E7
Herodsfoot Corn 4 E3
Herongate Essex 20 B3
Heronsford S Ayrs 54 A4
Herriard Hants 18 G3
Herringfleet Suff 39 F10
Herringswell Suff 30 A4
Hersden Kent 21 E9
Hersham Corn 6 F1
Hersham Sur 19 E8
Herstmonceux E Sus 12 E5
Herston Orkney 95 J5
Hertford Herts 29 G10
Hertford Heath Herts 29 G10
Hertingfordbury Herts 29 G10
Hesket Newmarket Cumb 56 C5
Hesketh Bank Lancs 49 G4
Hesketh Lane Lancs 50 E2
Heskin Green Lancs 49 H5
Hesleden Durham 58 C5
Hesleyside Northumb 62 E4
Heslington York 52 D2
Hessay York 51 D11
Hessenford Corn 4 F4
Hessett Suff 30 B6
Hessle E Yorks 52 G6
Hest Bank Lancs 49 C4
Heston London 19 D8
Hestwall Orkney 95 G3
Heswall Mers 42 D5
Hethe Oxon 28 F2
Hethersett Norf 39 E7
Hethersgill Cumb 61 G10
Hethpool Northumb 71 H7
Hett Durham 58 C3
Hetton N Yorks 50 D5
Hetton-le-Hole T&W 58 B4
Hetton Steads Northumb 71 G9
Heugh Northumb 62 F6
Heugh-head Aberds 82 B5
Heveningham Suff 31 A10
Hever Kent 12 B3
Heversham Cumb 49 A4
Hevingham Norf 39 C7
Hewas Water Corn 3 E8
Hewelsfield Glos 16 A2
Hewish N Som 15 E10
Hewish Som 8 D3
Heworth York 52 D2
Hexham Northumb 62 G5
Hextable Kent 20 D2
Hexton Herts 29 E8
Hexworthy Devon 5 D7
Hey Lancs 50 E4
Heybridge Essex 20 B3
Heybridge Essex 30 H5
Heybridge Basin Essex 30 H5
Heybrook Bay Devon 4 G6
Heydon Cambs 29 D11

Kinlocheil Highld 80 F1
Kinlochewe Highld 86 E3
Kinlochleven Highld 74 A4
Kinlochmoidart Highld 79 D10
Kinlochmorar Highld 79 B11
Kinlochmore Highld 74 A4
Kinlochspelve Argyll 79 J9
Kinloid Highld 79 C9
Kinloss Moray 87 E13
Kinmel Bay Conwy 42 D2
Kinmuck Aberds 83 B10
Kinmundy Aberds 83 B10
Kinnadie Aberds 89 D9
Kinnaird Perth 76 E5
Kinnaird Castle Angus 77 B9
Kinneff Aberds 83 F10
Kinnelhead Dumfries 60 C6
Kinnell Angus 77 B9
Kinnerley Shrops 33 C9
Kinnersley Hereford 25 D10
Kinnersley Worcs 26 D5
Kinnerton Powys 25 B9
Kinnesswood Perth 76 G4
Kinninvie Durham 58 D1
Kinnordy Angus 76 B6
Kinoulton Notts 36 B2
Kinross Perth 76 G4
Kinrossie Perth 76 D4
Kinsbourne Green Herts 29 G8
Kinsey Heath Ches E 34 A2
Kinsham Hereford 25 B10
Kinsham Worcs 26 E6
Kinsley W Yorks 45 A8
Kinson Bmouth 9 E9
Kintbury W Berks 17 E10
Kintessack Moray 87 E12
Kintillo Perth 76 F4
Kintocher Aberds 83 C7
Kinton Hereford 25 A11
Kinton Shrops 33 D9
Kintore Aberds 83 B9
Kintour Argyll 64 C5
Kintra Argyll 64 D4
Kintra Argyll 78 J6
Kintraw Argyll 73 C7
Kinuachdrachd Argyll 72 D6
Kinveachy Highld 81 B11
Kinver Staffs 34 G4
Kippax W Yorks 51 F10
Kippen Stirling 68 A5
Kippford or Scaur Dumfries 55 D11
Kirbister Orkney 95 F7
Kirbister Orkney 95 H4
Kirbuster Orkney 95 F3
Kirby Bedon Norf 39 E8
Kirby Bellars Leics 36 D3
Kirby Cane Norf 39 F9
Kirby Cross Essex 31 F9
Kirby Grindalythe N Yorks 52 C5
Kirby Hill N Yorks 51 C9
Kirby Hill N Yorks 58 F2
Kirby Knowle N Yorks 58 H5
Kirby-le-Soken Essex 31 F9
Kirby Misperton N Yorks 52 B3
Kirby Muxloe Leics 35 E11
Kirby Row Norf 39 F9
Kirby Sigston N Yorks 58 G5
Kirby Underdale E Yorks 52 D4
Kirby Wiske N Yorks 51 A9
Kirdford W Sus 11 B9
Kirk Highld 94 E4
Kirk Bramwith S Yorks 45 A10
Kirk Deighton N Yorks 51 D9
Kirk Ella E Yorks 52 G6
Kirk Hallam Derbys 35 A10
Kirk Hammerton N Yorks 51 D10
Kirk Ireton Derbys 44 G6
Kirk Langley Derbys 35 B8
Kirk Merrington Durham 58 C3
Kirk Michael IoM 48 C3
Kirk of Shotts N Lanark 69 D7
Kirk Sandall S Yorks 45 B10
Kirk Smeaton N Yorks 51 H11
Kirk Yetholm Borders 71 H7
Kirkabister Shetland 96 K6
Kirkandrews Dumfries 55 E9
Kirkandrews upon Eden Cumb 61 H9
Kirkbampton Cumb 61 H9
Kirkbean Dumfries 60 H5
Kirkbride Cumb 61 H8
Kirkbuddo Angus 77 C8
Kirkburn Borders 69 G11
Kirkburn E Yorks 52 D5
Kirkburton W Yorks 44 A5
Kirkby Lincs 46 C4
Kirkby Mers 43 C7
Kirkby N Yorks 59 F6
Kirkby Fleetham N Yorks 58 G3
Kirkby Green Lincs 46 G4
Kirkby In Ashfield Notts 45 G9
Kirkby-in-Furness Cumb 49 A2
Kirkby la Thorpe Lincs 46 H5
Kirkby Lonsdale Cumb 50 B2
Kirkby Malham N Yorks 50 C4
Kirkby Mallory Leics 35 E10
Kirkby Malzeard N Yorks 51 B8
Kirkby Mills N Yorks 59 H8
Kirkby on Bain Lincs 46 F6
Kirkby Overflow N Yorks 51 E9
Kirkby Stephen Cumb 57 F9
Kirkby Thore Cumb 57 D8
Kirkby Underwood Lincs 37 C6
Kirkby Wharfe N Yorks 51 E11
Kirkbymoorside N Yorks 59 H7
Kirkcaldy Fife 69 A11
Kirkcambeck Cumb 61 G11
Kirkcarswell Dumfries 55 E10
Kirkcolm Dumfries 54 C3
Kirkconnel Dumfries 60 B3
Kirkconnell Dumfries 60 G5
Kirkcowan Dumfries 54 C6
Kirkcudbright Dumfries 55 D9
Kirkdale Mers 42 C6
Kirkfieldbank S Lanark 69 F7
Kirkgunzeon Dumfries 55 C11
Kirkham Lancs 49 F4
Kirkham N Yorks 52 C3
Kirkhamgate W Yorks 51 G8
Kirkharle Northumb 62 E6
Kirkheaton Northumb 62 F6
Kirkheaton W Yorks 51 H7
Kirkhill Angus 77 A9
Kirkhill Highld 87 G8
Kirkhill Midloth 69 D11
Kirkhill Moray 88 E2
Kirkhope Borders 61 A9
Kirkhouse Borders 70 G2
Kirkiboll Highld 93 D8
Kirkibost Highld 85 G10
Kirkinch Angus 76 C6
Kirkinner Dumfries 55 D7
Kirkintilloch E Dunb 68 C5
Kirkland Cumb 56 E2
Kirkland Cumb 57 C8
Kirkland Dumfries 60 B3
Kirkland Dumfries 60 D4
Kirkleatham Redcar 59 D6
Kirklevington Stockton 58 F5
Kirkley Suff 39 F11
Kirklington N Yorks 51 A9
Kirklington Notts 45 G10
Kirklinton Cumb 61 G10
Kirkliston Edin 69 C10
Kirkmaiden Dumfries 54 F4
Kirkmichael Perth 76 B3
Kirkmichael S Ayrs 66 F6
Kirkmuirhill S Lanark 68 F6
Kirknewton Northumb 71 G8
Kirknewton W Loth 69 D10
Kirkney Aberds 88 E5
Kirkoswald Cumb 57 B7
Kirkoswald S Ayrs 66 F5
Kirkpatrick Durham Dumfries 60 F3
Kirkpatrick-Fleming Dumfries 61 F8
Kirksanton Cumb 49 A1
Kirkstall W Yorks 51 F8
Kirkstead Lincs 46 F5
Kirkstile Aberds 88 E5
Kirkstyle Highld 94 C5
Kirkton Aberds 83 A8
Kirkton Aberds 89 D6
Kirkton Angus 77 C7
Kirkton Angus 77 D7
Kirkton Borders 61 B11
Kirkton Dumfries 60 E5
Kirkton Fife 76 E6
Kirkton Highld 85 F13
Kirkton Highld 86 G2
Kirkton Highld 87 B10
Kirkton Highld 87 F10
Kirkton Perth 76 F2
Kirkton S Lanark 60 A5
Kirkton Stirling 75 G8
Kirkton Manor Borders 69 G11
Kirkton of Airlie Angus 76 B6
Kirkton of Auchterhouse Angus 76 D6
Kirkton of Auchterless Aberds 89 D7
Kirkton of Barevan Highld 87 G11
Kirkton of Bourtie Aberds 89 F8
Kirkton of Collace Perth 76 D4
Kirkton of Craig Angus 77 B10
Kirkton of Culsalmond Aberds 89 E6
Kirkton of Durris Aberds 83 D9
Kirkton of Glenbuchat Aberds 82 B5
Kirkton of Glenisla Angus 76 A5
Kirkton of Kingoldrum Angus 76 B6
Kirkton of Largo Fife 77 G7
Kirkton of Lethendy Perth 76 C4
Kirkton of Logie Buchan Aberds 89 F9
Kirkton of Maryculter Aberds 83 D10
Kirkton of Menmuir Angus 77 A8
Kirkton of Monikie Angus 77 D8
Kirkton of Oyne Aberds 83 A8
Kirkton of Rayne Aberds 83 A8
Kirkton of Skene Aberds 83 C10
Kirkton of Tough Aberds 83 B8
Kirktonhill Borders 70 E3
Kirktown Aberds 89 C10
Kirktown of Alvah Aberds 89 B6
Kirktown of Deskford Moray 88 B5
Kirktown of Fetteresso Aberds 83 E10
Kirktown of Mortlach Moray 88 E3
Kirktown of Slains Aberds 89 F10
Kirkurd Borders 69 F10
Kirkwall Orkney 95 G5
Kirkwhelpington Northumb 62 E5
Kirmington N Lincs 46 A5
Kirmond le Mire Lincs 46 C5
Kirn Argyll 73 F10
Kirriemuir Angus 76 B6
Kirstead Green Norf 39 F8
Kirtlebridge Dumfries 61 F8
Kirtleton Dumfries 61 E8
Kirtling Cambs 30 C3
Kirtling Green Cambs 30 C3
Kirtlington Oxon 27 G11
Kirtomy Highld 93 C10
Kirton Lincs 37 B9
Kirton Notts 45 F10
Kirton Suff 31 E9
Kirton End Lincs 37 A8
Kirton Holme Lincs 37 A8
Kirton in Lindsey N Lincs 46 C3
Kislingbury Northants 28 C3
Kites Hardwick Warks 27 B11
Kittisford Som 7 D9
Kittle Swansea 23 H10
Kitt's Green W Mid 35 G7
Kitt's Moss Gtr Man 44 D2
Kittybrewster Aberdeen 83 C11
Kitwood Hants 10 A5
Kivernoll Hereford 25 E11
Kiveton Park S Yorks 45 D8
Knaith Lincs 46 D2
Knaith Park Lincs 46 D2
Knap Corner Dorset 9 B7
Knaphill Sur 18 F6
Knapp Perth 76 D5
Knapp Som 8 B2
Knapthorpe Notts 45 G11
Knapton Norf 39 B9
Knapton York 52 D1
Knapton Green Hereford 25 C11
Knapwell Cambs 29 B10
Knaresborough N Yorks 51 D9
Knarsdale Northumb 57 A8
Knauchland Moray 88 C5
Knaven Aberds 89 D8
Knayton N Yorks 58 H5
Knebworth Herts 29 F9
Knedlington E Yorks 52 G3
Kneesall Notts 45 F11
Kneesworth Cambs 29 D10
Kneeton Notts 45 H11
Knelston Swansea 23 H9
Knenhall Staffs 34 B5
Knettishall Suff 38 G5
Knightacott Devon 6 C5
Knightcote Warks 27 C10
Knightley Dale Staffs 34 C4
Knighton Devon 4 G6
Knighton Leicester 36 E1
Knighton = Tref-y-Clawdd Powys 25 A9
Knighton Staffs 34 A3
Knighton Staffs 34 C3
Knightswood Glasgow 68 D4
Knightwick Worcs 26 C4
Knill Hereford 25 B9
Knipton Leics 36 B4
Knitsley Durham 58 B2
Kniveton Derbys 44 G6
Knock Argyll 79 H8
Knock Cumb 57 D8
Knock Moray 88 C5
Knockally Highld 94 H3
Knockan Highld 92 H5
Knockandhu Moray 82 A4
Knockando Moray 88 D1
Knockando Ho. Moray 88 D2
Knockbain Highld 87 F9
Knockbreck Highld 84 B7
Knockbrex Dumfries 55 E8
Knockdee Highld 94 D3
Knockdolian S Ayrs 66 H4
Knockenkelly N Ayrs 66 D3
Knockentiber E Ayrs 67 C6
Knockespock Ho. Aberds 83 A7
Knockfarrel Highld 87 F8
Knockglass Dumfries 54 D3
Knockholt Kent 19 F11
Knockholt Pound Kent 19 F11
Knockie Lodge Highld 80 B6
Knockin Shrops 33 C9
Knockinlaw E Ayrs 67 C7
Knocklearn Dumfries 60 F3
Knocknaha Argyll 65 G7
Knocknain Dumfries 54 C2
Knockrome Argyll 72 F4
Knocksharry IoM 48 D2
Knodishall Suff 31 B11
Knolls Green Ches E 44 E2
Knolton Wrex 33 B9
Knolton Bryn Wrex 33 B9
Knook Wilts 16 G6
Knossington Leics 36 E4
Knott End-on-Sea Lancs 49 E3
Knotting Bedford 29 B7
Knotting Green Bedford 29 B7
Knottingley W Yorks 51 G11
Knotts Cumb 56 D6
Knotts Lancs 50 D3
Knotty Ash Mers 43 C7
Knotty Green Bucks 18 B6
Knowbury Shrops 26 A2
Knowe Dumfries 54 B6
Knowehead Dumfries 67 G9
Knowes of Elrick Aberds 88 C6
Knowesgate Northumb 62 E5
Knoweton N Lanark 68 E6
Knowhead Aberds 89 C9
Knowl Hill Windsor 18 D5
Knowle Bristol 16 D3
Knowle Devon 6 C3
Knowle Devon 7 F6
Knowle Devon 7 H9
Knowle Shrops 26 A2
Knowle W Mid 35 H7
Knowle Green Lancs 50 F2
Knowle Park W Yorks 51 E6
Knowlton Dorset 9 C9
Knowlton Kent 21 F9
Knowsley Mers 43 C7
Knowstone Devon 7 D7
Knox Bridge Kent 13 B6
Knucklas Powys 25 A9
Knuston Northants 28 B6
Knutsford Ches E 43 E10
Knutton Staffs 44 H2
Knypersley Staffs 44 G2
Kuggar Corn 2 H6
Kyle of Lochalsh Highld 85 F12
Kyleakin Highld 85 F12
Kylerhea Highld 85 F12
Kylesknoydart Highld 79 B11
Kylesku Highld 92 F5
Kylesmorar Highld 79 B11
Kylestrome Highld 92 F5
Kyllachy House Highld 81 A9
Kynaston Shrops 33 C9
Kynnersley Telford 34 D2
Kyre Magna Worcs 26 B3

L

La Fontenelle Guern 11
La Planque Guern 11
Labost W Isles 91 C7
Lacasaidh W Isles 91 E8
Lacasdal W Isles 91 D9
Laceby NE Lincs 46 B6
Lacey Green Bucks 18 B5
Lach Dennis Ches W 43 E10
Lackford Suff 30 A4
Lacock Wilts 16 E6
Ladbroke Warks 27 C11
Laddingford Kent 20 G3
Lade Bank Lincs 47 G7
Ladock Corn 3 D7
Lady Orkney 95 D7
Ladybank Fife 76 F6
Ladykirk Borders 71 F7
Ladysford Aberds 89 B9
Laga Highld 79 E9
Lagalochan Argyll 73 B7
Lagavulin Argyll 64 D5
Lagg Argyll 72 F4
Lagg N Ayrs 66 D2
Laggan Argyll 64 C3
Laggan Highld 79 D10
Laggan Highld 80 D4
Laggan Highld 81 D8
Laggan S Ayrs 54 A5
Lagganulva Argyll 78 G7
Laide Highld 91 H13
Laigh Fenwick E Ayrs 67 B7
Laigh Glengall S Ayrs 66 E6
Laighmuir E Ayrs 67 B7
Laindon Essex 20 C3
Lair Highld 86 G3
Lairg Highld 93 J8
Lairg Lodge Highld 93 J8
Lairg Muir Highld 93 J8
Lairgmore Highld 87 H8
Laisterdyke W Yorks 51 F7
Laithes Cumb 56 C6
Lake IoW 10 F4
Lake Wilts 17 H8
Lakenham Norf 39 E8
Lakenheath Suff 38 G3
Lakesend Norf 37 F11
Lakeside Cumb 56 H5
Laleham Sur 19 E7
Laleston Bridgend 14 D4
Lamarsh Essex 30 E5
Lamas Norf 39 C8
Lambden Borders 70 F6
Lamberhurst Kent 12 C5
Lamberhurst Quarter Kent 12 C5
Lamberton Borders 71 E8
Lambeth London 19 D10
Lambhill Glasgow 68 D4
Lambley Northumb 62 H2
Lambley Notts 45 H10
Lamborough Hill Oxon 17 A11
Lambourn W Berks 17 D10
Lambourne End Essex 19 B11
Lambs Green W Sus 19 H9
Lambston Pembs 22 E4
Lambton T&W 58 A3
Lamerton Devon 4 D5
Lamesley T&W 63 H8
Laminess Orkney 95 E7
Lamington Highld 87 D10
Lamington S Lanark 69 G8
Lamlash N Ayrs 66 C3
Lamloch Dumfries 67 G8
Lamonby Cumb 56 C6
Lamorna Corn 2 G3
Lamorran Corn 3 E7
Lampardbrook Suff 31 B9
Lampeter = Llanbedr Pont Steffan Ceredig 23 B10
Lampeter Velfrey Pembs 22 E6
Lamphey Pembs 22 F5
Lamplugh Cumb 56 D2
Lamport Northants 28 A4
Lamyatt Som 16 H3
Lana Devon 6 G2
Lanark S Lanark 69 F7
Lancaster Lancs 49 C4
Lanchester Durham 58 B2
Lancing W Sus 11 D10
Landbeach Cambs 29 B11
Landcross Devon 6 D3
Landerberry Aberds 83 C9
Landford Wilts 10 C1
Landford Manor Wilts 10 B1
Landimore Swansea 23 G9
Landkey Devon 6 C4
Landore Swansea 14 B2
Landrake Corn 4 E4
Landscove Devon 5 E8
Landshipping Pembs 22 E5
Landshipping Quay Pembs 22 E5
Landulph Corn 4 E5
Landwade Suff 30 B3
Lane Corn 3 C7
Lane End Bucks 18 B5
Lane End Cumb 56 G3
Lane End Dorset 9 E7
Lane End Hants 10 B4
Lane End IoW 10 F5
Lane End Lancs 50 E4
Lane Ends Lancs 50 D3
Lane Ends Lancs 50 F3
Lane Ends N Yorks 50 E5
Lane Head Derbys 44 E5
Lane Head Durham 58 E2
Lane Head Gtr Man 43 C9
Lane Head W Yorks 44 B5
Lane Side Lancs 50 G3
Laneast Corn 4 C3
Laneham Notts 46 E2
Lanehead Durham 57 B10
Lanehead Northumb 62 E3
Lanercost Cumb 61 G11
Laneshaw Bridge Lancs 50 E5
Lanfach Caerph 15 B8
Langar Notts 36 B3
Langbank Renfs 68 C2
Langbar N Yorks 51 D6
Langburnshiels Borders 61 C11
Langcliffe N Yorks 50 C4
Langdale Highld 93 E9
Langdale End N Yorks 59 G10
Langdon Corn 4 C4
Langdon Beck Durham 57 C10
Langdon Hills Essex 20 C3
Langdyke Fife 76 G6
Langenhoe Essex 31 G7
Langford C Beds 29 D8
Langford Devon 7 F9
Langford Essex 30 H5
Langford Notts 46 G2
Langford Oxon 17 A9
Langford Budville Som 7 D10
Langham Essex 31 E7
Langham Norf 38 A6
Langham Rutland 36 D4
Langham Suff 30 B6
Langhaugh Borders 69 G11
Langho Lancs 50 F3
Langholm Dumfries 61 E9
Langleeford Northumb 62 A5
Langley Ches E 44 E3
Langley Hants 10 D3
Langley Herts 29 F9
Langley Kent 20 F5
Langley Northumb 62 G4
Langley Slough 19 D7
Langley W Sus 11 B7
Langley Warks 27 B8
Langley Burrell Wilts 16 D6
Langley Common Derbys 35 B8
Langley Heath Kent 20 F5
Langley Lower Green Essex 29 E11
Langley Marsh Som 7 D9
Langley Park Durham 58 B3
Langley Street Norf 39 E9
Langley Upper Green Essex 29 E11
Langney E Sus 12 F5
Langold Notts 45 D9
Langore Corn 4 C4
Langport Som 8 B3
Langrick Lincs 46 H6
Langridge Bath 16 E4
Langridge Ford Devon 6 D4
Langrigg Cumb 56 B3
Langrish Hants 10 B6
Langsett S Yorks 44 B6
Langshaw Borders 70 G4
Langside Perth 75 F10
Langskaill Orkney 95 D5
Langstone Hants 10 D6
Langstone Newport 15 B9
Langthorne N Yorks 58 G3
Langthorpe N Yorks 51 C9
Langthwaite N Yorks 58 F1
Langtoft E Yorks 52 C6
Langtoft Lincs 37 D7
Langton Durham 58 E2
Langton Lincs 46 F6
Langton Lincs 47 E7
Langton N Yorks 52 C3
Langton by Wragby Lincs 46 E5
Langton Green Kent 12 C4
Langton Green Suff 31 A8
Langton Herring Dorset 8 F5
Langton Matravers Dorset 9 G9
Langtree Devon 6 E3
Langwathby Cumb 57 C7
Langwell Ho. Highld 94 H3
Langwell Lodge Highld 92 J4
Langwith Derbys 45 F9
Langwith Junction Derbys 45 F9
Langworth Lincs 46 E4
Lanivet Corn 3 C9
Lanlivery Corn 4 F1
Lanner Corn 2 F6
Lanreath Corn 4 F2
Lansallos Corn 4 F2
Lansdown Glos 26 F6
Lanteglos Highway Corn 4 F2
Lanton Borders 62 A2
Lanton Northumb 71 G8
Lapford Devon 7 F6
Laphroaig Argyll 64 D4
Lapley Staffs 34 D4
Lapworth Warks 27 A8
Larachbeg Highld 79 G9
Larbert Falk 69 B7
Larden Green Ches E 43 G8
Largie Aberds 88 E6
Largiemore Argyll 73 E8
Largoward Fife 77 G7
Largs N Ayrs 73 H11
Largybeg N Ayrs 66 D3
Largymore N Ayrs 66 D3
Larkfield Invclyd 73 F11
Larkhall S Lanark 68 E6
Larkhill Wilts 17 G8
Larling Norf 38 G5
Larriston Borders 61 D11
Lartington Durham 58 E1
Lary Aberds 82 C5
Lasham Hants 18 G3
Lashenden Kent 13 B7
Lassington Glos 26 F4
Lassodie Fife 69 A10
Lastingham N Yorks 59 G8
Latcham Som 15 G10
Latchford Herts 29 F10
Latchford Warr 43 D9
Latchingdon Essex 20 A5
Latchley Corn 4 D5
Lately Common Warr 43 C9
Lathbury M Keynes 28 D5
Latheron Highld 94 G3
Latheronwheel Highld 94 G3
Latheronwheel Ho. Highld 94 G3
Lathones Fife 77 G7
Latimer Bucks 19 B7
Latteridge S Glos 16 C3
Lattiford Som 8 B5
Latton Wilts 17 B7
Latton Bush Essex 29 H11
Lauchintilly Aberds 83 B9
Lauder Borders 70 F4
Laugharne Carms 23 E8
Laughterton Lincs 46 E2
Laughton E Sus 12 E4
Laughton Leics 36 G2
Laughton Lincs 37 B6
Laughton Lincs 46 C2
Laughton Common S Yorks 45 D9
Laughton en le Morthen S Yorks 45 D9
Launcells Corn 6 F1
Launceston Corn 4 C4
Launton Oxon 28 F3
Laurencekirk Aberds 83 F9
Laurieston Dumfries 55 C9
Laurieston Falk 69 C8
Lavendon M Keynes 28 C6
Lavenham Suff 30 D6
Laverhay Dumfries 61 D7
Laversdale Cumb 61 G10
Laverstock Wilts 9 A10
Laverstoke Hants 17 G11
Laverton Glos 27 E7
Laverton N Yorks 51 B8
Laverton Som 16 F4
Lavister Wrex 42 G6
Law S Lanark 69 E7
Lawers Perth 75 D9
Lawers Perth 75 E10
Lawford Essex 31 E7
Lawhitton Corn 4 C4
Lawkland N Yorks 50 C3
Lawley Telford 34 E2
Lawnhead Staffs 34 C4
Lawrenny Pembs 22 F5
Lawshall Suff 30 C5
Lawton Hereford 25 C11
Laxey IoM 48 D4
Laxfield Suff 31 A9
Laxfirth Shetland 96 H6
Laxfirth Shetland 96 J6
Laxford Bridge Highld 92 E5
Laxo Shetland 96 G6
Laxobigging Shetland 96 F6
Laxton E Yorks 52 G3
Laxton Northants 36 F5
Laxton Notts 45 F11
Laycock W Yorks 50 E6
Layer Breton Essex 30 G6
Layer de la Haye Essex 30 G6
Layer Marney Essex 30 G6
Layham Suff 31 D7
Laylands Green W Berks 17 E10
Laytham E Yorks 52 F3
Layton Blackpool 49 F3
Lazenby Redcar 59 D6
Lazonby Cumb 57 C7
Le Planel Guern 11
Le Skerne Haughton Darl 58 E4
Le Villocq Guern 11
Lea Derbys 45 G7
Lea Hereford 26 F3
Lea Lincs 46 D2
Lea Shrops 33 E10
Lea Shrops 33 G9
Lea Wilts 16 C6
Lea Marston Warks 35 F8
Lea Town Lancs 49 F4
Leabrooks Derbys 45 G8
Leac a Li W Isles 90 H6
Leachkin Highld 87 G9
Leadburn Midloth 69 E11
Leaden Roding Essex 30 G2
Leadenham Lincs 46 G3
Leadgate Cumb 57 B9
Leadgate Durham 58 A2
Leadgate T&W 63 H7
Leadhills S Lanark 60 B4
Leafield Oxon 27 G10
Leagrave Luton 29 F7
Leake N Yorks 58 G5
Leake Commonside Lincs 47 G7
Lealholm N Yorks 59 F8
Lealt Argyll 72 D5
Lealt Highld 85 B10
Leamington Hastings Warks 27 B11
Leamonsley Staffs 35 E7
Leamside Durham 58 B4
Leanaig Highld 87 F8
Leargybreck Argyll 72 F4
Leasgill Cumb 49 A4
Leasingham Lincs 46 H4
Leasingthorne Durham 58 D3
Leasowe Mers 42 C5
Leatherhead Sur 19 F8
Leatherhead Common Sur 19 F8
Leathley N Yorks 51 E8
Leaton Shrops 33 D10
Leaveland Kent 21 F7
Leavening N Yorks 52 C3
Leaves Green London 19 E11
Leazes Durham 63 H7
Lebberston N Yorks 53 A6
Lechlade-on-Thames Glos 17 B9
Leck Lancs 50 B2
Leckford Hants 17 H10
Leckfurin Highld 93 D10
Leckgruinart Argyll 64 B3
Leckhampstead Bucks 28 E4
Leckhampstead W Berks 17 D11
Leckhampstead Thicket W Berks 17 D11
Leckhampton Glos 26 G6
Leckie Highld 86 E3
Leckmelm Highld 86 B4
Leckwith V Glam 15 D7
Leconfield E Yorks 52 E6
Ledaig Argyll 74 D2
Ledburn Bucks 28 F6
Ledbury Hereford 26 E4
Ledcharrie Stirling 75 E8
Ledgemoor Hereford 25 C11
Ledicot Hereford 25 B11
Ledmore Highld 92 H5
Lednagullin Highld 93 C10
Ledsham Ches W 42 E6
Ledsham W Yorks 51 G10
Ledston W Yorks 51 G10
Ledston Luck W Yorks 51 F10
Ledwell Oxon 27 F11
Lee Argyll 78 J7
Lee Devon 6 B3
Lee Hants 10 C2
Lee Lancs 50 D1
Lee Shrops 33 B10
Lee Brockhurst Shrops 33 C11
Lee Clump Bucks 18 A6
Lee Mill Devon 5 F7
Lee Moor Devon 5 E6
Lee-on-the-Solent Hants 10 D4
Leeans Shetland 96 J5
Leebotten Shetland 96 L6
Leebotwood Shrops 33 F10
Leece Cumb 49 C2
Leechpool Pembs 22 E4
Leeds Kent 20 F5
Leeds W Yorks 51 F8
Leedstown Corn 2 F5
Leek Staffs 44 G3
Leek Wootton Warks 27 B9
Leekbrook Staffs 44 G3
Leeming N Yorks 58 H3
Leeming Bar N Yorks 58 G3
Lees Derbys 35 B8
Lees Gtr Man 44 B3
Lees W Yorks 50 F6
Leeswood Flint 42 F5
Legbourne Lincs 47 D7
Legerwood Borders 70 F4
Legsby Lincs 46 D5
Leicester Leicester 36 E1
Leicester Forest East Leics 35 E11
Leigh Dorset 8 D5
Leigh Glos 26 F5
Leigh Gtr Man 43 B9
Leigh Kent 20 G2
Leigh Shrops 33 E9
Leigh Sur 19 G9
Leigh Wilts 17 B7
Leigh Worcs 26 C4
Leigh Beck Essex 20 C5
Leigh Common Som 8 B6
Leigh Delamere Wilts 16 D5
Leigh Green Kent 13 C8
Leigh on Sea Southend 20 C5
Leigh Park Hants 10 D6
Leigh Sinton Worcs 26 C4
Leigh upon Mendip Som 16 G3
Leigh Woods N Som 16 D2
Leighswood W Mid 35 E6
Leighterton Glos 16 B5
Leighton N Yorks 51 B7
Leighton Powys 33 E8
Leighton Shrops 34 E2
Leighton Som 16 G4
Leighton Bromswold Cambs 37 H7
Leighton Buzzard C Beds 28 F6
Leinthall Earls Hereford 25 B11
Leinthall Starkes Hereford 25 B11
Leintwardine Hereford 25 A11
Leire Leics 35 F11
Leirinmore Highld 92 C7
Leiston Suff 31 B11
Leitfie Perth 76 C5
Leith Edin 69 C11
Leitholm Borders 70 F6
Lelant Corn 2 F4
Lelley E Yorks 53 F8
Lem Hill Worcs 26 A4
Lemmington Hall Northumb 63 B7
Lempitlaw Borders 70 G6
Lenchwick Worcs 27 D7
Lendalfoot S Ayrs 66 H4
Lendrick Lodge Stirling 75 G8
Lenham Kent 20 F5
Lenham Heath Kent 20 G6
Lennel Borders 71 F7
Lennoxtown E Dunb 68 C5
Lenton Lincs 36 B6
Lenton Nottingham 36 B1
Lentran Highld 87 G8
Lenwade Norf 39 D6
Leny Ho. Stirling 75 G9
Lenzie E Dunb 68 C5
Leoch Angus 76 D6
Leochel-Cushnie Aberds 83 B7
Leominster Hereford 25 C11
Leonard Stanley Glos 16 A5
Leorin Argyll 64 D4
Lepe Hants 10 E3
Lephin Highld 84 D6
Lephinchapel Argyll 73 D8
Lephinmore Argyll 73 D8
Leppington N Yorks 52 C3
Lepton W Yorks 51 H8
Lerryn Corn 4 F2
Lerwick Shetland 96 J6
Lesbury Northumb 63 B8
Leslie Aberds 83 A7
Leslie Fife 76 G5
Lesmahagow S Lanark 69 G7
Lesnewth Corn 4 B2
Lessendrum Aberds 88 D5
Lessingham Norf 39 C9
Lessonhall Cumb 56 A4
Leswalt Dumfries 54 C3
Letchmore Heath Herts 19 B8
Letchworth Herts 29 E9
Letcombe Bassett Oxon 17 C10
Letcombe Regis Oxon 17 C10
Letham Angus 77 C8
Letham Falk 69 B7
Letham Fife 76 F6
Letham Perth 76 E3
Letham Grange Angus 77 C9
Lethenty Aberds 89 D8
Letheringham Suff 31 C9
Letheringsett Norf 39 B6
Lettaford Devon 5 C8
Lettan Orkney 95 D8
Letterewe Highld 86 D2
Letterfearn Highld 85 F13
Letterfinlay Highld 80 D4
Lettermorar Highld 79 C10
Lettermore Argyll 78 G7
Letters Highld 86 C4
Letterston Pembs 22 D4
Lettoch Highld 82 B2
Lettoch Highld 87 H13
Letton Hereford 25 A10
Letton Hereford 25 D10
Letton Green Norf 38 E5
Letty Green Herts 29 G9
Letwell S Yorks 45 D9
Leuchars Fife 77 E7
Leuchars Ho. Moray 88 B2
Leumrabhagh W Isles 91 F8
Levan Invclyd 73 F11
Levaneap Shetland 96 G6
Levedale Staffs 34 D4
Leven E Yorks 53 E7
Leven Fife 76 G6
Levencorroch N Ayrs 66 D3
Levens Cumb 57 H6
Levens Green Herts 29 F10
Levenshulme Gtr Man 44 C2
Levenwick Shetland 96 L6
Leverburgh = An t-Ob W Isles 90 J5
Leverington Cambs 37 D10
Leverton Lincs 47 H8
Leverton Highgate Lincs 47 H8
Leverton Lucasgate Lincs 47 H8
Leverton Outgate Lincs 47 H8
Levington Suff 31 E9
Levisham N Yorks 59 G9
Levishie Highld 80 B6
Lew Oxon 27 H10
Lewannick Corn 4 C3
Lewdown Devon 4 C5
Lewes E Sus 12 E3
Leweston Pembs 22 D4
Lewisham London 19 D10
Lewiston Highld 81 A7
Lewistown Bridgend 14 C5
Lewknor Oxon 18 B4
Leworthy Devon 6 C5
Leworthy Devon 6 F2
Lewtrenchard Devon 4 C5
Lexden Essex 30 F6
Ley Aberds 83 B7
Ley Corn 4 E2
Leybourne Kent 20 F3
Leyburn N Yorks 58 G2
Leyfields Staffs 35 E8
Leyhill Bucks 18 A6
Leyland Lancs 49 G5
Leylodge Aberds 83 B9
Leymoor W Yorks 51 H7
Leys Aberds 89 C10
Leys Perth 76 D5
Leys Castle Highld 87 G9
Leys of Cossans Angus 76 C6
Leysdown-on-Sea Kent 21 D7
Leysmill Angus 77 C9
Leysters Pole Hereford 26 B2
Leyton London 19 C10
Leytonstone London 19 C10
Lezant Corn 4 D4
Leziate Norf 38 D2
Lhanbryde Moray 88 B2
Liatrie Highld 86 H5
Libanus Powys 24 F6
Libberton S Lanark 69 F8
Liberton Edin 69 D11
Liceasto W Isles 90 H6
Lichfield Staffs 35 E7
Lickey Worcs 34 H5
Lickey End Worcs 26 A6
Lickfold W Sus 11 B8
Liddel Orkney 95 K5
Liddesdale Highld 79 F10
Liddington Swindon 17 C9
Lidgate Suff 30 C4
Lidget S Yorks 45 B10
Lidget Green W Yorks 51 F7
Lidgett Notts 45 F10
Lidlington C Beds 28 E6
Lidstone Oxon 27 F10
Lieurary Highld 94 D2
Liff Angus 76 D6
Lifton Devon 4 C4
Liftondown Devon 4 C4
Lighthorne Warks 27 C10
Lightwater Sur 18 E6
Lightwood Stoke 34 A5
Lightwood Green Ches E 34 A2
Lightwood Green Wrex 33 A9
Lilbourne Northants 36 H1
Lilburn Tower Northumb 62 A6
Lilleshall Telford 34 D3
Lilley Herts 29 F8
Lilley W Berks 17 D11
Lilliesleaf Borders 61 A11
Lillingstone Dayrell Bucks 28 E4
Lillingstone Lovell Bucks 28 D4
Lillington Dorset 8 C5
Lillington Warks 27 B10
Lilliput Poole 9 E9
Lilstock Som 7 B10
Lilyhurst Shrops 34 D3
Limbury Luton 29 F7
Limebrook Hereford 25 B10
Limefield Gtr Man 44 A2
Limekilnburn S Lanark 68 E6
Limekilns Fife 69 B9
Limerigg Falk 69 C7
Limerstone IoW 10 F3
Limington Som 8 B4
Limpenhoe Norf 39 E9
Limpley Stoke Wilts 16 E4
Limpsfield Sur 19 F11
Limpsfield Chart Sur 19 F11
Linby Notts 45 G9
Linchmere W Sus 11 A7
Lincluden Dumfries 60 F5
Lincoln Lincs 46 E3
Lincomb Worcs 26 B5
Lincombe Devon 5 F8
Lindal in Furness Cumb 49 B2
Lindale Cumb 49 A4
Lindean Borders 70 G3
Lindfield W Sus 12 D2
Lindford Hants 18 H5
Lindifferon Fife 76 F6
Lindley W Yorks 51 H7
Lindley Green N Yorks 51 E8
Lindores Fife 76 F5
Lindridge Worcs 26 B3
Lindsell Essex 30 F3
Lindsey Suff 30 D6
Linford Hants 9 D10
Linford Thurrock 20 D3
Lingague IoM 48 E2
Lingards Wood W Yorks 44 A4
Lingbob W Yorks 51 F6
Lingdale Redcar 59 E7
Lingen Hereford 25 B10
Lingfield Sur 12 B2
Lingreabhagh W Isles 90 J5
Lingwood Norf 39 E9
Linicro Highld 85 B8
Linkenholt Hants 17 F10
Linkhill Kent 13 D7
Linkinhorne Corn 4 D4
Linklater Orkney 95 K5
Linksness Orkney 95 H3
Linktown Fife 69 A11
Linley Shrops 33 F9
Linley Green Hereford 26 C3
Linlithgow W Loth 69 C9
Linlithgow Bridge W Loth 69 C8
Linshiels Northumb 62 C4
Linsiadar W Isles 90 D7
Linsidemore Highld 87 B8
Linslade C Beds 28 F6
Linstead Parva Suff 39 H9
Linstock Cumb 61 H10
Linthwaite W Yorks 44 A5
Lintlaw Borders 71 E7
Lintmill Moray 88 B5
Linton Borders 70 H6
Linton Cambs 30 D2
Linton Derbys 35 D8
Linton Hereford 26 F3
Linton Kent 20 G4
Linton N Yorks 50 C5
Linton Northumb 63 D8
Linton W Yorks 51 E9
Linton-on-Ouse N Yorks 51 C10
Linwood Hants 9 D10
Linwood Lincs 46 D5
Linwood Renfs 68 D3
Lionacleit W Isles 84 D2
Lional W Isles 91 A10
Liphook Hants 11 A7
Liscard Mers 42 C6
Liscombe Som 7 C7
Liskeard Corn 4 E3
L'Islet Guern 11
Liss Hants 11 B6
Liss Forest Hants 11 B6
Lissett E Yorks 53 D7
Lissington Lincs 46 D5
Lisvane Cardiff 15 C7
Liswerry Newport 15 C9
Litcham Norf 38 D4
Litchborough Northants 28 C3
Litchfield Hants 17 F11
Litherland Mers 42 C6
Litlington Cambs 29 D10
Litlington E Sus 12 F4
Little Abington Cambs 30 D2
Little Addington Northants 28 A6
Little Alne Warks 27 B8
Little Altcar Mers 42 B6
Little Asby Cumb 57 F8
Little Assynt Highld 92 G4
Little Aston Staffs 35 E6
Little Atherfield IoW 10 F3
Little Ayre Orkney 95 J4
Little-ayre Shetland 96 G5
Little Ayton N Yorks 59 E6
Little Baddow Essex 30 H4
Little Badminton S Glos 16 C5
Little Ballinluig Perth 76 B2
Little Bampton Cumb 61 H8
Little Bardfield Essex 30 E3
Little Barford Bedford 29 C8
Little Barningham Norf 39 B7
Little Barrington Glos 27 G9
Little Barrow Ches W 43 F7
Little Barugh N Yorks 52 B3
Little Bavington Northumb 62 F5
Little Bealings Suff 31 D9
Little Bedwyn Wilts 17 E9
Little Bentley Essex 31 F8
Little Berkhamsted Herts 29 H9
Little Billing Northants 28 B5
Little Birch Hereford 26 E2
Little Blakenham Suff 31 D8
Little Blencow Cumb 56 C6
Little Bollington Ches E 43 D10
Little Bookham Sur 19 F8
Little Bowden Leics 36 G3
Little Bradley Suff 30 C3
Little Brampton Shrops 33 G9
Little Brechin Angus 77 A8
Little Brickhill M Keynes 28 E6
Little Brington Northants 28 B3
Little Bromley Essex 31 F7
Little Broughton Cumb 56 C2
Little Budworth Ches W 43 F8
Little Burstead Essex 20 B3
Little Bytham Lincs 36 D6
Little Carlton Lincs 47 D7
Little Carlton Notts 45 G11
Little Casterton Rutland 36 E6
Little Cawthorpe Lincs 47 D7
Little Chalfont Bucks 18 B6
Little Chart Kent 20 G6
Little Chesterford Essex 30 D2
Little Cheverell Wilts 16 F6
Little Chishill Cambs 29 E11
Little Clacton Essex 31 G8
Little Clifton Cumb 56 D2
Little Colp Aberds 89 D7
Little Comberton Worcs 26 D6
Little Common E Sus 12 F6
Little Compton Warks 27 E9
Little Cornard Suff 30 E5
Little Cowarne Hereford 26 C3
Little Coxwell Oxon 17 B9
Little Crakehall N Yorks 58 G3
Little Cressingham Norf 38 F4
Little Crosby Mers 42 B6
Little Dalby Leics 36 D3
Little Dawley Telford 34 E2
Little Dens Aberds 89 D10
Little Dewchurch Hereford 26 E2
Little Downham Cambs 37 G11
Little Driffield E Yorks 52 D6
Little Dunham Norf 38 D4
Little Dunkeld Perth 76 C3
Little Dunmow Essex 30 F3
Little Easton Essex 30 F3
Little Eaton Derbys 35 A9
Little Eccleston Lancs 49 E4
Little Ellingham Norf 38 F6
Little End Essex 20 A2
Little Eversden Cambs 29 C10
Little Faringdon Oxon 17 A9
Little Fencote N Yorks 58 G3
Little Fenton N Yorks 51 F11
Little Finborough Suff 31 C7
Little Fransham Norf 38 D5
Little Gaddesden Herts 28 G6
Little Gidding Cambs 37 G7
Little Glemham Suff 31 C10
Little Glenshee Perth 76 D2
Little Gransden Cambs 29 C9
Little Green Som 16 G4
Little Grimsby Lincs 47 C7
Little Gruinard Highld 86 C2
Little Habton N Yorks 52 B3
Little Hadham Herts 29 F11
Little Hale Lincs 37 A7
Little Hallingbury Essex 29 G11
Little Hampden Bucks 18 A5
Little Harrowden Northants 28 A5
Little Haseley Oxon 18 A3
Little Hatfield E Yorks 53 E7
Little Hautbois Norf 39 C8
Little Haven Pembs 22 E3
Little Hay Staffs 35 E7
Little Hayfield Derbys 44 D4
Little Haywood Staffs 34 C6
Little Heath W Mid 35 G9
Little Hereford Hereford 26 B2
Little Horkesley Essex 30 E6
Little Horsted E Sus 12 E3
Little Horton W Yorks 51 F7
Little Horwood Bucks 28 E4
Little Houghton Northants 28 C5
Little Houghton S Yorks 45 B8
Little Hucklow Derbys 44 E5
Little Hulton Gtr Man 43 B10
Little Humber E Yorks 53 G7
Little Hungerford W Berks 18 D2
Little Irchester Northants 28 B6
Little Kimble Bucks 28 H5
Little Kineton Warks 27 C10
Little Kingshill Bucks 18 B5
Little Langdale Cumb 56 F5
Little Langford Wilts 17 H7
Little Laver Essex 30 H2
Little Leigh Ches W 43 E9
Little Leighs Essex 30 G4
Little Lever Gtr Man 43 B10
Little London Bucks 28 G3
Little London E Sus 12 E4
Little London Hants 17 G10
Little London Hants 18 F3
Little London Lincs 37 C10
Little London Lincs 37 C8
Little London Norf 39 C7
Little London Powys 32 G6
Little Longstone Derbys 44 E5
Little Lynturk Aberds 83 B7
Little Malvern Worcs 26 D4
Little Maplestead Essex 30 E5
Little Marcle Hereford 26 E3
Little Marlow Bucks 18 C5
Little Marsden Lancs 50 F4
Little Massingham Norf 38 C3
Little Melton Norf 39 E7
Little Mill Mon 15 A9
Little Milton Oxon 18 A3
Little Missenden Bucks 18 B6
Little Musgrave Cumb 57 E9
Little Ness Shrops 33 D10
Little Neston Ches W 42 E5
Little Newcastle Pembs 22 D4
Little Newsham Durham 58 E2
Little Oakley Essex 31 F9
Little Oakley Northants 36 G4
Little Orton Cumb 61 H9
Little Ouseburn N Yorks 51 C10
Little Paxton Cambs 29 B8
Little Petherick Corn 3 B8
Little Pitlurg Moray 88 D4
Little Plumpton Lancs 49 F3
Little Plumstead Norf 39 D9
Little Ponton Lincs 36 B5
Little Raveley Cambs 37 H8
Little Reedness E Yorks 52 G4
Little Ribston N Yorks 51 D9
Little Rissington Glos 27 G8
Little Ryburgh Norf 38 C5
Little Ryle Northumb 62 B6
Little Salkeld Cumb 57 C7
Little Sampford Essex 30 E3
Little Sandhurst Brack 18 E5
Little Saxham Suff 30 B4
Little Scatwell Highld 86 F6
Little Sessay N Yorks 51 B10
Little Shelford Cambs 29 C11
Little Singleton Lancs 49 F3
Little Skillymarno Aberds 89 C9
Little Smeaton N Yorks 51 H11
Little Snoring Norf 38 B5
Little Sodbury S Glos 16 C4
Little Somborne Hants 10 A2
Little Somerford Wilts 16 C6
Little Stainforth N Yorks 50 C4
Little Stainton Darl 58 D4
Little Stanney Ches W 43 E7
Little Staughton Bedford 29 B8
Little Steeping Lincs 47 F8
Little Stoke Staffs 34 B5
Little Stonham Suff 31 B8
Little Stretton Leics 36 E2
Little Stretton Shrops 33 F10
Little Strickland Cumb 57 E7
Little Stukeley Cambs 37 H8
Little Sutton Ches W 42 E6
Little Tew Oxon 27 F10
Little Thetford Cambs 37 H11
Little Thirkleby N Yorks 51 B10
Little Thurlow Suff 30 C3
Little Thurrock Thurrock 20 D3
Little Torboll Highld 87 B10
Little Torrington Devon 6 E3
Little Totham Essex 30 G5
Little Toux Aberds 88 C5
Little Town Cumb 56 E4
Little Town Lancs 50 F2
Little Urswick Cumb 49 B2
Little Wakering Essex 20 C6
Little Walden Essex 30 D2
Little Waldingfield Suff 30 D6
Little Walsingham Norf 38 B5
Little Waltham Essex 30 G4
Little Warley Essex 20 B3
Little Weighton E Yorks 52 F5
Little Weldon Northants 36 G5
Little Welnetham Suff 30 B5
Little Wenlock Telford 34 E2
Little Whittingham Green Suff 39 H8
Little Wilbraham Cambs 30 C2
Little Wishford Wilts 17 H7
Little Witley Worcs 26 B4
Little Wittenham Oxon 18 B2
Little Wolford Warks 27 E9
Little Wratting Suff 30 D3
Little Wymington Bedford 28 B6
Little Wymondley Herts 29 F9
Little Wyrley Staffs 34 E6
Little Yeldham Essex 30 E4
Littlebeck N Yorks 59 F9
Littleborough Gtr Man 50 H5
Littleborough Notts 46 D2
Littlebourne Kent 21 F9
Littlebredy Dorset 8 F4
Littlebury Essex 30 E2
Littlebury Green Essex 29 E11
Littledean Glos 26 G3
Littleferry Highld 87 B11
Littleham Devon 5 C11
Littleham Devon 6 D3
Littlehampton W Sus 11 D9
Littlehempston Devon 5 E9
Littlehoughton Northumb 63 B8
Littlemill Aberds 82 D5
Littlemill E Ayrs 67 E7
Littlemill Highld 87 F12
Littlemill Northumb 63 B8
Littlemoor Dorset 8 F5
Littlemore Oxon 18 A2
Littleover Derby 35 B9
Littleport Cambs 38 G1
Littlestone on Sea Kent 13 D9
Littlethorpe Leics 35 F11
Littlethorpe N Yorks 51 C9
Littleton Ches W 43 F7
Littleton Hants 10 A3
Littleton Perth 76 D5
Littleton Som 8 A3
Littleton Sur 18 G6
Littleton Sur 19 E7
Littleton Drew Wilts 16 C5
Littleton-on-Severn S Glos 16 C2
Littleton Pannell Wilts 17 F7
Littletown Durham 58 B4
Littlewick Green Windsor 18 D5
Littleworth Bedford 29 D7
Littleworth Glos 16 A5
Littleworth Oxon 17 B10
Littleworth Staffs 34 D6
Littleworth Worcs 26 C5
Litton Derbys 44 E5
Litton N Yorks 50 B5
Litton Som 16 F2
Litton Cheney Dorset 8 E4
Liurbost W Isles 91 E8
Liverpool Mers 42 C6
Liverpool Airport Mers 43 D7
Liversedge W Yorks 51 G8
Liverton Devon 5 D9
Liverton Redcar 59 E8
Livingston W Loth 69 D9
Livingston Village W Loth 69 D9
Lixwm Flint 42 E4
Lizard Corn 2 H6
Llaingoch Anglesey 40 B4
Llaithddu Powys 33 G6
Llan Powys 32 E4
Llan Ffestiniog Gwyn 41 F9
Llan-y-pwll Wrex 42 G6
Llanaber Gwyn 32 D2
Llanaelhaearn Gwyn 40 F5
Llanafan Ceredig 24 A3
Llanafan-fawr Powys 24 C6
Llanallgo Anglesey 40 B6
Llanandras = Presteigne Powys 25 B10
Llanarmon Gwyn 40 G6
Llanarmon Dyffryn Ceiriog Wrex 33 B7
Llanarmon-yn-Ial Denb 42 G4
Llanarth Ceredig 23 A9
Llanarth Mon 25 G10
Llanarthne Carms 23 D10
Llanasa Flint 42 D4
Llanbabo Anglesey 40 B5
Llanbadarn Fawr Ceredig 32 G2
Llanbadarn Fynydd Powys 33 H7
Llanbadarn-y-Garreg Powys 25 D8
Llanbadoc Mon 15 B9
Llanbadrig Anglesey 40 A5
Llanbeder Newport 15 B9
Llanbedr Gwyn 32 C1
Llanbedr Powys 25 D8
Llanbedr Powys 25 F9
Llanbedr-Dyffryn-Clwyd Denb 42 G4
Llanbedr Pont Steffan = Lampeter Ceredig 23 B10
Llanbedr-y-cennin Conwy 41 D9
Llanbedrgoch Anglesey 41 B7
Llanbedrog Gwyn 40 G5
Llanberis Gwyn 41 D7
Llanbethêry V Glam 14 E6
Llanbister Powys 25 A8
Llanblethian V Glam 14 D5
Llanboidy Carms 23 D7
Llanbradach Caerph 15 B7
Llanbrynmair Powys 32 E4
Llancarfan V Glam 14 D6
Llancayo Mon 15 A9
Llancloudy Hereford 25 F11
Llancynfelyn Ceredig 32 F2
Llandaff Cardiff 15 D7
Llandanwg Gwyn 32 C1
Llandarcy Neath 14 B3
Llandawke Carms 23 E7
Llanddaniel Fab Anglesey 40 C6
Llanddarog Carms 23 E10
Llanddeiniol Ceredig 24 A2
Llanddeiniolen Gwyn 41 D7
Llandderfel Gwyn 32 B5
Llanddeusant Anglesey 40 B5
Llanddeusant Carms 24 F4
Llanddew Powys 25 E7
Llanddewi Swansea 23 H9
Llanddewi-Brefi Ceredig 24 C3
Llanddewi Rhydderch Mon 25 G10
Llanddewi Velfrey Pembs 22 E6
Llanddewi'r Cwm Powys 25 D7
Llanddoged Conwy 41 D10
Llanddona Anglesey 41 C7
Llanddowror Carms 23 E7
Llanddulas Conwy 42 E2
Llanddwywe Gwyn 32 C1
Llanddyfynan Anglesey 41 C7
Llandefaelog Fach Powys 25 E7
Llandefaelog-tre'r-graig Powys 25 F8
Llandefalle Powys 25 E8
Llandegai Gwyn 41 C7
Llandegfan Anglesey 41 C7
Llandegla Denb 42 G4
Llandegley Powys 25 B8
Llandegveth Mon 15 B9
Llandegwning Gwyn 40 G4
Llandeilo Carms 24 F3
Llandeilo Graban Powys 25 D7
Llandeilo'r Fan Powys 24 E5
Llandeloy Pembs 22 D3
Llandenny Mon 15 A10
Llandevenny Mon 15 C10
Llandewednock Corn 2 H6
Llandewi Ystradenny Powys 25 B8
Llandinabo Hereford 26 F2
Llandinam Powys 32 G6
Llandissilio Pembs 22 D6
Llandogo Mon 15 A11
Llandough V Glam 14 D5
Llandough V Glam 15 D7
Llandovery = Llanymddyfri Carms 24 E4
Llandow V Glam 14 D5
Llandre Carms 24 D3
Llandre Ceredig 32 G2
Llandrillo Denb 32 B6
Llandrillo-yn-Rhos Conwy 41 B10
Llandrindod = Llandrindod Wells Powys 25 B7
Llandrindod Wells = Llandrindod Powys 25 B7
Llandrinio Powys 33 D8
Llandudno Conwy 41 B9
Llandudno Junction = Cyffordd Llandudno Conwy 41 C9
Llandwrog Gwyn 40 E6
Llandybie Carms 24 G3
Llandyfaelog Carms 23 E9
Llandyfan Carms 24 G3
Llandyfriog Ceredig 23 B8
Llandyfrydog Anglesey 40 B6
Llandygwydd Ceredig 23 B7
Llandynan Denb 42 H4
Llandyrnog Denb 42 F4
Llandysilio Powys 33 D8
Llandyssil Powys 33 F7
Llandysul Ceredig 23 B9
Llanedeyrn Cardiff 15 C8
Llanedi Carms 23 F10
Llaneglwys Powys 25 E7
Llanegryn Gwyn 32 E1
Llanegwad Carms 23 D10
Llaneilian Anglesey 40 A6
Llanelian-yn-Rhos Conwy 41 C10
Llanelidan Denb 42 G4
Llanelieu Powys 25 E8
Llanellen Mon 25 G10
Llanelli Carms 23 G10
Llanelltyd Gwyn 32 D3
Llanelly Mon 25 G9
Llanelly Hill Mon 25 G9
Llanelwedd Powys 25 C7
Llanelwy = St Asaph Denb 42 E3
Llanenddwyn Gwyn 32 C1
Llanengan Gwyn 40 H4
Llanerchymedd Anglesey 40 B6
Llanerfyl Powys 32 E6
Llanfachraeth Anglesey 40 B5
Llanfachreth Gwyn 32 C3
Llanfaelog Anglesey 40 C5
Llanfaelrhys Gwyn 40 H4
Llanfaenor Mon 25 G11
Llanfaes Anglesey 41 C8
Llanfaes Powys 25 F7
Llanfaethlu Anglesey 40 B5
Llanfaglan Gwyn 40 D6
Llanfair Gwyn 32 C1
Llanfair-ar-y-bryn Carms 24 E5
Llanfair Caereinion Powys 33 E7
Llanfair Clydogau Ceredig 24 C3
Llanfair-Dyffryn-Clwyd Denb 42 G4
Llanfair Kilgheddin Mon 25 H10
Llanfair-Nant-Gwyn Pembs 22 C6
Llanfair Talhaiarn Conwy 42 E2
Llanfair Waterdine Shrops 33 H8
Llanfair-ym-Muallt = Builth Wells Powys 25 C7
Llanfairfechan Conwy 41 C8
Llanfairpwll-gwyngyll Anglesey 41 C7
Llanfairyneubwll Anglesey 40 C5
Llanfairynghornwy Anglesey 40 A5
Llanfallteg Carms 22 E6
Llanfaredd Powys 25 C7
Llanfarian Ceredig 32 H1
Llanfechain Powys 33 C7
Llanfechan Powys 24 C6
Llanfechell Anglesey 40 A5
Llanfendigaid Gwyn 32 E1
Llanferres Denb 42 F4
Llanfflewyn Anglesey 40 B5
Llanfihangel-ar-arth Carms 23 C9
Llanfihangel-Crucorney Mon 25 F10
Llanfihangel Glyn Myfyr Conwy 42 H2
Llanfihangel Nant Bran Powys 24 E6
Llanfihangel-nant-Melan Powys 25 C8
Llanfihangel Rhydithon Powys 25 B8
Llanfihangel Rogiet Mon 15 C10
Llanfihangel Tal-y-llyn Powys 25 F8
Llanfihangel-uwch-Gwili Carms 23 D9
Llanfihangel-y-Creuddyn Ceredig 32 H2
Llanfihangel-y-pennant Gwyn 32 E2
Llanfihangel-y-pennant Gwyn 41 F7
Llanfihangel-y-traethau Gwyn 41 G7
Llanfihangel-yn-Ngwynfa Powys 33 D6
Llanfihangel yn Nhowyn Anglesey 40 C5
Llanfilo Powys 25 E8
Llanfoist Mon 25 G9
Llanfor Gwyn 32 B5
Llanfrechfa Torf 15 B9
Llanfrothen Gwyn 41 F8
Llanfrynach Powys 25 F7
Llanfwrog Anglesey 40 B5
Llanfwrog Denb 42 G4
Llanfyllin Powys 33 D7
Llanfynydd Carms 23 D10
Llanfynydd Flint 42 G5
Llanfyrnach Pembs 23 C7
Llangadfan Powys 32 D6
Llangadog Carms 24 F4
Llangadwaladr Anglesey 40 D5
Llangadwaladr Powys 33 B7
Llangaffo Anglesey 40 D6
Llangain Carms 23 E8
Llangammarch Wells Powys 24 D6
Llangan V Glam 14 D5
Llangarron Hereford 26 F2
Llangasty Talyllyn Powys 25 F8
Llangathen Carms 23 D10
Llangattock Powys 25 G9
Llangattock Lingoed Mon 25 F10
Llangattock nigh Usk Mon 25 H10
Llangattock-Vibon-Avel Mon 25 G11
Llangedwyn Powys 33 C7
Llangefni Anglesey 40 C6
Llangeinor Bridgend 14 C5
Llangeitho Ceredig 24 C3
Llangeler Carms 23 C8
Llangelynin Gwyn 32 E1
Llangendeirne Carms 23 E9
Llangennech Carms 23 F10
Llangennith Swansea 23 G9
Llangenny Powys 25 G9
Llangernyw Conwy 41 D10
Llangian Gwyn 40 H4
Llanglydwen Carms 22 D6
Llangoed Anglesey 41 C8
Llangoedmor Ceredig 22 B6
Llangollen Denb 33 A8
Llangolman Pembs 22 D6
Llangors Powys 25 F8
Llangovan Mon 25 H11
Llangower Gwyn 32 B5
Llangrannog Ceredig 23 A8
Llangristiolus Anglesey 40 C6
Llangrove Hereford 26 G2
Llangua Mon 25 F10
Llangunllo Powys 25 A9
Llangunnor Carms 23 E9
Llangurig Powys 32 H5
Llangwm Conwy 32 A5
Llangwm Mon 15 A10
Llangwm Pembs 22 F4
Llangwnnadl Gwyn 40 G4
Llangwyfan Denb 42 F4
Llangwyfan-isaf Anglesey 40 D5
Llangwyllog Anglesey 40 C6
Llangwyryfon Ceredig 24 A2
Llangybi Ceredig 24 C3
Llangybi Gwyn 40 F6
Llangybi Mon 15 B9
Llangyfelach Swansea 14 B2
Llangynhafal Denb 42 F4
Llangynidr Powys 25 G8
Llangynin Carms 23 E7
Llangynog Carms 23 E8
Llangynog Powys 33 C6
Llangynwyd Bridgend 14 C4
Llanhamlach Powys 25 F7
Llanharan Rhondda 14 C6
Llanharry Rhondda 14 C6
Llanhennock Mon 15 B9
Llanhiledd = Llanhilleth Bl Gwent 15 A8
Llanhilleth = Llanhiledd Bl Gwent 15 A8
Llanidloes Powys 32 G5
Llaniestyn Gwyn 40 G4
Llanifyny Powys 32 G4
Llanigon Powys 25 E9
Llanilar Ceredig 24 A3
Llanilid Rhondda 14 C5
Llanilltud Fawr = Llantwit Major V Glam 14 E5
Llanishen Cardiff 15 C7
Llanishen Mon 15 A10
Llanllawddog Carms 23 D9
Llanllechid Gwyn 41 D8
Llanllowell Mon 15 B9
Llanllugan Powys 33 E6
Llanllwch Carms 23 E8
Llanllwchaiarn Powys 33 F7
Llanllwni Carms 23 C9
Llanllyfni Gwyn 40 E6
Llanmadoc Swansea 23 G9
Llanmaes V Glam 14 E5
Llanmartin Newport 15 C9
Llanmihangel V Glam 14 D5
Llanmorlais Swansea 23 G10
Llannefydd Conwy 42 E2
Llannon Carms 23 F10
Llannor Gwyn 40 G5
Llanon Ceredig 24 B2
Llanover Mon 25 H10
Llanpumsaint Carms 23 D9
Llanreithan Pembs 22 D3
Llanrhaeadr Denb 42 F3
Llanrhaeadr-ym-Mochnant Powys 33 C7
Llanrhian Pembs 22 C3
Llanrhidian Swansea 23 G9
Llanrhos Conwy 41 B9
Llanrhyddlad Anglesey 40 B5
Llanrhystud Ceredig 24 B2
Llanrosser Hereford 25 E9
Llanrothal Hereford 25 G11
Llanrug Gwyn 41 D7
Llanrumney Cardiff 15 C8
Llanrwst Conwy 41 D10
Llansadurnen Carms 23 E7
Llansadwrn Anglesey 41 C7
Llansadwrn Carms 24 E3
Llansaint Carms 23 F8
Llansamlet Swansea 14 B2
Llansannan Conwy 42 F2
Llansannor V Glam 14 D5
Llansantffraed Ceredig 24 B2
Llansantffraed Powys 25 F8
Llansantffraed Cwmdeuddwr Powys 24 B6
Llansantffraed-in-Elvel Powys 25 C7
Llansantffraid-ym-Mechain Powys 33 C8
Llansawel Carms 24 E3
Llansilin Powys 33 C8
Llansoy Mon 15 A10
Llanspyddid Powys 25 F7
Llanstadwell Pembs 22 F4
Llansteffan Carms 23 E8
Llanstephan Powys 25 D8
Llantarnam Torf 15 B9
Llanteg Pembs 22 E6
Llanthony Mon 25 F9
Llantilio Crossenny Mon 25 G10
Llantilio Pertholey Mon 25 G10
Llantood Pembs 22 B6
Llantrisant Anglesey 40 B5
Llantrisant Mon 15 B9
Llantrisant Rhondda 14 C6
Llantrithyd V Glam 14 D6
Llantwit Fardre Rhondda 14 C6
Llantwit Major = Llanilltud Fawr V Glam 14 E5
Llanuwchllyn Gwyn 41 G10
Llanvaches Newport 15 B10

122 Lla–Mol

Llanvair Discoed Mon 15 B10
Llanvapley Mon 25 G10
Llanvetherine Mon 25 G10
Llanveynoe Hereford 25 E10
Llanvihangel Gobion Mon 25 H10
Llanvihangel-Ystern-Llewern Mon 25 G11
Llanwarne Hereford 26 F2
Llanwddyn Powys 32 D6
Llanwenog Ceredig 23 B9
Llanwern Newport 15 C9
Llanwinio Carms 23 D7
Llanwnda Gwyn 40 E6
Llanwnda Pembs 22 C4
Llanwnnen Ceredig 23 B10
Llanwnog Powys 32 F6
Llanwrda Carms 24 E4
Llanwrin Powys 32 E3
Llanwrthwl Powys 24 B6
Llanwrtud = Llanwrtyd Wells Powys 24 D5
Llanwrtyd Powys 24 D5
Llanwrtyd Wells = Llanwrtud Powys 24 D5
Llanwyddelan Powys 33 E6
Llanyblodwel Shrops 33 C8
Llanybri Carms 23 E8
Llanybydder Carms 23 B10
Llanycefn Pembs 22 D5
Llanychaer Pembs 22 C4
Llanycil Gwyn 32 B5
Llanycrwys Carms 24 D3
Llanymawddwy Gwyn 32 D5
Llanymddyfri = Llandovery Carms 24 E4
Llanymynech Powys 33 C8
Llanynghenedl Anglesey 40 B5
Llanynys Denb 42 F4
Llanyre Powys 25 B7
Llanystumdwy Gwyn 40 G6
Llanywern Powys 25 F8
Llawhaden Pembs 22 E5
Llawnt Shrops 33 B8
Llawr Dref Gwyn 40 H4
Llawryglyn Powys 32 F5
Llay Wrex 42 G6
Llechcynfarwy Anglesey 40 B5
Llecheiddior Gwyn 40 F6
Llechfaen Powys 25 F7
Llechryd Caerph 25 H8
Llechryd Ceredig 23 B7
Llechrydau Powys 33 B8
Lledrod Ceredig 24 A3
Llenmerewig Powys 33 F7
Llethrid Swansea 23 G10
Llidiad Nenog Carms 23 C10
Llidiardau Gwyn 41 G10
Llidiart-y-parc Denb 33 A7
Llithfaen Gwyn 40 F5
Llong Flint 42 F5
Llowes Powys 25 D8
Llundain-fach Ceredig 23 A10
Llwydcoed Rhondda 14 A5
Llwyn Shrops 33 G8
Llwyn-du Mon 25 G9
Llwyn-hendy Carms 23 G10
Llwyn-têg Carms 23 F10
Llwyn-y-brain Carms 22 E6
Llwyn-y-groes Ceredig 23 A10
Llwyncelyn Ceredig 23 A9
Llwyndafydd Ceredig 23 A8
Llwynderw Powys 33 E8
Llwyndyrys Gwyn 40 F5
Llwyngwril Gwyn 32 E1
Llwynmawr Wrex 33 B8
Llwynypia Rhondda 14 B5
Llynclys Shrops 33 C8
Llynfaes Anglesey 40 C6
Llys-y-frân Pembs 22 D5
Llysfaen Conwy 41 C10
Llyswen Powys 25 E8
Llysworney V Glam 14 D5
Llywel Powys 24 E5
Loan Falk 69 C8
Loanend Northumb 71 E8
Loanhead Midloth 69 D11
Loans S Ayrs 66 C6
Loans of Tullich Highld 87 D11
Lobb Devon 6 C3
Loch a Charnain W Isles 84 D3
Loch a' Ghainmhich W Isles 91 E7
Loch Baghasdail = Lochboisdale W Isles 84 G2
Loch Choire Lodge Highld 93 F9
Loch Euphoirt W Isles 84 B3
Loch Head Dumfries 54 E6
Loch Loyal Lodge Highld 93 E9
Loch nam Madadh = Lochmaddy W Isles 84 B4
Loch Sgioport W Isles 84 E3
Lochailort Highld 79 C10
Lochaline Highld 79 G9
Lochanhully Highld 81 A11
Lochans Dumfries 54 D3
Locharbriggs Dumfries 60 E5
Lochassynt Lodge Highld 92 G4
Lochavich Ho Argyll 73 B8
Lochawe Argyll 74 E4
Lochboisdale = Loch Baghasdail W Isles 84 G2
Lochbuie Argyll 79 J9
Lochcarron Highld 85 E13
Lochdhu Highld 93 E13
Lochdochart House Stirling 75 E7
Lochdon Argyll 79 H10
Lochdrum Highld 86 D5
Lochead Argyll 72 F6
Lochearnhead Stirling 75 E8
Lochee Dundee 76 D6
Lochend Highld 87 H8
Lochend Highld 94 D4
Locherben Dumfries 60 D5
Lochfoot Dumfries 60 F4
Lochgair Argyll 73 D8
Lochgarthside Highld 81 B7
Lochgelly Fife 69 A10
Lochgilphead Argyll 73 E7
Lochgoilhead Argyll 74 G5
Lochhill Moray 88 B2
Lochindorb Lodge Highld 87 H12
Lochinver Highld 92 G3
Lochlane Perth 75 E11
Lochluichart Highld 86 E6
Lochmaben Dumfries 60 E6
Lochmaddy = Loch nam Madadh W Isles 84 B4
Lochmore Cottage Highld 94 F2
Lochmore Lodge Highld 92 F5
Lochore Fife 76 H4
Lochportain W Isles 84 A4
Lochranza N Ayrs 66 A2
Lochs Crofts Moray 88 B3
Lochside Aberds 77 A10
Lochside Highld 87 F11
Lochside Highld 92 D7
Lochside Highld 93 F11
Lochslin Highld 87 C11
Lochstack Lodge Highld 92 E5
Lochton Aberds 83 D9
Lochty Angus 77 A8
Lochty Fife 77 G8
Lochty Perth 76 E3
Lochuisge Highld 79 F10
Lochurr Dumfries 60 E3
Lochwinnoch Renfs 68 E2
Lochwood Dumfries 60 D6
Lochyside Highld 80 F3
Lockengate Corn 3 C9
Lockerbie Dumfries 61 E7
Lockeridge Wilts 17 E8
Lockerley Hants 10 B1
Locking N Som 15 F9
Lockinge Oxon 17 C11
Lockington E Yorks 52 E5
Lockington Leics 35 C10
Lockleywood Shrops 34 C2
Locks Heath Hants 10 D4
Lockton N Yorks 59 G9
Lockwood W Yorks 51 H7
Loddington Leics 36 E3
Loddington Northants 36 H4
Loddiswell Devon 5 G8
Loddon Norf 39 F9
Lode Cambs 30 B2
Loders Dorset 8 E3
Lodsworth W Sus 11 B8
Lofthouse N Yorks 51 B7
Lofthouse W Yorks 51 G9
Loftus Redcar 59 E8
Logan E Ayrs 67 D8
Logan Mains Dumfries 54 E3
Loganlea W Loth 69 D8
Loggerheads Staffs 34 B3
Logie Angus 77 A9
Logie Fife 77 E7
Logie Moray 87 F13
Logie Coldstone Aberds 82 C6
Logie Hill Highld 87 D10
Logie Newton Aberds 89 E6
Logie Pert Angus 77 A9
Logiealmond Lodge Perth 76 D2
Logierait Perth 76 B2
Login Carms 22 D6
Lolworth Cambs 29 B10
Lonbain Highld 85 C11
Londesborough E Yorks 52 E4
London Colney Herts 19 A8
Londonderry N Yorks 58 H4
Londonthorpe Lincs 36 B5
Londubh Highld 91 J13
Lonemore Highld 87 C10
Long Ashton N Som 15 D11
Long Bennington Lincs 36 A4
Long Bredy Dorset 8 E4
Long Buckby Northants 28 B3
Long Clawson Leics 36 C3
Long Common Hants 10 C4
Long Compton Staffs 34 C4
Long Compton Warks 27 E9
Long Crendon Bucks 28 H3
Long Crichel Dorset 9 C8
Long Ditton Sur 19 E8
Long Drax N Yorks 52 G2
Long Duckmanton Derbys 45 E8
Long Eaton Derbys 35 B10
Long Green Worcs 26 E5
Long Hanborough Oxon 27 G11
Long Itchington Warks 27 B11
Long Lawford Warks 35 H10
Long Load Som 8 B3
Long Marston Herts 28 G5
Long Marston N Yorks 51 D11
Long Marston Warks 27 D8
Long Marton Cumb 57 D8
Long Melford Suff 30 D5
Long Newnton Glos 16 B6
Long Newton E Loth 70 D4
Long Preston N Yorks 50 D4
Long Riston E Yorks 53 E7
Long Sight Gtr Man 44 B3
Long Stratton Norf 39 F7
Long Street M Keynes 28 D4
Long Sutton Hants 18 G4
Long Sutton Lincs 37 C10
Long Sutton Som 8 B3
Long Thurlow Suff 31 B7
Long Whatton Leics 35 C10
Long Wittenham Oxon 18 B2
Longbar N Ayrs 66 A6
Longbenton T&W 63 G8
Longborough Glos 27 F8
Longbridge W Mid 34 H6
Longbridge Warks 27 B9
Longbridge Deverill Wilts 16 G5
Longburton Dorset 8 C5
Longcliffe Derbys 44 G6
Longcot Oxon 17 B9
Longcroft Falk 68 C6
Longden Shrops 33 E10
Longdon Staffs 35 D6
Longdon Worcs 26 E5
Longdon Green Staffs 35 D6
Longdon on Tern Telford 34 D2
Longdown Devon 7 G7
Longdowns Corn 2 F6
Longfield Kent 20 E3
Longfield Shetland 96 M5
Longford Derbys 35 B8
Longford Glos 26 F5
Longford London 19 D7
Longford Shrops 34 B2
Longford Telford 34 D3
Longford W Mid 35 G9
Longfordlane Derbys 35 B8
Longforgan Perth 76 E6
Longformacus Borders 70 E5
Longframlington Northumb 63 C7
Longham Dorset 9 E9
Longham Norf 38 D5
Longhaven Aberds 89 E11
Longhill Aberds 89 C9
Longhirst Northumb 63 E8
Longhope Glos 26 G3
Longhope Orkney 95 J4
Longhorsley Northumb 63 D7
Longhoughton Northumb 63 B8
Longlane Derbys 35 B8
Longlane W Berks 17 D11
Longlevens Glos 26 F5
Longley W Yorks 44 B5
Longley Green Worcs 26 C4
Longmanhill Aberds 89 B7
Longmoor Camp Hants 11 A6
Longmorn Moray 88 C2
Longnewton Borders 70 H4
Longnewton Stockton 58 E4
Longney Glos 26 G4
Longniddry E Loth 70 C3
Longnor Shrops 33 E10
Longnor Staffs 44 F4
Longparish Hants 17 G11
Longport Stoke 44 H2
Longridge Lancs 50 F2
Longridge Staffs 34 D5
Longridge W Loth 69 D8
Longriggend N Lanark 69 C7
Longsdon Staffs 44 G3
Longshaw Gtr Man 43 B8
Longside Aberds 89 D10
Longstanton Cambs 29 B10
Longstock Hants 17 H10
Longstone Pembs 22 F6
Longstowe Cambs 29 C10
Longthorpe Pboro 37 F7
Longthwaite Cumb 56 D6
Longton Lancs 49 G4
Longton Stoke 34 A5
Longtown Cumb 61 G9
Longtown Hereford 25 F10
Longview Mers 43 C7
Longville in the Dale Shrops 33 F11
Longwick Bucks 28 H4
Longwitton Northumb 62 E6
Longwood Shrops 34 E2
Longworth Oxon 17 B10
Longyester E Loth 70 D4
Lonmay Aberds 89 C10
Lonmore Highld 84 D7
Looe Corn 4 F3
Loose Kent 20 F4
Loosley Row Bucks 18 A5
Lopcombe Corner Wilts 17 H9
Lopen Som 8 C3
Loppington Shrops 33 C10
Lopwell Devon 4 E5
Lorbottle Northumb 62 C6
Lorbottle Hall Northumb 62 C6
Lornty Perth 76 C4
Loscoe Derbys 45 H8
Losgaintir W Isles 90 H5
Lossiemouth Moray 88 A2
Lossit Argyll 64 C2
Lostford Shrops 34 B2
Lostock Gralam Ches W 43 E9
Lostock Green Ches W 43 E9
Lostock Hall Lancs 49 G5
Lostock Junction Gtr Man 43 B9
Lostwithiel Corn 4 F2
Loth Orkney 95 E7
Lothbeg Highld 93 H12
Lothersdale N Yorks 50 E5
Lothmore Highld 93 H12
Loudwater Bucks 18 B6
Loughborough Leics 35 D11
Loughor Swansea 23 G10
Loughton Essex 19 B11
Loughton M Keynes 28 E5
Loughton Shrops 34 G2
Lound Lincs 37 D6
Lound Notts 45 D10
Lound Suff 39 F11
Lount Leics 35 D9
Louth Lincs 47 D7
Love Clough Lancs 50 G4
Lovedean Hants 10 C5
Lover Wilts 9 B11
Loversall S Yorks 45 C9
Loves Green Essex 20 A3
Lovesome Hill N Yorks 58 G4
Loveston Pembs 22 F5
Lovington Som 8 A4
Low Ackworth W Yorks 51 H10
Low Barlings Lincs 46 E4
Low Bentham N Yorks 50 C2
Low Bradfield S Yorks 44 C6
Low Bradley N Yorks 50 E6
Low Braithwaite Cumb 56 B6
Low Brunton Northumb 62 F5
Low Burnham N Lincs 45 B11
Low Burton N Yorks 51 A8
Low Buston Northumb 63 C8
Low Catton E Yorks 52 D3
Low Clanyard Dumfries 54 F4
Low Coniscliffe Darl 58 E3
Low Crosby Cumb 61 H10
Low Dalby N Yorks 59 H9
Low Dinsdale Darl 58 E4
Low Ellington N Yorks 51 A8
Low Etherley Durham 58 D2
Low Fell T&W 63 H8
Low Fulney Lincs 37 C8
Low Garth N Yorks 59 F8
Low Gate Northumb 62 G5
Low Grantley N Yorks 51 B8
Low Habberley Worcs 34 H4
Low Ham Som 8 B3
Low Hesket Cumb 56 B6
Low Hesleyhurst Northumb 62 D6
Low Hutton N Yorks 52 C3
Low Laithe N Yorks 51 C7
Low Leighton Derbys 44 D4
Low Lorton Cumb 56 D3
Low Marishes N Yorks 52 B4
Low Marnham Notts 46 F2
Low Mill N Yorks 59 G7
Low Moor Lancs 50 E3
Low Moor W Yorks 51 G7
Low Moorsley T&W 58 B4
Low Newton Cumb 49 A4
Low Newton-by-the-Sea Northumb 63 A8
Low Row Cumb 56 C5
Low Row Cumb 61 G11
Low Row N Yorks 57 G11
Low Salchrie Dumfries 54 C3
Low Smerby Argyll 65 F8
Low Torry Fife 69 B9
Low Worsall N Yorks 58 F4
Low Wray Cumb 56 F5
Lowbridge House Cumb 57 F7
Lowca Cumb 56 D1
Lowdham Notts 45 H10
Lowe Shrops 33 B11
Lowe Hill Staffs 44 G3
Lower Aisholt Som 7 C11
Lower Arncott Oxon 28 G3
Lower Ashton Devon 5 C9
Lower Assendon Oxon 18 C4
Lower Badcall Highld 92 E4
Lower Bartle Lancs 49 F4
Lower Basildon W Berks 18 D3
Lower Beeding W Sus 11 B11
Lower Benefield Northants 36 G5
Lower Boddington Northants 27 C11
Lower Brailes Warks 27 E10
Lower Breakish Highld 85 F11
Lower Broadheath Worcs 26 C5
Lower Bullingham Hereford 26 E2
Lower Cam Glos 16 A4
Lower Chapel Powys 25 E7
Lower Chute Wilts 17 F10
Lower Cragabus Argyll 64 D4
Lower Crossings Derbys 44 D4
Lower Cumberworth W Yorks 44 B6
Lower Cwm-twrch Powys 24 G4
Lower Darwen Blackburn 50 G2
Lower Dean Bedford 29 B7
Lower Diabaig Highld 85 B12
Lower Dicker E Sus 12 E4
Lower Dinchope Shrops 33 G10
Lower Down Shrops 33 G9
Lower Drift Corn 2 G3
Lower Dunsforth N Yorks 51 C10
Lower Egleton Hereford 26 D3
Lower Elkstone Staffs 44 G4
Lower End C Beds 28 F6
Lower Everleigh Wilts 17 F8
Lower Farringdon Hants 18 H4
Lower Foxdale IoM 48 E2
Lower Frankton Shrops 33 B9
Lower Froyle Hants 18 G4
Lower Gledfield Highld 87 B8
Lower Green Norf 38 B5
Lower Hacheston Suff 31 C10
Lower Halistra Highld 84 C7
Lower Halstow Kent 20 E5
Lower Hardres Kent 21 F8
Lower Hawthwaite Cumb 56 H4
Lower Heath Ches E 44 F2
Lower Hempriggs Moray 87 E14
Lower Hergest Hereford 25 C9
Lower Heyford Oxon 27 F11
Lower Higham Kent 20 D4
Lower Holbrook Suff 31 E8
Lower Hordley Shrops 33 C9
Lower Horsebridge E Sus 12 E4
Lower Killeyan Argyll 64 D3
Lower Kingswood Sur 19 F9
Lower Kinnerton Ches W 42 F6
Lower Langford N Som 15 E10
Lower Largo Fife 77 G7
Lower Leigh Staffs 34 B6
Lower Lemington Glos 27 E9
Lower Lenie Highld 81 A7
Lower Lydbrook Glos 26 G2
Lower Lye Hereford 25 B11
Lower Machen Newport 15 C8
Lower Maes-coed Hereford 25 E10
Lower Mayland Essex 20 A6
Lower Midway Derbys 35 C9
Lower Milovaig Highld 84 C6
Lower Moor Worcs 26 D6
Lower Nazeing Essex 29 H10
Lower Netchwood Shrops 34 F2
Lower Ollach Highld 85 E10
Lower Penarth V Glam 15 D7
Lower Penn Staffs 34 F4
Lower Pennington Hants 10 E2
Lower Peover Ches W 43 E10
Lower Pexhill Ches E 44 E2
Lower Place Gtr Man 44 A3
Lower Quinton Warks 27 D8
Lower Rochford Worcs 26 B3
Lower Seagry Wilts 16 C6
Lower Shelton C Beds 28 D6
Lower Shiplake Oxon 18 D4
Lower Shuckburgh Warks 27 B11
Lower Slaughter Glos 27 F8
Lower Stanton St Quintin Wilts 16 C6
Lower Stoke Medway 20 D5
Lower Stondon C Beds 29 E8
Lower Stow Bedon Norf 38 F5
Lower Street Norf 39 B8
Lower Street Norf 39 D9
Lower Strensham Worcs 26 D6
Lower Stretton Warr 43 D9
Lower Sundon C Beds 29 F7
Lower Swanwick Hants 10 D3
Lower Swell Glos 27 F8
Lower Tean Staffs 34 B6
Lower Thurlton Norf 39 F10
Lower Tote Highld 85 B10
Lower Town Pembs 22 C4
Lower Tysoe Warks 27 D10
Lower Upham Hants 10 C4
Lower Vexford Som 7 C10
Lower Weare Som 15 F10
Lower Welson Hereford 25 C9
Lower Whitley Ches W 43 E9
Lower Wield Hants 18 G3
Lower Winchendon Bucks 28 G4
Lower Withington Ches E 44 F2
Lower Woodend Bucks 18 C5
Lower Woodford Wilts 9 A10
Lower Wyche Worcs 26 D4
Lowesby Leics 36 E3
Lowestoft Suff 39 F11
Loweswater Cumb 56 D3
Lowford Hants 10 C3
Lowgill Cumb 57 G8
Lowgill Lancs 50 C2
Lowick Northants 36 G5
Lowick Northumb 71 G9
Lowick Bridge Cumb 56 H4
Lowick Green Cumb 56 H4
Lowlands Torf 15 B8
Lowmoor Row Cumb 57 D8
Lownie Moor Angus 77 C7
Lowsonford Warks 27 B8
Lowther Cumb 57 D7
Lowthorpe E Yorks 53 C6
Lowton Gtr Man 43 C9
Lowton Common Gtr Man 43 C9
Loxbeare Devon 7 E8
Loxhill Sur 19 H7
Loxhore Devon 6 C5
Loxley Warks 27 C9
Loxton N Som 15 F9
Loxwood W Sus 11 A9
Lubcroy Highld 92 J6
Lubenham Leics 36 G3
Luccombe Som 7 B8
Luccombe Village IoW 10 G4
Lucker Northumb 71 G10
Luckett Corn 4 D4
Luckington Wilts 16 C5
Lucklawhill Fife 77 E7
Luckwell Bridge Som 7 C8
Lucton Hereford 25 B11
Ludag W Isles 84 G2
Ludborough Lincs 46 C6
Ludchurch Pembs 22 E6
Luddenden W Yorks 50 G6
Luddenden Foot W Yorks 50 G6
Luddesdown Kent 20 E3
Luddington N Lincs 52 H4
Luddington Warks 27 C8
Luddington in the Brook Northants 37 G7
Lude House Perth 81 G10
Ludford Lincs 46 D6
Ludford Shrops 26 A2
Ludgershall Bucks 28 G3
Ludgershall Wilts 17 F9
Ludgvan Corn 2 F4
Ludham Norf 39 D9
Ludlow Shrops 26 A2
Ludwell Wilts 9 B8
Ludworth Durham 58 B4
Luffincott Devon 6 G2
Lugar E Ayrs 67 D8
Lugg Green Hereford 25 B11
Luggate Burn E Loth 70 C5
Luggiebank N Lanark 68 C6
Lugton E Ayrs 67 A7
Lugwardine Hereford 26 D2
Luib Highld 85 F10
Lulham Hereford 25 D11
Lullenden Sur 12 B3
Lullington Derbys 35 D8
Lullington Som 16 F4
Lulsgate Bottom N Som 15 E11
Lulsley Worcs 26 C4
Lumb W Yorks 50 G6
Lumby N Yorks 51 F10
Lumloch E Dunb 68 D5
Lumphanan Aberds 83 C7
Lumphinnans Fife 69 A10
Lumsdaine Borders 71 D7
Lumsden Aberds 82 A6
Lunan Angus 77 B9
Lunanhead Angus 77 B7
Luncarty Perth 76 E3
Lund E Yorks 52 E5
Lund N Yorks 52 F2
Lund Shetland 96 C7
Lunderton Aberds 89 D11
Lundie Angus 76 D5
Lundie Highld 80 B3
Lundin Links Fife 77 G7
Lunga Argyll 72 C6
Lunna Shetland 96 G6
Lunning Shetland 96 G7
Lunnon Swansea 23 H10
Lunsford's Cross E Sus 12 E6
Lunt Mers 42 B6
Luntley Hereford 25 C10
Luppitt Devon 7 F10
Lupset W Yorks 51 H9
Lupton Cumb 50 A1
Lurgashall W Sus 11 B8
Lusby Lincs 47 F7
Luson Devon 5 G7
Luss Argyll 68 A2
Lussagiven Argyll 72 E5
Lusta Highld 85 C7
Lustleigh Devon 5 C8
Luston Hereford 25 B11
Luthermuir Aberds 83 G8
Luthrie Fife 76 F6
Luton Devon 5 D10
Luton Luton 29 F7
Luton Medway 20 E4
Lutterworth Leics 35 G11
Lutton Devon 5 F6
Lutton Lincs 37 C10
Lutton Northants 37 G7
Lutworthy Devon 7 E6
Luxborough Som 7 C8
Luxulyan Corn 4 F1
Lybster Highld 94 G4
Lydbury North Shrops 33 G9
Lydcott Devon 6 C5
Lydd Kent 13 D9
Lydd on Sea Kent 13 D9
Lydden Kent 21 G9
Lyddington Rutland 36 F4
Lyde Green Hants 18 F4
Lydeard St Lawrence Som 7 C10
Lydford Devon 4 C6
Lydford-on-Fosse Som 8 A4
Lydgate W Yorks 50 G5
Lydham Shrops 33 F9
Lydiard Green Wilts 17 C7
Lydiard Millicent Wilts 17 C7
Lydiate Mers 42 B6
Lydlinch Dorset 8 C6
Lydney Glos 16 A3
Lydstep Pembs 22 G5
Lye W Mid 34 G5
Lye Green Bucks 18 A6
Lye Green E Sus 12 C4
Lyford Oxon 17 B10
Lymbridge Green Kent 13 B10
Lyme Regis Dorset 8 E2
Lyminge Kent 21 G8
Lymington Hants 10 E2
Lyminster W Sus 11 D9
Lymm Warr 43 D9
Lymore Hants 10 E1
Lympne Kent 13 C10
Lympsham Som 15 F9
Lympstone Devon 5 C10
Lynchat Highld 81 C9
Lyndale Ho. Highld 85 C8
Lyndhurst Hants 10 D2
Lyndon Rutland 36 E5
Lyne Sur 19 E7
Lyne Down Hereford 26 E3
Lyne of Gorthleck Highld 81 A7
Lyne of Skene Aberds 83 B9
Lyneal Shrops 33 B10
Lyneham Oxon 27 F9
Lyneham Wilts 17 D7
Lynemore Highld 82 A2
Lynemouth Northumb 63 D8
Lyness Orkney 95 J4
Lyng Norf 39 D6
Lyng Som 8 B2
Lynmouth Devon 7 B6
Lynsted Kent 20 E6
Lynton Devon 6 B6
Lyon's Gate Dorset 8 D5
Lyonshall Hereford 25 C10
Lytchett Matravers Dorset 9 E8
Lytchett Minster Dorset 9 E8
Lyth Highld 94 D4
Lytham Lancs 49 G3
Lytham St Anne's Lancs 49 G3
Lythe N Yorks 59 E9
Lythes Orkney 95 K5

M

Mabe Burnthouse Corn 3 F6
Mabie Dumfries 60 F5
Mablethorpe Lincs 47 D9
Macclesfield Ches E 44 E3
Macclesfield Forest Ches E 44 E3
Macduff Aberds 89 B7
Mace Green Suff 31 D8
Macharioch Argyll 65 H8
Machen Caerph 15 C8
Machrihanish Argyll 65 F7
Machynlleth Powys 32 E3
Machynys Carms 23 G10
Mackerel's Common W Sus 11 B9
Mackworth Derbys 35 B9
Macmerry E Loth 70 C3
Madderty Perth 76 E2
Maddiston Falk 69 C8
Madehurst W Sus 11 C8
Madeley Staffs 34 A3
Madeley Telford 34 E2
Madeley Heath Staffs 43 H10
Madeley Park Staffs 34 A3
Madingley Cambs 29 B10
Madley Hereford 25 E11
Madresfield Worcs 26 D5
Madron Corn 2 F3
Maen-y-groes Ceredig 23 A8
Maenaddwyn Anglesey 40 B6
Maenclochog Pembs 22 D5
Maendy V Glam 14 D6
Maentwrog Gwyn 41 F8
Maer Staffs 34 B3
Maerdy Conwy 32 A6
Maerdy Rhondda 14 B5
Maes-Treylow Powys 25 B9
Maesbrook Shrops 33 C8
Maesbury Shrops 33 C9
Maesbury Marsh Shrops 33 C9
Maesgwyn-Isaf Powys 33 D7
Maesgwynne Carms 23 D7
Maeshafn Denb 42 F5
Maesllyn Ceredig 23 B8
Maesmynis Powys 25 D7
Maesteg Bridgend 14 B4
Maestir Ceredig 23 B10
Maesy cwmmer Caerph 15 B7
Maesybont Carms 23 E10
Maesycrugiau Carms 23 B9
Maesymeillion Ceredig 23 B9
Magdalen Laver Essex 30 H2
Maggieknockater Moray 88 D3
Magham Down E Sus 12 E5
Maghull Mers 43 B6
Magor Mon 15 C10
Magpie Green Suff 39 H6
Maiden Bradley Wilts 16 H5
Maiden Law Durham 58 B2
Maiden Newton Dorset 8 E4
Maiden Wells Pembs 22 G4
Maidencombe Torbay 5 E10
Maidenhall Suff 31 D8
Maidenhead Windsor 18 C5
Maidens S Ayrs 66 F5
Maiden's Green Brack 18 D5
Maidensgrave Suff 31 D9
Maidenwell Corn 4 D2
Maidenwell Lincs 47 E7
Maidford Northants 28 C3
Maids Moreton Bucks 28 E4
Maidstone Kent 20 F4
Maidwell Northants 36 H3
Mail Shetland 96 L6
Main Powys 33 D7
Maindee Newport 15 C9
Mains of Airies Dumfries 54 C2
Mains of Allardice Aberds 83 F10
Mains of Annochie Aberds 89 D9
Mains of Ardestie Angus 77 D8
Mains of Balhall Angus 77 A8
Mains of Ballindarg Angus 77 B7
Mains of Balnakettle Aberds 83 F8
Mains of Birness Aberds 89 E9
Mains of Burgie Moray 87 F13
Mains of Clunas Highld 87 G11
Mains of Crichie Aberds 89 D9
Mains of Dalvey Highld 87 H14
Mains of Dellavaird Aberds 83 E9
Mains of Drum Aberds 83 D10
Mains of Edingight Moray 88 C5
Mains of Fedderate Aberds 89 D8
Mains of Inkhorn Aberds 89 E9
Mains of Mayen Moray 88 D5
Mains of Melgund Angus 77 B8
Mains of Thornton Aberds 83 F8
Mains of Watten Highld 94 E4
Mainsforth Durham 58 C4
Mainsriddle Dumfries 60 H5
Mainstone Shrops 33 G8
Maisemore Glos 26 F5
Malacleit W Isles 84 A2
Malborough Devon 5 H8
Malcoff Derbys 44 D4
Maldon Essex 30 H5
Malham N Yorks 50 C5
Maligar Highld 85 B9
Mallaig Highld 79 B9
Malleny Mills Edin 69 D10
Malling Stirling 75 G8
Malltraeth Anglesey 40 D6
Mallwyd Gwyn 32 D4
Malmesbury Wilts 16 C6
Malmsmead Devon 7 B6
Malpas Ches W 43 H7
Malpas Corn 3 E7
Malpas Newport 15 B9
Malswick Glos 26 F4
Maltby S Yorks 45 C9
Maltby Stockton 58 E5
Maltby le Marsh Lincs 47 D8
Malting Green Essex 30 F6
Maltman's Hill Kent 13 B8
Malton N Yorks 52 B3
Malvern Link Worcs 26 D4
Malvern Wells Worcs 26 D4
Mamble Worcs 26 A3
Man-moel Caerph 15 A7
Manaccan Corn 3 G6
Manafon Powys 33 E7
Manais W Isles 90 J6
Manar Ho. Aberds 83 A9
Manaton Devon 5 C8
Manby Lincs 47 D7
Mancetter Warks 35 F9
Manchester Gtr Man 44 C2
Manchester Airport Gtr Man 44 D2
Mancot Flint 42 F6
Mandally Highld 80 C4
Manea Cambs 37 G10
Manfield N Yorks 58 E3
Mangaster Shetland 96 F5
Mangotsfield S Glos 16 D3
Mangurstadh W Isles 90 D5
Mankinholes W Yorks 50 G5
Manley Ches W 43 E8
Mannal Argyll 78 G2
Mannerston W Loth 69 C9
Manningford Bohune Wilts 17 F8
Manningford Bruce Wilts 17 F8
Manningham W Yorks 51 F7
Mannings Heath W Sus 11 B11
Mannington Dorset 9 D9
Manningtree Essex 31 E7
Mannofield Aberdeen 83 C11
Manor London 19 C11
Manor Estate S Yorks 45 D7
Manorbier Pembs 22 G5
Manordeilo Carms 24 F3
Manorhill Borders 70 G5
Manorowen Pembs 22 C4
Mansel Lacy Hereford 25 D11
Manselfield Swansea 23 H10
Mansell Gamage Hereford 25 D10
Mansergh Cumb 50 A2
Mansfield E Ayrs 67 E9
Mansfield Notts 45 F9
Mansfield Woodhouse Notts 45 F9
Mansriggs Cumb 49 A2
Manston Dorset 9 C7
Manston Kent 21 E10
Manston W Yorks 51 F9
Manswood Dorset 9 D8
Manthorpe Lincs 36 B5
Manthorpe Lincs 37 D6
Manton N Lincs 46 B3
Manton Notts 45 E9
Manton Rutland 36 E4
Manton Wilts 17 E8
Manuden Essex 29 F11
Maperton Som 8 B5
Maple Cross Herts 19 B7
Maplebeck Notts 45 F11
Mapledurham Oxon 18 D3
Mapledurwell Hants 18 F3
Maplehurst W Sus 11 B10
Maplescombe Kent 20 E2
Mapleton Derbys 44 H5
Mapperley Derbys 35 A10
Mapperley Park Nottingham 36 A1
Mapperton Dorset 8 E4
Mappleborough Green Warks 27 B7
Mappleton E Yorks 53 E8
Mappowder Dorset 8 D6
Mar Lodge Aberds 82 D2
Maraig W Isles 90 G6
Marazanvose Corn 3 D7
Marazion Corn 2 F4
Marbhig W Isles 91 F9
Marbury Ches E 43 H8
March Cambs 37 F10
March S Lanark 60 B5
Marcham Oxon 17 B11
Marchamley Shrops 34 C1
Marchington Staffs 35 B7
Marchington Woodlands Staffs 35 C7
Marchroes Gwyn 40 H5
Marchwiel Wrex 42 H6
Marchwood Hants 10 C2
Marcross V Glam 14 E5
Marden Hereford 26 D2
Marden Kent 12 B6
Marden T&W 63 F9
Marden Wilts 17 F7
Marden Beech Kent 12 B6
Marden Thorn Kent 13 B6
Mardy Mon 25 G10
Marefield Leics 36 E3
Mareham le Fen Lincs 46 F6
Mareham on the Hill Lincs 46 F6
Marehay Derbys 45 H7
Marehill W Sus 11 C9
Maresfield E Sus 12 D3
Marfleet Hull 53 G7
Marford Wrex 42 G6
Margam Neath 14 C3
Margaret Marsh Dorset 9 C7
Margaret Roding Essex 30 G2
Margaretting Essex 20 A3
Margate Kent 21 D10
Margnaheglish N Ayrs 66 C3
Margrove Park Redcar 59 E7
Marham Norf 38 D3
Marhamchurch Corn 4 A3
Marholm Pboro 37 E7
Mariandyrys Anglesey 41 B8
Marianglas Anglesey 41 B7
Mariansleigh Devon 7 D6
Marionburgh Aberds 83 C9
Marishader Highld 85 B9
Marjoriebanks Dumfries 60 E6
Mark Dumfries 54 D4
Mark S Ayrs 54 B3
Mark Som 15 G9
Mark Causeway Som 15 G9
Mark Cross E Sus 12 C4
Mark Cross E Sus 12 E3
Markbeech Kent 12 B3
Markby Lincs 47 E8
Market Bosworth Leics 35 E10
Market Deeping Lincs 37 E7
Market Drayton Shrops 34 B2
Market Harborough Leics 36 G3
Market Lavington Wilts 17 F7
Market Overton Rutland 36 D4
Market Rasen Lincs 46 D5
Market Stainton Lincs 46 E6
Market Warsop Notts 45 F9
Market Weighton E Yorks 52 E4
Market Weston Suff 38 H5
Markethill Perth 76 D5
Markfield Leics 35 D10
Markham Caerph 15 A7
Markham Moor Notts 45 E11
Markinch Fife 76 G5
Markington N Yorks 51 C8
Marks Tey Essex 30 F6
Marksbury Bath 16 E3
Markyate Herts 29 G7
Marland Gtr Man 44 A2
Marlborough Wilts 17 E8
Marlbrook Hereford 26 C2
Marlbrook Worcs 26 A6
Marlcliff Warks 27 C7
Marldon Devon 5 E9
Marlesford Suff 31 C10
Marley Green Ches E 43 H8
Marley Hill T&W 63 H8
Marley Mount Hants 10 E1
Marlingford Norf 39 E7
Marloes Pembs 22 F2
Marlow Bucks 18 C5
Marlow Hereford 33 H10
Marlow Bottom Bucks 18 C5
Marlpit Hill Kent 19 G11
Marlpool Derbys 45 H8
Marnhull Dorset 9 C6
Marnoch Aberds 88 C5
Marnock N Lanark 68 D6
Marple Gtr Man 44 D3
Marple Bridge Gtr Man 44 D3
Marr S Yorks 45 B9
Marrel Highld 93 H13
Marrick N Yorks 58 G1
Marrister Shetland 96 G7
Marros Carms 23 F7
Marsden T&W 63 G9
Marsden W Yorks 44 A4
Marsett N Yorks 57 H11
Marsh Devon 8 C1
Marsh W Yorks 50 F6
Marsh Baldon Oxon 18 B2
Marsh Gibbon Bucks 28 F3
Marsh Green Devon 7 G9
Marsh Green Kent 12 B3
Marsh Green Staffs 44 G2
Marsh Lane Derbys 45 E8
Marsh Street Som 7 B8
Marshall's Heath Herts 29 G8
Marshalsea Dorset 8 D2
Marshalswick Herts 29 H8
Marsham Norf 39 C7
Marshaw Lancs 50 D1
Marshborough Kent 21 F10
Marshbrook Shrops 33 G10
Marshchapel Lincs 47 C7
Marshfield Newport 15 C8
Marshfield S Glos 16 D4
Marshgate Corn 4 B2
Marshland St James Norf 37 E11
Marshside Mers 49 H3
Marshwood Dorset 8 E2
Marske N Yorks 58 F2
Marske-by-the-Sea Redcar 59 D7
Marston Ches W 43 E9
Marston Hereford 25 C10
Marston Lincs 36 A4
Marston Oxon 28 H2
Marston Staffs 34 C5
Marston Staffs 34 D4
Marston Warks 35 F8
Marston Wilts 16 F6
Marston Doles Warks 27 C11
Marston Green W Mid 35 G7
Marston Magna Som 8 B4
Marston Meysey Wilts 17 B8
Marston Montgomery Derbys 35 B7
Marston Moretaine C Beds 28 D6
Marston on Dove Derbys 35 C8
Marston St Lawrence Northants 28 D2
Marston Stannett Hereford 26 C2
Marston Trussell Northants 36 G2
Marstow Hereford 26 G2
Marsworth Bucks 28 G6
Marten Wilts 17 F9
Marthall Ches E 44 E2
Martham Norf 39 D10
Martin Hants 9 C9
Martin Kent 21 G10
Martin Lincs 46 F6
Martin Lincs 46 G5
Martin Dales Lincs 46 F5
Martin Drove End Hants 9 B9
Martin Hussingtree Worcs 26 B5
Martin Mill Kent 21 G10
Martinhoe Devon 6 B5
Martinhoe Cross Devon 6 B5
Martinscroft Warr 43 D9
Martinstown Dorset 8 F5
Martlesham Suff 31 D9
Martlesham Heath Suff 31 D9
Martletwy Pembs 22 E5
Martley Worcs 26 C4
Martock Som 8 C3
Marton Ches E 44 F2
Marton E Yorks 53 F7
Marton Lincs 46 D2
Marton Mbro 58 E6
Marton N Yorks 51 C10
Marton N Yorks 52 A3
Marton Shrops 33 C10
Marton Shrops 33 E8
Marton Warks 27 B11
Marton-le-Moor N Yorks 51 B9
Martyr Worthy Hants 10 A4
Martyr's Green Sur 19 F7
Marwick Orkney 95 F3
Marwood Devon 6 C4
Mary Tavy Devon 4 D6
Marybank Highld 86 F7
Maryburgh Highld 87 F8
Maryhill Glasgow 68 D4
Marykirk Aberds 83 G8
Marylebone Gtr Man 43 B8
Marypark Moray 88 E1
Maryport Cumb 56 C2
Maryport Dumfries 54 F4
Maryton Angus 77 B9
Marywell Aberds 83 D7
Marywell Aberds 83 D11
Marywell Angus 77 C9
Masham N Yorks 51 A8
Mashbury Essex 30 G3
Masongill N Yorks 50 B2
Masonhill S Ayrs 67 D6
Mastin Moor Derbys 45 E8
Mastrick Aberdeen 83 C10
Matching Essex 30 G2
Matching Green Essex 30 G2
Matching Tye Essex 30 G2
Matfen Northumb 62 F6
Matfield Kent 12 B5
Mathern Mon 15 B11
Mathon Hereford 26 D4
Mathry Pembs 22 C3
Matlaske Norf 39 B7
Matlock Derbys 44 F6
Matlock Bath Derbys 44 G6
Matson Glos 26 G5
Matterdale End Cumb 56 D5
Mattersey Notts 45 D10
Mattersey Thorpe Notts 45 D10
Mattingley Hants 18 F4
Mattishall Norf 39 D6
Mattishall Burgh Norf 39 D6
Mauchline E Ayrs 67 D7
Maud Aberds 89 D9
Maugersbury Glos 27 F9
Maughold IoM 48 C4
Mauld Highld 86 H7
Maulden C Beds 29 E7
Maulds Meaburn Cumb 57 E8
Maunby N Yorks 58 H4
Maund Bryan Hereford 26 C2
Maundown Som 7 D9
Mautby Norf 39 D10
Mavis Enderby Lincs 47 F7
Maw Green Ches E 43 G10
Mawbray Cumb 56 B2
Mawdesley Lancs 43 A7
Mawdlam Bridgend 14 C4
Mawgan Corn 2 G6
Mawla Corn 2 E6
Mawnan Corn 3 G6
Mawnan Smith Corn 3 G6
Mawsley Northants 36 H4
Maxey Pboro 37 E7
Maxstoke Warks 35 G8
Maxton Borders 70 G5
Maxton Kent 21 G10
Maxwellheugh Borders 70 G6
Maxwelltown Dumfries 60 F5
Maxworthy Corn 6 G1
May Bank Staffs 44 H2
Mayals Swansea 14 B2
Maybole S Ayrs 66 F6
Mayfield E Sus 12 D4
Mayfield Midloth 70 D2
Mayfield Staffs 44 H5
Mayfield W Loth 69 D8
Mayford Sur 18 F6
Mayland Essex 20 A6
Maynard's Green E Sus 12 E4
Maypole Mon 25 G11
Maypole Scilly 2 C3
Maypole Green Essex 30 F6
Maypole Green Norf 39 F10
Maypole Green Suff 31 B9
Maywick Shetland 96 L5
Meadle Bucks 28 H5
Meadowtown Shrops 33 E9
Meaford Staffs 34 B4
Meal Bank Cumb 57 G7
Mealabost W Isles 91 D9
Mealabost Bhuirgh W Isles 91 B9
Mealsgate Cumb 56 B4
Meanwood W Yorks 51 F8
Mearbeck N Yorks 50 C4
Meare Som 15 G10
Meare Green Som 8 B2
Mears Ashby Northants 28 B5
Measham Leics 35 D9
Meath Green Sur 12 B1
Meathop Cumb 49 A4
Meaux E Yorks 53 F6
Meavy Devon 4 E6
Medbourne Leics 36 F3
Medburn Northumb 63 F7
Meddon Devon 6 E1
Meden Vale Notts 45 F9
Medlam Lincs 47 G7
Medmenham Bucks 18 C5
Medomsley Durham 58 A2
Medstead Hants 18 H3
Meer End W Mid 27 A9
Meerbrook Staffs 44 F3
Meers Bridge Lincs 47 D8
Meesden Herts 29 E11
Meeth Devon 6 F4
Meggethead Borders 61 A7
Meidrim Carms 23 D7
Meifod Denb 42 G3
Meifod Powys 33 D7
Meigle N Ayrs 73 G10
Meigle Perth 76 C5
Meikle Earnock S Lanark 68 E6
Meikle Ferry Highld 87 C10
Meikle Forter Angus 76 A4
Meikle Gluich Highld 87 C9
Meikle Pinkerton E Loth 70 C6
Meikle Strath Aberds 83 F8
Meikle Tarty Aberds 89 F9
Meikle Wartle Aberds 89 E7
Meikleour Perth 76 D4
Meinciau Carms 23 E9
Meir Stoke 34 A5
Meir Heath Staffs 34 A5
Melbourn Cambs 29 D10
Melbourne Derbys 35 C9
Melbourne E Yorks 52 E3
Melbourne S Lanark 69 F9
Melbury Abbas Dorset 9 B7
Melbury Bubb Dorset 8 D4
Melbury Osmond Dorset 8 D4
Melbury Sampford Dorset 8 D4
Melby Shetland 96 H3
Melchbourne Bedford 29 B7
Melcombe Bingham Dorset 9 D6
Melcombe Regis Dorset 8 F5
Meldon Devon 6 G4
Meldon Northumb 63 E7
Meldreth Cambs 29 D10
Meldrum Ho. Aberds 89 F8
Melfort Argyll 73 B7
Melgarve Highld 81 D6
Meliden Denb 42 D3
Melin-y-coed Conwy 41 D10
Melin-y-ddôl Powys 33 E6
Melin-y-grug Powys 33 E6
Melin-y-Wig Denb 42 H3
Melinbyrhedyn Powys 32 F4
Melincourt Neath 14 A4
Melkinthorpe Cumb 57 D7
Melkridge Northumb 62 G3
Melksham Wilts 16 E6
Melldalloch Argyll 73 F8
Melling Lancs 50 B1
Melling Mers 43 B6
Melling Mount Mers 43 B7
Mellis Suff 31 A8
Mellon Charles Highld 91 H13
Mellon Udrigle Highld 91 H13
Mellor Gtr Man 44 D3
Mellor Lancs 50 F2
Mellor Brook Lancs 50 F2
Mells Som 16 G4
Melmerby Cumb 57 C8
Melmerby N Yorks 51 B9
Melmerby N Yorks 58 H1
Melplash Dorset 8 E3
Melrose Borders 70 G4
Melsetter Orkney 95 K3
Melsonby N Yorks 58 F2
Meltham W Yorks 44 A5
Melton Suff 31 C9
Melton Constable Norf 38 B6
Melton Mowbray Leics 36 D3
Melton Ross N Lincs 46 A4
Meltonby E Yorks 52 D3
Melvaig Highld 91 J12
Melverley Shrops 33 D9
Melverley Green Shrops 33 D9
Melvich Highld 93 C11
Membury Devon 8 D1
Memsie Aberds 89 B9
Memus Angus 77 B7
Menabilly Corn 4 F1
Menai Bridge = Porthaethwy Anglesey 41 C7
Mendham Suff 39 G8
Mendlesham Suff 31 B8
Mendlesham Green Suff 31 B7
Menheniot Corn 4 E3
Mennock Dumfries 60 C4
Menston W Yorks 51 E7
Menstrie Clack 75 H11
Menthorpe N Yorks 52 F2
Mentmore Bucks 28 G6
Meoble Highld 79 C10
Meole Brace Shrops 33 D10
Meols Mers 42 C5
Meonstoke Hants 10 C5
Meopham Kent 20 E3
Meopham Station Kent 20 E3
Mepal Cambs 37 G10
Meppershall C Beds 29 E8
Merbach Hereford 25 D10
Mere Ches E 43 D10
Mere Wilts 9 A7
Mere Brow Lancs 49 H4
Mere Grn. W Mid 35 F7
Mereclough Lancs 50 F4
Mereside Blackpool 49 F3
Mereworth Kent 20 F3
Mergie Aberds 83 E9
Meriden W Mid 35 G8
Merkadale Highld 85 E8
Merkland Dumfries 60 F3
Merkland S Ayrs 66 G5
Merkland Lodge Highld 92 G7
Merley Poole 9 E9
Merlin's Bridge Pembs 22 E4
Merrington Shrops 33 C10
Merrion Pembs 22 G4
Merriott Som 8 C3
Merrivale Devon 4 D6
Merrow Sur 19 F7
Merrymeet Corn 4 E3
Mersham Kent 13 C9
Merstham Sur 19 F9
Merston W Sus 11 D7
Merstone IoW 10 F4
Merther Corn 3 E7
Merthyr Carms 23 D8
Merthyr Cynog Powys 24 E6
Merthyr-Dyfan V Glam 15 E7
Merthyr Mawr Bridgend 14 D4
Merthyr Tudful = Merthyr Tydfil M Tydf 25 H7
Merthyr Tydfil = Merthyr Tudful M Tydf 25 H7
Merthyr Vale M Tydf 14 B6
Merton Devon 6 E4
Merton London 19 D9
Merton Norf 38 F5
Merton Oxon 28 G2
Mervinslaw Borders 62 B2
Meshaw Devon 7 E6
Messing Essex 30 G5
Messingham N Lincs 46 B2
Metfield Suff 39 G8
Metheringham Lincs 46 F4
Methil Fife 76 H6
Methlem Gwyn 40 G3
Methley W Yorks 51 G9
Methlick Aberds 89 E8
Methven Perth 76 E3
Methwold Norf 38 F3
Methwold Hythe Norf 38 F3
Mettingham Suff 39 G9
Mevagissey Corn 3 E9
Mewith Head N Yorks 50 C3
Mexborough S Yorks 45 B8
Mey Highld 94 C4
Meysey Hampton Glos 17 B8
Miabhag W Isles 90 G5
Miabhag W Isles 90 H6
Miabhig W Isles 90 D5
Michaelchurch Hereford 26 F2
Michaelchurch Escley Hereford 25 E10
Michaelchurch on Arrow Powys 25 C9
Michaelston-le-Pit V Glam 15 D7
Michaelston-y-Fedw Newport 15 C8
Michaelstow Corn 4 D1
Michealston-super-Ely Cardiff 15 D7
Micheldever Hants 18 H2
Michelmersh Hants 10 B2
Mickfield Suff 31 B8
Mickle Trafford Ches W 43 F7
Micklebring S Yorks 45 C9
Mickleby N Yorks 59 E9
Mickleham Sur 19 F8
Mickleover Derby 35 B9
Micklethwaite W Yorks 51 E7
Mickleton Durham 57 D11
Mickleton Glos 27 D8
Mickletown W Yorks 51 G9
Mickley N Yorks 51 B8
Mickley Square Northumb 62 G6
Mid Ardlaw Aberds 89 B9
Mid Auchinlech Invclyd 68 C2
Mid Beltie Aberds 83 C8
Mid Calder W Loth 69 D9
Mid Cloch Forbie Aberds 89 C7
Mid Clyth Highld 94 G4
Mid Lavant W Sus 11 D7
Mid Main Highld 86 H7
Mid Urchany Highld 87 G11
Mid Walls Shetland 96 H4
Mid Yell Shetland 96 D7
Midbea Orkney 95 D5
Middle Assendon Oxon 18 C4
Middle Aston Oxon 27 F11
Middle Barton Oxon 27 F11
Middle Cairncake Aberds 89 D8
Middle Claydon Bucks 28 F4
Middle Drums Angus 77 B8
Middle Handley Derbys 45 E8
Middle Littleton Worcs 27 D7
Middle Maes-coed Hereford 25 E10
Middle Mill Pembs 22 D3
Middle Rasen Lincs 46 D4
Middle Rigg Perth 76 G3
Middle Tysoe Warks 27 D10
Middle Wallop Hants 17 H9
Middle Winterslow Wilts 9 A11
Middle Woodford Wilts 17 H8
Middlebie Dumfries 61 F8
Middleforth Green Lancs 49 G5
Middleham N Yorks 58 H2
Middlehope Shrops 33 G10
Middlemarsh Dorset 8 D5
Middlemuir Aberds 89 F9
Middlesbrough Mbro 58 D5
Middleshaw Cumb 57 H7
Middleshaw Dumfries 61 F7
Middlesmoor N Yorks 51 B6
Middlestone Durham 58 C3
Middlestone Moor Durham 58 C3
Middlestown W Yorks 51 H8
Middlethird Borders 70 F5
Middleton Aberds 83 B10
Middleton Argyll 78 G2
Middleton Cumb 57 H8
Middleton Derbys 44 F5
Middleton Derbys 44 G6
Middleton Essex 30 E5
Middleton Gtr Man 44 B2
Middleton Hants 17 G11
Middleton Hereford 26 B2
Middleton Lancs 49 D4
Middleton Midloth 70 E2
Middleton N Yorks 51 E7
Middleton N Yorks 59 H8
Middleton Norf 38 D2
Middleton Northants 36 G4
Middleton Northumb 62 E6
Middleton Northumb 71 G10
Middleton Perth 76 C4
Middleton Perth 76 G4
Middleton Shrops 33 C9
Middleton Shrops 33 F8
Middleton Shrops 33 H11
Middleton Suff 31 B11
Middleton Swansea 23 H9
Middleton W Yorks 51 G8
Middleton Warks 35 F7
Middleton Chene Northants 27 D11
Middleton Green Staffs 34 B5
Middleton Hall Northumb 71 H8
Middleton-in-Teesdale Durham 57 D11
Middleton Moor Suff 31 B11
Middleton-on-Leven N Yorks 58 F5
Middleton-on-Sea W Sus 11 D8
Middleton on the Hill Hereford 26 B2
Middleton-on-the-Wolds E Yorks 52 E5
Middleton One Row Darl 58 E4
Middleton Priors Shrops 34 F2
Middleton Quernham N Yorks 51 B9
Middleton St George Darl 58 E4
Middleton Scriven Shrops 34 G2
Middleton Stoney Oxon 28 F2
Middleton Tyas N Yorks 58 F3
Middletown Cumb 56 F1
Middletown Powys 33 D9
Middlewich Ches E 43 F9
Middlewood Green Suff 31 B7
Middlezoy Som 8 A2
Middridge Durham 58 D3
Midfield Highld 93 C8
Midge Hall Lancs 49 G5
Midgeholme Cumb 62 H2
Midgham W Berks 18 E2
Midgley W Yorks 44 A6
Midgley W Yorks 50 G6
Midhopestones S Yorks 44 C6
Midhurst W Sus 11 B7
Midlem Borders 70 H4
Midmar Aberds 83 C8
Midsomer Norton Bath 16 F3
Midton Invclyd 73 F11
Midtown Highld 91 J13
Midtown Highld 93 C8
Midtown of Buchromb Moray 88 D3
Midville Lincs 47 G7
Midway Ches E 44 D3
Migdale Highld 87 B9
Migvie Aberds 82 C6
Milarrochy Stirling 68 A3
Milborne Port Som 8 C5
Milborne St Andrew Dorset 9 E7
Milborne Wick Som 8 B5
Milbourne Northumb 63 F7
Milburn Cumb 57 D8
Milbury Heath S Glos 16 B3
Milcombe Oxon 27 E11
Milden Suff 30 D6
Mildenhall Suff 30 A4
Mildenhall Wilts 17 E9
Mile Cross Norf 39 D8
Mile Elm Wilts 16 E6
Mile End Essex 30 F6
Mile End Glos 26 G2
Mile Oak Brighton 11 D11
Milebrook Powys 25 A10
Milebush Kent 20 G4
Mileham Norf 38 D5
Milesmark Fife 69 B9
Milfield Northumb 71 G8
Milford Derbys 45 H7
Milford Devon 6 D1
Milford Powys 33 F6
Milford Staffs 34 C5
Milford Sur 18 G6
Milford Wilts 9 B10
Milford Haven = Aberdaugleddau Pembs 22 F4
Milford on Sea Hants 10 E1
Milkwall Glos 26 H2
Milkwell Wilts 9 B8
Mill Bank W Yorks 50 G6
Mill Common Suff 39 G10
Mill End Bucks 18 C4
Mill End Herts 29 E10
Mill Green Essex 20 A3
Mill Green Norf 39 G7
Mill Green Suff 30 D6
Mill Hill London 19 B9
Mill Lane Hants 18 F4
Mill of Kingoodie Aberds 89 F8
Mill of Muiresk Aberds 89 D6
Mill of Sterin Aberds 82 D5
Mill of Uras Aberds 83 E10
Mill Place N Lincs 46 B3
Mill Side Cumb 49 A4
Mill Street Norf 39 D6
Milland W Sus 11 B7
Millarston Renfs 68 D3
Millbank Aberds 89 D11
Millbank Highld 94 D3
Millbeck Cumb 56 D4
Millbounds Orkney 95 E6
Millbreck Aberds 89 D10
Millbridge Sur 18 G5
Millbrook C Beds 29 E7
Millbrook Corn 4 F5
Millbrook Soton 10 C2
Millburn S Ayrs 67 D7
Millcombe Devon 5 G9
Millcorner E Sus 13 D7
Milldale Staffs 44 G5
Millden Lodge Angus 83 F7
Milldens Angus 77 B8
Millerhill Midloth 70 D2
Miller's Dale Derbys 44 E5
Miller's Green Derbys 44 G6
Millgreen Shrops 34 C2
Millhalf Hereford 25 D9
Millhayes Devon 7 F11
Millhead Lancs 49 B4
Millheugh S Lanark 68 E6
Millholme Cumb 57 G7
Millhouse Argyll 73 F8
Millhouse Cumb 56 C5
Millhouse Green S Yorks 44 B6
Millhousebridge Dumfries 61 E7
Millhouses S Yorks 45 D7
Millikenpark Renfs 68 D3
Millin Cross Pembs 22 E4
Millington E Yorks 52 D4
Millmeece Staffs 34 B4
Millom Cumb 49 A1
Millook Corn 4 B2
Millpool Corn 4 D2
Millport N Ayrs 66 A4
Millquarter Dumfries 55 A9
Millthorpe Lincs 37 B7
Millthrop Cumb 57 G8
Milltimber Aberdeen 83 C10
Milltown Corn 4 F2
Milltown Derbys 45 F7
Milltown Devon 6 C4
Milltown Dumfries 61 F9
Milltown of Aberdalgie Perth 76 E3
Milltown of Auchindoun Moray 88 D3
Milltown of Craigston Aberds 89 C7
Milltown of Edinvillie Moray 88 D2
Milltown of Kildrummy Aberds 82 B6
Milltown of Rothiemay Moray 88 D5
Milltown of Towie Aberds 82 B6
Milnathort Perth 76 G4
Milner's Heath Ches W 43 F7
Milngavie E Dunb 68 C4
Milnrow Gtr Man 44 A3
Milnshaw Lancs 50 G3
Milnthorpe Cumb 49 A4
Milo Carms 23 E10
Milson Shrops 26 A3
Milstead Kent 20 F6
Milston Wilts 17 G8
Milton Angus 76 C6
Milton Cambs 29 B11
Milton Cumb 61 G11
Milton Derbys 35 C9
Milton Dumfries 54 D5
Milton Dumfries 60 E4
Milton Dumfries 60 F4
Milton Highld 86 F6
Milton Highld 86 H7
Milton Highld 87 D10
Milton Highld 87 G8
Milton Highld 94 E5
Milton Moray 88 B5
Milton N Som 15 E9
Milton Notts 45 E11
Milton Oxon 17 B11
Milton Oxon 27 E11
Milton Pembs 22 F5
Milton Perth 76 F2
Milton Ptsmth 10 E5
Milton Stirling 75 G8
Milton Stoke 44 G3
Milton W Dunb 68 C3
Milton Abbas Dorset 9 D7
Milton Abbot Devon 4 D5
Milton Bridge Midloth 69 D11
Milton Bryan C Beds 28 E6
Milton Clevedon Som 16 H3
Milton Coldwells Aberds 89 E9
Milton Combe Devon 4 E5
Milton Damerel Devon 6 E2
Milton End Glos 17 A8
Milton Ernest Bedford 29 C7
Milton Green Ches W 43 G7
Milton Hill Oxon 17 B11
Milton Keynes M Keynes 28 E5
Milton Keynes Village M Keynes 28 E5
Milton Lilbourne Wilts 17 E8
Milton Malsor Northants 28 C4
Milton Morenish Perth 75 D9
Milton of Auchinhove Aberds 83 C7
Milton of Balgonie Fife 76 G6
Milton of Buchanan Stirling 68 A3
Milton of Campfield Aberds 83 C8
Milton of Campsie E Dunb 68 C5
Milton of Corsindae Aberds 83 C8
Milton of Cushnie Aberds 83 B7
Milton of Dalcapon Perth 76 B2
Milton of Edradour Perth 76 B2
Milton of Gollanfield Highld 87 F10
Milton of Lesmore Aberds 82 A6
Milton of Logie Aberds 82 C6
Milton of Murtle Aberdeen 83 C10
Milton of Noth Aberds 83 A7
Milton of Tullich Aberds 82 D5
Milton on Stour Dorset 9 B6
Milton Regis Kent 20 E6
Milton under Wychwood Oxon 27 G9
Miltonduff Moray 88 B1
Miltonhill Moray 87 E13
Miltonise Dumfries 54 B4
Milverton Som 7 D10
Milverton Warks 27 B10
Milwich Staffs 34 B5
Minard Argyll 73 D8
Minchinhampton Glos 16 A5
Mindrum Northumb 71 G7
Minehead Som 7 B8
Minera Wrex 42 G5
Minety Wilts 17 B7
Minffordd Gwyn 32 D3
Minffordd Gwyn 41 C7
Minffordd Gwyn 41 G7
Miningsby Lincs 47 F7
Minions Corn 4 D3
Minishant S Ayrs 66 E6
Minllyn Gwyn 32 D4
Minnes Aberds 89 F9
Minngearraidh W Isles 84 F2
Minnigaff Dumfries 55 C7
Minnonie Aberds 89 B7
Minskip N Yorks 51 C9
Minstead Hants 10 C1
Minsted W Sus 11 B7
Minster Kent 20 D6
Minster Kent 21 E10
Minster Lovell Oxon 27 G10
Minsterley Shrops 33 E9
Minsterworth Glos 26 G4
Minterne Magna Dorset 8 D5
Minting Lincs 46 E5
Mintlaw Aberds 89 D10
Minto Borders 61 A11
Minton Shrops 33 F10
Minwear Pembs 22 E5
Minworth W Mid 35 F7
Mirbister Orkney 95 F4
Mirehouse Cumb 56 E1
Mireland Highld 94 D5
Mirfield W Yorks 51 H8
Miserden Glos 26 H6
Miskin Rhondda 14 C6
Misson Notts 45 C10
Misterton Leics 36 G1
Misterton Notts 45 C11
Misterton Som 8 D3
Mistley Essex 31 E8
Mitcham London 19 E9
Mitchel Troy Mon 25 G11
Mitcheldean Glos 26 G3
Mitchell Corn 3 D7
Mitcheltroy Common Mon 25 H11
Mitford Northumb 63 E7
Mithian Corn 2 D6
Mitton Staffs 34 D4
Mixbury Oxon 28 E3
Moat Cumb 61 F10
Moats Tye Suff 31 C7
Mobberley Ches E 43 E10
Mobberley Staffs 34 A6
Moccas Hereford 25 D10
Mochdre Conwy 41 C10
Mochdre Powys 33 G6
Mochrum Dumfries 54 E6
Mockbeggar Hants 9 D10
Mockerkin Cumb 56 D2
Modbury Devon 5 F7
Moddershall Staffs 34 B5
Moelfre Anglesey 41 B7
Moelfre Powys 33 C7
Moffat Dumfries 60 C6
Moggerhanger C Beds 29 D8
Moira Leics 35 D9
Mol-chlach Highld 85 G9
Molash Kent 21 F7
Mold = Yr Wyddgrug Flint 42 F5
Moldgreen W Yorks 51 H7

Molehill Green Essex 30 F2
Molescroft E Yorks 52 E6
Molesden Northumb 63 E7
Molesworth Cambs 37 H6
Moll Highld 85 E10
Molland Devon 7 D7
Mollington Ches W 43 E6
Mollington Oxon 27 D11
Mollinsburn N Lanark 68 C6
Monachty Ceredig 24 B2
Monachylemore Stirling 75 F7
Monar Lodge Highld 86 G5
Monaughty Powys 25 B9
Monboddo House Aberds 83 F9
Mondynes Aberds 83 F9
Monevechadan Argyll 74 G4
Monewden Suff 31 C9
Moneydie Perth 76 E3
Moniaive Dumfries 60 D3
Monifieth Angus 77 D7
Monikie Angus 77 D7
Monimail Fife 76 F5
Monington Pembs 22 B6
Monk Bretton S Yorks 45 B7
Monk Fryston N Yorks 51 G11
Monk Sherborne Hants 18 F3
Monk Soham Suff 31 B9
Monk Street Essex 30 F3
Monken Hadley London 19 B9
Monkhopton Shrops 34 F2
Monkland Hereford 25 C11
Monkleigh Devon 6 D3
Monknash V Glam 14 D5
Monkokehampton Devon 6 F4
Monks Eleigh Suff 30 D6
Monk's Gate W Sus 11 B11
Monks Heath Ches E 44 E2
Monks Kirby Warks 35 G10
Monks Risborough Bucks 18 A5
Monkseaton T&W 63 F9
Monkshill Aberds 89 D7
Monksilver Som 7 C9
Monkspath W Mid 35 H7
Monkswood Mon 15 A9
Monkton Devon 7 F10
Monkton Kent 21 E9
Monkton Pembs 22 F4
Monkton S Ayrs 67 D6
Monkton Combe Bath 16 E4
Monkton Deverill Wilts 16 H5
Monkton Farleigh Wilts 16 E5
Monkton Heathfield Som 8 B1
Monkton Up Wimborne Dorset 9 C9
Monkwearmouth T&W 63 H9
Monkwood Hants 10 A5
Monmouth = Trefynwy Mon 26 G2
Monmouth Cap Mon 25 F10
Monnington on Wye Hereford 25 D10
Monreith Dumfries 54 E6
Monreith Mains Dumfries 54 E6
Mont Saint Guern 11
Montacute Som 8 C3
Montcoffer Ho. Aberds 89 B6
Montford Argyll 73 G10
Montford Shrops 33 D10
Montford Bridge Shrops 33 D10
Montgarrie Aberds 83 B7
Montgomery = Trefaldwyn Powys 33 F8
Montrave Fife 76 G6
Montrose Angus 77 B10
Montsale Essex 21 B7
Monxton Hants 17 G10
Monyash Derbys 44 F5
Monymusk Aberds 83 B8
Monzie Perth 75 E11
Monzie Castle Perth 75 E11
Moodiesburn N Lanark 68 C5
Moonzie Fife 76 F6
Moor Allerton W Yorks 51 F8
Moor Crichel Dorset 9 D8
Moor End E Yorks 52 F4
Moor End York 52 D2
Moor Monkton N Yorks 51 D11
Moor of Granary Moray 87 F13
Moor of Ravenstone Dumfries 54 E6
Moor Row Cumb 56 E2
Moor Street Kent 20 E5
Moorby Lincs 46 F6
Moordown Bmouth 9 E9
Moore Halton 43 D8
Moorend Glos 16 A4
Moorends S Yorks 52 H2
Moorgate S Yorks 45 C8
Moorgreen Notts 45 H8
Moorhall Derbys 45 E7
Moorhampton Hereford 25 D10
Moorhead W Yorks 51 F7
Moorhouse Cumb 61 H9
Moorhouse Notts 45 F11
Moorlinch Som 15 H9
Moorsholm Redcar 59 E7
Moorside Gtr Man 44 B3
Moorthorpe W Yorks 45 A8
Moortown Hants 9 D10
Moortown IoW 10 F3
Moortown Lincs 46 C4
Morangie Highld 87 C10
Morar Highld 79 B9
Morborne Cambs 37 F7
Morchard Bishop Devon 7 F6
Morcombelake Dorset 8 E3
Morcott Rutland 36 E5
Morda Shrops 33 C8
Morden Dorset 9 E8
Morden London 19 E9
Mordiford Hereford 26 E2
Mordon Durham 58 D4
More Shrops 33 F9
Morebath Devon 7 D8
Morebattle Borders 62 A3
Morecambe Lancs 49 C4
Morefield Highld 86 B4
Moreleigh Devon 5 F8
Morenish Perth 75 D8
Moresby Cumb 56 D1
Moresby Parks Cumb 56 E1
Morestead Hants 10 B4
Moreton Dorset 9 F7
Moreton Essex 30 H2
Moreton Mers 42 C5
Moreton Oxon 18 A3
Moreton Staffs 34 D3
Moreton Corbet Shrops 34 C1
Moreton-in-Marsh Glos 27 E9
Moreton Jeffries Hereford 26 D3
Moreton Morrell Warks 27 C10
Moreton on Lugg Hereford 26 D2
Moreton Pinkney Northants 28 D2
Moreton Say Shrops 34 B2
Moreton Valence Glos 26 H4
Moretonhampstead Devon 5 C8
Morfa Carms 23 E10
Morfa Carms 23 G10
Morfa Bach Carms 23 E8
Morfa Bychan Gwyn 41 G7
Morfa Dinlle Gwyn 40 E6
Morfa Glas Neath 24 H5
Morfa Nefyn Gwyn 40 F4
Morfydd Denb 42 H4
Morgan's Vale Wilts 9 B10
Moriah Ceredig 32 H2
Morland Cumb 57 D7
Morley Derbys 35 A9
Morley Durham 58 D2
Morley W Yorks 51 G8
Morley Green Ches E 44 D2
Morley St Botolph Norf 39 F6
Morningside Edin 69 C11
Morningside N Lanark 69 E7
Morningthorpe Norf 39 F8
Morpeth Northumb 63 E8
Morphie Aberds 77 A10
Morrey Staffs 35 D7
Morris Green Essex 30 E4
Morriston Swansea 14 B2
Morston Norf 38 A6
Mortehoe Devon 6 B3
Mortimer W Berks 18 E3
Mortimer West End Hants 18 E3
Mortimer's Cross Hereford 25 B11
Mortlake London 19 D9
Morton Cumb 56 A5
Morton Derbys 45 F8
Morton Lincs 37 C6
Morton Lincs 46 C2
Morton Lincs 46 F2
Morton Norf 39 D7
Morton Notts 45 G11
Morton S Glos 16 B3
Morton Shrops 33 C8
Morton Bagot Warks 27 B8
Morton-on-Swale N Yorks 58 G4
Morvah Corn 2 F3
Morval Corn 4 F3
Morvich Highld 80 A1
Morvich Highld 93 J10
Morville Shrops 34 F2
Morville Heath Shrops 34 F2
Morwenstow Corn 6 E1
Mosborough S Yorks 45 D8
Moscow E Ayrs 67 B7
Mosedale Cumb 56 C5
Moseley W Mid 34 F5
Moseley W Mid 35 G6
Moseley Worcs 26 C5
Moss Argyll 78 G2
Moss Highld 79 E9
Moss S Yorks 45 A9
Moss Wrex 42 G6
Moss Bank Mers 43 C8
Moss Edge Lancs 49 E4
Moss End Brack 18 D5
Moss of Barmuckity Moray 88 B2
Moss Pit Staffs 34 C5
Moss-side Highld 87 F11
Moss Side Lancs 49 F3
Mossat Aberds 82 B6
Mossbank Shetland 96 F6
Mossbay Cumb 56 D1
Mossblown S Ayrs 67 D7
Mossbrow Gtr Man 43 D10
Mossburnford Borders 62 B2
Mossdale Dumfries 55 B9
Mossend N Lanark 68 D6
Mosser Cumb 56 D3
Mossfield Highld 87 D9
Mossgiel E Ayrs 67 D7
Mosside Angus 77 B7
Mossley Ches E 44 F2
Mossley Gtr Man 44 B3
Mossley Hill Mers 43 D6
Mosstodloch Moray 88 C3
Mosston Angus 77 C8
Mossy Lea Lancs 43 A8
Mosterton Dorset 8 D3
Moston Gtr Man 44 B2
Moston Shrops 34 C1
Moston Green Ches E 43 F10
Mostyn Flint 42 D4
Mostyn Quay Flint 42 D4
Motcombe Dorset 9 B7
Mothecombe Devon 5 G7
Motherby Cumb 56 D6
Motherwell N Lanark 68 E6
Mottingham London 19 D11
Mottisfont Hants 10 B2
Mottistone IoW 10 F3
Mottram in Longdendale Gtr Man 44 C3
Mottram St Andrew Ches E 44 E2
Mouilpied Guern 11
Mouldsworth Ches W 43 E8
Moulin Perth 76 B2
Moulsecoomb Brighton 12 F2
Moulsford Oxon 18 C2
Moulsoe M Keynes 28 D6
Moulton Ches W 43 F9
Moulton Lincs 37 C9
Moulton N Yorks 58 F3
Moulton Northants 28 B4
Moulton Suff 30 B3
Moulton V Glam 14 D6
Moulton Chapel Lincs 37 D8
Moulton Eaugate Lincs 37 D9
Moulton St Mary Norf 39 E9
Moulton Seas End Lincs 37 C9
Mounie Castle Aberds 83 A9
Mount Corn 3 D6
Mount Corn 4 E2
Mount Highld 87 G12
Mount Bures Essex 30 E6
Mount Canisp Highld 87 D10
Mount Hawke Corn 2 E6
Mount Pleasant Ches E 44 G2
Mount Pleasant Derbys 35 D8
Mount Pleasant Derbys 45 H7
Mount Pleasant Flint 42 E5
Mount Pleasant Hants 10 E1
Mount Pleasant W Yorks 51 G8
Mount Sorrel Wilts 9 B9
Mount Tabor W Yorks 51 G6
Mountain W Yorks 51 F6
Mountain Ash = Aberpennar Rhondda 14 B6
Mountain Cross Borders 69 F10
Mountain Water Pembs 22 D4
Mountbenger Borders 70 H2
Mountfield E Sus 12 D6
Mountgerald Highld 87 E8
Mountjoy Corn 3 C7
Mountnessing Essex 20 B3
Mounton Mon 15 B11
Mountsorrel Leics 36 D1
Mousehole Corn 2 G3
Mousen Northumb 71 G10
Mouswald Dumfries 60 F6
Mow Cop Ches E 44 G2
Mowhaugh Borders 62 A4
Mowsley Leics 36 G2
Moxley W Mid 34 F5
Moy Highld 80 E6
Moy Highld 87 H10
Moy Hall Highld 87 H10
Moy Ho. Moray 87 E13
Moy Lodge Highld 80 E6
Moyles Court Hants 9 D10
Moylgrove Pembs 22 B6
Muasdale Argyll 65 D7
Much Birch Hereford 26 E2
Much Cowarne Hereford 26 D3
Much Dewchurch Hereford 25 E11
Much Hadham Herts 29 G11
Much Hoole Lancs 49 G4
Much Marcle Hereford 26 E3
Much Wenlock Shrops 34 E2
Muchalls Aberds 83 D11
Muchelney Som 8 B3
Muchlarnick Corn 4 F3
Muchrachd Highld 86 H5
Muckernich Highld 87 F8
Mucking Thurrock 20 C3
Muckleford Dorset 8 E5
Mucklestone Staffs 34 B3
Muckleton Shrops 34 C1
Muckletown Aberds 83 A7
Muckley Corner Staffs 35 E6
Muckton Lincs 47 D7
Mudale Highld 93 F8
Muddiford Devon 6 C4
Mudeford Dorset 9 E10
Mudford Som 8 C4
Mudgley Som 15 G10
Mugdock Stirling 68 C4
Mugeary Highld 85 E9
Mugginton Derbys 35 A8
Muggleswick Durham 58 B1
Muie Highld 93 J9
Muir Aberds 82 E2
Muir of Fairburn Highld 86 F7
Muir of Fowlis Aberds 83 B7
Muir of Ord Highld 87 F8
Muir of Pert Angus 77 D7
Muirden Aberds 89 C7
Muirdrum Angus 77 D8
Muirhead Angus 76 D6
Muirhead Fife 76 G5
Muirhead N Lanark 68 D5
Muirhead S Ayrs 66 C6
Muirhouselaw Borders 70 H5
Muirhouses Falk 69 B9
Muirkirk E Ayrs 68 H5
Muirmill Stirling 68 B6
Muirshearlich Highld 80 E3
Muirskie Aberds 83 D10
Muirtack Aberds 89 E9
Muirton Highld 87 E10
Muirton Perth 76 E4
Muirton Perth 76 F2
Muirton Mains Highld 86 F7
Muirton of Ardblair Perth 76 C4
Muirton of Ballochy Angus 77 A9
Muiryfold Aberds 89 C7
Muker N Yorks 57 G11
Mulbarton Norf 39 E7
Mulben Moray 88 C3
Mulindry Argyll 64 C4
Mullardoch House Highld 86 H5
Mullion Corn 2 H5
Mullion Cove Corn 2 H5
Mumby Lincs 47 E9
Munderfield Row Hereford 26 C3
Munderfield Stocks Hereford 26 C3
Mundesley Norf 39 B9
Mundford Norf 38 F4
Mundham Norf 39 F9
Mundon Essex 20 A5
Mundurno Aberdeen 83 B11
Munerigie Highld 80 C4
Muness Shetland 96 C8
Mungasdale Highld 86 B2
Mungrisdale Cumb 56 C5
Munlochy Highld 87 F9
Munsley Hereford 26 D3
Munslow Shrops 33 G11
Murchington Devon 5 C7
Murcott Oxon 28 G2
Murkle Highld 94 D3
Murlaggan Highld 80 D2
Murlaggan Highld 80 E5
Murra Orkney 95 H3
Murrayfield Edin 69 C11
Murrow Cambs 37 E9
Mursley Bucks 28 F5
Murthill Angus 77 B7
Murthly Perth 76 D3
Murton Cumb 57 D9
Murton Durham 58 B4
Murton Northumb 71 F8
Murton York 52 D2
Musbury Devon 8 E1
Muscoates N Yorks 52 A2
Musdale Argyll 74 E2
Musselburgh E Loth 70 C2
Muston Leics 36 B4
Muston N Yorks 53 B6
Mustow Green Worcs 26 A5
Mutehill Dumfries 55 E9
Mutford Suff 39 G10
Muthill Perth 75 F11
Mutterton Devon 7 F9
Muxton Telford 34 D3
Mybster Highld 94 E3
Myddfai Carms 24 F4
Myddle Shrops 33 C10
Mydroilyn Ceredig 23 A9
Myerscough Lancs 49 F4
Mylor Bridge Corn 3 F7
Mynachlog-ddu Pembs 22 C6
Myndtown Shrops 33 G9
Mynydd Bach Ceredig 32 H3
Mynydd-bach Mon 15 B10
Mynydd Bodafon Anglesey 40 B6
Mynydd-isa Flint 42 F5
Mynyddygarreg Carms 23 F9
Mynytho Gwyn 40 G5
Myrebird Aberds 83 D9
Myrelandhorn Highld 94 E4
Myreside Perth 76 E5
Myrtle Hill Carms 24 E4
Mytchett Sur 18 F5
Mytholm W Yorks 50 G5
Mytholmroyd W Yorks 50 G6
Myton-on-Swale N Yorks 51 C10
Mytton Shrops 33 D10

N

Na Gearrannan W Isles 90 C6
Naast Highld 91 J13
Naburn York 52 E1
Nackington Kent 21 F8
Nacton Suff 31 D9
Nafferton E Yorks 53 D6
Nailbridge Glos 26 G3
Nailsbourne Som 7 D11
Nailsea N Som 15 D10
Nailstone Leics 35 E10
Nailsworth Glos 16 B5
Nairn Highld 87 F11
Nalderswood Sur 19 G9
Nancegollan Corn 2 F5
Nancledra Corn 2 F3
Nanhoron Gwyn 40 G4
Nannau Gwyn 32 C3
Nannerch Flint 42 F4
Nanpantan Leics 35 D11
Nanpean Corn 3 D8
Nanstallon Corn 3 C9
Nant-ddu Powys 25 G7
Nant-glas Powys 24 B6
Nant Peris Gwyn 41 E8
Nant Uchaf Denb 42 G3
Nant-y-Bai Carms 24 D4
Nant-y-cafn Neath 24 H5
Nant-y-derry Mon 25 H10
Nant-y-ffin Carms 23 C10
Nant-y-moel Bridgend 14 B5
Nant-y-pandy Conwy 41 C8
Nanternis Ceredig 23 A8
Nantgaredig Carms 23 D9
Nantgarw Rhondda 15 C7
Nantglyn Denb 42 F3
Nantgwyn Powys 32 H5
Nantlle Gwyn 41 E7
Nantmawr Shrops 33 C8
Nantmel Powys 25 B7
Nantmor Gwyn 41 F8
Nantwich Ches E 43 G9
Nantycaws Carms 23 E9
Nantyffyllon Bridgend 14 B4
Nantyglo Bl Gwent 25 G8
Naphill Bucks 18 B5
Nappa N Yorks 50 D4
Napton on the Hill Warks 27 B11
Narberth = Arberth Pembs 22 E6
Narborough Leics 35 F11
Narborough Norf 38 D3
Nasareth Gwyn 40 E6
Naseby Northants 36 H2
Nash Bucks 28 E4
Nash Hereford 25 B10
Nash Newport 15 C9
Nash Shrops 26 A3
Nash Lee Bucks 28 H5
Nassington Northants 37 F6
Nasty Herts 29 F10
Nateby Cumb 57 F9
Nateby Lancs 49 E4
Natland Cumb 57 H7
Naughton Suff 31 D7
Naunton Glos 27 F8
Naunton Worcs 26 E5
Naunton Beauchamp Worcs 26 C6
Navenby Lincs 46 G3
Navestock Heath Essex 20 B2
Navestock Side Essex 20 B2
Navidale Highld 93 H13
Nawton N Yorks 52 A2
Nayland Suff 30 E6
Nazeing Essex 29 H11
Neacroft Hants 9 E10
Neal's Green Warks 35 G9
Neap Shetland 96 H7
Near Sawrey Cumb 56 G5
Neasham Darl 58 E4
Neath = Castell-Nedd Neath 14 B3
Neath Abbey Neath 14 B3
Neatishead Norf 39 C9
Nebo Anglesey 40 A6
Nebo Ceredig 24 B2
Nebo Conwy 41 E10
Nebo Gwyn 40 E6
Necton Norf 38 E4
Nedd Highld 92 F4
Nedderton Northumb 63 E8
Nedging Tye Suff 31 D7
Needham Norf 39 G8
Needham Market Suff 31 C7
Needingworth Cambs 29 A10
Needwood Staffs 35 C7
Neen Savage Shrops 34 H2
Neen Sollars Shrops 26 A3
Neenton Shrops 34 G2
Nefyn Gwyn 40 F5
Neilston E Renf 68 E3
Neinthirion Powys 32 E5
Neithrop Oxon 27 D11
Nelly Andrews Green Powys 33 E8
Nelson Caerph 15 B7
Nelson Lancs 50 F4
Nelson Village Northumb 63 F8
Nemphlar S Lanark 69 F7
Nempnett Thrubwell N Som 15 E11
Nene Terrace Lincs 37 E8
Nenthall Cumb 57 B9
Nenthead Cumb 57 B9
Nenthorn Borders 70 G5
Nerabus Argyll 64 C3
Nercwys Flint 42 F5
Nerston S Lanark 68 E5
Nesbit Northumb 71 G8
Ness Ches W 42 E6
Nesscliffe Shrops 33 D9
Neston Ches W 42 E5
Neston Wilts 16 E5
Nether Alderley Ches E 44 E2
Nether Blainslie Borders 70 F4
Nether Booth Derbys 44 D5
Nether Broughton Leics 36 C2
Nether Burrow Lancs 50 B2
Nether Cerne Dorset 8 E5
Nether Compton Dorset 8 C4
Nether Crimond Aberds 89 F8
Nether Dalgliesh Borders 61 C8
Nether Dallachy Moray 88 B3
Nether Exe Devon 7 F8
Nether Glasslaw Aberds 89 C8
Nether Handwick Angus 76 C6
Nether Haugh S Yorks 45 C8
Nether Heage Derbys 45 G7
Nether Heyford Northants 28 C3
Nether Hindhope Borders 62 B3
Nether Howecleuch S Lanark 60 B6
Nether Kellet Lancs 49 C5
Nether Kinmundy Aberds 89 D10
Nether Langwith Notts 45 E9
Nether Leask Aberds 89 E10
Nether Lenshie Aberds 89 D6
Nether Monynut Borders 70 D6
Nether Padley Derbys 44 E6
Nether Park Aberds 89 C10
Nether Poppleton York 52 D1
Nether Silton N Yorks 58 G5
Nether Stowey Som 7 C10
Nether Urquhart Fife 76 G4
Nether Wallop Hants 17 H10
Nether Wasdale Cumb 56 F3
Nether Whitacre Warks 35 F8
Nether Worton Oxon 27 E11
Netheravon Wilts 17 G8
Netherbrae Aberds 89 C7
Netherbrough Orkney 95 G4
Netherburn S Lanark 69 F7
Netherbury Dorset 8 E3
Netherby Cumb 61 F9
Netherby N Yorks 51 E9
Nethercote Warks 28 B2
Nethercott Devon 6 C3
Netherend Glos 16 A2
Netherfield E Sus 12 E6
Netherhampton Wilts 9 B10
Netherlaw Dumfries 55 E10
Netherley Aberds 83 D10
Netherley Mers 43 D7
Nethermill Dumfries 60 E6
Nethermuir Aberds 89 D9
Netherplace E Renf 68 E4
Netherseal Derbys 35 D8
Netherthird E Ayrs 67 E8
Netherthong W Yorks 44 B5
Netherthorpe S Yorks 45 D9
Netherton Angus 77 B8
Netherton Devon 5 D9
Netherton Hants 17 F10
Netherton Mers 42 B6
Netherton Northumb 62 C5
Netherton Oxon 17 B11
Netherton Perth 76 B4
Netherton Stirling 68 C4
Netherton W Mid 34 G5
Netherton W Yorks 44 A5
Netherton W Yorks 51 H8
Netherton Worcs 26 D6
Nethertown Cumb 56 F1
Nethertown Highld 94 C5
Netherwitton Northumb 63 D7
Netherwood E Ayrs 68 H5
Nethy Bridge Highld 82 A2
Netley Hants 10 D3
Netley Marsh Hants 10 C2
Netteswell Essex 29 G11
Nettlebed Oxon 18 C4
Nettlebridge Som 16 G3
Nettlecombe Dorset 8 E4
Nettleden Herts 29 G7
Nettleham Lincs 46 E4
Nettlestead Kent 20 F3
Nettlestead Green Kent 20 F3
Nettlestone IoW 10 E5
Nettlesworth Durham 58 B3
Nettleton Lincs 46 B5
Nettleton Wilts 16 D5
Neuadd Carms 24 F3
Nevendon Essex 20 B4
Nevern Pembs 22 B5
New Abbey Dumfries 60 G5
New Aberdour Aberds 89 B8
New Addington London 19 E10
New Alresford Hants 10 A4
New Alyth Perth 76 C5
New Arley Warks 35 G8
New Ash Green Kent 20 E3
New Barn Kent 20 E3
New Barnetby N Lincs 46 A4
New Barton Northants 28 B5
New Bewick Northumb 62 A6
New-bigging Angus 76 C5
New Bilton Warks 35 H10
New Bolingbroke Lincs 47 G7
New Boultham Lincs 46 E3
New Bradwell M Keynes 28 D5
New Brancepeth Durham 58 B3
New Bridge Wrex 33 A8
New Brighton Flint 42 F5
New Brighton Mers 42 C6
New Brinsley Notts 45 G8
New Broughton Wrex 42 G6
New Buckenham Norf 39 F6
New Byth Aberds 89 C8
New Catton Norf 39 D8
New Cheriton Hants 10 B4
New Costessey Norf 39 D7
New Cowper Cumb 56 B3
New Cross Ceredig 32 H2
New Cross London 19 D10
New Cumnock E Ayrs 67 E9
New Deer Aberds 89 D8
New Delaval Northumb 63 F8
New Duston Northants 28 B4
New Earswick York 52 D2
New Edlington S Yorks 45 C9
New Elgin Moray 88 B2
New Ellerby E Yorks 53 F7
New Eltham London 19 D11
New End Worcs 27 C7
New Farnley W Yorks 51 F8
New Ferry Mers 42 D6
New Fryston W Yorks 51 G10
New Galloway Dumfries 55 B9
New Gilston Fife 77 G7
New Grimsby Scilly 2 C2
New Hainford Norf 39 D8
New Hartley Northumb 63 F9
New Haw Sur 19 E7
New Hedges Pembs 22 F6
New Herrington T&W 58 A4
New Hinksey Oxon 18 A2
New Holkham Norf 38 B4
New Holland N Lincs 53 G6
New Houghton Derbys 45 F8
New Houghton Norf 38 C3
New Houses N Yorks 50 B4
New Humberstone Leicester 36 E2
New Hutton Cumb 57 G7
New Hythe Kent 20 F4
New Inn Carms 23 C9
New Inn Mon 15 A10
New Inn Pembs 22 C5
New Inn Torf 15 B9
New Invention Shrops 33 H8
New Invention W Mid 34 E5
New Kelso Highld 86 G2
New Kingston Notts 35 C11
New Lanark S Lanark 69 F7
New Lane Lancs 43 A7
New Lane End Warr 43 C9
New Leake Lincs 47 G8
New Leeds Aberds 89 C9
New Longton Lancs 49 G5
New Luce Dumfries 54 C4
New Malden London 19 E9
New Marske Redcar 59 D7
New Marton Shrops 33 B9
New Micklefield W Yorks 51 F10
New Mill Aberds 83 E9
New Mill Herts 28 G6
New Mill W Yorks 44 B5
New Mill Wilts 17 E8
New Mills Ches E 43 D10
New Mills Corn 3 D7
New Mills Derbys 44 D3
New Mills Powys 33 E6
New Milton Hants 9 E11
New Moat Pembs 22 D5
New Ollerton Notts 45 F10
New Oscott W Mid 35 F6
New Park N Yorks 51 D8
New Pitsligo Aberds 89 C8
New Polzeath Corn 3 B8
New Quay = Ceinewydd Ceredig 23 A8
New Rackheath Norf 39 D8
New Radnor Powys 25 B9
New Rent Cumb 56 C6
New Ridley Northumb 62 H6
New Road Side N Yorks 50 E5
New Romney Kent 13 D9
New Rossington S Yorks 45 C10
New Row Ceredig 24 A4
New Row Lancs 50 F2
New Row N Yorks 59 E7
New Sarum Wilts 9 A10
New Silksworth T&W 58 A4
New Stevenston N Lanark 68 E6
New Street Staffs 44 G4
New Street Lane Shrops 34 B2
New Swanage Dorset 9 F9
New Totley S Yorks 45 E7
New Town E Loth 70 C3
New Tredegar = Tredegar Newydd Caerph 15 A7
New Trows S Lanark 69 G7
New Ulva Argyll 72 E6
New Walsoken Cambs 37 E10
New Waltham NE Lincs 46 B6
New Whittington Derbys 45 E7
New Wimpole Cambs 29 D10
New Winton E Loth 70 C3
New Yatt Oxon 27 G10
New York Lincs 46 G6
New York N Yorks 51 C7
Newall W Yorks 51 E7
Newark Orkney 95 D8
Newark Pboro 37 E8
Newark-on-Trent Notts 45 G11
Newarthill N Lanark 68 E6
Newbarns Cumb 49 B2
Newbattle Midloth 70 D2
Newbiggin Cumb 49 C2
Newbiggin Cumb 56 D6
Newbiggin Cumb 56 G2
Newbiggin Cumb 57 B7
Newbiggin Cumb 57 D8
Newbiggin Durham 57 D11
Newbiggin N Yorks 57 G11
Newbiggin N Yorks 57 H11
Newbiggin-by-the-Sea Northumb 63 E9
Newbiggin-on-Lune Cumb 57 F9
Newbigging Angus 77 D7
Newbigging Angus 77 D7
Newbigging S Lanark 69 F9
Newbold Derbys 45 E7
Newbold Leics 35 D10
Newbold on Avon Warks 35 H10
Newbold on Stour Warks 27 D9
Newbold Pacey Warks 27 C9
Newbold Verdon Leics 35 E10
Newborough Anglesey 40 D6
Newborough Pboro 37 E8
Newborough Staffs 35 C7
Newbottle Northants 28 E2
Newbottle T&W 58 A4
Newbourne Suff 31 D9
Newbridge Caerph 15 B8
Newbridge Ceredig 23 A10
Newbridge Corn 2 F3
Newbridge Corn 4 E4
Newbridge Dumfries 60 F5
Newbridge Edin 69 C10
Newbridge Hants 10 C1
Newbridge IoW 10 F3
Newbridge Pembs 22 C4
Newbridge Green Worcs 26 E5
Newbridge-on-Usk Mon 15 B9
Newbridge on Wye Powys 25 C7
Newbrough Northumb 62 G4
Newbuildings Devon 7 F6
Newburgh Aberds 89 C9
Newburgh Aberds 89 F9
Newburgh Borders 61 B9
Newburgh Fife 76 F5
Newburgh Lancs 43 A7
Newburn T&W 63 G7
Newbury W Berks 17 E11
Newbury Park London 19 C11
Newby Cumb 57 D7
Newby Lancs 50 E4
Newby N Yorks 50 B3
Newby N Yorks 58 E6
Newby N Yorks 59 G11
Newby Bridge Cumb 56 H5
Newby East Cumb 61 H10
Newby West Cumb 56 A5
Newby Wiske N Yorks 58 H4
Newcastle Mon 25 G11
Newcastle Shrops 33 G8
Newcastle Emlyn = Castell Newydd Emlyn Carms 23 B8
Newcastle-under-Lyme Staffs 44 H2
Newcastle Upon Tyne T&W 63 G8
Newcastleton or Copshaw Holm Borders 61 E10
Newchapel Pembs 23 C7
Newchapel Powys 32 G5
Newchapel Staffs 44 G2
Newchapel Sur 12 B2
Newchurch Carms 23 D8
Newchurch IoW 10 F4
Newchurch Kent 13 C9
Newchurch Lancs 50 F4
Newchurch Mon 15 B10
Newchurch Powys 25 C9
Newchurch Staffs 35 C7
Newcott Devon 7 F11
Newcraighall Edin 70 C2
Newdigate Sur 19 G8
Newell Green Brack 18 D5
Newenden Kent 13 D7
Newent Glos 26 F4
Newerne Glos 16 A3
Newfield Durham 58 C3
Newfield Highld 87 D10
Newford Scilly 2 C3
Newfound Hants 18 F2
Newgale Pembs 22 D3
Newgate Norf 39 A6
Newgate Street Herts 19 A10
Newhall Ches E 43 H9
Newhall Derbys 35 C8
Newhall House Highld 87 E9
Newhall Point Highld 87 E10
Newham Northumb 71 H10
Newham Hall Northumb 71 H10
Newhaven Derbys 44 G5
Newhaven E Sus 12 F3
Newhaven Edin 69 C11
Newhey Gtr Man 44 A3
Newholm N Yorks 59 E9
Newhouse N Lanark 68 D6
Newick E Sus 12 D3
Newingreen Kent 13 C10
Newington Kent 20 E5
Newington Kent 21 E10
Newington Kent 21 H8
Newington Notts 45 C10
Newington Oxon 18 B3
Newington Shrops 33 G10
Newland Glos 26 H2
Newland Hull 53 F6
Newland N Yorks 52 G2
Newland Worcs 26 D4
Newlandrig Midloth 70 D2
Newlands Borders 61 D11
Newlands Highld 87 G10
Newlands Moray 88 C3
Newlands Northumb 62 H6
Newland's Corner Sur 19 G7
Newlands of Geise Highld 94 D2
Newlands of Tynet Moray 88 B3
Newlands Park Anglesey 40 B4
Newlandsmuir S Lanark 68 E5
Newlot Orkney 95 G6
Newlyn Corn 2 G3
Newmachar Aberds 83 B10
Newmains N Lanark 69 E7
Newmarket Suff 30 B3
Newmarket W Isles 91 D9
Newmill Borders 61 B10
Newmill Corn 2 F3
Newmill Moray 88 C4
Newmill of Inshewan Angus 77 A7
Newmills of Boyne Aberds 88 C5
Newmiln Perth 76 D4
Newmilns E Ayrs 67 C8
Newnham Cambs 29 C11
Newnham Glos 26 G3
Newnham Hants 18 F4
Newnham Herts 29 E9
Newnham Kent 20 F6
Newnham Northants 28 C2
Newnham Bridge Worcs 26 B3
Newpark Fife 77 F7
Newport Devon 6 C4
Newport E Yorks 52 F4
Newport Essex 30 E2
Newport Highld 94 H3
Newport IoW 10 F4
Newport = Casnewydd Newport 15 C9
Newport Norf 39 D11
Newport = Trefdraeth Pembs 22 C5
Newport Telford 34 D3
Newport-on-Tay Fife 77 E7
Newport Pagnell M Keynes 28 D5
Newpound Common W Sus 11 B9
Newquay Corn 3 C7
Newsbank Ches E 44 F2
Newseat Aberds 89 D10
Newseat Aberds 89 E7
Newsham N Yorks 51 A9
Newsham N Yorks 58 E2
Newsham Northumb 63 F9
Newsholme E Yorks 52 G3
Newsholme Lancs 50 D4
Newsome W Yorks 44 A5
Newstead Borders 70 G4
Newstead Northumb 71 H10
Newstead Notts 45 G9
Newthorpe N Yorks 51 F10
Newton Argyll 73 D9
Newton Borders 62 A1
Newton Bridgend 14 D4
Newton Cambs 29 D11
Newton Cambs 37 D10
Newton Cardiff 15 D8
Newton Ches W 43 E8
Newton Ches W 43 F7
Newton Ches W 43 G8
Newton Cumb 49 B2
Newton Derbys 45 G8
Newton Dorset 9 C6
Newton Dumfries 61 D7
Newton Dumfries 61 F8
Newton Gtr Man 44 C3
Newton Hereford 25 E10
Newton Hereford 26 C2
Newton Highld 87 E10
Newton Highld 87 G10
Newton Highld 92 F5
Newton Highld 94 F5
Newton Lancs 49 F4
Newton Lancs 50 B1
Newton Lancs 50 D2
Newton Lincs 36 B6
Newton Moray 88 B1
Newton Norf 38 D4
Newton Northants 36 G4
Newton Northumb 62 G6
Newton Notts 36 A2
Newton Perth 75 D11
Newton S Lanark 68 D5
Newton S Lanark 69 G8
Newton S Yorks 45 B9
Newton Staffs 34 C6
Newton Suff 30 D6
Newton Swansea 14 C2
Newton W Loth 69 C9
Newton Warks 35 H11
Newton Wilts 9 B11
Newton Abbot Devon 5 D9
Newton Arlosh Cumb 61 H7
Newton Aycliffe Durham 58 D3
Newton Bewley Hrtlpl 58 D5
Newton Blossomville M Keynes 28 C6
Newton Bromswold Northants 28 B6
Newton Burgoland Leics 35 E9
Newton by Toft Lincs 46 D4
Newton Ferrers Devon 4 G6
Newton Flotman Norf 39 F8
Newton Hall Northumb 62 G6
Newton Harcourt Leics 36 F2
Newton Heath Gtr Man 44 B2
Newton Ho. Aberds 83 A8
Newton Kyme N Yorks 51 E10
Newton-le-Willows Mers 43 C8
Newton-le-Willows N Yorks 58 H3
Newton Longville Bucks 28 E5
Newton Mearns E Renf 68 E4
Newton Morrell N Yorks 58 F3
Newton Mulgrave N Yorks 59 E8
Newton of Ardtoe Highld 79 D9
Newton of Balcanquhal Perth 76 F4
Newton of Falkland Fife 76 G5
Newton on Ayr S Ayrs 66 D6
Newton on Ouse N Yorks 51 D11
Newton-on-Rawcliffe N Yorks 59 G9
Newton-on-the-Moor Northumb 63 C7
Newton on Trent Lincs 46 E2
Newton Park Argyll 73 G10
Newton Poppleford Devon 7 H9
Newton Purcell Oxon 28 E3
Newton Regis Warks 35 E8
Newton Reigny Cumb 57 C6
Newton St Cyres Devon 7 G7
Newton St Faith Norf 39 D8
Newton St Loe Bath 16 E4
Newton St Petrock Devon 6 E3
Newton Solney Derbys 35 C8
Newton Stacey Hants 17 G11
Newton Stewart Dumfries 55 C7
Newton Tony Wilts 17 G9
Newton Tracey Devon 6 D4
Newton under Roseberry Redcar 59 E6
Newton upon Derwent E Yorks 52 E3
Newton Valence Hants 10 A6
Newtonairds Dumfries 60 E4
Newtongrange Midloth 70 D2
Newtonhill Aberds 83 D11
Newtonhill Highld 87 G8
Newtonmill Angus 77 A9
Newtonmore Highld 81 D9
Newtown Argyll 73 C9
Newtown Ches W 43 E8
Newtown Corn 2 G6
Newtown Cumb 56 B2
Newtown Cumb 61 G11
Newtown Derbys 44 D3
Newtown Devon 7 D6
Newtown Glos 16 A3
Newtown Glos 26 E6
Newtown Hants 10 B2
Newtown Hants 10 C4
Newtown Hants 10 C1
Newtown Hants 10 C5
Newtown Hants 10 D3
Newtown Hants 17 E11
Newtown Hereford 26 D3
Newtown Highld 80 C5
Newtown IoM 48 E3
Newtown IoW 10 E3
Newtown Northumb 62 C6
Newtown Northumb 71 G8
Newtown Northumb 71 H9
Newtown Poole 9 E9
Newtown = Y Drenewydd Powys 33 F7
Newtown Shrops 33 B10
Newtown Staffs 44 F4
Newtown Staffs 44 F3
Newtown Wilts 9 B8
Newtown Linford Leics 35 E11
Newtown St Boswells Borders 70 G4
Newtown Unthank Leics 35 E10
Newtyle Angus 76 C5
Neyland Pembs 22 F4
Niarbyl IoM 48 E2
Nibley S Glos 16 C3
Nibley Green Glos 16 B4
Nibon Shetland 96 F5
Nicholashayne Devon 7 E10
Nicholaston Swansea 23 H10
Nidd N Yorks 51 C9
Nigg Aberdeen 83 C11
Nigg Highld 87 D11
Nigg Ferry Highld 87 E10
Nightcott Som 7 D7
Nilig Denb 42 G3
Nine Ashes Essex 20 A2
Nine Mile Burn Midloth 69 E10
Nine Wells Pembs 22 D2
Ninebanks Northumb 57 A9
Ninfield E Sus 12 E6
Ningwood IoW 10 F2
Nisbet Borders 70 H5
Nisthouse Orkney 95 G4
Nisthouse Shetland 96 G7
Niton IoW 10 G4
Nitshill Glasgow 68 D4
No Man's Heath Ches W 43 H8
No Man's Heath Warks 35 E8
Noak Hill London 20 B2
Noblethorpe S Yorks 44 B6
Nobottle Northants 28 B3
Nocton Lincs 46 F4
Noke Oxon 28 G2
Nolton Pembs 22 E3
Nolton Haven Pembs 22 E3
Nomansland Devon 7 E7
Nomansland Wilts 10 C1
Noneley Shrops 33 C10
Nonikiln Highld 87 D9
Nonington Kent 21 F9
Noonsbrough Shetland 96 H4
Norbreck Blackpool 49 E3
Norbridge Hereford 26 D4
Norbury Ches E 43 H8
Norbury Derbys 35 A7
Norbury Shrops 33 F9
Norbury Staffs 34 C3
Nordelph Norf 38 E1
Norden Gtr Man 44 A2
Norden Heath Dorset 9 F8
Nordley Shrops 34 F2
Norham Northumb 71 F8
Norley Ches W 43 E8
Norleywood Hants 10 E2
Norman Cross Cambs 37 F7
Normanby N Lincs 52 H4
Normanby N Yorks 52 A3
Normanby Redcar 59 E6
Normanby-by-Spital Lincs 46 D4
Normanby by Stow Lincs 46 D2
Normanby le Wold Lincs 46 C5
Normandy Sur 18 F6
Norman's Bay E Sus 12 F5
Norman's Green Devon 7 F9
Normanstone Suff 39 F11
Normanton Derby 35 B9
Normanton Leics 36 A4
Normanton Lincs 46 H3
Normanton Notts 45 G11
Normanton Rutland 36 E5
Normanton W Yorks 51 G9
Normanton le Heath Leics 35 D9
Normanton on Soar Notts 35 C11
Normanton-on-the-Wolds Notts 36 B2
Normanton on Trent Notts 45 F11
Normoss Lancs 49 F3
Norney Sur 18 G6
Norrington Common Wilts 16 E5
Norris Green Mers 43 C6
Norris Hill Leics 35 D9
North Anston S Yorks 45 D9
North Aston Oxon 27 F11
North Baddesley Hants 10 C2
North Ballachulish Highld 74 A3
North Barrow Som 8 B5
North Barsham Norf 38 B5
North Benfleet Essex 20 C4
North Bersted W Sus 11 D8
North Berwick E Loth 70 B4
North Boarhunt Hants 10 C5
North Bovey Devon 5 C8
North Bradley Wilts 16 F5
North Brentor Devon 4 C5
North Brewham Som 16 H4
North Buckland Devon 6 B3
North Burlingham Norf 39 D9
North Cadbury Som 8 B5
North Cairn Dumfries 54 B2
North Carlton Lincs 46 E3
North Carrine Argyll 65 H7
North Cave E Yorks 52 F4
North Cerney Glos 27 H7
North Charford Wilts 9 C10
North Charlton Northumb 63 A7
North Cheriton Som 8 B5
North Cliff E Yorks 53 E8
North Cliffe E Yorks 52 F4
North Clifton Notts 46 E2
North Cockerington Lincs 47 C7
North Coker Som 8 C4
North Collafirth Shetland 96 E5
North Common E Sus 12 D2
North Connel Argyll 74 D2
North Cornelly Bridgend 14 C4
North Cotes Lincs 47 B7
North Cove Suff 39 G10
North Cowton N Yorks 58 F3
North Crawley M Keynes 28 D6
North Cray London 19 D11
North Creake Norf 38 B4
North Curry Som 8 B2
North Dalton E Yorks 52 D5
North Dawn Orkney 95 H5
North Deighton N Yorks 51 D9
North Duffield N Yorks 52 F2
North Elkington Lincs 46 C6
North Elmham Norf 38 C5
North Elmshall W Yorks 45 A8
North End Bucks 28 F5
North End E Yorks 53 F8
North End Essex 30 G3
North End Hants 17 E11
North End Lincs 37 A8
North End N Som 15 E10
North End Ptsmth 10 D5
North End Som 8 B1
North End W Sus 11 D10
North Erradale Highld 91 J12
North Fambridge Essex 20 B5
North Fearns Highld 85 E10
North Featherstone W Yorks 51 G10
North Ferriby E Yorks 52 G5
North Frodingham E Yorks 53 D7
North Gluss Shetland 96 F5
North Gorley Hants 9 C10
North Green Norf 39 G8
North Green Suff 31 B10
North Greetwell Lincs 46 E4
North Grimston N Yorks 52 C4
North Halley Orkney 95 H6
North Halling Medway 20 E4
North Hayling Hants 10 D6
North Hazelrigg Northumb 71 G9
North Heasley Devon 7 C6
North Heath W Sus 11 B9
North Hill Cambs 37 H10
North Hill Corn 4 D3
North Hinksey Oxon 27 H11
North Holmwood Sur 19 G8
North Howden E Yorks 52 F3
North Huish Devon 5 F8
North Hykeham Lincs 46 F3
North Johnston Pembs 22 E4
North Kelsey Lincs 46 B4
North Kelsey Moor Lincs 46 B4
North Kessock Highld 87 G9
North Killingholme N Lincs 53 H7
North Kilvington N Yorks 58 H5
North Kilworth Leics 36 G2
North Kirkton Aberds 89 C11
North Kiscadale N Ayrs 66 D3
North Kyme Lincs 46 G5
North Lancing W Sus 11 D10
North Lee Bucks 28 H5
North Leigh Oxon 27 G10
North Leverton with Habblesthorpe Notts 45 D11
North Littleton Worcs 27 D7
North Lopham Norf 38 G6
North Luffenham Rutland 36 E5
North Marden W Sus 11 C7
North Marston Bucks 28 F4
North Middleton Midloth 70 E2
North Middleton Northumb 62 A6
North Molton Devon 7 D6
North Moreton Oxon 18 C2
North Mundham W Sus 11 D7
North Muskham Notts 45 G11
North Newbald E Yorks 52 F5
North Newington Oxon 27 E11
North Newnton Wilts 17 F8
North Newton Som 8 A1
North Nibley Glos 16 B4
North Oakley Hants 18 F2
North Ockendon London 20 C2
North Ormesby Mbro 58 D6
North Ormsby Lincs 46 C6
North Otterington N Yorks 58 H4
North Owersby Lincs 46 C4
North Perrott Som 8 D3
North Petherton Som 8 A1
North Petherwin Corn 4 C3
North Pickenham Norf 38 E4
North Piddle Worcs 26 C6
North Poorton Dorset 8 E4
North Port Argyll 74 E3
North Queensferry Fife 69 B10
North Radworthy Devon 7 C6
North Rauceby Lincs 46 H4
North Reston Lincs 47 D7
North Rigton N Yorks 51 E8
North Rode Ches E 44 F2
North Roe Shetland 96 E5
North Runcton Norf 38 D2
North Sandwick Shetland 96 D7
North Scale Cumb 49 C1
North Scarle Lincs 46 F2
North Seaton Northumb 63 E8
North Shian Argyll 74 C2
North Shields T&W 63 G9
North Shoebury Southend 20 C6
North Shore Blackpool 49 F3
North Side Cumb 56 D2
North Side Pboro 37 F8
North Skelton Redcar 59 E7
North Somercotes Lincs 47 C8
North Stainley N Yorks 51 B8
North Stainmore Cumb 57 E10
North Stifford Thurrock 20 C3
North Stoke Bath 16 E4
North Stoke Oxon 18 C3
North Stoke W Sus 11 C9
North Street Hants 10 A5
North Street Kent 21 F7
North Street Medway 20 D5
North Street W Berks 18 D3
North Sunderland Northumb 71 G11
North Tamerton Corn 6 G2
North Tawton Devon 6 F5
North Thoresby Lincs 46 C6
North Tidworth Wilts 17 G9
North Togston Northumb 63 C8
North Tuddenham Norf 38 D6
North Walbottle T&W 63 G7
North Walsham Norf 39 B8
North Waltham Hants 18 G2
North Warnborough Hants 18 F4
North Water Bridge Angus 83 G8
North Watten Highld 94 E4
North Weald Bassett Essex 19 A11
North Wheatley Notts 45 D11
North Whilborough Devon 5 E9
North Wick Bath 16 E2
North Willingham Lincs 46 D5
North Wingfield Derbys 45 F8
North Witham Lincs 36 C5
North Woolwich London 19 D11
North Wootton Dorset 8 C5
North Wootton Norf 38 C2
North Wootton Som 16 G2
North Wraxall Wilts 16 D5
North Wroughton Swindon 17 C8
Northacre Norf 38 F5
Northallerton N Yorks 58 G4
Northam Devon 6 D3
Northam Soton 10 C3
Northampton Northants 28 B4
Northaw Herts 19 A9
Northbeck Lincs 37 A6
Northborough Pboro 37 E7
Northbourne Kent 21 F10
Northbridge Street E Sus 12 D6
Northchapel W Sus 11 B8
Northchurch Herts 28 H6
Northcott Devon 6 G2
Northdown Kent 21 D10
Northdyke Orkney 95 F3
Northend Bath 16 E4
Northend Bucks 18 B4
Northend Warks 27 C10
Northenden Gtr Man 44 C2
Northfield Aberdeen 83 C11
Northfield Borders 71 D8
Northfield E Yorks 52 G6
Northfield W Mid 34 H6
Northfields Lincs 36 E6
Northfleet Kent 20 D3
Northgate Lincs 37 C7
Northhouse Borders 61 C10
Northiam E Sus 13 D7
Northill C Beds 29 D8
Northington Hants 18 H2
Northlands Lincs 47 G7
Northlea Durham 58 A5
Northleach Glos 27 G8
Northleigh Devon 7 G10
Northlew Devon 6 G4
Northmoor Oxon 17 A11
Northmoor Green or Moorland Som 8 A2
Northmuir Angus 76 B6
Northney Hants 10 D6
Northolt London 19 C8
Northop Flint 42 F5
Northop Hall Flint 42 F5
Northorpe Lincs 37 B8
Northorpe Lincs 37 D6
Northorpe Lincs 46 C2
Northover Som 8 B4
Northover Som 15 H10
Northowram W Yorks 51 G7
Northport Dorset 9 F8
Northpunds Shetland 96 L6
Northrepps Norf 39 B8
Northtown Orkney 95 J5
Northway Glos 26 E6
Northwich Ches W 43 E9
Northwick S Glos 16 C2
Northwold Norf 38 F3
Northwood Derbys 44 F6
Northwood IoW 10 E3
Northwood Kent 21 E10
Northwood London 19 B7
Northwood Shrops 33 B10
Northwood Green Glos 26 G4
Norton E Sus 12 F3
Norton Glos 26 F5
Norton Halton 43 D8
Norton Herts 29 E9
Norton IoW 10 F2
Norton Mon 25 G11
Norton Northants 28 B3
Norton Notts 45 E9
Norton Powys 25 B10
Norton S Yorks 51 H11
Norton Shrops 33 G10
Norton Shrops 34 E1
Norton Shrops 34 E3
Norton Stockton 58 D5
Norton Suff 30 B6
Norton W Sus 11 D8
Norton W Sus 11 E7
Norton Wilts 16 C5
Norton Worcs 26 C5
Norton Worcs 27 D7
Norton Bavant Wilts 16 G6
Norton Bridge Staffs 34 B4
Norton Canes Staffs 34 E6
Norton Canon Hereford 25 D10
Norton Corner Norf 39 C6
Norton Disney Lincs 46 G2
Norton East Staffs 34 E6
Norton Ferris Wilts 16 H4
Norton Fitzwarren Som 7 D10
Norton Green IoW 10 F2
Norton Hawkfield Bath 16 E2
Norton Heath Essex 20 A3
Norton in Hales Shrops 34 B3
Norton-in-the-Moors Stoke 44 G2
Norton-Juxta-Twycross Leics 35 E9
Norton-le-Clay N Yorks 51 B10
Norton Lindsey Warks 27 B9
Norton Malreward Bath 16 E3
Norton Mandeville Essex 20 A2
Norton-on-Derwent N Yorks 52 B3
Norton St Philip Som 16 F4
Norton sub Hamdon Som 8 C3
Norton Woodseats S Yorks 45 D7
Norwell Notts 45 F11
Norwell Woodhouse Notts 45 F11
Norwich Norf 39 E8
Norwick Shetland 96 B8
Norwood Derbys 45 D8
Norwood Hill Sur 19 G9
Norwoodside Cambs 37 F10
Noseley Leics 36 F3
Noss Shetland 96 M5
Noss Mayo Devon 4 G6
Nosterfield N Yorks 51 A8
Nostie Highld 85 F13
Notgrove Glos 27 F8
Nottage Bridgend 14 D4
Nottingham Nottingham 36 B1
Nottington Dorset 8 F5
Notton W Yorks 45 A7
Notton Wilts 16 E6
Nounsley Essex 30 G4
Noutard's Green Worcs 26 B4
Novar House Highld 87 E9
Nox Shrops 33 D10
Nuffield Oxon 18 C3
Nun Hills Lancs 50 G4
Nun Monkton N Yorks 51 D11
Nunburnholme E Yorks 52 E4
Nuncargate Notts 45 G9
Nuneaton Warks 35 F9
Nuneham Courtenay Oxon 18 B2
Nunney Som 16 G4
Nunnington N Yorks 52 B2
Nunnykirk Northumb 62 D6
Nunsthorpe NE Lincs 46 B6
Nunthorpe Mbro 59 E6
Nunthorpe York 52 D2
Nunton Wilts 9 B10
Nunwick N Yorks 51 B9
Nupend Glos 26 H4
Nursling Hants 10 C2
Nursted Hants 11 B6
Nutbourne W Sus 11 C9
Nutbourne W Sus 11 D6
Nutfield Sur 19 F10
Nuthall Notts 35 A11
Nuthampstead Herts 29 E11
Nuthurst W Sus 11 B10
Nutley E Sus 12 D3
Nutley Hants 18 G3
Nutwell S Yorks 45 B10
Nybster Highld 94 D5
Nyetimber W Sus 11 E7
Nyewood W Sus 11 B7
Nymet Rowland Devon 6 F6
Nymet Tracey Devon 7 F6
Nympsfield Glos 16 A5
Nynehead Som 7 D10
Nyton W Sus 11 D8

O

Oad Street Kent 20 E5
Oadby Leics 36 E2
Oak Cross Devon 6 G4
Oakamoor Staffs 35 A6
Oakbank W Loth 69 D9
Oakdale Caerph 15 B7
Oake Som 7 D10
Oaken Staffs 34 E4
Oakenclough Lancs 49 E5
Oakengates Telford 34 D3
Oakenholt Flint 42 E5
Oakenshaw Durham 58 C3
Oakenshaw W Yorks 51 G7
Oakerthorpe Derbys 45 G7
Oakes W Yorks 51 H7
Oakfield Torf 15 B9
Oakford Ceredig 23 A9
Oakford Devon 7 D8
Oakfordbridge Devon 7 D8
Oakgrove Ches E 44 F3
Oakham Rutland 36 E4
Oakhanger Hants 18 H4
Oakhill Som 16 G3
Oakhurst Kent 20 F2
Oakington Cambs 29 B11
Oaklands Herts 29 G9
Oaklands Powys 25 C7
Oakle Street Glos 26 G4
Oakley Bedford 29 C7
Oakley Bucks 28 G3
Oakley Fife 69 B9
Oakley Hants 18 F2
Oakley Oxon 18 A4
Oakley Poole 9 E9
Oakley Suff 39 H7
Oakley Green Windsor 18 D6
Oakley Park Powys 32 G5
Oakmere Ches W 43 F8
Oakridge Glos 16 A6
Oakridge Hants 18 F3
Oaks Shrops 33 E10
Oaks Green Derbys 35 B7
Oaksey Wilts 16 B6
Oakthorpe Leics 35 D9
Oakwoodhill Sur 19 H8
Oakworth W Yorks 50 F6
Oape Highld 92 J7
Oare Kent 21 E7
Oare Som 7 B7
Oare W Berks 18 D2
Oare Wilts 17 E8
Oasby Lincs 36 B6
Oathlaw Angus 77 B7
Oatlands N Yorks 51 D9
Oban Argyll 79 J11
Oban Highld 79 C11
Oborne Dorset 8 C5
Obthorpe Lincs 37 D6
Occlestone Green Ches W 43 F9
Occold Suff 31 A8
Ochiltree E Ayrs 67 D8
Ochtermuthill Perth 75 F11
Ochtertyre Perth 75 E11
Ockbrook Derbys 35 B10
Ockham Sur 19 F7
Ockle Highld 79 D8
Ockley Sur 19 H8
Ocle Pychard Hereford 26 D2
Octon E Yorks 52 C6
Octon Cross Roads E Yorks 52 C6
Odcombe Som 8 C4
Odd Down Bath 16 E4
Oddendale Cumb 57 E7
Odder Lincs 46 E3
Oddingley Worcs 26 C6
Oddington Glos 27 F9
Oddington Oxon 28 G2
Odell Bedford 28 C6
Odie Orkney 95 F7
Odiham Hants 18 F4
Odstock Wilts 9 B10
Odstone Leics 35 E9
Offchurch Warks 27 B10
Offenham Worcs 27 D7
Offham E Sus 12 E2
Offham Kent 20 F3
Offham W Sus 11 D9
Offord Cluny Cambs 29 B9
Offord Darcy Cambs 29 B9
Offton Suff 31 D7
Offwell Devon 7 G10
Ogbourne Maizey Wilts 17 D8
Ogbourne St Andrew Wilts 17 D8
Ogbourne St George Wilts 17 D9
Ogil Angus 77 A7
Ogle Northumb 63 F7
Ogmore V Glam 14 D4
Ogmore-by-Sea V Glam 14 D4
Ogmore Vale Bridgend 14 B5
Okeford Fitzpaine Dorset 9 C7
Okehampton Devon 6 G4
Okehampton Camp Devon 6 G4
Okraquoy Shetland 96 K6
Old Northants 28 A4
Old Aberdeen Aberdeen 83 C11
Old Alresford Hants 10 A4
Old Arley Warks 35 F8
Old Basford Nottingham 35 A11
Old Basing Hants 18 F3
Old Bewick Northumb 62 A6
Old Bolingbroke Lincs 47 F7
Old Bramhope W Yorks 51 E8
Old Brampton Derbys 45 E7
Old Bridge of Tilt Perth 81 G10
Old Bridge of Urr Dumfries 55 C10
Old Buckenham Norf 39 F6
Old Burghclere Hants 17 F11
Old Byland N Yorks 59 H6
Old Cassop Durham 58 C4
Old Castleton Borders 61 D11
Old Catton Norf 39 D8
Old Clee NE Lincs 46 B6
Old Cleeve Som 7 B9
Old Clipstone Notts 45 F10
Old Colwyn Conwy 41 C10
Old Coulsdon London 19 F10
Old Crombie Aberds 88 C5
Old Dailly S Ayrs 66 G5
Old Dalby Leics 36 C2
Old Deer Aberds 89 D9
Old Denaby S Yorks 45 C8
Old Edlington S Yorks 45 C9
Old Eldon Durham 58 D3
Old Ellerby E Yorks 53 F7
Old Felixstowe Suff 31 E10
Old Fletton Pboro 37 F7
Old Glossop Derbys 44 C4
Old Goole E Yorks 52 G3
Old Hall Powys 32 G5
Old Heath Essex 31 F7
Old Heathfield E Sus 12 D4
Old Hill W Mid 34 G5
Old Hunstanton Norf 38 A2
Old Hurst Cambs 37 H8
Old Hutton Cumb 57 H7
Old Kea Corn 3 E7
Old Kilpatrick W Dunb 68 C3
Old Kinnernie Aberds 83 C9
Old Knebworth Herts 29 F9
Old Langho Lancs 50 F3
Old Laxey IoM 48 D4
Old Leake Lincs 47 G8
Old Malton N Yorks 52 B3
Old Micklefield W Yorks 51 F10
Old Milton Hants 9 E11
Old Milverton Warks 27 B9
Old Monkland N Lanark 68 D6
Old Netley Hants 10 D3
Old Philpstoun W Loth 69 C9
Old Quarrington Durham 58 C4
Old Radnor Powys 25 C9
Old Rattray Aberds 89 C10
Old Rayne Aberds 83 A8
Old Romney Kent 13 D9
Old Sodbury S Glos 16 C4
Old Somerby Lincs 36 B5
Old Stratford Northants 28 D4
Old Thirsk N Yorks 51 A10
Old Town Cumb 50 A1
Old Town Cumb 57 B6
Old Town Northumb 62 D4
Old Town Scilly 2 C3
Old Trafford Gtr Man 44 C2
Old Tupton Derbys 45 F7
Old Warden C Beds 29 D8
Old Weston Cambs 37 H6
Old Whittington Derbys 45 E7
Old Wick Highld 94 E5
Old Windsor Windsor 18 D6
Old Wives Lees Kent 21 F7
Old Woking Sur 19 F7
Old Woodhall Lincs 46 F6
Oldany Highld 92 F4
Oldberrow Warks 27 B8
Oldborough Devon 7 F6
Oldbury Shrops 34 F3
Oldbury W Mid 34 G5
Oldbury Warks 35 F9
Oldbury-on-Severn S Glos 16 B3
Oldbury on the Hill Glos 16 C5
Oldcastle Bridgend 14 D5
Oldcastle Mon 25 F10
Oldcotes Notts 45 D9
Oldfallow Staffs 34 D5
Oldfield Worcs 26 B5
Oldford Som 16 F4
Oldham Gtr Man 44 B3
Oldhamstocks E Loth 70 C6
Oldland S Glos 16 D3
Oldmeldrum Aberds 89 F8
Oldshore Beg Highld 92 D4
Oldshoremore Highld 92 D5
Oldstead N Yorks 51 A11
Oldtown Aberds 83 A7
Oldtown of Ord Aberds 88 C6
Oldway Swansea 23 H10
Oldways End Devon 7 D7
Oldwhat Aberds 89 C8
Olgrinmore Highld 94 E2
Oliver's Battery Hants 10 B3
Ollaberry Shetland 96 E5
Ollerton Ches E 43 E10
Ollerton Notts 45 F10